thomson.com

changing the way the world learns

To get extra value from this book for no additional cost, go to:

http://www.thomson.com/wadsworth.html

thomson.com is the World Wide Web site for Wadsworth/ITP and is your direct source to dozens of on-line resources. *thomson.com* helps you find out about supplements, experiment with demonstration software, search for a job, and send e-mail to many of our authors. You can even preview new publications and exciting new technologies.

thomson.com: *It's where you'll find us in the future.*

FROM THE WADSWORTH SERIES IN MASS COMMUNICATION AND JOURNALISM

General Mass Communication

Communications Law: Liberties, Restraints, and the Modern Media, 2nd Ed., by John D. Zelezny

Communications Media in the Information Society, Updated Edition, by Joseph Straubhaar & Robert LaRose

Ethics in Media Communications: Cases and Controversies, 2nd Ed., by Louis Day

International Communications: History, Conflict, and Control of the Global Metropolis, by Robert S. Fortner

The Interplay of Influence, 4th Ed., by Kathleen Hall Jamieson & Karlyn Kohrs Campbell

Media/Impact: An Introduction to Mass Media, 3rd Ed., by Shirley Biagi

Media/Reader: Perspectives on Media Industries, Effects, and Issues, 3rd Ed., by Shirley Biagi

Mediamerica, Mediaworld: Form, Content, and Consequence of Mass Communication, Updated 5th Ed., by Edward Jay Whetmore

Women and Media: Content, Careers, and Criticism, by Cynthia Lont

Journalism

Creative Editing for Print Media, 2nd Ed., by Dorothy Bowles & Diane L. Borden

Free-Lancer and Staff Writer, 5th Ed., by William Rivers

News Writing, by Peter Berkow

The Search: Information Gathering for the Mass Media, by Lauren Kessler & Duncan McDonald

When Worlds Collide: A Media Writer's Guide to Grammar and Style, 4th Ed., by Lauren Kessler and Duncan McDonald

Writing and Reporting News: A Coaching Method, 2nd Ed., by Carole Rich

Photography and Design

Design Principles for Desktop Publishers, 2nd Ed., by Tom Lichty

Desktop Computing Workbook: A Guide to Fifteen Programs in Macintosh and Windows Formats, by Paul Martin Lester

Introduction to Photography, 4th Ed., by Marvin J. Rosen & David L. DeVries

Visual Communication: Images with Messages, by Paul Martin Lester

Public Relations and Advertising

Advertising and Marketing to the New Majority: A Case Study Approach, by Gail Baker Woods

Creative Strategy in Advertising, 5th Ed., by A. Jerome Jewler

Electronic Public Relations, by Eugene Marlow

International Advertising: Communicating Across Cultures, by Barbara Mueller

Public Relations Cases, 3rd Ed., by Jerry A. Hendrix

Public Relations Writing: Form and Style, 4th Ed., by Doug Newsom & Bob Carrell

This Is PR: The Realities of Public Relations, 6th Ed., by Doug Newsom, Judy VanSlyke Turk & Dean Kruckeberg

Research and Theory

Communication Research: Strategies and Sources, 4th Ed., by Rebecca B. Rubin, Alan M. Rubin & Linda J. Piele

Mass Communication Theory: Foundations, Ferment and Future, by Stanley Baran & Dennis Davis

Mass Media Research: An Introduction, 5th Ed., by Roger D. Wimmer & Joseph R. Dominick

The Practice of Social Research, 7th Ed., by Earl Babbie

Surveying Public Opinion, by Sondra Miller Rubenstein

FIFTH
EDITION

MASS MEDIA
RESEARCH

AN INTRODUCTION

ROGER D. WIMMER
Wimmer–Hudson
Research & Development

JOSEPH R. DOMINICK
University of Georgia

Wadsworth Publishing Company
ITP® An International Thomson Publishing Company

Belmont • Albany • Bonn • Boston • Cincinnati • Detroit • London • Madrid • Melbourne
Mexico City • New York • Paris • San Francisco • Singapore • Tokyo • Toronto • Washington

To MMM and Meaghan—neither wrote a word, but both provided the incentive.

Communications & Media Studies Editor:
 Todd R. Armstrong
Assistant Editor: Lewis DeSimone
Editorial Assistant: Michael Gillespie
Production: Greg Hubit Bookworks
Composition: Thompson Type

Print Buyer: Barbara Britton
Interior Design: Vargas / Williams / Design
Cover Design: Paul C. Uhl/Design Associates
Cover Photograph: Pelton & Assoc./Westlight
Printer: Quebecor/Fairfield

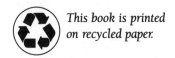

*This book is printed
on recycled paper.*

For more information, contact Wadsworth Publishing Company:

Wadsworth Publishing Company
10 Davis Drive
Belmont, California 94002, USA

International Thomson Publishing Europe
Berkshire House 168-173
High Holborn
London, WC1V 7AA, England

Thomas Nelson Australia
102 Dodds Street
South Melbourne 3205
Victoria, Australia

Nelson Canada
1120 Birchmount Road
Scarborough, Ontario
Canada M1K 5G4

International Thomson Editores
Campos Eliseos 385, Piso 7
Col. Polanco
11560 México D.F. México

International Thomson Publishing GmbH
Königswinterer Strasse 418
53227 Bonn, Germany

International Thomson Publishing Asia
221 Henderson Road
#05-10 Henderson Building
Singapore 0315

International Thomson Publishing Japan
Hirakawacho Kyowa Building, 3F
2-2-1 Hirakawacho
Chiyoda-ku, Tokyo 102, Japan

Preface

▯ ▯ ▯ ▯ ▯ ▮ ▯ ▯ ▯ ▯ ▯ ▮ ▯ ▯ ▯ ▯ ▯ ▮ ▯ ▯ ▯ ▯ ▯ ▮ ▯ ▯ ▯ ▯ ▯ ▮ ▯ ▯ ▯ ▯ ▯ ▮ ▯ ▯ ▯ ▯ ▮

In the preface to the fourth edition in 1994, we stated that "Writing this book over the past decade has been both exciting and frustrating: It is exciting to be able to publish ideas about topics and procedures we teach and use every day, but it is frustrating that many of the things we write about become outdated as soon as the edition is published." The statement continues to be true.

Since the fourth edition was published, several fundamental changes have impacted mass media and mass media research: new Arbitron and Nielsen ratings' procedures, on-line newspaper delivery systems, a proliferation of talk shows on radio and television, database marketing to allow the print media and others to produce materials for specifically targeted audiences, satellite delivery of radio and television to homes, intriguing public relations campaigns (related to the O. J. Simpson trial witnesses), and a tremendous increase in the use of research by mass media decision makers.

Many of these changes are attributable to rapid developments in the high tech field, especially computers. Almost every day brings an announcement of a new computer, new software, or a new peripheral device. While new products, services, and enhancements make mass media research easier to conduct, the problem is staying abreast of all the changes. Although we include a chapter about using the computer in mass media research, we know that it will be out of date by the time you read this book. But that's what makes this field fun—there aren't many days that are the same.

Our goal in this edition is the same as it has always been: introduce the reader to mass media research using a minimum of technical terms and a maximum of practical guidelines. Drawing on comments from reviewers, teachers, students, and professional media people who have used our book in the past, we have updated all of the chapters.

We would like to thank the following people who were involved in the production of this fifth edition: Betty Blosser, San Francisco State University; Jennings Bryant, University of Houston; Joanne Cantor, University of Wisconsin–Madison; Fiona Chew, Syracuse University; David Clark, Christian Broadcast Network; Susan Tyler Eastman, Indiana University; Edward A. Johnson, University of Alabama; Jack McLeod, University of Wisconsin–Madison; L. John Martin, University of Maryland; Allan Mussehl, Middle Tennessee State University; Joseph Philport, The Arbitron Company; John Robinson, Cox Enterprises, Inc.; Alan Rubin, Kent State University; Barry Sherman, University of Georgia; Dilnawaz A. Siddiqui, Clarion University of Pennsylvania; James Smith, SUNY–New Paltz; Linda Steiner, Rutgers University; Robert L. Stevenson, University of North Carolina; William Todd-Mancillas, California State University–Chico; Edward P. Trotter, California State University–Fullerton; Lauren Tucker, University of South Carolina; Charles Whitney, University of Texas–Austin.

And as we have stated in the previous editions, if you find a serious error in the text, please call one of the authors—he will be happy to give you the other author's home telephone number. If you access the Internet, you can reach us at our e-mail addresses.

Have fun with the book. The mass media research field is a great place to be!

Roger Wimmer
Denver, Colorado
E-mail: Roger_Wimmer@prodigy.com

Joseph Dominick
Athens, Georgia
E-mail: joedom@uga.cc.uga.edu

Brief Contents

Contents

। ।

PART THREE   DATA ANALYSIS   205

PART FOUR   RESEARCH APPLICATIONS   265

PART FIVE   ANALYZING AND REPORTING DATA   379

CHAPTER 17
THE COMPUTER AS A RESEARCH TOOL   380

CHAPTER 18
RESEARCH REPORTING, ETHICS, AND FINANCIAL SUPPORT   398

APPENDIXES   419

THE RESEARCH PROCESS

Chapter

1

SCIENCE
AND RESEARCH

At some point in our lives we have heard someone say, "Some things never change." This statement is particularly appropriate to the average person's perception of mass media research. It is the authors' experience that the perception of research is the same today as it was in 1979, when the first edition of this book was published. What is the perception of mass media research?

In the introduction to their book, *No Way: The Nature of the Impossible,* Davis and Park (1987) state:

- It is impossible to translate a poem.
- It is impossible for the president of the United States to be less than 35 years old.
- It is impossible to send a message into the past.
- It is impossible for a door to be open and closed simultaneously.

In reference to research, some people would add:

- It is impossible to learn how to conduct mass media research.

Davis and Park address the nature of the impossible in several areas. Their book is a collection of essays by authors who explain how some seemingly impossible statements and situations are not what they appear to be. For example, they say that the last item in their list (the open/closed door) sounds like pure logic, but it isn't. A revolving door is evidence that the "pure logic" is incorrect. The authors of this book contend that "it is impossible to learn how to conduct mass media research" may sound like pure logic, but isn't. What is required is an understanding of the basics of research.

THE "MEANING" OF RESEARCH

Many years ago Richard Weaver (1953), a communications scholar, identified the differences between "god" terms and "devil" terms. A god term is positive and has connotations of strength, goodness, and significance. For example, *knowledge, democracy, innovation,* and *freedom* are god terms in the United States. A devil term, on the other hand, represents a negative image and connotes weakness, evil, or impending doom, such as *disease, drug cartel, loser,* and *inferior.*

One term that transcends both categories is **research**. For example, advertisers use research as a god term to communicate a message to consumers about products, services, and ideas. Broadcast commercials and print advertisements include statements such as "Research shows that 6 out of 10 doctors . . ." and "According to a recent survey of Harley-Davidson owners, 95 out of 100 preferred . . ." The intent of these types of statements is to associate with the product a degree of importance based only on research; the research results alone should convince consumers of the need for a product.

Research can also be a devil term, especially to those mass media students who consider statistics and research as detours on the road to receiving a college degree. This book may help dispel the "devil" connotation of the term *research* and demonstrate that mass media research is not impossible. Indeed, research is an important part of the mass media field and should be viewed positively. As Tom McClendon, Vice-President of Cox Broadcasting, states:

> Proper research is essential in business today in order to maintain or gain a competitive edge. Unless business operators know what the customer wants, then failure is predictable. Research is the tool to enable success. Many business people feel that they know what their customers want without research, and they are left wondering what happened when a competitor steals their customers with the use of research. Research alone cannot guarantee success, but it is a necessary tool to aid in proper decision-making.

Research is an essential tool in all areas of mass media. Virtually all departments and positions in mass media are involved in research of some kind.

GETTING STARTED

This chapter contains discussions of the development of mass media research during the past several decades and the methods used to collect and analyze information; it also includes an expanded discussion of the scientific method of research. The intent of this chapter is to provide a foundation for the topics discussed in greater detail in later chapters.

Two basic questions a beginning researcher must learn to answer are *how* and *when* to use research methods and statistical procedures. Although developing methods and procedures are valuable tasks, the focus for most research students should be on applications. This book supports the approach of the applied data analyst (researcher), not the statistician; it is not intended to help the reader become a statistician because the "real world" of mass media research does not require specific knowledge of high-level statistics. After conducting

thousands of mass media research projects over almost 25 years, the authors have concluded that those who wish to become mass media researchers should spend time learning *what to do* with the research methods, not *how they work*.

Although both statisticians and researchers are involved in producing research results, their functions are quite different. (Keep in mind that one person sometimes serves in both capacities.)

Among other complex activities, statisticians generate statistical procedures, or formulas, called **algorithms**; researchers use these algorithms to investigate research questions and hypotheses. The results of this cooperative effort are used to advance our understanding of the mass media.

For example, users of radio and television ratings (mainly produced by Arbitron and A. C. Nielsen) continually complain about the instability of ratings information. The ratings and shares (Chapter 14) for radio and television stations in a given market often vary dramatically from one survey period to the next without any logical explanation. Users of ratings periodically ask statisticians and the ratings companies to help determine why this problem occurs and to offer suggestions for making syndicated media audience information more reliable. As recently as the spring of 1996, media statisticians recommended larger samples and more refined methods of selecting respondents to correct the instability. Although the problems have not been solved, it is clear that statisticians and researchers can work together.

Since the early part of the 20th century, when there was no interest in the size of an audience or in the types of people that comprised the audience, mass media leaders have come to rely on research results for nearly every major decision they make. As stated in the first edition of this book, the increased demand for information has created a need for more researchers, both public and private. And within the research field are many specializations.

There are research directors who plan and supervise studies and act as liaisons to management; methodological specialists who provide statistical support; research analysts who design and interpret studies; and computer specialists who provide hardware and software support in data analysis.

Research in mass media can be used to verify or nullify gut feelings or intuition when making decisions. Although common sense is often accurate, media decision makers need additional objective information to evaluate problems, especially when significant decisions are made (which usually involve large sums of money). The past 50 years have witnessed the evolution of a decision-making approach that combines research and intuition to produce a higher probability of success.

Research, however, is not limited only to decision-making situations. It is also widely used in theoretical areas to attempt to describe the media, to analyze media effects on consumers, to understand audience behavior, and so on. No day goes by without some reference in the media to audience surveys, public opinion polls, growth projections or status reports of one medium or another, or advertising or public relations campaigns. As philosopher Suzanne Langer (1967) said, "Most new discoveries are suddenly-seen things that were always there." As stated in previous editions of this book, mass media researchers still have a great deal to "see."

There is absolutely no question that media research and the need for qualified researchers will continue to grow at a phenomenal rate. However, it is becoming more and more difficult to find qualified researchers who can work in both the public and private sectors.

THE DEVELOPMENT OF MASS MEDIA RESEARCH

Mass media research has evolved in definable steps, and similar patterns have been followed in each medium's needs for research (see Figure 1.1).* In Phase 1 of the research, there is an interest in the medium itself. What is it? How does it work? What technology does it involve? How is it similar to or different from what we already have? What functions or services does it provide? Who will have access to the new medium? How much will it cost?

Phase 2 research begins once the medium is developed. In this phase, specific information about the uses and the users of the medium is accumulated. How do people use the medium in real life? Do they use it for information only, to save time, for entertainment, or for some other reason? Do children use it? Do adults use it? Why? What gratifications does the new medium provide? What other types of information and entertainment does the new medium replace? Were original projections about the use of the medium correct? What uses are evident other than those that were projected in initial research?

Phase 3 includes investigations of the social, psychological, and physical effects of the medium. How much time do people spend with the medium? Does it change people's perspectives about anything? What do the users of the medium want and expect to hear or see? Are there any harmful effects related to using the medium? Does the technology cause any harm? How does the medium help in people's lives? Can the medium be combined with other media or technology to make it even more useful?

Phase 4 includes research related to how the medium can be improved, either in its use or through technological developments. Can the medium provide information or entertainment to more types of people? How can new technology be used to perfect or enhance the sight or sound of the medium? Is there a way to change the content (programming) to be more valuable or entertaining?

---

*Note how research concerning the Internet is following these phases.

FIGURE 1.1   Research Phases in Mass Media

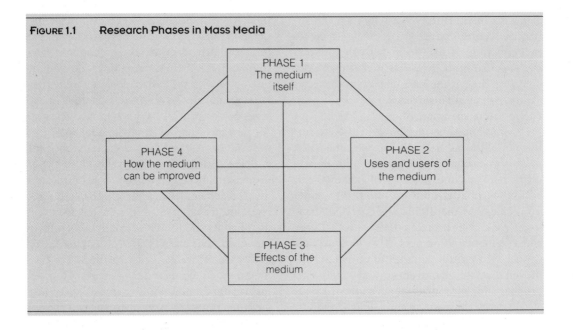

The design of Figure 1.1 is not intended to suggest that the research phases are linear—that when one phase is over, it is never considered again. In reality, once a medium is developed and established, research may be conducted simultaneously in all four phases. For example, though television has been around for over 50 years, researchers are still investigating the medium itself (satellite-delivered digital audio and video), the uses of TV (pay-per-view programming), effects (violent programming), and improvements (flat-screen TV).

Research is a never-ending process. In most instances a research project designed to answer one series of questions merely produces a new set of questions no one thought of before. This failure to produce a closure may be troublesome to some people, yet it is the essential nature of research.

Figure 1.1 depicts four phases of research. However, in some instances, as in private sector research, an additional element permeates every phase: How can the medium make money? The largest percentage of research conducted in the private sector relates in some way to money—

how to save it, make more of it, or take it away from others. This may not "sit well" with people who view the media as products of artistic endeavor, but this is how the "real world" operates.

At least four major events or social forces have contributed to the growth of mass media research. The first was World War I, which prompted a need to further understand the nature of propaganda. Researchers working from a stimulus-response point of view attempted to uncover the effects of the media on people (Lasswell, 1927). The media at that time were thought to exert a very powerful influence over their audiences, and several assumptions were made about what the media could and could not do. One theory of mass media, later named the "hypodermic needle" model of communication, basically suggested that mass communicators need only "shoot" messages at an audience and that those messages would produce preplanned and almost universal effects. The belief was that all people behave in very similar ways when they encounter media messages, though we know now that individual differences among people rule out this rather simplistic view. However, as DeFleur and Ball-Rokeach (1989) note:

> These assumptions may not have been explicitly formulated at the time, but they were drawn from fairly elaborate theories of human nature, as well as the nature of the social order. . . . It was these theories that guided the thinking of those who saw the media as powerful.

A second contributor to the development of mass media research was the realization by advertisers in the 1950s and 1960s that research data were useful in devising ways to persuade potential customers to buy products and services. Consequently, they encouraged studies of message effectiveness, audience demographics and size, placement of advertising to achieve the highest level of exposure (efficiency), frequency of advertising necessary to persuade potential customers, and selection of the medium that offered the best chance of reaching the target audience.

A third contributing social force was the increasing interest of citizens in the effects of the media on the public, especially on children. The direct result was an interest in research related to violence and sexual content in television programs and in commercials aired during children's programs. Researchers have expanded their focus to include the positive (prosocial) as well as the negative (antisocial) effects of television (Chapter 16). In the past several years there has been a heated debate over rap music lyrics and videos shown on video channels; in 1992, for example, the release of the song "Cop Killer" by Ice T triggered strong reactions, as did some music videos in 1995 that depicted violence against women.

Increased competition among the media for advertising dollars has been a fourth contributor to the growth of research. Most media managers are now very sophisticated and use long-range plans, management by objectives, and an increasing dependency on data to support the decision-making process. Even pro-gram producers, such as Rysher Entertainment in Hollywood, seek relevant research data, a task usually assigned to the creative side of program development. In addition, the mass media are geared toward *audience fragmentation*, which means that the masses of people have been divided into small groups, or *niches* (technically referred to as the "demassification" of the mass media).

The competition among the media for audiences and advertising dollars continues to reach new levels of complexity. The media "survival kit" today includes information about consumers' changing values and tastes, shifts in demographic patterns, and developing trends in lifestyles. Audience fragmentation increases the need for trend studies (fads, new behavior patterns), image studies (people's perceptions of the media and their environment), and segmentation studies (explanations of types or groups of people). Major research organizations, consultants, and media owners and operators conduct research that was previously considered the sole property of the marketing, psychology, and sociology disciplines. With the advent of increased competition and audience fragmentation, media managers are more frequently using marketing strategies in an attempt to discover their position in the marketplace. When this position is identified, the medium is packaged as an "image" rather than a product. (Similarly, the producers of consumer goods such as soap and toothpaste try to sell the "image" of these products since the products themselves are very similar, if not the same, from company to company.)

This packaging strategy involves determining what the members of the audience think, how they use language, how they occupy their spare time, and so on. Information on these ideas and behaviors is then woven into the merchandising effort to make the medium seem to be part of the audience. Positioning thus involves taking information from the audience and interpreting the data to use in marketing the medium. (For more information about positioning companies and products in the business and consumer worlds, see Ries & Trout, 1986a, 1986b.)

Much of the media research up to the early 1960s originated in psychology and sociology departments at colleges and universities. Researchers with backgrounds in the media were rare because the media themselves were young. But this situation has changed. Media departments in colleges and universities grew rapidly in the 1960s, and media researchers entered the scene. Today the field is dominated by mass media researchers, and now the trend is to encourage cross-disciplinary studies in which media researchers invite participation from sociologists, psychologists, and political scientists. Because of the pervasiveness of the media, researchers from all areas of science are now actively involved in attempting to answer media-related questions.

In recent years, mass media research has entered new areas of inquiry. These areas include the various psychological and sociological aspects of mass media, such as physiological and emotional responses to television programs, commercials, or music played by radio stations. In addition, computer modeling and other sophisticated computer analyses are now commonplace in media research to determine such things as the potential success of television programs (network or syndicated). Once considered eccentric by some, mass media research is now a legitimate and esteemed field.

MEDIA RESEARCH AND THE SCIENTIFIC METHOD

Kerlinger (1986) defines scientific research as a systematic, controlled, empirical, and critical investigation of hypothetical propositions about the presumed relations among observed phenomena. This definition contains the basic terms necessary to define the scientific research method and describes a procedure that has been accepted for centuries. In the 16th century, for example, Tycho Brahe (pronounced *Tee'-kóh Brah'-uh*) conducted years of systematic and controlled observation to refute many of Aristotle's theories of the universe.

Whether we realize it or not, we all conduct various types of research in our day-by-day lives. We do this whenever we start with an idea and then test it. Children conduct "studies" to determine which items are hot and which are cold, how to ride a bicycle or a snowboard, and which persuasive methods work best with parents. Teenagers "test" ideas about driving, dating, and working; and adults "test" ideas about family, finance, and survival.

All research, whether formal or informal, begins with a basic question or proposition about a specific phenomenon. For example, why do viewers select one television program over another? Which sections of the newspaper do people read most often? Which types of magazine covers attract the most readers? Which types of advertising are most effective in selling products and services? These questions can be answered to some degree with well-designed research studies. The difficulty, sometimes, is to determine which data collection method can most appropriately provide answers to specific questions.

There are several possible approaches in answering research questions. Kerlinger (1986), using definitions provided nearly a century ago by C. S. Peirce, discussed four approaches to finding answers, or "methods of knowing": tenacity, intuition, authority, and science.

A user of the **method of tenacity** follows the logic that something is true because it has always been true. An example is the store owner who says, "I don't advertise because my parents did not believe in advertising." The idea is that nothing changes; what was good, bad, or successful before will continue to be so in the future.

In the **method of intuition,** or *a priori* approach, a person assumes that something is true because it is "self-evident" or "stands to reason." Some creative people in advertising agencies resist efforts to test their advertising methods because they believe they know what will attract customers. To these people, scientific research is a waste of time.

The **method of authority** promotes a belief in something because a trusted source, such as a parent, a news correspondent, or a teacher, says it is true. The emphasis is on the source, not on the methods the source may have used to gain the information. For example, the claim that "Consumers will pay hundreds of dollars for a new satellite dish to receive hundreds of television channels because producers of satellite dish companies say so" is based on the method of authority. (During 1994 and 1995, this was shown not to be true. Consumers did not flock to the stores to buy the new delivery system, and research had to be conducted to find out what failed. Changes were made in both product and marketing, and sales quickly took off.

The **scientific method** approaches learning as a series of small steps. That is, one study or one source provides only an *indication* of what may or may not be true; the "truth" is found only through a series of objective analyses. This means that the scientific method is self-correcting in that changes in thought or theory are appropriate when errors in previous research are uncovered. For example, in the mid-1990s scientists changed their ideas about the planets in the solar system, ulcers (caused by a virus), and lasers when they uncovered errors in earlier observations. In communications, researchers discovered that the early perceptions of the power of the media (the "hypodermic needle" theory) were incorrect and, after numerous studies, concluded that behavior and ideas are changed by a combination of communication sources and that people may react to the same message in different ways. Isaac Asimov (1990, p. 42) stated, "One of the glories of scientific endeavor is that any scientific belief, however firmly established, is constantly being tested to see if it is truly universally valid."

The scientific method may be inappropriate in many areas of life—for instance, in evaluating works of art, choosing a religion, or forming friendships—but it has been valuable in producing accurate and useful data in mass media research. The following section provides a more detailed look at this method of knowing. Also see R. K. Tucker (1996) for a discussion of how a person's personality, temperament, or approach to life can affect the way people learn things.

CHARACTERISTICS OF THE SCIENTIFIC METHOD

Five basic characteristics, or tenets, distinguish the scientific method from other methods of knowing. A research approach that does not follow these tenets cannot be considered to be a scientific approach.

1. *Scientific research is public.* Scientific advancement depends on freely available information. Researchers (especially in the academic sector) cannot plead private knowledge, methods, or data in arguing for the accuracy of their findings; scientific research information must be freely communicated from one researcher to another. As Nunnally (1994) noted:

> Science is a highly public enterprise in which efficient communication among scientists is essential. Each scientist builds on what has been learned in the past, day by day his or her findings must be compared with those of other scientists working on the same types of problems. . . . The rate of scientific progress in a particular area is limited by the efficiency and fidelity with which scientists can communicate their results to one another.

Researchers, therefore, must take great care in published reports to include information on sampling methods, measurements, and data-gathering procedures. Such information allows other researchers to independently verify a given study and support or refute the initial research findings. This process of replication (discussed in Chapter 2) allows for correction and verification of previous research findings. Although not related to media research, the importance of replication in scientific research was underscored in 1992, when physicists were unable to duplicate the fantastic claim made by two University of Utah chemists who said they had produced fusion at room temperature.

Researchers also need to save their descriptions of observations (data) and their research materials so that information not included in a formal report can be made available to other researchers on request. Nunnally (1994) said: "A key principle of science is that any statement of fact made by one scientist should be independently verifiable by other scientists." Researchers can verify results only if they have access to the original data. It is common practice to keep all raw research materials for at least 5 years. This material is usually provided free as a courtesy to other researchers, or for a nominal fee if photocopying or additional materials are required.

2. *Science is objective.* Science tries to rule out eccentricities of judgment by researchers. When a study is undertaken, explicit rules and procedures are constructed and the researcher is bound to follow them, letting the chips fall where they may. Rules for classifying behavior are used so that two or more independent observers can classify particular behavior patterns in the same manner. For example, if the appeal of a television commercial is being measured, researchers might count the number of times a viewer switches channels while the commercial is shown. This is considered to be an objective measure because a change in channel would be reported by any competent observer. Conversely, to measure appeal by observing how many viewers make negative facial expressions while the ad is shown would be a subjective approach, since observers may have

different ideas of what constitutes a negative expression. However, an explicit definition of the term *negative facial expression* might eliminate the coding error.

Objectivity also requires that scientific research deal with facts rather than interpretations of facts. Science rejects its own authorities if their statements conflict with direct observation. As the noted psychologist B. F. Skinner (1953) wrote: "Research projects do not always come out as one expects, but the facts must stand and the expectations fall. The subject matter, not the scientist, knows best." Mass media researchers have often encountered situations in which media decision makers reject the results of a research project because the study did not produce the anticipated results. (In such a case, one might wonder why the research was conducted at all.)

3. *Science is empirical.* Researchers are concerned with a world that is knowable and potentially measurable. (*Empiricism* derives from the Greek word for "experience.") They must be able to perceive and classify what they study and to reject metaphysical and nonsensical explanations of events. For example, a newspaper publisher's claim that declining subscription rates are "God's will" would be rejected by scientists—such a statement cannot be perceived, classified, or measured. (Scientists whose areas of research rely on superstition and other nonscientific methods of knowing are said to practice "bad science." For a fascinating discussion on astrology, UFOs, and pseudoscience, see Seeds, 1992.)

This does not mean that scientists evade abstract ideas and notions—they encounter them every day. But they recognize that concepts must be strictly defined to allow for observation and measurement. Scientists must link abstract concepts to the empirical world through observations, which may be made either directly or indirectly via various measurement instruments. Typically, this linkage is accomplished by framing an operational definition.

Operational definitions are important in science, and a brief introduction necessitates some backtracking. There are basically two kinds of definitions. A constitutive definition defines a word by substituting other words or concepts for it. For example, the following statement provides a **constitutive definition** of the concept "artichoke": "An artichoke is a green leafy vegetable, a tall composite herb of the *Cynara scolymus* family." In contrast, an operational definition specifies procedures that will allow one to experience or measure a concept—for example, "Go to the grocery store and find the produce aisle; look for a sign that says 'Artichokes'; what's underneath the sign is an artichoke." Although an operational definition assures precision, it does not guarantee validity—a stock clerk may mistakenly stack lettuce under the artichoke sign. This possibility for error underscores the importance of considering both the constitutive definition *and* the operational definition of a concept to evaluate the trustworthiness of any measurement. Carefully examining the constitutive definition of artichoke would indicate that the operational definition might be faulty. (For more information about definitions in general, see Langer, 1967.)

Operational definitions can help dispel some of the strange questions raised in philosophical discussions. For instance, if you have taken a philosophy course, you may have encountered the question, "How many angels can stand on the head of a pin?" The debate ends quickly when the retort is, "Give me an operational definition of an angel, and I'll give you the answer." Literally any question can be answered as long as there are operational definitions for the independent or dependent variables. For further discussion of operational definitions, see *Psychometric Theory* (Nunnally, 1994) and *The Practice of Social Research,* 7th edition (Babbie, 1994).

4. *Science is systematic and cumulative.* No single research study stands alone, nor does it rise or fall by itself. Astute researchers always use previous studies as building blocks for their own work. One of the first steps in conducting research is the review of available scientific literature on the topic so that the current study will draw on the heritage of past research (Chapter 2). This review is valuable for identifying problem areas and important factors that might be relevant to the current study.

In addition, scientists attempt to search for order and consistency among their findings. In its ideal form, scientific research begins with a single, carefully observed event and progresses ultimately to the formulation of theories and laws. A **theory** is a set of related **propositions** that presents a systematic view of phenomena by specifying relationships among concepts. Researchers develop theories by searching for patterns of uniformity to explain the data that have been collected. When relationships among variables are invariant (always the same) under given conditions, researchers may formulate a law. Both theories and laws help researchers search for and explain consistency in behavior, situations, and phenomena.

5. *Science is predictive.* Science is concerned with relating the present to the future. In fact, scientists strive to develop theories because, among other reasons, they are useful in predicting behavior. A theory's adequacy lies in its ability to predict a phenomenon or event successfully. A theory that suggests predictions that are not borne out by data analysis must be carefully reexamined and perhaps discarded. Conversely, a theory that generates predictions that are supported by the data can be used to make predictions in other situations.

RESEARCH PROCEDURES

The purpose of the scientific method of research is to provide an objective, unbiased evaluation of data. To investigate research questions and hypotheses systematically, both academic and private sector researchers follow a basic eight-step set of procedures. However, merely following the eight research steps does not guarantee that the research is good, valid, reliable, or useful. An almost countless number of intervening variables (influences) can destroy even the best-planned research project. The situation is analogous to that of someone assuming he or she can bake a cake by just following the recipe. The cake may be ruined by an oven that doesn't work properly, spoiled ingredients, high or low altitude, or numerous other problems. The typical research process consists of the following eight steps:

1. Select a problem.
2. Review existing research and theory (when relevant).
3. Develop hypotheses or research questions.
4. Determine an appropriate methodology/research design.
5. Collect relevant data.
6. Analyze and interpret the results.
7. Present the results in an appropriate form.
8. Replicate the study (when necessary).

Step 4 includes the decision of whether to use **qualitative research** (such as focus groups or one-on-one interviews) with small samples or **quantitative research** (such as telephone interviews), in which large samples are used to allow results to be generalized to the population under study (see Chapter 7 for a discussion of qualitative research).

Steps 2 and 8 are optional in the private sector because in many instances research is conducted to answer a specific and unique question related to a future decision, such as whether to invest a large sum of money in a developing medium. In this type of project there generally is no previous research to consult, and there seldom is a reason to replicate the study because a decision will be made on the basis of the first analysis. However, if the research provides inconclusive results, the study would be revised and replicated.

Each step in the eight-step process depends on all the others to produce a maximally efficient research study. For example, before a literature search is possible, a clearly stated research problem is required; to design the most efficient method of investigating a problem, the researcher must know what types of studies have been conducted; and so on. Moreover, all the steps are interactive—a literature search may refine and even alter the initial research problem, or a study conducted previously by another company or business in the private sector might expedite (or complicate) the current research effort.

TWO SECTORS OF RESEARCH: ACADEMIC AND PRIVATE

The practice of research is divided into two major sectors, academic and private, which are sometimes called "basic" and "applied," respectively. However, these terms are not used in this text since research in both sectors can be basic or applied. The two sectors are equally important, and in many cases work together to solve mass media problems.

Academic sector research is conducted by scholars from colleges and universities. Generally, this research has a theoretical or scholarly approach—that is, the results are intended to help explain the mass media and their effects on individuals. Some popular research topics in the theoretical area include use of media and various media-related items, such as video games and multiple-channel cable systems; differences in consumer lifestyles; effects of media "overload" on consumers; and effects of various types of programming on children.

Private sector research is conducted by nongovernmental companies or their research consultants. It is generally applied research—that is, the results are intended to be used for decision making. Typical research topics in the private sector include media content and consumer preferences; acquisitions of additional businesses or facilities; analysis of on-air talent; advertising and promotional campaigns; public relations approaches to solving specific informational problems; sales forecasting; and image studies of the properties owned by the company.

There are other differences between academic research and private sector research. For instance, academic research is public. Any other researcher or research organization that wishes to use the information gathered by academic researchers should be able to do so merely by asking the original researcher for the raw data. Most private sector research, on the other hand, generates **proprietary data** that is considered to be the sole property of the sponsoring agency and generally cannot be obtained by other researchers. Some private sector research, however, is released to the public soon after it has been conducted (for example, public opinion polls and projections concerning the future of the media). Other studies may be released only after several years, though this practice is the exception rather than the rule.

Another difference between academic research and private sector research involves the amount of time allowed to conduct the work. Academic researchers generally do not have specific deadlines for their research projects (except when research grants are received). Academicians usually conduct their research at a pace that accommodates their teaching schedules. Private sector researchers, however, nearly always operate under some type of deadline. The time frame may be imposed by management or by an outside agency or client that requires a decision from the company or business. For example, on October 10, 1995, at approximately 9:00 a.m. (MST), The Eagle Group (where the senior author is president) received a request from a television station in Pittsburgh to conduct a 400-person telephone study to find out if viewers wanted the station to run the special NBC news interview of O. J.

Simpson a few days after he was found "not guilty" in the deaths of Nicole Simpson and Ron Goldman. The station wanted the results on the morning of October 11. Although the project was completed on time, NBC decided not to air the program. This type of project would not be encountered by an academic researcher. Private sector researchers can rarely afford to pursue research questions in a leisurely manner; typically a decision must be made quickly on the basis of the research.

Also, academic research is generally less expensive to conduct than research in the private sector. This is not to say that academic research is "cheap"—in many cases it is not. But academicians do not need to have enormous sums of money to cover overhead costs for office rent, equipment, facilities, computer analysis, subcontractors, and personnel. Private sector research must take such expenses into account, regardless of whether the research is conducted within the company or contracted out to a research supplier. The lower cost of academic researchers sometimes motivates large media companies and groups to use them rather than professional research firms.

Despite these differences, it is important for beginning researchers to understand that academic research and private sector research are not completely independent of each other. Academicians perform many studies for industry, and private sector groups conduct research that can be classified as theoretical. (For example, the television networks have departments that conduct social research.) Similarly, many college and university professors act as consultants to (and often conduct private sector research for) the media industry.

It is also important for all researchers to refrain from attaching to academic or private sector research stereotypical labels such as *unrealistic, inappropriate, pedantic,* and *limited in scope.* Research in both sectors, though occasionally differing in terms of cost and scope, uses similar methodologies and statistical analyses. In addition, the two sectors have common research goals: to understand problems and to predict the future.

In conducting a study according to the scientific method, researchers must have a clear understanding of what they are investigating, how the phenomenon can be measured or observed, and what procedures are required to test the observations or measurements. Answering a research question or hypothesis requires a conceptualization of the research problem in question and a logical development of the procedural steps. Chapter 2 discusses research procedures in more detail.

SUMMARY

Media research evolved from the fields of psychology and sociology and is now a well-established field in its own right. It is not necessary to be a statistician in order to be a successful researcher; it is more important to know how to conduct research and what research procedures can do.

In an effort to understand any phenomenon, researchers can follow one of several methods of inquiry. Of the procedures discussed in this chapter, the scientific approach is most applicable to the mass media because it involves a systematic, objective evaluation of information. Researchers first identify a problem, then investigate it using a prescribed set of procedures known as the scientific method. The scientific method is the only learning approach that allows for self-correction of research findings; one study does not stand alone but must be supported or refuted by others.

The proliferation of mass media research is mainly attributable to the rapidly developing technology of the media industry. Because of this growth in research, both applied and theoretical approaches have taken on more significance in the decision-making process of the mass media and in our understanding of the media. At the same time, there is a severe shortage of good researchers in both the academic and private sectors.

QUESTIONS AND PROBLEMS FOR FURTHER IINVESTIGATION

1. Obtain a recent issue of *Journal of Broadcasting and Electronic Media, Journalism Quarterly,* or *Public Opinion Quarterly*. How many articles fit into the research phases outlined in Figure 1.1?

2. What are some potential research questions that might be of interest to both academic researchers and private sector researchers?

3. How might the scientific research approach be abused by researchers?

4. In developing solid bodies of information, theories are used as springboards to investigation. However, there are only a few universally recognized theories in mass media research. Why do you think this is true?

5. During the past several years, some citizens' groups have claimed that television has a significant effect on viewers, especially the violence and sexual content of some programs. How might these groups collect data to support their claims? Which method of knowing can such groups use to support their claims?

6. Investigate how research is used to support or refute an argument outside the field of mass media. For example, how do various groups use research to support or refute the idea that motorcycle riders should be required to wear protective helmets? (You may wish to refer to publications such as *Motorcycle Consumer News*.)

REFERENCES AND SUGGESTED READINGS

Anderson, J. A. (1987). *Communication research: Issues and methods*. New York: McGraw-Hill.

Asimov, I. (1990). Exclusion principle survives another stab at its heart. *Rocky Mountain News*, December 9, 1990, p. 42.

Babbie, E. R. (1994). The practice of social research (7th ed.). Belmont, CA: Wadsworth.

Bowers, J. W., & Courtright, J. A. (1984). *Communication research methods*. Glenview, IL: Scott, Foresman.

Brown, J. A. (1980). Selling airtime for controversy: NAB self regulation and Father Coughlin. *Journal of Broadcasting, 24* (2), 199–224.

Carroll, R. L. (1980). The 1948 Truman campaign: The threshold of the modern era. *Journal of Broadcasting, 24* (2), 173–188.

Davis, P. J., & Park, D. (1987). *No way: The nature of the impossible*. New York: W. H. Freeman.

DeFleur, M. L., & Ball-Rokeach, S. (1989). *Theories of mass communication* (5th ed.). New York: Longman.

Ferris, T. (1988). *Coming of age in the Milky Way*. New York: William Morrow.

Herzog, H. (1944). *What do we really know about daytime serial listeners?* In P. Lazarsfeld & F. Stanton (Eds.), *Radio research 1943–44*. New York: Duell, Sloan, & Pearce.

Hough, D. L. (1995). Are you hanging it out too far? *Motorcycle Consumer News, 26*(9), 38–41.

Hsia, H. J. (1988). *Mass communication research methods: A step-by-step approach*. Hillsdale, NJ: Lawrence Erlbaum.

Katz, E., & Lazarsfeld, P. F. (1955). *Personal influence*. New York: Free Press.

Kerlinger, F. N. (1986). *Foundations of behavioral research* (3rd ed.). New York: Holt, Rinehart & Winston.

Klapper, J. (1960). *The effects of mass communication*. New York: Free Press.

Langer, S. K. (1967). *Philosophy in a new key: A study in the symbolism of reason, rite, and art*. (3rd ed.). Cambridge: Harvard University Press.

Lasswell, H. D. (1927). *Propaganda technique in the World War*. New York: Alfred A. Knopf.

Lazarsfeld, P., Berelson, B., & Gaudet, H. (1948). *The people's choice*. New York: Columbia University Press.

Lowery, S., & DeFleur, M. L. (1995). *Milestones in mass communication research* (3rd ed.). White Plains, NY: Longman.

McClendon, Tom. Personal correspondence. August 21, 1995.

Murphy, J. H., & Amundsen, M. S. (1981). The communication effectiveness of comparative advertising for a new brand on users of the dominant brand. *Journal of Advertising, 10*(1), 14–20.

Nesselroade, J. R., & Cattell, R. B. (Eds.). (1988). *Handbook of multivariate experimental psychology* (2nd ed). New York: Plenum Press.

Nunnally, J. C. (1994). *Psychometric theory* (3rd ed.). New York: McGraw-Hill.

Ries, A., & Trout, J. (1986a). *Marketing warfare*. New York: McGraw-Hill.

Ries, A., & Trout, J. (1986b). *Positioning: The battle for your mind*. New York: McGraw-Hill.

Seeds, M. A. (1992). *Foundations of astronomy*. Belmont, CA: Wadsworth.

Sharp, N. W. (1988). *Communications research: The challenge of the information age*. Syracuse, NY: Syracuse University Press.

Skinner, B. F. (1953). *Science and human behavior*. New York: Macmillan.

Sybert, P. J. (1980). MBS and the Dominican Republic. *Journal of Broadcasting, 24*(2), 189–198.

Tucker, R.K. (1996) S.O.B.s: *The Handbook for Handling Super Difficult People*. Bowling Green, OH: OptimAmerica, Ltd.

Weaver, R. M. (1953). *The ethics of rhetoric*. Chicago: Henry Regnery.

Williams, F. (1988). *Research methods and the new media*. New York: Free Press.

Chapter

2

RESEARCH PROCEDURES

The scientific evaluation of any problem must follow a sequence of steps to increase the probability of producing relevant data. Researchers who do not follow a prescribed set of steps do not subscribe to the scientific method of inquiry and simply increase the amount of error present in a study. This chapter describes the process of scientific research, from identifying and developing a topic for investigation to replicating the results. The first section briefly introduces the steps in the development of a research topic.

Objective, rigorous observation and analysis are characteristic of the scientific method. To meet this goal, researchers must follow the prescribed steps shown in Figure 2.1. This research model is appropriate to all areas of scientific research.

SELECTING A RESEARCH TOPIC

Selecting a research topic is not a concern for all researchers—some are able to choose and concentrate on a research area interesting to them. Many come to be identified with studies of specific types, such as those concerning children and media violence, newspaper readership, magazine advertising, or communications law. These researchers investigate small pieces of a puzzle to obtain a broad picture of their research area. In addition, some researchers become identified with specific approaches to research such as focus groups or historical analysis. In the private sector, researchers generally do not have the flexibility of selecting topics or questions to investigate. Instead, they

conduct studies to answer questions raised by management, or they address the problems and questions for which they are hired, as is the case with full-service research companies.

Although some private sector researchers are limited in the amount of input they can contribute in terms of topic selection, they are usually given total control over how the question should be answered (that is, what methodology should be used). The goal of private sector researchers is to develop a method that is fast, inexpensive, reliable, and valid. If all these criteria are met, the researcher has performed a valuable task.

However, selecting a topic is a concern for many beginning researchers, especially those writing term papers, theses, and dissertations. The problem is knowing where to start. Fortunately, there is an unlimited number of sources available for research topics—academic journals, periodicals, newsweeklies, and everyday encounters provide a wealth of ideas. This section highlights some primary sources.

PROFESSIONAL JOURNALS

Academic communication journals, such as the *Journal of Broadcasting and Electronic Media, Journalism Quarterly,* and others listed in this section, are excellent sources for information. Although academic journals tend to publish research that is 12 to 24 months old (due to review procedures and backlog of articles), the articles may provide ideas for research topics. Most authors conclude their research by discussing problems they encountered during the study and suggesting topics that need further investigation. In addition, some journal editors build issues around individual research themes, which often can help in   17

FIGURE 2.1   Steps in the Development of a Research Project

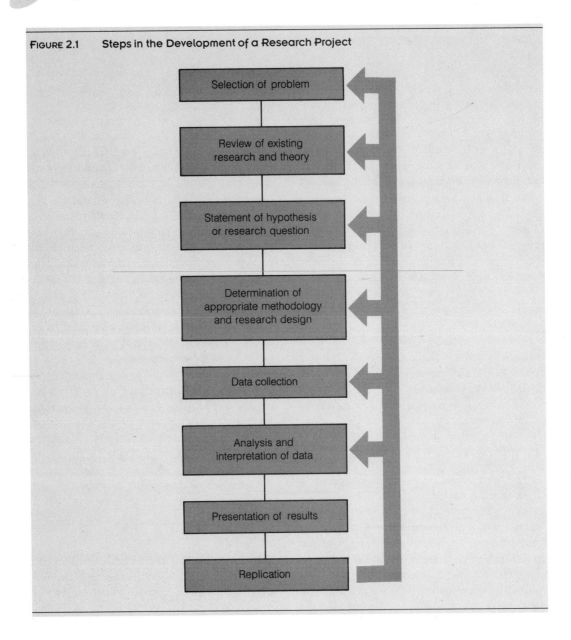

formulating research plans. Many high-quality journals cover various aspects of research; some specialize in mass media research, and others include media research occasionally. The journals listed on page 19 provide a starting point in using academic journals for research ideas.

In addition to academic journals, professional trade publications offer a wealth of in-formation relevant to mass media research. These include *Broadcasting & Cable, Radio & Records, Advertising Age, Electronic Media, Television/Radio Age, Media Decisions, Editor & Publisher, CableVision,* and *Media and Marketing Management.* Other excellent sources for identifying current topics in mass media are the weekly newsletters such as *Media Industry*

Journals That Specialize in Mass Media Research

- *Critical Studies in Mass Communication*
- *Journalism Quarterly*
- *Journal of Advertising*
- *Journal of Advertising Research*

- *Journal of Broadcasting and Electronic Media*
- *Journal of Consumer Research*
- *Public Relations Review*

Journals That Occasionally Publish Mass Media Research

- *American Psychologist*
- *Communication Education*
- *Communication Monographs*
- *Communication Research*
- *Feedback* (from the Broadcast Education Association)
- *Human Communication Research*
- *Journalism Educator*

- *Journal of Communication*
- *Journal of Marketing*
- *Journal of Marketing Research*
- *Multivariate Behavioral Research*
- *Public Opinion Quarterly*
- *Public Relations Quarterly*
- *Quarterly Journal of Speech*

Newsletter, Cable Digest, and several publications from Paul Kagan and Associates.

Research abstracts, located in most college and university libraries, are also valuable sources for research topics. These volumes contain summaries of research articles published in nearly every academic journal. Of particular interest to media researchers are *Communication Abstracts, Psychological Abstracts, Sociological Abstracts,* and *Dissertation Abstracts.*

MAGAZINES AND PERIODICALS

While some educators feel that publications other than professional journals contain only "watered-down" articles written for the general public, these articles tend to eliminate tedious technical jargon and are often good sources for problems and hypotheses. In addition, more and more articles written by highly trained communications professionals appear in weekly and monthly publications such as *TV Guide, Time,* and *Newsweek.* These sources often provide interesting perspectives on complex problems in communication and many times raise interesting questions that media researchers can pursue.

RESEARCH SUMMARIES

Professional research organizations periodically publish summaries that provide a close look at the major research areas in various fields. These summaries are often useful for obtaining information about research topics, since they survey a wide variety of studies. Good examples of summary research (also known as "meta-research") in communication include *Television and Human Behavior,* by George Comstock and others; *The Effects of Mass Communication on Political Behavior,* by Sydney Kraus and Dennis Davis; and *Mass Communication: A Research Bibliography,* by Donald Hansen and J. Hershel Parsons.

EVERYDAY SITUATIONS

Each day we are confronted with various types of communication via radio, television, newspapers, magazines, movies, personal discussions, and so forth. These confrontations can be excellent sources of topics for the researchers who take an active role in analyzing them. With this in mind, consider the following questions:

- Why do advertisers use specific types of messages in broadcasting or print?
- Why is "Entertainment Tonight," "Jeopardy," or "Wheel of Fortune" so popular?
- How do commercials affect the audience's enjoyment of a movie on television?
- How effective are billboards in advertising products?
- What types of people listen to the Rush Limbaugh radio program?
- How many commercials in a row can people watch on television or hear on the radio before the commercials are no longer effective?
- Why do some people faithfully watch soap operas while others find them silly?
- Why do commercials on radio and television always sound louder than the regular programming?
- Will there be any long-term changes in viewing television based on the O.J. Simpson trial coverage?
- Why do viewers purchase items from the television shopping channels?
- Does anyone *really* watch the Weather Channel?

These and other questions may help develop a research idea. Significant studies based on questions arising from everyday encounters with the media and other forms of mass communication have covered investigations of television violence, layout of newspaper advertisements, advisory warnings on television programs, and approaches to public relations campaigns. Pay attention to things around you and to conversations with others—these contacts can produce a wealth of questions to investigate.

ARCHIVE DATA

Data archives, such as the Inter-University Consortium for Political Research (ICPR) at the University of Michigan, the Simmons Target Group Index (TGI), the Gallup and Roper organizations, and the collections of Arbitron and Nielsen ratings data (Chapter 14), are valuable sources of ideas for researchers. The historical data are used to investigate questions different from those that the data were originally intended to address. For example, ratings books provide information about audience size and composition for a particular period in time, but other researchers may use the data for historical tracking, prediction of audiences in the future, changes in popularity of types of stations and/or programs, and the relationship between audience ratings and advertising revenue generated by individual stations or an entire market. This process, known as secondary analysis, is a marvelous research approach because of the time and resource savings it affords.

Secondary analysis provides an opportunity for researchers to evaluate otherwise unavailable data. Becker (1981, p. 240) defines secondary analysis as

> [the] reuse of social science data after they have been put aside by the researcher who gathered them. The reuse of the data can be by the original researcher or someone uninvolved in any way in the initial research project. The research questions examined in the secondary analysis can be related to the original research endeavor or quite distinct from it.

Advantages of Secondary Analysis. Ideally, every researcher should conduct a research project of some magnitude to learn about design, data collection, and analysis. Unfortunately, this ideal situation does not exist. Modern research is simply too expensive. In addition, because survey methodology has become so complex, it is rare to find one researcher, or even a small group of researchers, who are experts in all phases of large studies.

Secondary analysis is one research alternative that solves some of these problems. Using available data is very inexpensive—there are no questionnaires or measurement instruments to construct and validate; salaries for interviewers and other personnel are nonexistent; and there are no costs for subjects and special equipment. The only expenses entailed in secondary analysis are those for duplicating materials—some organizations provide their data free of charge—and computer time. Data archives are valuable sources for empirical data. In many cases, archive data provide researchers with information that can be used to help answer significant media problems and questions.

Although novice researchers (usually students) can derive some benefits from developing questionnaires and conducting a research project using a small and often unrepresentative sample of subjects, this type of analysis rarely produces results that are externally valid (discussed later in this chapter). Instead of conducting a small study that has limited (if any) value to other situations, these people can benefit from using data that have been previously collected. Researchers have more time to understand and analyze the data (Tukey, 1969). All too often researchers collect data that are quickly analyzed for publication or reported to management and never touched again. It is difficult to completely analyze all data from any research study in just one analysis; yet researchers in both the academic and private sectors are guilty of this practice.

Tukey (1969, p. 89) argues for data reanalysis, especially for graduate students, but his statement applies to all researchers:

There is merit in having a Ph.D. thesis encompass all the admitted steps of the research process. Once we recognize that research is a continuing, more or less cyclic process, however, we see that we can segment it in many places. Why should not at least a fair proportion of theses start with a careful analysis of previously collected and presumably already lightly analyzed data, a process usefully spread out over considerable time. Instant data analysis is—and will remain—an illusion.

Arguments for secondary analysis come from a variety of researchers (Glenn, 1972; Hyman, 1972; Tukey, 1969). It is clear that the research method provides excellent opportunities to produce valuable knowledge. The procedure, however, is not universally accepted.

Disadvantages of Secondary Analysis. Researchers who use secondary analysis are limited to the types of hypotheses or research questions that can be investigated. The data already exist, and since there is no way to go back for further information, researchers must keep their analyses within the boundaries of the type of data originally collected.

Researchers conducting secondary analysis may also be confronted with data that were poorly collected, inaccurate, fabricated, or flawed. Many studies do not include information about research design, sampling procedures, weighting of subjects' responses, or other peculiarities. Although individual researchers in mass media have made their data more readily available (Reid, Soley, & Wimmer, 1981; Wimmer & Reid, 1982), not all follow adequate scientific procedures. This may seriously affect a secondary analysis.

Although there are criticisms of using secondary analysis, it has rightfully become an acceptable research method, and detailed justifications for using it are no longer required. As the Nike ad campaign says, "Just do it."

DETERMINING TOPIC RELEVANCE

Once a basic research idea has been chosen or assigned, the next step is to ensure that the topic has merit. This step can be accomplished by answering eight basic questions.

QUESTION 1: IS THE TOPIC TOO BROAD?

Most research studies concentrate on one small area of a field; few researchers attempt to analyze an entire field in one study. There is a tendency, however, for researchers to choose topics that are too broad to cover in one study—for example, "the effects of television violence on children" or "the effects of mass media information on voters in a presidential election." To avoid this problem, researchers usually write down their proposed title as a visual starting point and attempt to dissect the topic into a series of questions.

QUESTION 2: CAN THE PROBLEM REALLY BE INVESTIGATED?

Aside from considerations of broadness, a topic might prove unsuitable for investigation simply because the question being asked has no answer or at least cannot be answered with the facilities and information available. For example, a researcher who wants to know how people who have no television receiver react to everyday interpersonal communication situations must consider the problem of finding subjects without at least one television set in the home. A few such subjects may exist in remote parts of the country, but the question is basically unanswerable due to the current saturation of television. Thus the researcher must attempt to reanalyze the original idea in conformity with practical considerations. A. S. Tan (1977) solved this particular dilemma by choosing to investigate what people do when their television sets are turned off for a period of time. He persuaded subjects not to watch television for one week and to record their use of other media, their interactions with their family and friends, and so on. (The authors have observed that subjects involved in these types

of media-deprivation studies usually cheat and use the medium before the end of the project.)

Another point to consider is whether all the terms of the proposed study are definable. Remember that all measured variables must be operationally defined (Chapter 3). A researcher who is interested in examining youngsters' use of the media must develop a working definition of the word *youngsters* to avoid confusion. Problems can be eliminated if an operational definition is stated: "Youngsters are children between the ages of 3 and 7 years."

One final consideration is to review available literature to determine whether the topic has been investigated. Were there any problems in previous studies? What methods were used to answer the research questions? What conclusions were drawn?

QUESTION 3: ARE THE DATA SUSCEPTIBLE TO ANALYSIS?

A topic does not lend itself to productive research if it requires collecting data that cannot be measured reliably and validly (Chapter 3). In other words, a researcher who wants to measure the effects of not watching television should consider whether the information about the subjects' behavior will be adequate and reliable, whether the subjects will answer truthfully, what value the data will have once gathered, and so forth. Researchers also need to have enough data to make the study worthwhile. It would be inadequate to analyze only 10 subjects in the "television turn-off" example, since the results could not be generalized to the entire population.

Another consideration is the researcher's previous experience with the statistical method selected to analyze the data—that is, does he or she really understand the proposed statistical analysis? Researchers need to know how the statistics work and how to interpret the results. All too often researchers design studies involving advanced statistical procedures they have never used. This tactic invariably creates errors in computation and interpretation. Research methods and statistics should not be selected because they happen to be popular or because a research director suggests a given method, but because they are appropriate for a given study and are understood by the person conducting the analysis. A common error made by beginning researchers—selecting a statistical method without understanding what the method produces—is called the *law of the instrument*. It is much wiser to use simple frequencies and percentages and understand the results than to try to use a high-level statistic and end up totally confused.

QUESTION 4: IS THE PROBLEM SIGNIFICANT?

Before a study is conducted, the researcher must determine its merit—that is, whether the results will have practical or theoretical value. The first question to ask is, Will the results add knowledge to information already available in the field? The goal of research is to help further the understanding of the problems and questions in the field of study; if a study does not do this, it has little value beyond the experience the researcher acquires from conducting it. This does not mean that all research has to be earth-shattering. Many researchers, however, waste valuable time trying to develop monumental projects when in fact the smaller problems are of more concern.

A second question is, What is the *real* purpose of the study? This question is important because it helps focus ideas. Is the study intended for a class paper, a thesis, a journal article, or a management decision? Each of these projects requires different amounts of background information, levels of explanation, and details about the results generated. For example, applied researchers need to consider whether any useful action based on the data will prove to be feasible, as well as whether the study will answer the question(s) posed by management.

QUESTION 5: CAN THE RESULTS OF THE STUDY BE GENERALIZED?

If a research project is to have practical value—to be significant beyond the immediate analysis—it must have **external validity**; that is, one must be able to generalize from it to other situations. For example, a study of the effects of a small-town public relations campaign might be appropriate if plans are made to analyze such effects in several small towns, or if it is a case study not intended for generalization; however, such an analysis has little external validity.

QUESTION 6: WHAT COSTS AND TIME ARE INVOLVED IN THE ANALYSIS?

In many cases the cost of a research study is the sole determinant of the feasibility of a project. A researcher may have an excellent idea, but if costs would be prohibitive the project is abandoned. A cost analysis must be completed very early on. It does not make sense to develop the specific designs and the data-gathering instrument for a project that will be canceled because of lack of funds. Sophisticated research is particularly expensive—the cost of one project can easily exceed $50,000.

A carefully itemized list of all materials, equipment, and other facilities required is necessary before beginning a research project. If the costs seem prohibitive, the researcher must determine whether the same goal can be achieved if costs are shaved in some areas. Another possibility to consider is financial aid from graduate schools, funding agencies, local governments, or other groups that subsidize research projects. In general, private sector researchers are not severely constrained by expenses; however, they must adhere to budget specifications set by management.

Time is also an important consideration in research planning. Research studies must be designed so that they can be completed in the amount of time available. Many studies fail because the researchers do not allot enough time for each research step, and in many cases the pressure of deadlines creates problems in producing reliable and valid results (for example, failure to provide alternatives if the correct sample of people cannot be located).

QUESTION 7: IS THE PLANNED APPROACH APPROPRIATE TO THE PROJECT?

The best research idea may be greatly, and often needlessly, hindered by a poorly planned method of approach. For example, a researcher might wish to measure any change in television viewing that may have accompanied an increase in time on the Internet. This researcher could mail questionnaires to a large number of people to determine how their television habits have changed during the past several months. However, the costs of printing and mailing questionnaires, plus follow-up letters and possibly phone calls to increase the response rate, might prove prohibitive.

Could the study be planned differently to eliminate some of the expense? Possibly, depending on its purpose and the types of questions planned. For example, the researcher could collect the data by telephone interviews to eliminate printing and postage costs. Although some questions might need reworking to fit the telephone procedure, the essential information could be collected. A close look at every study is required to plan the best approach. Every procedure in a research study should be considered from the standpoint of the parsimony principle, or Occam's razor. The principle, attributed to 14th-century philosopher William of Occam (also spelled Ockham), states that a person should not increase, beyond what is necessary, the number of entities required to explain anything, or make more assumptions than the minimum needed. Applying this to media research suggests that *the simplest research approach is always the most efficient.*

QUESTION 8: IS THERE ANY POTENTIAL HARM TO THE SUBJECTS?

Researchers must carefully analyze whether the project may cause physical or psychological harm to the subjects under evaluation—for example, will respondents be frightened in any way? Will they be required to answer embarrassing questions or perform embarrassing acts that may create adverse reactions? Is there a chance that the exposure to the research conditions will have lasting effects? Prior to the start of most public sector research projects involving human subjects, detailed statements explaining the exact procedures involved in the research are required to ensure that the subjects will not be injured in any way. These statements are intended to protect unsuspecting subjects from exposure to harmful research methods.

Underlying all eight steps in the research topic selection process is the necessity for validity (Chapter 3). In other words, are all the steps (from the initial idea to data analysis and interpretation) the correct ones to follow in trying to answer the question(s)?

So how should you respond if, after carefully selecting a research project and convincing yourself that it is something you want to do, someone confronts you with this reaction: "It's a good idea, but it can't be done; the topic is too broad, the problem cannot really be investigated, the data cannot be analyzed, the problem is not significant, the results cannot be generalized, it will cost too much, and the approach is wrong—two thumbs down!"? First, consider the criticisms carefully to make sure that you have not overlooked anything. If you are convinced you're on the right track and no harm will come to any subject or respondent, go ahead with the project. It is better to do the study and find nothing than to back off because of someone's criticism. (Almost every major inventor in the past 100 years has probably been the target of jokes and ridicule.)

REVIEWING THE LITERATURE

Researchers who conduct studies under the guidelines of scientific research *never* begin a research project without first consulting available literature to learn about what has been done, how it was done, and what results were generated. Experienced researchers consider the literature review to be one of the most important steps in the research process. It not only allows them to learn from (and eventually add to) previous research but also saves time, effort, and money. Failing to conduct a literature review is as detrimental to a project as failing to address any of the other steps in the research process.

Before any project is attempted, researchers should ask the following questions:

1. What type of research has been done in the area?
2. What has been found in previous studies?
3. What suggestions do other researchers make for further study?
4. What has not been investigated?
5. How can the proposed study add to our knowledge of the area?
6. What research methods were used in previous studies?

Answers to these questions will usually help define a specific hypothesis or research question.

STATING A HYPOTHESIS OR RESEARCH QUESTION

After a general research area has been identified and the existing literature reviewed, the researcher must state the problem as a workable **hypothesis** or **research question**. A hypothesis is a formal statement regarding the relationship between variables and is tested directly. The predicted relationship between the variables is either true or false. On the other hand, a research question is a formally stated question intended to provide indications about something, and it is not limited to investigating relationships between variables. Research questions are generally used when a researcher is unsure about the nature of the problem under investigation. Although the intent is merely to gather preliminary data, testable hypotheses are often developed from information gathered during the research question phase of a study.

For example, Singer and Singer (1981) provide an example of how a topic is narrowed, developed, and stated in simple terms. Interested in whether television material enhances or inhibits a child's capacity for symbolic behavior, Singer and Singer reviewed available literature and then narrowed their study to three basic research questions:

1. Does television content enrich a child's imaginative capacities by offering materials and ideas for make-believe play?
2. Does television lead to distortions of reality for children?
3. Can intervention and mediation by an adult while a child views a program, or immediately afterward, evoke changes in make-believe play or stimulate make-believe play?

The information collected from this type of study could provide data to create testable hypotheses. For example, Singer and Singer might have collected enough valuable information from their preliminary study to test the hypotheses suggested below:

1. The amount of time a child spends in make-believe play is directly related to the amount of time spent viewing make-believe play on television.
2. A child's level of distortion of reality is directly related to the amount and type of television program the child views.
3. Parental discussions with children about make-believe play before, during, and after

a child watches television programs involving make-believe play will increase the child's time involved in make-believe play.

The difference between the two sets of statements is that the research questions pose only general areas of investigation, whereas the hypotheses are testable statements about the relationship(s) between the variables. The only intent in the research question phase is to gather information to help the researchers define and test hypotheses in later projects.

RESEARCH SUPPLIERS AND FIELD SERVICES

Most media researchers do not conduct every phase of every project they supervise. Although they usually design research projects, determine the sample to be studied, and prepare the measurement instruments, researchers generally do not actually make telephone calls or interview respondents in on-site locations. Instead, the researchers contract with a **research supplier** or a **field service** to perform these tasks.

Research suppliers provide a variety of services. A full-service supplier participates in the design of a study, supervises data collection, tabulates the data, and analyzes the results. The company may work in any field (such as mass media, medical and hospital, or banking), or may specialize in only one type of research work. In addition, some companies can execute any type of research method—telephone surveys, one-on-one interviews, **shopping center interviews** (intercepts), or **focus groups**—while others may concentrate on only one method.

Field services usually specialize in conducting telephone interviews, mall intercepts, and one-on-one interviews; and in recruiting respondents for **group administration** (**central location testing**, or **CLT**) projects (Chapter 7)

and focus groups. The latter projects are called **prerecruits** (the company prerecruits respondents to attend a research session). Although some field services offer help in questionnaire design and data tabulation, most concentrate on telephone interviews, mall interviews, and prerecruiting.

Field services usually have focus group rooms available (with one-way mirrors to allow clients to view the session), and test kitchens for projects involving food and cooking. While some field service facilities are gorgeous and elaborate, others look as though the company just filed for bankruptcy protection. Many field services lease space (or lease the right to conduct research) in shopping malls to conduct intercepts. Some field services are actually based in shopping malls.

Hiring a research supplier or field service is a simple process. The researcher calls the company, explains the project, and is given a price quote. A contract or project confirmation letter is usually signed. In some cases, the price quote is a flat fee for the total project, or a fee plus or minus about 10% depending on the eventual difficulty of the project. Sometimes costs are based on the **cost per interview** (**CPI**), which will be discussed shortly.

Another term that plays an important role in the research process is **incidence**, which is used to describe how easily qualified respondents or subjects can be found for a research project. Incidence is expressed as a percentage of 100—the lower the incidence, the more difficult it is to find a qualified respondent or group of respondents. **Gross incidence** is the percentage of qualified respondents reached of *all* contacts made (such as telephone calls), and **net incidence** refers to the number of respondents or subjects who actually participate in a project.

For example, assume that a telephone research study requires 100 female respondents between the ages of 18 and 49 who listen to the radio for at least 1 hour per day. The estimated gross incidence is 10%. (Radio and television incidence figures can be estimated by using Arbitron and Nielsen ratings books; in many cases, however, an incidence is merely a guess on the part of the researcher.) A total of about 1,818 calls will have to be made to recruit the 100 females, not 1,000 calls as some people may think. The number of calls required is not computed as the target sample size (100 in this example) divided by incidence (.10), or 1,000. The number of calls computed for gross incidence (1,000) must then be divided by the **acceptance rate,** or the percentage of the target sample that agrees to participate in the study.

The total calls required is 1,000 divided by .55 (a *generally* used acceptance percentage), or 1,818. Of the 1,818 telephone calls made, 10% (182) will qualify for the interview, but only 55% of those (100) will actually agree to complete the interview (net incidence).

Field services and research suppliers base their charges on net incidence, not gross incidence. Many novice researchers fail to take this into account when they plan the financial budget for a project.

There is no "average" incidence rate in research. The actual rate depends on the complexity of the sample desired, the length of the research project, the time of year when the study is conducted, and a variety of other factors. The lower the incidence, the higher the cost for a research project. In addition, prices quoted by field services and research suppliers are based on an estimated incidence rate. Costs are adjusted after the project is completed and the actual incidence rate is known. As mentioned earlier, a quote from a field service is usually given with a plus or minus 10% "warning." Some people may think that understanding how a CPI is computed is unnecessary, but the concept is vitally important to any researcher who subcontracts work to a field service or research supplier.

Returning to the CPI discussion, let's assume that a researcher wants to conduct a 400-person telephone study with adults who are between the ages of 18 and 49. A representative of the company first asks for the researcher's estimated incidence and the length of the interview (in minutes). The two figures determine the CPI. Most field services and research suppliers use a chart to compute the CPI, such as the one shown in Table 2.1.

The table is easy to use. To find a CPI, first read across the top of the table for the length of the interview, then down the left-hand side for incidence. For example, the CPI for a 20-minute interview with an incidence of 10% is $30. A researcher conducting a 400-person telephone study with these "specs" will owe the field service or research supplier $12,000 (400 × $30) *plus* any costs for photocopying the questionnaire, mailing, and data tabulation (if requested). If the company analyzes the data and writes a final report, the total cost would be between $20,000 and $30,000.

Research projects involving prerecruits, such as focus groups and group administration, involve an additional cost—respondent co-op fees, or incentives. A telephone study respondent generally receives no payment for answering questions. However, when respondents are asked to leave their home to participate in a project, they are usually paid a co-op fee—normally between $25 and $100.

Costs escalate quickly in a prerecruit project. For example, assume that a researcher wants to conduct a group session with 400 respondents instead of using a telephone approach. Instead of paying a field service or a research supplier a CPI for a telephone interview, the payment is for recruiting respondents to attend a project conducted at a specific location. Although most companies have separate rate cards for prerecruiting (they are usually a bit higher than the card used for telephone interviewing), assume that the costs are the same. Recruiting costs, then, are $12,000 (400 × $30 CPI), with another $10,000 (minimum) for respondent co-op (400 × $25). Total costs so far are $22,000, about twice as much as a telephone study. Moreover, other costs must be added to this figure: a rental fee

TABLE 2.1   CPI Chart

Incidence	Minutes					
	5	10	15	20	25	30
5	44.25	45.50	46.50	47.75	49.00	50.00
6	38.00	39.25	40.50	41.75	42.75	44.00
7	34.00	35.00	36.25	37.50	38.50	39.75
8	30.75	32.00	33.00	34.25	35.50	36.50
9	28.50	29.50	30.75	32.00	33.00	34.25
10	26.50	27.75	29.00	30.00	31.25	32.50
20	14.25	15.50	16.75	17.75	19.00	20.25
30	10.25	11.50	12.50	13.75	15.00	16.25
40	8.25	9.50	10.50	11.75	13.00	14.25
50	7.00	8.25	9.50	10.50	11.75	13.00
60	6.50	7.75	9.00	10.00	11.25	12.50
70	6.00	7.25	8.50	9.50	10.75	11.75
80	5.75	7.00	8.00	9.25	10.50	11.50
90	5.50	6.75	8.00	9.00	10.25	11.00
100	5.00	6.50	7.75	9.00	10.00	10.50

for the room where the study will be conducted, refreshments for respondents, fees for assistants to check in respondents, and travel expenses (another $1,000–$4,000).

In addition, to ensure that 400 people show up (4 sessions of 100 each), it is necessary to overrecruit since not every respondent will "show." In prerecruit projects, field services and research suppliers overrecruit 25% to 100%. In other words, for a 400 "show rate," a company must prerecruit between 500 and 800 people. However, rarely does a prerecruit session hit the target sample size exactly. In many cases, the show rate falls short and a "make-good" session is required. (When this occurs, the project is repeated at a later date with another group of respondents to meet the target sample size.) In some cases, more respondents than required show for the study, which means that projected research costs may skyrocket.

In most prerecruit projects, field services and research suppliers are paid on a "show basis" only. That is, they receive payment only for respondents who show, not for the number who are recruited. If the companies were paid on a recruiting basis, they could recruit thousands of respondents for each project. The show-basis payment procedure also adds incentive for the companies to ensure that those who are recruited actually show up for the research session.

Although various problems with hiring and working with research suppliers and field services are discussed in Chapter 7, two important points are introduced here to help novice researchers when they begin to use these support companies.

1. *All suppliers and field services are not equal.* Regardless of qualifications, any person or group can form a research supply company

or field service. There are no formal requirements, no tests to take, and no national, state, or regional licenses to acquire. All that's required are a "shingle on the door," advertising in marketing and research trade publications, and (optional) membership in one or more of the *voluntary* research organizations. Thus it is the sole responsibility of researchers to determine which of the hundreds of suppliers available are capable of conducting a professional, scientifically based research project. Over time, experienced researchers develop a list of qualified companies that are professional and trustworthy. This list is developed from experience with a company or from the recommendations of other researchers. In any event, it is important to check the credentials of a research supplier or field service. The senior author has encountered several instances of research supplier and field service fraud during the past 20+ years in the industry.

2. *The researcher must maintain close supervision over the project.* This is true even with the very good companies, not because their professionalism cannot be trusted, but rather, to be sure that the project is answering the questions that were posed. Because of security considerations, a research supplier may never completely understand why a particular project is being conducted, and the researcher needs to be sure that the project will provide the exact information required.

DATA ANALYSIS AND INTERPRETATION

The time and effort required for data analysis and interpretation depend on the study's purpose and the methodology used. Analysis and interpretation may take from several days to several months. In many private sector research studies involving only a single question, however, data analysis and interpretation may be completed in a few minutes. For example, a radio station may be interested in finding out its listeners' perceptions of the morning show team. After a survey is conducted, that question may be answered by summarizing only one or two items on the questionnaire. The summary then may determine whether the morning show team "stays" or "goes."

Every analysis should be carefully planned and performed according to specific guidelines. Once the computations have been completed, the researcher must "step back" and consider what has been discovered. The results must be analyzed with reference to their external validity and the likelihood of their accuracy. Here, for example, is an excerpt from the conclusion drawn by Singer and Singer (1981, p. 385):

> Television by its very nature is a medium that emphasizes those very elements that are generally found in imagination: visual fluidity, time and space flexibility and make-believe. . . . Very little effort has emerged from producers or educators to develop age-specific programming. . . . It is evident that more research for the development of programming and adult mediation is urgently needed.

Researchers must determine through analysis whether their work is valid internally and externally. This chapter has touched briefly on the concept of external validity—an externally valid study is one whose results can be generalized to the population. To assess **internal validity**, on the other hand, one asks, Does the study really investigate the proposed research question?

INTERNAL VALIDITY

Control over research conditions is necessary to enable researchers to rule out plausible but incorrect explanations of results. If, for example, a researcher is interested in verifying that "y is a function of x," or $y = f(x)$, control over the research conditions is necessary to eliminate the possibility of finding that $y = f(b)$, where b is an extraneous variable. Any such variable that creates a plausible but incorrect explanation of results is called an **artifact** (also referred to as an extraneous, or confounding, variable). The presence of an artifact indicates a lack of internal validity—that is, the study has failed to investigate its hypothesis.

Suppose, for example, that researchers discover through a study that children who view television for extended lengths of time have lower grade point averages in school than children who watch only a limited amount of television. Could an artifact have created this finding? It may be that children who view fewer hours of television also receive parental help with their school work; parental help (the artifact), not hours of television viewed, may be the reason for the difference in grade point averages between the two groups.

Artifacts in research may arise from several sources. Those most frequently encountered are described below. Researchers should be familiar with these sources to achieve internal validity in the experiments they conduct (Campbell & Stanley, 1963; Cook & Campbell, 1979).

1. *History.* Various events occurring during a study may affect the subjects' attitudes, opinions, and behavior. For example, to analyze an oil company's public relations campaign for a new product, researchers first *pretest* subjects concerning their attitudes toward the company. The subjects are next exposed to an experimental promotional campaign (the *experimental treatment*); then a *posttest* is administered to determine whether changes in attitude occurred as a result of the campaign. Suppose the results indicate that the public relations campaign was a complete failure—that the subjects displayed a very poor perception of the oil company in the posttest. Before the results are reported, the researchers must determine whether an intervening variable could have caused the poor perception. An investigation discloses that during the period between tests, subjects learned from a television news story that a tanker owned by the oil company just spilled millions of gallons of crude oil in the North Atlantic. News of the oil spill—not the public relations campaign—may have acted as an artifact that created the poor perception. The longer the time between a pretest and a posttest, the greater the possibility that history might confound the study.

The effects of history in a study can be devastating, as was shown during the late 1970s and early 1980s, when several broadcast companies and other private businesses perceived a need to develop Subscription Television (STV) in various markets throughout the country where cable television penetration was thought to be very low. An STV service allows a household, using a special antenna, to receive pay television services similar to Home Box Office or Showtime. Several cities became prime targets for STV because both Arbitron and Nielsen reported very low cable penetration. Several companies conducted research in these cities, and results supported the Arbitron and Nielsen data. In addition, the research found that people who did not have access to cable television were very receptive to the idea of STV. However, it was discovered later that even as some studies were being conducted, cable companies in the target areas were expanding very rapidly and had wired many previously non-wired neighborhoods. What were once prime targets for STV soon became accessible to cable television. The major problem was that researchers attempting to determine the feasibility of STV failed to consider the historical changes (wiring of the cities) that could affect the results of their research. The result was that many companies lost millions of dollars and STV soon faded away.

2. *Maturation.* Subjects' biological and psychological characteristics change during the course of a study. Growing hungry or tired or becoming older may influence the manner in which subjects respond to a research study. An example of how maturation can affect a research project was seen in the early 1980s,

when radio stations around the country began to test their music playlist in auditorium sessions (Chapter 14). Some unskilled research companies tested as many as 600 songs in one session and wondered why the songs after about the 400th one tested dramatically different from the others. Without a great deal of investigation, researchers discovered that the respondents were physically and emotionally drained once they reached 400 songs (about 70 minutes of testing time), and they merely wrote down any number just to complete the project. (The presentation of too many songs in an auditorium music test continues to be a problem in the mid-1990s.)

3. *Testing.* Testing in itself may be an artifact, particularly when subjects are given similar pretests and posttests. A pretest may sensitize subjects to the material and improve their posttest scores regardless of the type of experimental treatment given to them. This is especially true when the same test is used for both situations. Subjects learn how to answer questions and to anticipate researchers' demands. To guard against the effects of testing, different pretests and posttests are required. Or, instead of being given a pretest, subjects can be tested for similarity (homogeneity) by means of a variable or set of variables that differs from the experimental variable. The pretest is not the only way to establish a *point of prior equivalency* (the point at which the groups were equal before the experiment) between groups—this also can be done through sampling (randomization and matching). For further discussion on control of confounding variables within the context of an experiment, see Chapter 5.

4. *Instrumentation.* Also known as **instrument decay,** this term refers to the deterioration of research instruments or methods over the course of a study. Equipment may wear out, observers may become more casual in recording their observations, and interviewers who memorize frequently asked questions may fail to present them in the proper order. Some college entrance tests, such as the SAT

and ACT, are targets of debate by many researchers and/or statisticians. The complaints mainly address the concern that the current tests do not adequately measure knowledge of *today,* but rather what was *once* considered necessary and important.

5. *Statistical regression.* Subjects who achieve either very high or very low scores on a test tend to regress to the sample or population mean during subsequent testing sessions. Often *outliers* (subjects whose pretest scores are far from the mean) are selected for further testing or evaluation. Suppose, for example, that researchers develop a series of television programs designed to teach simple mathematical concepts, and they select only subjects who score very low on a mathematical aptitude pretest. An experimental treatment is designed to expose these subjects to the new television series, and a posttest is given to determine whether the programs increased the subjects' knowledge of simple math concepts. The experimental study may show that indeed, after only one or two exposures to the new programs, math scores increased. But the higher scores on the posttest may not be due to the television programs; they may be a function of statistical regression. That is, regardless of whether the subjects viewed the programs, the scores in the sample may have increased merely because of statistical regression to the mean. The programs should be tested with a variety of subjects, not just those who score low on a pretest. (The significance of regression toward the mean is relevant to a variety of areas such as stock market prices and standings of professional sports teams.)

6. *Experimental mortality.* All research studies face the possibility that subjects will drop out for one reason or another. Especially in long-term studies, subjects may refuse to continue with the project, become ill, move away, drop out of school, or quit work. This **mortality,** or loss of subjects, is sure to have an effect on the results of a study, since most research methods and statistical analyses make

assumptions about the number of subjects used. It is always better, as mentioned in Chapter 4, to select more subjects than are actually required—within the budget limits of the study. It is not uncommon to lose 50% or more of the subjects from one testing period to another (Wimmer, 1995)

7. *Sample selection.* Most research designs compare two or more groups of subjects to determine whether differences exist on the dependent measurement. These groups must be randomly selected and tested for homogeneity to ensure that results are not due to the type of sample used (Chapter 5).

8. *Demand characteristics.* The term *demand characteristics* is used to describe subjects' reactions to experimental conditions. Orne (1969) suggested that, under some circumstances, subjects' awareness of the experimental purpose may be the sole determinant of how they behave; that is, subjects who recognize the purpose of a study may produce only "good" data for researchers.

Novice researchers quickly learn about the many variations of demand characteristics. For example, research studies seeking to find out about respondents' listening and viewing habits always find subjects who report high levels of PBS listening and viewing. However, when the same subjects are asked to name their favorite PBS programs, many cannot recall a single one. (In other words, the respondents are not telling the truth.)

Cross-validating questions are often necessary to verify subjects' responses; by giving subjects the opportunity to answer the same question phrased in different ways, the researcher can spot discrepant, potentially error-producing responses. In addition, researchers can help control demand characteristics by disguising the real purpose of the study; however, researchers should use caution when employing this technique (Chapter 18).

In addition, most respondents who participate in research projects are eager to provide the information the researcher requests. They are flattered to be asked for their opinions. Unfortunately, this means that they will answer any type of question, even if the question is totally ambiguous, misleading, vague, or absolutely uninterpretable. For example, this book's senior author conducted a telephone study in the early 1990s with respondents in area code 717 of Pennsylvania. An interviewer mistakenly called area code 714 (Orange County, California). For nearly 20 minutes, the respondent in California answered questions about radio stations with *W* call letters—stations impossible for her to pick up on any radio. The problem was discovered during questionnaire validation.

9. *Experimenter bias.* Rosenthal (1969) discussed a variety of ways in which a researcher may influence the results of a study. Bias can enter through mistakes made in observation, data recording, mathematical computations, and interpretation. Whether experimenter errors are intentional or unintentional, they usually support the researcher's hypothesis and are considered to be biased (Walizer & Wienir, 1978).

Experimenter bias can also enter into any phase of a research project if the researcher becomes swayed by a client's wishes for a project's end results. Such a situation can cause significant problems for researchers if they do not remain totally objective throughout the entire project, especially when they are hired by individuals or companies to "prove a point" or to provide "supporting information" for a decision (this is usually unknown to the researcher). For example, the news director at a local television station may dislike a particular news anchor and want information to justify the dislike (in order to fire the anchor). A researcher is hired under the guise of finding out whether the audience likes or dislikes the anchor. In this case, it is easy for the news director to intentionally or unintentionally sway the results just through conversations with the researcher in the planning stages of the study. It is possible for a researcher, either intentionally or unintentionally, to interpret the results in order to support the program director's desire to eliminate the anchor. The researcher may, for instance, have like/dislike numbers that are very close, but may give the "edge" to dislike because of the news director's influence.

Experimenter bias is a potential problem in all phases of research, and those conducting the study must be aware of problems caused by outside influences. Several procedures can help to reduce experimenter bias. For example, individuals who provide instructions to subjects and make observations should not be informed of the purpose of the study; experimenters and others involved in the research should not know whether subjects belong to the experimental group or the **control group** (called a **double-blind experiment**); and automated devices such as tape recorders should be used whenever possible to provide uniform instructions to subjects. (See Chapter 9 for more information about control groups.)

Researchers can also ask clients not to discuss the intent of a research project beyond what type of information is desired. In the example above, the program director should say only that information is desired about the like/dislike of the program and should not discuss what decisions will be made following the research. In cases where researchers *must* be told about the purpose of the project, or where the researcher is conducting the study independently, experimenter bias must be repressed at every phase.

10. *Evaluation apprehension.* Rosenberg's (1965) concept of **evaluation apprehension** is similar to demand characteristics, but it emphasizes that subjects are essentially *afraid* of being measured or tested. They are interested in receiving only positive evaluations from the researcher and from the other subjects involved in the study. Most people are hesitant to exhibit behavior that differs from the norm and will tend to follow the group, though they may totally disagree with the others. The researcher's task is to try to eliminate this passiveness by letting subjects know that their individual responses are important.

11. *Causal time order.* The organization of an experiment may create problems with data collection and/or interpretation. It may be that an experiment's results are not due to the stimulus (independent) variable, but rather to the effect of the dependent variable. For example, respondents in an experiment that is attempting to determine how magazine advertising layouts influence their purchasing behavior may change their opinions when they read or complete a questionnaire after viewing several ads.

12. *Diffusion or imitation of treatments.* In situations where respondents participate at different times during one day or over several days, or where groups of respondents are studied one after another, respondents may have the opportunity to discuss the project with someone else and contaminate the research project. This is a special problem with focus groups when one group leaves the focus room while a new group enters.

13. *Compensation.* Sometimes individuals who work with a control group (the one that receives no experimental treatment) may unknowingly treat the group differently since the group was "deprived" of something. In this case, the control group is no longer legitimate.

14. *Compensatory rivalry.* In some situations, subjects who know they are in a control group may work harder or perform differently to out-perform the experimental group.

15. *Demoralization.* Control group subjects may literally lose interest in a project because they are not experimental subjects. These people may give up or fail to perform normally because they may feel demoralized or angry that they are not in the experimental group.

The sources of internal invalidity are complex and may arise in all phases of research.

For this reason, it is easy to see why the results from a single study cannot be used to refute or support a theory or hypothesis. In attempting to control these artifacts, researchers use a variety of experimental designs and try to keep strict control over the research process so that subjects and researchers do not intentionally or unintentionally influence the results. As Hyman (1954) recognized:

> All scientific inquiry is subject to error, and it is far better to be aware of this, to study the sources in an attempt to reduce it, and to estimate the magnitude of such errors in our findings, than to be ignorant of the errors concealed in our data.

EXTERNAL VALADITY

External validity refers to how well the results of a study can be generalized across populations, settings, and time (Cook & Campbell, 1979). The external validity of a study can be severely affected by the interaction in an analysis of variables such as subject selection, instrumentation, and experimental conditions (Campbell & Stanley, 1963). A study that lacks external validity cannot be projected to other situations. The study is valid only for the sample tested.

Most procedures used to guard against external invalidity relate to sample selection. Cook and Campbell (1979) describe three considerations:

1. Use random samples.
2. Use heterogeneous samples and replicate the study several times.
3. Select a sample that is representative of the group to which the results will be generalized.

Using random samples rather than convenience or available samples allows researchers to gather information from a variety of subjects rather than from those who may share similar attitudes, opinions, and lifestyles. As discussed in Chapter 4, a random sample means that everyone (within the guidelines of the project) has an equal chance of being selected for the research study.

Several replicated research projects using samples with a variety of characteristics (heterogeneous) allow researchers to test hypotheses and research questions and not worry that the results will relate to only one type of subject.

Selecting a sample that is representative of the group to which the results will be generalized is basic common sense. For example, the results from a study of a group of high school students cannot be generalized to a group of college students.

A fourth way to increase external validity is to conduct research over a long period of time. Mass media research is often designed as short-term projects that expose subjects to an experimental treatment and then immediately test or measure them. However, in many cases, the immediate effects of a treatment are negligible. In advertising, for example, research studies designed to measure brand awareness are generally based on only one exposure to a commercial or advertisement. It is well known that persuasion and attitude change rarely take place after only one exposure; they require multiple exposures over time. Logically, then, such measurements should be made over a period of weeks or months to take into account the "sleeper" effect: that attitude change may be minimal or nonexistent in the short run and still prove significant in the long run.

PRESENTING RESULTS

The format used to present results depends on the purpose of the study. Research intended for publication in academic journals follows a format prescribed by each journal; research conducted for management in the private sector tends to be reported in simpler terms, often excluding detailed explanations of sampling, methodology, and review of literature. However, all presentations of results must be written in a clear and concise manner appropriate to both the research question and the individuals who will read the report. A more detailed discussion of reporting is included in Chapter 18.

REPLICATION

One important point mentioned throughout this book is that the results of any single study are, by themselves, only *indications* of what might exist. A study provides information that says, in effect, "This is what may be the case." To be relatively certain of the results of any study, the research must be replicated. Too often, researchers conduct one study and report the results as if they are providing the basis for a theory or a law. The information presented in this chapter, and in other chapters that deal with internal and external validity, argues that this cannot be true.

A research question or hypothesis must be investigated from many different perspectives before any significance can be attributed to the results of one study. Research methods and designs must be altered to eliminate design-specific results—that is, results that are based on, hence specific to, the design used. Similarly, subjects with a variety of characteristics should be studied from many angles to eliminate sample-specific results; and statistical analyses need to be varied to eliminate method-specific results. In other words, every effort must be made to ensure that the results of any single study are not created by or dependent on a methodological factor; studies must be replicated.

Researchers overwhelmingly advocate the use of replication to establish scientific fact. Lykken (1968) and Kelly, Chase, and Tucker (1979) have identified four basic types of replication that can be used to help validate a scientific test:

- **Literal replication** involves the exact duplication of a previous analysis, including the sampling procedures, experimental conditions, measuring techniques, and methods of data analysis.
- **Operational replication** attempts to duplicate only the sampling and experimental procedures of a previous analysis, to test whether the procedures will produce similar results.
- **Instrumental replication** attempts to duplicate the dependent measures used in a previous study and to vary the experimental conditions of the original study.
- **Constructive replication** tests the validity of methods used previously by deliberately not imitating the earlier study; both the manipulations and the measures used differ from those used in the first study. The researcher simply begins with a statement of empirical "fact" uncovered in a previous study and attempts to find the same "fact."

Despite the obvious need to conduct research replications, mass media researchers generally ignore this important step, probably because many feel that replications are not as glamorous or important as original research. The wise researcher will recognize that, while replications may lack glamour, they most certainly do not lack importance.

SUPPLEMENT ON INCIDENCE RATES AND CPI

Incidence rate is an important concept in research because it determines both the difficulty and the cost of a research project. Table 2.1 (on page 28) illustrates a standard CPI rate chart. The specific rates shown on the chart are computed through a complicated series of steps. Without going into exact detail, this supplement explains the general procedure of how each CPI is computed.

TABLE 2.2   Determining a CPI

Step		Explanation
1. Gross incidence	1,000	100 ÷ .10
2. Acceptance rate	55%	Standard figure used. Use acceptance rate to determine how many calls are needed.
3. Actual contacts necessary	1,818	1,000 ÷ .55
4. Minutes per contact	4	Number of minutes to find correct respondent (bad numbers, busy lines, etc.)
5. Total contact minutes	7,272	4 × 1,818
6. Productive minutes per hour	40	Average number of minutes interviewers usually work in 1 hour (net of breaks, etc.)
7. Total contact hours	182	7,272 ÷ 40
8. Total interview hours	33	100 × 20 minutes
9. Total hours	215	Contact hours + interview hours
10. Hourly rate	$15	Industry standard
11. Total cost	$3,225	215 × $15
12. CPI	$32.25	$3,225 ÷ 100 interviews

As mentioned earlier, CPI is based on incidence and interview length. In prerecruiting, only incidence is considered, but CPIs are basically the same as those for telephone interviews. To determine a CPI, let us assume we wish to conduct a 100-person telephone study, with an incidence of 10% and an interview length of 20 minutes. The computation and an explanation of each step is shown in Table 2.2. As shown in the table, 1,818 contacts must be made. Of these, 10% will qualify for the interview (182) and 55% of these will accept (100). The total number of hours required to conduct the 100-person survey is 215, with a CPI of $32.25.

SUMMARY

This chapter has described the processes involved in identifying and developing a topic for research investigation. It was suggested that researchers consider several sources for potential ideas, including a critical analysis of everyday situations. The steps in developing a topic for investigation naturally become easier with experience; the beginning researcher needs to pay particular attention to material already available. He or she should not attempt to tackle broad research questions, but should try to isolate a smaller, more practical subtopic for study. The researcher should develop an appropriate method of analysis and then proceed, through data analysis and interpretation, to a clear and concise presentation of results.

The chapter stresses that the results of a single survey or other research approach provide only indications of what may or may not exist. Before the researcher can claim support for a research question or hypothesis, the study must be replicated a number of times to eliminate dependence on extraneous factors.

While conducting research studies, the investigator must be constantly aware of potential sources of error that may create spurious results. Phenomena that affect an experiment in this way are sources of breakdowns in internal validity. Only if differing and rival hypotheses are ruled out can researchers validly say that the treatment was influential in creating differences between the experimental group and the control group. A good explanation of research results rules out intervening variables; every plausible alternative explanation should be considered. However, even when this is accomplished, the results of one study can be considered only as indications of what may or may not exist. Support for a theory or hypothesis can be made only after the completion of several studies that produce similar results.

In addition, if a study is to be helpful in understanding mass media, its results must be generalizable to subjects and groups other than those involved in the experiment. External validity can be best achieved through random sampling (Chapter 4).

QUESTIONS AND PROBLEMS FOR FURTHER IINVESTIGATION

1. The focus of this chapter is on developing a research topic by defining a major problem area and narrowing the topic to a manageable study. Develop two different research projects in an area of mass media research. Use either an outline format or a flowchart format.

2. Replication has long been a topic of debate in scientific research, but until recently mass media researchers have not paid much attention to it. Read the articles by Reid, Soley, and Wimmer (1981) and Wimmer and Reid (1982). Explain in your own words why replication has not been a major factor in mass media research. What could be done to correct the current situation in replication?

3. An analysis of the effects of television viewing revealed that the fewer hours of television students watched per week, the higher were their scores in school. What alternative explanations or artifacts might explain such differences? How could these variables be controlled?

4. The fact that some respondents will answer any type of question, whether it is a legitimate question or not, may surprise some novice researchers until they encounter it firsthand. Try posing the following question to a friend in another class or at a party: What effects do you think the sinking of Greenland into the Labrador Sea will have on the country's fishing industry?

REFERENCES AND SUGGESTED READINGS

Achenback, J. (1991). *Why things are*. New York: Ballantine Books.

Agostino, D. (1980). Cable television's impact on the audience of public television. *Journal of Broadcasting, 24*(3), 347–366.

Anderson, J. A. (1987). *Communication research: Issues and methods*. New York: McGraw-Hill.

Babbie, E. R. (1994). *The practice of social research* (5th ed.). Belmont, CA: Wadsworth.

Becker, L. B. (1981). Secondary analysis. In G. H. Stempel & B. H. Westley (Eds.), *Research methods in mass communications*. Englewood Cliffs, NJ: Prentice-Hall.

Becker, L. B., Beam, R., & Russial, J. (1978). Correlates of daily newspaper performance in New England. *Journalism Quarterly, 55*(1), 100–108.

Berliner, B. (1990). *The book of answers*. New York: Prentice Hall Press.

Burman, T. (1975). *The dictionary of misinformation*. New York: Thomas Crowell.

Campbell, D. T., & Stanley, J. C. (1963). *Experimental and quasi-experimental designs for research*. Skokie, IL: Rand McNally.

Cohen, J. (1965). Some statistical issues in psychological research. In B. B. Wolman (Ed.), *Handbook of clinical psychology*. New York: McGraw-Hill.

Comstock, G., Chaffee, S., Katzman, N., McCombs, M., & Roberts, D. (1978). *Television and human behavior*. New York: Columbia University Press.

Cook, T. D., & Campbell, D. T. (1979). *Quasi-experimentation: Designs and analysis for field studies*. Skokie, IL: Rand McNally.

Feldman, D. (1990). *Why do dogs have wet noses?* New York: HarperCollins Publishers.

Glenn, N. (1972). Archival data on political attitudes: Opportunities and pitfalls. In D. Nimmo & C. Bonjean (Eds.), *Political attitudes and public opinion*. New York: David McKay.

Graedon, J., and Graedon, T. (1991). *Graedons' best medicine*. New York: Bantam Books.

Gribben, J., & Rees, M. (1989). *Cosmic coincidences: Dark matter, mankind, and anthropic cosmology*. New York: Bantam Books.

Haskins, J. B. (1968). *How to evaluate mass communication*. New York: Advertising Research Foundation.

Hirsch, E. D., Kett, J. F., & Trefil, J. (1988). *Dictionary of cultural literacy: What every American needs to know*. New York: Houghton Mifflin.

Hyman, H. H. (1954). *Interviewing in social research*. Chicago: University of Chicago Press.

Hyman, H. H. (1972). *Secondary analysis of sample surveys*. New York: John Wiley.

Kelly, C. W., Chase, L. J., & Tucker, R. K. (1979). Replication in experimental communication research: An analysis. *Human Communication Research, 5,* 338–342.

Kraus, S., & Davis, D. (1967). *The effects of mass communication on political behavior*. University Park: Pennsylvania State University Press.

Lykken, D. T. (1968). Statistical significance in psychological research. *Psychological Bulletin, 21,* 151–159.

Orne, M. T. (1969). Demand characteristics and the concept of quasi-controls. In R. Rosenthal & R. L. Rosnow (Eds.), *Artifact in behavioral research*. New York: Academic Press.

Poundstone, W. (1986). *Bigger secrets*. New York: Houghton Mifflin.

Reid, L. N., Soley, L. C., & Wimmer, R. D. (1981). *Replication in advertising research: 1977, 1978, 1979. Journal of Advertising, 10,* 3–13.

Rensberger, B. (1986). *How the world works*. New York: Quill.

Rosenberg, M. J. (1965). When dissonance fails: On eliminating evaluation apprehension from attitude measurement. *Journal of Personality and Social Psychology, 1,* 28–42.

Rosenthal, R. (1969). *Experimenter effects in behavioral research*. New York: Appleton-Century-Crofts.

Rubin, R. B., Rubin, A. M., & Piele, L. J. (1985). *Communication research: Strategies and sources*. Belmont, CA: Wadsworth.

Singer, D. G., & Singer, J. L. (1981). Television and the developing imagination of the child. *Journal of Broadcasting, 25,* 373–387.

Sutton, C. (1984). *How did they do that?* New York: Quill.

Tan, A. S. (1977). Why TV is missed: A functional analysis. *Journal of Broadcasting, 21,* 371–380.

True, J. A. (1989). *Finding out: Conducting and evaluating social research* (2nd ed.). Belmont, CA: Wadsworth.

Tukey, J. W. (1969). Analyzing data: Sanctification or detective work? *American Psychologist, 24,* 83–91.

Tuleja, T. (1982). *Fabulous fallacies: More than 300 popular beliefs that are not true*. New York: Harmony Books.

Walizer, M. H., & Wienir, P. L. (1978). *Research methods and analysis: Searching for relationships*. New York: Harper & Row.

Wimmer, R. D. (1995). *Los Angeles Radio Listening: A Panel Study*. The Eagle Group.

Wimmer, R. D., & Reid, L. N. (1982). Willingness of communication researchers to respond to replication requests. *Journalism Quarterly, 59,* 317–319.

Whitcomb, J., and Whitcomb, C. (1987). *Oh say can you see: Unexpected anecdotes about American history*. New York: Quill.

Chapter

3

ELEMENTS OF RESEARCH

Chapters 1 and 2 presented a brief overview of the research process. In this chapter, four basic elements of this process are defined and discussed: concepts and constructs, measurement, variables, and scales. A clear understanding of these elements is essential to conducting precise and meaningful research.

CONCEPTS AND CONSTRUCTS

A **concept** is a term that expresses an abstract idea formed by generalizing from particulars and summarizing related observations. For example, a researcher might observe that a public speaker becomes restless, starts to perspire, and continually fidgets with a pencil just before giving an address. The researcher might summarize these observed patterns of behavior and label them "speech anxiety." On a more prosaic level, the word *table* is a concept that represents a wide variety of observable objects, ranging from a plank supported by concrete blocks to a piece of furniture commonly found in dining rooms. Typical concepts in mass media research include terms such as *message length, media usage,* and *readability.*

Concepts are important for at least two reasons. First, they simplify the research process by combining particular characteristics, objects, or people into more general categories. For example, a researcher may study families that own personal computers, modems, VCRs, CD players, cellular phones, and DAT players. To make it easier to describe these families, the researcher calls them "Taffies" and categorizes them under the concept of "technologically ad-

vanced families." Now, instead of describing each of the characteristics that make these families unique, the researcher has a general term that is more inclusive and convenient to use.

Second, concepts facilitate communication among those who have a shared understanding of them. Researchers use concepts to organize their observations into meaningful summaries and to transmit this information to their colleagues. Researchers who use the concept of "agenda setting" to describe a complicated set of audience and media activities find that their colleagues understand what is being discussed. Note that individuals must share an understanding of a concept if it is to be useful. For example, when teenagers use 'he word *dweeb* to describe some of their acquaintances, most of their peers understand perfectly what is meant by the concept (although many adults may not).

A **construct** is a concept that has three distinct characteristics. First, it is an abstract notion that is usually broken down into dimensions represented by lower-level concepts. In other words, a construct is a combination of concepts. Second, because of its abstraction, a construct usually cannot be directly observed. Third, a construct is usually designed for some particular research purpose so that its exact meaning relates only to the context in which it is found. For example, the construct "involvement" has been used in many advertising studies (Pokrywczynski, 1986). It is a construct that is difficult to see directly, and it includes the concepts of attention, interest, and arousal. Researchers can only observe its likely or presumed manifestations. In some contexts, involvement means product involvement; in others it refers to involvement with the message or even with the medium. Its precise meaning depends on the research context.

To take another example, in mass communication research, the term *authoritarianism* represents a construct defined to describe a certain type of personality; it comprises nine different concepts, including conventionalism, submission, superstition, and cynicism. Authoritarianism itself cannot be seen; its presence must be determined by some type of questionnaire or standardized test. The results of such tests indicate what authoritarianism might be and whether it is present under given conditions, but the tests do not provide exact definitions for the construct itself.

The empirical counterpart of a construct or concept is called a **variable**. Variables are important because they link the empirical world with the theoretical; they are the phenomena and events that can be measured or manipulated in research. Variables can have more than one value along a continuum. For example, the variable "satisfaction with cable TV programs" can take on different values—a person can be satisfied a lot, a little, or not at all—reflecting in the empirical world what the concept "satisfaction with cable TV programs" represents in the theoretical world.

Researchers attempt to test a number of associated variables to develop an underlying meaning or relationship among them. After suitable analysis, the most important variables are retained and the others are discarded. These important variables are labeled **marker variables** since they seem to define or highlight the construct under study. After further analysis, new marker variables may be added to increase understanding of the construct and to permit more reliable predictions.

Concepts and constructs are valuable tools in theoretical research. But, as noted in Chapter 1, researchers also function at the observational, or empirical, level. To understand how this is done, it is necessary to examine variables and to know how they are measured.

INDEPENDENT AND DEPENDENT VARIABLES

Variables are classified in terms of their relationship with one another. It is customary to talk about **independent** and **dependent variables**: Independent variables are systematically varied by the researcher, and dependent variables are observed and their values presumed to depend on the effects of the independent variables. In other words, the dependent variable is what the researcher wishes to explain. For example, assume that an investigator is interested in determining how the angle of a camera shot affects an audience's perception of the credibility of a television newscaster. Three versions of a newscast are videotaped: one shot from a very low angle, another from a high angle, and a third from eye level. Groups of subjects are randomly assigned to view one of the three versions and to complete a questionnaire that measures the newscaster's credibility. In this experiment, the camera angle is the independent variable. Its values are systematically varied by the experimenter, who selects only three of the camera angles possible. The dependent variable to be measured is the perceived credibility of the newscaster. If the researcher's assumption is correct, the newscaster's credibility will vary according to the camera angle. (Note that the values of the dependent variable are not manipulated; they are simply observed or measured.)

Keep in mind that the distinction between types of variables depends on the purposes of the research. An independent variable in one study may be a dependent variable in another. Also, a research task may involve examining the relationship of more than one independent variable to a single dependent variable. For example, the researcher in the previous example could investigate the effects not only of camera angles but also of closing styles on the newscaster's credibility (as perceived by the viewers). Moreover, in many instances multiple dependent variables are measured in a single study. This type of study, called a *multivariate analysis*, is discussed in Appendix 2.

OTHER TYPES OF VARIABLES

In nonexperimental research, where there is no active manipulation of variables, different terms are sometimes substituted for independent and dependent variables. The variable that is used for predictions or is assumed to be causal (analogous to the independent variable) is sometimes called the predictor, or **antecedent variable**. The variable that is predicted or assumed to be affected (analogous to the dependent variable) is sometimes called the **criterion variable**.

Researchers often wish to account for or control variables of certain types in order to eliminate unwanted influences. These control variables are used to ensure that the results of the study are due to the independent variables, not to another source. However, a control variable need not always be used to eliminate an unwanted influence. On occasion, researchers use a control variable such as age, gender, or socioeconomic status to divide subjects into specific, relevant categories. For example, in studying the relationship between newspaper readership and reading ability, it is apparent that IQ will affect the relationship and must be controlled; thus, subjects may be selected on the basis of IQ scores or placed in groups with similar scores.

One of the most difficult aspects of any type of research is identifying all the variables that may create spurious or misleading results. Some researchers refer to this problem as "noise." Noise can occur even in very simple research projects. For example, a researcher might design a telephone survey that asks respondents to name the local radio station they listened to most during the past week. The researcher uses an open-ended question—that is, no specific response choices are provided—and the interviewer writes down each respon-

dent's answer. When the completed surveys are tabulated, the researcher notices that several people mentioned radio station WAAA. But if the city has a WAAA-AM and a WAAA-FM, which station gets the credit? The researcher cannot arbitrarily assign credit to the AM station or to the FM station; nor can credit be split, because such a practice may distort the description of the actual listening pattern.

Interviewers could attempt callbacks to everyone who said "WAAA," but this method is not suggested for two reasons: (1) the likelihood of reaching all the people who gave that response is low; and (2) even if the first condition is met, some respondents may not recall which station they originally mentioned. The researcher, therefore, is unable to provide a reliable analysis of the data because not all possible intervening variables were considered. (The researcher should have foreseen this problem, and the interviewers should have been instructed to find out in each case whether WAAA meant the AM or the FM station.)

Another type of research noise is created by people who unknowingly provide false information. For example, people who keep diaries for radio and television surveys may err in recording the station or channel they tune in; that is, they may listen to or watch station KAAA but incorrectly record "KBBB." (This problem is partially solved by the use of people meters—see Chapter 14.) In addition, people often answer a multiple-choice or yes/no research question at random because they do not wish to appear ignorant or uninformed. To minimize this problem, researchers should construct their measurement instruments with great care. Noise is always present, but a large and representative sample should decrease the effects of some research noise. (In later chapters, noise is referred to as "error.")

Many simplistic problems in research are solved with experience. In many situations, however, researchers understand that total control over all aspects of the research is impossible, and the impossibility of achieving perfect control is accounted for in the interpretation of results.

DEFINING VARIABLES OPERATIONALLY

In Chapter 2, it was stated that an operational definition specifies procedures to be followed in experiencing or measuring a concept. Research depends on observations, and observations cannot be made without a clear statement of what is to be observed. An **operational definition** is such a statement.

Operational definitions are indispensable in scientific research because they enable investigators to measure relevant variables. In any study, it is necessary to provide operational definitions for both independent variables and dependent variables. Table 3.1 contains examples of such definitions taken from research studies in mass communication.

Kerlinger (1986) identified two types of operational definitions, measured and experimental. A measured operational definition specifies how to measure a variable. For instance, a researcher investigating *dogmatism* and media use might operationally define the term *dogmatism* as a subject's score on the Twenty-Item Short Form Dogmatism Scale. An experimental operational definition explains how an investigator has manipulated a variable. Obviously, this type of definition is used when defining the independent variable in a laboratory setting. For example, in a study concerning the impact of television violence, the researcher might manipulate media violence by constructing two 8-minute films. The first film, labeled "the violent condition," could contain scenes from a boxing match. The second film, labeled "the nonviolent condition," could depict a swimming race. Similarly, source credibility might be manipulated by alternately attributing an article on health to the *New England Journal of Medicine* and to the *National Enquirer*.

Operationally defining a variable forces the researcher to express abstract concepts in concrete terms. Occasionally, after unsuccessfully grappling with the task of making a key variable operational, the researcher may conclude that the variable as originally conceived is too vague or ambiguous and must be redefined. Because operational definitions are expressed so concretely, they can communicate *exactly* what the terms represent. For instance, a researcher might define political knowledge as the number of correct answers on a 20-item true/false test. Although it is possible to argue over the validity of the definition, there is no confusion as to what the statement "Women possess more political knowledge than men" actually means.

Finally, there is no single infallible method for operationally defining a variable. No operational definition satisfies everybody. The investigator must decide which method is best suited for the research problem at hand.

MEASUREMENT

Mass media research, like all research, can be qualitative or quantitative. **Qualitative research** refers to several methods of data collection, which include focus groups, field observation, in-depth interviews, and case studies. Although there are substantial differences among these techniques, all involve what some writers refer to as "getting close to the data" (Chadwick, Bahr, & Albrecht, 1984).

Qualitative research has certain advantages. In most cases, it allows a researcher to view behavior in a natural setting without the artificiality that sometimes surrounds experimental or survey research. In addition, qualitative techniques can increase a researcher's depth of understanding of the phenomenon under investigation. This is especially true when the phenomenon has not been previously investigated. Finally, qualitative methods are flexible and allow the researcher to pursue new areas of

TABLE 3.1   **Examples of Operational Definitions**

Study	Variable	Operational Definition
Whitmore and Tiene (1994)	Current events knowledge	Scores on the Associated Press Weekly News Quiz
Jacobs (1995)	Consumer satisfaction with cable system	15-item scale designed to tap subscribers' evaluations of cable systems
Kaid, Chanslor and Hovind (1992)	Image evaluation of political candidate	Summated ratings on a 12-item semantic differential
Shah and Gayatri (1994)	Development news	Any news item related to development priorities outlined in the fifth Indonesian Five-Year Plan, 1989–1994
Demers (1994)	Organizational size of daily newspapers	Newspapers' daily circulation figures

interest. A questionnaire is unlikely to provide data about questions that were not asked, but a person conducting a field observation or focus group might discover facets of a subject that were not considered before the study began.

There are, however, some disadvantages associated with qualitative methods. First of all, sample sizes are generally too small (sometimes as small as one) to allow the researcher to generalize the data beyond the sample selected for the particular study. For this reason, qualitative research is often the preliminary step to further investigation rather than the final phase of a project. The information collected from qualitative methods is often used to prepare a more elaborate quantitative analysis, although the qualitative data may in fact constitute all the information needed for a particular study.

Reliability of the data can also be a problem, since single observers are describing unique events. Because a person doing qualitative re-

search must become closely involved with the respondents, loss of objectivity when collecting data is possible. If the researcher becomes too close to the study, the necessary professional detachment may be lost.

Finally, if qualitative research is not properly planned, the project may produce nothing of value. Qualitative research appears to be easy to conduct, but projects must be carefully planned to ensure that they focus on key issues. Although this book is primarily concerned with quantitative research, several qualitative methods are discussed in Chapter 5. For those who wish to know more about the other research techniques that make up qualitative analysis, two sources are suggested, Anderson (1987) and Lindlof (1987).

Quantitative research requires that the variables under consideration be measured. This form of research is concerned with how often a variable is present and generally uses numbers to communicate this amount. Quantitative research has certain advantages. One is that the use of numbers allows greater precision in reporting results. For example, the Violence Index (Gerbner, Gross, Morgan, & Signorielli, 1980), a quantitative measuring device, makes it possible to report the exact increase or decrease in violence from one television season to another, whereas qualitative research could describe only whether violence went up or down. Another advantage is that quantitative research permits the use of powerful methods of mathematical analysis. The importance of mathematics to mass media research is difficult to overemphasize. As pointed out by measurement expert J. P. Guilford (1954, p. 1):

> The progress and maturity of a science are often judged by the extent to which it has succeeded in the use of mathematics. . . . Mathematics is a universal language that any science or technology may use with great power and convenience. Its vocabulary of terms is unlimited. . . . Its rules of operation . . . are unexcelled for logical precision.

For the past several years, some friction has existed in the mass media field and in other disciplines between those who favor quantitative methods and those who prefer qualitative methods. Recently, however, most researchers have come to realize that both methods are important in understanding any phenomenon. In fact, the term **triangulation**, commonly used by marine navigators, frequently crops up in conversations about communication research. If a ship picks up signals from only one navigational aid, it is impossible to know the vessel's precise location. If, however, signals from more than one source are detected, elementary geometry can be used to pinpoint the ship's location. In this book, the term _triangulation_ refers to the use of both qualitative methods and quantitative methods to fully understand the nature of a research problem.

For example, an investigation by Krugman and Johnson (1991) illustrates the use of trian-

gulation. The purpose of their investigation was to determine the differences in viewer involvement when subjects viewed standard broadcast television programs as opposed to VCR movie rentals. Using a combination of focus groups, mail surveys, and in-home observations, the authors found that respondents viewing VCR rentals showed a higher level of undistracted viewing and were more involved than when they were viewing standard broadcast television programs.

Although most of this book is concerned with skills relevant to quantitative research, it is not implied that quantitative research is in any sense "better" than qualitative research. Obviously, each technique has value, and different research questions and goals may make one or the other more appropriate in a given application. Over the past 30 years, however, quantitative research has become more common in mass media research. Consequently, it is increasingly important for beginning researchers to familiarize themselves with common quantitative techniques.

THE NATURE OF MEASUREMENT

The idea behind **measurement** is a simple one: A researcher assigns numerals to objects, events, or properties according to certain rules. Examples of measurement are everywhere: "She or he is a 10," or "Unemployment increased by 1%," or "The earthquake measured 5.5 on the Richter scale." Note that the definition contains three central concepts: numerals, assignment, and rules. A numeral is a symbol, such as V, X, C, or 5, 10, 100. A _numeral_ has no implicit quantitative meaning. When it is given quantitative meaning, it becomes a number and can be used in mathematical and statistical computations. _Assignment_ is the designation of numerals or numbers to certain objects or events. A simple measurement system might entail assigning the numeral 1 to the people who obtain most of their news from television, the numeral 2 to those who get most of their news from a newspaper, and the numeral 3 to those who receive most of their news from some other source.

Rules specify the way that numerals or numbers are to be assigned. Rules are at the heart of any measurement system; if they are faulty, the system will be flawed. In some situations, the rules are obvious and straightforward. To measure reading speed, a stopwatch and a standardized message may be sufficient. In other instances, the rules are not so apparent. Measuring certain psychological traits such as "source credibility" or "attitude toward violence" calls for carefully explicated measurement techniques.

Additionally, in mass media research and in much of social science research, investigators usually measure indicators of the properties of individuals or objects, rather than the individuals or objects themselves. Concepts such as "authoritarianism" or "motivation for reading the newspaper" cannot be directly observed; they must be inferred from presumed indicators. Thus, if a person endorses statements such as "Orders from a superior should always be followed without question," and "Law and order are the most important things in society," it can be deduced that he or she is more authoritarian than someone who disagrees with the same statements.

Measurement systems strive to be isomorphic to reality. **Isomorphism** means identity or similarity of form or structure. In some research areas, such as the physical sciences, isomorphism is not a problem since there is usually a direct relationship between the objects being measured and the numbers assigned to them. For example, if an electrical current travels through Substance A with less resistance than it does through Substance B, it can be deduced that A is a better conductor than B. Testing more substances can lead to a ranking of conductors, where the numbers assigned indicate the degree of conductivity. The measurement system is isomorphic to reality.

In mass media research, the correspondence is seldom that obvious. For example,

imagine that a researcher is trying to develop a scale to measure the "persuasibility" of people in connection with a certain type of advertisement. She devises a test and administers it to five people. The scores are displayed in Table 3.2. Now, imagine that an omniscient being is able to disclose the "true" persuasibility of the same five people. These scores are also shown in Table 3.2. For two people, the test scores correspond exactly to the "true" scores. The other three scores miss the "true" scores, but there is a correspondence between the rank orders. Also note that the "true" persuasibility scores range from 0 to 12 and that the measurement scale ranges from 1 to 8. To summarize, there is a general correspondence between the test and reality, but the test is far from an exact measure of what actually exists.

Unfortunately, the degree of correspondence between measurement and reality is rarely known in research. In some cases, researchers are not even sure they are actually measuring what they are trying to measure. In any event, researchers must carefully consider the degree of isomorphism between measurement and reality. This topic is discussed in greater detail later in the chapter.

LEVELS OF MEASUREMENT

Scientists have distinguished four different ways to measure things, or four different levels of measurement, depending upon the rules that are used to assign numbers to objects or events. The operations that can be performed with a given set of scores depend on the level of measurement achieved. The four levels of measurement are nominal, ordinal, interval, and ratio.

The **nominal level** is the weakest form of measurement. In nominal measurement, numerals or other symbols are used to classify persons, objects, or characteristics. For example, in the physical sciences, rocks can generally be classified into three categories: igneous, sedimentary, and metamorphic. A geologist who assigns a 1 to igneous, a 2 to sedimentary,

TABLE 3.2   Illustration of Isomorphism

Person	Test score	"True" score
A	1	0
B	3	1
C	6	6
D	7	7
E	8	12

and a 3 to metamorphic has formed a nominal scale. Note that the numerals are simply labels that stand for the respective categories; they have no mathematical significance. A rock that is placed in Category 3 does not have more "rockness" than those in Categories 2 and 1. Other examples of nominal measurement are numbers on football jerseys and license plates and social security numbers. An example of nominal measurement in mass media would be classifying respondents according to the medium they depend on most for news. Those depending most on TV would be in Category 1; those depending most on newspapers would be in Category 2; those depending on magazines in Category 3; and so on.

The nominal level, like all levels, possesses certain formal properties. Its basic property is that of equivalence. If an object is placed in Category 1, it is considered equal to all other objects in that category. Suppose a researcher is attempting to classify all the advertisements in a magazine according to primary appeal. If an ad has economic appeal, it is placed in Category 1; if it uses an appeal to fear, it is placed in Category 2; and so on. Note that all ads using "fear appeal" are equal even though they may differ on other dimensions such as product type or size, or use of illustrations.

Another property of nominal measurement is that all categories are exhaustive and mutually exclusive. This means that each measure accounts for every possible option and that each measurement is appropriate to only one category. For instance, in the example of primary appeals in magazine advertisements, all possible appeals would need to be included in the analysis (exhaustive): economic, fear, morality, religion, and so on. Each advertisement would be placed in one and only one category (mutually exclusive).

Nominal measurement is frequently used in mass media research. Hinkle and Elliot (1989) divided science coverage by supermarket tabloids and mainstream newspapers into medical coverage and hard technology stories and discovered that tabloids had far more medical stories. Weinberger and Spotts (1989) divided the use of humorous devices in British and American ads into six nominal categories—pun, understatement, joke, ludicrous, satire, and irony—and found that the use of humor was similar in both countries.

Even when it is measured at the nominal level, a variable may be used in higher-order statistics by *converting* it into another form. The result of this conversion process is known as **dummy variables**. For example, political party affiliation could be coded as follows:

Republican	1
Democrat	2
Independent	3
Other	4

However, this measurement scheme can be interpreted incorrectly to imply that a person classified as "Other" is three units "better" than a person classified as a "Republican." To measure political party affiliation and use the data in higher-order statistics, the variable must be converted into a more neutral form.

One way of converting the variable to give equivalent value to each option is to recode it as a dummy variable that creates an "either/or" situation for each option; in this example, a person is either a "Republican" or something else. For example, a binary coding scheme could be used:

Republican	001
Democrat	010
Independent	100
Other	000

This scheme treats each affiliation equivalently and allows the variable to be used in higher-order statistical procedures. Note that the final category "Other" is coded using all zeros. A complete explanation for this practice is beyond the scope of this book; basically, however, its purpose is to avoid redundancy, since the number of individuals classified as "Other" is known from the data on the first three options. If, in a sample of 100 subjects, 25 are found to belong in each of the first three options, it is obvious that there will be 25 in the "Other" option. (For more information on the topic of dummy variable coding, see Kerlinger & Pedhazur, 1986.)

Objects measured at the **ordinal level** are generally ranked along some dimension, usually in a meaningful way, from smaller to greater. For example, one might measure the variable "socioeconomic status" by categorizing families according to class: lower, lower middle, middle, upper middle, or upper. A rank of 1 is assigned to lower, 2 to lower middle, 3 to middle, and so forth. In this situation, the numbers have some mathematical meaning: Families in Category 3 have a higher socio-economic status than those in Category 2. Note that nothing is specified with regard to the distance between any two rankings. Ordinal measurement often has been compared to a horse race without a stopwatch. The order in which the horses finish is relatively easy to determine, but it is difficult to calculate the difference in time between the winner and the runner-up.

An ordinal scale possesses the property of *equivalence*; thus in the previous example, all families placed in a category are treated equally, even though some might have greater incomes than others. It also possesses the property of *order* among the categories. Any given category can be defined as being higher or lower than any other category. Common examples of ordinal scales include rankings of football or basketball teams, military ranks, restaurant ratings, and beauty pageant finishing orders.

Ordinal scales are frequently used in mass communication research. Schweitzer (1989) ranked 16 factors that were important to the success of mass communication researchers. In a study of electronic text news, Heeter, Brown, Soffin, Stanley, and Salwen (1989) rank-ordered audience evaluations of the importance of 25 different issues in the news and found little evidence of an effect on content, known as agenda-setting.

When a scale has all the properties of an ordinal scale and the intervals between adjacent points on the scale are of equal value, the scale is at the **interval level.** The most obvious example of an interval scale is temperature. The same amount of heat is required to warm an object from 30 to 40 degrees as to warm it from 50 to 60 degrees. Interval scales incorporate the formal property of *equal differences*; that is, numbers are assigned to the positions of objects on an interval scale in such a way that one may carry out arithmetic operations on the differences between them.

One disadvantage of an interval scale is that it lacks a true zero point, or condition of nothingness. For example, it is difficult to conceive of a person having zero intelligence or zero personality. The absence of a true zero point means that a researcher cannot make statements of a proportional nature; for example, someone with an IQ of 100 is not twice as smart as someone with an IQ of 50, and a person who scores 30 on a test of aggression is not three times as aggressive as a person who scores 10. Despite this disadvantage, interval scales are frequently used in mass communication research. Zohoori (1988) constructed a "motivations for using TV" scale by presenting respondents with a list of 11 reasons for viewing television. The response options ranged from "not at all like me," coded 1; "a little like me," coded 2; and "a lot like me," coded 3. Baran, Mok, Land, and Kang (1989) developed a five-point agree/disagree interval scale to measure a person's worth as seen by others by eliciting responses to seven statements such as "It's likely that I'd have this woman/man as a friend" and "It's fairly likely that this man/woman is punctual."

Scales at the **ratio level** of measurement have all the properties of interval scales plus one more: the existence of *true zero point*. With the introduction of this fixed zero point, ratio judgments can be made. For example, since time and distance are ratio measures, one can say that a car traveling at 50 miles per hour is going twice as fast as a car traveling at 25. Ratio scales are relatively rare in mass media research, although some variables, such as time spent watching television or number of words per story, are ratio measurements. For example, Gantz (1978) measured news recall ability by asking subjects to report whether they had seen or heard 10 stories taken from the evening news. Scores could range from 0 to 10 on this test. Giffard (1984) counted the length of wire service reports related to 101 developed or developing nations. Theoretically, scores could range from zero (no coverage) to hundreds of words.

As we shall see in Chapter 12, researchers who use interval or ratio data can use parametric statistics, which are specifically designed for these data. Procedures designed for use with "lower" types of data can also be used with data at a higher level of measurement. Statistical procedures designed for higher-level data, however, are generally more powerful than those designed for use with nominal or ordinal levels of measurement. Thus, if an investigator has achieved the interval level of measurement, parametric statistics should generally be employed. Statisticians disagree about the importance of the distinction between ordinal scales and interval scales and about the legitimacy of using interval statistics with data that may in fact be ordinal. Without delving too deeply into these arguments, it appears that the safest procedure is to assume interval measurement unless there is clear evidence to the contrary, in which case ordinal statistics should be employed. For example, for a research task in which a group of subjects ranks a set of objects, ordinal statistics should be used. If, on the other hand, subjects are given an attitude score constructed by rating responses to various questions, the researcher would be justified in using parametric procedures.

Most statisticians seem to feel that statistical analysis is performed on the numbers yielded by the measures, not on the measures themselves, and that the properties of interval scales belong to the number system (Nunnally, 1978; Roscoe, 1975). Additionally, there have been several studies in which various types of data have been subjected to different statistical analyses. These studies suggest that the distinction between ordinal data and interval data is not particularly crucial in selecting an analysis method (McNemar, 1969).

DISCRETE AND CONTINUOUS VARIABLES

Two forms of variables are used in mass media investigation. A **discrete variable** includes only a finite set of values; it cannot be divided into subparts. For instance, the number of children in a family is a discrete variable because the unit is a person. It would not make much sense to talk about a family size of 2.24 because it is hard to conceptualize 0.24 of a person. Political affiliation, population, and sex are other discrete variables.

A **continuous variable** can take on any value (including fractions) and can be meaningfully broken into smaller subsections. Height is a continuous variable. If the measurement tool is sophisticated enough, it is possible to distinguish between one person 72.113 inches tall and another 72.114 inches tall. Time spent watching television is another example; it is perfectly meaningful to say that Person A spent 3.12115 hours viewing while Person B watched 3.12114 hours. The average number of children in a family is a continuous variable; thus in this context, it may be perfectly meaningful to refer to 0.24 of a person.

When dealing with continuous variables, it is sometimes necessary to keep in mind the distinction between the variable and the measure of the variable. If a child's attitude toward television violence is measured by counting his or her positive responses to six questions, there are only seven possible scores: 0, 1, 2, 3, 4, 5, and 6. It is entirely likely, however, that the underlying variable is continuous even though the measure is discrete. In fact, even if a fractionalized scale was developed, it would still be limited to a finite number of scores. As a generalization, most of the measures in mass media research tend to be discrete approximations of continuous variables.

Variables measured at the nominal level are always discrete variables. Variables measured at the ordinal level are generally discrete, though there may be some underlying continuous measurement dimension. Variables measured at the interval or ratio level can be either discrete (number of magazine subscriptions in a household) or continuous (number of minutes per day spent reading magazines). Both the level of measurement and the type of variable under consideration are important in developing useful measurement scales.

SCALES

A scale represents a composite measure of a variable; it is based on more than one item. Scales are generally used with complex variables that do not easily lend themselves to single-item or single-indicator measurements. Some items, such as age, newspaper circulation, or number of radios in the house, can be adequately measured without scaling techniques. Measurement of other variables, such as attitude toward TV news or gratification received from moviegoing, generally requires the use of scales.

Several scaling techniques have been developed over the years. This section discusses only the better known methods.

THURSTONE SCALES

Thurstone scales are also called *equal-appearing interval scales* because of the technique used to develop them. They are typically used to measure the attitude toward a given concept or construct. To develop a Thurstone scale, a researcher first collects a large number of statements (Thurstone recommended at least 100) that relate to the concept or construct to be measured. Next, judges rate these statements along an 11-category scale in which each category expresses a different degree of favorableness toward the concept. The items are then ranked according to the mean or median ratings assigned by the judges and are used to construct a questionnaire of 20–30 items that are chosen more or less evenly from across the range of ratings. The statements are worded so that a person can agree or disagree with them. The scale is then administered to a sample of respondents whose scores are determined by computing the mean or median value of the items agreed with. A person who disagrees with all the items has a score of zero.

One advantage of the Thurstone method is that it is an interval measurement scale. On the downside, this method is time-consuming and labor-intensive. Thurstone scales are not often used in mass media research, but are common in psychology and education research.

GUTTMAN SCALING

Guttman scaling, also called *scalogram analysis*, is based on the idea that items can be arranged along a continuum in such a way that a person who agrees with an item or finds an item acceptable will also agree with or find acceptable all other items expressing a less extreme position. For example, here is a hypothetical four-item Guttman scale:

1. Indecent programming on TV is harmful to society.
2. Children should not be allowed to watch indecent TV shows.
3. Television station managers should not allow indecent programs on their stations.
4. The government should ban indecent programming from TV.

Presumably, a person who agrees with Statement 4 will also agree with Statements 1–3. Further, assuming the scale is valid, a person who agrees with Statement 2 will also agree with Statement 1, but will not necessarily agree with Statements 3 and 4. Because each score represents a unique set of responses, the number of items a person agrees with is the person's total score on a Guttman scale.

A Guttman scale also requires a great deal of time and energy to develop. Although they do not appear often in mass media research, Guttman scales are fairly common in political science, sociology, public opinion research, and anthropology.

LIKERT SCALES

Perhaps the most commonly used scale in mass media research is the **Likert scale**, also called the *summated rating approach*. A number of statements are developed with respect to a topic, and respondents can strongly agree, agree, be neutral, disagree, or strongly disagree with the statements (see Figure 3.1). Each response option is weighted, and each subject's responses are added to produce a single score on the topic.

The basic procedure for developing a Likert scale is as follows:

1. Compile a large number of statements that relate to a specific dimension. Some statements are positively worded; some are negatively worded.
2. Administer the scale to a randomly selected sample of respondents.
3. Code the responses consistently so that high scores indicate stronger agreement with the attitude in question.
4. Analyze the responses and select for the final scale those statements that most clearly differentiate the highest from the lowest scorers.

SEMANTIC DIFFERENTIAL SCALES

Another commonly used scaling procedure is the **semantic differential** technique. As originally conceived by Osgood, Suci, and Tannenbaum (1957), this technique is used to measure the meaning an item has for an individual. Research indicated that three general factors—activity, potency, and evaluation—were measured by the semantic differential. Communication researchers were quick to adapt the evaluative dimension of the semantic differential for use as a measure of attitude.

To use the technique, a name or a concept is placed at the top of a series of seven-point scales anchored by bipolar attitudes. Figure 3.2 shows an example of this technique as used to measure attitudes toward *Time* magazine. The bipolar adjectives that typically "anchor" such evaluative scales are *pleasant/unpleasant, valuable/worthless, honest/dishonest, nice/awful, clean/dirty, fair/unfair,* and *good/bad*. It is recommended, however, that a unique set of anchoring adjectives be developed for each particular measurement situation. For example, Markham (1968), in his study of the credibility of tele-

---

FIGURE 3.1   Sample of Likert Scale Items

1. Only U.S. citizens should be allowed to own broadcasting stations.

Response	Score Assigned
_____ Strongly agree	5
_____ Agree	4
_____ Neutral	3
_____ Disagree	2
_____ Strongly disagree	1

2. Prohibiting foreign ownership of broadcasting stations is bad for business.

Response	Score Assigned
_____ Strongly agree	1
_____ Agree	2
_____ Neutral	3
_____ Disagree	4
_____ Strongly disagree	5

Note: To maintain attitude measurement consistency, the scores are reversed for a negatively worded item. Question 1 is a positive item; Question 2 is a negative item.

vision newscasters, used 13 variable sets, including *deep/shallow, ordered/chaotic, annoying/pleasing,* and *clear/hazy.* Robinson and Shaver (1973) present a collection of scales commonly used in social science research.

Strictly speaking, the semantic differential technique attempts to place a concept in semantic space through the use of an advanced statistical procedure called factor analysis. When researchers borrow parts of the technique to measure attitudes, or images or perceptions of objects, persons, or concepts, they are not using the technique as originally developed. Consequently, perhaps a more appropriate name for this technique might be bipolar rating scales.

RELIABILITY AND VALIDITY

Using any scale without prior testing results in poor research. At least one pilot study should be conducted for any newly developed scale to ensure its reliability and validity. To be useful, a measurement must possess these two related qualities. A measure is reliable if it consistently gives the same answer. Reliability in measurement is the same as reliability in any other context. For example, a reliable person is one who is dependable, stable, and consistent over time. An unreliable person is unstable and unpredictable and may act one way today and another way tomorrow. Similarly, if measurements are consistent from one session to another, they are

FIGURE 3.2   **Sample Form for Applying the Semantic Differential Technique**

Time Magazine

Biased _____:___:_____:_____:_____:_____:_____ Unbiased

Trustworthy _____:___:_____:_____:_____:_____:_____ Untrustworthy

Valuable _____:___:_____:_____:_____:_____:_____ Worthless

Unfair _____:___:_____:_____:_____:_____:_____ Fair

reliable and can be believed to some degree.

In understanding measurement **reliability**, it is helpful to think of a measure as containing two components. The first represents an individual's "true" score on the measuring instrument. The second represents random error and does not provide an accurate assessment of what is being measured. Error can slip into the measurement process from several sources. Perhaps a question has been ambiguously worded, or a person's pencil slipped as he or she was filling out a measuring instrument. Whatever the cause, all measurement is subject to some degree of random error. Figure 3.3 illustrates this concept. As is evident, Measurement Instrument 1 is highly reliable because the ratio of the true component of the score to the total score is high. Measurement Instrument 2 is unreliable because the ratio of the true component to the total is low.

A completely unreliable measurement measures nothing at all. If a measure is repeatedly given to individuals and each person's responses at a later session are unrelated to his or her earlier responses, the measure is useless. If the responses are identical or nearly identical each time the measure is given, the measure is reliable—it at least measures something, though not necessarily what the researcher intended. (This problem is discussed below.)

The importance of reliability should be obvious now. Unreliable measures cannot be used

to detect relationships between variables. When the measurement of a variable is unreliable, it is composed mainly of random error, and random error is seldom related to anything else.

Reliability is not a unidimensional concept. It consists of three different components: stability, internal consistency, and equivalency.

Stability is the easiest of the components to understand. It refers to the consistency of a result or of a measure at different points in time. For example, suppose that a test designed to measure proofreading ability is administered during the first week of an editing class and again during the second week. The test possesses stability if the two results are consistent. Caution should be used whenever stability is used as a measure of reliability, since people and things can change over time. To use the previous example, it is entirely possible for a person to score higher the second time because some people might actually have improved their ability from Week 1 to Week 2. In this case the measure is not really unstable; actual change has occurred.

An assessment of reliability is necessary in all mass media research and should be reported along with other facets of the research as an aid in interpretation and evaluation. One commonly used statistic for assessing reliability takes the form of a correlation coefficient denoted as r_{xx}. Chapter 10 provides a more detailed examination of the correlation coeffi-

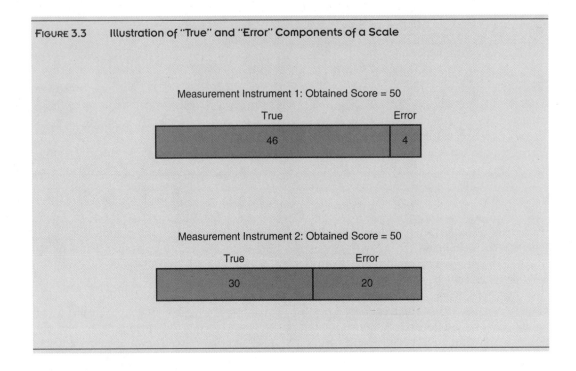

FIGURE 3.3   Illustration of "True" and "Error" Components of a Scale

cient; for now let's say only that r_{xx} is a number ranging from -1.00 to $+1.00$ and is used to gauge the strength of a relationship between two variables. When r_{xx} is high—that is, approaching $+1.00$—the relationship is strong. A negative number indicates a negative relationship (high scores on one variable are associated with low scores on the other), and a positive number indicates a positive relationship (a high score goes with another high score). In measuring reliability, a high, positive r_{xx} is desired.

One method that uses correlation coefficients to compute reliability is the *test-retest* method. This procedure measures the stability component of reliability. The same people are measured at two different points in time, and a coefficient between the two scores is computed. An r_{xx} that approaches $+1.00$ indicates that a person's score at Time A was similar to his or her score at Time B, showing consistency over time. There are two limitations to the test-

retest technique. First, the initial administration of the measure might affect scores on the second testing. If the measuring device is a questionnaire, a person might remember responses from session to session, thus falsely inflating reliability. Second, the concept measured may change from Time A to Time B, thus lowering the reliability estimate.

Internal consistency involves examining the consistency of performance among the items composing a scale. If separate items on a scale assign the same values to the concept being measured, the scale possesses internal consistency. For instance, suppose a researcher designs a 20-item scale to measure attitudes toward newspaper reading. For the scale to be internally consistent, the total score on the first half of the test should highly correlate with the score on the second half of the test. This method of determining reliability is called the *split-half technique*. Only one administration of the measuring instrument is made, but the test is split into halves and scored separately. For example, if the test is in the form of a questionnaire, the even-numbered items might constitute one half, and the odd-numbered items the other half. A correlation coefficient is then computed between the two sets of scores. Since this coefficient is computed from a test that is only half as long as the final form, it is corrected by using the following formula:

$$r_{xx} = \frac{2(r_{oe})}{1 + r_{oe}}$$

where r_{oe} is the correlation between the odd items and the even items.

Another common reliability coefficient is *alpha* (sometimes referred to as Cronbach's alpha), which uses the analysis of variance approach (Chapter 10) to assess the internal consistency of a measure.

The **equivalency** component of reliability, sometimes referred to as cross-test reliability, assesses the relative correlation between two parallel forms of a test. Two instruments using different scale items or different measurement techniques are developed to measure the same concept. The two versions are then administered to the same group of people during a single time period, and the correlation between the scores on the two forms of the test is taken as a measure of the reliability. The major problem with this method, of course, is developing two forms of a scale that are perfectly equivalent. The less parallel the two forms, the lower the reliability.

A special case of the equivalency component occurs when two or more observers judge the same phenomenon, as is the case in content analysis (Chapter 8). This type of reliability is called **intercoder reliability** and is used to assess the degree to which a result can be achieved or reproduced by other observers. Ideally, two individuals using the same operational measure and the same measuring instrument should end up with the same results. For example, if two researchers try to identify acts of violence in television content based on a given operational definition of *violence,* the degree to which their results are consistent is a measure of intercoder reliability. Disagreements reflect a difference either in perception or in the way the original definition was interpreted. Special formulas for computing intercoder reliability are discussed in Chapter 6.

In addition to being reliable, a measurement must be valid if it is to be of use in studying variables. A valid measuring device measures what it is supposed to measure. Or, to put it another way, determining validity requires an evaluation of the congruence between the operational definition of a variable and its conceptual or constitutive definition. Assessing validity requires some degree of judgment on the part of the researcher. In the following discussion of the major types of measurement validity, note that each one depends at least in part on the judgment of the researcher. Also, validity is almost never an all-or-none proposition; it is usually a matter of degree. A measurement rarely turns out to be totally valid or invalid. Typically it winds up somewhere in the middle.

In regard to measurement, there are four major types of validity, and each has a corresponding technique for evaluating the measurement method. They are face validity, predictive validity, concurrent validity, and construct validity.

The simplest and most basic kind of validity, *face validity,* is achieved by examining the measurement device to see whether, on the face of it, it measures what it appears to measure. For example, a test designed to measure proofreading ability could include accounting problems, but this measure would lack face validity. A test that asks people to read and correct certain paragraphs has more face validity as a measure of proofreading skill. Whether a measure possesses face validity depends to some degree on subjective judgment. To minimize subjectivity, the relevance of a given measurement should be independently judged by several experts.

Predictive validity is assessed by checking a measurement instrument against some future outcome. For example, scores on a test to predict whether a person will vote in an upcoming election can be checked against actual voting behavior. If the test scores allow the researcher to predict with a high degree of accuracy which people will actually vote and which will not, the test has predictive validity. Note that it is possible for a measure to have predictive validity and at the same time lack face validity. The sole factor in determining validity in the predictive method is the measurement's ability to correctly forecast future behavior. The concern is not with what is being measured but with whether the measurement instrument can predict something. Thus, a test to determine whether a person will become a successful mass media researcher could conceivably consist of geometry problems. If it predicts the ultimate success of a researcher reasonably well, the test has predictive validity but little face validity. The biggest problem associated with predictive validity is determining the criteria against which test scores are to be checked. What, for example, constitutes a "successful mass media researcher"? One who obtains an advanced degree? One who publishes research articles? One who writes a book?

Concurrent validity is closely related to predictive validity. In this method, however, the measuring instrument is checked against some present criterion. For example, it is possible to validate a test of proofreading ability by administering the test to a group of professional proofreaders and to a group of nonproofreaders. If the test discriminates well between the two groups, it can be said to have concurrent validity. Similarly, a test of aggression might discriminate between one group of children who are frequently detained after school for fighting and another group who have never been reprimanded for antisocial behavior.

The fourth type of validity, *construct validity,* is the most complex. In simplified form, construct validity involves relating a measuring instrument to some overall theoretic frame-work to ensure that the measurement is logically related to other concepts in the framework. Ideally, a researcher should be able to suggest various relationships between the property being measured and the other variables. For construct validity to exist, the researcher must show that these relationships are in fact present. For example, an investigator might expect the frequency with which a person views a particular television newscast to be influenced by his or her attitude toward that program. If the measure of attitudes correlates highly with frequency of viewing, there is some evidence for the validity of the attitude measure. By the same token, construct validity is evidenced if the measurement instrument under consideration does *not* relate to other variables when there is no theoretic reason to expect such a relationship. Thus, if an investigator finds a relationship between a measure and other variables that is predicted by a theory and fails to find other relationships that are not predicted by a theory, there is evidence for construct validity. For example, Milavsky, Kessler, Stipp, and Rubens (1982) established the validity of their measure of respondent aggression by noting that, as expected, boys scored higher than girls and that high aggression scores were associated with high levels of parental punishment. In addition, aggression was negatively correlated with scores on a scale measuring prosocial behavior. Figure 3.4 summarizes the various types of validity.

Before closing this discussion, it should be pointed out that reliability and validity are related. Reliability is necessary to establish validity, but it is not a sufficient condition—a reliable measure is not necessarily a valid one. Figure 3.5 shows this relationship. An X represents a test that is both reliable and valid; the scores are consistent from session to session and lie close to the true value. An ◯ represents a measure that is reliable but not valid; the scores are stable from session to session but they are not close to the true score. A + represents a test that is neither valid nor reliable;

FIGURE 3.4   Types of Validity

Judgment-based	Criterion-based	Theory-based
Face validity	Predictive validity	Construct validity
	Concurrent validity	

FIGURE 3.5   Relationship of Reliability and Validity

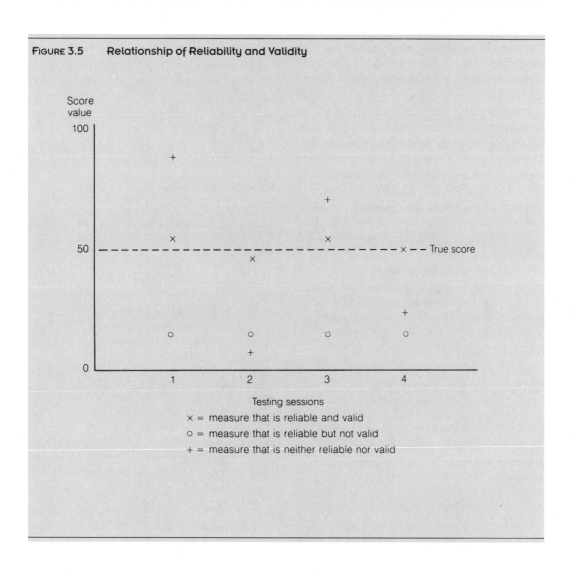

Testing sessions

× = measure that is reliable and valid
○ = measure that is reliable but not valid
+ = measure that is neither reliable nor valid

scores vary widely from session to session and are not close to the true score.

SUMMARY

Understanding empirical research requires a basic knowledge of concepts, constructs, variables, and measurement. Concepts summarize related observations and express an abstract notion that has been formed by generalizing from particulars. Connections among concepts form propositions that, in turn, are used to build theories. Constructs consist of combinations of concepts and are also useful in building theories.

Variables are phenomena or events that take on one or more different values. Independent variables are manipulated by the researcher, whereas dependent variables are what the researcher attempts to explain. All variables are related to the observable world by operational definitions.

Researchers frequently use scales to measure complex variables. Thurstone, Guttman, Likert, and semantic differential scales are used in mass media research.

Measurement is the assignment of numerals to objects, events, or properties according to certain rules. There are four levels of measurement: nominal, ordinal, interval, and ratio. To be useful, a measurement must be both reliable and valid.

QUESTIONS AND PROBLEMS FOR FURTHER IINVESTIGATION

1. Provide conceptual and operational definitions for the following items:
   a. Violence
   b. Artistic quality
   c. Programming appeal
   d. Sexual content
   e. Objectionable song lyrics
   Compare your definitions to those of others in the class. Would there be any difficulty in conducting a study using these definitions? Might you have demonstrated why so much contro-

versy surrounds the topics, for example, of sex and violence on television?

2. What type of data (nominal, ordinal, interval, or ratio) does each of the following concepts or measurements represent?
   a. Baseball team standings
   b. A test of listening comprehension
   c. A. C. Nielsen's list of the top 10 television programs
   d. Frequency of heads versus tails on coin flips
   e. Baseball batting averages
   f. A scale measuring intensity of attitudes toward violence
   g. VHF channels 2–13
   h. A scale for monitoring your weight over time

3. Try to develop a measurement technique that would examine each of the following concepts:
   a. Newspaper reading
   b. Aggressive tendencies
   c. Brand loyalty (in purchasing products)
   d. Television viewing

REFERENCES AND SUGGESTED READINGS

Anderson, J. A. (1987). *Communication research: Issues and methods.* New York: McGraw-Hill.

Baran, S. B., Mok, J. J., Land, M., & Kang, T. Y. (1989). You are what you buy. *Journal of Communication, 39*(2), 46–55.

Bergen, L. A., & Weaver, D. (1988). Job satisfaction of daily newspaper journalists and organization size. *Newspaper Research Journal, 9*(2), 1–14.

Bloom, M. (1986). *The experience of research.* New York: Macmillan.

Carroll, R. (1989). Market size and TV news values. *Journalism Quarterly, 66*(1), 48–56.

Chadwick, B., Bahr, H., & Albrecht, S. (1984). *Social science research methods.* Englewood Cliffs, NJ: Prentice-Hall.

Demers, D. (1994). Effect of organizational size on job satisfaction of top editors at U.S. dailies. *Journalism Quarterly, 71*(4), 914–925.

Emmert, P., & Barker, L. L. (1989). *Measurement of communication behavior.* White Plains, NY: Longman.

Fischer, P. M., Richards, J. V., Berman, E. J., & Krugman, D. M. (1989). Recall and eye-tracking study of adolescents viewing tobacco advertisements. *Journal of the American Medical Association, 261*, 840–889.

Gantz, W. (1978). How uses and gratifications affect recall of television news. *Journalism Quarterly, 55*(4), 664–672.

Gerbner, G., Gross, L., Morgan, M., & Signorielli, N. (1980). The mainstreaming of America: Violence profile no. 11. *Journal of Communication, 30*(3), 10–29.

Giffard, C. (1984). Developed and developing nations' news in U.S. wire service files to Asia. *Journalism Quarterly, 61*(1), 14–19.

Guilford, J. P. (1954). *Psychometric methods.* New York: McGraw-Hill.

Heeter, C., Brown, N., Soffin, S., Stanley, C., & Salwen, M. (1989). Agenda setting by electronic text news. *Journalism Quarterly, 66*(1), 101–106.

Hinkle, G., & Elliot, W. R. (1989). Science coverage in three newspapers and three supermarket tabloids. *Journalism Quarterly, 66*(2), 353–358.

Hsia, H. J. (1988). *Mass communication research methods: A step-by-step approach.* Hillsdale, NJ: Lawrence Erlbaum.

Jacobs, R. (1995). Exploring the determinants of cable television subscriber satisfaction. *Journal of Broadcasting and Electronic Media, 39*(2), 262–274.

Kaid, L., Chanslor, M. & Hovind, M. (1992). The influence of program and commercial type on political advertising effectiveness. *Journal of Broadcasting and Electronic Media, 36*(3), 303–320.

Kerlinger, F. N. (1986). *Foundations of behavioral research* (3rd ed.). New York: Holt, Rinehart & Winston.

Kerlinger, F. N., & Pedhazur, E. (1986). *Multiple regression in behavioral research* (2nd ed.). New York: Holt, Rinehart & Winston.

Krugman, D. M., & Johnson, K. F. (1991). Differences in the consumption of traditional broadcast and VCR movie rentals. *Journal of Broadcasting and Electronic Media, 35*(2), 213–232.

Lin, C. A., & Atkin, D. J. (1989). Parental mediation and rulemaking for adolescent use of television and VCRs. *Journal of Broadcasting and Electronic Media, 33*(1), 53–69.

Lindlof, T. R. (Ed.). (1987). *Natural audiences: Qualitative research of media uses and effects.* Norwood, NJ: Ablex.

Markham, D. (1968). The dimensions of source credibility for television newscasters. *Journal of Communication, 18*(1), 57–64.

Mason, E. J., & Bramble, W. J. (1989). *Understanding and conducting research* (2nd ed.). New York: McGraw-Hill.

McNemar, Q. (1969). *Psychological statistics.* (4th ed.). New York: John Wiley.

Milavsky, J., Kessler, R., Stipp, H., & Rubens, W. (1982). Television and aggression. New York: Academic Press.

Nunnally, J. C., & Bernstein, I. H. (1978). *Psychometric theory.* (3rd ed.). New York: McGraw-Hill.

Osgood, C., Suci, G., & Tannenbaum, P. (1957). *The measurement of meaning.* Urbana: University of Illinois Press.

Pokrywczynski, J. (1986). *Advertising effects and viewer involvement with televised sports.* Unpublished doctoral dissertation, University of Georgia, Athens.

Robinson, J., & Shaver, P. (1973). *Measures of social psychological attitudes* (2nd ed.). Ann Arbor, MI: Institute for Social Research.

Roscoe, J. (1975). *Fundamental research statistics for the behavioral sciences.* New York: Holt, Rinehart & Winston.

Schweitzer, J. C. (1989). Factors affecting scholarly research among mass communication faculty. *Journalism Quarterly, 66*(2), 410–417.

Shah, H. & Gayatri, G. (1994). Development news in elite and non-elite newspapers in Indonesia. *Journalism Quarterly, 71*(2), 411–420.

Smith, M. J. (1988). *Contemporary communication research methods.* Belmont, CA: Wadsworth.

Wanta, W., & Leggett, D. (1988). Hitting paydirt: Capacity theory and sports announcers' use of clichés. *Journal of Communication, 38*(4), 82–89.

Weinberger, M. G., & Spotts, H. E. (1989). Humor in U.S. versus U.K. TV commercials. *Journal of Advertising, 18*(2), 39–44.

Whitmore, E., & Tiene D. (1994). Viewing Channel One: Awareness of current events by teenagers. *Mass Comm Review, 21*(1/2), 67–75.

Williams, F., Rice, R. E., & Rogers, E. M. (1988). *Research methods and the new media.* New York: Free Press.

Zohoori, A. R. (1988). A cross-cultural analysis of children's television use. *Journal of Broadcasting and Electronic Media, 32*(1), 105–113.

Chapter

4

SAMPLING

This chapter describes the basics of the sampling methods that are used in mass media research. However, considering that sampling theory has become a distinct discipline in itself, there are some studies, such as nationwide surveys, that require a consultation of more technical discussions of sampling (for example, Cochran, 1977; Kish, 1965).

POPULATION AND SAMPLE

One goal of scientific research is to describe the nature of a **population**—that is, a group or a class of subjects, variables, concepts, or phenomena. In some cases, this can be done by investigating an entire class or group, such as a study of prime time television programs during the week of September 10–16. The process of examining every member of such a population is called a **census**. In many situations, however, an entire population cannot be examined due to time and resource constraints. Studying every member of a population is also generally cost-prohibitive and may in fact confound the research because measurements of large numbers of people often affect measurement quality.

The usual procedure in these instances is to take a sample from the population. A **sample** is a subset of the population that is representative of the entire population. An important word in this definition is *representative*. A sample that is not representative of the population, regardless of its size, is inadequate for testing purposes because the results cannot be generalized.

The sample selection process is illustrated using a Venn diagram (see Figure 4.1); the population is represented by the larger of the two spheres. A census would test or measure every element in the population (A), whereas a sample would measure or test a segment of the population (A_1). Although in Figure 4.1 it might seem that the sample is drawn from only one portion of the population, it is actually selected from every portion. Assuming that a sample is chosen according to proper guidelines and is representative of the population, the results from a study using the sample can be generalized to the population. However, results must be generalized with some caution because of the error that is inherent in all sample-selection methods. Theoretically, when a population is studied, only measurement error (that is, inconsistencies produced by the instrument used) will be present. However, when a sample is drawn from the population, the procedure introduces the likelihood of sampling error (that is, the degree to which measurements of the units or subjects selected differ from those of the population as a whole). Because a sample does not provide the exact data that a population would, the potential error must be taken into account.

A classic example of how sampling error can affect the results of a research study occurred during the 1936 presidential campaign. *Literary Digest* had predicted, based on the results of a sample survey, that Alf Landon would beat Franklin D. Roosevelt. Although the *Digest* sample included more than a million voters, it was composed mainly of affluent Republicans. Consequently, it inaccurately represented the population of eligible voters in the election. The researchers who conducted the study had failed to consider the population parameters

---

FIGURE 4.1   A Venn Diagram, As Used in the Process of Sample Selection

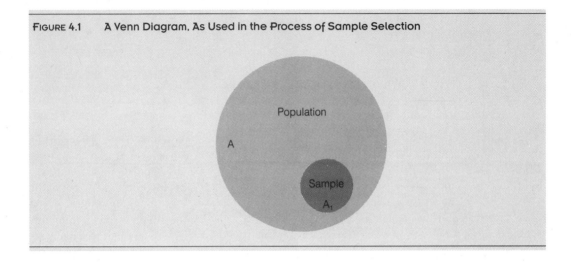

(characteristics) before selecting their sample. Of course, FDR was reelected in 1936, and it may be no coincidence that the *Literary Digest* went out of business shortly thereafter. (This 1936 research fiasco was the focus of many discussions about political polls by both George Bush and Bill Clinton during the 1992 presidential campaign.)

Have the "pollsters" improved? The following list shows the results from the five national media-sponsored polls conducted through November 1 for the 1992 presidential contest between Bill Clinton (Democrat), George Bush (Republican), and Ross Perot (Independent) as reported by *USA Today* shortly after the election. *USA Today* allocated undecided voters equally among the three candidates.

Poll	Clinton	Bush	Perot
Actual Vote	**43%**	**38%**	**19%**
USA Today/CNN/ Gallup	49	37	14
The Harris Poll	44	38	17
ABC News	44	37	16
NBC News/*Wall Street Journal*	44	36	15
CBS/*New York Times*	44	35	15
Washington Post	43	35	16

It is clear that researchers have become better at predicting the outcome of elections.

PROBABILITY AND NONPROBABILITY SAMPLES

A **probability sample** is selected according to mathematical guidelines whereby the chance for selection of each unit is known. A **nonprobability sample** does not follow the guidelines of mathematical probability. However, the most significant characteristic distinguishing the two types of samples is that probability sampling allows researchers to calculate the amount of sampling error present in a research study; nonprobability sampling does not.

A researcher should consider four points when deciding whether to use a probability or nonprobability sample:

1. *Purpose of the study.* Some research studies are not designed to be generalized to the population, but rather to investigate variable relationships or collect exploratory data for designing questionnaires or measurement instruments. A nonprobability sample is often appropriate in these situations.

2. *Cost versus value.* The sample should produce the greatest value for the least invest-

ment. If the cost of a probability sample is too high in relation to the type and quality of information collected, a nonprobability sample is a possible alternative.

3. *Time constraints.* In many cases researchers collecting preliminary information operate under time constraints imposed by sponsoring agencies, management directives, or publication guidelines. Since probability sampling is often time-consuming, a nonprobability sample may meet the need temporarily.

4. *Amount of acceptable error.* In preliminary or pilot studies, where error control is not a prime concern, a nonprobability sample is usually adequate.

While nonprobability sampling may have merit in some cases, it is always best to use a probability sample when the results will be generalized to the population. Any research study conducted to support or refute a significant question or a hypothesis should use a probability sample.

Probability sampling generally incorporates some type of systematic selection procedure, such as a table of random numbers, to ensure that each unit has an equal chance of being selected. However, it does not always guarantee a representative sample from the population, even when systematic selection is followed. It is possible to randomly select 50 members of the student body at a university in order to determine the average number of hours the students spend watching television during a typical week and, by extraordinary coincidence, end up with 50 students who do not own a TV set. Such an event is unlikely, but it is possible, and this possibility underscores the need to replicate any study.

TYPES OF NONPROBABILITY SAMPLES

Nonprobability sampling is frequently used in mass media research, particularly in the form of available samples, samples using volunteer subjects, and purposive samples. Mall intercepts (Chapter 7) use nonprobability sampling. An **available sample** (also known as a **convenience sample**) is a collection of readily accessible subjects for study, such as a group of students enrolled in an introductory mass media course or shoppers in a mall. Although available samples can be helpful in collecting exploratory information and may produce useful data in some instances, the samples are problematic because they contain unknown quantities of error. Researchers need to consider the positive and negative qualities of available samples before using them in a research study.

Available samples are a subject of heated debate in many research fields. Critics argue that regardless of what results they may generate, available samples do not represent the population and therefore have no external validity. (This problem was discussed in Chapter 2.) Proponents of the available sample procedure claim that if a phenomenon, characteristic, or trait does in fact exist, it should exist in any sample. Available samples can be useful in pretesting questionnaires or other preliminary (pilot study) work. They often help eliminate potential problems in research procedures, testing, and methodology before the final research study is attempted.

Subjects who constitute a *volunteer sample* also form a nonprobability sample, since the individuals are not selected mathematically. There is concern in all areas of research that persons who willingly participate in research projects differ greatly from nonvolunteers and may consequently produce erroneous research results. Rosenthal and Rosnow (1969) identified the characteristics of volunteer subjects on the basis of several studies and found that such subjects, in comparison with nonvolunteers, tend to exhibit higher educational levels, higher occupational status, greater need for approval, higher intelligence levels, and lower authoritarianism levels. They seem to be more sociable, more "arousal-seeking," and more unconventional; they are more likely to be first children; and they are generally younger.

Volunteer Samples

Some people involved in research claim that the worry about volunteer samples is a waste of time. Their claim is that all research conducted in mass media (as well as all behavioral research) uses volunteer samples all of the time—that in fact there are probably few, if any, behavioral research projects conducted with a truly random sample. Why? Because respondents in research projects must agree to participate. We cannot force a person to answer questions. Some critics say that because researchers ask questions of only those people who agree (volunteer) to answer them, the argument about using a random sample is moot.

These characteristics mean that use of volunteer subjects may significantly bias the results of a research study and may lead to inaccurate estimates of various population parameters (Rosenthal & Rosnow, 1969). Also, available data seem to indicate that volunteers may, more often than nonvolunteers, provide data to support a researcher's hypothesis. In some cases volunteer subjects are necessary—for example, in comparison tests of products or services. However, volunteers should be used carefully because, as with available samples, there is an unknown quantity of error present in the data.

Although volunteer samples have been shown to be inappropriate in scientific research, the media have begun to legitimize volunteers through the various polls conducted on radio and television stations and on the television networks. Local television news programs and radio station morning shows, for example, often report the results of the latest viewer or listener poll about some local concern. Even though announcers occasionally say that the polls are not intended to be scientific, the results are presented as such. Unwary listeners and viewers are being deceived by the media. These types of "studies" should be disallowed by the FCC.

A **purposive sample** includes subjects selected on the basis of specific characteristics or qualities and eliminates those who fail to meet these criteria. Purposive samples are often used in advertising studies; researchers select subjects who use a particular type of product and ask them to compare it with a new product. A purposive sample is chosen with the knowledge that it is not representative of the general population. In a similar method, the **quota sample**, subjects are selected to meet a predetermined or known percentage. For example, a researcher interested in finding out how VCR owners differ from non-VCR owners in their use of television may know that 40% of a particular population owns a VCR. The sample the researcher selects, therefore, would be composed of 40% VCR owners and 60% non-VCR owners (to reflect the population characteristics).

Another nonprobability sampling method is to select subjects haphazardly on the basis of appearance or convenience, or because they seem to meet certain requirements (for example, the subjects "look" like they qualify for the study in progress). Haphazard selection involves researcher subjectivity and introduces error. Some haphazard samples give the illusion of a probability sample; these must be carefully approached. For example, interviewing every 10th person who walks by in a shopping center is haphazard, since not everyone in the population has an equal chance of walking by that particular location. Some people live across town; some shop in other centers; and so on.

Some researchers, research suppliers, and field services try to work around the problems associated with convenience samples in mall intercepts by using a procedure based on what is called "The Law of Large Numbers." Essentially, the researchers interview *thousands* of respondents instead of hundreds. The presumption (and sales approach used on clients) is that the large number of respondents eliminates the problems of convenience sampling and somehow compensates for the fact that the sample is not random. *It does not*. The large number approach is a *convenience sample*. It is not a random sample, which is described below.

TYPES OF PROBABILITY SAMPLES

The most basic type of probability sampling is the simple **random sample** for which each subject or unit in the population has an equal chance of being selected. If a subject or unit is drawn from the population and removed from subsequent selections, the procedure is known as random sampling *without replacement*—the most widely used random sampling method. Random sampling *with replacement* involves returning the subject or unit into the population so that it has a chance of being chosen another time. Sampling with replacement is often used in more complicated research studies such as nationwide surveys (Raj, 1972).

Researchers usually use a table of random numbers to generate a simple random sample. For example, a researcher who wants to analyze 10 prime time television programs out of a population of 100 programs to determine how the medium portrays elderly people can take a random sample from the 100 programs by numbering each show from 00 to 99, then selecting 10 numbers from a table of random numbers, such as the brief listing in Table 4.1. First, a starting point in the table is selected at random. There is no specific way to choose a starting point; it is an arbitrary decision. The researcher then selects the remaining 9 numbers by going up, down, left, or right on the table—or even randomly throughout the table. For example, if the researcher decides to go

down the table from the starting point of 44 until a sample of 10 has been drawn, the sample would include television programs numbered 44, 85, 46, 71, 17, 50, 66, 56, 03, and 49.

Simple random samples for use in telephone surveys are often obtained by a process called **random digit dialing**. One method involves randomly selecting four-digit numbers (usually generated by a computer or through the use of a random numbers table) and adding them to the three-digit exchange prefixes in the city in which the survey is conducted. A single four-digit series may be used once, or it may be added to all the prefixes.

Unfortunately, a large number of the telephone numbers generated by this method of random digit dialing are invalid because some phones have been disconnected, some numbers generated have not yet been assigned, and so on. Therefore, it is advisable to produce at least three times the number of telephone numbers needed; if a sample of 100 is required, at least 300 numbers should be generated to allow for invalid numbers.

A second random digit dialing method that tends to decrease the occurrence of invalid numbers involves adding from one to three random digits to a telephone number selected from a phone directory or a list of phone numbers. One first selects a number from a list of telephone numbers (a directory or list purchased from a supplier). Assume that the number 448–3047 was selected from the list. The researcher could simply add a predetermined number, say 6, to produce 448–3053; or a predetermined two-digit number, say 21, to get 448–3068; or even a three-digit number, say 112, to produce 448–3159. Each variation of the method helps to eliminate many of the invalid numbers produced in pure random number generation, since telephone companies tend to distribute telephone numbers in series, or blocks. In this example, the block "30__" is in use, and there is a good chance that random add-ons to this block will be residential telephone numbers.

TABLE 4.1   Random Numbers

38	71	81	39	18	24	33	94	56	48	80	95	52	63	01	93	62
27	29	03	62	76	85	37	00	44	11	07	61	17	26	87	63	79
34	24	23	64	18	79	80	33	98	94	56	23	17	05	96	52	94
32	44	31	87	37	41	18	38	01	71	19	42	52	78	80	21	07
41	88	20	11	60	81	02	15	09	49	96	38	27	07	74	20	12
95	65	36	89	80	51	03	64	87	19	06	09	53	69	37	06	85
77	66	74	33	70	97	79	01	19	44	06	64	39	70	63	46	86
54	55	22	17	35	56	66	38	15	50	77	94	08	46	57	70	61
33	95	06	68	60	97	09	45	44	60	60	07	49	98	78	61	88
83	48	36	10	11	70	07	00	66	50	51	93	19	88	45	33	23
34	35	86	77	88	40	03	63	36	35	73	39	(44)	06	51	48	84
58	35	66	95	48	56	17	04	44	99	79	87	85	01	73	33	65
98	48	03	63	53	58	03	87	97	57	16	38	46	55	96	66	80
83	12	51	88	33	98	68	72	79	69	88	41	71	55	85	50	31
56	66	06	69	44	70	43	49	35	46	98	61	17	63	14	55	74
68	07	59	51	48	87	64	79	19	76	46	68	50	55	01	10	61
20	11	75	63	05	16	96	95	66	00	18	86	66	67	54	68	06
26	56	75	77	75	69	93	54	47	39	67	49	56	96	94	53	68
26	45	74	77	74	55	92	43	37	80	76	31	03	48	40	25	11
73	39	44	06	59	48	48	99	72	90	88	96	49	09	57	45	07
34	36	64	17	21	39	09	97	33	34	40	99	36	12	12	53	77
26	32	06	40	37	02	11	83	79	28	38	49	44	84	94	47	32
04	52	85	62	24	76	53	83	52	05	14	14	49	19	94	62	51
33	93	35	91	24	92	47	57	23	06	33	56	07	94	98	39	27
16	29	97	86	31	45	96	33	83	77	28	14	40	43	59	04	79

As indicated here, random number generation is possible via a variety of methods. However, two rules are always applicable: (1) each unit or subject in the population must have an equal chance of being selected, and (2) the selection procedure must be free from subjective intervention by the researcher. The purpose of random sampling is to reduce sampling error; violating random sampling rules only increases the chance of introducing such error into a study.

Similar in some ways to simple random sampling is a procedure called **systematic random sampling** in which every nth subject or unit is selected from a population. For example, to obtain a sample of 20 from a population of 100, or a sampling rate of $\frac{1}{5}$, a researcher randomly selects a starting point and a **sampling interval**. Thus, if the number 11 is chosen, the sample will include the 20 subjects or items numbered 11, 16, 21, 26, and so on. To add further randomness to the process, the researcher may randomly select both the starting point and the interval. For example, an interval of 11 together with a starting point of 29 would generate the numbers 40, 51, 62, 73, and so on.

Systematic samples are frequently used in mass media research. They often save time, re-

---

Simple Random Sampling

Advantages

1. Detailed knowledge of the population is not required.
2. External validity may be statistically inferred.
3. A representative group is easily obtainable.
4. The possibility of classification error is eliminated.

Disadvantages

1. A list of the population must be compiled.
2. A representative sample may not result in all cases.
3. The procedure can be more expensive than other methods.

---

sources, and effort when compared to simple random samples. In fact, since the procedure so closely resembles a simple random sample, many researchers consider systematic sampling as effective as the random procedure. The method is widely used in selecting subjects from lists such as telephone directories, *Broadcasting/Cablecasting Yearbook,* and *Editor & Publisher.*

The degree of accuracy of systematic sampling depends on the adequacy of the **sampling frame,** or complete list of members in the population. Telephone directories are inadequate sampling frames in most cases, since not all phone numbers are listed, and some people do not have telephones at all. However, lists that include all the members of a population have a high degree of precision. Before deciding to use systematic sampling, one should consider the goals and purpose of a study, and the availability of a comprehensive list of the population. If such a list is not available, systematic sampling is probably ill advised.

One major problem associated with systematic sampling is that the procedure is susceptible to **periodicity**; that is, the arrangements or order of the items in the population list may bias the selection process. For example, consider the problem mentioned earlier of analyzing television programs to determine how the elderly are portrayed. Quite possibly, every 10th program listed may have been aired by ABC; the result would be a nonrepresentative sampling of the three networks.

Periodicity also causes problems when telephone directories are used to select samples. The alphabetical listing does not allow each person or household an equal chance of being selected. One way to solve the problem is to cut each name from the directory, place them all in a "hat," and draw names randomly. Obviously, this would take days to accomplish and it is not a real alternative. An easier way to use a directory is to tear the pages loose, mix them up, randomly select pages, and then randomly select names. Although this procedure does not totally solve the problem, it is generally accepted when simple random sampling is impossible. If periodicity is eliminated, systematic sampling can be an excellent sampling methodology.

Although a simple random sample is the usual choice in most research projects, some researchers do not wish to rely on randomness. In some projects, researchers want to *guarantee* that a specific subsample of the population

---

Systematic Sampling

Advantages

1. Selection is easy.
2. Selection can be more accurate than in a simple random sample.
3. The procedure is generally inexpensive.

Disadvantages

1. A complete list of the population must be obtained.
2. Periodicity may bias the process.

---

is adequately represented. No such guarantee is possible using a simple random sample. A **stratified sample** is the approach used when adequate representation of a subsample is desired. The characteristics of the subsample (strata or segment) may include almost any variable: age, sex, religion, income level, or even individuals who listen to specific radio stations or read certain magazines. The strata may be defined by an almost unlimited number of characteristics; however, each additional variable or characteristic makes the subsample more difficult to find. Therefore, incidence drops.

Stratified sampling ensures that a sample is drawn from a homogeneous subset of the population—that is, from a population with similar characteristics. Homogeneity helps researchers to reduce sampling error. For example, consider a research study on subjects' attitudes toward two-way, interactive cable television. The investigator, knowing that cable subscribers tend to have higher achievement levels, may wish to stratify the population according to education. Before randomly selecting subjects, the researcher divides the population into three levels: grade school, high school, and college. Then, if it is determined that 10% of the population completed college, a random sample proportional to the population should contain

10% of the population who meet this standard. As Babbie (1995) notes:

> Stratified sampling ensures the proper representation of the stratification variables to enhance representation of other variables related to them. Taken as a whole, then, a stratified sample is likely to be more representative on a number of variables than a simple random sample.

Stratified sampling can be applied in two different ways. **Proportionate stratified sampling** includes strata with sizes based on their proportion in the population. If 30% of the population is comprised of adults 18–24, then 30% of the total sample will be subjects in this age group. This procedure is designed to give each person in the population an equal chance of being selected. **Disproportionate stratified sampling** is used to over-sample or over-represent a particular stratum. The approach is used basically because the stratum is considered important for marketing, advertising, or other similar reasons. For example, a radio station that targets 25- to 54-year-olds may have ratings problems with the 25- to 34-year-old group. In a telephone study of 500 respondents, the station management may wish to have the sample represented as follows: 70% in the 24–34 group, 20% in the 35–49 group, and 10% in the 50–54 group.

Stratified Sampling

Advantages

1. Representativeness of relevant variables is ensured.
2. Comparisons can be made to other populations.
3. Selection is made from a homogeneous group.
4. Sampling error is reduced.

Disadvantages

1. A knowledge of the population prior to selection is required.
2. The procedure can be costly and time-consuming.
3. It can be difficult to find a sample if incidence is low.
4. Variables that define strata may not be relevant.

This distribution would allow researchers to break the 25–34 group into smaller groups such as males, females, fans of specific stations, and other subcategories and still have reasonable sample sizes.

The usual sampling procedure is to select one unit or subject at a time, but this requires the researcher to have a complete list of the population. In some cases there is no way to obtain such a list. One way to avoid this problem is to select the sample in groups or categories; this procedure is known as **cluster sampling**. For example, analyzing magazine readership habits of people in Wisconsin would be time-consuming and complicated if individual subjects were randomly selected. With cluster sampling, one can divide the state into districts, counties, or zip code areas and select groups of people from these areas.

Cluster sampling creates two types of errors: errors in defining the initial clusters and errors in selecting from the clusters. For example, a zip code area may comprise mostly residents of a low socioeconomic status who are unrepresentative of the remainder of the state; if selected for analysis, such a group may confound the research results. To help control

such error, it is best to use small areas or clusters, both to decrease the number of elements in each cluster and to maximize the number of clusters selected (Babbie, 1995).

In many nationwide studies, researchers use a form of cluster sampling called **multistage sampling**, in which individual households or persons (not groups) are selected. Figure 4.2 demonstrates a four-stage sequence for a nationwide survey. First, a cluster of counties (or another specific geographic area) in the United States is selected. This cluster is narrowed by randomly selecting a county, district, or block group within the principal cluster. Next, individual blocks are selected within each area. Finally, a convention such as "the third household from the northeast corner" is established, and then the individual households in the sample can be identified by applying the selection formula in the stages just described.

In many cases researchers also need to randomly select an individual in a given household. In most cases researchers cannot count on being able to interview the person who happens to answer the telephone. Usually *demographic quotas* are established for a research

---

Cluster Sampling

Advantages

1. Only part of the population need be enumerated.
2. Costs are reduced if clusters are well defined.
3. Estimates of cluster parameters are made and compared to the population.

Disadvantages

1. Sampling errors are likely.
2. Clusters may not be representative of the population.
3. Each subject or unit must be assigned to a specific cluster.

---

study, which means that a certain percentage of all respondents must be of a certain sex or age. In this type of study, researchers determine which person in the household should answer the questionnaire by using a form of random numbers table, as illustrated in Table 4.2.

To get a random selection of individuals in the selected households, the interviewer simply asks each person who answers the telephone, "How many people are there in your home who are age 12 or older?" If the first respondent answers "Five," the interviewer asks to speak to the fifth-oldest (in this case the youngest) person in the home. Each time a call is completed, the interviewer checks off on the table the number representing the person questioned. If the next household called also has five family members, the interviewer would move to the next number in the 5 column and ask to talk to the third-oldest person in the home.

The same table can be used to select respondents by gender—that is, the interviewer could ask, "How many males who are age 12 or older live in your home?" The interviewer could then ask for the nth oldest male, or female, according to the requirements of the survey.

Since the media are complex systems, researchers frequently encounter complicated

sampling methods. These are known as *hybrid* situations. Consider some researchers attempting to determine the potential for videotext distribution of a local newspaper to cable subscribers. This problem requires investigating readers and nonreaders of the newspaper in addition to cable subscribers and nonsubscribers. The research, therefore, requires random sampling from the following four groups:

Group A	Subscribers/Readers
Group B	Subscribers/Nonreaders
Group C	Nonsubscribers/Readers
Group D	Nonsubscribers/Nonreaders

The researcher must identify each subject as belonging to one of these four groups. If three variables were involved, sampling from eight groups would be required, and so on. In other words, researchers are often faced with very complicated sampling situations that involve numerous steps.

SAMPLE SIZE

Determining an adequate sample size is one of the most controversial aspects of sampling.

FIGURE 4.2   Census Tracts

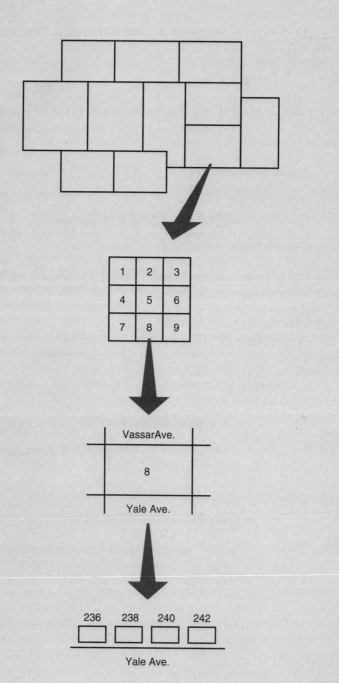

TABLE 4.2   Example of Matrix for Selecting Respondents at Random

	Number of people in household						
	1	**2**	**3**	**4**	**5**	**6**	**7**
Person to interview:	1	2	1	3	5	5	7
		1	3	4	3	2	6
			2	2	1	4	1
				1	2	6	4
					4	1	3
						3	2
							5

How large must a sample be to provide the desired level of confidence in the results? Unfortunately, there is no simple answer. There are suggested sample sizes for various statistical procedures, but no single sample-size formula or method is available for every research method or statistical procedure. For this reason, it is advisable to consult sampling texts for information concerning specific techniques (Cochran, 1977; Raj, 1972). The size of the sample required for a study depends on at least one or more of the following seven factors: (1) project type, (2) project purpose, (3) project complexity, (4) amount of error willing to be tolerated, (5) time constraints, (6) financial constraints, and (7) previous research in the area. (An eighth factor in private sector research is how much the client is *willing to spend*.) Research designed as a preliminary investigation to search for general indications generally does not require a large sample. However, projects intended to answer significant questions (those designed to provide information for decisions involving large sums of money or decisions that may affect people's lives) require high levels of precision and, therefore, large samples.

A few general principles guide researchers in determining an acceptable sample size. These suggestions are not based on mathematical or statistical theory, but they should provide a starting point in most cases.

1. A primary consideration in determining sample size is the research method used. Focus groups (Chapter 5) use samples of 6–12 people, but the results are not intended to be generalized to the population from which the respondents were selected. Samples with a total of 10–50 subjects are commonly used for pretesting measurement instruments and pilot studies, and for conducting studies that will be used only for heuristic value.

2. A sample of 50, 75, or 100 subjects per group (such as adults 18–24 years old) is often used by researchers. This base figure is used to "back in" to a total sample size. For example, assume a researcher is planning to conduct a telephone study with adults 18–54. Using the normal mass media age spans of 18–24, 25–34, 35–44, and 45-54, the researcher would probably consider a total sample of 400 as satisfactory (100 per age group, or "cell"). However, the client may also wish to investigate the differences in opinions and attitudes among men and women, which produces a total of eight age cells. In this case, a sample of 800 would be used—100 for each of the cell possibilities. Realistically, however, not many clients in private sector research would be willing to pay for a study with a sample of 800 respondents

(approximately $56,000 for a 20-minute telephone interview). More than likely, the client would accept 50 respondents in each of the eight cells, producing a total sample of 400 (8 × 50).

3. Sample size is always controlled by cost and time. Although researchers may wish to use a sample of 1,000 for a survey, the economics of such a sample are usually prohibitive. Research with 1,000 respondents can *easily* exceed $70,000. Most research is conducted using a sample that conforms to the project's budget. If a smaller sample is forced on a researcher by someone else (a client or a project manager), the results must be interpreted accordingly—that is, with caution. However, considering the fact that reducing a sample size from 1,000 to 400 (for example) reduces sampling error by only a small percentage, it may be wise to consider using smaller samples for most research projects.

4. Multivariate studies (Appendix 2) always require larger samples than do univariate studies because they involve the analysis of multiple response data (several measurements on the same subject). One guideline recommended for multivariate studies is as follows: 50 = very poor; 100 = poor; 200 = fair; 300 = good; 500 = very good; 1,000 = excellent (Comrey, 1973). Other researchers suggest using a sample of 100 *plus* 1 subject for each dependent variable in the analysis (Gorsuch, 1983).

5. As for panel studies, central location testing, focus groups, and other prerecruit projects, researchers should always select a larger sample than is actually required. The larger sample will compensate for those subjects who drop out of research studies for one reason or another, and allowances must be made for this in planning the sample selection. High dropout rates are especially prevalent in panel studies, where the same group of subjects is tested or measured frequently over a long period of time. Usually, researchers can expect 10%–25% of the sample to drop out of a study before it is completed, and 50% or more is not uncommon.

6. Information about sample size is available in published research. Consulting the work of other researchers provides a base from which to start. If a survey is planned and similar research indicates that a representative sample of 400 has been used regularly with reliable results, a sample larger than 400 may be unnecessary.

7. Generally speaking, the larger the sample used, the better. However, a large unrepresentative sample ("Law of Large Numbers") is as meaningless as a small unrepresentative sample, so researchers should not consider numbers alone. Quality is always more important in sample selection than mere size. During their 25 years of research, the authors have found that a sample size of less than 30 in a given cell (such as Females, 18–24) produces results that are unstable. For more information about sampling, see Tukey, 1986.

SAMPLING ERROR

Since researchers deal with samples from a population, there must be some way for them to compare the results of (or make inferences about) what was found in the sample to what *exists* in the target population. The comparison allows researchers to determine the accuracy of their data and involves the computation of error. All research involves error, be it sampling error, measurement error, or random error (also called unknown, or uncontrollable, error). Sampling error is also known as standard error. The different sources of error are additive; that is, total error is the sum of the three different sources. This section discusses sampling error in mass media research.

Sampling error occurs when measurements taken from a sample do not correspond to what exists in the population. For example, assume we wish to measure attitudes toward a new television program by 18–24-year-old viewers in Denver, Colorado. Further assume that all the viewers produce an average score of 6 on a 10-point program appeal measurement scale. Some viewers may dislike the program and rate the show 1, 2, or 3; some may find it mediocre and rate it 4, 5, 6, or 7; and the remaining viewers may like the show a lot and rate it 8, 9, or 10. The differences among the 18–24-year-old viewers provide an example of how sampling error may occur. If we asked each viewer to rate the show in a separate study and each one rated the program a 6, then no error exists. However, an error-free sample is highly unlikely.

Respondent differences do exist; some dislike the program, and others like it. Although the average program rating is 6 in the hypothetical example, it is possible to select a sample from the target population that does not match the average rating. A sample could be selected that includes only viewers who dislike the program. This would misrepresent the population because the average appeal score would be lower than the mean score. Computing the rate of sampling error allows researchers to assess the risk involved in accepting research findings as "real."

Computing sampling error is appropriate only with probability samples. Sampling error cannot be computed with research using nonprobability samples because not everyone has an equal chance of being selected. This is one reason nonprobability samples are used only in preliminary research or in studies where error rates are not considered important.

Sampling error computations are essential in research and are based on the concept of the **central limit theorem**. In its simplest form, the theorem states that the sum of a large number of independent and identically distributed random variables (or **sampling distributions**) has an **approximate normal distribution**. A theoretical sampling distribution is the set of all possible samples of a given size. This distribution of values is described by a bell-shaped curve, or *normal curve* (also known as a *Gaussian distribution,* after German mathematician and astronomer Karl F. Gauss, who used the

concept to analyze observational errors). The normal distribution is important in computing sampling error because sampling errors (a sampling distribution) made in repeated measurements tend to be normally distributed.

Computing standard error is a process of determining, with a certain amount of confidence, the difference between a sample and the target population. Error can occur by chance or through some fault of the research procedure. However, when probability sampling is used, the incidence of error can be determined because of the relationship between the sample and the normal curve. A normal curve, as shown in Figure 4.3, is symmetrical about the mean or midpoint, which indicates that an equal number of scores lies on either side of the midpoint.

CONFIDENCE LEVEL AND CONFIDENCE INTERVAL

Sampling error involves two concepts: **confidence level** and **confidence interval**. After a research project has been conducted, the researcher estimates the accuracy of the results in terms of a level of confidence that the results lie within a specified interval. For example, a researcher may say he is 95% confident (confidence level) that his finding—in which 50% of his study's respondents named "ER" as their favorite TV program—is within ± 5% (confidence interval) of the *true* population percentage.

In every normal distribution, the standard deviation defines a standard unit of distance from the midpoint of the distribution to the outer limits of the distribution. These standard deviation interval units (values) are used in establishing the confidence interval that is accepted in a research project. In addition, the standard deviation units indicate the amount of standard error. For example, using an interval (confidence interval) of −1 or +1 standard deviation unit—1 standard error—says that the probability is that 68% of the sample selected from the population will produce esti-

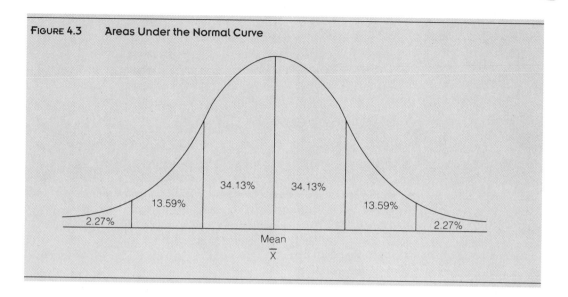

FIGURE 4.3   Areas Under the Normal Curve

34.13%   34.13%

13.59%   13.59%

2.27%   2.27%

Mean
$\overline{X}$

mates within that distance from the population value (1 standard deviation unit).

Researchers use a number of different confidence intervals. Greater confidence in results is achieved when the data are tested at higher levels, such as 95%. Research projects that are preliminary in nature or whose results are not intended to be used for significant decision making can and should use more conservative confidence levels, such as 68%. Conducting research that deals with human subjects is difficult enough on its own, without further complicating the work with highly restrictive confidence levels. The researcher must balance necessity with practicality. For instance, a researcher might need to ask whether her investigation concerning tastes and preferences in music needs to be tested at a confidence level of 95% or 99%. The answer is, No. In fact, the necessity for confidence levels and confidence intervals in behavioral research is under debate. Research is often judged as good or bad depending on whether a study is "statistically significant," not on whether the study contributed anything to the advancement of knowledge. Statistical significance

alone does not anoint a research project as scientific; a nonsignificant finding is as important to knowledge as a study that "finds" statistical significance. For more information about the misguided nature of statistical significance, see Tukey, 1986.

The areas under the normal curve in Table 3 of Appendix 1 are used to determine other confidence intervals. For example, the 90% confidence interval (.45 on either side of the mean) corresponds to 1.645 standard errors; the 95% interval corresponds to 1.96 standard errors; and the 99% interval corresponds to 2.576 standard errors. If the statistical data from the sample falls within the range set by the researcher, the results are considered significant.

COMPUTING STANDARD ERROR

The essence of statistical hypothesis testing is to draw a sample from a target population, compute some type of statistical measurement, and compare the results to the theoretical sampling distribution. The comparison determines the frequency with which sample values of a statistic are expected to occur.

TABLE 4.3	Finding Error Rate Using a Rating of 20		
Sample size	Error	Lower limit	Upper limit
600	±1.63	18.37	21.63
700	±1.51	18.49	21.51
800	±1.41	18.59	21.41
900	±1.33	18.67	21.33
1,000	±1.26	18.74	21.26
1,500	±1.03	18.97	21.03

The *expected value* of a statistic is the mean of the sampling distribution. The standard error is the standard deviation of the sampling distribution. There are several ways to compute standard (sampling) error, but no single method is appropriate for all sample types or for all situations. In addition, error formulas vary in complexity. One error formula, designed for estimating audience sizes during certain time periods or for certain programs and for measuring cumulative audiences (see Chapter 15), uses the standard error of a percentage derived from a simple random sample. If the sample percentage is designated as p, the size of the sample as n, and the estimated, or standard, error of the sample percentage as SEp, the formula is as follows:

$$SE(p) = \sqrt{\frac{p(100 - p)}{n}}$$

Suppose a random sample of 500 households produces a rating (or estimate of the percentage of viewers—see Chapter 14) of 20 for a particular show. This means that 20% of those households were tuned to that channel at that time. The formula can be used to calculate the standard error as follows:

$$SE(p) = \sqrt{\frac{20\,(80)}{500}}$$

$$SE(p) = \sqrt{\frac{1,600}{500}}$$

$$= \sqrt{3.2}$$

$$= \pm 1.78$$

That is, the rating of 20 computed in the survey is subject to an error of ±1.78 points; the actual rating could be as low as 18.22 or as high as 21.78.

Standard error is directly related to sample size. The error figure improves as the sample size is increased, but in decreasing increments. Thus, an increase in sample size does not provide a big gain, as illustrated by Table 4.3. As can be seen, even with a sample of 1,500, the standard error is only .75 better than with the sample of 500 computed above. A researcher would need to determine whether the increase in time and expense caused by an additional 1,000 subjects would justify such a proportionally small increase in precision.

Table 4.4 shows the amount of error at the 95% confidence level for measurements that contain dichotomous variables (such as "yes/no"). For example, with a sample of 1,000 and a 30% "yes" response to a question, the probable error due to sample size alone is ±2.9. This means that we are 95% sure that our values for this particular question fall between 27.1% and 32.9%.

Sampling error is an important concept in all research areas because it provides an indication of the degree of accuracy of the research. Research studies published by large audience measurement firms such as Arbitron and A. C.

Nielsen are required by the Electronic Media Ratings Council (EMRC) to include simplified charts to assist in determining sampling error. In addition, each company provides some type of explanation about error, such as the Arbitron statement contained in every ratings book section entitled "Description of Methodology":

> Arbitron estimates are subject to statistical variances associated with all surveys which use a sample of the universe . . . the accuracy of Arbitron estimates, data and reports and their statistical evaluators cannot be determined to any precise mathematical value or definition.

Statistical error due to sampling is found in all research studies. Researchers must pay specific attention to the potential sources of error in any study. Producing a study riddled with error is tantamount to never having conducted the study at all. If the magnitude of error were subject to accurate assessment, researchers could simply determine the source of error and correct it. Since this is not possible, they must accept error as part of the research process, attempt to reduce its effects to a minimum, and remember always to consider its presence when interpreting their results.

SAMPLE WEIGHTING

In an ideal research study, a researcher has enough respondents or subjects with the required demographic, psychographic (why people behave in specific ways), or lifestyle characteristics. The ideal sample, however, is rare, due to the time and budget constraints of most research. Instead of canceling a research project because of sampling inadequacies, most researchers utilize a statistical procedure known as **weighting**, or *sample balancing*. That is, when subject totals in given categories do not reach the necessary population percentages, subjects' responses are multiplied (weighted) to allow for the shortfall. A single subject's responses may be

multiplied by 1.3, 1.7, 2.0, or any other figure to reach the predetermined required level.

Subject weighting is a controversial data manipulation technique, especially in the area of broadcast ratings. The major question is just how much one subject's responses can be weighted and still be representative. Weighting is discussed in greater detail in Chapter 14.

SUMMARY

To make predictions about events, concepts, or phenomena, researchers must perform detailed, objective analyses. One procedure to use in such analyses is a census, in which every member of the population is studied. Conducting a census for each research project is impractical, however, and researchers must resort to alternative methods. The most widely used alternative is to select a random sample from the population, examine it, and make predictions from it that can be generalized to the population. There are several procedures for identifying the units that are to compose a random sample.

If the scientific procedure is to provide valid and useful results, researchers must pay close attention to the methods they use in selecting a sample. This chapter has described several types of samples commonly used in mass media research. Some are elementary and do not require a great deal of time or resources; others entail great expense and time. Researchers must decide whether costs and time are justified in relation to the results generated.

Sampling procedures must not be taken lightly in the process of scientific investigation. It makes no sense to develop a research design for testing a valuable hypothesis or research question and then nullify this effort by neglecting correct sampling procedures. These procedures must be continually scrutinized to ensure that the results of an analysis are not sample-specific—that is, that the results are not based on the type of sample used in the study.

TABLE 4.4   Sampling Error at .95 Confidence Interval

Survey result is:		1% or 99%	5% or 95%	10% or 90%	15% or 85%	20% or 80%
Sample of:	25	4.0	8.7	12.0	14.3	16.0
	50	2.8	6.2	8.5	10.1	11.4
	75	2.3	5.0	6.9	8.2	9.2
	100	2.0	4.4	6.0	7.1	8.0
	150	1.6	3.6	4.9	5.9	6.6
	200	1.4	3.1	4.3	5.1	5.7
	250	1.2	2.7	3.8	4.5	5.0
	300	1.1	2.5	3.5	4.1	4.6
	400	.99	2.2	3.0	3.6	4.0
	500	.89	2.0	2.7	3.2	3.6
	600	.81	1.8	2.5	2.9	3.3
	800	.69	1.5	2.1	2.5	2.8
	1,000	.63	1.4	1.9	2.3	2.6
	2,000	.44	.96	1.3	1.6	1.8
	5,000	.28	.62	.85	1.0	1.1

QUESTIONS AND PROBLEMS FOR FURTHER IINVESTIGATION

1. The use of available samples in research has long been a target for heated debate. Some researchers say that available samples are inaccurate representations of the population; others claim that if a concept or phenomenon exists, it should exist in an available sample as well as in a random sample. Which argument do you agree with? Explain your answer.

2. Many research studies use small samples. What are the advantages or disadvantages of this practice? Can any gain other than cost savings be realized by using a small sample in a research study?

3. What sampling technique might be appropriate for the following research projects?
   a. A pilot study to test whether people understand the directions to a telephone questionnaire
   b. A study to determine who buys videocassette recorders
   c. A study to determine the demographic makeup of the audience for a local television show
   d. A content analysis of commercials during Saturday morning children's programs
   e. A survey examining the differences between newspaper readership in high-income households and low-income households

REFERENCES AND SUGGESTED READINGS

Babbie, E. R. (1995). *The practice of social research* (7th ed.). Belmont, CA: Wadsworth.

Blalock, H. M. (1972). *Social statistics.* New York: McGraw-Hill.

Cochran, W. G. (1977). *Sampling techniques.* (3rd ed.). New York: John Wiley.

Comrey, A. L., & Lee, H. B. (1973). *A first course in factor analysis.* (2nd ed.). Hillsdale, N. J.: L. Erlbaum Associates.

Fletcher, J. E. (Ed.). (1981). *Handbook of radio and TV broadcasting.* New York: Van Nostrand Reinhold.

TABLE 4.4   Continued

Survey result is:	25% or 75%	30% or 70%	35% or 65%	40% or 60%	45% or 55%	50%
Sample of:	17.3	18.3	19.1	19.6	19.8	20.0
	12.3	13.0	13.5	13.9	14.1	14.2
	10.0	10.5	11.0	11.3	11.4	11.5
	8.7	9.2	9.5	9.8	9.9	10.0
	7.1	7.5	7.8	8.0	8.1	8.2
	6.1	6.5	6.8	7.0	7.0	7.1
	5.5	5.8	6.0	6.2	6.2	6.3
	5.0	5.3	5.5	5.7	5.8	5.8
	4.3	4.6	4.8	4.9	5.0	5.0
	3.9	4.1	4.3	4.4	4.5	4.5
	3.6	3.8	3.9	4.0	4.1	4.1
	3.0	3.2	3.3	3.4	3.5	3.5
	2.8	2.9	3.1	3.1	3.2	3.2
	1.9	2.0	2.1	2.2	2.2	2.2
	1.2	1.3	1.4	1.4	1.4	1.4

Gorsuch, R. L. (1983). *Factor analysis.* (2nd ed.). Philadelphia: W. B. Saunders.

Kish, L. (1965). *Survey sampling.* New York: John Wiley.

Nunnally, J. C., & Bernstein, I. H. (1994). *Psychometric theory* (3rd ed.). New York: McGraw-Hill.

Raj, D. (1972). *The design of sample surveys.* New York: McGraw-Hill.

Rosenthal, R., & Rosnow, R. L. (1969). *Artifact in behavioral research.* New York: Academic Press.

Tukey, J. W. (1986). *The collected works of John W. Tukey,* Vols. III and IV. Belmont, CA: Wadsworth and Brooks Cole.

Walizer, M. H., & Wienir, P. L. (1978). *Research methods and analysis: Searching for relationships.* New York: Harper & Row.

Chapter

5

Qualitative Research Methods

Part II on research approaches proceeds from the more general to the more specific research techniques. This first chapter discusses qualitative analysis, which mainly relies on the analysis of words that reflect everyday experience. This is followed by a chapter on content analysis, which also focuses on words and other message characteristics but is conducted in a more systematic and measured way. The next chapter discusses survey research, which relies on greater quantification and greater measurement sophistication than either qualitative research or content analysis. This sophistication, however, comes with a price: Increasing quantifiability also narrows the types of research questions that can be addressed. Or to put it another way, research depth is sacrificed to gain research breadth. The survey chapter is followed by a chapter on longitudinal research, since most longitudinal research is based on surveys. Finally, this part concludes with a discussion of experimental methods, which are among the most precise, complex, and intricate of methodologies.

Cooper, Potter and Dupagne (1994) document the importance of qualitative methods in the field. They report that although almost 60% of published mass communication research studies conducted since 1971 have used quantitative methods, qualitative techniques were used either exclusively (33%) or partially in the other 40%.

Qualitative research and its advantages and disadvantages were introduced in Chapter 3. This chapter outlines the major differences between the two methods and examines the most frequently used techniques in qualitative research.

AIMS AND PHILOSOPHY

The term *qualitative research* covers a wide range of research techniques. Erickson (1986) provides a definition that may help students understand better what the process is all about. Erickson suggests that qualitative research has four distinctive characteristics:

1. Intensive, long-term participation in a field setting
2. Careful recording of what happens in that setting through field notes and other types of documentary evidence
3. Analysis of the field data
4. Reporting of results, including detailed descriptions, quotes, and commentary

Qualitative research differs from quantitative research along three main dimensions. First, the two methods have a different philosophy of reality. For the quantitative researcher, reality is objective; it exists apart from researchers and can be seen by all. In other words, it is out there. For the qualitative researcher, there is no single reality. Each observer creates reality as part of the research process; it is subjective and exists only in reference to the observer. Further, the quantitative researcher believes that reality can be divided into component parts, and that he or she gains knowledge of the whole by looking at these parts. On the other hand, the qualitative researcher examines the entire process, believing that reality is holistic and cannot be subdivided.

Second, the two methods have different views of the individual. The quantitative researcher believes all human beings are basically

83

In My Room: A Qualitative Approach to Studying Teen Identities

One of the advantages of the qualitative approach is that it allows for great flexibility during the research process. For example, Brown, Dykers, Steele, and White (1994) originally started out to study the best way to construct health messages to reach adolescents. In the course of their study, the researchers conducted interviews with several teenagers in the teens' bedrooms. The interviewers were struck by the wide variation in the general appearance of the bedrooms and the way the walls were decorated.

Subsequent investigation led to the notion of "room culture," which analyzed how bedrooms and the things they contain helped teens relate to the world and create their own identities. A big part of the study of room culture concerned the way media were used as a source of cultural options. Pictures were taken of each room and analyzed to see what they suggested about how the young people were using the media.

The investigators also found that having teens talk about their bedrooms was a good way to establish rapport for subsequent interviews and helped convince the teens to keep journals and diaries about their use of the media. All in all, this study shows the great versatility of the qualitative method.

---

similar and looks for general categories to summarize their behaviors or feelings. The qualitative investigator believes that human beings are fundamentally different and cannot be pigeonholed.

Third, quantitative researchers aim to generate general laws of behavior and explain many things across many settings. In contrast, qualitative scholars attempt to produce a unique explanation about a given situation or individual. Whereas quantitative researchers strive for breadth, qualitative researchers strive for depth. The practical differences between these approaches are perhaps most apparent in the research process. The following five major research areas describe significant differences between quantitative research and qualitative research:

1. *Role of the researcher.* The quantitative researcher strives for objectivity and is separated from the data. The qualitative researcher is an integral part of the data; in fact, without the active participation of the researcher, no data exist.

2. *Design.* In quantitative methods, the design of a study is determined before it begins. In qualitative research, the design evolves during the research; it can be adjusted or changed as the research progresses.

3. *Setting.* The quantitative researcher tries to limit contaminating and/or confounding variables by conducting investigations in controlled settings. The qualitative researcher conducts studies in the field, in natural surroundings, trying to capture the normal flow of events without controlling extraneous variables.

4. *Measurement instruments.* In quantitative research, measurement instruments exist apart from the researcher; another party could use the instruments to collect data in the researcher's absence. In qualitative research, the researcher is the instrument; no other individual can substitute for the qualitative researcher.

5. *Theory building.* Whereas the quantitative researcher uses research to test, support, or reject theory, the qualitative researcher develops theories as part of the research process—theory is "data driven" and emerges as part of

the research process, evolving from the data as they are collected.

Despite these differences, many researchers are now using a combination of the quantitative and qualitative approaches in order to fully understand the phenomenon they are studying. As Miles and Huberman (1984, p. 20) state:

> It is getting harder to find any methodologists solidly encamped in one epistemology or the other. More and more "quantitative" methodologists . . . are using naturalistic and phenomenological approaches to complement tests, surveys, and structured interviews. On the other side, an increasing number of ethnographers and qualitative researchers are using predesigned conceptual frameworks and prestructured instrumentation. . . . Most people now see the world with more ecumenical eyes.

Although qualitative research can be an excellent method to collect and analyze data, researchers must keep in mind that the results of such studies have interpretational limits. In most cases, qualitative research studies use small samples: respondents or units that are not representative of the population from which they are drawn. Qualitative research is a useful mass media research tool only when its limitations are recognized. All too often the results from small-sample qualitative projects are interpreted as though they had been collected via large-sample quantitative techniques. This approach can only cause problems in the long run: Incorrect decisions are highly likely if they are based on small-sample research.

DATA ANALYSIS IN QUALITATIVE RESEARCH

Before examining some specific types of qualitative research, let's discuss qualitative data and methods of analysis in general.

Qualitative data come in a variety of forms, such as notes made while observing in the field, interview transcripts, documents, diaries, and journals. In addition, a researcher accumulates a great deal of data during the course of a study. Organizing, analyzing, and making sense of all this information poses special challenges for the qualitative researcher.

Unlike the quantitative approach, which waits until all the numbers are in before beginning analysis, data analysis in qualitative studies is done early in the collection process and continues throughout the project. In addition, quantitative researchers generally follow a deductive model in data analysis: Hypotheses are derived prior to the study, and relevant data are then collected and analyzed to determine whether the hypotheses were confirmed or not confirmed.

On the other hand, qualitative researchers use an inductive method: Data are collected relevant to some topic and are grouped into appropriate and meaningful categories; explanations emerge from the data themselves.

PREPARING THE DATA

To facilitate working with the large amounts of data generated by a qualitative analysis, the researcher generally first organizes the information along a temporal dimension. In other words, the data are arranged in chronological order according to the sequence of events that occurred during the investigation. Further, each piece of information should be coded to identify the source. Multiple photocopies of the notes, transcripts, and other documents should also be made.

The data are then organized into a preliminary category system. These categories might arise from the data themselves, or they might be suggested by prior research or theory. Many researchers prefer to do a preliminary run-through of the data and jot possible category assignments in the margins. For example, a qualitative study of teenage radio listening might produce many pages of interview transcripts. The researcher would read the comments and might write "peer group pressure" next to one section and "escape" next to another. When the process was finished a preliminary category system would have emerged from the data. Other researchers prefer to make many multiple copies of the data, cut them into coherent units of analysis, and physically sort them into as many categories as might be relevant. Finally, there are several software programs available that help organize qualitative data.

Moreover, many qualitative researchers like to have a particular room or other space that is specially suited for the analysis of qualitative data. Typically, this room has bulletin boards or other arrangements that allow for the visual display of data. Photocopies of notes, observations written on index cards, large flow charts, and marginal comments can then be conveniently arrayed so that the analysis task is simplified. This "analytical wallpaper" approach is particularly helpful when several members of the research team are working on the project because it is an efficient way to display the data to several people at once.

Finally, since the researcher is the main instrument in qualitative data collection and analysis, he or she must also do some preparation before beginning the task of investigation. Maykut and Morehouse (1994) describe this preparation as *epoche,* the process by which the researcher tries to remove or at least become aware of prejudices, viewpoints, or assumptions that might interfere with the analysis. *Epoche* helps the researcher put aside his or her personal viewpoints so that the phenomenon under study may be seen for itself.

ANALYSIS TECHNIQUES

There are many different analysis techniques that can be brought to bear on qualitative data. This section will discuss two of the best known:

the constant comparative technique and the analytical induction technique.

The **constant comparative technique** was first articulated by Glaser and Strauss (1967) and has been refined in more recent years (Lincoln & Guba, 1985). At a general level, the process consists of four steps:

1. Comparative assignment of incidents to categories
2. Elaboration and refinement of categories
3. Searching for relationships and themes among categories
4. Simplifying and integrating data into a coherent theoretical structure

Each step will be discussed in turn.

After the data have been prepared for analysis, the researcher groups each unit of analysis into a set of provisional categories. As each new unit is examined, it is constantly compared to other units previously assigned to that category to see if its inclusion is appropriate. It is possible that some initial categories may have only one or two incidents assigned to them while others may have a large number. If some units of analysis do not fit any preexisting category, new classifications may have to be created. Some units may fit in more than one category. These should be copied and included where relevant. Throughout the process, the emphasis is on comparing units and finding similarities among the units that fit into the category.

For example, suppose a researcher is doing a qualitative study about why individuals subscribe to on-line services such as CompuServe or America Online. Interviews are conducted with several people and transcribed. The researcher then defines each individual assertion as the unit of analysis and writes each statement on an index card. The first two cards selected for analysis mention getting news faster from on-line services. The researcher places both of these into a category tentatively labeled "news." The next statement talks about e-mail;

Personal Computers in Qualitative Research

Quantitative researchers have made extensive use of personal computers (PCs) in compiling and summarizing statistics. Similarly, qualitative researchers have discovered that the PC can aid them in their work as well. For instance, before the use of PCs became commonplace, field notes were either handwritten or typed and stored in file folders or boxes. Today, however, a researcher can store field notes as text with a text editing or word processing program and can structure data as text files. The availability of notebook computers enables researchers to word process field notes on location. Without a computer, creating typologies and concepts from the text was a laborious process. Using a PC, however, a researcher can cut and paste, move, scan, and search field notes for key words and phrases. In addition, key items or sections of text in notes can be flagged or specially coded for easy retrieval or indexing. When researchers worked without computers, the number of times a particular event or theme occurred had to be manually counted and summarized. PCs can scan text for codes and count and display frequencies. Many specific programs have been written for the qualitative researcher and many more are in the works. For more specifics, see Brent and Anderson (1990).

---

it does not seem to belong to the first category and is set aside. The next card mentions chat lines; the researcher decides this reason is similar to the one that mentioned e-mail and creates a new category called "interpersonal communication." The process is then repeated with every unit of analysis, which can be a long and formidable task. At some point during the process, however, the researcher begins to fine-tune and refine the categories.

During the category refinement stage the researcher writes rules or propositions that attempt to describe the underlying meaning that defines the category. Some rules for inclusion might be rewritten and revised throughout the study. These rules not only help to focus the study but also allow the researcher to start to explore the theoretical dimensions of the emerging category system. The ultimate value of these rules, however, is that they reveal what you are learning about your chosen topic and will help you determine your research outcome.

In the example mentioned above, after scanning all the data cards that were placed in the "interpersonal communication" category, a researcher might write a proposition such as

"People subscribe to on-line services in order to expand their circle of casual friends." Other similar statements would be written for the other categories.

The third phase of the method involves searching for relationships and common patterns across categories. The researcher examines the propositional statements and looks for meaningful connections. Some propositions will probably be strong enough to stand alone; others might be related in several important ways. Whatever the situation, the goal of this phase is to generate assertions that can explain and further clarify the phenomenon under study.

In our on-line example, the researcher might note that several propositions refer to the notion of expansion. People might use on-line services to expand their shopping opportunities, to enlarge their pool of potential chess opponents, or to have a greater number of news sources. The analyst might then generalize that the expansion of one's informational space is a key reason for subscribing.

In the final phase of the process, the report summarizing the research is written. All the results of the foregoing analyses are integrated into some coherent explanation of the phenomenon. The researcher attempts to offer a brief explanation but in sufficient detail to convey an idea of the scope of the project. The goal of this phase of the project is to arrive at an understanding of the people and/or the events being studied.

The **analytic induction strategy** blends together hypothesis construction and data analysis. It consists of the following steps (adapted from Stainback & Stainback, 1988):

1. Define a topic of interest and develop a hypothesis.
2. Study a case to see if the hypothesis works. If it doesn't work, reformulate it.
3. Study other cases until the hypothesis is in refined form.
4. Look for "negative cases" that might disprove the hypothesis. Reformulate again.
5. Continue until the hypothesis is adequately tested.

Note that in this method, an explanation for the phenomenon in the form of a hypothesis is generated at the beginning of the study. This is in contrast to the constant comparative technique, in which an explanation is derived as the end result of the research.

Perhaps the best way to demonstrate how this approach works is to use a simplified example. Let's suppose that a researcher is interested in explaining why people watch home shopping channels. Colleagues tell the researcher that the answer is obvious: People watch because they want to buy the merchandise. The researcher is not convinced of this but decides to use this explanation as an initial hypothesis. He/she seeks out a person who is known to be a heavy viewer of these channels. During the interview the person says that although she has ordered a couple of things off the air, her primary reason for watching is to find out about new and unusual products.

Armed with this information, the researcher reformulates the hypothesis: People watch the

home shopping channels to buy and find out about new products. Another viewer is interviewed and reports essentially the same reasons but also adds that she uses the prices advertised on the channel to comparison shop. Once again, the hypothesis is refined. The researcher posits that the home shopping channels are viewed for practical consumer-related reasons: finding bargains, learning about products, and comparing prices.

At this point, the researcher tries to find cases that might not fit the new hypothesis. A colleague points out that all of the people interviewed so far have been affluent with substantial disposable income and that perhaps people who are less well-off economically might watch the home shopping channels for other reasons. The researcher interviews a viewer from a different economic background and discovers that this person watches because he finds the people who do the selling entertaining to watch. Once again, the initial hypothesis is modified to take this finding into account.

The researcher then seeks out other cases from different economic levels to check the validity of this new hypothesis and continues to gather data until no further cases can be located that do not fit the hypothesis.

RELIABILITY AND VALIDITY IN QUALITATIVE DATA

The concepts of reliability and validity have different connotations for qualitative data. As discussed earlier, quantitative methods use distinct and precise ways to calculate indices of reliability and several articulated techniques that help establish validity. Although envisioned differently, reliability and validity are no less important in qualitative research. They help the reader determine how much confidence can be placed in the outcomes of the study and whether we can believe the researcher's conclusions.

Rather than emphasizing reliability and validity, Maykut and Morehouse (1994) address the trustworthiness of a qualitative research project. They summarize four factors that help build credibility:

1. *Multiple methods of data collection.* This is similar to the notion of triangulation that was discussed in Chapter 3. The use of interviews along with field observations and analysis of existing documents suggests that the topic was examined from several different perspectives, which helps build confidence in the findings.

2. *Audit trail.* This is essentially a permanent record of the original data used for analysis and the researcher's comments and analysis methods. The audit trail allows others to examine the thought processes involved in your work and allows them to assess the accuracy of your conclusions.

3. *Member checks.* In this technique you ask research participants to read your notes and conclusions and ask them if you have accurately described what they told you.

4. *Research team.* This method assumes that team members keep one another honest and on target when describing and interpreting their data. Sometimes an outside person is asked to observe the process and raise questions of possible bias or misinterpretation where appropriate.

The balance of this chapter discusses four common qualitative techniques: field observations, focus groups, intensive interviews, and case studies.

FIELD OBSERVATIONS

Field observation was rarely used in mass media research before 1980. Lowry (1979) re-

ported that only 2%–3% of the articles published in journalism and broadcasting journals used this technique. In the study mentioned above, Cooper, Potter and Dupagne (1994) found that about 2% of all published studies from 1965 to 1989 relied on observation. Recently, however, field observations have become more common in the research literature (Anderson, 1987; Lindlof, 1987, 1991, 1995).

Field observation is useful for collecting data and for generating hypotheses and theories. Like all qualitative techniques, it is concerned more with description and explanation than with measurement and quantification. Figure 5.1 shows that field observations are classified along two major dimensions: (1) the degree to which the researcher participates in the behavior under observation; and (2) the degree to which the observation is concealed.

Quadrant 1 in Figure 5.1 represents overt observation. In this situation, the researcher is identified when the study begins and those under observation are aware that they are being studied. Further, the researcher's role is only to observe, refraining from participation in the process under observation. Quadrant 2 represents overt participation. In this arrangement, the researcher is also known to those being observed, but unlike the situation represented in Quadrant 1, the researcher goes beyond the observer role and becomes a participant in the situation. Quadrant 3 represents the situation where the researcher's role is limited to that of observer, but those under observation are not aware they are being studied. Quadrant 4 represents a study in which the researcher participates in the process under investigation but is not identified as a researcher.

To illustrate the difference between the various approaches, assume that a researcher wants to observe and analyze the dynamics of writing comedy for television. The researcher could choose the covert observer technique and pretend to be doing something else (such as fixing a computer) while actually observing the TV writing team at work. Or, the researcher could

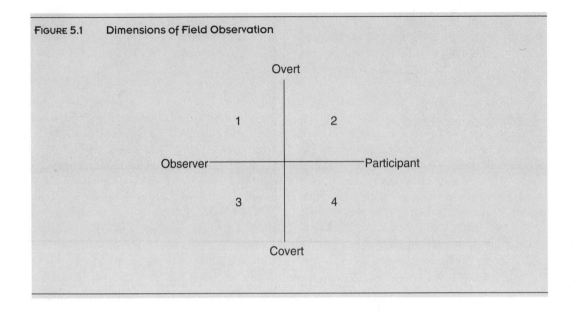

FIGURE 5.1   Dimensions of Field Observation

be introduced as someone doing a study of comedy writing and allowed to watch the team in action. If the research question is best answered by active participation, the researcher might be introduced as a researcher but would still participate in the writing process. If the covert participant strategy is used, the researcher might be introduced as a new writer just joining the group (such an arrangement might be made with the head writer, who would be the only person to know the identity of the researcher). The choice of technique depends upon the research problem, the degree of cooperation available from the group or individual observed, and ethical considerations. Covert participation may affect subjects' behavior and raise the ethical question of deception. On the other hand, the information gathered may be more valid if subjects are unaware of being scrutinized.

Some examples of field observation studies in mass media research include Gieber's (1956) classic study of gatekeeping (information flow) in the newsroom and Epstein's (1974) description of network news operations. Browne (1991) observed the operations at 11

Swiss radio stations for his study of localism in Swiss radio programming. Pekurny (1980) was an overt participant in his study of NBC's "Saturday Night Live." He was given access to all phases of the program, including discussions with writers about joke structure and the suitability of material for broadcast. Lemish (1987) used overt observation in her study of television viewing by infants and toddlers. Researchers visited the homes of 16 families and observed the viewing behavior of infants during 1- to 2–hour periods. Lull (1982) conducted a mass observation study of the TV viewing habits of more than 90 families. Observers spent 2 days with the families and then returned to conduct interviews with each person they observed. Note that, by using the two data sources (observations and interviews), Lull was "triangulating" to gain additional perspective on his data. He found that the interview data were only partially supported by the observations. Observers noted that the father was the primary controller of the TV set, but the interviews suggested the father's influence was somewhat less. Similarly, Moriarty and

Everett (1994) conducted a study where researchers observed family members watching television and recorded their behaviors on a moment-to-moment basis during several 45-minute viewing episodes.

ADVANTAGES OF FIELD OBSERVATIONS

Although field observation is not an appropriate technique for every research question because of the lack of control and quantification, it does possess several unique advantages. For one thing, many mass media problems and questions cannot be studied using any other methodology. Field observation often helps the researcher to define basic background information necessary to frame a hypothesis and to isolate independent and dependent variables. For example, a researcher interested in how creative decisions in advertising are made could observe several decision-making sessions to see what happens. Field observations often make excellent pilot studies because they identify important variables and provide useful preliminary information. In addition, since the data are gathered firsthand, observation is not dependent on the subjects' ability or willingness to report their behavior. For example, young children may lack the reading or verbal skills necessary to respond to a questionnaire concerning their television viewing behavior, but such data are easily gathered by the observational technique.

A field observation is not always used as a preliminary step to other approaches. Sometimes it alone is the only appropriate approach, especially when quantification is difficult. Field observation is particularly suitable for a study of the gatekeeping process in a network television news department because quantification of gatekeeping is difficult.

Field observation may also provide access to groups that would otherwise be difficult to observe or examine. For example, a questionnaire sent to a group of producers of X-rated movies is not likely to have a high return rate. An observer, however, may be able to establish enough mutual trust with such a group to persuade them to respond to rigorous questioning.

Field observation is usually inexpensive. In most cases, it requires only writing materials or a small tape recorder. Expenses increase if the problem under study requires several observers, extensive travel, or special equipment (such as video recording machines).

Perhaps the most noteworthy advantage of field observation is that the study takes place in the natural setting of the activity being observed and thus can provide data rich in detail and subtlety. Many mass media situations, such as a family watching television, are complex and constantly subjected to intervening influences. Field observation, because of the opportunity for careful examination, allows observers to identify these otherwise unknown variables.

DISADVANTAGES OF FIELD OBSERVATIONS

On the negative side, field observation is a poor choice if the researcher is concerned with external validity. This difficulty is partly due to the potentially questionable representativeness of the observations made and partly due to problems in sampling. Observing the television viewing behavior of a group of children at a day care center can provide valuable insights into the social setting of television viewing, but it probably has little correlation to what preschoolers do in other places and under different circumstances. Besides, since field observation relies heavily on a researcher's perceptions and judgments and on preconceived notions about the material under study, experimenter bias may unavoidably favor specific preconceptions of results, while observations to the contrary are ignored or distorted. This, primarily, is why only one observer is rarely used in a field observation study. Observations need to be *cross-validated* by second or third observers.

Finally, field observations suffer from the problem of reactivity. The very process of being observed may influence the behavior under study. Of course, reactivity can be a problem with other research methods, but it is most often mentioned as a criticism of field observation (Chadwick, Bahr, & Albrecht, 1984). Lull (1985) provides perspective on observer effects using data taken from an observational study of families' TV viewing behavior. He found that the presence of an observer in the house did have some impact on family members. About 20% of parents and 25% of children reported that their overall behavior was affected by the presence of an observer. Most of those who were affected thought that they became nicer or more polite and formal because of the observer's presence. As for differences in the key behavior under study, 87% said that the observer's presence had no effect on their TV viewing activity. Additionally, among those who reported an observer effect, there were no systematic differences in the distribution of changes. About the same number said that they watched more because of the observer as said they watched less. Obviously, additional studies of different groups in different settings are needed before this problem is fully understood, but Lull's data suggest that, though reactivity is a problem with observational techniques, its impact may not be as drastic as some suggest.

In any case, at least two strategies are available to diminish the impact of selective perception and reactivity. One is to use several observers to cross-validate the results. A second strategy relates to triangulating, or supplementing observational data with data gathered by other means (for example, questionnaires or existing records). Accuracy is sought by using multiple data collection methods.

FIELD OBSERVATION TECHNIQUES

There are at least six stages in a typical field observation study: choosing the research site, gaining access, sampling, collecting data, analyzing data, and exiting.

Choosing the Research Site. The nature of the research question or area of inquiry usually suggests a behavior or a phenomenon of interest. Once identified, the next step is to select a setting where the behavior or phenomenon occurs with sufficient frequency to make observation worthwhile. The settings also should fit the recording forms and instruments the observer plans to use. For example, videotaping requires adequate lighting for the camera to operate.

Possible research venues can be identified from personal experience, from talking with other researchers, from interviews with people who frequent the site, or from newspaper and magazine stories. Anderson (1987) suggests that the researchers should select two or three research sites and then "hang around" (Anderson's terminology) each one to discover their main advantages and disadvantages. He cautions researchers that the site must be permanent and stable enough to permit observations over a period of time. Lindlof (1995) suggests a similar process that he labels "casing the scene." He suggests that researchers should gain an understanding of what is possible from a site and make sure that the site holds the potential for fruitful data collection.

Qualitative researchers should avoid choosing sites where they are well known or have some involvement. Studying one's own workplace, for example, would be difficult since the researcher's preconceptions might preclude more objective observations. Further, at a site where the researcher is a familiar figure, other individuals might find it difficult to relate to a colleague or friend in the new role of researcher.

Gaining Access. Once the site is selected, the next step is to establish contact. Williamson, Karp, and Dalphin (1977) note that the degree of difficulty faced by researchers in gaining access to settings depends on two factors: (1)

how public the setting is, and (2) the willingness of the subjects in the setting to be observed. The easiest setting to enter is one that is open to the public and that gives people little reason to keep their behavior secret (for example, a place in which people are watching TV in public—an airport, a bar, a dormitory viewing room). The most difficult setting to enter is one in which entry is restricted because participants have good reason to keep their activities secret (for example, a place in which one could observe the behavior of hostage takers).

Observing a formal group (such as a film production crew) often requires permission from management and perhaps union officials. School systems and other bureaucracies usually have a special unit to handle requests from researchers and to help them obtain necessary permissions.

Gaining permission to conduct field observation research requires persistence and public relations skills. Researchers must decide how much to disclose about the nature of the research. Usually it is not necessary to provide a complete explanation of the hypothesis and procedures unless there are objections to sensitive areas. Researchers interested in observing which family member actually controls the television set might explain that they are studying patterns of family communication. After the contact is made, rapport must be established with the subject(s). Bogdan and Taylor (1984) suggest the following techniques for building rapport: establish common interests with the participants; start relationships slowly; if appropriate, participate in common events and activities; and do not disrupt participants' normal routines.

Lindlof (1995) suggests several ways of gaining access:

- Identify the scene's gatekeeper and attempt to persuade him/her of the project's relevance.
- Find a sponsor who can vouch for the usefulness of the project and can help locate participants.
- Negotiate an agreement with participants.

Sampling.   Sampling in field observation is more ambiguous than in most other research approaches. First, there is the problem of how many individuals or groups to observe. If the focus of the study is communication in the newsroom, how many newsrooms should be observed? If the topic is family viewing of television, how many families should be included? Unfortunately, there are no guidelines to help answer these questions. The research problem and the goals of the study are indicators of the appropriate sample size; for example, if the results are intended for generalization to a population, one subject or group is inadequate.

Another problem is deciding what behavior episodes or segments to sample. The observer cannot be everywhere and see everything, so what is observed becomes a de facto sample of what is not observed. If an observer views one staff meeting in the newsroom, this meeting represents other, unobserved meetings; one conversation at the coffee machine represents all such conversations. Representativeness must be considered even when researchers cannot follow the principles of probability sampling.

Most field observations use purposive sampling, where observers draw on their knowledge of the subject(s) under study and sample only from the relevant behaviors or events. Sometimes previous experience and study of the activity in question will suggest what needs to be examined. In a study of newsroom decision making, for example, researchers would want to observe staff meetings, since they are an important part of the process. However, restricting the sampling to observations of staff meetings would be a mistake since many decisions are made at the water fountain, at lunch, and in the hallways. Experienced observers tend not to isolate a specific situation but instead to consider even the most insignificant situation for analysis. For most field observations, researchers need to spend some time simply getting the feel of the situation and absorbing the pertinent aspects of the environment before beginning a detailed analysis.

Some sampling strategies that might be used include (Lindlof, 1995):

- *Maximum variation sampling:* Settings, activities, events, and informants are chosen purposefully to yield as many different and varied situations as possible.
- *Snowball sampling:* A participant refers the researcher to another person who can provide information. This person, in turn, mentions another, and so forth.
- *Typical case sampling:* In contrast to the maximum variation technique, the researcher chooses cases that seem to be most representative of the topic under study.

Collecting Data. The traditional data collection tools—notebook and pencil—have been supplemented if not supplanted by other instruments in recent years. For example, Bechtel, Achelpohl, and Akers (1972) installed television cameras in a small sample of households to document families' television-viewing behavior. Two cameras, automatically activated when the television set was turned on, videotaped the scene in front of the set. However, even though a camera can record more information than an observer, Bechtel reported that the project was difficult because of problems in finding consenting families, maintaining the equipment, and interpreting tapes shot at low light levels.

Similarly, Anderson (1987) notes that though the advantages offered by audio and video recording are tempting, there are five major drawbacks to their use:

1. Recording devices take time away from the research process because they need regular calibration and adjustment to work properly.
2. The frame of the recording is different from the frame of the observer; a human observer's field of view is about 180°, whereas a camera's is about 60°.
3. Recordings have to be cataloged, indexed, and transcribed, adding extra work to the project.
4. Recordings take behavior out of context.
5. Recordings tend to fragment behavior and distract attention from the overall process.

Consequently, researchers must weigh the pros and cons carefully before deciding to use recording equipment for observations.

Note taking in the covert participant situation requires special attention. Continually scribbling away on a notepad is certain to draw attention and suspicion to the note taker and might expose the study's real purpose. In this type of situation, researchers should make mental notes and transcribe them at the first opportunity. If a researcher's identity is known initially, the problem of note taking is eliminated. Regardless of the situation, it is not wise for a researcher to spend a lot of time taking notes; subjects are already aware of being observed, and note taking could make them uneasy. Brief notes jotted down during natural breaks in a situation attract a minimum of attention and can be expanded later.

The field notes constitute the basic corpus of data in any field study. In these notes, the observers record not only what happened and what was said, but also personal impressions, feelings, and interpretations of what was observed. A useful procedure is to separate personal opinions from the descriptive narrative by enclosing the former in brackets.

How much should be recorded? It is always better to record too much information than too little. A seemingly irrelevant observation made during the first viewing session might become significant later on in the project. If the material is sensitive or if the researcher does not wish it known that research is taking place, notes may be written in abbreviated form or in code.

In addition to firsthand observation, three other data collection techniques are available to field researchers: diary keeping, unobtrusive measures, and document analysis. With the first technique, an investigator routinely supplements his or her field notes by keeping a research diary. This diary consists of personal feelings, sentiments, occasional reflections, and other private thoughts about the research process itself; the writings augment and help interpret the raw data contained in the field notes. Moreover, the researcher may also ask the individuals under study to keep a diary for a specified length of time. This enables the researcher to learn about behaviors that take place out of his or her sight and extends the horizontal dimension of the observation. Individuals may be instructed to track certain habits—such as the reading of books or magazines during a specific time of day—or to record general feelings and thoughts—such as the way they felt while watching commercials on TV.

One form of diary keeping actually provides researchers with a glimpse of the world as seen through the eyes of the subject(s). The researcher gives the subjects still cameras and asks them to make photographic essays or to keep photographic diaries. Analysis of these photographs might help determine how the subjects perceive reality and what they find important. To illustrate, Ziller and Smith (1977) asked current and former students of the University of Florida to take photographs that described the school. The perceptions of the two groups were different: Current students brought in pictures of buildings, and former students brought in pictures of people.

A second data collection technique available to the field researcher is unobtrusive measurement. This technique helps overcome the problem of reactivity by searching out naturally occurring phenomena relevant to the research task. The people who provide data through unobtrusive measurement are unaware that they are providing information for a research project. Covert observation, as previously mentioned, is obviously a technique of this type, but there are also other very subtle ways to collect data in this way. It might be possible, for example, to determine the popularity of radio stations in a given market by asking auto mechanics to keep track of the dial positions of the radio push buttons of cars brought in for repair. Or, in another case, an investigator might use the parking lot at an auto race to discover which brand of tires appears most often on cars owned by people attending the race. Such information might enable tire companies to determine whether their sponsorship of various races has an impact.

Webb, Campbell, Schwartz, and Secrest (1968) identify two general types of unobtrusive measurements: erosion and accretion. The first type, *erosion,* estimates wear and tear on a specific object or material. For example, to determine what textbooks are heavily used by students, a researcher might note how many passages in the text are highlighted, how many pages are dog-eared, whether the book's spine is creased, and so on. *Accretion,* on the other hand, quantifies deposits that have built up over time, such as the amount of dust that has built up on the cover of a textbook.

Accretion and erosion measurement methods, however, do have drawbacks. First, they are passive measures and out of the control of the researcher. Second, other factors might influence what is being observed. Compulsively neat students, for example, might dust their books every day, whether or not they open them, thus providing a misleading accretion measurement. For these reasons, unobtrusive measurements are usually used to support or corroborate findings from other observational methods rather than to draw conclusions.

Finally, existing documents may represent a fertile source of data for the qualitative researcher. In general terms, there are two varieties of documents available for analysis: public and private. Public documents include police reports, newspaper stories, transcripts of TV shows, data archives, and so on. Other items may be less recognizable as public documents; however, messages on computer bulletin boards, company newsletters, tombstones, posters, graffiti, and bumper stickers can all fit into this category. Any of these messages may represent a rich source of data for the qualitative researcher. Shamp (1991), for example, received messages that had been left on computer bulletin boards to examine users' perceptions of their communication partners. Priest (1992) used transcripts of the "Donahue" TV program to structure in-depth interviews with people who appeared on the show.

Private documents, on the other hand, include personal letters, diaries, memos, faxes, home movies and videos, telephone logs, appointment books, reports, and so on. For example, a public relations researcher interested in examining the communication flow among executives in an organization might find copies of memos, faxes, appointments, and phone logs of special interest.

Much like unobtrusive measurements, however, document analysis also has occasional disadvantages: missing documents; subjects unwilling to make private documents available; ethical problems with the use of private records such as diaries and letters; and so on. To reduce the possibility of error when working with archival data, Berg (1995) urges researchers to use a number of data collection methods.

Analyzing Data. Some general considerations of qualitative data analysis were discussed above. With regard to the specific technique of field observation, data analysis consists primarily of filing the information and analyzing its content. Constructing a filing system is an important step in observation. The purpose of the filing system is to arrange raw field data in an orderly format to enable systematic retrieval later. (The precise filing categories are determined by the data.) Using the hypothetical study of decision making in the newsroom, filing categories might include the headings "Relationships," "Interaction—Horizontal," "Interaction—Vertical," and "Disputes." An observation may be placed in more than one category. It is a good idea to make multiple copies of notes; periodic filing of notes during the observation period will save time and confusion later.

Once all the notes have been assigned to their proper files, a rough content analysis is performed to search for consistent patterns. Perhaps, for example, most decisions in the newsroom are made in informal settings such as hallways rather than in formal settings such as conference rooms. Perhaps most decisions are made with little superior–subordinate consultation. At the same time, deviations from the norm should be investigated. Perhaps all reporters except one are typically asked their opinions on the newsworthiness of events; why the exception?

The overall goal of data analysis in field observation is to arrive at a general understanding of the phenomenon under study. In this regard, the observer has the advantage of flexibility. In laboratory and other research approaches, investigators must at some point commit themselves to a particular design or questionnaire. If it subsequently becomes apparent that a crucial variable was left out, there is little that can be done. In field observation, however, the researcher can analyze data during the course of the study and change the research design accordingly.

Exiting. A participant also must have a plan for leaving the setting or the group under study. Of course, if the participant is known to everyone, exiting will not be a problem. Exiting from a setting that participants regularly enter and leave is also not a problem. Exiting can be difficult, however, when participation is covert. In some instances, the group may have become dependent on the researcher in some way, and the departure may have a negative effect on the group as a whole. In other cases, the sudden revelation that a group has been infiltrated or duped by an outsider might be unpleasant or distressing to some. The researcher has an ethical obligation to do everything possible to prevent psychological, emotional, or physical injury to those being studied. Consequently, leaving the scene must be handled with diplomacy and tact.

Focus Groups

The **focus group**, or group interviewing, is a research strategy for understanding audience/consumer attitudes and behavior. From 6 to 12 people are interviewed simultaneously, with a moderator leading the respondents in a relatively unstructured discussion about the focal topic. The identifying characteristic of the focus group is *controlled group discussion,* which is employed to gather preliminary information for a research project, to help develop questionnaire items for survey research, to understand the reasons behind a particular phenomenon, or to test preliminary ideas or plans. Appendix 3 contains a brief guide for conducting focus groups.

Advantages of Focus Groups

Focus groups allow for the collection of preliminary information about a topic or a phenomenon. They may be used in pilot studies to detect ideas that will be further investigated using another research method, such as a telephone survey, or another qualitative method.

A second important advantage is that focus groups can be conducted very quickly. Most of the time is spent recruiting the respondents. A field service that specializes in recruiting focus groups can usually recruit respondents in about 7–10 days, depending on the type of participant required.

The cost of focus groups also makes the approach an attractive research method. Most groups can be conducted for about $1,000–$4,000 per group, depending on the type of respondent required, the part of the country in which the group is conducted, and the moderator or company used to conduct the group. When respondents are difficult to recruit or when the topic requires a specially trained moderator, a focus group may cost much more. However, the cost is not excessive if the groups provide valuable data for further research studies.

Researchers also like focus groups because of the flexibility in question design and follow-up. In conventional surveys, interviewers work from a rigid series of questions and are instructed to follow explicit directions in asking the questions. A moderator in a focus group, however, works from a list of broad questions as well as more refined probe questions; hence, follow-up on important points raised by participants in the group is easy. The ability to clear up confusing responses from respondents makes the use of focus groups valuable in the research process.

Most professional focus group moderators use a procedure known as an *extended focus group,* whereby respondents are required to complete a written questionnaire before the group session begins. The pregroup questionnaire, which covers the material that will be discussed during the group session, forces the respondents to "commit" to a particular answer or position before entering the group. This commitment eliminates one potential problem created by group dynamics—namely, the person who does not wish to offer an opinion because he or she is in a minority.

Finally, focus group responses are often more complete and less inhibited than those from individual interviews. One respondent's remarks tend to stimulate others to pursue lines of thinking that might not have been elicited in a situation involving just one individual. With a competent moderator, the discussion can have a beneficial snowball effect, as one respondent comments on the views of another. A skilled moderator also can detect the opinions and attitudes of those who are less articulate by noting facial expressions and other nonverbal behavior while others are speaking.

Disadvantages of Focus Groups

Focus group research is not free of complications—the approach is far from perfect. Some

Telefocus

A recent development in qualitative research conducted with professionals (radio and television station owners and managers, newspaper and magazine editors, and so on) is the **telefocus** session. Conducted over the telephone, a telefocus session is used when a typical focus group cannot be arranged because of the difficulty of getting group members together in one location. Telefocus sessions are often conducted with individuals who live or work in several parts of the country.

The procedure for a telefocus session is simple: Individuals are recruited; a time convenient to all participants is arranged (the most difficult part of the procedure); and a conference call is made. The moderator conducts the conference call in the same manner as that of a typical focus group, and the conversation is audiotaped for review. After completing the discussion, the participants receive a co-op check (incentive money or payment for participation).

The telefocus session procedure has recently been modified to include one-on-one, open-ended interviews over the telephone. By investigating the preliminary aspects of a problem, these interviews are intended to generate questions for more detailed quantitative studies. Specifically, they are used when a researcher may know that a problem exists, but does not know which questions to ask. Enter the one-on-one telefocus: 10–20 specifically qualified respondents are called and, quite literally, a totally open-ended discussion is conducted. The individuals are told about the topics being investigated and asked their opinions and perceptions. This method requires highly trained and skilled professional interviewers, but always provides valuable information. The one-on-one telefocus provides researchers with information about what "real people" think.

of the problems are discussed here; others are addressed in Appendix 3.

Some groups become dominated by a self-appointed group leader who monopolizes the conversation and attempts to impose his or her opinion on other participants. Such a person usually draws the resentment of the other participants and may have an extremely adverse effect on the performance of the group. The moderator needs to control such situations tactfully before they get out of hand.

Gathering quantitative data is inappropriate for a focus group. If quantification is important, it is wise to supplement the focus group with other research tools that permit more specific questions to be addressed to a more representative sample. Many people unfamiliar with focus group research incorrectly assume that the method will answer questions of "how many" or "how much." In fact, focus group research is intended to gather qualitative data to answer questions such as "why" or "how." Many times people who hire a person or company to conduct a focus group are disgruntled with the results because they expected exact numbers and percentages. Focus groups do not provide such information. As suggested earlier, focus groups depend heavily on the skills of the moderator, who must know when to probe for further information, when to stop respondents from discussing irrelevant topics, and how to involve all respondents in the discussion. All these things must be accomplished with professionalism, since one sarcastic or inappropriate comment to a respondent may have a chilling effect on the group's performance.

There are other drawbacks as well. The small focus group samples are usually composed of volunteers and do not necessarily represent the population from which they were drawn; the recording equipment or other physical characteristics of the location may inhibit respondents; and if the respondents are allowed to stray too far from the topic under consideration, the data produced may not be useful.

METHODOLOGY OF FOCUS GROUPS

There are seven basic steps in focus group research:

1. *Define the problem.* This step is similar in all types of scientific research: A well-defined problem is established on the basis of previous investigation or out of curiosity. For example, television production companies that produce pilot programs for potential series often conduct 10–50 focus groups with target viewers to determine the groups' reactions to each concept.

2. *Select a sample.* Because focus groups are small, researchers must define a narrow audience for the study. The type of sample depends on the purpose of the focus group; the sample might consist of consumers who watch a particular type of television program, men aged 18–34 who listen to a certain type of music, or teenagers who purchase more than 10 record albums a year.

3. *Determine the number of groups necessary.* To help eliminate part of the problem of selecting a representative group, most researchers conduct two or more focus groups on the same topic. Results can then be compared to determine whether any similarities or differences exist; or one group may be used as a basis for comparison to the other group. A focus group study using only one group is rare, since there is no way to know whether the results are group-specific or characteristic of a wider audience.

4. *Prepare the study mechanics.* A more detailed description of the mechanical aspects of focus groups is presented in Appendix 3; suffice it to say here that this step includes arrang-

ing for the recruitment of respondents (by telephone or possibly by shopping center intercept); reserving the facilities at which the groups will be conducted; and deciding what type of recording (audio and/or video) will be used. The moderator must be selected and briefed about the purpose of the group. In addition, the researcher needs to determine the amount of co-op money each respondent will receive for participating. Respondents usually receive between $10 and $50 for attending, although professionals such as doctors and lawyers may require up to $100 or more for co-op.

5. *Prepare the focus group materials.* Each aspect of a focus group must be planned in detail; nothing should be left to chance—in particular, the moderator must not be allowed to "wing it." The screener questionnaire is developed to recruit the desired respondents; recordings and other materials the subjects will hear or see are prepared; any questionnaires the subjects will complete are produced (including the presession questionnaire); and a list of questions is developed for the presession questionnaire and the moderator's guide.

Generally a focus group session begins with some type of shared experience, so that the individuals have a common base from which to start the discussion. The members may listen to or view a tape or examine a new product, or they may simply be asked how they answered the first question on the presession questionnaire.

The existence of a moderator's guide (Appendix 3) does not mean that the moderator cannot ask questions not contained in the guide. Quite the opposite is true. The significant quality of a focus group is that it allows the moderator to probe respondents' comments during the session. A professional moderator is able to develop a line of questioning that no one thought about before the group began, and the questioning usually provides important information. Professional moderators who have this skill receive very substantial fees for conducting focus groups.

6. *Conduct the session.* Focus groups may be conducted in a variety of settings, from

professional conference rooms equipped with one-way mirrors to hotel rooms rented for the occasion. In most situations, a professional conference room is used. Hotel and motel rooms are used when a focus facility is not located close by.

7. *Analyze the data and prepare a summary report.* The written summary of focus group interviews depends on the needs of the study and the amount of time and money available. At one extreme, the moderator/researcher may simply write a brief synopsis of what was said and offer an interpretation of the subjects' responses. For a more elaborate content analysis or a more complete description of what happened, the sessions can be transcribed so that the moderator or researcher can scan the comments and develop a category system, coding each comment into the appropriate category. Focus groups conducted in the private sector rarely go beyond a summary of the groups; clients also have access to the audiotapes and videotapes if they desire.

INTENSIVE INTERVIEWS

Intensive interviews, or in-depth interviews, are essentially a hybrid of the one-on-one interview approach discussed in Chapter 7. Intensive interviews are unique in that they:

- Generally use smaller samples.
- Provide detailed background about the reasons why respondents give specific answers. Elaborate data concerning respondents' opinions, values, motivations, recollections, experiences, and feelings are obtained.
- Allow for lengthy observation of respondents' nonverbal responses.
- Are usually very long. Unlike personal interviews used in survey research that may last only a few minutes, an intensive interview may last several hours and may take more than one session.

- Are customized to individual respondents. In a personal interview, all respondents are usually asked the same questions. Intensive interviews allow interviewers to form questions based on each respondent's answers.
- Can be influenced by the interview climate. To a greater extent than with personal interviews, the success of intensive interviews depends on the rapport established between the interviewer and the respondent.

ADVANTAGES AND DISADVANTAGES OF INTENSIVE INTERVIEWS

The most important advantage of the in-depth interview is the wealth of detail that it provides. Further, when compared to more traditional survey methods, intensive interviewing provides more accurate responses on sensitive issues. The rapport between respondent and interviewer makes it easier to approach certain topics that might be taboo in other approaches. In addition, there may be certain groups for which intensive interviewing is the only practical technique. For example, a study of the media habits of U.S. senators would be hard to carry out as an observational study. Also, it would be difficult to get a sample of senators to take the time to respond to a survey questionnaire. But in some cases, such persons might be willing to talk to an interviewer.

On the negative side, generalizability is sometimes a problem. Intensive interviewing is typically done with a nonrandom sample. Further, since interviews are usually nonstandardized, each respondent may answer a slightly different version of a question. In fact, it is very likely that a particular respondent may answer questions not asked of any other respondent. Another disadvantage of in-depth interviews is that they are especially sensitive to interviewer bias. In a long interview, it is possible for a respondent to learn a good deal of information about the interviewer. Despite practice and training, some interviewers may inadvertently communicate their attitudes through loaded

---

Locating Respondents

In most cases, identifying and contacting respondents for intensive interviewing is not difficult. In a few cases, however, it can be a downright challenge. Consider the problems faced by
Priest (1992) in her study of self-disclosure on television. She wished to recruit subjects who
had appeared on TV talk shows and revealed something intimate and personal about themselves. For obvious reasons, the full names and addresses of such people are rarely given
when they appear. In addition, executive producers of "Oprah," "Donahue," and "Sally Jesse
Raphael" were unwilling to assist Priest in contacting guests. What to do?

   Priest taped several months of "Donahue" for clues about how to reach the show's guests.
On several occasions, a guest was identified by name and a place of residence was subsequently mentioned during the interview. One panel member mentioned the more tolerant
atmosphere in San Francisco. The researcher found her name in the San Francisco phone
book and called her. Some guests came with their therapists; since the therapists were usually
identified, Priest was able to call them and ask that her request for an interview be forwarded
to their patients. Potential respondents were given a toll-free number they could call. One
guest had mentioned that she worked at a McDonald's restaurant in a certain town. The
researcher called the various McDonald's in that area until the person was located. A couple
was reached by addressing a letter to them in care of the show. Another man had mentioned
frequenting a local bar in New York City. Priest wrote him a letter in care of the bar, and he
called the toll-free number. Eventually, the researcher was able to locate and interview 24
informants, including a transsexual lesbian, a sex priestess, an incest survivor, and a "swing-
ing" couple. Her experience suggests that qualitative researchers need imagination and perse-
verance when building their samples.

---

questions, nonverbal cues, or tone of voice.
The effect of this on the validity of a respondent's answers is difficult to gauge. Finally, intensive interviewing presents problems in data
analysis. A researcher given the same body of
data taken from an interview may wind up
with interpretations significantly different from
the original investigator.

PROCEDURES

The problem definition, respondent recruiting,
and data collection and analysis procedures for
conducting intensive interviews are similar to
those used in personal interviews. The primary
differences with intensive interviews are as
follows:

1. Co-op payments are usually higher, generally $50–$1,000.
2. The amount of data collected is tremendous. Analysis may take several weeks to
   several months.
3. Interviewers become extremely tired and
   bored. Interviews must be scheduled several hours apart, which lengthens the data
   collection effort.
4. Because of the time required it is very difficult to arrange intensive interviews. This is
   especially true for respondents who are
   professionals.
5. Small samples do not allow for generalization to the target population.

Berg (1995) provides further details concerning the in-depth interview technique.

EXAMPLES OF INTENSIVE INTERVIEWS

In their study of violence on television, Baldwin and Lewis (1972) conducted interviews that ranged from 1 to 4 hours with a sample of Hollywood writers, producers, and directors. They followed a semistructured approach and worked from an outline of topics. The subjects were people responsible for the content of a prime time series most likely to contain violence. The researchers sent letters explaining the project to the respondents and followed up with a phone call. None of their respondents refused an interview.

Graber (1988) conducted intensive interviews with 21 registered voters about their use of information media. The respondents were drawn randomly from the voter registration list and then contacted by the researchers. The final sample was selected to represent a fourfold typology based on the respondents' interest in politics and access to the media. Interviews averaged 2 hours in length, and each respondent was interviewed for a total of 20 hours.

Swenson (1989) recruited respondents for her study of TV news viewers by placing classified ads in the local newspapers. After finding eight individuals who fit the study criteria, the researcher then conducted five interview sessions averaging about 2–3 hours in length with each respondent. Priest (1992), as previously mentioned, personally interviewed people who had revealed highly intimate information about themselves on the "Donahue" TV show. Each of her 24 semistructured interviews lasted about 2 hours, and respondents were provided with a toll-free number they could call if they later wished to make further comments on or add to their interview. Pardun and Krugman (1994) report the results of a study that examined the influence of the architectural style of the home on television viewing. Two-hour interviews were conducted with a purposive sample of 20 families, 10 living in traditional homes and 10 in transitional homes. In addition, photos were taken of each room that housed a TV set. The results suggested that a home's architecture influenced the style of viewing that took place.

CASE STUDIES

The **case study** method is another common qualitative research technique. Simply put, a case study uses as many data sources as possible to systematically investigate individuals, groups, organizations, or events. Case studies are conducted when a researcher needs to understand or explain a phenomenon. They are frequently used in medicine, anthropology, clinical psychology, management science, and history. Sigmund Freud wrote case studies of his patients; economists wrote case studies of the cable TV industry for the FCC; the list is endless.

On a more formal level, Yin (1989) defines a case study as an empirical inquiry that uses multiple sources of evidence to investigate a contemporary phenomenon within its real-life context, in which the boundaries between the phenomenon and its context are not clearly evident. This definition highlights how a case study differs from other research strategies. For example, an experiment separates a phenomenon from its real-life context. The context is controlled by the laboratory environment. The survey technique tries to define the phenomenon under study narrowly enough to limit the number of variables to be examined. Case study research includes both single cases and multiple cases. Comparative case study research, frequently used in political science, is an example of the multiple case study technique.

Merriam (1988) lists four essential characteristics of case study research:

1. *Particularistic.* This means that the case study focuses on a particular situation, event, program, or phenomenon, making it a good method for studying practical, real-life problems.

2. *Descriptive.* The final result of a case study is a detailed description of the topic under study.

3. *Heuristic.* A case study helps people to understand what's being studied. New interpretations, new perspectives, new meaning, and fresh insights are all goals of a case study.

4. *Inductive.* Most case studies depend on inductive reasoning. Principles and generalizations emerge from an examination of the data. Many case studies attempt to discover new relationships rather than verify existing hypotheses.

ADVANTAGES OF CASE STUDIES

The case study method is most valuable when the researcher wants to obtain a wealth of information about the research topic. Case studies provide tremendous detail. Many times researchers want such detail when they do not know exactly what they are looking for. The case study is particularly advantageous to the researcher who is trying to find clues and ideas for further research (Simon, 1985). This is not to suggest, however, that case studies are to be used only at the exploratory stage of research. The method can also be used to gather descriptive and explanatory data.

The case study technique can suggest *why* something has occurred. For example, in many cities in the mid-1980s, cable companies asked to be released from certain promises made when negotiating for a franchise. To learn why this occurred, a multiple case study approach, examining several cities, could have been used. Other research techniques, such as the survey, might not be able to reveal all the possible reasons behind this phenomenon. Ideally, case studies should be used in combination with theory to achieve maximum understanding.

The case study method also affords the researcher the ability to deal with a wide spectrum of evidence. Documents, historical artifacts, systematic interviews, direct observations, and even traditional surveys can all be incor-

porated into a case study. In fact, the mo sources that can be brought to bear in a c the more likely it is that the study will be valid

DISADVANTAGES OF CASE STUDIES

There are three main criticisms. The first has to do with a general lack of scientific rigor in many case studies. Yin (1989) points out that "too many times, the case study researcher has been sloppy, and has allowed equivocal evidence or biased views to influence the . . . findings and conclusions" (p. 21). It is easy to do a sloppy case study; rigorous case studies require a good deal of time and effort.

The second criticism is that the case study is not amenable to generalization. If the main goal of the researcher is to make statistically based normative statements about the frequency of occurrence of a phenomenon in a defined population, some other method may be more appropriate. This is not to say that the results of all case studies are idiosyncratic and unique. In fact, if generalizing theoretic propositions is the main goal, the case study method is perfectly suited to the task.

Finally, like participant observation, case studies are often time-consuming and may occasionally produce massive quantities of data that are hard to summarize. Consequently, fellow researchers are forced to wait years for the results of the research, which too often are poorly presented. Some authors, however, are experimenting with nontraditional methods of reporting to overcome this last criticism (see Peters & Waterman, 1982).

CONDUCTING A CASE STUDY

The precise method of conducting a case study has not been as well documented as the more traditional techniques of the survey and the experiment. Nonetheless, there appear to be five distinct stages in carrying out a case study: design, pilot study, data collection, data analysis, and report writing.

ncern in case study de-
e case study is most ap-
that begin with "how"
estion that is clear and
mainder of the efforts
nd design concern is
nstitutes a "case"? In
case is an individual, several
individuals, or an event or events. If information is gathered about each relevant individual,
the results are reported in the single or multiple case study format; in other instances, however, the precise boundaries of the case are
harder to pinpoint. A case might be a specific
decision, a particular organization at a certain
time, a program, or some other discrete event.
One rough guide for determining what to use
as the unit of analysis is the available research
literature. Since researchers want to compare
their findings with the results of previous research, it is sometimes a good idea not to stray
too far from what was done in past research.

Pilot Study. Before the pilot study is conducted, the case study researcher must construct a **study protocol**. This document
contains the procedures to be used in the
study and also includes the data-gathering instrument or instruments. A good case study
protocol contains the procedures necessary for
gaining access to a particular person or organization and the methods for accessing records.
It also contains the schedule for data collection
and addresses logistical problems. For example, the protocol should note whether a copy
machine will be available in the field to duplicate records, whether office space is available
to the researchers, and what supplies will be
needed. The protocol should also list the questions central to the inquiry and the possible
sources of information to be tapped in answering these questions. If interviews are to be used
in the case study, the protocol should specify
the questions to be asked.

Once the protocol has been developed, the
researcher is ready to begin the pilot study. A
pilot study is used to refine both the research

design and the field procedures. Variables that
were not foreseen during the design phase can
crop up during the pilot study, and problems
with the protocol or with study logistics can
also be uncovered. The pilot study also allows
the researchers to try different data-gathering
approaches and to observe different activities
from several trial perspectives. The results of
the pilot study are used to revise and polish the
study protocol.

Data Collection. At least four sources of data
can be used in case studies. Documents, which
represent a rich data source, may take the form
of letters, memos, minutes, agendas, historical
records, brochures, pamphlets, posters, and so
on. A second source is the interview. Some case
studies make use of survey research methods
and ask respondents to fill out questionnaires;
others may use intensive interviewing.

Observation/participation is the third data
collection technique. The general comments
made about this technique earlier in this chapter apply to the case study method as well. The
fourth source of evidence used in case studies
is the physical artifact—a tool, a piece of furniture, or even a computer printout. Although
artifacts are commonly used as a data source in
anthropology and history, they are seldom used
in mass media case study research. (They are,
however, frequently used in legal research concerning the media.)

Most case study researchers recommend
using multiple sources of data, thus affording
triangulation of the phenomenon under study
(Rubin, 1984). In addition, multiple sources
help the case study researcher improve the reliability and validity of the study. Not surprisingly, a study of the case study method found
that the ones that used multiple sources of evidence were rated higher than those relying
on a single source (Yin, Bateman, & Moore,
1983).

Data Analysis. Unlike more quantitative research techniques, there are no specific formulas or "cookbook" techniques to guide the

researcher in analyzing the data. Consequently, this stage is probably the most difficult in the case study method. Although it is impossible to generalize to all case study situations, Yin (1989) has suggested three broad analytic strategies: pattern matching, explanation building, and time series.

(1) In the *pattern-matching* strategy, an empirically based pattern is compared with one or more predicted patterns. For instance, suppose a newspaper is about to initiate a new management tool: a regular series of meetings between top management and reporters, excluding editors. Based on organizational theory, a researcher might predict certain outcomes—namely, more stress between editors and reporters, increased productivity, weakened supervisory links, and so on. If analysis of the case study data indicates that these results did in fact occur, some conclusions about the management change can be made. If the predicted pattern did not match the actual one, the initial study propositions would have to be questioned. (2) In the analytic strategy of *explanation building*, the researcher tries to construct an explanation about the case by making statements about the cause or causes of the phenomenon under study. This method can take several forms. Typically, however, an investigator drafts an initial theoretical statement about some process or outcome, compares the findings of an initial case study against the statement, revises the statement, analyzes a second comparable case, and repeats this process as many times as necessary. Note that this technique is similar to the general approach of analytical induction discussed earlier. For example, to explain why some new communication technologies are failing, a researcher might suggest lack of managerial expertise as an initial proposition. But an investigator who examined the subscription television industry might find that lack of management expertise is only part of the problem, that inadequate market research is also a factor. Armed with the revised version of the explanatory statement, the researcher would next examine the direct broadcast satellite industry to see whether this explanation needs to be further refined, and so on, until a full and satisfactory answer is achieved.

In *time series* analysis, the investigator tries to compare a series of data points to some theoretic trend that was predicted before the research, or to some alternative trend. If, for instance, several cities have experienced newspaper strikes, a case study investigator might generate predictions about the changes in information-seeking behaviors of residents in these communities and conduct a case study to see whether these predictions were supported.

Report Writing. The case study report can take several forms. The report can follow the traditional research study format—problem, methods, findings, and discussion—or it can use a nontraditional technique. Some case studies are best suited to a chronological arrangement, whereas comparative case studies can be reported from that perspective. No matter what form is chosen, the researcher must consider the intended audience of the report. A case study report for policy makers would be written in a style different from one to be published in a scholarly journal.

EXAMPLES OF CASE STUDIES

Browne (1983) conducted a comparative case study of the newsroom practices at the Voice of America, the BBC, and Deutsche-Welle, three of the world's largest international radio stations. Browne's study illustrated how multiple sources of evidence are used in the case study technique. He interviewed 55 staff members of the three stations, observed actual newsroom practices, and had access to corporate documents. He found that the three stations had common problems, particularly in their relationships with their foreign language services.

Dimmick and Wallschlaeger (1986) conducted a case study of new media ventures by television network parent companies. They depended primarily upon published documents, particularly annual reports, to reach their

Qualitative Research and Ethnography

This discussion on qualitative research necessitates a brief explanation of terminology in relation to ethnography. The term *ethnographic research* is sometimes used as a synonym for *qualitative research* (Lindlof, 1991). Ethnography, however, is in fact a special kind of qualitative research. As first practiced by anthropologists and sociologists, ethnography referred to the process by which researchers spent long periods of time living with and observing other cultures in a natural setting. This immersion in the other culture helped the researcher understand another way of life seen from the native perspective. Recently, however, the notion of ethnography has been adapted to other areas: political science, education, social work, and communication. These disciplines were less interested in describing the way of life of an entire culture and more concerned with analyzing smaller units: subgroups, organizations, institutions, professions, audiences, and so on. To reduce confusion, Berg (1995) suggests referring to the traditional study of entire cultures as *macro-ethnography* and to the study of smaller units of analysis as *micro-ethnography*. The latter approach is the one most often used by mass communication researchers.

Regardless of whether it is focusing on an entire culture or on a cultural subunit, ethnography is characterized by several qualities:

1. It puts the researcher in the middle of the topic under study. The researcher goes to the data rather than the other way around.
2. It emphasizes studying an issue or topic from the participants' frame of reference.
3. It involves spending a considerable amount of time in the field.
4. It uses a variety of research techniques including observation, interviewing, diary keeping, analysis of existing documents, photography, videotaping, and so on.

Item 4 seems to distinguish ethnographic research from other forms of qualitative research; indeed, ethnographic research relies upon an assortment of data collection techniques.

Although other qualitative research projects can be adequately conducted using only one method, ethnographic research generally utilizes several of the four common qualitative techniques discussed in this chapter: field observations, intensive interviewing, focus groups, and case studies.

conclusion that companies most dependent on network television profits were most active in new media ventures. Stipp, Hill-Scott, and Dorr (1987) used the case study approach in their analysis of the making of the "Mr. T" cartoon series. Working with a social science advisory panel, the authors observed meetings with producers and writers and examined story treatments, scripts, and storyboards. Ad-

ditionally, the researchers were able to work directly with the series production staff.

Kaplan and Houlberg's (1990) case study involved television advertising for condoms on San Francisco's KRON-TV. The researchers conducted personal interviews with the executives involved in the decision to air the commercials, examined transcripts of the accepted ad, inspected station policy documents, and scrutinized local and national newspaper accounts of the event. Walsh-Childers (1994) conducted a case study of the effect on state health policy of an Alabama newspaper's series on infant mortality. She analyzed the relevant news reports and conducted interviews with editors, reporters, and health care officials as part of her analysis.

SUMMARY

Qualitative research differs from quantitative research along a number of dimensions. Qualitative data analysis requires special techniques. Two commonly used methods are constant comparison and analytic induction.

This chapter discussed four alternatives to laboratory and survey research: field observations, focus groups, intensive interviews, and case studies. *Field observation* involves the study of a phenomenon in natural settings. The researcher may be a detached observer or a participant in the process under study. The main advantage of this technique is its flexibility; it can be used to develop hypotheses, to gather preliminary data, or to study groups that would otherwise be inaccessible. Its biggest disadvantage is the difficulty in achieving external validity.

The *focus group,* or group interviewing, is used to gather preliminary information for a research study or to gather qualitative data concerning a research question. The advantages of the focus group method are the ease of data collection and the depth of information that can be gathered. Among the disadvantages, the quality of information gathered during focus groups depends heavily on the group moderators' skill, and focus groups can only complement other research because they provide qualitative, not quantitative, data.

Intensive interviewing is used to gather extremely detailed information from a small sample of respondents. The wealth of data that can be gathered with this method is its primary advantage. Because intensive interviewing is usually done with small, nonrandom samples, however, generalizability is sometimes a disadvantage. Interviewer bias can also be a disadvantage.

The *case study* method draws from as many data sources as possible to investigate an event. Case studies are particularly helpful when a researcher desires to explain or understand some phenomenon. Some problems with case studies are that they can lack scientific rigor, they can be time-consuming to conduct, and the data they provide can be difficult to generalize from and to summarize.

Ethnographic research is a special form of qualitative research that utilizes one or more of the techniques mentioned above.

QUESTIONS AND PROBLEMS FOR FURTHER IINVESTIGATION

1. Develop a research topic that would be appropriate for a study by
   a. Intensive interview
   b. Field observation
   c. Case study

2. Suggest three specific research topics that would be best studied by the technique of covert participation. Would any ethical problems be involved?

3. Select a research topic that is suitable for study using the focus group method, then assemble six or eight of your classmates or friends and conduct a sample interview. Select an appropriate method for analyzing the data.

4. Examine recent journals in the mass media research field and identify instances where the case study method was used. For each example, specify the sources of data used in the study, how the data were analyzed, and how the study was reported.

REFERENCES AND SUGGESTED READINGS

Anderson, J. A. (1987). *Communication research: Issues and methods.* New York: McGraw-Hill.

Babbie, E. R. (1995). *The practice of social research* (7th ed.). Belmont, CA: Wadsworth.

Baldwin, T., & Lewis, C. (1972). Violence in television: The industry looks at itself. In E. Rubinstein, G. Comstock, & J. Murray (Eds.), *Television and social behavior* (Vol. I). Washington, DC: U.S. Government Printing Office.

Bechtel, R., Achelpohl, C., & Akers, R. (1972). Correlates between observed behavior and questionnaire responses on television viewing. In E. Rubinstein, G. Comstock, & J. Murray (Eds.), *Television and social behavior* (Vol. IV). Washington, DC: U.S. Government Printing Office.

Berg, B. (1995). *Qualitative research methods*. Boston, MA: Allyn & Bacon.

Bickman, L., & Hency, T. (1972). *Beyond the laboratory: Field research in social psychology*. New York: McGraw-Hill.

Bogdan, R., & Taylor, S. (1984). *Introduction to qualitative research methods* (2nd ed.). New York: John Wiley.

Brent, E. E., & Anderson, R. E. (1990). *Computer applications in the social sciences*. Philadelphia, PA: Temple University Press.

Brown, J., Dykers, C., Steele, J. & White, A. (1994). Teenage room culture. *Communication Research, 21*(6), 813–827.

Browne, D. (1983). The international newsroom. *Journal of Broadcasting, 27*(3), 205–231.

Browne, D. (1991). Local radio in Switzerland. *Journal of Broadcasting and Electronic Media, 35*(4), 449–464.

Calder, B. J. (1977). Focus groups and the nature of qualitative marketing research. *Journal of Marketing Research, 14*, 353–364.

Chadwick, B., Bahr, H., & Albrecht, S. (1984). *Social science research methods*. Englewood Cliffs, NJ: Prentice-Hall.

Cooper, R., Potter, W., & Dupagne, M. (1994). A status report on methods used in mass communication research. *Journalism Educator, 48*(4), 54–61.

Cox, K. D., Higginbotham, J. B., & Burton, J. (1976). Applications of focus group interviewing in marketing. *Journal of Marketing, 40*, 77–80.

Dimmick, J., & Wallschlaeger, M. (1986). Measuring corporate diversification: A case study of new media ventures by television network parent companies. *Journal of Broadcasting and Electronic Media, 30*(1), 1–14.

Elliot, S. C. (1980). *Focus group research: A workbook for broadcasters*. Washington, DC: National Association of Broadcasters.

Epstein, E. J. (1974). *News from nowhere*. New York: Vintage.

Erickson, F. (1986). Qualitative methods in research on teaching. In M. C. Wittrock (Ed.), *Handbook of research on teaching*. New York: Macmillan.

Fletcher, A., & Bowers, T. (1991). *Fundamentals of advertising research* (4th ed.). Belmont, CA: Wadsworth.

Fletcher, J. E., & Wimmer, R. D. (1981). *Focus group interviews in radio research*. Washington, DC: National Association of Broadcasters.

Gieber, W. (1956). Across the desk: A study of 16 telegraph editors. *Journalism Quarterly, 33*, 423–432.

Glaser, B., & Strauss, A. (1967). *The discovery of grounded theory*. Chicago, IL: Aldine.

Graber, D. A. (1988). *Processing the news* (2nd ed.). White Plains, NY: Longman.

Kaplan, H., & Houlberg, R. (1990). Broadcast condom advertising: A case study. *Journalism Quarterly, 67*(1), 171–176.

Lemish, D. (1987). Viewers in diapers: The early development of television viewing. In T. R. Lindlof (Ed.), *Natural audiences*. Norwood, NJ: Ablex.

Lincoln, Y., & Guba, E. (1985). *Naturalistic inquiry*. Beverly Hills, CA: Sage.

Lindlof, T. R. (1987). *Natural audiences: Qualitative research of media uses and effects*. Norwood, NJ: Ablex.

Lindlof, T. R. (1991). The qualitative study of media audiences. *Journal of Broadcasting and Electronic Media, 35*(1) 23–42.

Lindlof, T. R. (1995). *Qualitative communication research methods*. Thousand Oaks, CA: Sage.

Lowry, D. (1979). An evaluation of empirical studies reported in seven journals in the '70s. *Journalism Quarterly, 56*, 262–268.

Lull, J. (1982). How families select television programs. *Journal of Broadcasting, 26*(4), 801–812.

Lull, J. (1985). Ethnographic studies of broadcast media audiences. In J. Dominick & J. Fletcher (Eds.), *Broadcasting research methods*. Boston: Allyn & Bacon.

Maykut, P., & Morehouse, R. (1994). *Beginning qualitative research*. Bristol, PA: The Falmer Press.

Merriam, S. B. (1988). *Case study research in education*. San Francisco: Jossey-Bass.

Miles, M. B., & Huberman, A. M. (1984). *Qualitative data analysis*. Beverly Hills, CA: Sage Publications.

Moriarty, S., & Everett, S. (1994). Commercial breaks: A viewing behavior study. *Journalism Quarterly, 71*(2), 346–355.

Pardun, C., & Krugman, D. (1994). How the architectural style of the home relates to family television viewing. *Journal of Broadcasting and Electronic Media, 38*(2), 145–162.

Pekurny, R. (1980). The production process and environment of NBC's *Saturday Night Live. Journal of Broadcasting, 24*, 91–100.

Peters, J. J., & Waterman, R. (1982). In search of excellence. New York: Harper & Row.

Pfaffenberger, B., (1988). *Microcomputer applications in qualitative research*. Beverly Hills, CA: Sage Publications.

Priest, P. J. (1992). *Self disclosure on television*. Unpublished doctoral dissertation, University of Georgia, Athens, Georgia.

Reid, L. N., Soley, L. C., & Wimmer, R. D. (1981). Replication in advertising research: 1977, 1978, 1979. *Journal of Advertising, 10*, 3–13.

Reynolds, F. D., & Johnson, D. K. (1978). Validity of focus group findings. *Journal of Advertising Research, 18*, 21–24.

Robertson, L., Kelley, A. B., O'Neill, B., Wixom, C. W., Elswirth, R. S., & Haddon, W. (1974). A controlled study of the effect of television messages of safety belt use. *American Journal of Public Health, 64*, 1074–1084.

Rubin, H. (1984). *Applied social research*. Columbus, OH: Charles E. Merrill.

Shamp, S. A. (1991). Mechanomorphism in perception of computer communication partners. *Computers in Human Behavior, 17*, 147–161.

Simon, J. (1985). *Basic research methods in social science* (3rd ed.). New York: Random House.

Stainback, S., & Stainback, W. (1988). *Understanding and conducting qualitative research*. Dubuque, IA: Kendall/Hunt.

Stipp, H., Hill-Scott, K., & Dorr, A. (1987). Using social science to improve children's television. *Journal of Broadcasting and Electronic Media, 31*(4), 461–473.

Swenson, J. D. (1989). *TV news viewers: Making sense out of Iran-Contra*. Unpublished doctoral dissertation, University of Chicago.

Szybillo, G., & Berger, R. (1979). What advertising agencies think of focus groups. *Journal of Advertising Research, 19*(3), 29–33.

Tull, D., & Hawkins, D. (1990). *Marketing research* (5th ed.). New York: Macmillan.

Walsh-Childers, K. (1994). A death in the family: A case study of newspaper influence on health policy development. *Journalism Quarterly, 71*(4), 820–829.

Webb, E. J., Campbell, D. T., Schwartz, R. D., and Sechrest, L. (1968). *Unobtrusive measures*. Chicago: Rand McNally.

Westley, B. H. (1989). The controlled experiment. In G. H. Stempel & B. H. Westley (Eds.), *Research methods in mass communication* (2nd ed.). Englewood Cliffs, NJ: Prentice-Hall.

Williamson, J. B., Karp, D. A., & Dalphin, J. R. (1977). *The research craft*. Boston: Little, Brown.

Wimmer, R. D., & Reid, L. N. (1982). Researchers' response to replication requests. *Journalism Quarterly, 59*(2), 317–320.

Woodside, A., & Fleck, R. (1979). The case approach to understanding brand choice. *Journal of Advertising Research, 19*(2), 23–30.

Woodward, B., & Bernstein, C. (1974). *All the president's men*. New York: Simon & Schuster.

Yin, R. (1989). *Case study research* (2nd ed.). Newbury Park, CA: Sage Publications.

Yin, R., Bateman, P., & Moore, G. (1983). *Case studies and organizational innovation*. Washington, DC: Cosmos Corporation.

Ziller, R. C., & Smith, D. C. (1977). A phenomenological utilization of photographs. *Journal of Phenomenological Psychology, 7*, 172–185.

Chapter

6

CONTENT ANALYSIS

Up to this point, the chapters in Part II have concentrated on the more general approaches used in mass media investigation. This chapter moves to a discussion of content analysis, a specific research approach used frequently in all areas of the media. The method is popular with mass media researchers because it provides an efficient way to investigate the content of the media, such as the number and types of commercials or advertisements in broadcasting or the print media. The beginning researcher will find content analysis a valuable tool in answering many mass media questions.

Modern content analysis can be traced back to World War II, when allied intelligence units painstakingly monitored the number and types of popular songs played on European radio stations. By comparing the music played on German stations with that on other stations in occupied Europe, the allies were able to measure with some degree of certainty the changes in troop concentration on the continent. In the Pacific theater, communications between Japan and various island bases were carefully tabulated; an increase in message volume to and from a particular base usually meant that some new operation involving that base was planned.

About this time, content analysis was used in attempts to verify the authorship of historical documents. These studies (Yule, 1944) were primarily concerned with counting words in documents of questionable authenticity and comparing their frequencies with the same words in documents whose authors were known. These literary detective cases demonstrated the usefulness of quantification in content analysis.

After the war, content analysis was used by researchers to study propaganda in newspapers and radio. In 1952 Bernard Berelson published *Content Analysis in Communication Research,* which signaled that the technique had gained recognition as a tool for media scholars.

In 1968, Tannenbaum and Greenberg reported that content analysis of newspapers was the largest single category of master's theses in mass communication. A later publication (Comstock, 1975) listed more than 225 content analyses of television programming. Concern over the portrayal of violence on television and the treatment of women and minority groups in print and television advertising and in music videos further popularized the content analysis technique among mass media researchers. From 1977 to 1985, 21% of the quantitative studies published in the *Journal of Broadcasting and Electronic Media* were content analyses (Moffett & Dominick, 1987). A study by Cooper, Potter, and Dupagne (1994) found that 25% of all quantitative studies in mass communication from 1965 to 1989 were content analyses. This popularity shows no signs of decreasing. *Communication Abstracts* listed more than 80 content analytic studies in 1993 and 1994, indicating that it is still a favored research technique.

Content analysis figured prominently in broadcasting and cable regulation in 1994 and 1995. In 1994, in response to congressional pressure, the four major TV networks commissioned a $1.5 million research project that included a content analysis of network entertainment programs. The results of the content analysis, released in 1995, found that only 10 network shows were rated as highly violent (Littleton, 1995). Also in 1995 a proposed bill to regulate telecommunications required that all TV sets be equipped with a V-chip that would block violent and sexually explicit programming. The bill gave the broadcasting and cable industries a year in which to devise a measurement system, presumably based on some method of content analysis, that would assign ratings to programs that could trigger the V-chip. If the industry is unable to come up with such a system, the FCC could then appoint a panel to do the analysis and assign a rating.

DEFINITION OF CONTENT ANALYSIS

Many definitions of content analysis exist. Walizer and Wienir (1978) define it as any systematic procedure devised to examine the content of recorded information; Krippendorf (1980) defines it as a research technique for making replicable and valid references from data to their context. Kerlinger's (1986) definition is fairly typical: Content analysis is a method of studying and analyzing communication in a systematic, objective, and quantitative manner for the purpose of measuring variables.

Kerlinger's definition involves three concepts that require elaboration. First, content analysis is *systematic*. This means that the content to be analyzed is selected according to explicit and consistently applied rules: sample selection must follow proper procedures, and each item must have an equal chance of being included in the analysis. Moreover, the evaluation process must be systematic: All content under consideration is to be treated in exactly the same manner. There must be uniformity in the coding and analysis procedures and in the length of time coders are exposed to the material. Systematic evaluation simply means that one and only one set of guidelines for evaluation is used throughout the study. Alternating procedures in an analysis is a sure way to confound the results.

Second, content analysis is *objective*. That is, the researcher's personal idiosyncrasies and biases should not enter into the findings; if replicated by another researcher, the analysis should yield the same results. Operational definitions and rules for classification of variables should be sufficiently explicit and comprehensive that other researchers who repeat the process will arrive at the same decisions. Unless a clear set of criteria and procedures is established that fully explains the sampling and categorization methods, the researcher does not meet the requirement of objectivity and the reliability of the results may be called into question. Perfect objectivity, however, is seldom achieved in a content analysis. The specification of the unit of analysis and the precise makeup and definition of relevant categories are areas in which individual researchers must exercise subjective choice. (Reliability, as it applies to content analysis, is discussed at length later in the chapter.)

Third, content analysis is *quantitative*. The goal of content analysis is the accurate representation of a body of messages. Quantification is important in fulfilling that objective, since it aids researchers in the quest for precision. The statement "Seventy percent of all prime time programs contain at least one act of violence," is more precise than "Most shows are violent." Additionally, quantification allows researchers to summarize results and to report them succinctly. If measurements are to be made over intervals of time, comparisons of the numerical data from one time period to another can help simplify and standardize the evaluation procedure. Finally, quantification gives researchers additional statistical tools that can aid in interpretation and analysis.

Note, however, that quantification should not blind the researcher to other ways of assessing the potential impact or effects of the content. The fact that some item or behavior was the most frequently occurring element in a body of content does not necessarily make that element the most important. For example, a content analysis of the news coverage of the urban violence in Los Angeles in 1992 might disclose that 90% of the coverage showed nonviolent scenes. The other 10% that contained violence, however, might have been so powerful and so sensational that its impact on the audience was far greater than the nonviolent coverage.

USES OF CONTENT ANALYSIS

Over the past decade, the symbols and messages contained in the mass media have become increasingly popular research topics in both the academic sector and the private sector. The American Broadcasting Company (ABC) conducts systematic comparative studies of the three networks' evening newscasts to determine how ABC's news coverage compares to its competitors'. The national Parent-Teachers Association has offered do-it-yourself training in rough forms of content analysis so that local members can monitor television violence levels in their viewing areas. Citizens groups, such as the National Coalition on Television Violence, keep track of TV content. Public relations firms use content analysis to monitor the subject matter of company publications, and some labor unions now conduct content analyses of the mass media to examine their images. The *Media Monitor* publishes periodic studies of how the media treat social and political issues.

Although it is difficult to classify and categorize studies as varied and diverse as those using content analysis, they are generally employed for one of five purposes. A discussion of these aims will help illustrate some ways in which this technique can be applied.

DESCRIBING COMMUNICATION CONTENT

Several recent studies have cataloged the characteristics of a given body of communication content at one or more points in time. These studies exemplify content analysis used in the traditional, descriptive manner: to identify what exists. For example, Glascock and La-Rose (1993) described the sexual content of 82 dial-a-porn numbers. Similarly, Bogaert, Turkovich, and Hafer (1993) analyzed the sexual explicitness and age of the models in *Playboy* centerfolds from 1953 to 1990. Note that one of the advantages of content analysis is its potential to identify trends occurring over long periods of time. Gross and Sheth (1989), for example, analyzed magazine ads from 1890 to 1988, and Siegelman and Bullock (1991) studied newspaper coverage of election campaigns from 1888 to 1988.

These descriptive studies also can be used to study societal change. For example, changing public opinion on various controversial issues could be gauged with a longitudinal study (see Chapter 8) of letters to the editor or newspaper editorials. Statements about what values are judged to be important by a society could be inferred by a study of the nonfiction books on the best-seller list at different points in time.

Chadwick, Bahr, and Albrecht (1984) suggest that content analysis is useful in the analysis of projective personality tests such as the Rorschach and the Thematic Apperception tests. Subjects' responses to these tests can be content analyzed for characteristics suggesting certain personality traits. For example, Attkisson, Handler, and Shrader (1969) used content analysis to assess the validity of the Draw-A-Man test in determining religious values. The size, position, and details of the drawings were compared with subjects' religious beliefs.

TESTING HYPOTHESES OF MESSAGE CHARACTERISTICS

A number of analyses attempt to relate certain characteristics of the source of a given body of message content to characteristics of the messages that are produced. As Holsti (1969) pointed out, this category of content analysis has been used in many studies that test hypotheses of form: "If the source has characteristic *A,* then messages containing elements *x* and *y* will be produced; if the source has characteristic *B,* then messages with elements *w* and *z* will be produced." Busby and Leichty (1993), for example, found that traditional women's magazines were more likely to portray women in decorative roles than were non-traditional magazines. Eaton and Dominick (1991) found that cartoons built around characters merchandised as toys (for example, G.I. Joe) had larger casts and contained more violence than did cartoons whose characters were not used in toy merchandising. Kenney and Simpson (1993) content analyzed the coverage of the 1988 presidential race and found that the *Washington Post's* coverage was balanced and neutral but that the *Washington Times'* coverage favored the Republicans. Soderlund, Surlin, and Romanow (1989) compared the gender of anchors and reporters on private and government-operated stations in Canada and found that females were far more likely to serve as anchors on the government stations.

COMPARING MEDIA CONTENT TO THE "REAL WORLD"

Many content analyses are reality checks, in which the portrayal of a certain group, phenomenon, trait, or characteristic is assessed against a standard taken from real life. The congruence of the media presentation and the actual situation is then discussed. Probably the earliest study of this type was by Davis (1951), who found that crime coverage in Colorado newspapers bore no relationship to changes in state crime rates. DeFleur (1964) compared television's portrayal of the work world with job data taken from the U.S. census. More recently, the National Commission on the Causes and Prevention of Violence used content analysis data collected by Gerbner (1969) to compare the world of television violence with real-life violence. Lester (1994) analyzed African-American photo coverage in four major U.S. newspapers from 1937 to 1990 and found

that although the overall percentage of photos containing African Americans increased, it was still less than national or statewide population percentages. Trujillo and Ekdom (1987) examined the portrayal of American industry on TV and found that, when compared to government statistics, the service and public administration industries were overrepresented, whereas the manufacturing segment was underrepresented. Finally, O'Callaghan and Duke (1992) matched media coverage of the caseload of the Supreme Court and found that civil rights and First Amendment issues were covered more than the actual number of cases would seem to justify. In contrast, economic developments received far less coverage than their numbers would warrant.

ASSESSING THE IMAGE OF PARTICULAR GROUPS IN SOCIETY

Ever-growing numbers of content analyses have focused on exploring the media image of certain minority or otherwise notable groups. In many instances, these studies are conducted to assess changes in media policy toward these groups, to make inferences about the media's responsiveness to demands for better coverage, or to document social trends. For example, as part of a license renewal challenge, Hennessee and Nicholson (1972) performed an extensive analysis of the image presented of women by a New York television station, and Greenberg (1983) completed a lengthy content analysis of the image of Mexican Americans in the mass media. More recently, Barber and Gandy (1990) studied the representation of African-American U.S. representatives in daily newspapers, and Greenwald (1990) analyzed the coverage of women in the business sections of two metropolitan newspapers. She found that women were the main subjects in only 5 of 180 stories. Taylor and Lee (1994) traced the portrayals of Asian Americans in magazine ads during the early 1990s and reported that only 4% of the ads featured an Asian-American model. Dupagne, Potter, and Cooper (1993) used content analysis to analyze the change in mass communication research articles published by women from 1965 to 1989 and found that the number more than doubled during that period.

ESTABLISHING A STARTING POINT FOR STUDIES OF MEDIA EFFECTS

The use of content analysis as a starting point for subsequent studies is relatively new. The best known example is **cultivation analysis,** whereby the dominant message and themes in media content are documented by systematic procedures and a separate study of the audience is conducted to see whether these messages are fostering similar attitudes among heavy media users. Gerbner, Gross, Signorielli, Morgan, and Jackson-Beeck (1979) discovered that heavy viewers of television tend to be more fearful of the world around them. In other words, television content—in this case, large doses of crime and violence—may cultivate attitudes more consistent with its messasages than with reality. Other work that has used a similar framework includes Morgan and Shanahan's (1991) analysis of television programming and the cultivation of political attitudes in Argentina, and Pfau, Mullen, Deidrich and Garrow's (1995) study of public perception of attorneys and the viewing of prime time television programs featuring lawyers.

LIMITATIONS OF CONTENT ANALYSIS

Content analysis alone cannot serve as a basis for making statements about the effects of content on an audience. A study of Saturday morning cartoon programs on television might reveal that 80% of these programs contain commercials for sugared cereal, but this finding alone does not allow researchers to

claim that children who watch these programs will want to purchase sugared cereals. To make such an assertion, an additional study of the viewers would be necessary (as in cultivation analysis). Content analysis cannot serve as the sole basis for claims about media effects.

Also, the findings of a particular content analysis are limited to the framework of the categories and definitions used in that analysis. Different researchers may use varying definitions and category systems to measure a single concept. In mass media research, this problem is most evident in studies of televised violence. Some researchers rule out comic or slapstick violence in their studies, whereas others consider it an important dimension. Obviously, great care should be exercised in comparing the results of different content analysis studies. Researchers who use different tools of measurement will naturally arrive at different conclusions.

Another potential limitation of content analysis is a lack of messages relevant to the research. Many topics or characters receive little exposure in the mass media. For example, a study of how Asians are portrayed in U.S. television commercials would be difficult because characters of this ethnicity are rarely seen (of course, this fact in itself might be a significant finding). A researcher interested in such a topic must be prepared to examine a large body of media content to find sufficient quantities for analysis.

Finally, content analysis is frequently time-consuming and expensive. The task of examining and categorizing large volumes of content is often laborious and tedious. Plowing through 100 copies of the *New York Times* or 50 issues of *Newsweek* involves time and patience. In addition, if television content is selected for analysis, there must be some means of preserving the programs for detailed examination. Typically, researchers videotape programs for analysis, but this requires access to a recorder and large supplies of videotape—materials not all researchers can afford.

STEPS IN CONTENT ANALYSIS

In general, a content analysis is conducted in several discrete stages. Although the steps are listed here in sequence, they need not be followed in the order given. In fact, the initial stages of analysis can easily be combined. Nonetheless, the following steps may be used as a rough outline:

1. Formulate the research question or hypothesis.
2. Define the population in question.
3. Select an appropriate sample from the population.
4. Select and define a unit of analysis.
5. Construct the categories of content to be analyzed.
6. Establish a quantification system.
7. Train coders and conduct a pilot study.
8. Code the content according to established definitions.
9. Analyze the collected data.
10. Draw conclusions and search for indications.

FORMULATING A RESEARCH QUESTION

One problem to avoid in content analysis is the "counting-for-the-sake-of-counting" syndrome. The ultimate goal of the analysis must be clearly articulated, to avoid aimless exercises in data collection that have little utility for mass media research. For example, by counting the punctuation marks that are used in the *New York Times* and *Esquire*, it would be possible to generate a statement such as "*Esquire* used 45% more commas, but 23% fewer semicolons than the *New York Times*." The value of such information for mass media theory or policy making, however, is dubious. Content analysis should not be conducted simply because the material exists and can be tabulated.

As with other methods of mass media research, content analyses should be guided by well-formulated research questions or hypotheses. A basic review of the literature is a required step. The sources for hypotheses are the same as for other areas of media research. It is possible to generate a research question based on existing theory, prior research, or practical problems, or as a response to changing social conditions. For example, a research question might ask whether the growing visibility of the women's movement has produced a change in the way women are depicted in advertisements. Or a content analysis might be conducted to determine whether the public affairs programming of group-owned television stations differs from that of other stations. Well-defined research questions or hypotheses enable the development of accurate and sensitive content categories, which in turn helps to produce more valuable data.

DEFINING THE UNIVERSE

This stage is not as grandiose as it sounds. To "define the universe" is to specify the boundaries of the body of content to be considered, which requires an appropriate operational definition of the relevant population. If researchers are interested in analyzing the content of popular songs, they must define what is meant by a *popular* song: all songs listed in *Billboard's* "Hot 100" chart or on the back page of *Radio & Records*? the top 50 songs? the top 10? They must also ask what time period will be considered: the past 6 months? this month only? A researcher who intends to study the image of minority groups on television must first define what the term *television* means. Does it include broadcast and cable networks? Pay television? Videocassettes? Is it evening programming, or does it also include daytime shows? Will the study examine news content, or confine itself to dramatic offerings? Basically, two dimensions are used to determine the appropriate universe for a content analysis—the topic area and the time period. The specification of the topic area should be logically consistent with the research question and related to the goals of the study. For example, if a researcher plans a study of the United States' involvement in Bosnia, should the sample period extend back to the time when Bosnia was part of Yugoslavia? Finally, the time period to be examined should be sufficiently long so that the phenomenon under study has ample chance to occur.

By clearly specifying the topic area and the time period, the researcher is providing a basic requirement of content analysis: a concise statement that spells out the parameters of the investigation. For example:

> This study considers TV commercials broadcast in prime time in the New York City area from September 1, 1993, to October 1, 1995.

Or

> This study considers the news content on the front pages of the *Washington Post* and the *New York Times,* excluding Sundays, from January 1 to December 31 of the past year.

SELECTING A SAMPLE

Once the universe has been defined, a sample is selected. Although many of the guidelines and procedures discussed in Chapter 4 are applicable here, the sampling of content involves some special considerations. On one hand, some analyses are concerned with a relatively finite amount of data, and it may be possible to conduct a census of the content. Thus, Wimmer and Haynes (1978) conducted a census of 7 years' worth of articles published in the *Journal of Broadcasting,* and Skill and Robinson (1994) analyzed a census of all television series that featured families from 1950 to 1989, a total of 497 different series. On the other hand, in the more typical situation, the researcher has such a vast amount of content available that a

census is not practical. Thus, a sample must be selected.

Most content analysis in mass media involves multistage sampling. This process typically consists of two stages (though it may entail three). The first stage is usually to take a sampling of content sources. For example, a researcher interested in the treatment of the environmental movement by American newspapers would first need to sample from among the 1,650 or so newspapers published each day. The researcher may decide to focus primarily on the way big-city dailies covered the story and opt to analyze only the leading circulation newspapers in the 10 largest American cities. To take another example, a researcher interested in the changing portrayal of elderly people in magazine advertisements would first need to sample from among the thousands of publications available. In this instance, the researcher might select only the top 10, 15, or 25 mass-circulation magazines. Of course, it is also possible to sample randomly if the task of analyzing all the titles is too overwhelming. A further possibility is to use the technique of stratified sampling discussed in Chapter 4. A researcher studying the environmental movement might wish to stratify the sample by circulation size and sample from within strata composed of big-city newspapers, medium-city newspapers, and small-city newspapers. The magazine researcher might stratify by type of magazine: news, women's interests, men's interests, and so on. A researcher interested in television content might stratify by network or by program type.

Once the sources have been identified, the dates can be selected. In many studies, the time period from which the issues are to be selected is determined by the goal of the project. If the goal is to assess the nature of news coverage of the 1996 election campaign, the sampling period is fairly well defined by the actual duration of the story. If the research question is directed toward changes in the media image of the Los Angeles police force following the O. J. Simpson trial, content should be sampled before, at the time of, and after the trial. But within this period, what editions of newspapers and magazines and which television programs should be selected for analysis? It would be a tremendous amount of work to analyze each copy of *Time, Newsweek,* and *U.S. News and World Report* over a 5-year period. It is possible to sample from within that time period and obtain a representative group of issues. A simple random sample of the calendar dates involved is one possibility: After a random start, every *n*th issue of a publication is selected for the sample. This method cannot be used without planning, however. For instance, if the goal is 50 edition dates, and an interval of 7 is used, the sample might include 50 Saturday editions (periodicity). Since news content is not randomly distributed over the days of the week, the sample will not be representative.

Another technique for sampling edition dates is stratification by week of the month and by day of the week. A sampling rule that no more than two days from one week can be chosen is one way to ensure a balanced distribution across the month. Another procedure is to construct a *composite week* for each month in the sample. For example, a study might use a sample of one Monday (drawn at random from the four or five possible Mondays in the month), one Tuesday (drawn from the available Tuesdays), and so on, until all weekdays have been included. How many edition dates should be selected? Obviously, this depends on the topic under study. If an investigator is trying to describe the portrayal of Mexican Americans on prime time television, several dates would have to be sampled to ensure a representative analysis. If there is an interest in analyzing the geographic sources of news stories, a smaller number of dates would be needed, since almost every story would be relevant. The number of dates should be a function of the incidence of the phenomenon in question: The lower the incidence, the more dates that must be sampled.

There are some rough guidelines for sampling in the media. Stempel (1952) drew separate samples of 6, 12, 18, 24, and 48 issues of a newspaper and compared the average content of each sample size in a single subject category against the total for the entire year. He found that each of the five sample sizes was adequate and that increasing the sample beyond 12 issues did not significantly improve sampling accuracy. More recently, Riffe, Aust, and Lacy (1993) demonstrated that a composite week sampling technique was superior to both a random sample and a consecutive day sample when dealing with newspaper content. In television, Gerbner, Gross, Jackson-Beeck, Jeffries-Fox, and Signorielli (1977) demonstrated that, at least for the purpose of measuring violent behavior, a sample of one week of fall programming and various sample dates drawn throughout the year will produce comparable results. As a general rule, however, the larger the sample the better—within reason, of course. If too few dates are selected for analysis, the possibility of an unrepresentative sample is increased. Larger samples, if chosen randomly, usually run less risk of being atypical.

There may be times, however, when purposive sampling is useful. As Stempel (1989) points out, a researcher might learn more about newspaper coverage of South Africa by examining a small sample of carefully selected papers (for example, those that subscribe to the international/national wire services and/or have correspondents in South Africa) than by studying a random sample of 100 newspapers.

Another problem that can arise during the sampling phase is systematic bias in the content itself. For example, a study of the amount of sports news in a daily paper might yield inflated results if the sampling were done only in April, when three or more professional sports are simultaneously in season. A study of marriage announcements in the Sunday *New York Times* for the month of June from 1932 to 1942 revealed no announcement of a marriage in a synagogue (Hatch & Hatch, 1947). It was later

---

FIGURE 6.1   Multistage Sampling in a Hypothetical Analysis Study

Research Question: Have there been changes in the types of products advertised in men's magazines from 1980 to 1995?

Sampling Stage 1: Selection of Titles
Men's magazines are defined as those magazines whose circulation figures show that 80% or more of their readers are men. These magazines will be divided into two groups: large and medium circulation.
    Large circulation: reaches more than 1,000,000 men.
    Medium circulation: reaches between 500,000 and 999,999 men.
From all the magazines that fall into these two groups, three will be selected at random from each division, for a total of six titles.

Sampling Stage 2: Selection of Dates
Three issues from each year will be chosen at random from clusters of four months. One magazine will be selected from the January, February, March, and April issues, and so on. This procedure will be followed for each magazine, yielding a final sample of 30 issues per magazine, or a total of 180 issues.

Sampling Stage 3: Selection of Content
Every other display ad will be tabulated, regardless of its size.

---

pointed out that the month of June usually falls within a period during which traditional Jewish marriages are prohibited. Researchers familiar with their topics can generally detect and guard against this type of distortion.

Once the sources and the dates have been determined, there may be one further stage of sampling. A researcher might wish to confine his or her attention to the specific content within an edition. For example, an analysis of the front page of a newspaper is valid for a study of general reporting trends but is probably inadequate for a study of social news coverage. Figure 6.1 provides an example of multistage sampling in content analysis.

The next step is to select the unit of analysis, which is the smallest element of a content analysis but also one of the most important. In written content, the unit of analysis might be a single word or symbol, a theme (a single assertion about one subject), or an entire article or story. In television and film analyses, units of analysis can be characters, acts, or entire programs. Specific rules and definitions are required for determining these units to ensure closer agreement between coders and fewer judgment calls.

Certain units of analysis are simpler to count than others. It is easier to determine the number of stories on the "CBS Evening News" that deal with international news than the number of acts of violence in a week of network television, because a story is a more readily distinguishable unit of analysis. The beginning and ending of a news story are fairly easy to discern, but suppose that a researcher trying to catalog violent content was faced with a long fistfight between three characters? Is the whole sequence one act of violence, or is every blow considered an act? What if a fourth character joins in? Does it then become a different act?

Operational definitions of the unit of analysis should be clear-cut and thorough; the criteria for inclusion should be apparent and easily observed. These goals cannot be accomplished without effort and some trial and error. As a preliminary step, researchers must form a rough draft of a definition and then sample representative content to see whether problems exist. This procedure usually results in further refinement and modification of the operational definition. Table 6.1 presents typical

TABLE 6.1   Operational Definitions of Units of Analysis

Researcher(s)	Topic	Universe	Sample	Unit of Analysis
Leslie (1995)	Advertising in *Ebony* magazine, 1957–1989	All issues of *Ebony,* 1957–1989	Randomly chosen magazines from the 1950s, 1970s, and 1980s	All full and one-quarter page ads
Lowry and Shidler (1995)	Network TV news bias in the 1992 campaign	All weeknight newscasts from Aug. 24–Oct. 30, 1992, on ABC, CBS, NBC, and CNN	99 newscasts chosen at random	Statements made on air by news source
Oliver (1994)	Portrayal of crime and aggression in reality-based TV police shows	All episodes of five reality-based police shows in 1991–1992	76 programs recorded from Fall 1991–January 1992	Characters portrayed as either a police officer or criminal suspect
Smith (1994)	Gender differences in children's ads	Network children's programming in 1991	All ads broadcast in one week of Feb. 1991 on ABC, Fox, CBS, and Nickelodeon	Gender-positioned ads
Vest (1992)	Gender representation in prime time pilots	TV pilots appearing during 1986–1987 season	Shooting scripts provided by producers	Each character with a name and speaking role

operational definitions of units of analysis taken from mass media research.

At the heart of any content analysis is the category system used to classify media content. The precise makeup of this system, of course, varies with the topic under study. As Berelson (1952, p. 147) pointed out, "Particular studies have been productive to the extent that the categories were clearly formulated and well-adapted to the problem and the content."

To be serviceable, all category systems should be mutually exclusive, exhaustive, and reliable. A category system is mutually exclusive if a unit of analysis can be placed in one and only one category. If the researcher discovers that certain units fall simultaneously into two categories, the definitions of those categories must be revised. For example, suppose researchers attempt to describe the ethnic makeup of prime time television characters using the following category system: (1) African American, (2) Jewish, (3) white, (4) Native American, and (5) other. Obviously, a Jewish person would fall into two categories at once, thus violating the exclusivity rule. Or, to take another example, a researcher might start with the following categories in an attempt to describe the types of programming on network television: (1) situation comedies, (2) children's shows, (3) movies, (4) documentaries, (5) action/adventure programs, (6) quiz and talk shows, and (7) general drama. This list might look acceptable at first glance, but a program such as "NYPD Blue" raises questions. Does it belong in the action/adventure category, or in the general drama category? Definitions must be highly specific to ensure accurate categorization.

In addition to exclusivity, content analysis categories must have the property of **exhaustivity**: There must be an existing slot into which every unit of analysis can be placed. If investigators suddenly find a unit of analysis that does not logically fit into a predefined category, they have a problem with their category system. Taken as a whole, the category system should account for every unit of analysis. Achieving exhaustivity is usually not difficult in mass media content analysis. If one or two unusual instances are detected, a category labeled "other" or "miscellaneous" usually solves the problem. (If too many items fall in this category, however, a reexamination of the original category definitions is called for; a study with 10% or more of its content in the "other" category is probably overlooking some relevant content characteristic.) An additional way to assure exhaustivity is to dichotomize or trichotomize the content: Attempts at problem solving might be defined as aggressive and nonaggressive, or statements might be placed in positive, neutral, and negative categories. The most practical way to determine whether a proposed categorization system is exhaustive is to pretest it on a sample of content. If unanticipated items appear, the original scheme requires changes before the primary analysis can begin.

The categorization system should also be reliable; that is, different coders should agree in the great majority of instances about the proper category for each unit of analysis. This agreement is usually quantified in content analysis and is called **intercoder reliability**. Precise category definitions generally increase reliability, while sloppily defined categories tend to lower it. Pretesting the category system for reliability is highly recommended before beginning to process the main body of content. Reliability is crucial in content analysis, as discussed in more detail later in this chapter.

The question of how many categories to include may arise in constructing category systems. Common sense, pretesting, and practice with the coding system are valuable guides to aid the researcher in steering between the two extremes of developing a system with too few categories (so that essential differences are obscured) or defining too many categories (so that only a small percentage falls into each, thus limiting generalizations). As an illustration of too few categories, consider Wurtzel's (1975) study of programming on public access television. One of the preliminary categories was labeled "informational," and the data indicated that more than 70% of the content fell into this classification. As a result, Wurtzel subdivided the category into seven informational headings (ethnic, community, health, consumer, and so on). An example of the opposite extreme is the attempt made by Dominick, Richman, and Wurtzel (1979) to describe the types of problems encountered by characters in prime time television shows popular with children. They originally developed seven categories, including problems that dealt with romance, problems between friends, and other emotional problems arising out of relationships (with siblings, coworkers, or others).

Preliminary analysis, however, indicated that only a small fraction of problems fell into the "friendship" and "other emotional" slots. Consequently, these three categories were combined into a single classification labeled "problems dealing with romance, sentiment, and other emotions." As a general rule, many researchers suggest that too many initial categories are preferable to too few, since it is usually easier to combine several categories than it is to subdivide a large one after the units have been coded.

ESTABLISHING A QUANTIFICATION SYSTEM

Quantification in content analysis can involve all four of the levels of data measurement discussed in Chapter 3, though usually only nominal, interval, and ratio data are used. At the nominal level, researchers simply count the frequency of occurrence of the units in each category. Thus, Signorielli, McLeod, and Healy (1994) analyzed commercials on MTV and found that 6.5% of the male characters were coded as wearing somewhat sexy clothing and none were coded as being dressed in very sexy outfits; among the female characters, however, the corresponding percentages were 24% and 29%. The topics of conversation on daytime television, the themes of newspaper editorials, and the occupation of prime time television characters can all be quantified by means of nominal measurement.

At the interval level, it is possible to develop scales for coders to use to rate certain attributes of characters or situations. For example, in a study dealing with the images of women in commercials, each character might be rated by coders on several scales, such as

Independent __:__:__:__:__ Dependent
Dominant __:__:__:__:__ Submissive

Scales such as these add depth and texture to a content analysis and are perhaps more interesting than the surface data obtained through nominal measurement. However, rating scales inject subjectivity into the analysis and may lower intercoder reliability unless careful training is undertaken. Chang (1975), for example, constructed an interval scale based on the degree of movie critics' like or dislike of certain films.

At the ratio level, measurements in mass media research are generally applied to space and time. In the print media, column-inch measurements are used to analyze editorials, advertisements, and stories about particular events or phenomena. In television and radio, ratio-level measurements are made concerning time: the number of commercial minutes, the types of programs on the air, the amount of the program day devoted to programs of various types, and so on. Interval and ratio data permit the researcher to use some powerful statistical techniques. For example, Gurian (1993) counted the number of column inches of news coverage devoted to the 1988 presidential primaries and developed a regression equation (see Chapter 12) to explain variations in coverage.

CODING THE CONTENT

Placing a unit of analysis into a content category is called **coding**. It is the most time-consuming and least glamorous part of a content analysis. Individuals who do the coding are called *coders*. The number of coders involved in a content analysis is typically small; a brief examination of a sampling of recent content analyses indicated that typically two to six coders are used.

Careful training of coders is an integral task in any content analysis and usually results in a more reliable analysis. Although the investigator may have a firm grasp of the operational definitions and the category schemes, coders may not share this close knowledge. Consequently, they must become thoroughly familiar

Coder Perception versus Audience Perception

One problem with using content analysis as a starting point for studies of audience effects is the possibility of falsely assuming that what trained coders see in a body of content is the same as what is perceived by audience members. For example, a study of the cultivation effects of TV content on viewers' attitudes toward sexual practices might start with an analysis of the sexual content on specific television programs. Coders might be trained to count how many provocatively dressed characters appear; how many instances of kissing, embracing, caressing, and other forms of sexual behavior occur; and so on. When they are finished with this aspect of the study, a list of TV programs could be rank-ordered with regard to their sexual content. Audience viewings of these shows could then be correlated with audience attitudes toward sexual matters. The trouble is that the researchers do not know whether the audience defines the term *sexual content* in the same manner as do the coders. For example, perhaps many in the audience might not define all forms of kissing as sexual. Or perhaps programs such as "Studs" or "Love Connection," where sexual activity is only talked about and implied rather than acted out, are also influential in shaping audience attitudes. Since these shows would probably score low on most of the measures used by coders to gauge sexual content, the influence of these shows might be overlooked.

Consequently, researchers who intend to use content analytic data as a starting point for audience effects studies need to consider how "normal" people perceive and interpret the content. Indeed, Kepplinger (1989) argues that a "reception analysis" should supplement many forms of content analysis, and Greenberg (1989) advocates including "fans" or experts on the content analysis coding team, to provide context and depth to the raw data. In any case, researchers need to be aware that not everybody will perceive the world in the same way.

with the study's mechanics and peculiarities. To this end, researchers should plan several lengthy training sessions in which sample content is examined and coded. These sessions are used to revise definitions, clarify category boundaries, and revamp coding sheets until the coders are comfortable with the materials and procedure. Detailed instruction sheets should also be provided to coders.

Next, a pilot study is done to check intercoder reliability. The pilot study should be conducted with a fresh set of coders who are given some initial training to impart familiarity with the instructions and the methods of the study. Some would argue that fresh coders are to be preferred for this task because intercoder reliability (among coders who have worked for long periods of time developing the coding

scheme) might be artificially high. As Lorr and McNair (1966, p. 133) suggest, "Interrater agreement for a new set of judges given a reasonable but practical amount of training . . . would represent a more realistic index of reliability."

To facilitate coding, standardized sheets are generally used. These sheets allow coders to classify the data by simply placing check marks or slashes in predetermined spaces. Figure 6.2 is an example of a standardized coding sheet, and Figure 6.3 illustrates the coder instruction sheet that accompanied it. If data are to be tabulated by hand, the coding sheets should be constructed to allow for rapid tabulation. Some studies code data on 4-by-6-inch index cards, with information recorded across the top of the card. This enables researchers to quickly sort the information into categories. Templates are

---

FIGURE 6.2   **Standardized Coding Sheet for Studying TV Cartoons**

Character Description Code Sheet

Program name _____

A. Character number _____

B. Character name
   or description _____

C. Role   1-Major   3-Other (individual)
            2-Minor   4-Other (group)

D. Species
   1-Human   4-Robot   7-Other (specify):
   2-Animal   5-Animated object
   3-Monster/Ghost 6-Indeterminate   _____

E. Sex

   1-Male   2-Female   3-Indeterminate   4-Mixed (group)

F. Race

   1-White   4-Robot   7-Other (specify):

   2-African American 5-Native American

   3-Animal   6-Indeterminate   _____

G. Age

   1-Child   3-Adult   5-Indeterminate

   2-Teenager   4-Mature adult   6-Mixed (group)

---

available to speed the measurement of newspaper space. Researchers who work with television generally videotape the programs and allow coders to stop and start the tape at their own pace while coding data.

When a computer is used in tabulating data, the data are usually transferred directly to computer coding sheets or perhaps to mark-sense forms or optical scan sheets (answer sheets scored by computer). These forms save time and reduce data errors.

Computers are useful not only in the data-tabulation phase of a content analysis, but also in the actual coding process. Computers will perform with unerring accuracy any coding task in which the classification rules are unambiguous. Computers can do simple tasks rapidly, such as recognizing words or even syllables as they occur in a sample of text. Dyer, Miller, and Boone (1991), for example, instructed a computer to recognize the name "Exxon" whenever it appeared in wire service copy. Simonton (1990) used a computer to analyze 154 of Shakespeare's sonnets in order to detect what lexical choices were related to the aesthetic success of the sonnet. The computer

FIGURE 6.3 **Coder Instruction Sheet That Accompanies Form Shown in Figure 6.2**

Character Description Code Sheet Instructions

Code all characters that appear on the screen for at least 90 seconds and/or speak more than 15 words (include cartoon narrator when applicable). Complete one sheet for each character to be coded.

A. Character number: code two-digit program number first (listed on page 12 of this instruction book), followed by two-digit character number randomly assigned to each character (starting with 01).

B. Character name: list all formal names, nicknames, or dual identity names (code dual identity behavior as one character's actions). List description of character if name is not identifiable.

C. Role
   1-*Major*: major characters share the majority of dialogue during the program, play the largest role in the dramatic action, and appear on the screen for the longest period of time during the program.
   2-*Minor*: all codeable characters that are not identified as major characters.
   3-*Other (individual)*: one character that does not meet coding requirements but is involved in a behavioral act that is coded.
   4-*Other (group)*: two or more characters that are simultaneously involved in a behavioral act but do not meet coding requirements.

D. Species
   1-*Human*: any character resembling man, even ghost or apparition if it appears in human form (e.g., the Ghostbusters)
   2-*Animal*: any character resembling bird, fish, beast, or insect; may or may not be capable of human speech (e.g., muppets, smurfs, Teddy Ruxpin)
   3-*Monster/Ghost*: any supernatural creature (e.g., my pet monster, ghosts)
   4-*Robot*: mechanical creature (e.g., transformers)
   5-*Animated object*: any inanimate object (e.g., car, telephone) that acts like a sentient being (speaks, thinks, etc.). Do not include objects that "speak" through programmed mechanical means (e.g., recorded voice playback through computer).
   6-*Indeterminate*
   7-*Other*: if species is mixed within group, code as mixed here and specify which of the species are represented.

E. 1-Male   2-Female   3-Indeterminate: use this   4-Mixed (group only)
                              category sparingly (if
                              animal has low masculine
                              voice, code as male).

Note: The remainder of the instructions continue in this format.

gauged the number of words, the number of different words, and the unique words, and it categorized the imagery used. Only a few years ago, this approach was laborious and tiring because the material had to be input by hand into a computer. Recent developments in computer technology, however, have eased this problem. Many documents and publications in on-line databases such as Vu/Text or Nexis can be searched for key topics and phrases in a matter of seconds. This ease of searching, however, comes with a price. As Kaufman, Dykers, and Caldwell (1993) discovered, an on-line content analysis conducted with Nexis and Vu/Text produced different results from a conventional hand-count content analysis of the same sources.

ANALYZING THE DATA

The descriptive statistics discussed in Chapters 10, 11, and 12 and in Appendix 2, such as percentages, means, modes, and medians, are appropriate for content analysis. If hypothesis tests are planned, common inferential statistics (whereby results are generalized to the population) are acceptable. The chi-square test is the most commonly used, since content analysis data tend to be nominal in form; however, if the data meet the requirements of interval or ratio levels, a t-test, ANOVA, or Pearson's r may be appropriate. Other statistical analyses are discussed by Krippendorf (1980), such as discriminant analysis, cluster analysis, and contextual analysis.

INTERPRETING THE RESULTS

If an investigator is testing specific hypotheses concerning the relationships between variables, the interpretation will be fairly evident. However, if the study is descriptive, questions about the meaning or importance of the results may arise. Researchers are often faced with a "fully/

only" dilemma. Suppose, for example, that a content analysis of children's television programs reveals that 30% of the commercials were for snacks and candy. What is the researcher to conclude? Is this a high amount or a low amount? Should the researcher report, "*Fully* 30% of the commercials fell into this category," or should the same percentage be presented as "*Only* 30% of the commercials fell into this category"? Clearly, the investigator needs some benchmark for comparison; 30% may indeed be a high figure when compared to commercials for other products or for those shown during adult programs.

In a study done by one of the authors, the amount of network news time devoted to the various states was tabulated. It was determined that California and New York receive 19% and 18% respectively, of non-Washington, D.C., national news coverage. By themselves, these numbers are interesting, but their significance is somewhat unclear. In an attempt to aid interpretation, each state's relative news time was compared to its population, and an "attention index" was created by subtracting the ratio of each state's population to the national population from its percentage of news coverage. This provided a listing of states that were either "overcovered" or "undercovered" (Dominick, 1977). To aid in their interpretation, Whitney, Fritzler, Jones, Mazzarella, and Rakow (1989) created a sophisticated "attention ratio" in their replication of this study.

RELIABILITY

The concept of reliability is crucial to content analysis. If a content analysis is to be objective, its measures and procedures must be reliable. Reliability is present when repeated measurement of the same material results in similar decisions or conclusions. Intercoder reliability refers to levels of agreement among independent coders who code the same content using the same coding instrument. If the results fail

Coding by Computer

There's no question that coding is the least glamorous part of a content analysis. Several researchers have suggested that it might be possible for the computer to take over some if not all of the more mundane types of coding. One question, however, that needed to be answered before relying on the computer as a coding tool concerned how a computerized content analysis compared to the traditional human-coded content analysis.

Morris (1994) provided an initial answer to this question. She had six human coders categorize the elements of corporate mission statements into nine categories. This content analysis was done using various units of analysis ranging from an individual sentence to an entire document. Once these results were obtained, the same analysis was done using a ZyIndex text management program.

The results indicated that content analysis by computer had both advantages and disadvantages. On the plus side, the reliability was higher, as one might expect, for the computer coding, and the computer was able to process large amounts of data more quickly. In addition, the computer was in general agreement with the human coders when the unit of analysis was a sentence or a paragraph. The computer did not agree with the human coders, however, when the unit of analysis was an entire document. Apparently, human coders were more sensitive to variations in the broader context of the document than was the computer. In any case, the results suggested that for certain tasks the computer holds promise as a coding device.

to achieve reliability, something is amiss with the coders, the coding instructions, the category definitions, the unit of analysis, or some combination of these. To achieve acceptable levels of reliability, the following steps are recommended:

1. *Define category boundaries with maximum detail.* A group of vague or ambiguously defined categories makes reliability extremely difficult to achieve. Examples of units of analysis and a brief explanation for each are necessary for coders to fully understand the procedure.

2. *Train the coders.* Before the data are collected, training sessions in using the coding instrument and the category system must be conducted. These sessions help eliminate methodological problems. During the sessions, the group as a whole should code sample material; afterward, they should discuss the results and the purpose of the study. Dis-

agreements should be analyzed as they occur. The end result of the training sessions is a "bible" of detailed instructions and coding examples, and each coder should receive a copy.

3. *Conduct a pilot study.* Select a subsample of the content universe under consideration and let independent coders categorize it. These data are useful for two reasons: Poorly defined categories can be detected, and chronically dissenting coders can be identified. To illustrate these problems, consider Tables 6.2 and 6.3.

In Table 6.2, the definitions for Categories I and IV appear to be satisfactory. All four coders placed Units 1, 3, 7, and 11 in the first category; in Category IV, Item 14 is classified consistently by three of the four coders and Items 4 and 9 by all four coders. The confusion apparently lies in the boundaries between Categories II and III. Three coders put Items 2, 6, and/or 13 in Category II, and three placed

TABLE 6.2   Detecting Poorly Defined Categories from Pilot Study Data*

	Categories			
Coders	**I**	**II**	**III**	**IV**
A	1,3,7,11	2,5,6,8,12,13	10	4,9,14
B	1,3,7,11	5,8,10,12	2,6,13	4,9,14
C	1,3,7,11	2,8,12,13	5,6,10	4,9,14
D	1,3,7,11	5,6	2,8,10,12,13,14	4,9

*Arabic numerals refer to items.

some or all of these numbers in Category III. The definitions of these two categories require reexamination and perhaps revision because of this ambiguity.

Table 6.3 illustrates the problem of the chronic disagreer. Although Coders A and B agree 7 of 8 times, Coders B and C agree only 2 of 8 times and Coders A and C agree only once. Obviously, Coder C is going to be a problem. As a rule, the investigator would carefully reexplain to this coder the rules used in cate-

TABLE 6.3   Identifying a Chronic Dissenter from Pilot Study Data*

	Coders		
Items	**A**	**B**	**C**
1	I	I	II
2	III	III	I
3	II	II	II
4	IV	IV	III
5	I	II	II
6	IV	IV	I
7	I	I	III
8	II	II	I

*Roman numerals refer to categories.

gorization and examine the reasons for his or her consistent deviation. If the problem persists it may be necessary to dismiss the coder from the analysis.

Assuming that the initial test of reliability yields satisfactory results, the main body of data is coded. When the coding is complete, it is recommended that a subsample of the data, probably between 10% and 25%, be reanalyzed by independent coders to calculate an overall intercoder reliability coefficient.

Intercoder reliability can be calculated by several methods. Holsti (1969) reported a formula for determining the reliability of nominal data in terms of percentage of agreement:

$$\text{Reliability} = \frac{2M}{N_1 + N_2}$$

where M is the number of coding decisions on which two coders agree, and N_1 and N_2 refer to the total number of coding decisions by the first and second coder, respectively. Thus, if two coders judge a subsample of 50 units and agree on 35 of them, the calculation is

$$\text{Reliability} \ \frac{2(35)}{50 + 50} = .70$$

This method is straightforward and easy to

apply, but it is criticized because it does not take into account the occurrence of some coder agreement strictly by chance, an amount that is a function of the number of categories in the analysis. For example, a two-category system should obtain 50% reliability simply by chance; a five-category system would generate a 20% agreement by chance; and so on. To take this into account, Scott (1955) developed the *pi* index, which corrects for the number of categories used and also for the probable frequency of use:

$$pi = \frac{\% \text{ observed agreement} - \% \text{ expected agreement}}{1 - \% \text{ expected agreement}}$$

A hypothetical example demonstrates the use of this index. Suppose that two coders are assigning magazine advertisements to the six categories shown and obtain the following matrix of agreement:

Coder A

		Categories	1	2	3	4	5	Marginal Totals
		1	42	2	1	3	0	48
		2	1	12	2	0	0	15
Coder B		3	0	0	10	0	2	12
		4	0	2	1	8	1	12
		5	2	0	1	2	8	13
Marginal Totals			45	16	15	13	11	100

The percentage of observed agreement is found by adding the numbers in the diagonals (42 + 12 + 10 + 8 + 8 = 80) and dividing by the N (80/100 = .80). The percentage of agreement expected by chance is a little more complicated. It is found by multiplying the marginal totals for each cell of the diagonal, dividing by the total N, summing across the cells, and converting the result to a percentage. For example, for the cell in row 1 and column 1: 45 × 48/100 = 21.6, or .216. For the cell in row 2 and column 2: 16 × 15/100 = 2.4, or .024, and so on for all the six cells along the diagonal of the matrix. This calculation yields an

expected proportion of .288. Now we can calculate Scott's pi:

$$pi = \frac{.80 - .288}{1 - .288} = .719$$

This same technique can be used to calculate reliability when there are more than two coders. In this instance, the statistic is called Cohen's kappa (Cohen, 1960; Fleiss, 1971), and the formula is slightly modified:

$$Kappa = \frac{\% \text{ observed} - \% \text{ expected}}{N \times M - \% \text{ expected}}$$

where N = the total number of objects coded and M = the number of coders.

Estimating reliability with interval data requires certain care. Several studies have used the correlation method called the Pearson r, a method that investigates the relationship between two items. The Pearson r can range from -1.00 to $+1.00$. In estimating reliability in content analysis, however, if this measure has a high value, it may indicate either that the coders were in agreement or that their ratings were associated in some systematic manner.

For example, suppose an interval scale ranging from 1 to 10 is used to score the degree of favorability of a news item to some person or topic. (A score of 1 represents very positive; 10 represents very negative.) Assume that two coders are independently scoring the same 10 items. Table 6.4 illustrates two possible outcomes. In Situation I, the coders agree on every item, and r equals 1.00. In Situation II, the coders disagree on every item by three scale positions, yet r still equals 1.00. Clearly, the uses of this estimate are not equally reliable in the two situations.

Krippendorf (1980) circumvents this dilemma by presenting what might be termed an "all-purpose reliability measure," *alpha*, which can be used for nominal, ordinal, interval, and ratio scales, and for more than one coder.

TABLE 6.4   False Equivalence as a Reliability Measure When *r* Is Used

	Situation I			Situation II	
Items	Coder 1	Coder 2	Items	Coder 1	Coder 2
1	1	1	1	1	4
2	2	2	2	2	5
3	3	3	3	3	6
4	3	3	4	3	6
5	4	4	5	4	7
6	5	5	6	5	8
7	6	6	7	6	9
8	6	6	8	6	9
9	7	7	9	7	10
10	7	7	10	7	10
	$r = 1.00$			$r = 1.00$	

Although somewhat difficult to calculate, *alpha* is the equivalent of Scott's *pi* at the nominal level with two coders and represents an improvement over *r* in the interval situation. Unfortunately, available computer software generally lacks programs that calculate intercoder reliability. Kang, Kara, Laskey, and Seaton (1993) have eased that problem somewhat by presenting a SAS MACRO that computes five different reliability coefficients including alpha and can be used in conjunction with many popular spreadsheet programs.

What is an acceptable level of intercoder reliability? This depends on the research context and the type of information coded. In some instances, little coder judgment is needed to place units into categories (for example, counting the number of words per sentence in a newspaper story or tabulating the number of times a network correspondent contributes a story to the evening news), and coding becomes a mechanical or clerical task. In this context, one would expect a fairly high degree of reliability, perhaps approaching 100%, since

coder disagreements would probably result only from carelessness or fatigue. If, however, a certain amount of interpretation is involved, reliability estimates are typically lower. In general, the greater the amount of judgmental leeway given to coders, the lower the reliability coefficients will be. As a rule of thumb, most published content analyses typically report a minimum reliability coefficient of about 90% or above when using Holsti's formula, and about .75 or above when using *pi* or *alpha*.

Note that the previous discussion assumed that at least two independent coders categorized the same content. In some situations, however, *intracoder* reliability also might be assessed. These circumstances occur most frequently when only a few coders are used because extensive training must be employed to ensure the detection of subtle message elements. To test intracoder reliability, the same individual codes a set of data twice, at different times, and the reliability statistics are computed using the two sets of results.

VALIDITY

In addition to being reliable, a content analysis must yield valid results. As indicated in Chapter 3, validity is usually defined as the degree to which an instrument actually measures what it sets out to measure. This raises special concerns in content analysis. In the first place, validity is intimately connected with the procedures used in the analysis. If the sampling design is faulty, if categories overlap, or if reliability is low, the results of the study probably possess little validity. Additionally, the adequacy of the definitions used in a content analysis bears directly on the question of validity. For example, a great deal of content analysis has focused on the depiction of televised violence; different investigators have offered different definitions of what constitutes a violent act. The question of validity emerges when one tries to decide whether each of the various definitions actually encompasses what one might logically refer to as violence. The continuing debate between Gerbner and the television networks vividly illustrates this problem. The definition of violence propounded by Gerbner and his associates in 1977 includes accidents, acts of nature, or violence that might occur in a fantasy or a humorous setting. However, network analysts do not consider these phenomena to be acts of violence (Blank, 1977). Both Gerbner and the networks offer arguments in support of their decisions. Which analysis is the more valid? The answer depends in part on the plausibility of the rationale that underlies the definitions.

This discussion relates closely to a technique traditionally called *face validity*. This validation technique assumes that an instrument adequately measures what it purports to measure if the categories are rigidly and satisfactorily defined and if the procedures of the analysis have been adequately conducted. Most descriptive content analyses usually rely on face validity, but other techniques are available.

The use of *concurrent validity* in content analysis is exemplified in a study by Clarke and Blankenburg (1972). These investigators attempted a longitudinal study of violence in television shows dating back to 1952. Unfortunately, few copies of the early programs were available, and the authors were forced to use program summaries in *TV Guide*. To establish that such summaries would indeed disclose the presence of violence, the authors compared the results of a subsample of programs coded from these synopses to the results obtained from a direct viewing of the same programs. The results were sufficiently related to convince the authors that their measurement technique was valid. However, this method of checking validity is only as good as the criterion measurement: If the direct-viewing technique is itself invalid, there is little value in showing that synopsis coding is related to it.

Only a few studies have attempted to document *construct validity*. One instance involves the use of sensationalism in news stories. This construct has been measured by semantic differentials and factor analysis (Appendix 2) in an attempt to isolate its underlying dimensions, and is related to relevant message characteristics (Tannenbaum, 1962; Tannenbaum & Lynch, 1960). Another technique that investigators occasionally use is *predictive validity*. For example, certain content attributes from wire stories might allow a researcher to predict which items will be carried by a newspaper and which will not.

In summary, several different methods are used in content analysis to assess validity. The most common is face validity, which is appropriate for some studies. It is recommended, however, that the content analyst also examine other methods to establish the validity of a given study.

EXAMPLES OF CONTENT ANALYSIS

Table 6.5, which summarizes four recent content analyses, lists the purpose of the analysis, the

TABLE 6.5   Summaries of Content Analysis Studies

Researcher(s)	Purpose of Study	Sample	Units of Analysis	Representative Categories	Statistics
Kahn and Goldberg (1991)	To examine differences in coverage of male and female U.S. Senate candidates	Newspaper coverage of 26 Senate races in 17 states	Any item mentioning either candidate	Paragraphs of coverage per candidate, type of coverage	t-tests
Molitor and Sapolsky (1993)	To examine violence and victimization in "slasher" films	10 most successful "slasher" films in 1980, 1985, and 1989	Violent, sexually violent, or sexual behavior	Violence outcome, duration of fear, subjective camera shots	F-test
Olson (1994)	To describe health issues in daytime serials	105 hours of network daytime soap opera programming in 1989–1990	Scenes containing explicit or implicit sexual behavior	Suggestiveness, erotic touching, aggressive sexual contact	Percentages
Reid, King, and Kreshel (1995)	To describe portrayals of Black and White models in cigarette and alcohol ads	Cigarette and alcohol ads published in 11 consumer magazines during one year	All ½-page or larger cigarette or alcohol ads	Ad themes, activity of models	Percentages X^2

sample, the unit of analysis, illustrative categories, and the type of statistic used for each study.

SUMMARY

Content analysis is a popular technique in mass media research. Many of the steps involved in laboratory and survey studies are also found in content analysis; in particular, sampling procedures need to be objective and detailed, and operational definitions are mandatory. Coders must be carefully trained to ensure accurate data. Interpreting a content analysis, however, requires more caution: No claims about the impact of the content can be drawn from an analysis of the message in the absence of a study that examines the audience. In the future, the computer will become an integral part of many content analyses.

QUESTIONS AND PROBLEMS FOR FURTHER INVESTIGATION

1. Define a unit of analysis that could be used in a content analysis of the following:
   a. Problem solving on television
   b. News emphasis in a daily newspaper and a weekly newspaper
   c. Changes in the values expressed by popular songs
   d. The role of women in editorial cartoons

2. Using the topics in question 1, define a sample-selection procedure appropriate for each.

3. Generate two content analyses that could be used as preliminary tests for an audience study.

4. Conduct a brief content analysis of one of the topics listed below. (Train a second individual in the use of the category system that you develop, and have this person independently code a subsample of the content.)
   a. Similarities and differences between local newscasts on two television stations
   b. Changes in the subject matter of movies from 1980 to 1995
   c. The treatment of the elderly on network television

5. Using the topic selected in question 4, compute a reliability coefficient for the items that were scored by both coders.

REFERENCES AND SUGGESTED READINGS

Attkisson, C. Handler, L., & Shrader, R. (1969). The use of figure drawing to assess religious values. *Journal of Psychology, 71,* 27–31.

Barber, J. T., & Gandy, O. H. (1990). Press portrayals of African American and white United States representatives. *Howard Journal of Communications, 2*(2), 213–225.

Berelson, B. (1952). *Content analysis in communication research.* New York: Free Press.

Blank, D. (1977). The Gerbner violence profile. *Journal of Broadcasting, 21,* 273–279.

Bogaert, A. F., Turkovich, D. A., & Hafer, C. (1993). A content analysis of *Playboy* centerfolds from 1953 to 1990. *Journal of Sex Research, 30*(2), 135–140.

Busby, L. J., & Leichty, G. (1993). Feminism and advertising in traditional and nontraditional women's magazines. *Journalism Quarterly, 70*(2), 247–265.

Chadwick, B., Bahr, H., & Albrecht, S. (1984). *Social science research methods.* Englewood Cliffs, NJ: Prentice-Hall.

Chang, W. (1975). A typology study of movie critics. *Journalism Quarterly, 52*(4), 721–725.

Clarke, D., & Blankenburg, W. (1972). Trends in violent content in selected mass media. In G. Comstock & E. Rubinstein (Eds.), *Television and social behavior: Media content and control.* Washington, DC: U.S. Government Printing Office.

Cohen, J. (1960). A coefficient of agreement for nominal scales. *Educational and Psychological Measurement, 20*(1), 37–46.

Comstock, G. (1975). *Television and human behavior: The key studies.* Santa Monica, CA: Rand Corporation.

Cooper, R., Potter, W. J., and Dupagne, M. (1994). A status report on methods used in mass communication research. *Journalism Educator, 48*(4), 54–61.

Davis, F. (1951). Crime news in Colorado newspapers. *American Journal of Sociology, 57,* 325–330.

DeFleur, M. (1964). Occupational roles as portrayed on television. *Public Opinion Quarterly, 28,* 57–74.

Dominick, J. (1977). Geographic bias in national TV news. *Journal of Communication, 27,* 94–99.

Dominick, J., Richman, S., & Wurtzel, A. (1979). Problem-solving in TV shows popular with children: Assertion vs. aggression. *Journalism Quarterly, 56,* 455–463.

Dupagne M., Potter, W. J., & Cooper, R. (1993). A content analysis of women's published mass communication research, 1965–1989. *Journalism Quarterly, 70*(4), 815–823.

Eaton, B. C., & Dominick, J. R. (1991). Product-related programming and children's TV. *Journalism Quarterly, 68*(½), 67–75.

Fleiss, J. L. (1971). Measuring nominal scale agreement among many raters. *Psychological Bulletin, 76,* 378–382.

Gerbner, G. (1969). The television world of violence. In D. Lange, R. Baker, & S. Ball (Eds.), *Mass media and violence.* Washington, DC: U.S. Government Printing Office.

Gerbner, G., Gross, L., Jackson-Beeck, M., Jeffries-Fox, S., & Signorielli, N. (1977). One more time: An analysis of the CBS "Final Comments on the Violence Profile." *Journal of Broadcasting, 21*, 297–304.

Gerbner, G., Gross, L., Signorielli, N., Morgan, M., & Jackson-Beeck, M. (1979). The demonstration of power: Violence profile no. 10. *Journal of Communication, 29*(3), 177–196.

Gerbner, G., Holsti, O., Krippendorf, K., Paisley, W., & Stone, P. (1969). *The analysis of communication content.* New York: John Wiley.

Glascock, J., & LaRose, R. (1993). Dial-a-porn recordings. *Journal of Broadcasting and Electronic Media, 37*(3), 313–324.

Greenberg, B. (1983). *Mexican-Americans and the mass media.* Norwood, NJ: Ablex.

Greenberg, B. (1989). On other perceptions toward message analysis. *American Behavioral Scientist, 33*(2), 183–186.

Greenwald, M. S. (1990). Gender representations in newspaper business sections. *Newspaper Research Journal, 11*(1), 68–79.

Gross, B. L., & Sheth, J. N. (1989). Time-oriented advertising: A content analysis of U.S. magazine advertising, 1890-1988. *Journal of Marketing, 53*(4), 76–83.

Gurian, P. (1993). The distribution of news coverage in presidential primaries. *Journalism Quarterly, 70*(2), 336–344.

Hatch, D., & Hatch, M. (1947). Criteria of social status as derived from marriage announcements in the *New York Times. American Sociological Review, 12*, 396–403.

Hennessee, J., & Nicholson, J. (1972, May 28). NOW says: TV commercials insult women. *New York Times Magazine,* pp. 12–14.

Hinkle, G., & Elliott, W. R. (1989). Science coverage in three newspapers and three supermarket tabloids. *Journalism Quarterly, 66*(2), 353–358.

Holsti, O. (1969). *Content analysis for the social sciences and humanities.* Reading, MA: Addison-Wesley.

Kahn, K. F., & Goldberg, E. (1991). Women candidates in the news. *Public Opinion Quarterly, 55*(2), 180–199.

Kang, N., Kara, A., & Lasky, A. (1993). A SAS macro for calculating intercoder agreement in content analysis. *Journal of Advertising, 22*(2), 17–29.

Kaufman, P., Dykers, C., & Caldwell, C. (1993). Why going online can reduce reliability. *Journalism Quarterly, 70*(4), 824–832.

Kenney, K., & Simpson, C. (1993). Was coverage of the 1988 presidential race by Washington's two major dailies biased? *Journalism Quarterly, 70*(2), 345–355.

Kepplinger, H. M. (1989). Content analysis and reception analysis. *American Behavioral Scientist, 33*(2), 175–182.

Kerlinger, F. N. (1986). *Foundations of behavioral research* (3rd ed.). New York: Holt, Rinehart & Winston.

Krippendorf, K. (1980). *Content analysis: An introduction to its methodology.* Beverly Hills, CA: Sage Publications.

Leslie, M. (1995). Advertising in *Ebony* magazine. *Journalism and Mass Communication Quarterly, 72*(2), 412–425.

Lester, P. (1994). African-American photo coverage in four U.S. newspapers, 1937–1990. *Journalism Quarterly, 71*(2), 380–394.

Littleton, C. (1995, Sept. 25). Violence study finds promising signs. *Broadcasting & Cable,* p. 20.

Lorr, M., & McNair, D. (1966). Methods relating to evaluation of therapeutic outcome. In L. Gottschalk & A. Auerbach (Eds.), *Methods of research in psychotherapy.* Englewood Cliffs, NJ: Prentice-Hall.

Lowry, D., & Shidler, J. (1995). The soundbites, the biters and the bitten: An analysis of network TV news bias in Campaign '92. *Journalism and Mass Communication Quarterly, 72*(1), 33–44.

Moffett, E. A., & Dominick, J. R. (1987). Statistical analysis in the Journal of Broadcasting, 1970–1985. *Feedback, 28*(2), 13–20.

Molitor, F., & Sapolsky, B. (1993). Sex, violence and victimization in slasher films. *Journal of Broadcasting and Electronic Media, 37*(2), 223–241.

Morgan, M., & Shanahan, J. (1991). Television and the cultivation of political attitudes in Argentina. *Journal of Communication, 41*(1), 88–103.

Morris, R. (1994). Computerized content analysis in management research. *Journal of Management, 20*(4), 903–931.

O'Callaghan, J., & Duke, J. (1992). Media coverage of the Supreme Court's caseload. *Journalism Quarterly, 69*(1), 195–203.

Oliver, M. A., (1994). Portrayals of crime, race, and aggression in reality-based police shows. *Jour-*

nal of Broadcasting and Electronic Media, 38(2), 179–192.

Olson, B. (1994). Sex and the soaps: A comparative content analysis of health issues. Journalism Quarterly, 71(4). 840–850.

Pfau, M., Mullen, L., Deidrich, T., & Garrow, K. (1995). Television viewing and public perceptions of attorneys. Human Communication Research, 21(3), 307–330.

Reid, L., King, K., & Kreshel, P. (1995). Black and white models and their activities in modern cigarette and alcohol ads. Journalism and Mass Communication Quarterly, 71(4), 873–886.

Riffe, D., Aust, C., & Lacy, S. (1993). The effectiveness of random, consecutive day and constructed week sampling in newspaper content analysis. Journalism Quarterly, 70(1), 133–139.

Scott, W. (1955). Reliability of content analysis: The case of nominal scale coding. Public Opinion Quarterly, 17, 321–325.

Siegelman, L., & Bullock, D. (1991). Candidates, issues, horse races and hoopla. American Political Quarterly, 19(1), 5–32.

Signorielli, N., McLeod, D., & Healy, E. (1994). Gender stereotypes in MTV commercials. Journal of Broadcasting and Electronic Media, 38(1), 91–101.

Simonton, D. K. (1990, August). Lexical choices and aesthetic success. Computers and the Humanities, 24, 251–265.

Skill, T., & Robinson, J. (1994). Four decades of families on television. Journal of Broadcasting and Electronic Media, 38(4), 449–464.

Smith, L. (1994). A content analysis of gender differences in children's advertising. Journal of Broadcasting and Electronic Media, 38(3), 323–338.

Soderlund, W. C., Surlin, S. H., & Romanow, W. I. (1989). Gender in Canadian local television news. Journal of Broadcasting and Electronic Media, 33(2), 187–196.

Stempel, G. H. (1952). Sample size for classifying subject matter in dailies. Journalism Quarterly, 29, 333–334.

Stempel, G. H. (1989). Content analysis. In G. H. Stempel & B. H. Westley, Research methods in mass communications. Englewood Cliffs, NJ: Prentice-Hall.

Tannenbaum, P. (1962). Sensationalism: Some objective message correlates. Journalism Quarterly, 39, 317–323.

Tannenbaum, P., & Greenberg, B. (1968). Mass communication. Annual Review of Psychology, 19, 351–386.

Tannenbaum, P., & Lynch, M. (1960). Sensationalism: The concept and its measurement. Journalism Quarterly, 37, 381–392.

Taylor, C. R., & Lee, J. (1994). Not in Vogue: Portrayals of Asian-Americans in magazine advertising. Journal of Public Policy and Marketing, 13(2), 239–245.

Trujillo, N., & Ekdom, L. R. (1987). A 40-year portrait of the portrayal of industry on prime-time television. Journalism Quarterly, 64(2), 368–375.

Vest, D. (1992). Prime time pilots: A content analysis of changes in gender representation. Journal of Broadcasting and Electronic Media, 36(1), 25–44.

Walizer, M. H., & Wienir, P. L. (1978). Research methods and analysis: Searching for relationships. New York: Harper & Row.

Whitney, D. C., Fritzler, M., Jones, S., Mazzarella, S., & Rakow, L. (1989). Source and geographic bias in network television news: 1982–1984. Journal of Broadcasting and Electronic Media, 33(2), 159–174.

Wilhoit, G., & Sherrill, K. (1968). Wire service visibility of U.S. Senators. Journalism Quarterly, 45, 42–48.

Wimmer, R., & Haynes, R. (1978). Statistical analyses in the Journal of Broadcasting, 22, 241–248.

Wurtzel, A. (1975). Public access cable television: Programming. Journal of Communication, 25, 15–21.

Yule, G. (1944). The statistical study of literary vocabulary. Cambridge, England: Cambridge University Press.

Chapter

7

SURVEY RESEARCH

Surveys have become ubiquitous in our society. Businesses, consumer and activist groups, politicians, and advertisers use them in their everyday decision-making processes. Firms such as Gallup, Harris, and The Eagle Group regularly conduct public opinion surveys on a full-time basis. Particularly during political campaigns, the public continually hears or reads about polls conducted to ascertain how candidates are perceived by the electorate.

The increased use of surveys has created changes in the way they are conducted and reported. More attention is now given to sample selection, questionnaire design, and error rates. This means that surveys require careful planning and execution; mass media studies using survey research must take into account a wide variety of decisions and problems. This chapter is designed to acquaint the beginning researcher with the basic steps of survey methodology.

DESCRIPTIVE AND ANALYTICAL SURVEYS

At least two major types of surveys are used by researchers: descriptive and analytical. A *descriptive survey* attempts to picture or document current conditions or attitudes—that is, to describe what exists at the moment. For example, the Department of Labor regularly conducts surveys on the amount of unemployment in the United States. Professional pollsters survey the electorate to learn its opinions of candidates or issues. Broadcast stations and networks continually survey their audiences to determine programming tastes, changing values, and lifestyle variations that might affect

programming. In descriptive surveys of this type, researchers are interested in discovering the current situation in a given area.

Analytical surveys attempt to describe and explain *why* certain situations exist. In this approach, two or more variables are usually examined to test research hypotheses. The results allow researchers to examine the interrelationships among variables and to draw explanatory inferences. For example, television station owners survey the market to determine how lifestyles affect viewing habits or to determine whether viewers' lifestyles can be used to predict the success of syndicated programming. On a broader scale, television networks conduct yearly surveys to determine how the public's tastes and desires are changing and how these attitudes relate to viewers' perceptions of the three commercial networks.

ADVANTAGES AND DISADVANTAGES OF SURVEY RESEARCH

Surveys have certain well-defined advantages. First, they can be used to investigate problems in realistic settings. Newspaper reading, television viewing, and consumer behavior patterns can be examined where they happen rather than in a laboratory or screening room under artificial conditions.

Second, the cost of surveys is reasonable considering the amount of information gathered. In addition, researchers can control expenses by selecting from four major types of surveys: mail, telephone, personal interview, and group administration.

A third advantage is that large amounts of data can be collected with relative ease from a variety of people. The survey technique allows researchers to examine many variables (demographic and lifestyle information, attitudes, motives, intentions, and so on) and to use multivariate statistics (Appendix 2) to analyze the data. Also, geographic boundaries do not limit most surveys.

Finally, data helpful to survey research already exist. Data archives, government documents, census materials, radio and television rating books, and voter registration lists can be used as *primary* sources (main sources of data) or as *secondary* sources (supportive data) of information. With archive data, it is possible to conduct an entire survey study without ever developing a questionnaire or contacting a single respondent.

Survey research, however, is not a perfect research methodology. The first and most important disadvantage is that independent variables cannot be manipulated the way they are in laboratory experiments. Without control over independent variables, the researcher cannot be certain whether the relationships between independent variables and dependent variables are causal or noncausal. That is, a survey may establish that A and B are related, but it is impossible to determine solely from the survey results that A causes B. Causality is difficult to establish because many intervening and extraneous variables are involved. Time series studies can sometimes help correct this problem.

A second disadvantage is that inappropriate wording or placement of questions within a questionnaire can bias results. The questions must be worded and placed unambiguously to elicit the desired information. This problem is discussed later in the chapter.

A third disadvantage of survey research, especially in telephone studies, is the potential problem of talking to the wrong people. For example, a respondent may claim to be 18 to 24 years old, but may in fact be well over 30 years old.

Finally, some survey research is becoming difficult to conduct. This is especially true with telephone surveys, where answering machines and respondents unwilling to participate are creating low incidence rates. Telemarketers (telephone salespeople) are destroying mass media research. More and more people refuse to participate in legitimate studies for fear of attempts by the interviewer to try to sell something.

Despite these problems, however, surveys can produce reliable and useful information. They are especially useful for collecting information on audiences and readership.

CONSTRUCTING QUESTIONS

Two basic considerations apply to the construction of good survey questions: (1) the questions must clearly and unambiguously communicate the desired information to the respondent, and (2) the questions should be worded to allow accurate transmission of respondents' answers to researchers.

Questionnaire design depends on the choice of data collection technique. Questions written for a **mail survey** must be easy to read and understand, since respondents are unable to obtain explanations. **Telephone surveys** cannot use questions with long lists of response options; the respondent may forget the first few responses by the time the last ones have been read. Questions written for **group administration** must be concise and easy for the respondents to answer. In a **personal interview**, interviewers must tread lightly with sensitive and personal questions, because his or her physical presence might make the respondent less willing to answer. (These procedures are discussed in greater detail later in this chapter.)

The design of a questionnaire must always reflect the basic purpose of the research. A complex research topic such as media use during a political campaign requires more detailed questions than does a survey to determine a favorite radio station or magazine. Nonetheless, there are several general guidelines to follow regarding wording of questions and question order and length.

TYPES OF QUESTIONS

Surveys can consist of two basic types of questions: open-ended and closed-ended. An **open-ended question** requires respondents to generate their own answers. For example:

What could your favorite radio station change so that you would listen more often?

_____

_____

What type of television program do you prefer?

_____

_____

Why do you subscribe to the *Daily Record*?

_____

_____

Open-ended questions allow respondents freedom in answering questions and an opportunity to provide in-depth responses. Furthermore, they give researchers the opportunity to ask, "Why did you say that?" or "Could you explain your answer in more detail?" The flexibility to follow up on, or *probe,* certain questions enables the interviewers to gather information about the respondents' feelings and the motives behind their answers.

Also, open-ended questions allow for answers that researchers did not foresee in designing the questionnaire—answers that may suggest possible relationships with other answers or variables. For example, in response to the question, "Which radio stations do you have programmed on the buttons in the vehicle you drive most often?" the manager of a local radio station might expect to receive a list of the local radio stations. However, a subject may give an unexpected response, such as, "I have no idea. I thought the stations were programmed by the car dealer" (The Eagle Group,

1995). This forces the manager to reconsider his or her perceptions of radio listeners.

Finally, open-ended questions are particularly useful in a pilot version of a study. Researchers may not know what types of responses to expect from subjects, so open-ended questions are used to allow subjects to answer in any way they wish. From the list of responses provided by the subjects, the researcher then selects the most often mentioned items and includes them in multiple-choice or forced-choice questions. Using open-ended questions in a pilot study generally saves time and resources, since all possible responses are more likely to be included on the final measurement instrument, obviating the need to reconduct the analysis.

The major disadvantage associated with open-ended questions is the amount of time needed to collect and analyze the responses. Open-ended responses require that interviewers spend time writing down answers. In addition, because there are so many types of responses, a content analysis (Chapter 6) of each open-ended question must be completed to produce data that can be tabulated. A content analysis groups common responses into categories, essentially making the question closed-ended. The content analysis results are then used to produce a codebook to code the open-ended responses. A **codebook** is a menu or list of quantified responses. For example, "I hate television" may be coded as a 5 for input into the computer.

In the case of **closed-ended questions**, respondents select an answer from a list provided by the researcher. These questions are popular because they provide greater uniformity of response and because the answers are easily quantified. The major disadvantage is that researchers often fail to include some important responses. Respondents may have an answer different from those that are supplied. One way to solve the problem is to include an "Other" response followed by a blank space to give respondents an opportunity to supply their own answer. The "Other" responses are then handled just like an open-ended question—a content analysis of the responses is completed to develop a codebook. A pilot study or pretest of a questionnaire usually solves most problems with closed-ended questions.

Problems in Interpreting Open-ended Questions. Open-ended questions often cause a great deal of frustration. In many cases, respondents' answers are bizarre. Sometimes respondents do not understand a question and provide answers that are not relevant to anything. Sometimes interviewers have difficulty understanding respondents, or they may have problems spelling what the respondents say. In these cases, researchers must interpret the answers and determine which code is appropriate.

The following examples are actual comments (called "verbatims") from telephone surveys and self-administered surveys conducted by the senior author. They show that even the best-planned survey questionnaire can produce a wide range of responses. The survey question asked, "How do you describe the programming on your favorite radio station?" Some responses were as follows:

1. The station is OK, but it's geared to Jerry Atrics.
2. I only listen to the station because my poodle likes it.
3. It sounds like it is run by people who don't know what they're doing.
4. The music is good, but sometimes it's too Tiny Booper.
5. I don't listen to that station because I live on Chinese time.
6. It's great. It has the best floormat in the city.
7. The station is good, but sometimes it makes me want to vomit.
8. It's my favorite, but I really don't like it since my mother does.
9. My parrot is just learning to talk, and the station teaches him a lot of words.
10. My kids hate it, so I turn it up real loud.
11. It sounds great with my car trunk open.
12. There is no way for me to answer that question before I eat dinner.

And then there was a woman who, when asked what her spouse does for a living, wrote "Arrow Space Engeneer." Research is not always easy to conduct, especially when trying to decipher comments made by respondents.

GENERAL GUIDELINES

Before examining specific types of questions appropriate in survey research, some general do's and don'ts about writing questions are in order:

1. *Make questions clear.* This should go without saying, but many researchers become so closely associated with a problem that they can no longer put themselves in the respondents' position. What might be perfectly clear to researchers might not be nearly as clear to persons answering the question. For example, after finding out which radio stations a respondent has been listening to more lately, the researcher might ask the question, "Why have you been listening to WXXX more lately?" and expect to receive an answer such as, "I like the music a lot more." But the respondents might say, "It's the only station my radio can pick up." The question would be much clearer to a respondent if asked in this form: "Which radio station, or stations, if any, do you *enjoy* listening to more lately as compared to a few months ago?" Questionnaire items must be phrased precisely so that respondents know what is being asked.

Making questions clear also requires avoiding difficult or specialized words, acronyms, and stilted language. In general, the level of vocabulary commonly found in newspapers or popular magazines is adequate for a survey. Questions should be phrased in everyday speech, and social science jargon and technical words should be eliminated. For example, "If you didn't have a premium channel, would you consider PPV?" might be better phrased, "If you didn't have a pay channel like Home Box Office or Showtime, would you consider a service where you pay a small amount for individual movies or specials you watch?"

The item, "Should the city council approve the construction of an interactive cable TV system?" assumes that respondents know what "interactive cable TV systems" are. A preferable option is, "An interactive cable television system is one in which viewers can send messages back to the cable company as well as receive normal television. Do you think the city council should approve such a system for this community?"

The clarity of a questionnaire item can be affected by double or hidden meanings in the words that are not apparent to investigators. For example, the question, "How many television shows do you think are a little too violent—most, some, few, or none?" contains such a problem. Some respondents who feel that all TV shows are extremely violent will answer "none" on the basis of the question's wording. These subjects reason that all shows are more than "a little too violent"; therefore, the most appropriate answer to the question is "none." (Deleting the phrase "a little" from the question helps avoid this pitfall.) In addition, the question inadvertently establishes the idea that at least some shows are violent. The question should read, "How many television shows, if any, do you think are too violent—most, some, few, or none?" Questions should be written so they are fair to all types of respondents.

2. _Keep questions short._ To be precise and unambiguous, researchers sometimes write long and complicated questions. Yet respondents who are in a hurry to complete a questionnaire are unlikely to take the time to study the precise intent of the person who drafted the items. Short, concise items that will not be misunderstood are best. A good question should not contain more than two short sentences.

3. _Remember the purposes of the research._ It is important to include in a questionnaire only items that directly relate to what is being studied. For example, if the occupational level of the respondents is not relevant to the purpose of the survey, the questionnaire should not ask about it. Beginning researchers often add questions for the sake of developing a longer questionnaire, or because the information "will be interesting to find out." Only relevant questions should be included.

4. _Do not ask double-barreled questions._ A **double-barreled question** is one that asks two or more questions in the same sentence. Whenever the word _and_ appears in a question, the sentence structure should be examined to see whether more than one question is being asked. For example, "The ABC network has programs that are funny and sexually explicit. Do you agree or disagree?" Since a program may be funny but not necessarily sexually explicit, a respondent could agree with the second part of the question even though he or she disagrees with the first part. This question should be divided into two items.

5. _Avoid biased words or terms._ Consider the following item: "In your free time, would you rather read a book or just watch television?" The word _just_ in this example injects a pro-book bias into the question because it implies that there is something less desirable about watching television. In like manner, "Where did you hear the news about the President's new economic program?" is mildly biased against newspapers; the word hear suggests that "radio," "television," or "other people" is a more appropriate answer. Questionnaire items that start with "Do you agree or disagree with so-and-so's proposal to . . ." almost always bias a question. If the name "Adolf Hitler" is inserted for "so-and-so," the item becomes overwhelmingly negative. Inserting "the President" creates a potential for both positive bias and negative bias. Any time a specific person or source is mentioned in a question, the possibility of introducing bias arises.

6. _Avoid leading questions._ A **leading question** is one that suggests a certain response

(either literally or by implication) or contains a hidden premise. For example, "Like most Americans, do you read a newspaper every day?" suggests that the respondent should answer in the affirmative or run the risk of being unlike most Americans. The question "Do you still use marijuana?" contains a hidden premise. This type of question is called a *double bind*: Regardless of how the respondent answers, an affirmative response to the hidden premise is implied—in this case, that he or she has used marijuana at some point.

7. *Do not use questions that ask for highly detailed information.* The question "In the past 30 days, how many hours of television have you viewed with your family?" is unrealistic. Few respondents could answer such a question. A more realistic approach would be to ask "How many hours did you spend watching television with your family yesterday?" A researcher interested in a 30-day period should ask respondents to keep a log or diary of family viewing habits.

8. *Avoid potentially embarrassing questions unless absolutely necessary.* Most surveys need to collect data of a confidential or personal nature, but an overly personal question may cause embarrassment and inhibit respondents from answering honestly. One common area with high potential for embarrassment is income. Many individuals are reluctant to tell their income to strangers doing a survey. A straightforward, "What is your annual income?" often prompts the reply, "None of your business." It is more prudent to preface a reading of the following list with the question, "Which of these categories includes your household's total annual income?"

    ____ More than $50,000
    ____ $25,000–$50,000
    ____ $20,000–$24,999
    ____ $15,000–$19,999
    ____ $10,000–$14,999
    ____ Under $10,000

The categories are broad enough to allow respondents some privacy, but narrow enough for statistical analysis. Moreover, the bottom category, "Under $10,000," was made artificially low so that individuals who fall into the $10,000–$14,999 slot would not be embarrassed by giving the lowest choice. The income classifications depend on the purpose of the questionnaire and the geographic and demographic distribution of the subjects. The $50,000 upper level in the example would be much too low in several parts of the country.

Other potentially sensitive areas include people's sex lives, drug use, religion, business practices, and trustworthiness. In all these areas, care should be taken to ensure respondents of confidentiality and anonymity, when possible.

The simplest type of closed-ended question is one that provides a *dichotomous response,* usually "agree/disagree" or "yes/no." For example:

Local television stations should have longer weather reports in the late evening news.

    ____ Agree
    ____ Disagree
    ____ No opinion

Although such questions provide little sensitivity to different degrees of conviction, they are the easiest to tabulate of all question forms. Whether they provide enough sensitivity or information in regard to the purpose of the research project are questions the researcher must seriously consider.

The *multiple-choice* question allows respondents to choose an answer from several options. For example:

In general, television commercials tell the truth . . .

    ____ All of the time
    ____ Most of the time
    ____ Some of the time

_____ Rarely
_____ Never

Multiple-choice questions should include all possible responses. A question that excludes any significant response usually creates problems. For example:

What is your favorite television network?

_____ ABC
_____ CBS
_____ NBC

Subjects who prefer PBS, Turner, or Fox (though they are not networks in the strictest sense of the word) cannot answer the question as presented.

Additionally, multiple-choice responses must be **mutually exclusive**: There should be only one response option per question for each respondent. For instance:

How many years have you been working in the newspaper industry?

_____ Less than 1 year
_____ 1–5 years
_____ 5–10 years

Which blank would a person with exactly 5 years of experience check? One way to correct this problem is to reword the responses, such as in the following item:

How many years have you been working in the newspaper industry?

_____ Less than 1 year
_____ Between 1 and 5 years
_____ More than 5 years

Rating scales are also widely used in mass media research (see Chapter 3). They can be arranged horizontally or vertically:

There are too many commercials on TV.

_____ Strongly agree (coded as a 5 for analysis)
_____ Agree (coded as a 4)
_____ Neutral (coded as a 3)
_____ Disagree (coded as a 2)
_____ Strongly disagree (coded as a 1)

What is your opinion of the local news on Channel 9?

Fair _____ _____ _____ _____ _____ Unfair
   (5) (4) (3) (2) (1)

Semantic differential scales (see Chapter 3) are another form of rating scale frequently used to rate persons, concepts, or objects. These scales use bipolar adjectives with seven scale points:

How do you perceive the term _public television_?

Uninteresting	_____ _____ _____ _____ _____ _____ _____	Interesting
Good	_____ _____ _____ _____ _____ _____ _____	Bad
Dull	_____ _____ _____ _____ _____ _____ _____	Exciting
Happy	_____ _____ _____ _____ _____ _____ _____	Sad

Researchers are often interested in the relative perception of several concepts or items. In such cases the *rank-ordering* technique is appropriate:

Here are several common occupations. Please rank them in terms of their prestige. Put a 1 next to the profession that has the most prestige, a 2 next to the one with the second most, and so on.

_____ Newspaper reporter
_____ Banker
_____ Dentist
_____ Lawyer
_____ Police officer
_____ Politician
_____ Newspaper writer
_____ Teacher
_____ Television news reporter

Asking respondents to rank more than a dozen objects is not recommended because the process can become tedious and the discriminations exceedingly fine. Furthermore, ranking data imposes limitations on the statistical analysis that can be performed.

The **checklist question** is often used in pilot studies to refine questions for the final project. For example:

What things do you look for in a new television set? (Check as many as apply.)

_____ Automatic fine tuning
_____ Picture within a picture (the ability to view more than one channel at a time)
_____ Remote control
_____ Cable ready
_____ Portable
_____ Stereo sound
_____ Other

In this case, the most frequently checked answers may be used to develop a multiple-choice question; the unchecked responses are dropped.

Forced-choice questions are frequently used in media studies designed to gather information about lifestyles, and they are always listed in pairs. Forced-choice questionnaires are usually very long—sometimes containing dozens of questions—and repeat questions (in a different form) on the same topic. The answers for each topic are analyzed for patterns, and a respondent's interest in that topic is scored. A typical forced-choice questionnaire might contain the following pairs.

Select one statement from each of the following pairs of statements:

_____ Advertising of any kind is a waste of time and money.
_____ I learn a lot from all types of advertising.

_____ Television program content should be regulated by the government.
_____ Television program content should not be regulated by the government.

_____ I listen to the radio every day.
_____ I only listen to the radio when I'm alone.

Respondents generally complain that neither of the responses to a forced-choice question is satisfactory, but they have to select one or the other. Through a series of questions on the same topic (violence, lifestyles, career goals), a pattern of behavior or attitude usually develops.

Fill-in-the-blank questions are used infrequently by survey researchers. However, some studies are particularly suited for fill-in-the-blank questions. In advertising copy testing, for example, they are often employed to test subjects' recall of a commercial. After seeing, hearing, or reading a commercial, subjects receive a script of the commercial in which a number of words have been randomly omitted (often every fifth or seventh word). Subjects are required to fill in the missing words to complete the commercial. Fill-in-the-blank questions also can be used in information tests. For example, "The local news anchors on Channel 4 are _____

FIGURE 7.1   A "Feeling Thermometer" for Recording a Subject's Degree of Like or Dislike

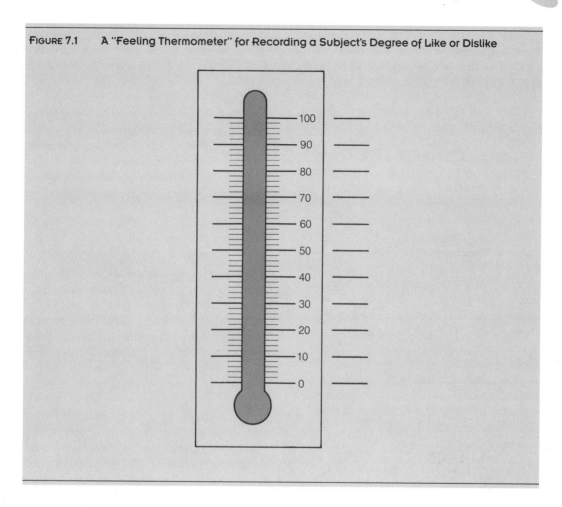

and _____ " or "The headline story on the front page was about _____ ."

Tables, graphs, and figures are also used in survey research. Some ingenious questioning devices have been developed to help respondents more accurately describe how they think and feel. For example, the University of Michigan Survey Research Center developed the **feeling thermometer**, with which subjects can rate an idea or object. The thermometer (see Figure 7.1), which is patterned after a normal mercury thermometer, offers an easy way for respondents to rate their degree of like or dislike in terms of "hot" or "cold." For example:

How would you rate the coverage your local newspaper provided on the recent school board campaign? (Place an X near the number on the thermometer that most accurately reflects your feelings; 100 indicates strong approval, and 0 reflects strong disapproval.)

Some questionnaires designed for children use other methods to collect information. Since young children have difficulty in assigning numbers to values, one logical alternative is to use pictures. For example, the interviewer might read the question, "How do you feel about

Saturday morning cartoons on television?" and present the faces in Figure 7.2 to elicit a response from a 5-year-old. Zillmann and Bryant (1975) present a similar approach with their "Yucky" scale.

QUESTIONNAIRE DESIGN

The approach used in asking questions as well as the physical appearance (in a self-administered questionnaire) can affect the response rate. Time and effort invested in developing a good questionnaire always pay off with more usable data. The following section offers some useful suggestions. [Note: Many of the suggestions about questionnaire design and layout discussed here are intended for paper questionnaires, not CATI (computer-aided telephone interviewing), which precludes problems such as skip patterns or rotation of questions. However, all researchers must understand all of the idiosyncrasies of questionnaire design in order to work with paper questionnaires or review a CATI-designed questionnaire.]

INTRODUCTION

One way to increase the response rate in any survey is to prepare a persuasive introduction to the survey. Backstrom and Hursh-Cesar (1981) suggest six principles for writing a successful introduction to a questionnaire; namely, the introduction should be short, realistically worded, nonthreatening, serious, neutral, and pleasant but firm.

Generally speaking, there is no need to explain the purpose or value of a survey to respondents, nor to tell them how long the survey will take to complete. In a telephone survey, telling the respondents that "the survey will take only a few minutes" gives them the opportunity to say they do not have that long to talk. The introduction should be short so that the respondent can begin writing answers

or the interviewer can start asking questions. An effective introduction for a telephone survey conducted by a field service is as follows:

> Hi, we're conducting an opinion survey about radio in the Chicago area and I'd like to ask you a few questions. My name is _____ with [INSERT COMPANY NAME]. We're not trying to sell anything, and this is not a contest or promotion. We're interested only in your opinions. Please tell me which of these age groups you belong to—under 18, 18 to 24, 25 to 34, 35 to 44, 45 to 54, or over 54? [TERMINATE IF UNDER 18 OR OVER 54.]

With some modifications, the same introduction is appropriate for a self-administered questionnaire. The introduction would include the first, third, and fourth sentences along with a final sentence that says, "Please answer the questions as completely and honestly as possible."

The goal of the introduction in telephone surveys is to get into the interview as quickly as possible so the respondent does not have a chance to say "No" and hang up. This may sound overly aggressive, but it works. The goal of the introduction in self-administered questionnaires is to make it as simple as possible.

Regardless of the survey approach used, a well-constructed introduction usually generates higher response rates than a simple "Please answer the following questions. . . ."

INSTRUCTIONS

All instructions necessary to complete the questionnaire should be clearly stated for respondents or interviewers. These instructions vary, depending on the type of survey conducted. Mail surveys and self-administered questionnaires usually require the most specific instructions, since respondents are not able to ask questions about the survey. Respondents and interviewers should understand whether the correct response consists of cir-

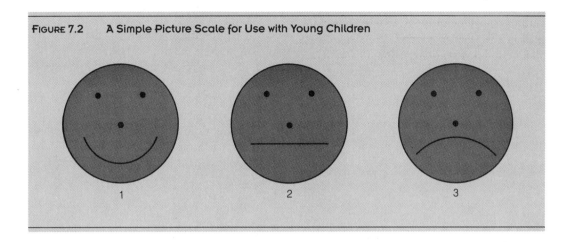

FIGURE 7.2   A Simple Picture Scale for Use with Young Children

cling, checking, placing items in a specific order, or skipping an item.

Procedural instructions for respondents are
often highlighted using a different typeface,
capital letters, or some graphic device, perhaps
arrows or lines. The following is an example
from a mail survey:

Do you have a favorite radio station that
you listen to most of the time?

_____ Yes   _____ No
        ↓

If yes, can you remember the names of
any of the disc jockeys who work for that
station? *WRITE THE NAMES IN THE SPACE
BELOW.*

_____

_____

Some questionnaires require respondents
to rank a list of items. In this case, the instructions must clearly describe which response
represents the highest value:

Please rate the following magazines in order of importance to you. Place a 1 next to
the magazine you prefer most, a 2 next to

the magazine in second place, and so on,
up to 5.

_____ *Better Homes and Gardens*
_____ *Consumer Reports*
_____ *Hot Rod Bikes*
_____ *Popular Science*
_____ *American Iron Magazine*

Fowler (1984) offered the following suggestions for putting together a self-administered
questionnaire:

1. Make the questionnaire self-explanatory.
2. Limit the questions to closed-ended items.
   Checking a box or circling an answer should
   be the only task required.
3. Use only a limited number of question
   forms.
4. Lay out and type the questionnaire in a
   clear and uncluttered way.
5. Limit the amount of instructions. Respondents can be confused easily by elaborate
   instructions.

Fowler's second suggestion is too strict. Respondents of most ages are usually able to answer open-ended questions with the same ease
(or complication) as closed-ended questions.

Whether open-ended or closed-ended, all questions should be tested in a pretest to determine whether the directions for answering them are clear.

Instructions for interviewers are usually typed in capital letters and enclosed in parentheses, brackets, or boxes. For example, instructions for a telephone survey might look like this:

We'd like to start by asking you some things about television. First, what are your favorite TV shows? [RECORD]

1. _____   3. _____

2. _____   4. _____

RECORD ALL NAMES OF TV SHOWS. PROBE WITH
"ARE THERE ANY MORE?" TO GET AT LEAST THREE SHOWS.

Screener questions, or **filter questions**, are used to eliminate unwanted respondents or to include only respondents who have specific characteristics or who answer questions in a specific manner. These questions often require respondents or interviewers to skip one or more questions. Skips must be clearly specified (recall that a CATI-designed questionnaire will automatically skip to the next question). For example:

In a typical week, do you listen to AM radio?

_____ Yes [ASK Q.16]

_____ No [SKIP TO Q.17]

A survey using this question might be designed to question only respondents who listen to AM radio. The screener question immediately determines whether the subject falls into this group. If the respondent says "No," the interviewer (or respondent if the survey is self-administered) may skip a certain number of questions or terminate the survey immediately.

When interviewers are used, as is the case in telephone and one-on-one interviews, the questionnaires must have easy-to-follow instructions (including how many responses to take for open-ended questions), simple skip patterns, and enough space to record answers (if survey responses are written). Telephone questionnaires must include everything an interviewer will say, including introductions, explanations, definitions, transitions, and pronunciations. The last point is particularly important because interviewers should sound like they know the topic. For example, the rock singer Sade should have a phonetic spelling in parentheses, ("Sha-Day"), following its first appearance in the questionnaire. Otherwise, an interviewer is *sure* to say something like, "Do you think music by the singer 'Say-dee' should be played on your favorite radio station?"

All instructions should be clear and simple. A confusing questionnaire impairs the effectiveness of the interviewer, lowers the number of respondents who complete the test, and, in the long run, increases costs.

QUESTION ORDER

All surveys flow better when the initial questions are simple and easy to answer. Researchers often include one or two "warm-up" questions about the topic under investigation so respondents become accustomed to answering questions and begin thinking about the survey topic. Preliminary questions can also serve as motivation to create interest in the questionnaire. Demographic data, personal questions, and other sensitive items should be placed at the end of the questionnaire to allow the interviewer to establish a rapport with each respondent, or, for a self-administered questionnaire, to allay any suspicions. Although some respondents may still refuse to answer personal items, or may hang up the telephone, at least the main body of data is already collected. Age and gender information are usually included in the first part of a questionnaire, so at least some respondent identification is possible.

The questionnaire should be organized in a logical sequence, proceeding from the general to the specific. Questions on similar topics should be grouped together, and the transitions between question sections should be clear and logical.

Poor question order may bias a respondent's answers. For example, suppose that, after several questions about the presence of violence in society, the respondent is asked to rank the major problems facing the country today from the following list:

_____ Corrupt government
_____ War
_____ Communism
_____ Violence on TV
_____ High prices

Violence on TV might receive a higher ranking than it would if the ranking question had been asked before the series of questions on violence. Or, to take another example, suppose a public relations researcher is attempting to discover the public's attitudes toward a large oil company. If the questionnaire that began with attitudinal questions concerning oil spills and inflated profits asked respondents to rate certain oil companies, it is likely that the ratings of all the companies would be lower, due to general impressions created by the earlier questions.

There is no easy solution for the problem of question "contamination." Obviously, some questions have to be asked before others. Perhaps the best approach for researchers is to be sensitive to the problem and test for it in a pretest. If they think question order A, B, C may have biasing effects, they should test another version using the order C, B, A. Completely neutral positioning is not always possible, however, and when bias may enter because of how responses are ordered, the list of items should be rotated. The command [ROTATE] after a question indicates that the interviewer

must alter the order of responses for each subject (performed automatically by a CATI-designed questionnaire). Different versions of question order can be printed for self-administered questionnaires.

LAYOUT

The physical design of the questionnaire is another important factor in survey research. A badly typed, poorly reproduced questionnaire is not likely to attract many responses in a mail survey. Nor does a cramped questionnaire with 40 questions to a page help to instill a positive attitude in respondents. Response categories should be adequately spaced and presented in a nonconfusing manner. For example, the following format might lead to problems:

There are too many commercials on television.

Do you Strongly agree _____ Agree _____ Have no opinion _____ Disagree _____ Strongly disagree _____ ?

A more effective and less confusing method is to provide a vertical ordering of the response choices:

There are too many commercials on television.

_____ Strongly agree
_____ Agree
_____ No opinion
_____ Disagree
_____ Strongly disagree

Some researchers recommend avoiding blanks altogether because respondents and interviewers tend to make large check marks or X's that cover more than one blank, making interpretation difficult. If blanks are perceived as a problem, boxes to check or numbers to circle are satisfactory. In any case, the response form should be consistent throughout the questionnaire. Format changes generally create confusion for both respondents and interviewers. Finally, each question must have enough space for answers. This is especially true for open-ended questions. Nothing is more discouraging to respondents and interviewers than to be confronted with a presentation like the following:

What would you change on your favorite radio station? _____

Why do you go to the movies? _____

Who are your favorite movie stars? _____

What are your favorite television shows?

_____

If a research budget limits the amount of paper for questionnaires, subjects can be asked to add further comments on the back of the survey.

QUESTIONNAIRE LENGTH

Questionnaire length is an important concern in any survey because it is directly related to completion rate. Long questionnaires cause fatigue, respondent mortality, and low completion rates. Shorter questionnaires guarantee higher completion rates.

Unfortunately, there are no strict guidelines to help in deciding how long a questionnaire should be. The length depends on a variety of factors including the following:

1. Amount of money in the research budget
2. Purpose of the survey
3. Type of problems or questions to be investigated
4. Age of respondents involved in the survey
5. Type and complexity of questions in the questionnaire
6. Location in the country where the study is conducted
7. Specific setting of the testing situation
8. Time of year
9. Time of day
10. Type of interviewer (professional or amateur)

In most cases, questionnaire length is determined by trial and error. A survey developed with significantly less than 100% respondent completion is too long. The authors' experience during the past 20 years has shown the following time limits as *maximum*:

Type of Survey	Maximum Time Limit
Self-administered mail survey	60 min.
Self-administered in a group situation supervised by a researcher	60 min.
One-on-one interviews	60 min.
Telephone	20 min.
Shopping center intercept	10 min.

Telephone interviewing can be a difficult approach to use because it takes talent to keep respondents answering questions on the phone. Professional interviewers can usually hold respondents' attention for about 20 minutes. There is a severe drop-off in incidence (due to *breakoffs*, where the respondent hangs up) when an interview lasts more than 20 minutes.

Two hints to researchers can make the questionnaire development process go much more smoothly: (1) read the questionnaire out loud or call up a friend and conduct the interview—errors are easier to detect; and (2) if possible, put the questionnaire aside for a day or two and come back to it—sometimes researchers become too deeply involved in questionnaire development and overlook a simple problem.

PRETESTING

Without a doubt, the best way to discover whether a research instrument is adequately designed is to pretest it—that is, conduct a ministudy with a small sample to determine whether the study approach is correct and to help refine the questions. Areas of misunderstanding or confusion can be easily corrected without wasting time or money.

There are several ways to pretest a questionnaire. When an acceptable draft of the questionnaire is completed, a focus group (Chapter 5) can be used to discuss the questionnaire with potential respondents. However, this is usually too expensive. The best pretest in telephone surveys is for interviewers to call 10–20 people and do a run-through. Any problems quickly emerge. Self-administered questionnaires should be pretested with the type of respondent who will participate in the actual study. Once again, any problems should be noted immediately.

In any type of pretesting situation, it is appropriate to discuss the project with respondents after the questionnaire is completed. They can be asked whether they understood the questions, whether the questions were simple to answer, and so on. Respondents are almost always willing to help researchers.

GATHERING SURVEY DATA

Once a questionnaire is developed and one or more pretests or pilot studies have been conducted, the next step is to gather data from an appropriate group of respondents. There are four basic methods for doing this: mail survey, telephone survey, personal interview, and group administration. Researchers can also use variations and combinations of these four methods, such as disk-by-mail surveys and mall interviews. Each procedure has definite advantages and disadvantages that must be considered before a choice is made. The remainder of this chapter highlights the characteristics of each method.

MAIL SURVEYS

Mail surveys involve mailing self-administered questionnaires to a sample of respondents. Stamped reply envelopes are enclosed to en-
courage respondents to mail completed questionnaires back to the researcher. Mail surveys are popular in some types of businesses because they can secure a great deal of data with a minimum expenditure of time and money. At the outset, however, researchers should be aware that respondents are often busy people with many demands on their time. Consequently, many people do not share the researcher's enthusiasm for questionnaires and often simply throw them away.

The general stages of a mail survey are discussed below. Although the steps are listed in numerical sequence, many of them are often accomplished in a different order or even simultaneously.

1. *Select a sample.* Sampling is generally done from a prepared frame (Chapter 4) that contains the names and addresses of potential respondents. The most common sampling frame used is the **mailing list,** a compilation of names and addresses in narrowly defined groupings that commercial sampling firms can prepare.

2. *Construct the questionnaire.* As discussed earlier, mail survey questionnaires must be concise and specific, since no interviewer is present to correct misunderstandings, answer questions, or give directions.

3. *Write a cover letter.* A brief note explaining the purpose and importance of the questionnaire usually increases response rates.

4. *Assemble the package.* The questionnaire, cover letter, and return envelope are stuffed into mailing envelopes. Researchers sometimes choose to use bulk mail with first-class return envelopes. An alternative method is to send questionnaires via first class mail and use business reply envelopes for responses. This method allows researchers to pay postage only for the questionnaires actually returned. Postal options always depend on the research budget.

5. *Mail the surveys.* Bulk-mail regulations require sorting envelopes into zip code areas.

6. *Closely monitor the return rates.*

7. *Send follow-up mailings.* The first follow-up should be sent 2 weeks after the initial

mailing, and a second (if necessary) 2 weeks after the first. The follow-up letter can be sent to the entire sample or only the subjects who fail to answer.

8. *Tabulate and analyze the data.*

Advantages. Mail surveys cover a wide geographic area for a rather reasonable cost. They are often the only way to gather information from people who live in hard-to-reach areas of the country (or in other countries). Mail surveys also allow for selective sampling through the use of specialized mailing lists. In addition to those mentioned, lists are available that include only people with annual incomes exceeding $50,000, consumers who have bought a car within the past year, subscribers to a particular magazine, or residents of a specific zip code area. If researchers need to collect information from a highly specialized audience, mail surveys are excellent.

Another advantage of the mail survey is that it provides anonymity—some respondents are more likely to answer sensitive questions candidly. Questionnaires can be completed at home or in the office, affording respondents a certain sense of privacy. People can answer questions at their own pace and have an opportunity to look up facts or check past information. Mail surveys also eliminate interviewer bias, since there is no personal contact.

Probably the biggest advantage of this method is its relatively low cost. Mail surveys do not require a large staff of trained workers. The only costs are for printing, mailing lists, envelopes, and postage. If the cost per completed questionnaire were to be computed, it is likely that the mail survey would prove to be the most inexpensive of all the survey methods. Researchers who are willing to spend the necessary time and money on a mail survey can usually ensure an above-average return rate.

Disdvantages. First, mail questionnaires must be self-explanatory. No interviewer is present to answer questions or to clear up misunder-

standings. Mail surveys are also the slowest form of data collection. Returns start to trickle in around a week or so after the initial mailing and continue to arrive for several weeks thereafter. However, it may be months before some responses are returned. Many researchers simply set a cutoff date, after which returns are not included in the analysis.

Another problem with mail surveys is that researchers never know exactly who answers the questions. A survey sent to corporate executives, for example, may be completed by assistants. Furthermore, replies are often received only from people who are interested in the survey, and this injects bias into the results. Most researchers agree, however, that the biggest disadvantage of the mail survey is the low return rate. A typical survey (depending on area and type of survey) will achieve a response rate of 10%–40%. This low return casts doubt on the reliability of the findings.

Increasing Response Rates. A number of ways to improve return rates have been investigated by survey researchers, but there are no hard and fast guarantees. In a *meta-analysis* (in which the findings of several studies are treated as independent observations and combined to calculate an overall or average effect) of numerous studies concerning mail surveys, Fox, Crask, and Kim (1989) found that, on the average, response rates can be increased in a variety of ways. In descending order of importance, the authors found the following procedures to increase mail survey response rates: university sponsorship; stamped return postage as opposed to business reply; written prenotification of the survey sent to the respondent; postcard follow-up; first-class outgoing postage; questionnaire color (green paper as opposed to white); notification of cutoff date; and stamped outgoing postage as compared to metered stamping.

In addition. mail surveys conducted by The Eagle Group in 1995 found the following to be very successful in increasing response rates (as much as 50%):

1. A drawing of some type that offers a prize of a color TV, stereo, or CD player
2. Telephone calling cards with 30 minutes of time (activated when the questionnaire is returned)
3. A $10 bill

TELEPHONE SURVEYS

Telephone surveys and personal interviews employ trained interviewers who ask questions orally and record the responses. The respondents generally do not see the actual questionnaire. Since telephone and personal interviewing techniques have certain similarities, much of what follows applies to personal interviews as well.

Telephone surveys fill a middle ground between mail surveys and personal interviews. They offer more control and higher response rates than most mail surveys but are limited in the types of questions that can be used. Telephone interviews are generally more expensive than mail surveys but less expensive than face-to-face interviews. Because of these factors, telephone surveys seem to represent a compromise between the other two techniques, and this may account for their enormous popularity in mass media research.

Interviewers are extremely important to both telephone surveys and personal surveys. An interviewer ideally should function as a neutral medium through which the respondents' answers are communicated to the researcher. The interviewer's presence and manner of speaking should not influence respondents' answers in any way. Adequate training and instruction can minimize bias that the interviewer might inject into the data. For example, if the interviewer shows disdain or shock over an answer, it is unlikely that the respondent will continue to answer questions in a totally honest manner. Showing agreement with certain responses might prompt similar answers to other questions. Skipping questions, carelessly asking questions, and being impatient

with the respondent might also cause problems. As an aid to minimizing interviewer bias, the National Association of Broadcasters has published the following recommendations for interviewers:*

1. Read the questions exactly as worded. Ask them in the exact order listed. Skip questions only when the instructions on the questionnaire tell you to. There are no exceptions to this.
2. Never suggest an answer, try to explain a question, or imply what kind of reply is wanted. Don't prompt in any way.
3. If a question is not understood, say, "Let me read it again," and repeat it slowly and clearly. If it is still not understood, report a "no answer."
4. Report answers and comments exactly as given, writing them out fully. If an answer seems vague or incomplete, probe with neutral questions, such as, "Will you explain that?" or, "How do you mean that?" Sometimes just waiting a bit will tell the respondent you want more information.
5. Act interested, alert, and appreciative of the respondent's cooperation. But never comment on his or her replies. Never express approval, disapproval, or surprise. Even an "Oh" can cause a respondent to hesitate or refuse to answer further questions. Never talk up or down to a respondent.
6. Follow all instructions carefully, whether you agree with them or not.
7. Thank each respondent. Leave a good impression for the next interviewer.
8. Discuss any communication problems immediately with the researcher in charge.

A general procedure for conducting a telephone survey follows. Again, the steps are

*From *A Broadcast Research Primer,* 1976, pp. 37–38. Reprinted with permission (edited).

FIGURE 7.3   Sample Telephone Interview Disposition Sheet

Phone number _____

Call #1 ____ #2 ____ #3 ____ #4 ____ #5 ____

    Date ____ Date ____ Date ____ Date ____ Date ____

    Time ____ Time ____ Time ____ Time ____ Time ____

Code

    1   Completed interview
    2   Answering machine
    3   Busy
    4   No answer
    5   Refusal
    6   Appointment to call again
        (when _____)
    7   Nonworking number (out of order, disconnected, nonexistent)
    8   Nonresidential number
    9   Reached but respondent not available (out of town, hospital, etc.)
    10 Reached but not interviewed (ineligible household, speech or physical
        problem, age disqualification)

---

presented in numerical order, but it is possible to address many tasks simultaneously.

1. *Select a sample.* Telephone surveys require researchers to clearly specify the geographic area to be covered and to identify the type of respondent to be interviewed in each household contacted. Many surveys are restricted to people over 18, heads of households, and so forth. The sampling procedure used depends on the purpose of the study (see Chapter 4).

2. *Construct the questionnaire.* Phone surveys require straightforward and uncomplicated response options. Ranking a long list of items is especially difficult over the telephone, and this task should be avoided. In addition, the length of the survey should not exceed 10 minutes for nonprofessional interviewers. Longer interviews require professionals who are capable of keeping people on the telephone.

3. *Prepare an interviewer instruction manual.* This document should cover the basic mechanics of the survey (what numbers to call,

when to call, how to record times, and so on). It should also specify which household member to interview and provide general guidelines on how to ask the questions and how to record the responses.

4. *Train the interviewers.* Interviewers need to practice going through the questionnaire to become familiar with all the items, response options, and instructions. It is best to train interviewers in a group using interview simulations that allow each person to practice asking questions. It is advisable to pretest interviewers as well as the questionnaire.

5. *Collect the data.* Data collection is most efficient when conducted from one central location (assuming enough telephone lines are available). Problems that develop are easier to remedy, and important questions raised by one interviewer can easily be communicated to the rest of the group. A central location also makes it easier for researchers to check (validate) the interviewers' work. The completion rate should also be monitored during this stage.

6. *Make necessary callbacks.* Additional calls (usually no more than two) should be made to respondents whose lines were busy or who did not answer during the first session. Callbacks on a different day or night tend to have a greater chance of reaching someone willing to be interviewed.

Backstrom and Hursh-Cesar (1981, p. 134) offer the following advice about callbacks:

> About 95% of all telephone interviews are successfully completed within three calls. However, we have rules for the number of callbacks to make if the first call results in a busy signal or a no answer. . . . We generally permit only three calls—one original and two callbacks—but if any of these calls produce busy signals or [future interview] appointments, we allow up to five calls total. . . .

Backstrom and Hursh-Cesar's comment that about 95% of the interviews are successfully completed with three calls is a bit optimistic. According to The Eagle Group data collected over several years, three callbacks will produce a contact about 75% of the time. In some cases, to achieve 95% as Backstrom and Hursh-Cesar said, six or more callbacks are required.

When the first call produces a busy signal, the rule is to wait one-half hour before calling again. If the first call produced a "no answer," wait 2 to 3 hours before calling again, assuming it will still be a reasonable hour to call. If evening calls produce no answer, call during the following day.

In addition, interviewers should keep track of the *disposition* or status of their sample numbers. Figure 7.3 contains a sample disposition sheet.

7. *Verify the results.* When all questionnaires have been completed, a small subsample of each interviewer's respondents should be called again to check that the information they provided was accurately recorded. Respondents should be told during the initial survey that they may receive an additional call at a later

date. This tends to eliminate any confusion when subjects receive a second call. A typical procedure is to ask the subject's first name in the interview so that it can be used later. The interviewer should ask, "Were you called a few days ago and asked questions about television viewing?" The verification can begin from there, and need consist of only two or three of the original questions (preferably open-ended and sensitive questions, since interviewers are most likely to omit these).

8. *Tabulate the data.* Along with the normal data analysis, telephone researchers generally compute response rates for the following items: completed interviews, initial refusals, unqualified respondents, busy signals, language barriers, no-answers, terminates, breakoffs, and disconnects.

Advantages. The cost of telephone surveys tends to be reasonable. The sampling involves minimal expense, and there are no significant transportation costs. Callbacks are simple and economical. The variety of telephone plans from AT&T, MCI, Sprint, and others enable researchers to conduct telephone surveys from any location.

Compared to mail surveys, telephone surveys can include more detailed questions, and, as stated earlier, interviewers can clarify misunderstandings that might arise during the administration of the questionnaire.

The response rates of telephone surveys about the media (once a qualified respondent is contacted) are generally high, especially when multiple callbacks are used. In addition, phone surveys are much faster than mail. A large staff of interviewers can collect the data from the designated sample in a relatively short time. In summary, phone surveys tend to be fast, easy, and relatively inexpensive.

Disadvantages. First of all, researchers must recognize that much of what is called survey "research" by telephone is not research at all, but an attempt to sell people something. Unfortunately, many companies disguise their sales pitch as a "survey." This has made respondents suspicious and even prompts some to terminate an interview before it has started. Additionally, it is impossible to include questions that involve visual demonstrations. A researcher cannot, for example, hold up a picture of a product and ask if the respondent remembers seeing it advertised. A potentially severe problem is that not everyone in a community is listed in the telephone directory, the most often used sampling frame. Not everyone has a phone, and many people have unlisted phone numbers; also, some numbers are listed incorrectly, and others are too new to be listed. These problems would not be serious if the people with no phones or with unlisted numbers were just like those listed in the phone book. Unfortunately, researchers generally have no way of checking for such similarities or differences, so it is possible that a sample obtained from a telephone directory may be significantly different from the population. (See Chapter 4 concerning random digit dialing.)

Finally, telephone surveys require a large number of "dialings" and contacts in order to successfully interview the number of respondents required for a study. To demonstrate this, the table below shows a summary of the telephone call "disposition sheets" from 75 randomly selected telephone studies conducted by The Eagle Group in Denver in 1995. The studies included respondents between the ages of 18 and 54 and investigated topics such as radio listening, television viewing, automotive purchases, and other nonmedia topics.

Disposition Summary

Call Breakdown	Number	Percent of Total
Noncontact	231,694	48.5%
Ineligible	65,621	13.7
Initial refusal	57,221	11.9
Disconnect/business	51,431	10.8
Answering machine	48,666	10.2
Qualified refusal	12,526	2.6
Language barrier	949	0.2
Completed	9,562	2.0
TOTAL	477,670	100%

The data show what a professional interviewer faces during a working day. Of nearly one-half million dialings, only 2% represented completed interviews; thus, of every 100 dialings made, only 2 will achieve success. There aren't many other jobs where a "success rate" is this low.

PERSONAL INTERVIEWS

Personal interviews usually involve inviting a respondent to a field service location or a research office (called a *one-on-one interview*). Sometimes interviews are conducted at a person's place of work or at home. There are two basic types of interviews, structured and unstructured. In a **structured interview**, standardized questions are asked in a predetermined order; relatively little freedom is given to interviewers. In an **unstructured interview**, broad questions are asked, which allows interviewers freedom in determining what further questions to ask to obtain the required information. Structured interviews are easy to tabulate and analyze but do not achieve the depth or expanse of unstructured interviews. Conversely, the unstructured type elicits more detail but takes a great deal of time to score and analyze.

The steps in constructing a personal interview survey are similar to those for a telephone survey. The following list discusses instances in which the personal interview differs substantially from the telephone method:

1. *Select a sample.* Drawing a sample for a personal interview is essentially the same as sample selection in any other research method. In one-on-one interviews, respondents are selected on the basis of a predetermined set of

screening requirements. In door-to-door interviews, a multistage sample is used to first select a general area, then a block or a neighborhood, and finally a random household from which a person will be chosen (Figure 4.2 on page 71).

2. *Construct the questionnaire.* Personal interviews are flexible: Detailed questions are easy to ask, and the time taken to complete the survey can be greatly extended. (Many personal interviews last 30–60 minutes.) Researchers can also make use of visual exhibits, lists, and photographs to ask questions, and respondents can be asked to sort photos or materials into categories, or to point to their answers on printed cards. Respondents can have privacy and anonymity by marking ballots, which can then be slipped into envelopes and sealed.

3. *Prepare an interviewer instruction guide.* The detail needed in an instruction guide depends on the type of interview. One-on-one interviewer guides are not very detailed because there is only one location, respondents are prerecruited by a field service, and interviewing times are prearranged. Door-to-door interviewer guides contain information about the household to select, the respondent to select, and an alternative action to take in the event the target respondent is not at home. Interviewer guides often contain information about how to conduct the interview, how to dress, how to record data, and how to ask questions.

4. *Train the interviewers.* Training is important because the questionnaires in a personal interview are longer and more detailed. Interviewers should receive instructions on establishing a rapport with subjects, on administrative details (for example, time and length of interviews, interviewer salaries, and so on), and on asking follow-up questions. Several practice sessions are necessary to ensure that the project's goal is met and that interviewers follow the established guidelines.

5. *Collect the data.* Personal interviews are both labor- and cost-intensive. These problems are why most researchers prefer to use telephone or mail surveys. A personal interview project can take several days to several weeks to complete because turnaround is slow. One interviewer can complete only a handful of surveys each day. In addition, costs for salaries and expenses escalate quickly. It is not uncommon for some research companies to charge as much as $1,000 per respondent in a one-on-one situation.

Data gathering is accomplished either by writing down answers or by audiotaping or videotaping the respondents' answers. Both methods are slow, and detailed transcriptions and editing are often necessary.

6. *Make necessary callbacks.* Each callback requires an interviewer to return to a household originally selected or the location used for the original interview. Additional salary, expenses, and time are required.

7. *Verify the results.* As with telephone surveys, a subsample of each interviewer's completed questionnaires is selected for verification. Respondents can be called on the phone or reinterviewed in person.

8. *Tabulate the data.* Data tabulation procedures for personal interviews are essentially the same as with any other research method. A codebook must be designed, questionnaires are coded, and data input into a computer.

Advantages. Many advantages of the personal interview technique have already been mentioned. It is the most flexible means of obtaining information, since the face-to-face situation lends itself easily to questioning in greater depth and detail. Also, some information can be observed by the interviewer during the interview without adding to the length of the questionnaire. Additionally, the interviewers can develop a rapport with the respondents and may be able to elicit replies to sensitive questions that would remain unanswered in a mail or phone survey. The identity of the respondent is known or can be controlled in the personal interview survey. Whereas in a mail survey it is possible that all members of a family might confer on an answer, this can usually be avoided in a face-to-face interview. Finally, once an interview has begun, it is harder for respondents to terminate the interview before all the questions have been asked. In a phone survey, the respondent can simply hang up the telephone.

Disadvantages.   As mentioned, time and costs are the major drawbacks to the personal interview technique. Another major disadvantage is the problem of interviewer bias. The physical appearance, age, race, sex, dress, nonverbal behavior, and/or comments of the interviewer may prompt respondents to answer questions untruthfully. Moreover, the organization necessary for recruiting, training, and administering a field staff of interviewers is much greater than that required for other data collection procedures. If large numbers of interviewers are needed, it is usually necessary to employ field supervisors to coordinate their work, which in turn will make the survey even more expensive. Finally, if personal interviews are conducted during the day, most of the respondents will not be employed outside the home. If it is desirable to interview respondents with jobs outside the home, interviews must be scheduled on the weekends or during the evening.

One alternative now used in personal interviews is a self-administered interview that respondents answer on a personal computer. Respondents are usually invited to the research company or field service to participate in the project by answering questions presented to them on the computer.

A hybrid of personal interviewing is intensive, or in-depth, interviewing, which is discussed in Chapter 5.

MALL INTERVIEWS

Although mall interviews are essentially a form of the personal interviews just discussed, their recent popularity and widespread use warrant individual consideration.

During the late 1980s, mall intercepts became one of the most popular research approaches among marketing and consumer researchers. Schleifer (1986) found that of all the people who participated in a survey in 1984, 33% were mall intercepts. In addition, *Marketing News* (1983) stated that 90% of the market researchers it surveyed in the United States use mall intercepts. Both figures have risen since the studies were conducted.

Although mall intercepts use convenience samples and sampling error cannot be determined, the method has become the standard for many researchers. It is rare to enter a shopping mall without seeing a man or a woman with a clipboard trying to interview a shopper. The method has become commonplace, and some shoppers resent the intrusion. In fact, it is common for shoppers to take paths to avoid the interviewers they can so easily detect.

The procedures involved in conducting mall intercepts are the same as those for personal interviews. The only major difference is that it is necessary to locate the field service that conducts research in the particular mall of interest. Field services pay license fees to mall owners to allow them to conduct research on the premises. Not just any field service can conduct research in any mall.

One recent trend in some mall-intercept research is the use of a personal computer for data collection. As with one-on-one interviews conducted in a field service, the respondents simply answer questions posed to them on the computer monitor.

Advantages.   Mall intercepts are a quick and inexpensive way to collect personal data.

Disadvantages.   Most of the disadvantages of mall intercepts have been discussed in other sections of this book. The three major problems are that convenience sampling restricts the generalizability of the results (not all people in a given area shop at the same mall); the length of interviews must be short (no more than about 10 minutes); and there is no control over data collection (researchers are at the mercy of the field service to conduct a proper interview).

DISK-BY-MAIL SURVEYS

During the late 1980s, a high-tech form of mail surveys appeared that offers great promise. The procedure is called **disk-by-mail surveys,** or **DBM.** The name of the survey approach essentially explains the procedure: Respondents are sent computer disks that contain a self-administered questionnaire, and they are asked to complete it by using a personal computer. This method obviously involves several new areas to consider when conducting a research project.

DBM surveys are essentially the same as a typical self-administered mail survey. The normal steps involved in problem definition, questionnaire design, and pretesting are used. However, there are several unique considerations researchers must address when using DBM.

Type of Study.   Most DBM surveys are conducted with professionals or other business-related samples. The reason is simple: Only about 20% of American households have personal computers. Sample selection would be time-consuming and costly. However, computer ownership will certainly increase in the future, and in-home DBM surveys may become commonplace. For the time being, DBM surveys are conducted with professionals who generally have access to personal computers in their workplace.

Sample Selection.   Locating qualified respondents for DBM surveys is the same as for any other research project, except that in addition to the other screener questions, there must be one about the availability of a personal computer.

Computer Hardware.   A typical self-administered mail survey requires only that the respondent have a writing instrument. DBM surveys complicate the process in several ways. First, computers can use one of several different operating systems, or languages, that run the computer (Chapter 17). Fortunately, the IBM and Apple systems are the most widely used. The problems with the two operating systems can be solved by preparing two different DBM disks, or by asking one of the groups of users to try to locate the other type of computer to complete the survey.

A second problem with the DBM method is whether to use a color or monochrome display to present the questionnaire. Not all color monitors are equal, and the color appearance may be drastically different from one monitor to another. A monochrome display is best to avoid problems.

The size of the disk drive presents a third problem. The screener must include questions about the size of the respondent's disk drive (that is, $5\frac{1}{4}$-inch or $3\frac{1}{2}$-inch) to ensure that the respondent receives the correct type of disk.

Another problem, and not necessarily the last, occurs in the form of physical risk to the floppy disks. Disks may be accidentally erased; they are also fragile and may be damaged in the disk-duplication process, in shipment, or by the respondent. Thus, replacement disks may have to be sent to some respondents.

Support.   Because computer problems may occur or respondents may be unable to complete the survey, most DBM surveys offer respondents a toll-free number to call for assistance. This service adds further costs to the project.

Reliability and Validity.   Significant questions are raised about these two areas in relation to DBM surveys. Who actually completes the surveys? Are responses more or less accurate than those provided to interviewers or in typical mail interviews? How does the novelty of the approach affect respondents?

As mentioned earlier, DBM surveys are a totally new approach in research. Not much is known about the procedure, but in all likelihood they will be used more frequently in the future.

GROUP ADMINISTRATION

Group administration combines some of the features of mail surveys and personal interviews. The group-administered survey takes place when a group of respondents is gathered together (prerecruited by a field service) and given individual copies of a questionnaire or asked to participate in a group interview (a large focus group). The session can take place in a natural setting, but it is usually held at a field service location or a hotel ballroom. For example, respondents may be recruited to complete questionnaires about radio or television stations; students in a classroom may complete questionnaires about their newspaper reading habits; or an audience may be asked to answer questions after viewing a sneak preview of a new film.

The interviewer in charge of the session may or may not read questions to respondents. Reading questions aloud may help respondents who have reading problems, but this is not always necessary. (It is possible to screen respondents for reading or language skills.) The best approach is for several interviewers to be present in the room so that individual problems can be resolved without disturbing the other respondents.

Some group-administered sessions include audio and/or video materials for respondents to analyze. The session allows respondents to proceed at their own pace, and in most cases interviewers allow respondents to ask questions, although this is not a requirement.

Advantages. The group administration technique has certain advantages. For example, a group-administered questionnaire can be longer than the typical questionnaire used in a mail survey. Since the respondents are usually assembled for the sole purpose of completing the questionnaire, the response rates are almost always quite high. The opportunity for researchers to answer questions and handle problems that might arise generally means that fewer items are left blank or answered incorrectly.

Disadvantages. On the negative side, if a group-administered survey leads to the perception that the study is sanctioned by some authority, respondents may become suspicious or uneasy. For example, if a group of teachers is brought together to fill out a questionnaire, some might think that the survey has the approval of the local school administration and that the results will be made available to their superiors. Also, the group environment makes interaction possible among the respondents; this can make the situation more difficult for the researcher to control. In addition, not all surveys can use samples that can be tested together in a group. Surveys often require responses from a wide variety of people, and mixing respondents together may bias the results.

Finally, group administration can be expensive. Costs usually include recruiting fees, co-op payments, hotel rental, refreshments, and salaries for interviewers. Typical costs for group sessions include the following:

CPI	$25–$1,000 per person
Co-op	$25–$150 per person
Hotel	$200–$1,000 per night
Refreshments	$0–$50 per person
Audio/video materials and rental	$0–thousands of dollars
Hostesses	$0–$100 per hostess
Parking fees	$0–$10 per person
Interviewers/assistants	$0–thousands of dollars
Travel expenses for researchers	$0–thousands of dollars

ACHIEVING A REASONABLE RESPONSE RATE

No matter what type of survey is conducted, it is virtually impossible to obtain a 100% response rate. Researchers have more control over the situation in some types of surveys (such as the personal interview) and less in others (such as the mail survey). But no matter what the situation, not all respondents will be available for interviews and not all will cooperate. Consequently, the researcher must try to achieve the highest response rate possible under the circumstances.

What constitutes an acceptable response rate? Obviously, the higher the response rate the better: As more respondents are sampled, response bias is less likely. But is there a minimum rate that should be achieved? Not everyone agrees on an answer to this question, but there are some helpful data available. Several studies have calculated the average response rates for surveys of various kinds. A comparison with these figures can at least tell a researcher if a given response rate is above or below the norm. For example, Dillman (1978) noted that response rates for face-to-face interviews have dropped sharply in recent years. In the 1960s, the average rate was 80%–85%. More recently, the completion rates of general population samples interviewed by the face-to-face technique are about 60%–65%. Yu and Cooper (1983) studied the completion rates reported in 93 social science journal articles from 1965 to 1981. They found the completion rate for personal interviews to be 82% and for telephone surveys about 72%. Mail surveys had an average completion rate of about 47%. (Note that many of the personal interviews included in the Yu and Cooper study were done in the 1960s and early 1970s. This should be kept in mind when comparing their figures to Dillman's.)

Regardless of how high the response rate is, the researcher is responsible for examining any possible biases in response patterns. Were females more likely to respond than males? Older respondents more likely than younger ones? Whites more likely than minorities? A significant lack of response from a particular group might weaken the strength of any inferences from the data to the population under study. To be on the safe side, the researcher should attempt to gather information from other sources about the people who did not respond; by comparing such additional data with those from respondents, it should be possible to determine whether underrepresentation introduced any bias into the results.

Using common sense will help increase the response rate. In phone surveys, respondents should be called when they are likely to be at home and receptive to interviewing. Do not call when people are likely to be eating or sleeping. In a one-on-one situation, the interviewer should be appropriately attired. In addition, the researcher should spend time tracking down some of the nonrespondents and asking them why they refused to be interviewed or why they did not fill out the questionnaire. Responses such as "The interviewer was insensitive and pushy," "The questionnaire was delivered with postage due," and "The survey sounded like a ploy to sell something" can be illuminating.

Along with common sense, certain elements of the research design can have a significant impact on response rates. Yu and Cooper (1983), in their survey of 93 published studies, discovered that:

1. Monetary incentives increased the response, with larger incentives being the most effective. Nonmonetary incentives (for example, ballpoint pens) were also helpful.
2. Preliminary notification, personalization of the questionnaire, a follow-up letter, and assertive "foot-in-the-door" personal interview techniques all significantly increased the response rate.

3. A cover letter, the assurance of anonymity, and a statement of a deadline did not significantly increase the response rate.
4. Stressing the social utility of the study and appealing to the respondent to help out the researcher did not affect response rates.

GENERAL PROBLEMS IN SURVEY RESEARCH

Although surveys are valuable tools in mass media research, several obstacles are frequently encountered. Experience in survey research confirms the following points:

1. Subjects or respondents are often unable to recall information about themselves or their activities. This inability may be caused by memory failure, nervousness related to being involved in a research study, confusion about the questions asked, or some other intervening factor. Questions that are glaringly simple to researchers may create severe problems for respondents.

For example, radio station managers often want to ask respondents which radio stations they have set on their vehicle's radio push buttons. The managers are surprised to discover the number of people who not only do not know which stations are programmed on their radio buttons, but do not know how many buttons are *on* their radio.

2. Due to a respondent's feelings of inadequacy or lack of knowledge about a particular topic, he or she may often provide "prestigious" answers rather than admit to not knowing something. This is called **prestige bias**. For example, as mentioned earlier in the book, some respondents claim to watch public TV and listen to public radio when, in fact, they do not.

3. Subjects may purposely deceive researchers by giving incorrect answers to questions. Almost nothing can be done about respondents who knowingly lie. A large sample may discount this type of response. However, there is no acceptable and valid method

to determine whether a respondent's answers are truthful; the answers must be accepted as they are given, although one way is to ask the same question two or three times throughout the survey (using different question approaches).

4. Respondents often give elaborate answers to simple questions because they try to "figure out" what the purpose of a study is and what the researcher is doing. People are naturally curious, but they become even more curious when they are the focus of a scientific research project.

5. Surveys are often complicated by the inability of respondents to explain their true feelings, perceptions, and beliefs—not because they do not have any, but because they cannot put them into words. The question, "Why do you like to watch soap operas?" may be particularly difficult for some people. They may watch them every day, but respond only by saying "Because I like them." Probing respondents for further information may help, but not in every case.

Survey research can be an exciting process. It is fun to find out why people think in certain ways or what they do in certain situations. But researchers must continually remain aware of obstacles that may hinder data collection, and they must deal with these problems. The United States is the most surveyed country in the world, and many citizens now refuse to take part in any type of research project. Researchers must convince respondents and subjects that their help is important in decision making and solving problems.

The face of survey research is continually changing. One-on-one and door-to-door interviews are now very difficult to carry out. This means there is a greater emphasis on mail surveys, mall intercepts, and electronic datagathering procedures. In telephone surveys, for example, **computer-assisted telephone interviewing (CATI)** is now common.

CATI uses video display terminals operated by interviewers to present questions and accept respondent answers, thus eliminating the need for the traditional pencil-and-paper questionnaires. The computer displays the proper questions in the proper order, eliminating the possibility of the interviewer making an error by asking the wrong questions or skipping the right ones. The respondent's answers are entered by the interviewer through the keyboard, making data coding much easier. Groves and Mathiowetz (1984) and Wimmer (1995) found that there is little difference in results from using CATI and non-CATI techniques. The response rates, reactions of the interviewers and respondents, and quality of data were virtually equivalent. CATI interviews tended to take slightly more time, but this was balanced by the presence of fewer interviewer errors due to skipping questions. As new software is developed in this area, it seems likely that a greater proportion of surveys will use the CATI technique.

Other areas of change include computer-generated, voice-synthesized surveys in which respondents answer by pushing Touch-Tone telephone buttons; 800 telephone numbers for recruited respondents to call to answer questions asked by an interviewer or computer; and various types of touch-sensitive TV screens that present questionnaires to respondents. Survey research is changing very quickly.

SUPPLEMENT ON CODEBOOK DEVELOPMENT

Since most research data are analyzed by computer, questionnaire responses must be quantified. A project codebook is a column-by-column explanation of the responses and their corresponding code numbers.

For example, the following codebook was prepared for the data used in Chapter 17 of this book. For those readers interested in conducting further analysis, the raw data for the study are included in Appendix 4.

Column(s)	Variable
1–3	Respondent number
4	Age and sex
	1 = Male 18–24
	2 = Male 25–34
	3 = Female 18–24
	4 = Female 25–34
5	WAAA Listen
	1 = Yes
	2 = No
6	WAAA Morning Show Listener
	1 = Frequently
	2 = Sometimes
	3 = Never
7	WBBB Listen
	1 = Yes
	2 = No
8	WBBB Morning Show Listener
	1 = Frequently
	2 = Sometimes
	3 = Never
9	WCCC Listen
	1 = Yes
	2 = No
10	WCCC Morning Show Listener
	1 = Frequently
	2 = Sometimes
	3 = Never
11	WDDD Listen
	1 = Yes
	2 = No
12	WDDD Morning Show Listener
	1 = Frequently
	2 = Sometimes
	3 = Never
13	WEEE Listen
	1 = Yes
	2 = No
14	WEEE Morning Show Listener
	1 = Frequently
	2 = Sometimes
	3 = Never
15	WFFF Listen
	1 = Yes
	2 = No

16	WFFF Morning Show Listener
	1 = Frequently
	2 = Sometimes
	3 = Never
17	Favorite Station
	1 = Don't know/No answer
	2 = Other
	3 = WAAA
	4 = WBBB
	5 = WCCC
	6 = WDDD
	7 = WEEE
	8 = WFFF
	9 = WGGG

The following columns relate to why respondents listen to station WCCC. The possible answers are: 1 = Agree; 2 = Disagree; 3 = Don't know/No answer.

18	Amount of new or current music
19	Quality of new or current music
20	Amount of older music
21	Quality of older music
22	Morning show
23	Upbeat/energetic feeling
24	Contests and prizes
25	Because friends listen
26	Afternoon announcers
27	Involvement in local activities
28	Hear favorite songs frequently
29	Attitude toward its listeners
30	Morning show announcers
31	Pace or tempo of station
32	News and information
33	Traffic reports
34	To hear new music and artists
35	Variety of music played
36	Source of local information
37	Amount of music

Coding questionnaires consists of reading each question, referring to the codebook, and assigning the appropriate code for the respondent's answer(s). These data are then input into the computer for analysis.

SUMMARY

Survey research is an important and useful method of data collection. The survey is also one of the most widely used methods of media research, primarily because of its flexibility. Surveys, however, involve a number of steps. Researchers must decide whether to use a descriptive or analytical approach; define the purpose of the study; review the available literature in the area; select the survey approach, questionnaire design, and sample; analyze and interpret the data; and finally, decide whether to publish or disseminate the results. These steps are not necessarily taken in that order, but all must be considered before a survey is conducted.

To ensure that all the steps in the survey process are in harmony, researchers should conduct one or more pilot studies to detect any errors in the approach. Pilot studies save time, money, and frustration, since an error that could void an entire analysis sometimes surfaces at this stage.

Questionnaire design is also a major step in any survey. In this chapter, examples have been provided to show how a question or an interviewing approach may elicit a specific response. The goal in questionnaire design is to avoid bias in answers. Question wording, length, style, and order may affect a respondent's answers. Extreme care must be taken when developing questions to ensure that they are neutral. To achieve a reasonable response rate, researchers should consider including an incentive, notifying survey subjects beforehand, and personalizing the questionnaire. Also, researchers should mention the response rate when they report the results of the survey.

Finally, researchers must select the most appropriate survey approach from among four basic types: mail, telephone, personal interview, and group administration. Each approach has advantages and disadvantages that must be weighed before a decision is made. The type of survey used will depend on the purpose of the study, the amount of time available to the researcher, and the funds available for the study. In the future, survey researchers may depend less on the face-to-face survey and more on computer-assisted telephone interviewing.

QUESTIONS AND PROBLEMS FOR FURTHER INVESTIGATION

1. Develop five questions or hypotheses that could be tested by survey research. What approaches could be used to collect data on these topics?

2. Nonresponse is a problem in all survey research. In addition, many people refuse to participate in surveys at all. Provide an example of a cover letter for a survey on television viewing habits.

3. Define a target group and design questions to collect information on the following topics:
   a. Political party affiliation
   b. Attitudes toward television soap operas
   c. Attitudes toward newspaper editorials
   d. Attitudes toward the frequency of television commercials
   e. Public television viewing habits

4. Locate one or more survey studies in journals related to mass media research. Answer the following questions in relation to the article(s):
   a. What was the purpose of the survey?
   b. How were the data collected?
   c. What type of information was produced?
   d. Did the data answer a particular research question or hypothesis?
   e. Were any problems evident with the survey and its approach?

5. Design a survey to collect data on a topic of your choice. Be sure to address the following points:
   a. What is the purpose of the survey? What is its goal?
   b. What research questions or hypotheses will be tested?
   c. Are any operational definitions required?
   d. Develop at least 10 questions relevant to the problem.
   e. Describe the approach to be used to collect data.
   f. Design a cover letter or an interview schedule for the study.
   g. Conduct a pretest to test the questionnaire.

REFERENCES AND SUGGESTED READINGS

Babbie, E. R. (1990). *Survey research methods* (2nd ed.). Belmont, CA: Wadsworth.

Backstrom, C., & Hursh-Cesar, G. (1981). *Survey research*. New York: John Wiley.

Beville, H. Jr. (1988). Audience ratings (Rev. ed.). Hillsdale, NJ: Lawrence Erlbaum.

Brighton, M. (1981). Data capture in the 1980s. *Communicare: Journal of Communication Science, 2*(1), 12–19.

Chaffee, S. H., & Choe, S. Y. (1980). Time of decision and media use during the Ford-Carter campaign. *Public Opinion Quarterly, 44,* 53–70.

Dillman, D. (1978). *Mail and telephone surveys.* New York: John Wiley.

Eagle Group, The (1995). Proprietary research conducted by the senior author.

Erdos, P. L. (1974). Data collection methods: Mail surveys. In R. Ferber (Ed.), *Handbook of marketing research.* New York: McGraw-Hill.

Fletcher, J. E., & Wimmer, R. D. (1981). *Focus group interviews in radio research.* Washington, DC: National Association of Broadcasters.

Fowler, F. (1993). *Survey research methods* (2nd ed.). Newbury Park, CA: Sage Publications.

Fox, R. J., Crask, M. R., & Kim, J. (1989). Mail survey response rate. *Public Opinion Quarterly, 52*(4), 467–491.

Groves, R., & Mathiowetz, N. (1984). Computer-assisted telephone interviewing: Effects on interviewers and respondents. *Public Opinion Quarterly, 48*(1), 356–369.

Hornik, J., & Ellis, S. (1989). Strategies to secure compliance for a mall intercept interview. *Public Opinion Quarterly, 52*(4), 539–551.

Hsia, H. J. (1988). *Mass communication research methods: A step-by-step approach.* Hillsdale, NJ: Lawrence Erlbaum.

Kerlinger, F. N. (1986). *Foundations of behavioral research* (3rd ed.). New York: Holt, Rinehart & Winston.

Lavrakas, P. J. (1993). *Telephone survey methods: Sampling, selection, and supervision* (2nd ed.). Newbury Park, CA: Sage Publications.

Marketing News. (1983). Inflation adjusted spending is on rise for consumer research. *Marketing News, 17*(1), 13.

Miller, D. C. (1991). *Handbook of research design and social measurement* (5th ed.). New York: Longman.

National Association of Broadcasters. (1976). *A broadcast research primer*. Washington, DC: NAB.

Oppenheim, A. N. (1992). *Questionnaire design and attitude measurement*. New York: Pinter.

Poindexter, P. M. (1979). Daily newspaper nonreaders: Why they don't read. *Journalism Quarterly, 56*, 764–770.

Rosenberg, M. (1968). *The logic of survey analysis*. New York: Basic Books.

Schleifer, S. (1986). Trends in attitudes toward and participation in survey research. *Public Opinion Quarterly, 50*(1), 17–26.

Sewell, W., & Shaw, M. (1968). Increasing returns in mail surveys. *American Sociological Review, 33*, 193.

Sharp, L., & Frankel, J. (1983). Respondent burden: A test of some common assumptions. *Public Opinion Quarterly, 47*(1), 36–53.

Singer, E., & Presser, S. (Eds.) (1989). *Survey research methods: A reader*. Chicago: University of Chicago Press.

Wakshlag, J. J., & Greenberg, B. S. (1979). Programming strategies and the popularity of television programs for children. *Journal of Communication, 6*, 58–68.

Walizer, M. H., & Wienir, P. L. (1978). *Research methods and analysis: Searching for relationships*. New York: Harper & Row.

Weisberg, H. F., & Bowen, B. D. (1989). *An introduction to survey research and data analysis* (2nd ed.). Glenview, IL: Scott, Foresman.

Williams, F., Rice, R. E., & Rogers, E. M. (1988). *Research methods and the new media*. New York: Free Press.

Wimmer, R. D. (1976). *A multivariate analysis of the uses and effects of the mass media in the 1968 presidential campaign*. Unpublished doctoral dissertation, Bowling Green University, Ohio.

Wimmer, R. D. (1995). *Comparison of CATI and non-CATI interviewing*. Unpublished company paper. Denver: The Eagle Group.

Winkler, R. L., & Hays, W. L. (1975). *Statistics: Probability, inference and decision* (2nd ed.). New York: Holt, Rinehart & Winston.

Yu, J., & Cooper, H. (1983). A quantitative review of research design effects on response rates to questionnaires. *Journal of Marketing Research, 20*(1), 36–44.

Zillmann, D., & Bryant, J. (1975). Viewers' moral sanctions of retribution in the appreciation of dramatic presentations. *Journal of Experimental Social Psychology, 11*, 572–582.

LONGITUDINAL RESEARCH

Most of the research discussed to this point has been cross-sectional. In **cross-sectional research,** data are collected from a representative sample at only one point in time. **Longitudinal research,** in contrast, involves the collection of data at different points in time. Although longitudinal investigations appear relatively infrequently in mass communication research, several longitudinal studies have been among the most influential and provocative in the field.

Of the 14 studies Lowery and DeFleur (1988) consider to be milestones in the evolution of mass media research, 4 represent the longitudinal approach: Lazarsfeld, Berelson, and Gaudet's *The People's Choice* (1944), which introduced the two-step flow model; Katz and Lazarsfeld's *Personal Influence* (1955), which examined the role of opinion leaders; the Surgeon General's Report on Television and Social Behavior, particularly as used in the study by Lefkowitz, Eron, Walder, and Huesmann (1972), which found evidence suggesting that viewing violence on television caused subsequent aggressive behavior; and the 10-year update of the Lefkowitz et al. report (Pearl, Bouthilet, & Lazar, 1982), which cited the longitudinal studies that further affirmed the link between TV violence and aggression. Other longitudinal studies also figure prominently in the field, including the elaborate panel study done for NBC by Milavsky, Kessler, Stipp, and Rubens (1982), the cross-national comparisons cited in Huesmann and Eron (1986), and the studies of mass media in elections as summarized by Peterson (1980). Thus, although it is not widely used, the longitudinal method can produce results that are both theoretically and socially important.

DEVELOPMENT

Longitudinal studies have a long history in the behavioral sciences. In psychology in particular, they have been used to trace the development of children and the clinical progress of patients. In medicine, longitudinal studies have been widely used to study the impact of disease and treatment methods. The pioneering work in political science was done by sociologists studying the 1924 election campaign. Somewhat later, Newcomb (1943) conducted repeated interviews of Bennington College students from 1935 to 1939 to examine the impact of a liberal college environment on respondents who came from conservative families.

In the mass communication area, the first major longitudinal study was that of Lazarsfeld, Berelson, and Gaudet (1944) during the 1940 presidential election. Lazarsfeld pioneered the use of the panel technique in which the same individuals are interviewed several times. Lazarsfeld also developed the use of the 16–fold table, one of the earliest statistical techniques to attempt to derive causation from longitudinal survey data. Another form of longitudinal research, **trend studies** (in which different people are asked the same question at different points in time) began showing up in mass media research in the 1960s. One of the most publicized trend studies was the continuing survey of media credibility done by the Roper organization. Trend studies by Gallup and Harris, among others, also gained notoriety during this time.

More recently, the notion of cohort analysis, a method of research developed by demographers, has achieved popularity. **Cohort analysis** involves the study of specific populations, usually all those born during a given period, as they change over time. Other significant developments in the longitudinal area have taken place as more sophisticated techniques for analyzing longitudinal data were developed. More technical information about advanced computational strategies for longitudinal data is contained in Magnusson, Bergman, Rudinger, and Torestad (1991) and Uncles (1988).

Cross-lagged correlation was widely discussed during the 1960s and 1970s. Cross-lagged correlations are done when information about two variables is gathered from the same sample at two different times. The correlations between variables at the same point in time are compared with the correlations at different points in time. Three other forms of analysis using advanced statistical techniques have had relevance in longitudinal studies: path analysis, log-linear models, and structural equations. Path analysis is used to chart directions in panel data. Log-linear models are used with categorical panel data and involve the analysis of multivariate contingency tables. LISREL (LInear Structural RELations), a model developed by Joreskog (1973), is another statistical technique that has broad application in longitudinal analysis.

TYPES OF LONGITUDINAL STUDIES

The three main types of longitudinal studies are trend study, cohort analysis, and panel study. Each is discussed in this section.

TREND STUDIES

The trend study is probably the most common longitudinal study in mass media research. Recall that a trend study samples different groups of people at different times from the same population. Trend studies are common around pres-

idential election time. Suppose that 3 months before an election a sample of adults is drawn; 57% report that they intend to vote for Candidate A and 43% for Candidate B. A month later a different sample drawn from the same population shows a change: 55% report that they are going to vote for A and 45% for B. This is a simple example of a trend study. Trend studies provide information about net changes at an aggregate level. In the example, we know that in the period under consideration, Candidate A lost 2% of his support. We do not know how many people changed from B to A or from A to B, nor do we know how many stayed with their original choice. We know only that the net result was a 2-point loss for A. To determine both the gross change and the net change, a panel study would be necessary.

Advantages. Trend studies are valuable in describing long-term changes in a population. They can establish a pattern over time to detect shifts and changes in some event. Broadcast researchers, for example, compile trend studies that chart fluctuations in viewing levels for the major networks. Another advantage of trend studies is that they can be based on a comparison of survey data originally constructed for other purposes. Of course in utilizing such data, the researcher needs to recognize any differences in question wording, context, sampling, or analysis techniques that might differ from one survey to the next. Hyman (1987) provides extensive guidance on the secondary analysis of survey data. The growing movement to preserve data archives and the ability of computer networks, such as the Internet, to make retrieval and sharing much easier suggest that this technique will gain in popularity. The Winter 1990 edition of *Public Opinion Quarterly* lists 19 data archives in the United States and other countries that are available for use by researchers. Secondary analysis saves time, money, and personnel; it also makes it possible to understand long-term change. In fact, mass media researchers might want to consider what socially significant data concerning media behaviors should be collected and archived at regular intervals. Economists have developed regular trend indicators to gauge the health of the economy, but mass communication scholars have developed almost no analogous social indicators of the media or audiences.

Disadvantages. Trend analysis is only as good as the underlying data. If data are unreliable, false trends will show up in the results. Moreover, to be most valuable, trend analysis must be based on consistent measures. Changes in the way indexes are constructed or the way questions are asked will produce results that are not comparable over time.

Examples of Trend Studies. Both university and commercial research firms have asked some of the same questions for many national and statewide trend studies. For example, in the United States, a question about satisfaction with the President's performance has been asked hundreds of times dating back to the administration of Harry Truman. *Public Opinion Quarterly* has a regular section entitled "The Polls" that allows researchers to construct trend data on selected topics. In recent issues the following trend data have appeared: (1) a 15-year sampling of public opinion about energy issues; (2) a 24-year sampling of attitudes toward congressional reform; and (3) an 8-year compilation of public attitudes toward AIDS. Of specific interest in the field of mass media research are the trend data on changing patterns of media credibility, compiled for more than 3 decades by the Roper organization (summarized in Mayer, 1993). Among other well-known trend studies are the Violence Index constructed by Gerbner and his associates (Gerbner, Gross, Signorielli, Morgan, & Jackson-Beeck, 1979); the 60-year study of trends in research about children and the mass media by Wartella and Reeves (1985); and the 6-year study of trends in network program shares of the audience and lead-in effects done

by Davis and Walker (1990). Another example is the recent trend study by Xiaoming (1994) that documents demographic trends in the television viewing habits of adults from the 1960s to the 1990s and Ader's (1995) use of Gallup poll results to document longitudinal trends in environmental pollution agendas. In the professional area, the local market diary surveys in radio and television done by Arbitron and Nielsen are also examples of trend studies.

COHORT ANALYSIS

To the Romans, a "cohort" was 1 of the 10 divisions of a military legion. For research purposes, a *cohort* is any group of individuals who are linked in some way or who have experienced the same significant life event within a given period. Usually the "significant life event" is birth, in which case the group is termed a *birth cohort*. There are, however, many other kinds of cohorts, including marriage (for example, all those married between 1980 and 1985), divorce (for example, all those divorced between 1985 and 1990), education (the class of 1990), and others (all those who attended college during the Vietnam era).

Any study in which there are measures of some characteristic of one or more cohorts at two or more points in time is a cohort analysis. Cohort analysis attempts to identify a *cohort effect*: Are changes in the dependent variable due to aging, or are they present because the sample members belong to the same cohort? To illustrate, suppose that 50% of college seniors reported that they regularly read news magazines, whereas only 10% of college freshmen in the same survey gave this answer. How might the difference be accounted for? One explanation is that freshmen change their reading habits as they progress through college. Another is that this year's freshman class is composed of people with reading habits different from those who were enrolled 3 years ago.

There are two ways to distinguish between these explanations. One way involves questioning the same students during their freshman year and again during their senior year and comparing their second set of responses to those of a group of current freshmen. (This is the familiar panel design, which is discussed in detail below.) Or a researcher can take two samples of the student population, at Time 1 and Time 2. Each survey has different participants—the same people are not questioned again, as in a panel study—but each sample represents the same group of people at different points in their college career. Although we have no direct information about which individuals changed their habits over time, we do have information on how the cohort of people who entered college at Time 1 had changed by the time they became seniors. If 15% of the freshmen at Time 1 read news magazines and if 40% of the seniors at Time 2 read them, we can deduce that students change their reading habits as they progress through college.

Typically, a cohort analysis involves data in more than one cohort, and a standard table for presenting the data from multiple cohorts was proposed by Glenn (1977). Table 8.1 is such a table. It displays news magazine readership for a number of birth cohorts. Note that the column variable (read down) is age, and the row variable (read across) is the year of data collection. Because the interval between any two periods of measurement (that is, surveys) corresponds to the age class intervals, cohorts can be followed over time. When the intervals are not equal, the progress of cohorts cannot be followed with precision.

Three types of comparisons can be made from such a table. Reading down a single column is analogous to a cross-sectional study and represents comparisons among different age cohorts at one point in time (intercohort differences). Trends at each age level that occur when cohorts replace one another can be seen by reading across the rows. Third, reading diagonally toward the right reveals changes in a single cohort from one time to another (an intracohort study). Thus, Table 8.1 suggests

TABLE 8.1   Percentage Who Regularly Read News Magazines

	Year		
Age	1982	1986	1990
18–21	15	12	10
22–25	34	32	28
26–29	48	44	35

that news magazine reading increases with age (reading down each column). In each successive time period, the percentage of younger readers has diminished (reading across the rows), and the increase in reading percentage as each cohort ages is about the same (reading diagonally to the right).

The variations in the percentages in the table can be categorized into three kinds of effects. (For the moment we will assume that there is no variation due to sampling error or to changing composition in each cohort as it ages.) First, there are the influences produced by the sheer fact of maturation, or growing older, called age effects. Second, there are the influences associated with members in a certain birth cohort (cohort effects). Finally, there are the influences associated with each particular time period (period effects).

To recognize these various influences at work, examine the hypothetical data in Tables 8.2, 8.3, and 8.4. Again, let us assume that the dependent variable is the percentage of the sample who regularly read a news magazine. Table 8.2 demonstrates a "pure" age effect. Note that the rows are identical and the columns show the same pattern of variation. Apparently it does not matter when a person was born or in which period he or she lived. As the individual becomes older, news magazine readership increases. For ease of illustration, Table 8.2

TABLE 8.2	Cohort Table Showing Pure Age Effect		
	Year		
Age	**1982**	**1986**	**1990**
18–21	15	15	15
22–25	20	20	20
26–29	25	25	25
Average	20	20	20

TABLE 8.3	Cohort Table Showing Pure Period Effect		
	Year		
Age	**1982**	**1986**	**1990**
18–21	15	20	25
22–25	15	20	25
26–29	15	20	25
Average	15	20	25

shows a linear effect, but this is not necessarily the only effect possible. For example, readership might increase from the first age interval to the next but not increase from the second to the third.

Table 8.3 shows a "pure" period effect. There is no variation by age at any period—the columns are identical, and the variations from one period to the next are identical. Furthermore, the change in each cohort (read diagonally to the right) is the same as the average change in the total population. The data in this table suggest that year of birth and maturation have little to do with news magazine reading. In this hypothetical case, the time period seems to be most important. Knowing when the survey was done enables the researcher to predict the variation in news magazine reading.

A "pure" cohort effect is illustrated in Table 8.4. Here the cohort diagonals are constant, and the variation from younger to older respondents is in the opposite direction from the variation from earlier to later survey periods. In this table, the key variable seems to be date of birth. Among those who were born between 1959 and 1962, news magazine readership was 15% regardless of their age or when they were surveyed.

Of course in actual data, these pure patterns rarely occur. Nonetheless an examination

of Tables 8.2, 8.3, and 8.4 can help develop a sensitivity to the patterns one can detect in analyzing cohort data. In addition, the tables illustrate the logic behind the analysis. Glenn (1977) and Mason, Mason, Winsborough, and Poole (1973) also present tables showing pure effects.

Advantages. Cohort analysis is an appealing and useful technique because it is highly flexible. It provides insight into the effects of maturation and social, cultural, and political change. In addition, it can be used with either original data or secondary data. In many instances, a

TABLE 8.4	Cohort Table Showing Pure Cohort Effect		
	Year		
Age	**1982**	**1986**	**1990**
18–21	15	10	5
22–25	20	15	10
26–29	25	20	15
Average	20	15	10

cohort analysis can be less expensive than experiments or surveys.

Disadvantages. The major disadvantage of cohort analysis is that the specific effects of age, cohort, and period are difficult to untangle through purely statistical analysis of a standard cohort table. In survey data, much of the variation in percentages among cells is due to sampling variability. There are no uniformly accepted tests of significance appropriate to a cohort table that allow researchers to estimate the probability that the observed differences are due to chance. Moreover, as a cohort grows older, many of its members die. If the remaining cohort members differ in regard to the variable under study, the variation in the cohort table may simply reflect this change. Finally, as Glenn (1977) points out, no matter how a cohort table is examined, three of the basic effects—namely age, cohort, and period—are confounded. Age and cohort effects are confounded in the columns; age and period effects in the diagonals; and cohort and period effects in each row. Even the patterns of variations in the "pure" cohort Tables 8.2, 8.3, and 8.4 could be explained by a combination of influences.

Several authors have developed techniques to try to sort out these effects. Three of the most useful are Palmore's (1978) triad method; the constrained multiple regression model (Rentz, Reynolds, & Stout, 1983); and the goodness-of-fit technique (Feinberg & Mason, 1980). If the researcher is willing to make certain assumptions, these methods can provide some tentative evidence about the probable influences of age, period, and cohort. Moreover, in many cases, there is only one likely or plausible explanation for the variation. Nonetheless, a researcher should exercise caution in attributing causation to any variable in a cohort analysis. Theory and evidence from outside sources should also be utilized in any interpretation. For example, in his study of the influences of television watching and newspaper reading on cohort differences in verbal

ability, Glenn (1994) assumed that there were no period effects on changes in adult vocabulary during the duration of his study. As a result, he was able to demonstrate a cohort effect that suggested that decreases in verbal ability were associated with a decline in newspaper reading and an increase in TV viewing.

A second disadvantage of the technique is sample mortality. If a long period is involved or if the specific sample group is difficult to reach, the researcher may have some empty cells in the cohort table or some that contain too few members for meaningful analysis.

Examples of cohort analysis. Cohort analysis is widely used in advertising and marketing research. For example, Rentz et al. (1983) conducted a cohort analysis of consumers born in four time periods: 1931–1940, 1941–1950, 1951–1960, and 1961–1970. Soft drink consumption was the dependent variable. Multiple regression analysis was employed to help separate the three possible sources of variation. The results indicated a large cohort effect, suggesting that soft drink consumption will not decrease as successive cohorts age. Cohort analysis is also useful in the study of public opinion. Wood (1986) outlined the use of cohort analysis in marketing and showed how *Time* examined cohort data to chart trends in its subscribership. Rosengren and Windahl (1989) used cohort analysis as part of their in-depth longitudinal study of TV usage by Swedish youngsters. Among other things, they found a slight cohort effect but noted that age seemed the prime determinant of habitual television viewing. Basil (1990) found a cohort effect in a person's choice of his or her primary news source. Older people relied more on newspapers than did younger cohorts. Zhu (1990) discovered a cohort effect in the attitudes of journalists toward adversarial reporting. Wilson (1994) found a cohort effect relating to the degree of tolerance that people expressed toward leftist and rightist groups. Finally, in his cohort analysis of newspaper readership patterns, Stevenson (1994) discovered

Cohorts and Shared Experiences

According to an ancient Arab proverb, "Children resemble the times more than they do their parents." A generational cohort is a group of people who were born over a contiguous and relatively short time period and who shared key events during their formative years. Demographers have divided the American public into six distinct generational cohorts: (1) the Depression Cohort, consisting of those coming of age between 1930 and 1939; (2) the World War II Cohort, those who came of age during 1940 to 1945; (3) the Post-War Cohort, coming of age between 1946 and 1963; (4) the Baby Boomer One Cohort, coming of age between 1963 and 1972; (5) the Baby Boomer Two Cohort, coming of age between 1973 and 1983; and (6) the Generation X cohort, coming of age from 1984 to 1995.

To illustrate just one of the areas where cohorts have an effect, consider popular music. When rock and roll first came on the scene during the 1950s and 1960s, young people loved it while older people hated it. Record companies thought that the rock and roll market would be limited to the young, reasoning that as young people became older their tastes would change to reflect those of their parents. Teens who listened to the Beatles, reasoned the record industry, would grow into adults who liked Mantovani, Victor Young, or Percy Faith. Not so. The Rolling Stones still enjoyed popularity during the 1990s because those in the Baby Boomer Cohort continued to like them even as the Boomers were approaching 50. A generation's taste in popular music doesn't change simply because that generation ages. With that in mind, readers of this book should probably hang on to their Hootie and the Blowfish and Nine-Inch Nails CDs. Thirty years from now, readers will still probably enjoy them.

both an age and a cohort effect: Readership increased with age, but within each age cohort readership declined over the 10-year period covered by the study.

PANEL STUDIES

Panel studies measure the same sample of respondents at different points in time. Unlike trend studies, panel studies can reveal information about both net change and gross change in the dependent variable. For example, a study of voting intentions might reveal that between Time 1 and Time 2, 20% of the panel switched from Candidate A to Candidate B and 20% switched from Candidate B to Candidate A. Whereas a trend study would show a net change of zero because the gross changes simply canceled each other out, the panel study would show a high degree of volatility in voting intention.

Similar to trend and cohort studies, panel studies can make use of mail questionnaires, telephone interviews, or personal interviews. Television networks, advertising agencies, and marketing research firms use panel studies to track changes in consumer behavior. Panel studies can reveal shifting attitudes and patterns of behavior that might go unnoticed with other research approaches; thus trends, new ideas, fads, and buying habits are among the variables investigated. For a panel study on the effectiveness of political commercials, for example, all members of the panel would be interviewed periodically during a campaign to determine whether and when each respondent makes a voting decision.

Depending on the purpose of the study, researchers can use either a *continuous panel,* consisting of members who report specific attitudes or behavior patterns on a regular basis, or an *interval panel,* whose members agree to complete a certain number of measurement instruments (usually questionnaires) only when the information is needed. Panel studies produce data suitable for sophisticated statistical analysis and enable researchers to predict cause-and-effect relationships.

Advantages.   Panel data are particularly useful in answering questions about the dynamics of change. For example, under what conditions do voters change political party affiliation? What are the respective roles of mass media and friends in changing political attitudes? Moreover, repeated contacts with the respondents may help reduce suspicions, so that later interviews yield more information than the initial encounters. Of course, the other side to this benefit is the sensitization effect, discussed below. Finally, panel studies help solve the problems normally encountered when defining a theory on the basis of a one-shot case study. Since the research progresses over a period of time, the researcher can allow for the influences of competing stimuli on the subject.

Disadvantages.   On the negative side, panel members are often difficult to recruit because of an unwillingness to fill out questionnaires or submit to interviews several times. The number of initial refusals in a panel study fluctuates, depending on the amount of time required, the prestige of the organization directing the study, and the presence or absence of some type of compensation. One analysis of the refusal rates in 12 marketing panel studies found a range of 15%–80%, with a median of about 40% (Carman, 1974). Wimmer (1995) found that even a cash incentive may not increase a respondent's willingness to participate in a panel study.

Once the sample has been secured, the problem of mortality emerges. Some panel members will drop out for one reason or another. Because the strength of panel studies lies in interviewing the same people at different times, this advantage diminishes as the sample size decreases. Another serious problem is that respondents often become sensitized to measurement instruments after repeated interviewing, thus making the sample atypical (Chapter 4). For example, panelists who know in advance that they will be interviewed about public television watching might alter their viewing patterns to include more PBS programs (or fewer). Menard (1991) suggests that a revolving panel design might overcome the sensitization problem. In this design, after the first measurement period, some of the original members of the panel are replaced by new members. For example, if the researcher is concerned that increased PBS viewing is the result of sensitization, he or she could interview 100 viewers during Week 1 and then replace 50 of the original sample with new panel members in Week 2. The viewing data from those who had been interviewed twice could then be compared with the data from those who participated in a single interview.

Finally, respondent error is always a problem in situations that depend on self-administered measurement instruments. If panelists are asked to keep a diary over a certain period, some may not fill it out until immediately before it is due. And, of course, panel studies require much more time and can be quite expensive.

Examples of Panel Studies.   Perhaps the most famous example of the panel technique in mass media research is the collection of national television audience data by the A. C. Nielsen Company. Nielsen's sample consists of approximately 4,500 households located across the United States. These homes are equipped with people meters—devices that record when the television set is turned on, which channel is tuned in, and who is watching. (See Chapter

14 for more information about people meters.) Other panels are maintained by such commercial research organizations as Market Facts, Inc., National Family Opinion, Inc., and the Home Testing Institute.

A study by Bolton and Drew (1991) illustrated the advantage in using a panel study to understand the process of change in a specific area. In their longitudinal study of the impact of changes in telephone service, they found that changes in the evaluation of individual components of telephone service (for example, absence of static, quality of voice) were influenced quickly by a service change but that changes in the general evaluations of telephone service were noticeable only after six months.

Outside the marketing area, a well-publicized panel study was carried out with the support of the National Broadcasting Company (Milavsky et al., 1982). The overall purpose of this study was to isolate any possible causal influence on aggression among young people from viewing violence on television. Three panel studies were conducted, with the most ambitious involving boys aged 7–12. In brief, the methodology in the study involved collecting data on aggression, TV viewing, and a host of sociological variables from children in Minneapolis, Minnesota, and Fort Worth, Texas, on six occasions. About 1,200 boys participated in the study. The time lags between each wave of data collection were deliberately varied so that the effects of TV viewing could be analyzed over different durations. Thus, there was a 5-month lag between Waves 1 and 2, a 4-month lag between Waves 2 and 3, and a 3-month lag between Waves 3 and 4. The lag between Waves 1 and 6 constituted the longest elapsed time (3 years). As is the case in all panel studies, the NBC study suffered from attrition. The particular design, however, magnified the effects of attrition. When respondents left the sixth grade, they frequently left the panel. Consequently, only a small number of children (58 of the 1,200 who participated) were available for observing and analyzing the long-term effects of viewing violence on TV.

The participant losses reported by the NBC team illustrate the impact of year-to-year attrition on a sample of this age group. About 7% of the sample was lost in the first year, approximately 37% in the first 2 years, and 63% over all 3 years.

The study also illustrates how a panel design influences the statistical analysis. The most powerful statistical test would have incorporated data from all six waves and simultaneously examined all the possible causal relationships. This was impossible, however, because due to the initial study design and subsequent attrition, the sample size fell below minimum standards. Instead, the investigators worked with each of the 15 possible wave pairs in the sample. The main statistical tests used the analytical technique of partial regression coefficients to remove the impact of earlier aggression levels. In effect, the researchers sought to determine whether TV viewing at an earlier time added to the predictability of aggression at a later time, once the aggression levels present before the test began had been statistically discounted. After looking at all the resulting coefficients for all the possible wave pairs, the investigators concluded that there was no consistent statistically significant relationship between watching violent TV programs and later acts of aggression. Nonetheless, they did find a large number of small but consistently positive coefficients that suggested the possibility of a weak relationship that might not have been detected by conventional statistical methods. Upon further analysis, however, the researchers concluded that these associations were due to chance.

Since their initial publication, the NBC data have been the topic of at least three reanalyses and reinterpretations (Cook, Kendizierski, & Thomas, 1983; Kenny, Milavsky, Kessler, Stipp, & Rubens, 1984; Turner, Hesse, & Peterson-Lewis, 1986). Concerns were raised over various aspects of the methodology and the appropriateness of conventional standards of statistical significance in light of the small samples and skewed aggression measures. It is likely that more reanalyses will follow. Nonetheless, this study has value for anyone interested in longitudinal research. Many of the problems encountered in panel studies and the compromises involved in doing a 3-year study are discussed in great detail.

The panel technique continues to be popular for studying the impact of TV violence. Singer, Singer, Desmond, Hirsch, and Nicol (1988) used this technique to examine the effects of family communication patterns, parental mediation, and TV viewing on children's perceptions of the world and their aggressive behavior. Ninety-one first and second graders were interviewed during the first phase of the study. One year later, 66 of the original sample were reinterviewed. Concerned about the effects of attrition, the researchers compared their final sample with the original on a wide range of demographic variables and found that attrition did not cause any significant differences between the two groups. Singer et al. found that family communication patterns during the first phase were strong predictors of children's cognitive scores, but were only weakly related to emotional and behavioral variables. The influence of TV viewing on aggression was greatest among heavy viewers who were least exposed to parental mediation.

The Rosengren and Windahl study (1989) mentioned earlier arrived at a similar conclusion. During their panel study of Swedish schoolchildren, the investigators interviewed the main panel participants in 1976, 1978, and 1980. This study is remarkable for its low attrition rate: About 86% of those in the original 1976 survey were also in the 1980 survey. The researchers found that the relationship between TV violence and antisocial behavior was greatest among those children who were heavy viewers (more than 15 hours a week) of TV.

Potter (1992) used a three-wave panel study across 5 years to examine how adolescents' perceptions of television's reality changed over time. The design was such that no respondent was present in all three waves. Of the 287 original respondents in Wave 1, 196 were tested again in Wave 2. Of the 443 original respondents in Wave 2, 115 were also measured in Wave 3. Valkenburg and Van Der Voort (1995) conducted a 1-year panel study of Dutch children to investigate the influence of television on children's daydreaming. They found that children's daydreaming styles in Year 1 did not influence television viewing behavior in Year 2 but that TV viewing in Year 1 did influence daydreaming in Year 2.

SPECIAL PANEL DESIGNS

Panel data can be expensive to obtain. Moreover, analysis cannot begin until at least two waves of data are available. For many panel studies, this may take years. Researchers who have limited time and resources might consider one of the alternatives discussed next.

Schulsinger, Mednick, and Knop (1981) outlined a research design called a **retrospective panel.** In this method, the respondent is asked to recall facts or attitudes about education, occupations, events, situations, and so on, from the past. These recalled factors are then compared with a later measure of the same variable, thus producing an instant longitudinal design. Belson (1978) used a variation of this design in his study of the effects of exposure to violent TV shows on the aggressive behavior of teenage boys when he asked his respondents to recall when they first started watching violent TV programs.

There are several problems with this technique. Many people have faulty memories; some will deliberately misrepresent the past; and others will try to give a socially desirable response. Only a few research studies have examined the extent to which retrospective panel data might be misleading. Powers, Goudy, and Keith (1978) reanalyzed data from a 1964 study of adult men. In 1974 all the original

---

FIGURE 8.1   Comparison of Retrospective, Follow-back, and Catch-up Designs

Retrospective panel
   Step 1: Select current sample.
   Step 2: Interview sample about past recollections concerning topic of interest.
   Step 3: Collect current data on topic of interest.
   Step 4: Compare data.

Follow-back panel
   Step 1: Select current sample.
   Step 2: Collect current data on topic of interest.
   Step 3: Locate archival data on sample regarding topic of interest.
   Step 4: Compare data.

Catch-up panel
   Step 1: Locate archival data on topic of interest.
   Step 2: Select current sample by locating as many respondents as possible for whom data exist in the archive.
   Step 3: Collect current data on topic of interest.
   Step 4: Compare data.

---

respondents who could be located were reinterviewed and asked about their answers to the 1964 survey. In most instances, the recall responses presented respondents in a more favorable light than did their original answers. Interestingly enough, using the 1974 recall data produced almost the same pattern of correlations as using the 1964 data, suggesting that recall data might be used, albeit with caution, in correlational studies. In 1974 Norlen (1977) reinterviewed about 4,700 persons originally questioned in 1968. Of those reinterviewed, 464 had originally reported that they had written a letter to the editor of a newspaper or magazine, but in 1974 about a third of this group denied ever having written to a newspaper or magazine. Auriat (1993) found that respondents were more likely to recall correctly the month of a major life event (in this case, a family move) than they were the year. In addition, women were slightly better than men at remembering exact dates. Clearly, the savings in time and money accrued by using retrospective data must be weighed against possible losses in accuracy.

A **follow-back panel** selects a cross-sectional sample in the present and uses archival data from an earlier point in time to create the longitudinal dimension of the study. The advantages of such a technique are clear: Changes that occurred over a great many years can be analyzed in a short time period. This design is also useful in studying dwindling populations, since the researcher can assemble a sample from baseline investigations conducted earlier, probably at great expense. The disadvantages are also obvious. The follow-back panel depends on archival data, and many variables that interest mass media researchers are not contained in archives. In addition, the resulting sample in a follow-back design may not represent all possible entities. For example, a follow-back study of the managerial practices of small radio stations will not represent stations that went out of business and no longer exist.

A **catch-up panel** involves selecting a cross-sectional study done in the past and locating all possible units of analysis for observation in the present. The catch-up design is particularly attractive if the researcher has a rich source of baseline data in the archive. Of course, this is usually not the case, since most data sources lack enough identifying information to allow the investigator to track down the respondents. When the appropriate data exist, however, the catch-up study can be highly useful. In effect, Lefkowitz et al. (1972) used a catch-up technique in their study of TV watching and child aggression. After a lapse of 10 years, the investigators tracked down 735 of 875 youths who had participated in a survey of mental health factors when they were in the third grade. These individuals were recontacted and asked questions similar to those they had answered as young children. Huesmann and his colleagues (Huesmann, 1986) caught up with this panel one more time when the panel members were 30 years old. After reinterviewing 409 subjects from the original pool of 875, the authors concluded that this 22-year panel study demonstrated that viewing media violence can have harmful lifelong consequences.

Another problem associated with the catch-up panel involves comparability of measures. If the earlier study was not constructed to be part of a longitudinal design, the original measurement instruments will have to be modified. For example, a study of 10-year-olds might have used teacher ratings to measure aggressiveness; however, such a measure would not be appropriate with 20-year-olds.

Finally, the researcher in the catch-up situation is confined to the variables measured in the original study. In the intervening time, new variables might have been identified as important, but if those variables were not measured during the original survey, they are unavailable to the researcher. Figure 8.1 shows the similar-

ities and differences in retrospective, follow-back, and catch-up panel designs.

ANALYZING CAUSATION IN PANEL DATA

The panel design provides an opportunity for the researcher to make statements about the causal ordering among different variables. There are three necessary conditions for determining cause and effect. The first is time order. Causation is present if and only if the cause precedes the effect. Second, causation can occur only if some tendency for change in A results in change in B. In other words, there is an association between the two variables. Third, before effects are attributed to causes, all other alternative causes must be ruled out. Cross-sectional surveys, for which the data are collected at a single point in time, can fulfill only two of these three criteria. A cross-sectional survey allows the researcher to say that Variables A and B are associated. A skillfully constructed questionnaire and statistical controls such as partial correlation can help the researcher rule out alternative explanations. Nonetheless, only if the time order between A and B is evident can statements of cause be inferred. For example, a person's education is typically acquired before his or her occupational status. Thus, the statement that education is a cause of occupational status (all other things being equal) can be inferred. If there is no distinguishable temporal sequence in the data (as is the case with viewing violence on TV and aggressive behavior), causal statements are conjectural. In a panel study, however, the variables are measured across time, making causal inferences more defensible.

Note, however, two important points: First, the interval between measurement periods must be long enough to allow the cause to produce an effect. For example, if it takes a full year for exposure to TV violence to have an effect on viewers' aggressive behavior, a panel

---

Trackdown

One of the most common causes of attrition in panel research is the inability to locate the original respondents for a follow-up study. The longer the time lag between the two waves of data collection, the more severe this problem becomes. There are, however, a variety of tracking strategies available for persistent researchers who wish to overcome this problem. Call, Otto, and Spenner (1982) offer the following suggestions for finding those missing respondents:

1. Use the Postal Service to find forwarding addresses.
2. Check with the phone company for new phone numbers.
3. Question family and relatives for current location.
4. Ask neighbors for current information.
5. Interview former classmates.
6. Enlist the aid of a high school class reunion committee.
7. Check with former employers.
8. Examine records of college alumni associations.
9. Inquire at churches in the area.
10. Examine driver's license registration records.
11. Utilize military locator services.
12. Hire a professional tracking company (such as Equifax or Tracers Company of America).

---

study with only six months between measurement periods will not discover any effect. On the other hand, if a cause produces an effect that does not remain stable over the long run, an overly long interval between measurement waves will also fail to discover an effect. Again continuing the above example, suppose that exposure to TV violence produces an effect that appears three months after exposure but quickly disappears. A panel survey with six months between waves will totally miss observing this effect. The hard part, of course, is determining proper time intervals. Most researchers rely on past research and appropriate theories for some guidelines.

Many statistical techniques are available for determining a causal sequence in panel data. A detailed listing and explanation of the computations that are involved is beyond the scope of this book. Nonetheless, some of the following references will be helpful to readers who desire more detailed information. Menard (1991) discusses common methods for analyzing panel data measured at the interval level. Similarly, Markus (1979) gives computational methods for data measured at the interval level and discusses ways to analyze dichotomous panel data, including the increasingly popular log-linear technique. Asher (1983) provides a detailed discussion of path analysis. Trumbo (1995) describes statistical methods for analyzing panel data including time series analysis and Granger verification and illustrates their use in a longitudinal study of agenda setting. Finally, the most mathematically sophisticated technique, linear structural equations, or LISREL, is discussed in Joreskog (1973), Long (1976), and Wheaton, Muthen, Alwin, and Summers (1977). Since it appears that the LISREL method has much to recommend it (it was used in the NBC panel study discussed previously), researchers who intend to do panel studies should be familiar with its assumptions and techniques.

LONGITUDINAL DESIGN IN EXPERIMENTS

Although the preceding discussion was concerned with survey research, experimental research has a longitudinal dimension that should not be overlooked. Many research designs are based on a single exposure to a message, with the dependent variable measured almost immediately afterward. This procedure might be appropriate in many circumstances, but a longitudinal treatment design may be necessary to measure subtle, cumulative media effects. Furthermore, delayed assessment is essential to decide the duration of the impact of certain media effects (for example, how long does it take a persuasive effect to disappear?).

Bryant, Carveth, and Brown (1981) illustrated the importance of the longitudinal design to the experimental approach. In investigating TV viewing and anxiety, they divided their subjects into groups and assigned to each a menu of TV shows that could be watched. Over a 6-week period, one group was assigned a light viewing schedule, and a second was directed to watch a large number of shows that depicted a clear triumph of justice. A third group was assigned to view several shows in which justice did not triumph. One of the dependent variables was also measured over time. The investigators obtained voluntary viewing data by having students fill out diaries for another 3 weeks. The results of this study indicated that the cumulative exposure to TV shows in which justice does not prevail seemed to make some viewers more anxious, thus offering some support to Gerbner's cultivation hypothesis.

A study by Zillmann and Bryant (1982) also showed the importance of the longitudinal dimension in assessing the cumulative effects

of continued exposure. One experimental group watched nearly 5 hours of pornographic films over a 6-week period. A second group saw about 2.5 hours over the same period, while a control group saw nonpornographic films. Those exposed to the larger dose of pornography showed less compassion toward women as rape victims and toward women in general. More recently, Wicks (1992) exposed 46 subjects to a TV newscast or newspaper account of several stories. Subjects were then told to think about the stories for 2 days. Upon retesting, the subjects had higher recall scores than they had immediately after viewing or reading, thus demonstrating the "hypernesia" effect. Clearly, the longitudinal design can be of great value in experimental research.

SUMMARY

Longitudinal research involves the collection of data at different points in time. There are three types of longitudinal study: trend, cohort, and panel. A trend study asks the same questions of different groups of people at different points in time. A cohort study measures some characteristic of a sample whose members share some significant life event (usually the same age range) at two or more points in time. In a panel study the same respondents are measured at least twice. One of the advantages of the panel design is that it allows the researcher to make statements about the causal ordering of the study variables, and several different statistical methods are available for this task.

QUESTIONS AND PROBLEMS FOR FURTHER INVESTIGATION

1. Search recent issues of scholarly journals for examples of longitudinal studies. Which of the three designs discussed in this chapter was used? Try to find additional longitudinal studies done by commercial research firms. What design was most used?

2. What are some mass media variables that would be best studied using the cohort method?

3. What are some possible measures of media or audience characteristics that might be regularly made and stored in a data archive for secondary trend analysis?

4. How might a panel study make use of laboratory techniques?

REFERENCES AND SUGGESTED READINGS

Ader, C. (1995). A longitudinal study of agenda setting for the issue of environmental pollution. *Journalism and Mass Communication Quarterly, 72*(2), 300–311.

Asher, H. (1983). *Causal modeling* (2nd ed.). Beverly Hills, CA: Sage Publications.

Auriat, N. (1993). A comparison of event dating accuracy between the wife, the husband, and the couple, and the Belgian population register. *Public Opinion Quarterly, 57*(2), 165–190.

Basil, M. D. (1990). Primary news source changes: Question wording, availability and cohort effects. *Journalism Quarterly, 67*(4), 708–722.

Belson, W. (1978). *Television violence and the adolescent boy*. Hampshire, England: Saxon House.

Bolton, R. N., & Drew, J. H. (1991, January). A longitudinal analysis of the impact of service changes on customer attitudes. *Journal of Marketing, 55*, 1–9.

Bryant, J., Carveth, R., & Brown, D. (1981). Television viewing and anxiety. *Journal of Communication, 31*(1), 106–119.

Call, V., Otto, L., & Spenner, K. (1982). *Tracking respondents*. Lexington, MA: Lexington Books.

Carman, J. (1974). Consumer panels. In R. Ferber (Ed.), *Handbook of marketing research*. New York: McGraw-Hill.

Cook, T., Kendizierski, D., & Thomas, S. (1983). The implicit assumptions of television research. *Public Opinion Quarterly, 47*(2), 161–201.

Davis, D. M., & Walker, J. R. (1990). Countering the new media: The resurgence of share maintenance in prime time network television. *Journal of Broadcasting and Electronic Media, 34*(4), 487–493.

Feinberg, S. E., & Mason, W. M. (1980). Identification and estimation of age-period-cohort models in the analysis of archival data. In K. F. Schuessler (Ed.), *Sociological Methodology*. San Francisco: Jossey-Bass.

Gerbner, G., Gross, L., Signorielli, N., Morgan, M., & Jackson-Beeck, M. (1979). The demonstration of power: Violence profile no. 10. *Journal of Communication, 29*(3), 177–196.

Glenn, N. (1977). *Cohort analysis*. Beverly Hills, CA: Sage Publications.

Glenn, N. (1994). Television watching, newspaper reading and cohort differences in verbal ability. *Sociology of Education, 67*(2), 216–230.

Huesmann, L. R. (1986). Psychological processes promoting the relation between exposure to media violence and aggressive behavior by the viewer. *Journal of Social Issues, 42*(3), 125–139.

Huesmann, L. R., & Eron, L. D. (1986). *Television and the aggressive child*. Hillsdale, NJ: Lawrence Erlbaum.

Hyman, H. H. (1987). *Secondary analysis of sample*. Middletown, NY: Wesleyan University Press.

Joreskog, K. (1973). A general method for estimating a linear structural equation system. In A. Goldberger & O. Duncan (Eds.), *Structural equations models in the social sciences*. New York: Seminar Press.

Katz, E., & Lazarsfeld, P. F. (1955). *Personal influence*. New York: Free Press.

Kenny, D., Milavsky, J. R., Kessler, R. C., Stipp, H. H., & Rubens, W. S. (1984). The NBC study and television violence. *Journal of Communication, 34*(1), 176–188.

Lazarsfeld, P., Berelson, B., & Gaudet, H. (1944). *The people's choice*. New York: Columbia University Press.

Lefkowitz, M., Eron, L. D., Walder, L. O., & Huesmann, L. R. (1972). *Television violence and child aggression*. In E. Rubinstein, G. Comstock, & J. Murray (Eds.), Television and adolescent aggressiveness. Washington, DC: U.S. Government Printing Office.

Long, J. (1976). Estimation and hypothesis testing in linear models containing measurement error. *Sociological Methods and Research, 5*, 157–206.

Lowery, S., & DeFleur, M. (1988). *Milestones in mass communication research* (2nd ed.). White Plains, NY: Longman.

Magnusson, D., Bergman, L., Rudinger, G, & Torestad, B. (1991). *Problems and methods in longitu-*

dinal research. Cambridge: Cambridge University Press.

Markus, G. (1979). *Analyzing panel data.* Beverly Hills, CA: Sage Publications.

Mason, K., Mason, W., Winsborough, H., & Poole, W. K. (1973, April). Some methodological issues in cohort analysis of archival data. *American Sociological Review*, pp. 242–258.

Mayer, W. (1993). Trends in media usage. *Public Opinion Quarterly, 57*(4), 593–610.

Menard, S. (1991). *Longitudinal research.* Newbury Park, CA: Sage Publications.

Milavsky, J., Kessler, R. C., Stipp, H. H., & Rubens, W. S. (1982). *Television and aggression.* New York: Academic Press.

Newcomb, T. (1943). *Personality and social change.* New York: Dryden.

Norlen, V. (1977). Response errors in the answers to retrospective questions. *Statistik Tidskrift, 4,* 331–341.

Palmore, E. (1978). When can age, period and cohort effects be separated? *Social Forces, 57,* 282–295.

Pearl, D., Bouthilet, L., & Lazar, J. (1982). *Television and behavior: Ten years of scientific progress and implications for the eighties.* Washington, DC: U.S. Government Printing Office.

Peterson, T. (1980). *The mass media election.* New York: Praeger.

Potter, W. J. (1992). How do adolescents' perceptions of television reality change over time? *Journalism Quarterly, 69*(2), 392–405.

Powers, E., Goudy, W., & Keith, P. (1978). Congruence between panel and recall data in longitudinal research. *Public Opinion Quarterly, 42*(3), 380–389.

Rentz, J., Reynolds, F., & Stout, R. (1983, February). Analyzing changing consumption patterns with cohort analysis. *Journal of Marketing Research, 20,* 12–20.

Rosengren, K. E., & Windahl, S. (1989). *Media matter.* Norwood NJ: Ablex.

Schulsinger, F., Mednick, S., & Knop, J. (1981). *Longitudinal research.* Boston: Nijhoff Publishing.

Singer, J. L., Singer, D. G., Desmond, R., Hirsch, B., & Nicol, A. (1988). Family mediation and children's cognition, aggression and comprehension of television. *Journal of Applied Developmental Psychology, 9*(3), 329–347.

Stevenson, R. (1994). The disappearing reader. *Newspaper Research Journal, 15*(3), 22–31.

Trumbo, C. (1995). Longitudinal modeling of public issues. *Journalism and Mass Communication Monographs, 152* (August, 1995), 1–53.

Turner, C. W., Hesse, B. W., & Peterson-Lewis, S. (1986). Naturalistic studies of the long-term effects of television violence. *Journal of Social Issues, 42*(3), 51–73.

Uncles, M. (1988). *Longitudinal data analysis: Methods and applications.* London: Pion Limited.

Valkenburg, P., & Van Der Voort, T. (1995). *Communication Research, 22*(3), 267–287.

Wartella, E., & Reeves, B. (1985). Historical trends in research on children and the media, 1900–1960. *Journal of Communication, 35*(2), 118–133.

Wheaton, B., Muthen, D., Alwin, D. F., & Summers, G. F. (1977). Assessing reliability and stability in panel models. In D. Heise (Ed.), *Sociological Methodology, 1977.* San Francisco: Jossey-Bass.

Wicks, R. (1992). Improvement over time in recall of media information. *Journal of Broadcasting and Electronic Media, 36*(3), 287–302.

Wilson, T. (1994). Trends in tolerance toward rightist and leftist groups, 1976–1988. *Public Opinion Quarterly, 58*(4), 539–556.

Wimmer, R. D. (1995) *An analysis of panel study participation methods.* The Eagle Group.

Wood, W. (1986, February). Get to know your cohort. *Marketing and Media Decisions,* 144–145.

Xiamong, H. (1994). Television viewing among American adults in the 1990s. *Journal of Broadcasting and Electronic Media, 38*(3), 353–360.

Zhu, J. H. (1990). Recent trends in adversarial attitudes among American newspaper journalists: A cohort analysis. *Journalism Quarterly, 67*(4), 992–1004.

Zillmann, D., & Bryant, J. (1982). Pornography, sexual callousness, and the trivialization of rape. *Journal of Communication, 32*(4), 10–21.

Chapter

9

EXPERIMENTAL RESEARCH

This chapter describes the experimental method of research and its use in mass media investigations. Experiments are used much more often in fields such as psychology than they are in media research. For example, a recent survey by Cooper, Potter and Dupagne (1994) found that from 1965 to 1989 only 15% of published quantitative studies used the experimental method. In contrast, nearly 50% relied on surveys (see Chapter 7). Nonetheless, the experimental method is the oldest approach in mass media research and continues to provide a wealth of information for researchers and critics of the media. Because of their relative infrequency, however, only the more basic techniques are examined in this chapter. Readers who wish to learn more about advanced experimental procedures should consult McBurney (1994) and Saslow (1994). This chapter will discuss controlled laboratory experiments, then examine quasi-experimental designs, and conclude with a consideration of field experiments.

ADVANTAGES AND DISADVANTAGES OF LABORATORY EXPERIMENTS

There are several reasons why mass media researchers might select the experimental method:

1. *Evidence of causality.* First, experiments help establish cause and effect. Although philosophers of science might argue whether we can ever really prove a cause-effect link between two variables, the experiment is undoubtedly the best social science research method for establishing causality. The researcher controls the time order of the presentation of two variables and thus makes sure that the cause actually precedes the effect. In addition, the experimental method allows the investigator to control other possible causes of the variable under investigation.

2. *Control.* As suggested previously, control is another advantage of the experimental method. Researchers have control over the environment, the variables, and the subjects. Laboratory research allows investigators to isolate a testing situation from the competing influences of normal activity. Researchers are free to structure the experimental environment in almost any way. Lighting and temperature levels, proximity of subjects to measuring instruments, soundproofing, and nearly every other aspect of the experimental situation can be arranged and altered. Environmental control, however, has its drawbacks, and the artificially created environment of the laboratory is one of the main disadvantages of the technique.

Laboratory studies also allow researchers to control the number and types of independent and dependent variables selected and the way these variables are manipulated. Variable control strengthens internal validity and helps eliminate confounding influences. Gilbert and Schleuder (1990), for example, were able to control almost every detail of their laboratory analysis of the effects of color and complexity in still photographs.

The experimental approach also allows researchers to control subjects. This includes control over the selection process, assignment to the control or the experimental group, and exposure to experimental treatment. Researchers can place limits on the number of subjects participating in a study and can choose specific types of subjects for exposure in varying degrees to the independent variable. For example, researchers may select subjects according to which medium they use for news information and vary each subject's exposure to commercials of different types to determine which is the most effective.

3. *Cost.* In relative terms, the cost of an experiment can be low when compared to other research methods. An advertising researcher, for example, can examine the impact of two different ad designs using an experimental design with as few as 40–50 subjects. A comparable test done in the field would be far more costly.

4. *Replication.* Finally, the experimental method aids in replication. The conditions of the study are typically clearly spelled out in the description of an experiment, which makes it easier for others to replicate. In fact, classic experiments are often repeated, sometimes under slightly different conditions, to ensure that the original results were not idiosyncratic.

The experimental technique, however, is not perfect. It has three major disadvantages:

1. *Artificiality.* Perhaps the biggest problem with using this technique is the artificial nature of the experimental environment. The behavior under investigation must be placed in circumstances that afford proper control. Unfortunately, much behavior of interest to mass media researchers is often altered when studied out of its natural environment. Critics claim that the sterile and unnatural conditions created in the laboratory produce results that have little direct application to real-world settings, where subjects are continually exposed to competing stimuli. Miller (1991) noted that critics of the laboratory method often resort to ambiguous and disjunctive arguments about the artificiality of the procedure, suggesting that contrasting the "real" world with the "unreal" world may, in fact, be merely a problem in semantics. The main point, he claimed, is that both the laboratory method and the field method investigate communication behavior,

and if viewed in this way, it is meaningless to speak of behavior as "real" or "unreal": All behavior is real.

Miller also noted, however, that it is unsatisfactory and unscientific to dodge the problem of artificiality in laboratory procedures by including a disclaimer in a study indicating that the findings are applicable only to a particular audience, to the environmental conditions of the analysis, and to the period during which the study was conducted. Since external validity is a major goal of scientific research, a disclaimer of this nature is counterproductive. If researchers are not willing to expand their interests beyond the scope of a single analysis, such studies have only heuristic value; they make little or no contribution to the advancement of knowledge in mass media.

Many researchers have conducted field experiments in an attempt to overcome the artificiality of the laboratory. Although they take place in more natural surroundings, field experiments are prone to problems with control.

2. *Experimenter bias.* Experiments can be impacted by experimenter bias (Chapter 2). Rosenthal and Jacobson (1966) discovered that experimenters who were told what findings were expected had results more in line with the research hypothesis than experimenters who were not told what to expect. To counteract this problem, some researchers use the double-blind technique, in which neither subjects nor researchers know whether a given subject belongs to the control group or the experimental group.

3. *Limited scope.* Finally, there are some research questions that simply don't lend themselves to the experimental approach. Many of the more interesting research topics in mass communication are concerned with the collective behavior of perhaps millions of people. Experiments on this scale would be much too massive to conduct. Consider for example, the cultivation effect (discussed in more detail in Chapter 16), which involves the long-term impact of television on society. Any experimental design that would "test" the cultiva-

tion effect would be too time-consuming, expensive, and ethically questionable to take place. Although it is possible to conduct some smaller-scale experiments on this topic with small groups of subjects, it is unclear how these experiments relate to the larger-scale phenomenon.

CONDUCTING EXPERIMENTAL RESEARCH

The experimental method involves both manipulation and observation. In the simplest form of an experiment, researchers manipulate the independent variable and then observe the responses of subjects on the dependent variable. Although every experiment is different, most researchers agree that the following eight steps should be followed when conducting an experiment:

1. *Select the setting.* Many experiments are best done in a laboratory or in another environment under the direct control of the researcher. Others are best done in more natural surroundings where the researcher has little, if any, control over the experimental situation. This latter type of experiment is discussed in more detail later in this chapter.

2. *Select the experimental design.* The appropriate design depends upon the nature of the hypothesis or the research question, types of variables to be manipulated or measured, availability of subjects, and amount of resources available.

3. *Operationalize the variables.* In the experimental approach, independent variable(s) are usually operationalized in terms of the manipulation used to create them. Dependent variables are operationalized by constructing scales or rules for categorizing observations of behavior.

4. *Decide how to manipulate the independent variable.* To manipulate the independent variable (or variables), a set of specific instructions, events, or stimuli are developed for presentation to the experimental subjects. There are two types of manipulations. In **straightforward manipulation**, written materials, verbal instructions, or other stimuli are presented to the subjects. For example, Baran, Mok, Land and Kang, (1989) used a straightforward manipulation of their independent variable—product positioning. One group of subjects was presented with a "generic" shopping list containing items such as ice cream, frozen dinner, mustard, and coffee. Another group saw the "practical" list with items such as Borden's ice cream, Swanson's frozen dinner, French's mustard, and Maxwell House coffee. A third group was presented with the "upscale" list consisting of Lean Cuisine frozen dinner, Grey Poupon mustard, General Foods International Coffees, and similar items. Each group was then asked to make judgments about the character of the person to whom the list belonged. As predicted by the experimenters, the shopping lists had an impact on the way subjects evaluated the general goodness and responsibility of the lists' authors.

In a **staged manipulation**, researchers construct events and circumstances that enable them to manipulate the independent variable. Staged manipulations can be relatively simple or rather elaborate. They frequently involve the use of a confederate, a person who pretends to be a subject but who is actually part of the manipulation.

For example, staged manipulations and confederates have been used in experiments that examine the impact of media portrayals of antisocial behavior. In their study of rock music videos, Hansen and Hansen (1990) showed half of their sample three music videos that depicted antisocial behavior; the other half of the sample viewed three rock videos depicting a more "neutral" type of behavior. The subjects then watched a videotaped job interview of a person applying for a position with the campus TV station's rock video program. One version of this tape showed the applicant (who was actually a confederate of the experimenters) making an obscene gesture while the interviewer's back was turned. Subjects who had previously viewed the rock videos depicting "neutral" behaviors evaluated the applicant's behavior more negatively than did the subjects who saw the videos depicting antisocial behaviors.

Hoyt (1977) investigated the effects of television coverage on courtroom behavior. In a staged manipulation of three groups of subjects, he separately questioned the groups about a film they had just viewed. One group answered questions in the presence of a TV camera at the front of the room; a second group answered questions with the camera concealed behind a full-length mirror; and a third group answered questions without being filmed. Hoyt found no differences in subjects' verbal behavior across the three conditions.

No matter what manipulation technique is used, a general principle for the experimenter to follow is to construct or choose a manipulation that is as strong as possible so that potential differences between the experimental groups are maximized. If, for example, an experimenter was trying to assess the effects of different degrees of newspaper credibility on audience perceptions of the accuracy of a story, one condition might attribute the story to the *New York Times* and another might attribute it to the *National Enquirer* or the *National Star*. A strong manipulation maximizes the chances that the independent variable will have an effect.

5. *Select and assign subjects to experimental conditions.* Recall from Chapter 2 that, to ensure external validity, experimental subjects should be selected randomly from the population under investigation. The various random sampling techniques discussed in Chapter 4 are also appropriate for selecting subjects for experimental studies.

6. *Conduct a pilot study.* A pilot study with a small number of subjects will reveal problems, and it will also allow the experimenter to

make a **manipulation check**—a test to see whether the manipulation of the independent variable will actually have the intended effect. For example, suppose a researcher wants to assess the effect of the viewer's involvement in a TV show on how well the viewer remembers the ads in the show. The experimenter constructs TV shows labeled "high involvement" (a cliff-hanger with lots of suspense), "medium involvement" (a family drama), and "low involvement" (a Senate committee hearing taped from C-SPAN). To check whether these programs actually differ in involvement, the experimenter must measure the degree to which subjects were actually involved with the programs under each of the conditions. Such a check might include a self-report, an observational report (such as counting the number of times a subject looked away from the screen), or even a physiological measure. If the check shows that the manipulation was not effective, the experimenter can revamp the manipulation before the main experiment is conducted. (It is also a good idea to include a manipulation check in the main experiment itself.)

7. *Administer the experiment.* After the bugs are out and the manipulation is checked, the main phase of data collection begins. Experimental manipulations can be carried out on either individuals or groups. The dependent variable is measured, and the subjects are debriefed. During debriefing, the experimenter explains the purpose and the implications of the research. If the manipulation required deception, the experimenter must explain why and how the deception was used. (See Chapter 18 for more about deception and other ethical problems of research.)

8. *Analyze and interpret the results.* The subjects' scores on the dependent variable(s) are tabulated, and the data are subjected to statistical analysis. Many statistics discussed in Chapters 10, 11, and 12 are used to analyze the results of experiments. Finally, the experimenter must decide what the results mean. In

some experiments, this may be the most difficult task to accomplish.

CONTROL OF CONFOUNDING VARIABLES

As previously discussed (Chapters 2 and 4), experimenters must ensure the internal validity of their research by controlling for the effects of extraneous, or confounding, variables that might contaminate their findings. Control of these variables can be managed through the environment, experimental manipulations, experimental design, or assignment of subjects; all of these items are under the experimenter's direct supervision. This section will concentrate on techniques for ensuring that the various groups in an experiment are comparable before the experimental treatment is administered. This is an important consideration because it helps to assure that all of the possible alternative explanations based on the natural differences among people are ruled out.

Perhaps an example will illustrate this point. Suppose an experimenter wants to determine whether different versions of a TV commercial's musical soundtrack have different impacts on what is remembered from that ad. The experimenter uses a media research class as the sample and assigns an ad with a rap soundtrack to the students in the first three rows. Students in the last three rows view the same ad but hear a heavy metal soundtrack. Both groups are then given a memory test, and the results show that the group hearing the rap soundtrack remembered more information from the ad. How confident should the researcher be of this conclusion? Not too confident: It is entirely possible that the people who sat in the first three rows of the class are different from those who sat in the back. The "fronters" might have chosen the front seats because they are more intelligent, more attentive, and more alert than the "backers,"

who might have sat in the rear of the room so they could sleep, talk, or otherwise amuse themselves. Consequently, the superior performance of the "fronters" might be due to these factors rather than to the effectiveness of the soundtrack.

How can experimenters assure that their groups are equivalent? There are three main techniques: randomization, matching, and including the confounding variable in the design.

RANDOMIZATION

A powerful technique for eliminating the influence of extraneous variables is randomization: randomly assigning subjects to various treatment groups. Random assignment means that each subject has an equal chance of being assigned to each treatment group. This method works because the variables to be controlled are distributed in approximately the same manner in all groups. In the above example, suppose that the experimenter had randomly assigned students to one group or the other instead of assigning them according to where they sat. It is highly probable that the average level of intelligence in the two groups would have been the same, as would have been their levels of attentiveness and alertness, thus ruling out those variables as alternative explanations. In addition, randomization would equalize some other confounding factors that the experimenter might have overlooked, such as the influence of gender on what was remembered.

Random assignment would also assure that a disproportionate number of males or females in one or the other group does not occur, thereby skewing the results. The same might be said for geographic background: Randomization would provide for proportionate numbers of urban versus rural residents in each group.

There are several ways that randomization can be achieved. If there are only two groups in the experiment, the experimenter might simply flip a coin. If heads comes up, the subject goes to Group 1; if tails, Group 2. Experimental designs with more than two groups might use a table of random numbers to assign subjects. In a four-group design, a two-digit random number might be assigned to each subject. Those assigned 00–24 are placed in Group 1; 25–49 in Group 2; 50–74 in Group 3; and 75–99 in Group 4.

Randomization, however, is not infallible. The smaller the size of the sample in the experiment, the more the risk that randomization will produce nonequivalent groups. This is another reason why researchers should use an adequate sample size in an experiment.

MATCHING

Another way to control for the impact of confounding variables is to match subjects on characteristics that might be related to the dependent variable. There are two chief methods of matching. The first, *matching by constancy,* makes a variable uniform for all of the experimental groups. For example, let's say a researcher is interested in assessing the impact of playing two types of video games on aggressiveness in children. Past research strongly suggests that gender will be related to the levels and types of aggressive acts performed. To match the sample by constancy, then, the researcher may decide to perform the experiment using only boys or only girls in the sample, thus controlling for gender effects.

The second type of matching involves *matching by pairing.* In this method, subjects are paired off on some similar value of a relevant variable before being assigned to different groups. Using the video game example from above, suppose the experimenter suspects that a subject's prior level of aggressive tendencies will have an impact on how that subject is affected by violent video games. The experimenter would administer a test of aggressiveness to all subjects and calculate their scores. For simplici-

ty's sake let us say that there are only three possible scores on this test: low, medium, and high. The experimenter would find two people who scored high on this test, pair them up, and then assign one at random to one treatment group and the other to the second. A similar procedure would be followed for those scoring low and medium. When finished, the researcher would be confident that equal numbers of high-, medium-, and low-aggression subjects were placed in each treatment group. This process, of course, is not necessarily restricted to pairs. If an experiment had three groups, it is entirely possible that subjects might be matched as triplets and then randomly assigned to groups.

In addition to helping gain control over confounding variables, matching subjects also increases the sensitivity of the experimental design. Since the treatment groups become more homogenous, smaller differences that might have been obscured by individual variations can be detected.

On the other hand, this method does have some disadvantages. Matching by constancy limits the generalizability of the study and restricts the size of the population available for sampling. Both forms of matching also require at least some prior knowledge about the subjects and may require the extra effort of a pretest.

INCLUDING THE CONFOUNDING VARIABLE IN THE DESIGN

Another way to control the impact of confounding variables from an experiment and to increase the sensitivity of the experiment is to incorporate the confounding variable(s) into the design. For instance, let us return to the video game example. Instead of controlling for the effects of gender by restricting the study to either only boys or only girls, the experimenter might include gender as an independent variable. After dividing the sample by gender, each male or female would be randomly assigned to

Importance of Pretesting

The importance of pretesting in an experiment is illustrated by the following scenario. A researcher was planning to conduct a study with high school students. After completing the laborious process of securing approval from the appropriate authorities, the researcher scheduled a date and showed up bright and early to collect the data. About 70 students were assembled in the auditorium, and the school's principal had given the researcher 45 minutes in which to collect the data. No problem, thought the researcher. The subjects merely had to listen to a few musical selections and fill out rating scales.

The researcher passed out the sheets containing the rating scales and told students to get their pencils or pens ready. At this point, the students looked perplexed, and many protested that they did not have pencils or pens with them. Unlike the college students that the researcher was used to, high school students do not routinely carry pens or pencils.

With the allotted time quickly running out, the researcher ran to the principal's office and asked to borrow pencils. Luckily, there were several boxes in the supply cabinet. The researcher hurried back into the auditorium and started to pass out the pencils when he suddenly discovered that they were not sharpened. A frenzied search of the auditorium revealed exactly one pencil sharpener that probably dated from the 1930s.

Needless to say, the experiment had to be rescheduled. Since that experience, the researcher has never failed to run a pretest before doing an experiment. And he *always* brings along plenty of pencils.

a condition. The resulting design would have four groups: males who play video game A, males who play video game B, females who play video game A, and females who play video game B. (Note that this is an example of the factorial design described later in this chapter.) An added benefit of this design is that it can provide information about the interaction—the combined effects of the confounding variable and independent variable of interest. Again, there are disadvantages to this method. Including another factor in the design increases the number of subjects needed for the experiment and also increases the time and energy necessary to complete it.

EXPERIMENTAL DESIGN

When used within the context of experimental research, the word *design* can have two differ-

ent meanings. In the first place, it can refer to the statistical procedures to be used to analyze the data. Hence, it is common to hear about an analysis of variance design or a repeated-measures *t*-test design. On the other hand, *design* can refer to the total experimental plan or structure of the research. Used in this sense, it means selecting and planning the entire experimental approach to a research problem. This chapter uses the latter meaning of *design*. The appropriate statistical techniques for the various experimental designs in this chapter are discussed in Part III.

An experimental design does not have to be a complicated series of statements, diagrams, and figures; it may be as simple as

Pretest > Experimental treatment > Posttest

Although other factors, such as variable and sample selection, control, and construction of a measurement instrument, enter into this design, the diagram does provide a legitimate starting point for research.

To facilitate the discussion of experimental design, the following notations are used to represent specific parts of a design (Campbell & Stanley, 1963):

- R represents a random sample or random assignment.
- X represents a treatment or manipulation of the independent variables so that the effects of these variables on the dependent variables can be measured.
- O refers to a process of observation or measurement; it is usually followed by a numerical subscript indicating the number of the observation (O_1 = Observation 1).

A left-to-right listing of symbols, such as R O_1 X O_2, represents the order of the experiment. In this case, subjects are randomly selected or assigned to groups (R) and then observed or measured (O_1). Next, some type of treatment or manipulation of the independent variable is performed (X), followed by a second observation or measurement (O_2). Each line in experimental notation refers to the experience of a single group. Consider the following design:

$$R \quad O_1 \quad X \quad O_2$$
$$R \quad O_1 \quad \quad O_2$$

This design indicates that the operations in the experiment are conducted simultaneously on two different groups. Notice that the second group, the control group, does not receive the experimental treatment.

BASIC EXPERIMENTAL DESIGNS

Each experimental design makes assumptions about the type of data the researcher wishes to collect, since different data require different research methods. Several questions need to be

answered by the researcher before any type of design is constructed:

1. What is the purpose of the study?
2. What is to be measured or tested?
3. How many factors (independent variables) are involved?
4. How many levels of the factors (degrees of the independent variables) are involved?
5. What type of data is desired?
6. What is the easiest and most efficient way to collect the data?
7. What type of statistical analysis is appropriate for the data?
8. How much will the study cost?
9. How can these costs be trimmed?
10. What facilities are available for conducting the study?
11. What types of studies have been conducted in the area?
12. What benefits will be received from the results of the study?

The answer to each question has a bearing on the sequence of steps a study should follow. For example, if a limited budget is available for the study, a complicated, four-group research design must be excluded. Or if previous studies have shown the "posttest only" design to be useful, another design may be unjustified.

Not all experimental designs are covered in this section; only the most widely used are considered. The sources listed at the end of the chapter provide more information about these and other designs.

Pretest-Posttest Control Group. The pretest-posttest control group design is a fundamental and widely used procedure in all research areas. The design controls many of the rival hypotheses generated by artifacts; the effects of maturation, testing, history, and other sources are controlled because each group faces the same circumstances in the study. As shown in Figure 9.1, subjects are to be randomly selected or assigned, and each group is to be given a

FIGURE 9.1	Pretest-Posttest Control Group Design

R O_1 X O_2
R O_1 O_2

FIGURE 9.2	Posttest-Only Control Group Design

R   X O_1

R O_2

pretest. Only the first group, however, is to receive the experimental treatment. The difference between O_1 and O_2 for Group 1 is compared to the difference between O_1 and O_2 for Group 2. If a significant statistical difference is found, it is assumed that the experimental treatment was the primary cause.

Posttest-Only Control Group.   When researchers are hesitant to use a pretest because of the possibility of subject sensitization to the posttest, the design in Figure 9.1 can be altered to describe a posttest-only control group (see Figure 9.2). Neither group has a pretest, but Group 1 is exposed to the treatment variable, followed by a posttest. The two groups are compared to determine whether a statistical significance is present.

The posttest-only control group design is also widely used to control rival explanations. Both groups are equally affected by maturation, history, and so on. Also, both normally call for a *t-test*, a test to compare the significance between two groups, to determine whether a significant statistical difference is present (Chapter 12).

Solomon Four-Group Design.   The Solomon four-group design (see Figure 9.3) combines the first two designs and is useful if pretesting is considered to be a negative factor. Each alternative for pretesting and posttesting is accounted for in the design, which makes it attractive to researchers. For example, consider the hypothetical data presented in Figure 9.4. The numbers in the figure represent college students' scores on a test of current events

knowledge. The X represents a program of regular newspaper reading.

To determine whether the newspaper reading had an effect, O_2 should be significantly different from O_1 and also significantly different from O_4. In addition, O_2 should be significantly different from O_6 and also from O_3. If we assume that the 20-point difference shown in Figure 9.4 is significant, it would appear that the independent variable in our example is indeed having an effect on current events knowledge. Note that other informative comparisons are also possible in this design. To assess the possible effects of pretesting, O_4 can be compared with O_6. Comparing O_1 and O_3 allows the experimenter to check on the efficacy of randomization, and any possible pretest-manipulation interaction can be detected by comparing O_2 and O_5.

The biggest drawback of the Solomon four-group design is a practical one. The design requires four separate groups, which means more subjects, more time, and more money. Further, some results produced from this design can be difficult to interpret. For example, what does it

FIGURE 9.3	Solomon Four-Group Design

R O_1 X O_2

R O_3 O_4

R   X O_5

R O_6

FIGURE 9.4   Hypothetical Data for Solomon Four-Group Design

Group				
1	R	20 (O_1)	X	40 (O_2)
2	R	20 (O_3)		20 (O_4)
3	R		X	40 (O_5)
4	R			20 (O_6)

mean if O_2 is significantly greater than O_4, even though O_5 is significantly less than O_6?

FACTORIAL STUDIES

Research studies involving the simultaneous analysis of two or more independent variables are called **factorial designs**, and each independent variable is called a *factor*. The approach saves time, money, and resources and allows researchers to investigate the interaction between the independent variables. That is, in many instances, it is possible that two or more variables are interdependent in the effects they produce on the dependent variable, a relationship that could not be detected if two simple randomized designs were used.

The term *two-factor design* indicates that two independent variables are manipulated; a three-factor design includes three independent variables; and so on. (A one-factor design is a simple random design because only one independent variable is involved.) A *factorial* design for a study must have at least two factors or independent variables.

Factors may also have two or more levels. Therefore, the 2 × 2 factorial design has two independent variables, each with two levels. A 3 × 3 factorial design has three levels for each of the two independent variables. A 2 × 3 × 3 factorial design has three independent variables: The first has two levels, and the second and third have three levels each.

To demonstrate the concept of levels, imagine that a television station manager would like to study the success of a promotional campaign for a new movie-of-the-week series. The manager plans to advertise the new series on radio and in newspapers. Subjects selected randomly are placed into one of the *cells* of the 2 × 2 factorial design in Figure 9.5. This allows for the testing of two levels of two independent variables—exposure to radio and exposure to newspapers.

Four groups are involved in the study: Group I is exposed to both newspaper material and radio material; Group II is exposed only to newspaper; Group III is exposed only to radio; and

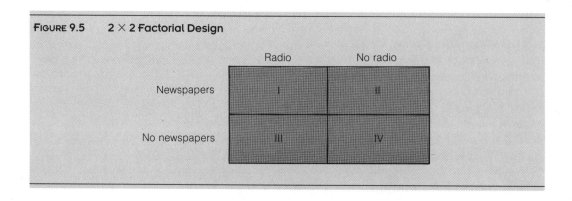

FIGURE 9.5   2 × 2 Factorial Design

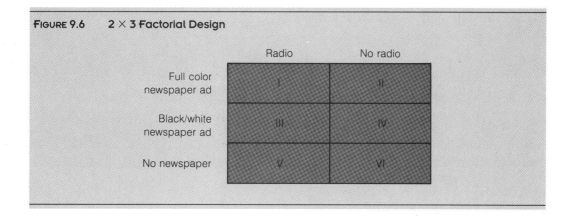

FIGURE 9.6 **2 × 3 Factorial Design**

	Radio	No radio
Full color newspaper ad	I	II
Black/white newspaper ad	III	IV
No newspaper	V	VI

Group IV serves as a control group and receives no exposure to either radio or newspaper. After the groups have undergone the experimental treatment, the manager can administer a short questionnaire to determine which medium, or combination of media, worked most effectively.

A 2 × 3 factorial design, which adds a third level to the second independent variable, is shown in Figure 9.6. This design demonstrates how the manager might investigate the relative effectiveness of full-color versus black-and-white newspaper advertisements while also measuring the impact of the exposure to radio material.

Say the television station manager wants to include promotional advertisements on television as well as use radio and newspaper. The third factor produces a 2 × 2 × 2 factorial design. This three-factor design (see Figure 9.7) shows the eight possibilities of a 2 × 2 × 2 factorial study. Note that the subjects in Group I are exposed to newspaper, radio, and television announcements, whereas those in Group VIII are not exposed to any of the announcements.

The testing procedure in the three-factor design is similar to that of previous methods. Subjects in all eight cells would be given some type of measurement instrument, and differ-

FIGURE 9.7 **2 × 2 × 2 Factorial Design**

	Radio		No radio	
	TV	No TV	TV	No TV
Newspaper	I	II	III	IV
No newspaper	V	V!	VII	VIII

ences between the groups would be tested for statistical significance.

OTHER EXPERIMENTAL DESIGNS

Research designs are as unique and varied as the questions and hypotheses they help answer. Designs of different types yield different types of information. If information about the effects of multiple manipulations is desired, a repeated-measures design (several measurements of the same subject) is appropriate. In this design, instead of assigning different people to different manipulations, the researcher exposes the same subjects to multiple manipulations. The effects of the various manipulations appear as variations within the same person's performance rather than as differences between groups of people.

One obvious advantage of the repeated-measures design is that fewer subjects are necessary since each subject participates in all conditions. Further, since each subject in effect acts as his or her own control, the design is quite sensitive to detecting treatment differences. On the other hand, repeated-measures designs are subject to carryover effects—the effects of one manipulation may still be present when the next manipulation is presented. Another possible disadvantage stems from the fact that subjects experience all of the various experimental conditions, and they may figure out the purpose behind the experiment. As a result, they may behave differently than they would if they were unaware of the study's goal.

If the experimenter thinks that the order of presentation of the independent variables in a repeated-measures design will be a problem, a Latin square design can be used. Figure 9.8 shows an example of a Latin square design for a repeated-measures experiment with four subjects. Note that each subject is exposed to all conditions and that each of the four conditions appears only once per row and once per column. The Latin square arrangement also can be used when repeated measures are made on

FIGURE 9.8	Latin Square Design			
Subjects	**Experimental conditions**			
A	1	2	3	4
B	2	3	4	1
C	3	4	1	2
D	4	1	2	3

independent groups rather than on individual subjects.

QUASI-EXPERIMENTAL DESIGNS

Sometimes the experimenter does not have the luxury of randomly assigning subjects to experimental conditions. Suppose, for example, a researcher knows that a local radio station is about to be sold and he or she is interested in determining the effects of this change of ownership on employee morale. The researcher measures the morale of a sample of employees at the station before and after the sale. At the same time, the researcher collects data on morale from a sample of employees at a comparable station in the same community. This design is similar to the pretest-posttest control group design discussed on page 192, but it does not involve random assignment of subjects to experimental groups. Using Campbell and Stanley's (1963) terminology, it is a **quasi-experiment**. Quasi-experiments represent a valuable source of information, but there are design faults that must be considered in the interpretation of the data.

This chapter discusses only two types of quasi-experimental designs: the pretest-posttest nonequivalent control group design and the interrupted time series design. For further information, consult Campbell and Stanley (1963) and Cook and Campbell (1979).

FIGURE 9.9   Pretest-Posttest Nonequivalent Control Group Design

$$O_1 \qquad X \qquad O_2$$

$$O_3 \qquad\qquad O_4$$

Note: The line dividing the two groups indicates that no random assignment occurred.

Pretest-Posttest Nonequivalent Control Group Design.   This approach, illustrated in Figure 9.9, is the one used by the hypothetical researcher studying employee morale at radio stations. In this design, one group is exposed to the experimental manipulation and is compared to a similar group that is not exposed. The pre- and posttest differences are compared to determine whether the experimental condition had an effect.

In the radio station example mentioned before, assume the pretest of employee morale showed that the workers at both radio stations had the same morale level before the sale. The posttest, however, showed that the morale of the employees at the sold station decreased significantly after the sale, but the morale level at the other (control) station remained constant. This indicates that the station sale had an impact on morale. However, this may not be true. The two groups might have been different on other variables at the time of the pretest. For example, suppose the two groups of employees were of different ages. It is possible that the effect of the station sale on older employees produced the difference. The quasi-experimental design does not rule out this alternative selection-treatment interaction explanation.

Interrupted Time Series Design.   In this arrangement, diagrammed in Figure 9.10, a series of periodic measurements is made of a group. The series of measurements is interrupted by the experimental treatment, and then measurements are continued.

This design can rule out several threats to internal validity. If there is a significant difference between O_5 and O_6, maturation can be ruled out by examining the scores for all the intervals prior to the manipulation. If maturation were occurring, it would probably produce differences between O_1 and O_2, O_2 and O_3, and so on. If the only difference is between O_5 and O_6, then maturation is not a plausible explanation. The same logic can be applied to rule out the sensitizing effects of testing. The biggest threat to the internal validity in this design is history. It is possible that any apparent changes occurring after the experimental manipulation might be due to some other event that occurred at the same time as the experimental treatment.

FIELD EXPERIMENTS

Experiments conducted in a laboratory can be disadvantageous for many research studies because of certain problems they present: They are performed in controlled conditions that are unlike natural settings; they are generally considered to lack external validity; and they usually necessitate subject awareness of the testing situation. Because of these shortcomings, many researchers prefer to use field experiments (Haskins, 1968).

The exact difference between laboratory experiments and field experiments has been a subject of debate for years, especially with regard to the "realism" of the situations involved. Many researchers consider field and laboratory experiments to be on opposite ends of the "realism" continuum. However, the main difference between the two approaches is the setting. As Westley (1989, p. 129) pointed out:

> The laboratory experiment is carried out on the experimenter's own turf, the subjects come into the laboratory. In the field experiment, the

FIGURE 9.10   Interrupted Time Series Design

$$O_1 \quad O_2 \quad O_3 \quad O_4 \quad O_5 \quad X \quad O_6 \quad O_7 \quad O_8 \quad O_9 \quad O_{10}$$

experimenter goes to the subject's turf. In general, the physical controls available in the laboratory are greater than those found in the field. For that reason, statistical controls are often substituted for physical controls in the field.

The two approaches can also be distinguished by the presence or absence of rules and procedures to control the conditions and the subjects' awareness or unawareness of being subjects. If the researcher maintains tight control over the subjects' behavior and the subjects are placed in an environment they perceive to be radically different from their everyday life, the situation is probably better described as a laboratory experiment. On the other hand, if the subjects function primarily in their everyday social roles with little investigator interference or environmental restructuring, the case is probably closer to a field experiment. Basically, the difference between laboratory experiments and field experiments is one of degree.

ADVANTAGES OF FIELD EXPERIMENTS

The major advantage of field experiments is their external validity: Since study conditions closely resemble natural settings, subjects usually provide a truer picture of their normal behavior and are not influenced by the experimental situation. For example, consider a laboratory study designed to test the effectiveness of two versions of a television commercial. One group views Version A, and the other group views Version B. Both groups are then given a questionnaire to measure their willingness to purchase the advertised product. On the basis

of these results, it may be concluded that Version B is more effective in selling the product. Although this may actually be the case, the validity of the experiment is questionable because the subjects knew they were being studied. (See the discussion of demand characteristics in Chapter 2.) Another problem is that answering a questionnaire cannot be equated to buying a product. Furthermore, viewing commercials in a laboratory setting is different from the normal viewing situation, in which competing stimuli (crying children, ringing telephones, and so on) are often present.

In a field experiment, these commercials might be tested by showing Version A in one market and Version B in a similar, but different, market. Actual sales of the product in both markets might then be monitored to determine which commercial was the more successful in persuading viewers to buy the product. As can be seen, the results of the field experiment have more relevance to reality, but the degree of control involved is markedly less than in the laboratory experiment.

Some field studies have the advantage of being nonreactive. Reactivity is the influence that a subject's awareness of being measured or observed has on his or her behavior. Laboratory subjects are almost always aware of being measured. Although this is also true of some field experiments, many can be conducted without the subjects' knowledge of their participation.

Field experiments are useful for studying complex social processes and situations. In their study of the effects of the arrival of television in an English community, Himmelweit, Oppenheim, and Vince (1958) recognized the advantages of the field experiment for examining such a complicated topic. Since television has an impact on several lifestyle variables, the researchers employed a range of analysis techniques, including diaries, personal interviews, direct observation, questionnaires, and teachers' ratings of students, to document this impact. A topic area as broad as this does not easily lend itself to laboratory research.

Field experiments can be inexpensive. Most studies require no special equipment or facilities. However, expenses increase rapidly with the size and scope of the study (Babbie, 1992). Finally, the field experiment may be the only research option to use. For example, suppose a researcher is interested in examining patterns of communication at a television station before and after a change in management—a problem difficult if not impossible to simulate in a laboratory. The only practical option is to conduct the study in the field—that is, at the station.

DISADVANTAGES OF FIELD EXPERIMENTS

The disadvantages of the field experiment are mostly practical ones. However, some research is impossible to conduct because of ethical considerations. The vexing question of the effects of television violence on young viewers provides a good example of this problem. Probably the most informative study that could be performed in this area would be a field experiment in which one group of children is required to watch violent television programs and another, similar group to watch only nonviolent programs. The subjects could be carefully observed over a number of years to check for any significant difference in the number of aggressive acts committed by the members of each group. However, the ethics involved in controlling the television-viewing behavior of children and in possibly encouraging aggressive acts are extremely questionable. Therefore, scientists have resorted to laboratory and survey techniques to study this problem.

On a more practical level, field experiments often encounter external hindrances that cannot be anticipated. For example, a researcher may spend weeks planning a study to manipulate the media use of students in a summer camp, only to have camp counselors or a group of parents scuttle the project because they do not want the children used as "guinea pigs." Also, it takes time for researchers to establish contacts, secure cooperation, and gain necessary permissions before beginning a field experiment. In many cases this phase of the process may take weeks or months to complete.

Finally, and perhaps most important, researchers cannot control all the intervening variables in a field experiment. The presence of those extraneous variables affects the precision of the experiment and the confidence of the researchers in its outcome.

TYPES OF FIELD EXPERIMENTS

There are two basic categories of field experiments: those in which the researcher manipulates the independent variable(s) and those in which independent variable manipulation occurs naturally as a result of other circumstances. To illustrate the first type, suppose that a researcher is interested in investigating the effects of not being able to read a newspaper. A possible approach would be to select two comparable samples and not allow one of the samples to read any newspapers for a period of time; the second sample (the control group) would continue to read the newspaper as usual. A comparison could then be made to determine whether abstinence from newspapers has any effect in other areas of life, such as in interpersonal communication. In this example, reading the newspaper is the independent variable that has been manipulated.

The second type of field experiment involves passive manipulation of independent variables. Suppose a community with no cable television system is scheduled to be wired for cable in the future. In an attempt to gauge the effects of cable on television viewing and other media use, a researcher might begin studying a large sample of television set owners in the community long before the cable service is available. A few months after it is introduced, the researcher could return to the original sample, sort out the households that subscribed to cable and those that did not, and then determine the effects of the cable service. In this case, there is no control over the independent variable (cable service); the researcher is merely taking advantage of existing conditions.

Note that in some field experiments, the experimenter is not able to randomly assign subjects to treatment groups. As a result, many field experiments are classified as quasi-experiments. As Cook and Campbell (1979) point out, the extent to which causal statements can be made from the results of these studies depends upon the ability to rule out alternative explanations. Consequently, researchers who use field experiments must pay close attention to threats to internal validity.

EXAMPLES OF FIELD EXPERIMENTS

Tan (1977) was interested in what people would do during a week without television. He recruited a sample of 51 adults and paid them each $4 a day not to watch television for an entire week. Before depriving these subjects of television, Tan requested that they watch television normally for a 1-week period and keep a detailed diary of all their activities. At the start of the experimental week, Tan's assistants visited the subjects' homes and taped up the electrical plugs on their television sets to lessen temptation. Again, the subjects were requested to record their activities for the week. To maintain some control over the experiment, the assistants visited the subjects' homes periodically during the week to ensure that television was not being viewed.

One week later, the diaries completed during the week of deprivation were collected, and the data were compared to the week of normal television viewing. Tan discovered that, when deprived of television, subjects turned more to radio and newspapers for entertainment and information. They also tended to engage in more social activities with their friends and family.

This study illustrates some of the strengths and weaknesses of field experiments. In the first place, they probably represent the only viable technique available to investigate this particular topic. A survey (Chapter 7) does not permit the researcher to control whether the subjects watch television, and it would be impossible in the United States to select a representative sample composed of people who do not own a television set. Nor would it be feasible to bring people into the laboratory for an entire week of television deprivation.

On the other hand, the ability of the field experimenter to control independent variables is not conclusively demonstrated here: Tan had no way to be sure that his sample subjects actually avoided television for the entire week. Subjects could have watched at friends' homes or at local bars, or even at home by untaping the plugs. Moreover, Tan mentioned that several individuals who fell into the initial sample refused to go without television for only $4 per day. As a result, the nonprobability sample did not accurately reflect the general makeup of the community.

Smith and Hand (1987) took advantage of a natural occurrence in their field experiment on the effects of viewing pornography. One XXX-rated film was shown every year at the small college that served as the site of the research. About one third of all the male students on campus typically attend this film at its annual showing. One week before the film was shown, the investigators surveyed 230 women students of the college about their contact with aggression. The same measurement was taken on the Monday following the film and then again a week later. The researchers then analyzed the amount of violence experienced by females whose male companions had seen the film as compared to females whose male companions had not seen the film. The results showed that there were no differences in the amount of violence experienced by the two groups of females.

This study represents one of the few times that the effects of exposure to pornographic films have been studied experimentally outside of the laboratory. Nonetheless, the study suffers from some common limitations of field experiments. First, the researchers were unable to make random assignments of sample subjects. As a consequence, this study is more accurately described as a quasi-experiment. The males who went to the film may have been different from those who stayed away. Second, the researchers had no control over the content of the film that was shown. The actual film may have been too mild to elicit much aggression. Third, the researchers could not control how many females or which particular females had contact with males who attended the movie. They were able to find only 38 of 230 whose companions saw the film. These 38 might not be typical of the rest of the population.

Williams (1986) and her colleagues conducted an elaborate field experiment on the impact of television on a community. In 1973, she was able to identify a Canadian town that, because of its peculiar geographic location, was unable to receive television. This particular town, however, was due to acquire television service within a year. Given this lead time, the researchers could match the town with two others that were similar in population, area, income, transportation systems, education, and other variables. Residents of the three towns completed questionnaires that measured a large number of variables including aggressive behavior, personality traits, reading ability, creativity, sex-role perceptions, intelligence, and vocabulary.

Two years later, the research team went back to the three communities, and residents completed a posttest with questions that measured the same variables as before. The design

FIGURE 9.11	Design of Canadian Field Experiment	
Town	**Time one**	**Time two**
A	No TV reception	One TV channel
B	One TV channel	Two TV channels
C	Four TV channels	Four TV channels

of this field experiment is illustrated in Figure 9.11. Note that it is a variation of the quasi-experimental, pretest-posttest nonequivalent control group design discussed earlier.

This field experiment provided a wealth of data. Among other things, the researchers found that the arrival of TV apparently slowed down the acquisition of reading skills, lowered attendance at outside social events, fostered more stereotypical attitudes toward sex roles, and increased children's verbal and physical aggression.

Two rather ambitious field experiments were conducted by Milgram and Shotland (1973) with the cooperation of the CBS television network. The researchers arranged to have three versions of the popular television series "Medical Center" constructed. One version depicted antisocial behavior that was punished by a jail sentence; another portrayed antisocial behavior that went unpunished; and a third contained prosocial (favorable) behavior. The antisocial behavior consisted of scenes of a distraught young man smashing a plastic charity collection box and pocketing the money.

In the first experiment, the researchers used two methods to recruit subjects—ads placed in New York City newspapers promised a free transistor radio to anyone willing to view a 1-hour television show, and business reply cards containing the same message were passed out to pedestrians near several subway stops. Subjects were asked to report to a special television theater to view the program; upon arrival, each person was randomly assigned to one of four groups, and each group was shown a different program (the three programs described above plus a different nonviolent show used as a control). After viewing the program (with no commercial interruptions) and completing a short questionnaire about it, the subjects were instructed to go to an office in a downtown building to receive their free radio.

The downtown office, monitored by hidden cameras, was part of the experiment. The office contained a plastic charity collection box with about $5 in it; a notice informed the subjects that no more transistor radios were available. Their behavior on reading the notice was to be the dependent variable: How many would emulate the antisocial act seen in the program and take the money from the charity box? Milgram and Shotland found no differences in antisocial behavior among the viewers of each group; no one broke into the charity box.

The second study tried to gauge the immediate effects of televised antisocial acts on viewers. Subjects were recruited from the streets of New York City's Times Square area and ushered into a room with a color television set and a plastic charity collection box containing $4.45. A hidden camera monitored the subjects' behavior, even though they were told that they would not be observed. Although this time some subjects broke into the box, once again no differences emerged between the groups.

These two studies also demonstrate several positive and negative aspects of field experiments. In the first place, Milgram and Shotland had to secure the cooperation of CBS to conduct their expensive experiments. Second, volunteer subjects were used, and it is reasonable to assume that the sample was unrepresentative of the general population. Third, in the first experiment, the researchers did not control for the amount of time that passed between viewing the program and arriving at the testing center. Some participants arrived 24 hours after watching "Medical Center," while others

came several days later. Clearly, the subjects' experiences during this interval may have influenced their responses. Finally, Milgram and Shotland reported that the second experiment had to be terminated early because some of the subjects started resorting to behavior that the researchers could not control. On the positive side, the first experiment clearly shows the potential of the field experiment to simulate natural conditions and to provide a nonreactive setting. Upon leaving the theater after seeing the program, subjects had no reason to believe that they would be participating in another phase of the research. Consequently, their behavior at the supposed gift center was probably genuine and not a reaction to the experimental situation.

The Milgram and Shotland studies also raise the important question of ethics in field experiments. Subjects were observed without their knowledge and apparently were never told about the real purpose of the study, nor even that they were involved in a research study. Does the use of a hidden camera constitute an invasion of privacy? Does the experimental situation constitute entrapment? How about the subjects who stole the money from the charity box? Have they committed a crime? Field experiments can sometimes pose difficult ethical considerations, and these points must be dealt with *before the experiment is conducted*, not afterward, when harm may already have been inflicted on the subjects (see Chapter 18).

Two recent field experiments concerned the impact of media on politics. Donsbach, Brosius, and Mattenklott (1993) compared the perceptions of people who attended a political event in person and those who saw different versions of the same event on television. They concluded that participants in the event and those who saw the television coverage did not differ significantly in their perceptions of the event and the people involved. Those who watched the TV versions, however, were more likely to hold polarized opinions than those who had seen the event in person. Cappella and Jamieson (1994) conducted a field experiment that evaluated the effects of adwatches—analyses by some TV networks of misleading political ads during the 1992 presidential election. The researchers recruited subjects from 12 cities across the country and paid respondents $10 per day for participating in the study. A total of 165 individuals provided useful data. Six groups of respondents were given video tapes that contained several news items and different versions of an adwatch report. The number of exposures per group was also manipulated. One group received a tape that contained only the news reports. All respondents were instructed to view the tapes at home. After exposure, each participant was asked a number of questions about the tapes including information about the particular adwatch he or she had viewed. Results showed that exposure to the adwatches had an impact on the perceived fairness and importance of the ad.

This study is another illustration of the complexity that can be involved in a field experiment. The experimental tapes were constructed with the cooperation of CNN; each research location had to have a research coordinator on site; participants had to be paid for their efforts, and so forth. In addition, it also points out some of the difficulties in control and generalization. Respondents were volunteers; they might not be a representative sample of the total population. The researchers could not control exposure to other sources of political information. Some sensitization to the study's purpose might have occurred. All in all, field experiments can go a long way toward providing more external validity but there can be substantial efforts involved in carrying out the study.

SUMMARY

Mass media researchers have a number of research designs from which to choose when analyzing a given topic. The laboratory experiment has been a staple in mass media research for several decades. Although criticized by many researchers as being artificial, the method offers a number of advantages that make it particularly useful to some researchers. Of specific importance is the researcher's ability to control the experimental situation and to manipulate experimental treatments.

This chapter also described the process of experimental design—the researcher's blueprint for conducting an experiment. The experimental design provides the steps the researcher will follow to accept or reject a hypothesis or research question. Some experimental designs are simple and take very little time to perform; others involve many different groups and numerous treatments.

Quasi-experimental designs are used when random selection and random assignment of subjects are not possible. Field experiments take place in natural settings, which aids the generalizability of the results but also introduces problems of control.

QUESTIONS AND PROBLEMS FOR FURTHER INVESTIGATION

1. Provide four research questions or hypotheses for any mass media area. Which of the designs described in this chapter is best suited to investigate the problems?

2. What are the advantages and/or disadvantages of each of the following four experimental designs?

   a. X O_1
            O_2
   b. R   X O_1
   c. R O_1 X O_2
       R   X O_3
   d. R O_1 X O_2

3. A good example of the experimental technique as it relates to mass communication research is Ward's (1992) study of the effectiveness of sidebar graphics on reader comprehension that appears in the Summer 1992 issue of *Journalism Quarterly*. Read this study and note how the independent variable was manipulated.

4. What research questions are best answered by field experiments?

REFERENCES AND SUGGESTED READINGS

Babbie, E. R. (1992). *The practice of social research* (6th ed.). Belmont, CA: Wadsworth.

Baran, S. B., Mok, J. J., Land, M., & Kang, T. Y. (1989). You are what you buy. *Journal of Communication, 39*(2), 46–55.

Bruning, J. L., & Kintz, B. L. (1987). *Computational handbook of statistics.* Chicago: Scott, Foresman.

Campbell, D. T., & Stanley, J. C. (1963). *Experimental and quasi-experimental designs and research.* Skokie, IL: Rand McNally.

Capella, J., & Jamieson, K. (1994). Broadcast adwatch effects. *Communication Research, 21*(3), 342–365.

Cook, T. D., & Campbell, D. T. (1979). *Quasiexperimentation: Designs and analysis for field studies.* Skokie, IL: Rand McNally.

Cooper, R., Potter, W., & Dupagne, M. (1994). A status report on methods used in mass communication research. *Journalism Educator, 48*(4), 54–61.

Donsbach, W., Brosius, H., & Mattenklott, A. (1993). How unique is the perspective of television? A field experiment. *Political Communication, 10*(1), 37–53.

Gilbert, K., & Schleuder, J. (1990). Effects of color and complexity in still photographs on mental effort and memory. *Journalism Quarterly, 67*(4), 749–756.

Hansen, C., & Hansen, R. (1990, Dec.). Rock music videos and antisocial behavior. *Basic and Applied Social Psychology, 11*, 357–369.

Haskins, J. B. (1968). *How to evaluate mass communication.* New York: Advertising Research Foundation.

Haskins, J. B. (1981). A precise notational system for planning and analysis. *Evaluation Review, 5*(1), 33–50.

Himmelweit, H., Oppenheim, A. N., & Vince, P. (1958). *Television and the child.* London: Oxford University Press.

Hoyt, J. L. (1977). Courtroom coverage: The effects of being televised. *Journal of Broadcasting, 21*(41), 487–496.

Keppel, G. (1991). *Design and analysis: A researcher's handbook* (3rd ed.). Englewood Cliffs, NJ: Prentice-Hall.

McBurney, D. H. (1990). *Experimental psychology.* Belmont, CA: Wadsworth.

McBurney, D. H. (1994). *Research methods.* Pacific Grove, CA: Brooks/Cole.

Milgram, S., & Shotland, R. (1973). *Television and antisocial behavior.* New York: Academic Press.

Miller, D. C. (1991). *Handbook of research design and social measurement* (5th ed.). White Plains, NY: Longman.

Nunnally, J. C. (1978). *Psychometric theory* (2nd ed.). New York: McGraw-Hill.

Roscoe, J. T. (1975). *Fundamental research statistics for the behavioral sciences.* New York: Holt, Rinehart & Winston.

Rosenberg, M. J. (1965). When dissonance fails: On eliminating evaluation apprehension from attitude measurement. *Journal of Personality and Social Psychology, 1*, 28–42.

Rosenthal, R. (1976). *Experimenter effects in behavioral research* (2nd ed.). New York: Irvington.

Rosenthal, R., & Jacobson, L. (1966). Teacher's expectancies: Determinants of pupils' IQ gains. *Psychological Reports, 19*, 115–118.

Rosenthal, R., & Rosnow, R. L. (1969). *Artifact in behavioral research.* New York: Academic Press.

Saslow, C. (1994). *Basic research methods.* New York: McGraw-Hill.

Smith, M. D., & Hand, C. (1987). The pornography/aggression linkage: Results from a field study. *Deviant Behavior, 8*(4), 389–400.

Tan, A. S. (1977). Why TV is missed: A functional analysis. *Journal of Broadcasting, 21*, 371–380.

Walizer, M. H., & Wienir, P. L. (1978). *Research methods and analysis: Searching for relationships.* New York: Harper & Row.

Ward, D. (1992). The effectiveness of sidebar graphics. *Journalism Quarterly, 69*(2), 318–328.

Westley, B. H. (1989). The controlled experiment. In G. H. Stempel & B. H. Westley (Eds.), *Research methods in mass communication.* Englewood Cliffs, NJ: Prentice-Hall.

Williams, T. B. (1986). *The impact of television.* New York: Academic Press.

three

DATA ANALYSIS

10

INTRODUCTION TO STATISTICS

Statistics is the science that uses mathematical methods to collect, organize, summarize, and analyze data. Statistics cannot perform miracles. If a research question or hypothesis is misdirected, poorly phrased, or ambiguous, or if a study uses sloppy measurement and design and contains numerous errors, statistics alone will not help. Statistics provide valid and reliable results only when the data collection and research methods follow established scientific procedures.

The science of statistics and the ease with which they can be used has changed dramatically since the development of mini- and microcomputers. Only a few decades ago, researchers spent weeks or months generating statistical data by writing out calculations; those calculations now take only seconds or minutes.

Much of the groundwork for statistics was developed in 1835 by Lambert Adolphe Quetelet ('kay-tuh-lay), a Belgian mathematician and astronomer, with his paper titled *On Man and the Development of His Faculties*. In addition to other techniques, Quetelet developed the ideas behind the normal distribution and developed the basics of probability theory from preliminary work by French mathematician and physicist Pierre-Simon Laplace (la-'plas) and others. Quetelet's background is similar to others who were instrumental in the development of statistics. Almost all were renaissance men who were involved in such disciplines as astronomy, mathematics, physics, and philosophy.

Part III focuses on the statistical procedures used by mass media researchers. This chapter provides an introduction to descriptive statistics.

DESCRIPTIVE STATISTICS

Descriptive statistics are intended to reduce data sets to allow for easier interpretation. If you asked 100 people how long they listened to the radio yesterday and then randomly recorded all 100 answers on a sheet of paper, you would be hard pressed to draw conclusions from a simple examination of that paper. Data analysis would be easier if the data were organized in some fashion. In this regard, descriptive statistics are useful.

During the course of a research study, investigators typically collect data that are the results of measurements or observations of the people or items in the sample. These data usually have little meaning or usefulness until they are displayed or summarized using one of the techniques of descriptive statistics. Mass media researchers use two primary methods to make their data more manageable: data distribution and summary statistics.

DATA DISTRIBUTION

One way researchers can display their data is by distributing them in tables or graphs. A **distribution** is simply a collection of numbers. Table 10.1 shows a hypothetical distribution of 20 respondents' answers to the question, "How many hours did you spend last week listening to the radio and watching TV?" The distribution may look nice, but it would be difficult to draw any conclusions or make any generalizations from this collection of unordered scores.

As a preliminary step toward making these numbers more manageable, the data may be arranged in a **frequency distribution**—that

TABLE 10.1   Distribution of Responses to "How Many Hours Did You Spend Last Week Listening to the Radio and Watching TV?"

Respondent	Hours	Respondent	Hours
A	12	K	14
B	9	L	16
C	18	M	23
D	8	N	25
E	19	O	11
F	21	P	14
G	15	Q	12
H	8	R	19
I	11	S	21
J	6	T	11

TABLE 10.2   Frequency Distribution of Responses to "How Many Hours Did You Spend Last Week Listening to the Radio and Watching TV?"

Hours	Frequency ($N = 20$)
6	1
8	2
9	1
11	3
12	2
14	2
15	1
16	1
18	1
19	2
21	2
23	1
25	1

is, a table of each score, ordered according to magnitude, and its actual frequency of occurrence. Table 10.2 presents the data from the hypothetical radio/TV survey in a frequency distribution.

Now the data begin to show a pattern. Note that the typical frequency distribution table consists of two columns. The column on the left contains all the values of the variable under study; the column on the right shows the number of occurrences of each value. The sum of the frequency column is the number (N) of persons or items that make up the distribution.

A frequency distribution can also be constructed using grouped intervals, each of which contains several score levels. Table 10.3 shows the data from the hypothetical survey with the scores grouped together in intervals. This table is a more compact frequency distribution than Table 10.2, but the scores have lost their individual identity.

Other columns can be included in frequency distribution tables. For example, the data can be transformed into proportions or percentages. To obtain the percentage of a response, simply divide the frequency of the in-

dividual responses by N—the total number of responses in the distribution. Percentages allow comparisons to be made between different frequency distributions that are based on different values of N.

Some frequency distributions include the cumulative frequency (cf). This column is constructed by adding the number of scores in

TABLE 10.3   Frequency Distribution of Radio and TV Listening and Viewing Hours Grouped in Intervals

Hours	Frequency
0–10	4
11–15	8
16–20	4
21–25	4

TABLE 10.4   Frequency Distribution with Added Columns for Percentage, Cumulative Frequency, and Cumulative Frequency as a Percentage of N

Hours	Frequency	Percentage	cf	cf percentage of N
6	1	5	1	5
8	2	10	3	15
9	1	5	4	20
11	3	15	7	35
12	2	10	9	45
14	2	10	11	55
15	1	5	12	60
16	1	5	13	65
18	1	5	14	70
19	2	10	16	80
21	2	10	18	90
23	1	5	19	95
25	1	5	20	100
	$N = 20$	100%		

one interval to the number of scores in the intervals above it. Table 10.4 displays the frequency distribution from Table 10.2 with the addition of a percentage column, a cumulative frequency column, and a column showing cumulative frequency as a percentage of N.

Sometimes it is desirable to present data in graph form. The graphs shown on the following pages contain the same information as frequency distributions. Graphs usually consist of two perpendicular lines, the x-axis, or abscissa (horizontal), and the y-axis, or ordinate (vertical). Over the years, statisticians have developed certain conventions regarding graphic format. One common convention is to list the scores along the x-axis and the frequency or relative frequency along the y-axis. Thus, the height of a line or bar indicates the frequency of a score. One common form of graph is the **histogram**, or **bar chart**, in which frequencies are represented by vertical bars. Figure 10.1 is a histogram constructed from the data in Table 10.1. Note that the scores on the x-axis are ac-

tually the scores (hours) listed from the lowest value to the highest; the y-axis shows the frequency of scores.

If a line is drawn from the *midpoint* of each interval at its peak along the y-axis to each adjacent midpoint/peak, the resulting graph is called a **frequency polygon**. Figure 10.2 shows a frequency polygon superimposed onto the histogram from Figure 10.1. As can be seen, the two figures display the same information.

A **frequency curve** is similar to a frequency polygon except that points are connected by a continuous, unbroken curve instead of by lines. Such a curve assumes that any irregularities shown in a frequency polygon are simply due to chance and that the variable being studied is distributed continuously over the population. Figure 10.3 superimposes a frequency curve onto the frequency polygon shown in Figure 10.2.

Frequency curves are described in relation to the **normal curve**, a symmetrical bell curve whose properties are discussed more fully later

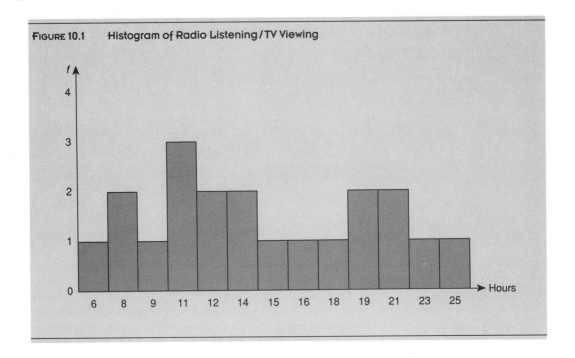

FIGURE 10.1   Histogram of Radio Listening/TV Viewing

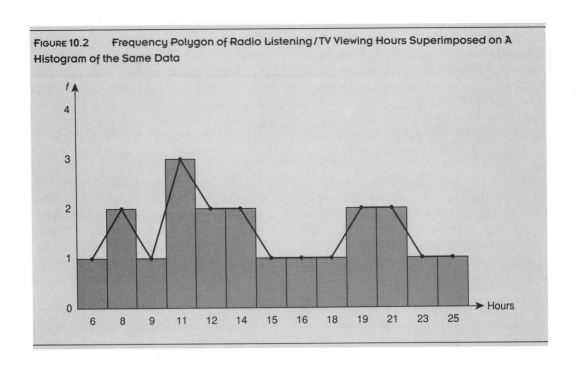

FIGURE 10.2   Frequency Polygon of Radio Listening/TV Viewing Hours Superimposed on A Histogram of the Same Data

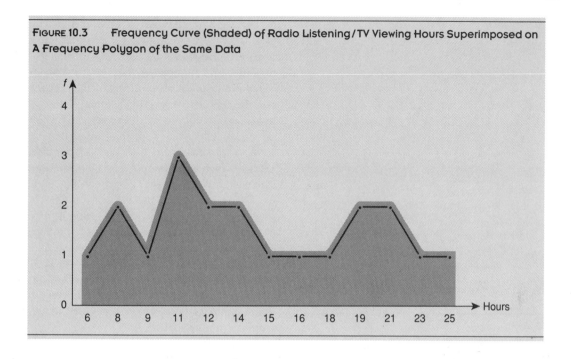

FIGURE 10.3   Frequency Curve (Shaded) of Radio Listening/TV Viewing Hours Superimposed on A Frequency Polygon of the Same Data

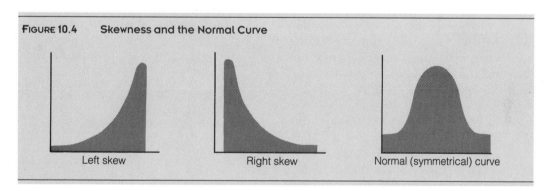

FIGURE 10.4   Skewness and the Normal Curve

Left skew   Right skew   Normal (symmetrical) curve

in this chapter. Figure 10.4 illustrates the normal curve and shows the ways in which a frequency curve can deviate from it. These patterns of deviation are called skewness.

Skewness refers to the concentration of scores around a particular point on the *x*-axis. If this concentration lies toward the low end of the scale, with the tail of the curve trailing off to the right, the curve is called a *right skew*.

Conversely, if the tail of the curve trails off to the left, it is a *left skew*. If the halves of the curve are identical, it is *symmetrical,* or normal.

A normal distribution of data is free from skewness. If data produce a curve that deviates substantially from the normal curve, the data may have to be transformed in some way (discussed later in this chapter) to achieve a more normal distribution.

TABLE 10.5 The Mode as a Potentially Misleading Statistic	
Score	f
70	2
35–69	0
34	1
33	1
32	1
31	1
30	1
29	1
28	1
27	1
26	1

SUMMARY STATISTICS

The data in Table 10.1 (page 208) can be condensed still further through the use of **summary statistics**. These statistics help make data more manageable by measuring two basic tendencies of distributions: central tendency and dispersion, or variability.

Central tendency statistics answer the question, What is a typical score? They provide information about the grouping of the numbers in a distribution by calculating a single number that is characteristic of the entire distribution. Exactly what constitutes a "typical" score depends on the level of measurement and the purpose for which the data will be used.

For every distribution, three types of characteristic numbers can be identified. One is the **mode (Mo)**, or the score or scores occurring most frequently. Calculation is not necessary to determine the mode; it is found by inspecting the distribution. For the data in Table 10.1, the mode is 11. Although easy to determine, the mode has some serious drawbacks as a descriptive statistic. It focuses attention on only one possible score and can thus camouflage impor-

tant facts about the data when considered in isolation. This is illustrated by the data in Table 10.5: The mode is 70, but the most striking feature about the numbers is the way they cluster around 30. Another serious drawback is that a distribution of scores can have more than one mode. When this happens, the mode does not provide an effective way of analyzing data.

A second characteristic score is the **median (Mdn)**, which is the midpoint of a distribution: Half the scores lie above it, and half lie below it. If the distribution has an odd number of scores, the median is the middle score; if there is an even number, the median is a hypothetical score halfway between the two middle scores. To determine the median, one must order the scores from smallest to largest and locate the midpoint by inspection. (The median in the sample data is 14.) Consider another example with nine scores:

0　2　2　5　⑥　17　18　19　67

The median score is 6, since there are four scores above this number and four below it. Now consider these numbers:

0　2　2　5　6　17　18　19　67　75
↑
11.5

No score neatly bisects this distribution; to determine the median, the two middle scores must be added and divided by 2:

$$\text{Mdn} = \frac{6 + 17}{2} = 11.5$$

When many scores in the distribution are the same, computing the median becomes more complicated. See *Statistics for the Behavioral Sciences* by Jaccard and Becker (1990) for a detailed description on how to compute the median when there are duplications of middle scores.

The third type of central tendency statistic is the **mean**. The mean is probably the most familiar summary statistic; it represents the average of a set of scores. Mathematically speaking, the mean is defined as the sum of all scores divided by N, or the total number of scores. Since the mean is widely used in both descriptive statistics and inferential statistics, it is described here in greater detail.

As a first step, some basic statistical notation is required:

X = any score in a series of scores
$\bar{X}$ = the mean (read "X-bar"; M is also commonly used to denote the mean)
Σ = the sum (symbol is Greek capital letter **sigma**)
N = the total number of scores in a distribution

Using these symbols, the formula for the calculation of the mean is

$$\bar{X} = \frac{\Sigma X}{N}$$

This equation indicates that the mean is the sum of all scores (ΣX) divided by the number of scores (N). Using the data in Table 10.1, the mean is

$$\bar{X} = \frac{293}{20}$$
$$= 14.65$$

If the data are contained in a frequency distribution, a slightly different formula is used to calculate the mean:

$$\bar{X} = \frac{\Sigma fX}{N}$$

In this case X represents the midpoint of any given interval, and f is the frequency of that interval. Table 10.6 uses this formula to calcu-

TABLE 10.6   Calculation of Mean from Frequency Distribution

Hours	Frequency	fx
6	1	6
8	2	16
9	1	9
11	3	33
12	2	24
14	2	28
15	1	15
16	1	16
18	1	18
19	2	38
21	2	42
23	1	23
25	1	25
	$N = 20$	$\Sigma fX = 293$

$$\bar{X} = \frac{293}{20} = 14.65$$

late the mean of the frequency distribution in Table 10.2.

Unlike the mode and the median, the mean takes into account all the values in the distribution, making it especially sensitive to extreme scores or "outliers." Extreme scores draw the mean in their direction. For example, suppose Table 10.1 contained another response, from Respondent U, who reported 100 hours of radio and television use. The new mean would then be approximately 18.71, an increase of about 28% due to the addition of only one large number.

The mean may be thought of as the score that would be assigned to each individual or element if the total were to be evenly distributed among all members of the sample. It is also the only measure of central tendency that can be defined algebraically. As will be seen later, this allows the mean to be used in a wide

TABLE 10.7	Calculation of Variance: X = Score		
X	$\bar{X}$	$X - \bar{X}$	$(X - \bar{X})^2$
6	14.65	−8.65	74.8
8	14.65	−6.65	44.2
8	14.65	−6.65	44.2
9	14.65	−5.65	31.9
11	14.65	−3.65	13.3
11	14.65	−3.65	13.3
11	14.65	−3.65	13.3
12	14.65	−2.65	7.0
12	14.65	−2.65	7.0
14	14.65	−0.65	0.4
14	14.65	−0.65	0.4
15	14.65	0.35	0.1
16	14.65	1.35	1.8
18	14.65	3.35	11.2
19	14.65	4.35	18.9
19	14.65	4.35	18.9
21	14.65	6.35	40.3
21	14.65	6.35	40.3
23	14.65	8.35	69.7
25	14.65	10.35	107.1
			558

$$S^2 = \frac{\Sigma(X - \bar{X})^2}{N - 1} = \frac{558}{19} = 29.4$$

Second, the purpose of the statistic is important. If the ultimate goal is to describe a set of data, the measure that is most typical of the distribution should be used. To illustrate, suppose the scores on a statistics exam were 100, 100, 100, 100, 0, and 0. To say that the mean grade was 67 does not accurately portray the distribution; the mode would provide a more characteristic description.

The second type of descriptive statistics is used to measure **dispersion**, or variation. Measures of central tendency determine the typical score of a distribution; dispersion measures describe the way in which the scores are spread out about this central point. Dispersion measures can be particularly valuable when comparing different distributions. For example, suppose the average grades for two classes in research methods are the same; however, one class has several excellent students and many poor students, while the other class has students who are all about average. A measure of dispersion must be used to reflect this difference. In many cases, an adequate description of a data set can be achieved by simply reporting a measure of central tendency (usually the mean) and an index of dispersion.

There are three measures of dispersion, or variation: range, variance, and standard deviation (some statisticians include a fourth measure—sum of squares). The simplest measure, **range** (R), is the difference between the highest and lowest scores in a distribution of scores. The formula used to calculate the range is

$$R = X_{hi} - X_{lo}$$

where X_{hi} = the highest score and X_{lo} = the lowest score. The range is sometimes reported simply as "the range among scores was 40."

Since the range uses only two scores out of the entire distribution, it is not particularly descriptive of the data set. Additionally, the range often increases with sample size, since larger samples tend to include more extreme values. For these reasons, the range is seldom used in

range of situations. It also suggests that the data used to calculate the mean should be at the interval or ratio level (Chapter 3).

Two factors must be considered when deciding which of the three measures of central tendency to report for a given set of data. First, the level of measurement used may determine the choice: If the data are at the nominal level, only the mode is meaningful; with ordinal data, either the mode or the median may be used. All three measures are appropriate for interval and ratio data, however, and it may be desirable to report more than one.

mass media research as the sole measure of dispersion.

A second measure, **variance**, provides a mathematical index of the degree to which scores deviate from, or are at variance with, the mean. A small variance indicates that most of the scores in the distribution lie fairly close to the mean; a large variance represents scores that are widely scattered. Thus, variance is directly proportional to the degree of dispersion.

To compute the variance of a distribution, the mean is first subtracted from each score; these *deviation scores* are then squared, and the squares are summed and divided by $N - 1$. The formula for variance (usually symbolized as S^2, although many textbooks use a different notation) is

$$S^2 = \frac{\Sigma(X - \bar{X})^2}{N - 1}$$

(In many texts, the expression $(X - \bar{X})^2$ is symbolized by x^2.) The numerator in this formula, $\Sigma(X - \bar{X})^2$, is called the *sum of squares*. Although this quantity is usually not reported as a descriptive statistic, the sum of squares is used in the calculation of several other statistics. An example using this variance formula is found in Table 10.7.

This equation may not be the most convenient formula for calculating variance, especially if N is large. A simpler, equivalent formula is

$$S^2 = \frac{\Sigma X^2}{N - 1} - \bar{X}^2$$

The expression X^2 means to square each score and sum the squared scores. (Note that this is not the same as $\Sigma(X)^2$, which means to sum all the scores and then square the sum.)

Variance is a commonly used and highly valuable measure of dispersion. In fact, it is at the heart of one powerful technique, analysis of variance (Chapter 12), which is widely used in inferential statistics. However, variance does

have one minor inconvenience: It is expressed in terms of squared deviations from the mean rather than in terms of the original measurements. To obtain a measure of dispersion that is calibrated in the same units as the original data, it is necessary to take the square root of the variance. This quantity, called the **standard deviation**, is the third type of dispersion measure. The standard deviation is a more meaningful term than variance since it is expressed in the same units as the measurement involved to compute it.

To illustrate, assume that a research project involves a question on household income that produces a variance of $90,000—interpreted as 90,000 "squared dollars." Because the concept of "squared dollars" is confusing to work with, a researcher would probably choose to report the standard deviation: 300 "regular dollars" ($300 = \sqrt{90,000}$). Usually symbolized as S (or SD), standard deviation is computed using either of the formulas shown below:

$$S = \sqrt{\frac{\Sigma(X - \bar{X})^2}{N - 1}}$$

$$S = \sqrt{\frac{\Sigma X^2}{N - 1} - \bar{X}^2}$$

Note that these two equations correspond to the respective variance formulas described above. Standard deviation represents a given distance of the scores from the mean of a distribution. This figure is especially helpful in describing the results of standardized tests. For example, modern intelligence tests are constructed to yield a mean of 100 and a standard deviation of 15. A person with a score of 115 falls 1 standard deviation above the mean; a person with a score of 85 falls 1 standard deviation below the mean.

The notions of variance and standard deviation are easier to understand if they are

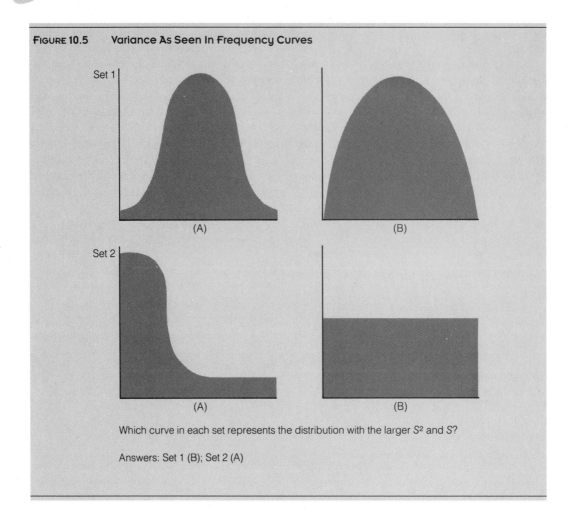

FIGURE 10.5   Variance As Seen In Frequency Curves

Set 1

(A)   (B)

Set 2

(A)   (B)

Which curve in each set represents the distribution with the larger S^2 and S?

Answers: Set 1 (B); Set 2 (A)

visualized. Figure 10.5 contains two sets of frequency curves. Which curve in each set would have the larger S^2 and S?

By determining the mean and standard deviation of a set of scores or measurements, it is possible to compute **standard scores** (*z scores*) for any distribution of data. Standard scores allow comparison of scores or measurements obtained from totally different methods—"apple and orange" comparisons. This is possible because all standard score computations are based on the same metric; they all have a mean of 0 and a standard deviation of 1.

Standard scores are easy to compute and interpret. The formula for computing standard scores is simply the score minus the mean, divided by the standard deviation:

$$z = \frac{X - \overline{X}}{S}$$

Interpretation is easy because each score simply represents how many standard deviation units an entity is above or below the mean.

The computation of standard scores and the ability to compare different measurements or methods can be demonstrated by a brief example. Suppose that two roommates are in different sections of a media research course. On a particular day, the two sections are given different exams, and both students score 73. However, the first roommate receives a letter grade of C, and the second roommate receives an A. How can this be? To understand how the professors arrived at the different grades, it is necessary to look at each section's standard scores.

Table 10.8 shows the hypothetical data for the two research sections. Each section contains 20 students. Scores in the first roommate's section range from a low of 68 to a high of 84 (range = 16), whereas the scores in the second roommate's section range from a low of 38 to a high of 73 (range = 35). The differences in scores can be due to a variety of things including the difficulty of the tests, the ability of students in each section, and the teaching approach used by the professors.

The mean score in the first roommate's section is 74.6, with a standard deviation of 4.9 (43.9 and 7.5, respectively, in the other section). Assuming that the professors strictly followed the normal curve (discussed later in the chapter), it is easy to see why a score of 73 can result in different grades. The first roommate's performance is about average in comparison to the other students in the section; the second roommate is clearly above the performance of the other students.

Note: The distribution of scores in each section is not normal (discussed later). In reality, the professors might transform (change to a different metric) the scores to produce a more normal distribution, or they might set grade cut-offs at other scores to spread the grades out.

When any collection of raw scores is transformed into z scores, the resulting distribution possesses certain characteristics. Any score below the mean becomes a negative z score, and any score above the mean is positive. The mean of a distribution of z scores is 0, which is also the z score assigned to a person whose raw score equals the mean. As mentioned, the variance and the standard deviation of a z-score distribution are both 1.00. (The mean is 0.) Standard scores are expressed in units of the standard deviation; thus, a z score of 3.00 means that the score is 3 standard deviation units above the mean.

Standard scores are used frequently in all types of research because they allow researchers to directly compare the performance of different subjects on tests using different measurements (assuming the distributions have similar shapes). Assume for a moment that the apple harvest for a certain year was 24 bushels per acre, compared to an average annual yield of 22 bushels per acre, with a standard deviation of 10. During the same year, the orange crop yielded 18 bushels per acre, compared to an average of 16 bushels, with a standard deviation of 8. Was it a better year for apples or oranges? The standard score formula reveals a z score of .20 for apples [(24 − 22)/10] and .25 for oranges [(18 − 16)/8]. Relatively speaking, oranges had a better year.

THE NORMAL CURVE

An important tool in statistical analysis is the normal curve, which was briefly introduced in Chapter 4. Standard scores not only enable comparisons to be made between dissimilar measurements, but, when used in connection with the normal curve, they also allow statements to be made regarding the frequency of occurrence of certain variables. Figure 10.6 shows an example of the familiar normal curve. The curve is symmetrical and achieves maximum height at its mean, which is also its median and its mode. Also note that the curve in Figure 10.6 is calibrated in standard score units. When the curve is expressed in this way, it is called a *standard normal curve* and possesses all the properties of a z-score distribution.

Statisticians have studied the normal curve closely to describe its properties. The most

TABLE 10.8   z-Score Hypothetical Data

	First Roommate's Section			Second Roommate's Section			
	Scores	(Computation)	z Score	Scores	(Computation)	z Score	
B grade	84	(84−74.6)/4.9 =	1.9	73	(73−43.9)/7.5 =	3.9	A grade
	81	(81−74.6)/4.9 =	1.3				
	81	(81−74.6)/4.9 =	1.3	50	(50−43.9)/7.5 =	.8	
				50	(50−43.9)/7.5 =	.8	
C grade	79	(79−74.6)/4.9 =	.9	47	(47−43.9)/7.5 =	.4	
	79	(79−74.6)/4.9 =	.9	46	(46−43.9)/7.5 =	.3	
	79	(79−74.6)/4.9 =	.9	45	(45−43.9)/7.5 =	.2	
	78	(78−74.6)/4.9 =	.7	43	(43−43.9)/7.5 =	−.1	
	77	(77−74.6)/4.9 =	.5	43	(43−43.9)/7.5 =	−.1	
	77	(77−74.6)/4.9 =	.5	42	(42−43.9)/7.5 =	−.2	
	75	(75−74.6)/4.9 =	.1	41	(41−43.9)/7.5 =	−.4	C grade
	73	(73−74.6)/4.9 =	−.3	41	(41−43.9)/7.5 =	−.4	
	71	(71−74.6)/4.9 =	−.7	41	(41−43.9)/7.5 =	−.4	
	71	(71−74.6)/4.9 =	−.7	40	(40−43.9)/7.5 =	−.5	
	71	(71−74.6)/4.9 =	−.7	40	(40−43.9)/7.5 =	−.5	
	70	(70−74.6)/4.9 =	−.9	40	(40−43.9)/7.5 =	−.5	
	70	(70−74.6)/4.9 =	−.9	40	(40−43.9)/7.5 =	−.5	
	70	(70−74.6)/4.9 =	−.9	40	(40−43.9)/7.5 =	−.5	
				39	(39−43.9)/7.5 =	−.6	
D grade	69	(69−74.6)/4.9 =	−1.1	38	(38−43.9)/7.5 =	−.8	
	68	(68−74.6)/4.9 =	−1.3	38	(38−43.9)/7.5 =	−.8	
	68	(68−74.6)/4.9 =	−1.3				

Mean 74.6
S 4.9

Mean 43.9
S 7.5

Note: The distribution of scores in each section is not normal (discussed later). In reality, the professors might transform the scores to produce a more normal distribution, or they might set grade cut-offs at other scores to spread the grades out.

important of these is the fact that a fixed proportion of the area below the curve lies between the mean and any unit of standard deviation. The area under a certain segment of the curve is representative of the frequency of the scores that fall therein. From Figure 10.7, which portrays the areas contained under the normal curve between several key standard deviation units, it can be determined that roughly 68% of the total area, hence of the scores, lies within the +1 and −1 standard deviations from the mean; about 95% lies within the +2 and −2

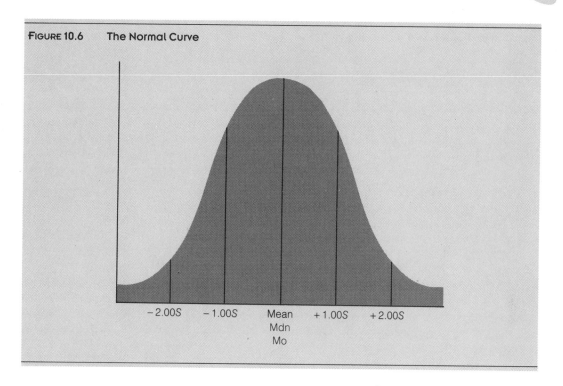

FIGURE 10.6   The Normal Curve

$-2.00S$ $-1.00S$ Mean Mdn Mo $+1.00S$ $+2.00S$

standard deviations, and so forth. This knowledge, together with the presence of a normal distribution, allows researchers to make useful predictive statements. For example, suppose that television viewing is normally distributed with a mean of 2 hours per day and a standard deviation of 0.5 hour. What proportion of the population watches between 2 and 2.5 hours of TV? First, the raw scores are changed to standard scores:

$$\frac{2-2}{0.5} = 0 \quad \text{and} \quad \frac{2.5-2}{0.5} = 1.00$$

Figure 10.7 shows that approximately 34% of the area below the curve is contained between the mean and 1 standard deviation. Thus, 34% of the population watches between 2 and 2.5 hours of television daily.

The same data can be used to find the proportion of the population that watches more than 3 hours of television per day. Again, the first step is to translate the raw figures into z scores. In this case, 3 hours corresponds to a z score of 2.00. A glance at Figure 10.7 shows that approximately 98% of the area under the curve falls below a score of 2.00 (50% in the left half of the curve plus about 48% from the mean to the 2.00 mark). Thus, only 2% of the population views more than 3 hours of television daily.

Table 3 in Appendix 1 contains all the areas under the normal curve between the mean of the curve and some specified distance. To use this table, we match the row and the column represented by some standard score. For example, let us assume that the standard score of a normally distributed variable is 1.79. In Table 3, first find the row labeled 1.7. Next find the column labeled .09. At the intersection of the 1.7 row and .09 column is the number .4633. The area between the mean of the curve (the

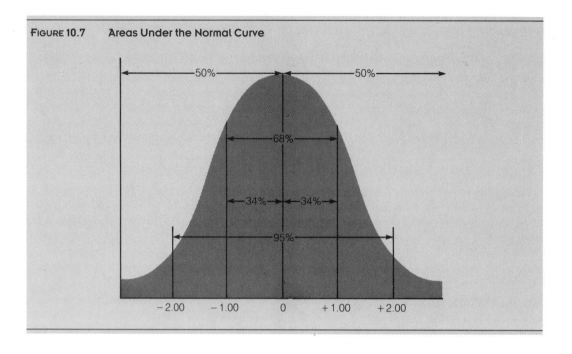

FIGURE 10.7   Areas Under the Normal Curve

midpoint) and a standard score of 1.79 is .4633, or roughly 46%. To take another example, what is the distance from the midpoint of the curve to the standard score of ±1.32? According to Table 3, 40.66% of the curve lies between these two values. Note that the area is always positive even though the standard score was expressed as a negative value.

To make this exercise more meaningful, let us go back to our example of the two roommates. Assume that the scores were normally distributed in the class that had a mean of 72 and a standard deviation of 5.0. The instructor decided to assign *C*s to 50% of the class. What numerical scores would receive these grades? To begin, remember that "50% of the grades" actually means "25% above the mean and 25% below the mean." What standard deviation unit corresponds to this distance? To answer this question, it is necessary to reverse the process performed above. Specifically, the first thing that we must do is examine the *body* of Table 3 in Appendix 1 for the value .2500. Unfortu-

nately, it does not appear. There are, however, two numbers bracketing it, .2486 and .2517. Since .2486 is a little closer to .2500, let's use it as our area. Examining the row and column that intersect at .2486, we find that it corresponds to 0.67 standard deviation unit. Now we can quickly calculate the scores that receive *C*s. First we find the upper limit of the *C* range by taking the mean (72) and adding it to .067 × 5, or 3.35. This yields 75.35, which represents the quarter of the area above the mean. To find the lower limit of the range, we take the mean (72) and subtract from it 0.67 × 5, or 72 − 3.35. This gives us 68.65. After rounding, we find that all students who scored 69–75 would receive the *C* grade.

The normal curve is important because many of the variables encountered by mass media researchers are distributed in a normal manner, or normally enough that minor departures can be overlooked. Furthermore, the normal curve is an example of a probability distribution that becomes important in inferential statistics. Finally, many of the more advanced statistics discussed in later chapters assume normal distribution of the variable(s) under consideration.

SAMPLE DISTRIBUTION

A **sample distribution** is the distribution of some characteristic measured on the individuals or other units of analysis that were part of a sample. If a random sample of 1,500 college students were asked how many movies they attended in the last month, the resulting distribution of the variable "number of movies attended" would be a sample distribution, with a mean ($\overline{X}$) and variance (S^2). It is theoretically possible (though not practical) to ask the same question of every college student in the United States. This would create a **population distribution** with a mean (μ) and a variance (σ^2). Ordinarily, the precise shape of the population distribution and the values of μ and σ^2 are unknown and are estimated from the sample. This estimate is called a **sampling distribution.**

In any sample drawn from a specified population, the mean of the sample, X, will probably differ somewhat from the population mean, μ. For example, suppose that the average number of movies seen by each college student in the United States during the past month was exactly 3.8. It is unlikely that a random sample of 10 students from this population would produce a mean of exactly 3.8. The amount that the sample mean differs from μ is called *sampling error* (Chapter 4). If more random samples of 10 were selected from this population,

the values calculated for X that are close to the population mean would become more numerous than the values of X that are greatly different from μ. If this process were duplicated an infinite number of times and each mean placed on a frequency curve, the curve would form a sampling distribution.

Once the sampling distribution has been identified, statements about the *probability* of occurrence of certain values are possible. There are many ways to define the concept of probability. Stated simply, the probability that an event will occur is equal to the relative frequency of occurrence of that event in the population under consideration (Roscoe, 1975). To illustrate, suppose a large urn contains 1,000 table tennis balls, of which 700 are red and 300 white. The probability of drawing a red ball at random is 700/1,000, or 70%. It is also possible to calculate probability when the relative frequency of occurrence of an event is determined theoretically. For example, what is the probability of randomly guessing the answer to a true/false question? One out of two, or 50%. What is the probability of guessing the right answer on a four-item multiple-choice question? One out of four, or 25%. Probabilities can range from zero (no chance) to one (a sure thing). The sum of all the probable events in a population must equal 1.00, which is also the sum of the probabilities that an event will and will not occur. For instance, when a coin is tossed, the probability of it landing face up ("heads") is .50, and the probability of it not landing face up ("tails") is .50 (.50 + .50 = 1.00).

There are two important rules of probability. The "addition rule" states that the proba-

Characteristic	Sample statistic	Population parameter
Average	$\overline{X}$ (or M)	μ (mu)
Variance	S^2	σ^2 (sigma squared)
Standard deviation	S (or SD)	σ (sigma)

bility that any one of a set of mutually exclusive events will occur is the sum of the probabilities of the separate events. (Two events are mutually exclusive if the occurrence of one precludes the other. In the table tennis ball example, the color of the ball is either red or white; it cannot be both.) To illustrate the addition rule, consider a population in which 20% of the people read no magazines per month, 40% read only one, 20% read two, 10% read three, and 10% read four. What is the probability of selecting at random a person who reads at least two magazines per month? The answer is .40 (.20 + .10 + .10), the sum of the probabilities of the separate events.

The "multiplication rule" states that the probability of a combination of independent events occurring is the product of the separate probabilities of the events. (Two events are independent when the occurrence of one has no effect on the other. For example, getting "tails" on a flip of a coin has no impact on the next flip.) To illustrate the multiplication rule, calculate the probability that an unprepared student will correctly guess the right answers to the first four questions on a true/false test. The answer is the product of the probabilities of each event: .5 (chance of guessing right on Question 1) × .5 (chance of guessing right on Question 2) × .5 (chance of guessing right on Question 3) × .5 (chance of guessing right on Question 4) = .0625.

The notion of probability is important in inferential statistics because sampling distributions are a type of probability distribution. When the concept of probability is understood, a formal definition of "sampling distribution" is possible. A sampling distribution is *a probability distribution of all possible values of a statistic that would occur if all possible samples of a fixed size from a given population were taken.* For each outcome, the sampling distribution determines the probability of occurrence. For example, assume that a population consists of six college students. Their film viewing for the last month was as follows:

Student	Number of films seen
A	1
B	2
C	3
D	3
E	4
F	5

$$\mu = \frac{1 + 2 + 3 + 3 + 4 + 5}{6} = 3.00$$

Suppose a study is made using a sample of two ($N = 2$) from this population. As is evident, there is a limit to the number of combinations that can be generated, assuming that sampling is done without replacement. Table 10.9 shows the possible outcomes.

The mean of this sampling distribution is equal to μ, the mean of the population. The likelihood of drawing a sample whose mean is 2.0 or 1.5 or any other value is found simply by reading the figure in the far right-hand column.

Table 10.9 is an example of a sampling distribution determined by empirical means. Many sampling distributions, however, are not derived by mathematical calculations but are determined theoretically. For example, sampling distributions often take the form of a normal curve. When this is the case, the researcher can make use of everything that is known about the properties of the normal curve. This can be illustrated by a hypothetical example using dichotomous data (data with only two possible values). (This type of data is chosen because it makes the mathematics less complicated. The same logic applies to continuous data, but the computations are elaborate.) Consider the case of a television rating firm attempting to estimate from the results of a sample the total number of people in the population who saw a given program. One sample of 100 people might produce an estimate of 40%, a second an estimate of 42%, and a third an estimate of 39%. If, after a large number of

TABLE 10.9   Generating a Sampling Distribution Population = (1,2,3,3,4,5) N = 2

$\overline{X}$	Number of possible sample combinations producing this $\overline{X}$	Probability of occurrence
1.5	2 (1,2) (2,1)	2/30 or .07
2.0	4 (1,3) (1,3) (3,1) (3,1)	4/30 or .13
2.5	6 (1,4) (2,3) (2,3) (3,2) (3,2) (4,1)	6/30 or .20
3.0	6 (1,5) (2,4) (3,3) (3,3) (4,2) (5,1)	6/30 or .20
3.5	6 (2,5) (3,4) (3,4) (4,3) (4,3) (5,2)	6/30 or .20
4.0	4 (3,5) (3,5) (5,3) (5,3)	4/30 or .13
4.5	2 (4,5) (5,4)	2/30 or .07
		1.00

Total number of possible sample combinations = 30

samples have been taken, the results are expressed as a sampling distribution, probability theory predicts that it would have the shape of the normal curve with a mean equal to μ. This distribution is shown in Figure 10.8. Interestingly, if a person draws samples of size N repeatedly from a given population, the sampling distribution of the means of these samples, assuming N is large enough, will almost always be normal. This holds even if the population itself is not normally distributed. Furthermore, the mean of the sampling distribution will equal the population mean—the parameter.

In earlier discussions of the normal curve, the horizontal divisions along the base of the curve were expressed in terms of standard deviation units. With sampling distributions, this unit is called the *standard error of the mean (SE)* and serves as a criterion for determining the probable accuracy of an estimate. As is the case with the normal curve, roughly 68% of the sample will fall within ±1 standard error of the population mean, and about 95% will fall within ±2 standard errors.

In most actual research studies, a sampling distribution is not generated by taking large numbers of samples and computing the probable outcome of each, and the standard error is not computed by taking the standard deviation of a sampling distribution of means. Instead, a researcher takes only one sample and uses it to estimate the population mean and the standard error. The process of inference from only one sample works in the following way: The sample mean is used as the best estimate of the population mean, and the standard error is calculated from the sample data. Suppose that in the foregoing example, 40 of a sample of 100 people were watching a particular program. The mean, in this case symbolized as *p* because the data are dichotomous, is 40% (dichotomous data require this unique formula). The formula for standard error in a dichotomous situation is calculated as

$$SE = \sqrt{\frac{pq}{N}}$$

where *p* = the proportion viewing, *q* = 1−*p*, and N = the number in the sample. In the example, the standard error is

FIGURE 10.8   Hypothetical Sampling Distribution

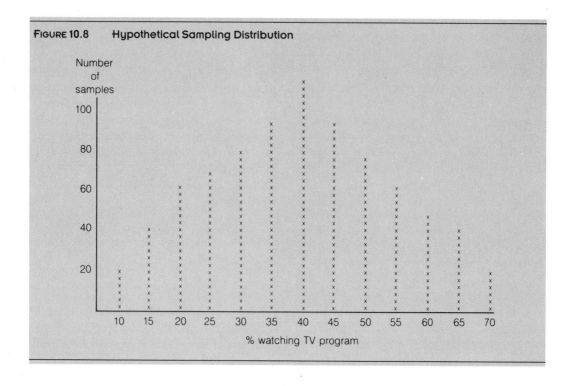

$$\sqrt{\frac{(.4)\,(.6)}{100}} = \sqrt{\frac{.24}{100}} = .048, \text{ or } 4.8\%$$

Standard error is used in conjunction with the **confidence interval** (CI) set by the researcher. Recall from Chapter 4 that a confidence interval establishes an interval in which researchers state, with a certain degree of probability, that the statistical result found will fall within. Using the previous example, this means that at the 68% confidence interval, 68% of all possible samples taken will fall within the interval of 35.2 (40 − 4.8) and 44.8 (40 + 4.8), and at the 95% confidence level, 95% of all samples will fall between 30.4 (40 − 9.6) and 49.6 (40 + 9.6).

The most commonly used confidence level is .95, which is expressed by the following formula:

$$.95CI = p \pm 1.96SE$$

where p is the proportion obtained in the sample, SE is the standard error, and 1.96 is the specific value to use for encompassing exactly 95% of the scores in a normal distribution.

As an example, consider that a television ratings firm sampled 400 people and found that 20% of the sample was watching a certain program. What is the .95 confidence interval estimate for the population mean? The standard error is equal to the square root of [(.20)(.80)]/400, or .02. Inserting this value into the formula above yields a confidence interval of .20 ± (1.96) (.02), or .16 − .24. In other words there is a .95 chance that the population average lies between 16% and 24%. There is also a 5% chance of error—that is, that μ lies outside this interval. If this 5% chance is too great a risk, it is possible to compute a .99 confidence interval estimate by substituting 2.58 for 2 in the formula. (In the normal curve, 99% of all scores fall within ± 2.58 standard errors of the mean.) For a discussion of confidence intervals using continuous data, the reader should consult Hays (1973).

The concept of sampling distribution is important to statistical inference. Confidence intervals represent only one way in which sampling distributions are used in inferential statistics. They are also important in *hypothesis testing*, where the probability of a specified sample result is determined under assumed population conditions (Chapter 11).

DATA TRANSFORMATION

Most statistical procedures are based on the assumption that the data are normally distributed. Although many statistical procedures are "robust," or conservative, in their requirement of normally distributed data, in some instances the results of studies using data that show a high degree of skewness may be invalid. The data used for any study should be checked for normality, a procedure accomplished very easily with most computer programs (Chapter 17).

Most nonnormal distributions are caused by outliers. When such anomalies arise, researchers can attempt to transform the data to try to achieve normality. Basically, transformation involves performing some type of mathematical adjustment to *each score* to try to bring the outliers closer to the group mean. This may take the form of multiplying or dividing each score by a certain number, or even taking the square root or log of the scores. It makes no difference what procedure is used (though some methods are more powerful than others), as long as the same method is used for all the data.

There is a variety of transformation methods from which to choose, depending on the type of distribution found in the data. Rummel (1970) describes these procedures in more detail.

SUMMARY

This chapter has introduced some of the more common descriptive and inferential statistics used by mass media researchers. Little attempt has been made to explain the mathematical derivations of the formulas and principles presented; rather, the emphasis here (as throughout the book) has been on understanding the reasoning behind these statistics and their applications. Unless researchers understand the logic underlying such concepts as mean, standard deviation, and standard error, the statistics themselves will be of little value.

QUESTIONS AND PROBLEMS FOR FURTHER INVESTIGATION

1. Find the mean, the variance, and the standard deviation for the following sets of data (answers appear at the end of the exercise):

   Group 1 5, 5, 5, 6, 7, 5, 4, 8, 4, 5, 8, 8, 7, 6, 3, 3, 2, 5, 4, 7
   Group 2 19, 21, 22, 27, 16, 15, 18, 24, 26, 24, 22, 27, 16, 15, 18, 21, 20

2. From a regular deck of playing cards, what is the probability of randomly drawing an ace? An ace *or* a nine? A spade *or* a face card?

3. Assume that scores on the Mass Media History Test are normally distributed in the population with a μ of 50 and a population standard deviation of 5. What is the probability that
   a. Someone picked at random will have a score between 50 and 55?
   b. Someone picked at random will score 2 standard deviations above the mean?
   c. Someone picked at random will have a score of 58 or higher?

4. Assume that a population of scores consists of the following: 2, 4, 5, 5, 7, and 9. Generate the sampling distribution of the mean if $N = 2$ (sampling without replacement).

Answers to Question 1:
   Group 1 $\overline{X} = 5.35, S^2 = 3.08, S = 1.76$
   Group 2 $\overline{X} = 20.6, S^2 = 16.2, S = 4.0$

REFERENCES AND SUGGESTED READINGS

Blalock, H. M. (1972). *Social statistics.* New York: McGraw-Hill.

Champion, D. J. (1981). *Basic statistics for social research.* (2nd ed.). New York: Macmillan.

Hays, W. L. (1973). *Statistics for the social sciences.* New York: Holt, Rinehart & Winston.

Jaccard, J., & Becker, M. A. (1990). *Statistics for the behavioral sciences.* Belmont, CA: Wadsworth.

Lehmann, E. L. (1991). *Testing statistical hypotheses* (2nd ed.). Belmont, CA: Wadsworth.

Nunnally, J. (1994). *Psychometric theory* (3rd ed.). New York: McGraw-Hill.

Rasmussen, S. (1992). *An introduction to statistics with data analysis.* Pacific Grove, CA: Brooks/Cole Publishing Company.

Roscoe, J. T. (1975). *Fundamental research statistics for the behavioral sciences.* New York: Holt, Rinehart & Winston.

Rummel, R. J. (1970). *Factor analysis.* Chicago: Northwestern University Press.

Siegel, S. (1988). *Nonparametric statistics for the behavioral sciences.* New York: McGraw-Hill.

Williams, F. (1992). *Reasoning with statistics* (2nd ed.). New York: Holt, Rinehart & Winston.

11

HYPOTHESIS TESTING

Scientists rarely begin a research study without a problem or a question to test. This would be similar to holding a cross-country race without telling the runners where to start. Both events need an initial step: The cross-country race needs a starting line, and the research study needs a question or statement to test. This chapter describes the procedures for developing research questions and the steps involved in testing them. (See the writings of John W. Tukey on the topics of exploratory and confirmatory research.)

RESEARCH QUESTIONS AND HYPOTHESES

Mass media researchers use a variety of approaches to answer questions. Some research is informal and seeks to solve relatively simple problems; some is based on theory and requires formally worded questions. All researchers, however, must start with some tentative generalization regarding a relationship between two or more variables. These generalizations may take two forms: *research questions* and *statistical hypotheses*. The two are identical except for the aspect of prediction—hypotheses predict an experimental outcome; research questions do not.

RESEARCH QUESTIONS

Researchers often use research questions in problem- or policy-oriented studies when they are not specifically interested in testing the statistical significance of their findings. For instance, researchers analyzing television program preferences or newspaper circulation would probably be concerned only with discovering general indications, not with gathering data for statistical testing. However, research questions can be tested for statistical significance. They are not merely weak hypotheses; they are valuable tools for many types of research.

Research questions are frequently used in areas that have been studied only marginally or not at all. Studies of this nature are classified as *exploratory research* because researchers have no idea what may be found. They do not have enough prior information to make predictions. Exploratory research is intended to search for data *indications* rather than to attempt to find *causality* (Tukey, 1962, 1986). The goal is to gather preliminary data, to be able to refine research questions, and possibly to develop hypotheses.

Research questions may be stated as simple questions about the relationship between two or more variables, or about the components of a phenomenon. As Tukey (1986) states, exploratory research responds to the question: What appears to be going on? For example, researchers might ask, "How do high-technology firms perceive and use advertising?" (Traynor & Traynor, 1989) or "How do television and radio programs influence children's creativity as measured by a standardized test?" (Runco & Pezdek, 1984). Slater and Thompson (1984) posed several research questions about the attitudes of parents concerning warning statements that precede some television shows: "Do parents indicate that they frequently see the warning statements?" "Do the warnings influence parents' decisions about the suitability of a program for their child's viewing?" "Do parents advocate the imposition of a movie-type rating system for TV programs?"

RESEARCH HYPOTHESES

In countless situations, researchers develop studies on the basis of existing theory and are thus able to make predictions about the outcome of the work. Tukey (1986) says that hypotheses ask, Do we have firm evidence that such-and-such is happening (has happened)? Brody (1984) hypothesized that access to the diverse offerings of cable television would produce a decline in borrowing books from the library. His data revealed support for this hypothesis in one cable market but not in another. Milliman, Fugate, and Rahim (1991, p. 53) investigated the advertising of legal services and tested the following three hypotheses:

- The level of price disclosure in advertising legal services on the radio will influence the public's perception of the legal services advertiser.
- The use (or nonuse) of a free first consultation in advertising legal services on the radio will influence the consuming public's perception of the legal services advertiser.
- The interaction between the different levels of price disclosure and the free consultation offer used in the advertisements tested in this experiment will influence the consumers' perceptions of legal services advertisers.

The authors found that advertisements including free consultation or price mentions were considered the least credible.

To facilitate the discussion of research testing, the remainder of this chapter uses only the word *hypothesis*. But recall that research questions and hypotheses are identical except for the absence of the element of prediction in the former.

PURPOSE OF HYPOTHESES

Hypotheses offer researchers a variety of benefits. First, they *provide direction* for a study. As indicated at the opening of the chapter, research begun without hypotheses offers no starting point; there is no indication of the sequence of steps to follow. Hypothesis development is usually the culmination of a rigorous literature review and emerges as a natural step in the research process. Without hypotheses, research would lack focus and clarity.

A second benefit of hypotheses is that they *eliminate trial-and-error research*—that is, the haphazard investigation of a topic in the hope of finding something significant. Hypothesis development requires researchers to isolate a specific area for study. Trial-and-error research is time-consuming and wasteful. The development of hypotheses eliminates this waste.

Hypotheses also *help rule out intervening and confounding variables*. Since hypotheses focus research to precise testable statements, other variables, whether relevant or not, are excluded. For instance, researchers interested in determining how the media are used to provide consumer information must develop a specific hypothesis stating what media are included, what products are being tested for what specific demographic groups, and so on. Through this process of narrowing, extraneous and intervening variables are eliminated or controlled. This does not mean that hypotheses eliminate all error in research; nothing can do that. Error in some form is present in every study (Chapter 4).

Finally, hypotheses *allow for quantification of variables*. As stated in Chapter 3, any concept or phenomenon is capable of quantification if it is put into an adequate operational definition. All terms used in hypotheses must have an operational definition. For example, to test the hypothesis, "There is a significant difference between recall of television commercials for subjects exposed to low-frequency broadcasts and that for subjects exposed to high-frequency

---

Purpose of Hypotheses

- Provide direction for a study
- Eliminate trial-and-error research
- Help rule out intervening and confounding variables
- Allow for quantification of variables

---

broadcasts," researchers would need operational definitions of *recall, low-frequency,* and *high-frequency.* Words incapable of quantification cannot be included in a hypothesis.

In addition, some concepts have a variety of definitions. One example of this is *violence.* The complaint of many researchers is not that violence cannot be quantified, but rather that it can be operationally defined in more than one way. Therefore, before comparing the results of studies of media violence, it is necessary to consider the definition of *violence* used in each study. Contradictory results may be due to the definitions used, not to the presence or absence of violence.

CRITERIA FOR GOOD HYPOTHESES

A useful hypothesis should possess at least four essential characteristics: It should be compatible with current knowledge in the area; it should follow logical consistency; it should be stated concisely; and it should be testable.

That hypotheses must be in harmony with current knowledge is obvious. If available literature strongly suggests one point of view, researchers who develop hypotheses that oppose this knowledge without basis only slow the development of the area. For example, it has been demonstrated beyond a doubt that most people obtain their news from television. It would be rather wasteful for a researcher to develop a hypothesis suggesting that this is not true. There is simply too much evidence to the contrary.

The criterion of logical consistency means that if a hypothesis suggests that $A = B$ and $B = C$, then A must also equal C. That is, if reading the *New York Times* implies a knowledge of current events, and a knowledge of current events means greater participation in social activities, then readers of the *New York Times* should exhibit greater participation in social activities. (Logical consistency relates to the concept of Aristotle's notion of an enthymeme, which produces such pop culture "logical consistencies" as: God is Love/Love is blind/Stevie Wonder is God.)

It should come as no surprise that hypotheses must be stated as succinctly as possible. A hypothesis such as "Intellectual and psychomotor creativity possessed by an individual positively coincides with the level of intelligence of the individual as indicated by standardized evaluative procedures measuring intelligence," is not exactly concise. Stated simply, the same hypothesis could read, "Psychomotor ability and IQ are positively related."

Most researchers would agree that developing an untestable hypothesis is unproductive. But there is a fine line between what is and what is not testable. The authors agree that untestable hypotheses will probably create a great deal of frustration, and the information collected and tested will probably add nothing to the development of knowledge. However, the situation here is similar to some teachers who say (and really mean) on the first day of class, "Don't ever be afraid to ask me a question because you think it's stupid. The only stupid question is the one that is not asked."

The authors consider hypothesis development in the same fashion. It is much better to form an untestable hypothesis than none at all. The developmental process itself is a valuable experience, and researchers will no doubt soon find their error. The untestable ("stupid") hypothesis may eventually become a respectable research project. The suggestion here is not to try to develop untestable hypotheses, but rather to accept the fact when it happens, correct it,

Criteria for Good Hypotheses
• Compatible with current knowledge
• Logically consistent
• Succinct
• Testable

and move on. Beginning researchers should not try to solve the problems of the world. Take small steps.

What are some unrealistic and/or untestable hypotheses? Read the list of hypotheses below (some relate to areas other than mass media) and determine what is wrong with each one. Feldman (1987) was used in preparing some of these statements.

1. Watching too many soap operas on television creates antisocial behavior.
2. Clocks run clockwise because most people are right-handed.
3. High school students with no exposure to television earn higher grades than those who watch television.
4. Students who give apples to teachers tend to earn higher grades.
5. People who read newspapers wash their hands more frequently than those who do not read newspapers.
6. Movies rated XXX are 10 times worse than movies rated XX, and 20 times worse than movies rated X.
7. College students who cut classes have more deceased relatives than students who attend classes.
8. Einstein's theory of relativity would not have been developed if he had access to television.
9. Sales of Fords in America would be higher if Lexus did not exist.
10. World opinion of the United States would be different if Richard Nixon had never been the president.

THE NULL HYPOTHESIS

The **null hypothesis** (also called the "hypothesis of no difference") asserts that the statistical differences or relationships being analyzed are due to chance or random error. The null hypothesis (H_0) is the logical alternative to the research hypothesis (H_1). For example, the hypothesis "The level of attention paid to radio commercials is positively related to the amount of recall of the commercial," has its logical alternative (null hypothesis): "The level of attention paid to radio commercials is *not* related to the amount of recall of the commercial."

In practice, researchers rarely state the null hypothesis. Since every research hypothesis does have its logical alternative, stating the null form is redundant (Williams, 1979). However, the null hypothesis is always present and plays an important role in the rationale underlying hypothesis testing.

TESTING HYPOTHESES FOR STATISTICAL SIGNIFICANCE

In hypothesis testing, or significance testing, the researcher either rejects or accepts the null hypothesis. That is, if H_0 is accepted (supported), it is assumed that H_1 is rejected; and if H_0 is rejected, H_1 must be accepted.

To determine the statistical significance of a research study, the researcher must set a **probability level**, or significance level, against which the null hypothesis is tested. If the results of the study indicate a probability lower than this level, the researcher can reject the null hypothesis. If the research outcome has a high probability, the researcher must support (or, more precisely, fail to reject) the null hypothesis. In reality, since the null hypothesis is not generally stated, acceptance and rejection apply to the research hypothesis, not to the null hypothesis.

The probability level is expressed by a lowercase letter p (indicating probability), followed by a "less than" or "less than or equal to" sign, and then a value. For example, "$p \leq .01$" means that the null hypothesis is being tested at the .01 level of significance and that the results will be considered statistically significant if the probability is equal to or lower than this level. A .05 level of significance indicates that the researcher has a 5% chance of making a wrong decision about rejecting the null hypothesis (or accepting the research hypothesis). Establishing a level of significance depends on the amount of error researchers are willing to accept (in addition to other factors peculiar to the particular research study). The question of error is discussed in greater detail later in the chapter.

It is common practice in mass media research studies to set the probability level at .01 or .05, which means that either one or five times out of 100, the results of the study are based on random error or chance. There is no logical reason for using these figures; the practice has been followed for many years, because Sir Ronald A. Fisher, who developed the concept of significance testing, formulated tables based on the areas under the normal curve defined by these points. In many research areas, however, the researchers set the significance level according to the purpose of the study rather than by general convention. Some studies use .10 or .20, depending on the goals of the research. In exploratory research especially, more liberal levels are generally used; these are made more restrictive as further information is gathered.

In a theoretical sampling distribution, the proportion of the area in which the null hypothesis is rejected is called the **region of rejection**. This area is defined by the level of significance chosen by the researcher. If the .05 level of significance is used, then 5% of the sampling distribution becomes the critical region. Conversely, the null hypothesis is retained in the region between the two rejection values (or levels).

As Figure 11.1 shows, the regions of rejection are located in the *tails*, or outer edges, of

the sampling distribution. The terms *one-tail testing* and *two-tail testing* refer to the type of prediction made in a research study. A one-tail test predicts that the results will fall in only one direction—either positive or negative. This approach is more stringent than the two-tail test, which does not predict a direction. Two-tail tests are generally used when little information is available about the research area. One-tail tests are used when researchers have more knowledge of the area and are able to more accurately predict the outcome of the study.

Consider, for example, a study of the math competency of a group of subjects who receive a special type of learning treatment, possibly a series of television programs on mathematics. The hypothesis is that the group, after viewing the programs, will have scores on a standardized math test significantly different from those of the remainder of the population, which has not seen the programs. The level of significance is set at .05, indicating that for the null hypothesis to be rejected, the mean test score of the sample must fall outside the boundaries in the normal distribution that are specified by the statement, "$p \leq .05$." These boundaries, or values, are determined by a simple computation. First, the critical values of the boundaries are found by consulting the normal distribution table (see Appendix 1, Table 3).

In Figure 11.1, the area from the middle of the distribution, or μ, the hypothesized mean (denoted by a dotted line) to the end of the tails is 50%. At the .05 level, using a two-tail test, there is a 2.5% (.0250) area of rejection tucked into each tail. Consequently, the area from the middle of the distribution to the region of rejection is equal to 47.5% (50% − 2.5% = 47.5%). It follows that the corresponding z values that will define the region of rejection are those that cut off 47.5% (.4750) of the area from μ to each end of the tail. To find this z value, use Table 3 of Appendix 1 (Areas Under the Normal Curve). This table provides a list of the proportions of various areas under the curve as measured from the midpoint of the curve out toward the tails. The far left column

---

FIGURE 11.1   Regions of Rejection for $p \leq .05$ (Two-Tail)

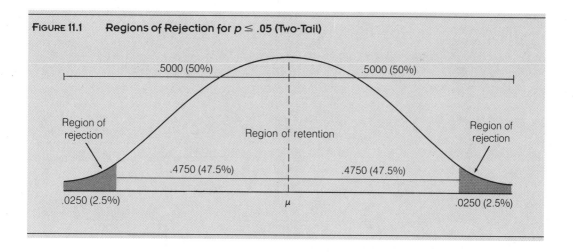

.5000 (50%)   .5000 (50%)

Region of
rejection   Region of retention   Region of
rejection

.4750 (47.5%)   .4750 (47.5%)

.0250 (2.5%)   μ   .0250 (2.5%)

---

displays the first two digits of the z value. The row across the top of the table contains the third digit. For example, find the 1.0 row in the left-hand column. Next, find the entry under the .08 column in this row. The table entry is .3599. This means that 35.99% of the curve is found between the midpoint and a z value of 1.08. Of course, another 35.99% lies in the other direction, from the midpoint to a z value of −1.08. In our current example, it is necessary to work backwards. We know the areas under the curve that we want to define (.4750 to the left and right of μ) and need to find the z values. An examination of the body of Table 3 shows that .4750 corresponds to a z value of ±1.96.

These values are then used to determine the region of rejection:

$$-1.96\,\alpha_m + \mu = \text{lower boundary}$$
$$+1.96\,\alpha_m + \mu = \text{upper boundary}$$

where α_m = the standard deviation of the distribution and μ = the population mean. Assume that the population mean for math competency is 100 and the standard deviation is 15. Thus, the sample must achieve a mean math competency score either lower than 70.60 or higher than 129.40 for the research study to be considered significant:

$$-1.96(15) + 100 = 70.60$$
$$+1.96(15) + 100 = 129.40$$

If a research study produces a result between 70.60 and 129.40, the null hypothesis cannot be rejected; the instructional television programs had no significant effect on math levels. Using the normal distribution to demonstrate these boundaries, the area of rejection is illustrated in Figure 11.2.

ERROR

As with all steps in the research process, testing for statistical significance involves error. Two types of error particularly relevant to hypothesis testing are called **Type I error** and **Type II error**. Type I error is the rejection of a null hypothesis that should be accepted, and Type II error is the acceptance of a null hypothesis that should be rejected. These error types are represented in Figure 11.3.

The probability of making a Type I error is equal to the established level of significance and is therefore under the direct control of the researcher. That is, to reduce the probability of Type I error, the researcher can simply set the level of significance closer to zero.

Type II error, often signified by the symbol β, is a bit more difficult to conceptualize. The

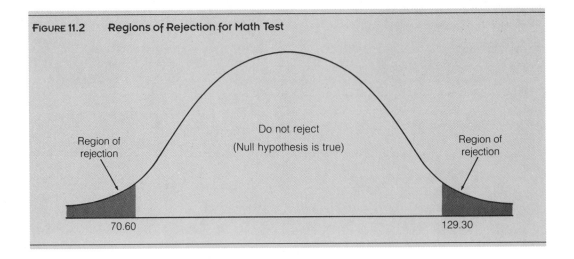

FIGURE 11.2   Regions of Rejection for Math Test

Do not reject
(Null hypothesis is true)

Region of
rejection

Region of
rejection

70.60

129.30

researcher does not have direct control over Type II error; instead, Type II error is controlled, though indirectly, by the design of the experiment. In addition, the level of Type II error is inversely proportional to the level of Type I error: As Type I error decreases, Type II error increases, and vice versa. The potential magnitude of Type II error depends in part on the probability level and in part on which of the possible alternative hypotheses actually is true. Figure 11.4 shows the inverse relationship between the two types of error.

As mentioned earlier, most research studies do not state the null hypothesis, since it is generally assumed. There is a way to depict Type I and Type II errors without considering the null hypothesis, however, and this approach may help to demonstrate the relationship between Type I and Type II errors.

As Figure 11.5 demonstrates, the research hypothesis is used to describe Type I and Type II errors instead of the null hypothesis. To use the table, start at the desired row on the left side and then read the column entry that completes the hypothesis to be tested. For example, "Significant difference found where none exists = Type I error."

One final way to explain Type I and Type II errors is by using a hypothetical example. Con-

sider a research study to determine the effects of a short-term public relations campaign promoting the use of safety belts in automobiles. Suppose that the effort was highly successful and indeed changed the behavior of a majority of subjects exposed to the campaign. (This information is of course unknown to the researcher.) If the researcher finds that a significant effect was created by the campaign, the conclusion is a correct one; if the researcher does not find a significant effect, a Type II error is committed. On the other hand, if the campaign actually had no effect but the researcher concludes that the campaign was successful, a Type I error is committed.

THE IMPORTANCE OF SIGNIFICANCE

The concept of significance testing causes problems for many people, primarily because too many researchers overemphasize the importance of significance. When researchers find that the results of a study are nonsignificant, it is common to "talk around" the results—to deemphasize the finding that the results were not significant. But there is really no need to follow this course of action.

There is no difference in value between a study that finds statistically significant results

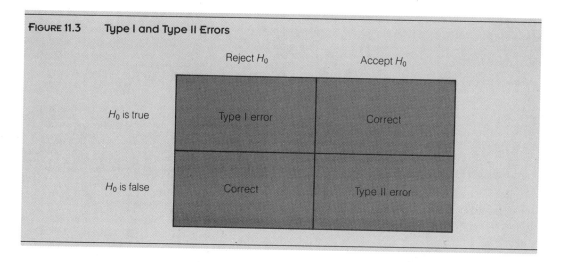

FIGURE 11.3   Type I and Type II Errors

	Reject H_0	Accept H_0
H_0 is true	Type I error	Correct
H_0 is false	Correct	Type II error

and a study that does not. Both studies provide valuable information. Discovering that some variables are not significant is just as important as determining which variables are significant. The nonsignificant study can save time for other researchers working in the same area by ruling out worthless variables. Nonsignificant research is important in collecting information about a theory or concept.

Also, there is nothing wrong with the idea of proposing a null hypothesis as the research hypothesis. For example, a researcher could formulate the following hypothesis: "There is no significant difference in comprehension of program content between a group of adults (age 18–49) with normal hearing that views a television program with closed-captioned phrases and a similar group that views the

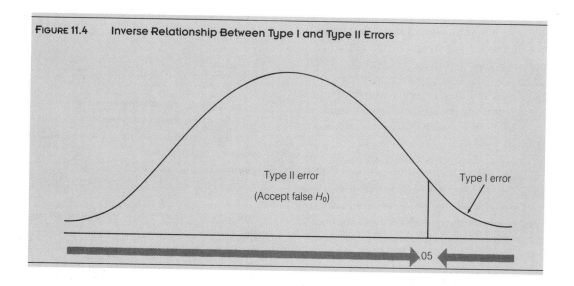

FIGURE 11.4   Inverse Relationship Between Type I and Type II Errors

Type II error
(Accept false H_0)

Type I error

.05

FIGURE 11.5   Use of the Research Hypothesis to Distinguish Between Type I and Type II Errors

	Where one exists	Where none exists
Significant difference found	Correct	Type I error
No significant difference found	Type II error	Correct

---

same program without captions." A scientific research study does not always have to test for significant relationships; it can also test for non-significance. However, sloppy research techniques and faulty measurement procedures can add to error variance in a study and contribute to the failure to reject a hypothesis of no difference as well as jeopardize the entire study. This is a danger in using a null hypothesis as a substantive hypothesis.

POWER

The concept of **power** is intimately related to Type I and Type II errors. Power refers to the probability of rejecting the null hypothesis when it is true. In other words, power indicates the probability that a statistical test of a null hypothesis will result in the conclusion that the phenomenon under study actually exists (Cohen, 1969).

Statistical power is a function of three parameters: probability level, sample size, and effects size. As we know, the *probability level* is under the direct control of the researcher and predetermines the probability of committing a Type I error. *Sample size* refers to the number of subjects used in an experiment. The most

difficult concept is the *effects size*. Basically, the effects size is the degree to which the null hypothesis is rejected; this can be stated either in general terms (such as *any* nonzero value) or in exact terms (such as .40). That is, when a null hypothesis is false, it is false to some degree; researchers can say the null hypothesis is false and leave it at that, or they can specify exactly how false it is. The larger the effects size, the greater the degree to which the phenomenon under study is present (Cohen, 1969). However, researchers seldom know the exact value of the effects size. When such precision is lacking, researchers can use one of three alternatives:

1. Estimate the effects size, based on knowledge in the area of investigation or indications from previous studies in the area, or simply state the size as "small," "medium," or "large." (Cohen describes these values in greater detail.)
2. Assume an effects size of "medium."
3. Select a series of effects sizes and experiment.

When the probability level, sample size, and effects size are known, researchers can consult power tables (published in statistics books) to determine the level of power present in their study. Power tables consist of sets of curves representing different sample sizes, levels of significance (.05 and so on), and types of tests (one- or two-tail). For example, in a two-tail test with a probability of .05 and sample of 10, the probability of rejecting the null hypothesis (that is, assume that it is false) is .37 (Type I error), and the probability of accepting or retaining the hypothesis is .63 (Type II error). The power tables show that by increasing the sample size to 20, the probability of rejecting the null hypothesis jumps to .62 and the probability of retaining the hypothesis drops to .38.

A determination of power is important for two reasons. First and most important, if a low power level prevents researchers from arriving at statistical significance, a Type II error may result. If the power of the statistical test is increased, however, the results may be made significant.

Second, the high power level may help in interpreting the research results. If an experiment just barely reaches the significance level but has high power, researchers can place more faith in the results. Without power figures, the researchers would have to be more hesitant in their interpretations.

Considerations of statistical power should be a step in all research studies. Although power is only an approximation, computation of the value helps control Type II error. In addition, as power increases, there is no direct effect on Type I error; power acts independently of Type I error. Since the mid-1970s, researchers have paid closer attention to statistical power.

Chase and Tucker (1975) conducted power analyses on articles published in nine communications journals. The authors found that 82% of the 46 articles analyzed had an average power for medium effects of less than .80 (the recommended minimum power value). In addition, more than half the articles had an average power of less than .50, which suggests a significant increase in the probability of Type II error.

SUMMARY

Hypothesis development in scientific research is important because the process refines and focuses the research by excluding extraneous variables and permitting variables to be quantified. Rarely will researchers conduct a project without developing some type of research question or hypothesis. Research without this focus usually proves to be a waste of time (though some people may argue that many inventions, theories, and new information have been found without the focus provided by a research question or hypothesis).

An applicable hypothesis must be compatible with current related knowledge, and it must be logically consistent. It should also be stated as simply as possible, and, generally speaking, it should be testable. Hypotheses must be tested for statistical significance. This testing involves error, particularly Type I and Type II error. Error must be considered in all research. An understanding of error such as Type I and Type II will not make research foolproof, but it will make the process somewhat easier because researchers must pay closer attention to the elements involved in the project.

Too much emphasis is often placed on significance testing. It is possible that a nonsignificant test may add information to an available body of knowledge simply by finding what "does not work" or "should not be investigated." However, some nonsignificant research projects may be more valuable if the statistical power is analyzed.

QUESTIONS AND PROBLEMS FOR FURTHER INVESTIGATION

1. Develop three research questions and three hypotheses in any mass media area that could be investigated or tested.

2. What is your opinion about using very conservative levels of significance (.10 or greater) in exploratory research?

3. Conduct a brief review of published research in mass media. What percentage of the studies report the results of a power analysis calculation?

4. Explain the relationship between Type I errors and Type II errors.

5. Under what circumstances might a researcher use a probability level of .001?

6. If a researcher's significance level is set at ≤.02 and the results of the experiment indicate that the null hypothesis cannot be rejected, what is the probability of a Type I error?

REFERENCES AND SUGGESTED READINGS

Benze, J., & Declerq, E. (1985). Content of television spot ads for female candidates. *Journalism Quarterly, 62*(2), 278–283.

Brody, E. (1984). Impact of cable television on library borrowing. *Journalism Quarterly, 61*(3), 686–688.

Chase, L. J., & Tucker, R. K. (1975). A power-analytic examination of contemporary communication research. *Speech Monographs, 42,* 29–41.

Cohen, J. (1988). *Statistical power analysis for the behavioral sciences.* New York: Academic Press.

Doolittle, J. C. (1979). News media use by older adults. *Journalism Quarterly, 56*(2), 311–317.

Feldman, D. (1987). *Why do clocks run clockwise?* New York: Harper & Row.

Holly, S. (1979). Women in management of weeklies. *Journalism Quarterly, 56*(4), 810–815.

Joslyn, R. A. (1981). The impact of campaign spot advertising on voting decisions. *Human Communication Research, 7*(4), 347–360.

Milliman, R. E., Fugate, D. L., and Rahim, M. A. (1991). An empirical investigation into the advertising of legal services. *Journal of Advertising Research, 31*(5), 51–54.

Roscoe, J. T. (1975). *Fundamental research statistics for the behavioral sciences.* New York: Holt, Rinehart & Winston.

Runco, M., & Pezdek, K. (1984). The effects of TV and radio on children's creativity. *Human Communication Research, 11*(1), 109–120.

Ryan, M. (1979). Reports, inferences and judgments in news coverage of social issues. *Journalism Quarterly, 56*(3), 497–503.

Slater, D., & Thompson, T. (1984). Attitudes of parents concerning televised warning statements. *Journalism Quarterly, 61*(4), 853–859.

Traynor, K., & Traynor, S. (1989). High-tech advertising: A status report. *Journal of Advertising Research, 29*(4), 30–36.

Tukey, J. W. (1962). The future of data analysis. 1–67.

Tukey, J. W. (1986). *The collected works of John W. Tukey, Vols III and IV.* Belmont, CA: Wadsworth.

Williams, F. (1979). *Reasoning with statistics* (2nd ed.). New York: Holt, Rinehart & Winston.

Basic Statistical Procedures

Researchers often wish to do more than merely describe a sample; they want to use their results to make inferences about the population from which the sample has been taken. Tukey (1986), in his typically nonpresumptuous manner, identifies four purposes of statistics:

1. To aid in summarization.
2. To aid in "getting at what is going on"
3. To aid in extracting "information" from the data.
4. To aid in communication.

Keeping these four purposes in mind, this chapter describes some of the basic inferential statistical methods used in mass media research and suggests ways in which these methods may help answer questions.

HISTORY OF SMALL-SAMPLE STATISTICS

Samples were used in scientific research as long ago as 1627, when Sir Francis Bacon published an account of tests he had conducted measuring wheat seed growth in various forms of fertilizer. In 1763 Arthur Young began a series of experiments to discover the most profitable method of farming; and in 1849 James Johnston published a book called *Experimental Agriculture,* in which he provided advice on scientific research (Cochran, 1976).

One of the best-known investigators of the early 20th century was William S. Gossett, who in 1908 attempted to quantify experimental results in a paper entitled "The Probable Error of the Mean." Under the pen name "Student," Gossett published the results of small-sample

investigations he had conducted while working in a Dublin brewery. The t-distribution statistics Gossett developed were not widely accepted at the time; in fact, it was more than 15 years before other researchers began to take an interest in his work. The t-test, however, as will be seen, is now one of the most widely used statistical procedures in all areas of research.

Sir Ronald Fisher provided a stepping stone from early work in statistics and sampling procedures to modern statistical inference techniques. It was Fisher who developed the concept of probability and established the use of the .01 and .05 levels of probability testing (Chapter 11). Until Fisher, statistical methods were not generally perceived as practical in areas other than agriculture, for which they were originally developed.

NONPARAMETRIC STATISTICS

Statistical methods are commonly divided into two broad categories: **parametric** and **nonparametric**. Historically, researchers recognized three primary differences between parametric statistics and nonparametric statistics:

1. Nonparametric statistics are appropriate only with nominal and ordinal data. Parametric statistics are appropriate for interval and ratio data.
2. Nonparametric results cannot be generalized to the population. This is possible only with parametric statistics.
3. Nonparametric statistics make no assumption about normally distributed data, whereas parametric statistics assume normality. Nonparametric statistics are said to be "distribution-free."

For the most part, the distinctions in items 1 and 2 have vanished. Most researchers argue that both parametric statistics and nonparametric statistics can be used successfully with all types of data and that both are appropriate for generalizing results to the population. The authors of this text agree with this position.

CHI-SQUARE GOODNESS OF FIT

Mass media researchers often compare *observed* frequencies of a phenomenon with the frequencies that might be *expected* or hypothesized. For example, a researcher who wanted to determine whether the sales of television sets by four manufacturers in the current year are the same as sales for the previous year might advance the following hypothesis: "Television set sales of four major manufacturers are significantly different this year from those of the previous year."

Suppose the previous year's television set sales were distributed as follows:

Manufacturer	Percent of sales
RCA	22
Sony	36
JVC	19
Mitsubishi	23

From these previous sales, the investigator can calculate the expected frequencies (using a sample of 1,000) for each manufacturer's sales by multiplying the percentage of each company's sales by 1,000. The expected frequencies are

Manufacturer	Expected frequency
RCA	220
Sony	360
JVC	190
Mitsubishi	230

Next, the researcher surveys a random sample of 1,000 households known to have purchased one of the four manufacturers' television sets during the current year. Assume that the data from this survey provide the following information:

Manufacturer	Expected frequency	Observed frequency
RCA	220	180
Sony	360	330
JVC	190	220
Mitsubishi	230	270

The researcher now must interpret these data to determine whether the change in frequency is actually *significant*. This can be done by reducing the data to a **chi-square statistic** and performing a test known as the chi-square "goodness of fit" test.

A chi-square (χ^2) is simply a value showing the relationship between expected frequencies and observed frequencies. It is computed by the following formula:

$$\chi^2 = \Sigma \frac{(O_i - E_i)^2}{E_i}$$

where O_i = the observed frequencies and E_i = the expected frequencies. This means that the difference between each expected and observed frequency must be squared and then divided by the expected frequency. The sum of the quotients is the chi-square for those frequencies. For the frequency distribution above, chi-square is calculated as follows:

$$\chi^2 = \frac{(O_1 - E_1)^2}{E_1} + \frac{(O_2 - E_2)^2}{E_2} + \frac{(O_3 - E_3)^2}{E_3}$$
$$+ \frac{(O_4 - E_4)^2}{E_4}$$
$$= \frac{(180 - 220)^2}{220} + \frac{(330 - 360)^2}{360}$$
$$+ \frac{(220 - 190)^2}{190} + \frac{(270 - 230)^2}{230}$$
$$= \frac{(-40)^2}{220} + \frac{(-30)^2}{360} + \frac{(30)^2}{190} + \frac{(40)^2}{230}$$
$$= \frac{1,600}{220} + \frac{900}{360} + \frac{900}{190} + \frac{1,600}{230}$$
$$= 7.27 + 2.50 + 4.73 + 6.95$$
$$= 21.45$$

Once the value of chi-square is known, the goodness of fit test is conducted to determine whether this value represents a significant difference in frequencies. To do this, two values are necessary: the first is the probability level, which is predetermined by the researcher; the second, called *degrees of freedom (df)*, is the number of scores in any particular test that are free to vary in value. For example, if one has three unknown values (x, y, and z) such that $x + y + z = 10$, there are two degrees of freedom: Any two of the three variables may be assigned any value without affecting the total, but the value of the third will then be predetermined. Thus, if $x = 2$ and $y = 5$, z must be 3. In the goodness of fit test, degrees of freedom are expressed in terms of $K - 1$, where K is the number of categories. In the case of the television sales study, $K = 4$, and $df = 4 - 1 = 3$. Next, a chi-square significance table is consulted (Appendix 1, Table 4). These tables are arranged by probability level and degrees of freedom. A portion of the chi-square table relevant to the hypothetical study has been adapted here to show how the table is used:

	Probability			
df	.10	.05	.01	.001
1	2.706	3.841	6.635	10.827
2	4.605	5.991	9.210	13.815
3	6.251	7.815	11.345	16.266
4	7.779	9.488	13.277	18.467

If the calculated chi-square value equals or exceeds the value found in the table, the differences in observed frequencies are considered to be statistically significant at the predetermined alpha level; if the calculated value is smaller, the results are nonsignificant.

In the television sales example, suppose the researcher finds a chi-square value of 21.45,

with a degree of freedom of 3, and has established a probability level of .05. The chi-square table shows a value of 7.815 at this level when $df = 3$. Since 21.45 is greater than 7.815, the frequency difference is significant, and the hypothesis is accepted or supported: Television set sales of the four manufacturers are significantly different in the current year from sales in the previous year.

The chi-square goodness of fit test can be used in a variety of ways to measure changes—for example, in studies of audience perceptions of advertising messages over time, in planning changes in television programming, or in analyzing the results of public relations campaigns. Idsvoog and Hoyt (1977) used a chi-square test to analyze the professionalism and performance of television journalists. The authors attempted to determine whether "professionalism" was related to several other characteristics, including the desire to look for employment, educational level, and job satisfaction. The results indicated that journalists classified on the basis of questionnaire responses differed significantly from those classified as "medium" or "low" professionals.

There are limitations to the use of the goodness of fit test, however. Since this is a nonparametric statistical procedure, the variables must be measured at the nominal or ordinal level. The categories must be mutually exclusive, and each observation in each category must be independent from all others. Additionally, because the chi-square distribution is sharply skewed (Chapter 10) for small samples, Type II error may occur: Small samples may not produce significant results in cases that could have yielded significant results if a larger sample had been used. To avoid this problem, most researchers suggest that each category contain at least five observations. Other researchers suggest that 20% of the cells should have an expected frequency of at least 5, and none should have expected frequencies of 0.

As an alternative to the chi-square goodness of fit test, some researchers prefer the

Kolomogorov-Smirnov test, which is considered to be more powerful than the chi-square approach. In addition, a minimum number of expected frequencies in each cell is not required, as in the chi-square test. (See Winkler & Hays, 1975, for more information about the Kolomogorov-Smirnov test.)

CONTINGENCY TABLE ANALYSIS

Another nonparametric procedure often used in mass media research is the contingency table analysis, frequently called **cross-tabulation**, or, simply, **crosstabs**. Crosstab analysis is basically an extension of the goodness of fit test, the primary difference being that two or more variables can be tested simultaneously. Consider a study to determine the relationship between a person's gender and his or her media-usage habits in regard to obtaining information on new products. Suppose the researcher selects a random sample of 210 adults and obtains the information displayed in Figure 12.1.

The next step is to calculate the expected frequencies for each cell. This procedure is similar to that used in the goodness of fit test, but it involves a slightly more detailed formula:

$$E_{ij} = \frac{R_i C_j}{N}$$

where E_{ij} = expected frequency for cell in row i, column j; R_i = sum of frequencies in row i, C_j = sum of frequencies in column j; and N = sum of frequencies for all cells. Using this formula, the researcher in the hypothetical example can calculate the expected frequencies as follows:

$$\text{Male/radio} = \frac{100 \times 21}{210} = \frac{2,100}{210} = 10$$

$$\text{Female/radio} = \frac{110 \times 21}{210} = \frac{2,310}{210} = 11$$

and so forth. Each expected frequency is placed in a small square in the upper right-hand corner of the appropriate cell, as illustrated in Figure 12.2.

After the expected frequencies have been calculated, the investigator must compute the chi-square, using the following formula:

$$\chi^2 = \Sigma \frac{(O_{ij} - E_{ij})^2}{E_{ij}}$$

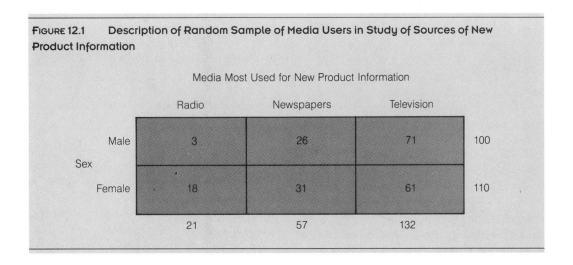

FIGURE 12.1   Description of Random Sample of Media Users in Study of Sources of New Product Information

Media Most Used for New Product Information

		Radio	Newspapers	Television	
	Male	3	26	71	100
Sex					
	Female	18	31	61	110
		21	57	132	

FIGURE 12.2   Random Sample of Media Users Showing Expected Frequencies

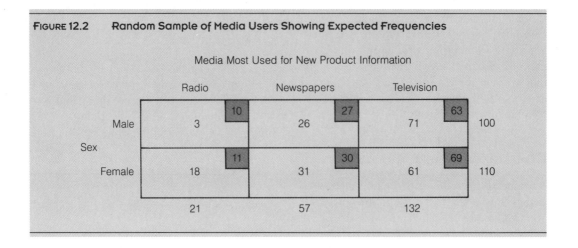

Using the same example:

$$\chi^2 = \frac{(3 - 10)^2}{10} + \frac{(26 - 27)^2}{27} + \frac{(71 - 63)^2}{63}$$

$$+ \frac{(18 - 11)^2}{11} + \frac{(31 - 30)^2}{30}$$

$$+ \frac{(61 - 69)^2}{69}$$

$$= \frac{49}{10} + \frac{1}{27} + \frac{64}{63} + \frac{49}{11} + \frac{1}{30} + \frac{64}{69}$$

$$= 4.90 + 0.04 + 1.01 + 4.45 + 0.03$$

$$+ 0.92$$

$$= 11.35$$

To determine statistical significance, the researcher must now consult the chi-square table. In a crosstab analysis, the degrees of freedom are expressed as $(R - 1)(C - 1)$, where R is the number of rows and C is the number of columns. If $p \leq .05$, the chi-square value is listed in Table 4 of Appendix 1 as 5.991, which is lower than the calculated value of 11.35. Thus, there is a significant relationship between the gender of the respondent and the media used to

acquire new product information. The test indicates that the two variables are somehow related, but it does not tell exactly how. To find this out, it is necessary to go back and examine the original crosstab data (Figure 12.1). Looking at the distribution, it is easy to see that females use radio more and television less than do males.

For a 2 × 2 crosstab (where $df = 1$), computational effort is saved when the corresponding cells are represented by the letters A, B, C, and D, such as

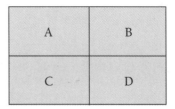

The following formula can then be used to compute the chi-square:

$$\chi^2 = \frac{N(AD - BC)^2}{(A + B)(C + D)(A + C)(B + D)}$$

Crosstab analysis has become a widely used analytical technique in mass media research, especially since the development of computer programs such as the Statistical Package for the Social Sciences (SPSS-X). In addition to chi-square, various other statistics can be used in crosstabs to determine whether the variables are statistically related.

PARAMETRIC STATISTICS

The sections that follow discuss parametric statistical methods usually used with higher-level data (interval and ratio). Recall that these methods assume that data are normally distributed. The most basic parametric statistic is the *t*-test, a procedure widely used in all areas of mass media research.

THE *t*-TEST

In many research studies, two groups of subjects are tested: One group receives some type of treatment, and the other serves as the control. After the treatment has been administered, both groups are tested, and the results are compared to determine whether a statistically significant difference exists between the groups. That is, did the treatment have an effect on the results of the test? In cases such as this, the mean score for each group is compared with a *t*-test.

The *t*-test is the most elementary method for comparing two groups' mean scores. A variety of *t*-test alternatives are available, depending on the problem under consideration and the situation of a particular research study. Variations of the *t*-test are available for testing independent groups, related groups, and cases in which the population mean is either known or unknown (Champion, 1981; Roscoe, 1975).

The *t*-test assumes that the variables in the populations from which the samples are drawn are normally distributed (Chapter 10). The test

also assumes that the data have homogeneity of variance—that is, that they deviate equally from the mean.

The basic formula for the *t*-test is relatively simple. The numerator of the formula is the difference between the sample mean and the hypothesized population mean, divided by the estimate of the standard error of the mean (S_m):

$$t = \frac{\overline{X} - \mu}{S_m}$$

where

$$S_m = \sqrt{\frac{SS}{n-1}} \text{ and } SS = \Sigma(X - \overline{X})^2$$

One of the more commonly used forms of the *t*-test is the test for independent groups or means. This procedure is used in studying two independent groups for differences (the type of study described at the beginning of this section). The formula for the independent *t*-test is

$$t = \frac{\overline{X}_1 - \overline{X}_2}{S_{\bar{x}_1 - \bar{x}_2}}$$

where $\overline{X}_1$ = the mean for Group 1, $\overline{X}_2$ = the mean for Group 2, and $S_{\bar{x}_1 - \bar{x}_2}$ = the standard error for the groups. The standard error is an important part of the *t*-test formula and is computed as follows:

$$S_{\bar{x}_1 - \bar{x}_2} = \sqrt{\left(\frac{SS_1 + SS_2}{n_1 + n_2 - 2}\right)\left(\frac{1}{n_1} + \frac{1}{n_2}\right)}$$

where SS_1 = the sum of squares for Group 1, SS_2 = the sum of squares for Group 2, n_1 = the sample size for Group 1, and n_2 = the sample size for Group 2.

To illustrate a *t*-test, consider a research problem to determine the recall of two groups of subjects with regard to a television commercial for a new household cleaner. One group consists of 10 males, and the other consists of 10 females. Each group views the commercial once and then completes a 15-item questionnaire. The hypothesis predicts a significant difference between the recall scores of males and females. The data are shown below. Using the t-test formula, the next step is to compute the standard error for the groups by using the previous formula:

$$S_{\bar{x}_1 - \bar{x}_2} = \sqrt{\left(\frac{110 + 106}{10 + 10 - 2}\right)\left(\frac{1}{10} + \frac{1}{10}\right)}$$

$$= 1.55$$

The researcher then substitutes this standard error value in the t-test formula:

$$t = \frac{8 - 6}{1.55}$$

$$= 1.29$$

To determine whether the t value of 1.29 is statistically significant, a t-distribution table is consulted. The t-distribution is a family of curves closely resembling the normal curve. The portion of the t-distribution table relevant to the sample problem is reproduced in Table 12.1. Again, to interpret the table, two values are required: degrees of freedom and level of probability. (For a complete t-distribution table, see Appendix 1, Table 2.)

For purposes of the t-test, degrees of freedom are equal to $n_1 + n_2 - 2$, where n_1 and n_2 represent the sizes of the respective groups. In the example of advertising recall, $df = 18$ (10 + 10 − 2). If the problem is tested at the .05 level of significance, a t value of 2.101 is required for the research to be considered statistically significant. However, since the sample problem is a "two-tail test" (the hypothesis predicts only a difference between the two groups, not that one particular group will have the higher mean score), the required values are actually $t \leq -2.101$ or $t \geq +2.101$. The conclusion of the hypothetical problem is that there is no significant difference between the recall scores of the female group and the recall scores of the male group, because calculated t does not equal or exceed the table values.

Female recall scores			Male recall scores		
X	x	x²(SS)	X	x	x²(SS)
4	−4	16	2	−4	16
4	−4	16	3	−3	9
5	−3	9	4	−2	4
7	−1	1	4	−2	4
8	0	0	6	0	0
9	1	1	6	0	0
9	1	1	8	2	4
12	4	16	10	4	16
15	7	49	13	7	49
80		110	60		106
$\bar{X} = 8$			$\bar{X} = 6$		

TABLE 12.1   Portion of the *t*-Distribution Table for the Two-Tail Test

		Probability		
n	.10	.05	.01	.001
1	6.314	12.706	63.657	636.619
2	2.920	4.303	9.925	31.598
•				
•				
•				
17	1.740	2.110	2.898	3.965
18	1.734	2.101	2.878	3.992
19	1.729	2.093	2.861	3.883
•				
•				
•				

There are many examples of the *t*-test in mass media research that demonstrate the versatility of the method. For example, Garramone (1985) investigated political advertising by exploring the roles of the commercial sponsor (the source of the message) and the rebuttal commercial (a message that charges as false the claims of another commercial). Among six separate hypotheses that were tested, Garramone predicted that

H_1 Viewers of a negative political commercial will perceive an independent sponsor as more trustworthy than a candidate sponsor.

H_2 Viewers of an independent commercial opposing a candidate will demonstrate
  a. more negative perceptions of the target's image.
  b. lesser likelihood of voting for the target than viewers of a candidate commercial.

H_3 Viewers of an independent commercial opposing a candidate will demonstrate

  a. more positive perceptions of the target's opponent.
  b. greater likelihood of voting for the target's opponent than viewers of a candidate commercial.

Among other findings, Garramone concluded that

The first hypothesis . . . was not supported. [However] hypotheses 2 and 3 . . . were supported. Viewers of an independent commercial opposing a candidate demonstrated a more negative perception of the target's image, $t(110) = 2.41, p \leq .01$, and a lesser likelihood of voting for the target, $t(110) = 1.83, p \leq .05$, than did viewers of a candidate commercial. Also as predicted, viewers of an independent commercial demonstrated a more positive perception of the target's opponent, $t(110) = 1.89, p \leq .05$, and a greater likelihood of voting for the target's opponent, $t(110) = 2.45, p \leq .01$, than did viewers of a candidate commercial.

ANALYSIS OF VARIANCE

The *t*-test allows researchers to investigate the effects of one independent variable upon two samples of people, such as the effect of room temperature on subjects' performance on a research exam. One group may take the test in a room at 70° F while another group takes the same test in a room at 100° F. The mean test scores for each group are used to calculate *t*. However, in many situations, researchers want to investigate several *levels* of an independent variable (rooms set at 70°, 80°, 90°, and 100° F), or possibly several independent variables (heat and light), and possibly several different groups (freshmen, sophomores, and so on). A *t*-test is inappropriate in these cases because the procedure is valid only for one single comparison. What may be required is an analysis of variance (ANOVA).

ANOVA is essentially an extension of the *t*-test. The advantage of ANOVA is that it can be used to simultaneously investigate several independent variables, also called *factors*. An ANOVA is named according to the number of factors involved in the study: A *one-way* ANOVA investigates one independent variable, a *two-way* ANOVA investigates two independent variables, and so on. An additional naming convention is used to describe an ANOVA that involves different levels of an independent variable. A 2 × 2 ANOVA studies two independent variables, each with two levels. For example, using the room temperature study just described, an ANOVA research project may include two levels of room temperature (70° and 100° F) and two levels of room lighting (dim and bright). This provides four different effects possibilities on test scores: 70°, dim lighting; 70°, bright lighting; 100°, dim lighting; and 100°, bright lighting. ANOVA allows the researcher in this example to look at four unique situations at one time. ANOVA is a versatile statistic that is widely used in mass media research. However, the name of the statistic is somewhat misleading because the most common form of ANOVA tests for significant differences between two or more group means and has nothing to do with the analysis of variance differences. Additionally, ANOVA breaks down the total variability in a set of data into its different *sources of variation*— that is, it "explains" the sources of variance in a set of scores on one or more independent variables.

An ANOVA identifies or explains two types of variance: systematic and error. **Systematic variance** in data is attributable to a known factor that predictably increases or decreases all the scores it influences. One such factor commonly identified in mass media research is gender: Often an increase or decrease in a given score can be predicted simply by determining whether a subject is male or female. **Error variance** in data is created by an unknown factor that most likely has not been examined or controlled in the study. A primary goal of all research is to eliminate or control as much error variance as possible (a task that is generally easier to do in the laboratory—see Chapter 9).

The ANOVA model assumes (1) that each sample is normally distributed, (2) that variances for each group are equal, (3) that the subjects are randomly selected from the population, and (4) that the scores are statistically independent—that they have no concomitant relationship with any other variable or score.

The ANOVA procedure begins with the selection of two or more random samples. Samples may be from the same or different populations. Each group is subjected to different experimental treatments, followed by some type of test or measurement. The scores from the measurements are then used to calculate a ratio of variance, known as the *F ratio* (*F*).

To understand this calculation, it is necessary to examine in greater detail the procedure known as sum of squares (discussed briefly in Chapter 10). In the sum of squares procedure, raw scores or deviation scores are squared and summed, to eliminate the need for dealing with negative numbers. The squaring process does not change the meaning of the data as long as the same procedure is used on all the data; it simply converts the data into a more easily interpreted set of scores.

In ANOVA, sums of squares are computed *between groups* (of subjects), *within groups* (of subjects), and *in total* (the sum of the between and within figures). The sums of squares between groups and within groups are divided by their respective degrees of freedom (as will be illustrated) to obtain a *mean square*: mean squares between (MS_b) and mean squares within (MS_w). The F ratio is then calculated using the following formula:

$$F = \frac{MS_b}{MS_w}$$

where $MS_b df = K - 1$; $MS_w df = N - K$; $K =$ the number of groups; and $N =$ the total sample. The F ratio derived from the data is then compared to the value in the F-distribution table (Table 5 in Appendix 1) that corresponds to the appropriate degrees of freedom and the desired probability level. If the calculated value equals or exceeds the tabled value, the ANOVA is considered to be statistically significant. The F table is similar to the t table and the chi-square table except that two different degrees of freedom are used, one for the numerator of the F ratio and one for the denominator.

The ANOVA statistic can be demonstrated by using an example from advertising. Suppose that three groups of five subjects each are randomly selected to determine the credibility of a newspaper advertisement for a new laundry detergent. The groups are exposed to versions of the advertisement that reflect varying degrees of design complexity: easy, medium, and difficult. The subjects are then asked to rate the advertisement on a scale of 1 to 10, with 10 indicating believable and 1 indicating not believable. The null hypothesis is advanced: "There is no signif-

icant difference in credibility among the three versions of the ad."

To test this hypothesis, the researchers must first calculate the three sums of squares: total, within, and between. The formulas for sums of squares (*SS*) are

$$Total_{ss} = \Sigma X^2 - \frac{(\Sigma X)^2}{N}$$

$$Within_{ss} = \Sigma X^2 - \frac{\Sigma\,(\Sigma X)^2}{N}$$

$$Between_{ss} = T_{ss} - W_{ss}$$

The scores for the three groups furnish the data shown on page 250.

By inserting the figures so obtained in the formulas, the researchers are able to calculate the sums of squares as follows:

$$T_{ss} = \Sigma X^2 - \frac{(\Sigma X)^2}{n_k} = 537 - \frac{(83)^2}{15}$$

$$= 537 - 459.2 = 77.8$$

$$W_{ss} = \Sigma X^2 - \frac{\Sigma(\Sigma X)^2}{n}$$

$$= 537 - \frac{16^2}{5} - \frac{29^2}{5} - \frac{38^2}{5}$$

$$= 537 - 508.2 = 28.8$$

$$B_{ss} = T_{ss} - W_{ss} = 77.8 - 28.8 = 49$$

With this information, the research team can calculate the mean squares between and within groups (*SS/df*), which can then be divided (MS_b /MS_w) to obtain the value of the F ratio. These results are displayed in Figure 12.3.

Assuming a significance level of .05, the F-distribution data (Table 5, Appendix 1) for degrees of freedom of 2 and 12 indicate that the F ratio must be 3.89 or greater to show statistical significance. Since the calculated value of 10.2 is greater than 3.89, a significant difference in credibility among the three types of advertisements does exist, and the researchers must reject the null hypothesis.

TWO-WAY ANOVA

Researchers often examine more than one independent variable in a study. For example, if the researchers in the preceding example had wished to investigate simultaneously a second independent variable, product knowledge, they could have used a two-way ANOVA. In a two-

way ANOVA, the researchers gather the data and organize them in table form, as with the one-way ANOVA, but the two-way table has both rows *and* columns, where each row and column represents an independent variable. The dependent variable score, represented by the letter X for each subject, is entered into each cell of the table. This procedure is demonstrated in Figure 12.4.

The two-way ANOVA can save time and resources, since studies for each independent variable are being conducted simultaneously. In ad-

Group A (easy)		Group B (medium)		Group C (difficult)	
X	X^2	X	X^2	X	X^2
1	1	4	16	6	36
2	4	5	25	7	49
4	16	6	36	7	49
4	16	6	36	8	64
5	25	8	64	10	100
16	62	29	177	38	298

$$\Sigma X = (16 + 29 + 38) = 83$$

$$\Sigma X^2 = (62 + 177 + 298) = 537$$

FIGURE 12.3 Values for One-Way ANOVA Example

Sources of variation	df	Sums of squares	Mean square	F
Between groups	2 $(K-1)$	49	24.50	10.19
Within groups	12 $(n-K)$	28.8	2.4	xxxx
Total	14 $(n-1)$	77.8	xxxx	

dition, it enables researchers to calculate two types of independent variable effects on the dependent variable: main effects and interactions. (One-way ANOVA tests only for main effects.) A **main effect** is simply the influence of an independent variable on the dependent variable. **Interaction** refers to the concomitant influence of two or more independent variables on the single dependent variable. For example, it may be found that a subject's educational background has no effect on media used for entertainment, but education and socioeconomic status may interact to create a significant effect.

The main effects plus interaction in a two-way ANOVA create a summary table slightly different from that shown for the one-way ANOVA, as illustrated by comparing Figures 12.3 and 12.4. Instead of computing only one F ratio as in one-way ANOVA, a two-way ANOVA will compute four F ratios, each of which is tested for statistical significance on the F distribution table (Between columns, Between rows, Interaction, Within cells). "Between columns" (a main effect) represents the test of the independent variable levels located in the columns of a two-way ANOVA. (From the preceding example, this would be a test for the differences between groups "easy," "medium," and "hard".) "Between rows" is another main effects test; it represents the significance between levels of the independent variable identified in the rows of the two-way ANOVA (product knowledge and no product knowledge). The "Interaction" section is the test for interaction between both independent variables in the study, and "Within cells" tests for significant differences between each cell in the study to determine how each individual group performed in the analysis. F ratios are not computed for the "Total," which accounts for the X's in the mean square and F columns.

BASIC CORRELATIONAL STATISTICS

Assume that a researcher hypothesizes an association between the number of pictures on

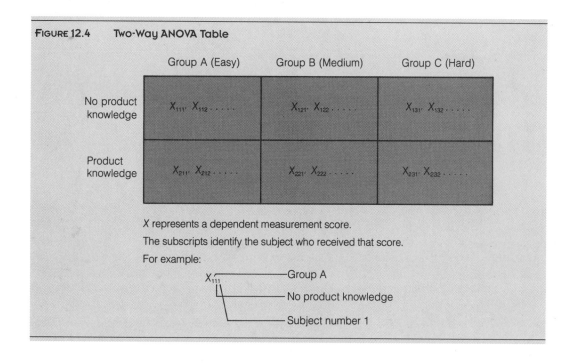

FIGURE 12.4   Two-Way ANOVA Table

	Group A (Easy)	Group B (Medium)	Group C (Hard)
No product knowledge	$X_{111}, X_{112} \ldots$	$X_{121}, X_{122} \ldots$	$X_{131}, X_{132} \ldots$
Product knowledge	$X_{211}, X_{212} \ldots$	$X_{221}, X_{222} \ldots$	$X_{231}, X_{232} \ldots$

X represents a dependent measurement score.
The subscripts identify the subject who received that score.
For example:

X_{111} ——— Group A
——— No product knowledge
——— Subject number 1

the front page of a newspaper and the total number of copies sold at newsstands. If the observations reveal that the more pictures there are, the more papers are sold, a relationship may exist between the two variables. Numerical expressions of the degree to which two variables change in relation with one another are called *measures of association,* or *correlation.* When making two different measurements of the same person, it is common to designate one measure as the *X variable* and the other as the *Y variable.* For example, in determining whether a relationship exists between the size of a subject's family and the frequency with which that person reads a newspaper, the measure of family size could be the *X* variable and the measure of newspaper reading the *Y* variable. Note that each subject in the group under study must be measured for both variables.

Figure 12.5 contains hypothetical data collected from a study of eight subjects. The *Y* variable is the number of times per week the news-

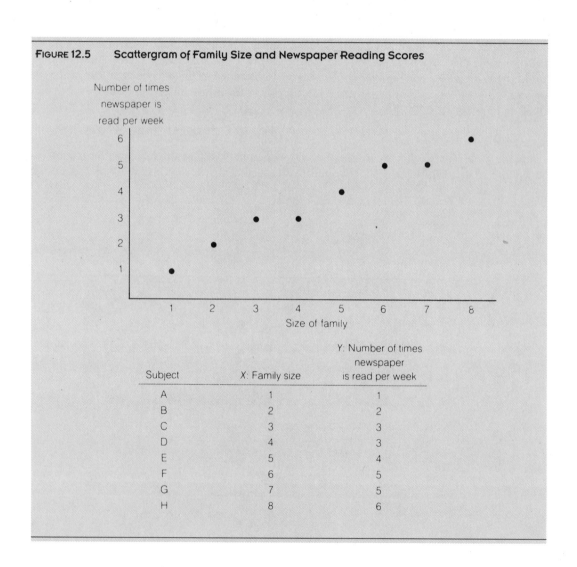

FIGURE 12.5   Scattergram of Family Size and Newspaper Reading Scores

Subject	X: Family size	Y: Number of times newspaper is read per week
A	1	1
B	2	2
C	3	3
D	4	3
E	5	4
F	6	5
G	7	5
H	8	6

paper is read; the X variable is the number of persons in the household. The two scores for each subject are plotted on a **scattergram**, a graphic technique for portraying a relationship between two or more variables. As indicated, family size and newspaper reading increase together. This is an example of a *positive relationship*.

An *inverse* (or *negative*) *relationship* exists when one variable increases while the other decreases. Sometimes the relationship between two variables is positive up to a point and then becomes inverse (or vice versa). When this happens, the relationship is said to be curvilinear. When

there is no tendency for a high score on one variable to be associated with a high or low score on another variable, the two are said to be uncorrelated. Figure 12.6 illustrates these relationships.

There are many statistics available to measure the degree of relationship between two variables, but the most commonly used is the Pearson product-moment correlation, commonly symbolized as r. It varies between -1.00 and $+1.00$. A correlation coefficient of $+1.00$ indicates a perfect positive correlation: X and Y are completely covariant. A Pearson r of -1.00 indicates a perfect relationship in the negative

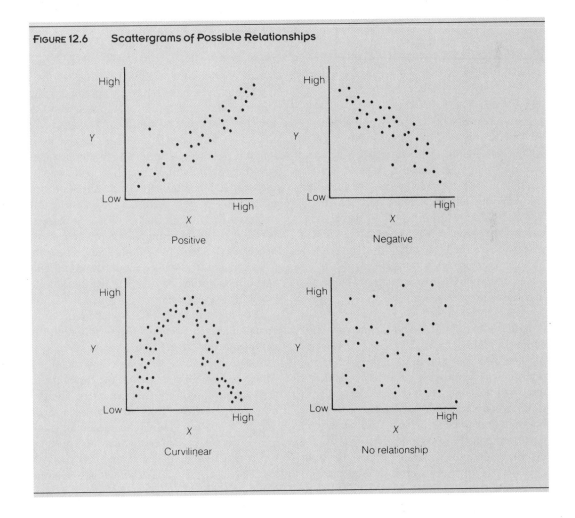

FIGURE 12.6   Scattergrams of Possible Relationships

direction. The lowest value that the Pearson r can achieve is 0.00. This represents absolutely no relationship between two variables. Thus, the Pearson r contains two pieces of information: (1) an estimate of the strength of the relationship, as indicated by the number, and (2) a statement about the direction of the relationship, as shown by the sign. Keep in mind that the strength of the relationship depends solely on the number; strength of relationship must be interpreted in terms of absolute value. A correlation of $-.83$ is a stronger relationship than one of $+.23$.

The formula for calculating r looks foreboding; actually, however, it includes only one new expression:

$$r = \frac{N\Sigma XY - \Sigma X \Sigma Y}{\sqrt{[N\Sigma X^2 - (\Sigma X)^2]\,[N\Sigma Y^2 - (\Sigma Y)^2]}}$$

where X and Y stand for the original scores, N is the number of pairs of scores, and Σ again is the summation symbol. The only new term is ΣXY, which stands for the sum of the products of each X and Y. To find this quantity, simply multiply each X variable by its corresponding Y variable and add the results. Table 12.2 demonstrates a computation of r. (The use of a calculator or computer is recommended when N is large, since the calculation of r can be tedious when many observations are involved.)

A correlation coefficient is a pure number—it is not expressed in feet, inches, or pounds, nor is it a proportion or percent. The Pearson r is independent of the size and units of measurement of the original data. (In fact, the original scores do not have to be expressed in the same units.) Because of its abstract nature, r must be interpreted with care. In particular, it is not as easy as it sounds to determine whether a correlation is large or small. Some writers have suggested various adjectives to describe certain ranges of r. For example, an r between .40 and .70 might be called a "moderate" or "substantial" relationship, while an r of .71 to

.90 might be termed "very high." These labels are helpful, but they may lead to confusion. The best advice is to consider the nature of the study. For example, an r of .70 between frequency of viewing television violence and frequency of arrest for violent crimes would be more than substantial; it would be phenomenal. Conversely, a correlation of .70 between two coders' timings of the length of news stories on the evening news is low enough to call the reliability of the study into question. Additionally, correlation does not in itself imply causation. Newspaper reading and income might be strongly related, but this does not mean that earning a high salary causes people to read the newspaper. Correlation is just one factor in determining causality.

Furthermore, a large r does not necessarily mean that the two sets of correlated scores are equal. What it does mean is that there is a high likelihood of being correct when predicting the value of one variable by examining another variable that correlates with it. For example, there may be a correlation of .90 between the amount of time people spend reading newspapers and the amount of time they spend watching television news. That is, the amount of time reading newspapers correlates with the amount of time watching television news. The correlation figure says nothing about the *amount* of time spent with each medium. It suggests only that there is a strong likelihood that people who spend time reading newspapers also spend time watching television news.

Perhaps the best way to interpret r is in terms of the **coefficient of determination**, or the proportion of the total variation of one measure that can be determined by the other. This is calculated by squaring the Pearson r to arrive at a ratio of the two variances: The denominator of this ratio is the total variance of one of the variables, while the numerator is the part of the total variance that can be attributed to the other variable. For example, if $r = .40$, then $r^2 = .16$. One variable explains 16% of the variation in the other. Or to put it another way,

TABLE 12.2   Calculation of r

Subject	X	X^2	Y	Y^2	XY
A	1	1	1	1	1
B	2	4	2	4	4
C	3	9	3	9	9
D	4	16	3	9	12
E	4	16	4	16	16
F	5	25	5	25	25
G	6	36	5	25	30
H	8	64	6	36	48
$N = 8$	$\Sigma X = 33$	$\Sigma X^2 = 171$	$\Sigma Y = 29$	$\Sigma Y^2 = 125$	$\Sigma XY = 145$

$$(\Sigma X)^2 = 1{,}089$$
$$(\Sigma Y)^2 = \ \ 841$$

$$r = \frac{(8)(145) - (33)(29)}{\sqrt{[(8)(171) - 1{,}089][(8)(125) - 841]}}$$

$$= \frac{203}{\sqrt{(279)(159)}} = \frac{203}{(16.7)(12.6)}$$

$$= \frac{203}{210.62} = .964$$

r formula:
$$\frac{N\Sigma XY - \Sigma X \Sigma Y}{\sqrt{[N\Sigma X^2 - (\Sigma X)^2][N\Sigma Y^2 - (\Sigma Y)^2]}}$$

16% of the information necessary to make a perfect prediction from one variable to another is known. Obviously, if $r = 1.00$, then $r^2 = 100\%$; one variable allows perfect predictability of the other. The quantity $1 - r^2$ is usually called the **coefficient of nondetermination** because it represents that proportion of the variance left unaccounted for or unexplained.

Suppose that a correlation of .30 is found between a child's aggression and the amount of television violence the child views. This would mean that 9% of the total variance in aggression is accounted for by television violence. The other 91% of the variation is unexplained (except to the extent that it is not accounted for by the television variable). Note that the coefficient of determination is not measured on an equal interval scale: .80 is twice as large as .40, but this does not mean that an r of .80 represents twice as great a relationship between two variables as an r of .40. In fact, the r of .40 explains 16% of the variance, while the r of .80 explains 64%—four times as much.

The Pearson r can be computed between any two sets of scores. For the statistic to be a valid description of the relationship, however, several assumptions must be made: (1) that the data represent interval or ratio measurements;

(2) that the relationship between X and Y is linear, not curvilinear; and (3) that the distributions of the X and Y variables are symmetrical and comparable. (Pearson's r can also be used as an inferential statistic. When this is the case, it is necessary to assume that X and Y come from normally distributed populations with similar variances.) If these assumptions cannot validly be made, the researcher must use another kind of correlation coefficient, such as Spearman's rho or Kendall's W. For a thorough discussion of these and other correlation coefficients, the reader should consult Nunnally (1978).

PARTIAL CORRELATION

Partial correlation is a method researchers use when they believe that a confounding or spurious variable may affect the relationship between the independent variables and the dependent variable: If such an influence is perceived, they can "partial out" or control the confounding variable. For example, consider a study of the relationship between exposure to television commercials and purchase of the advertised products. The researchers select two commercials for a liquid laundry detergent (a "straight sell" version, with no special video or audio effects, and a "hard sell" version that does use special effects) and show them to two groups of subjects: people who use only powdered detergent and people who use only liquid detergent. The study design is shown in Figure 12.7.

If the results show a very low correlation, indicating that any prediction made on the basis of these two variables would be very tenuous, the researchers should suspect the presence of a confounding variable. An examination might reveal, for example, that the technicians had problems adjusting the color definition of the recording equipment; instead of its natural blue color, the detergent appeared dingy brown on the television screen. The study could be repeated to control (statistically eliminate) this variable by filming new commercials with the color controls properly adjusted. The design for the new study is shown in Figure 12.8.

The partial correlation statistical procedure would enable the researchers to determine the influence of the controlled variable. Using the new statistical method, the correlation might increase from the original study.

Cutler and Danowski (1981) used partial correlation in their study of older persons' use of

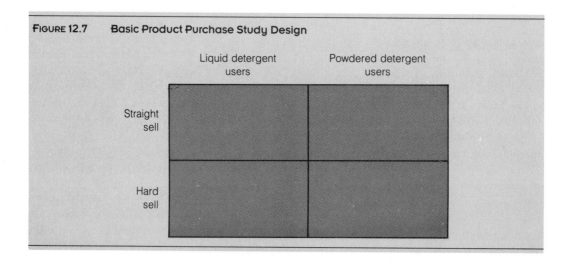

FIGURE 12.7   Basic Product Purchase Study Design

Liquid detergent users   Powdered detergent users

Straight sell

Hard sell

television. The authors found it necessary, on the basis of suggestions from previous analyses, to control for gender and education when determining the correlation between political interest and television use. When these variables were partialed out (controlled), they found that media use varied with the subject's age and when the media were used during the campaign.

SIMPLE LINEAR REGRESSION

Simple correlation involves the measurement of the relationship between two variables. Simple linear regression is used to determine the degree to which one variable changes with a given change in another variable. Thus, linear regression is a way of using the association between two variables as a method of prediction. Let us take the simplest case to illustrate the logic behind this technique. Suppose two variables are perfectly related ($r = 1.00$). Knowledge of a person's score on one variable will allow the researcher to determine the score on the other. Figure 12.9 is a scattergram that portrays such a situation. Note that all the points

lie on a straight line, the regression line. Unfortunately, relationships are never this simple, and scattergrams more often resemble the one portrayed in Figure 12.10(a). Obviously, no single line can be drawn straight through all the points in the scattergram. It is possible, however, to mathematically construct a line that best represents all the observations in the figure. This line will come the closest to all the dots, though it might not pass through any of them. Mathematicians have worked out a technique to calculate such a line. This procedure, known as the "least squares" method, was developed in 1794 by German mathematician Karl Gauss, who used it successfully to relocate Ceres, the first recorded asteroid, after it was tracked for 41 days.

The least squares technique produces a line that is the best summary description of the relationship between two variables. For example, Figure 12.10(a) shows data points representing the relationship between eight x and y variables. The principle of least squares determines the line equation for the data points such that the line passes through, or near, the greatest

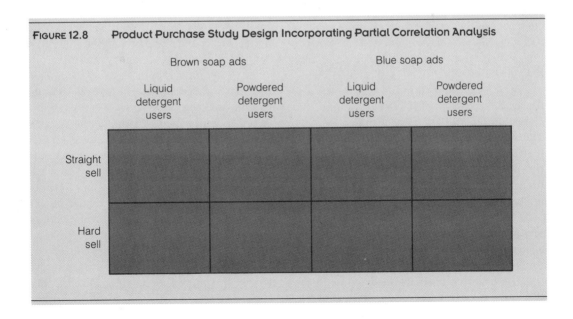

FIGURE 12.8   Product Purchase Study Design Incorporating Partial Correlation Analysis

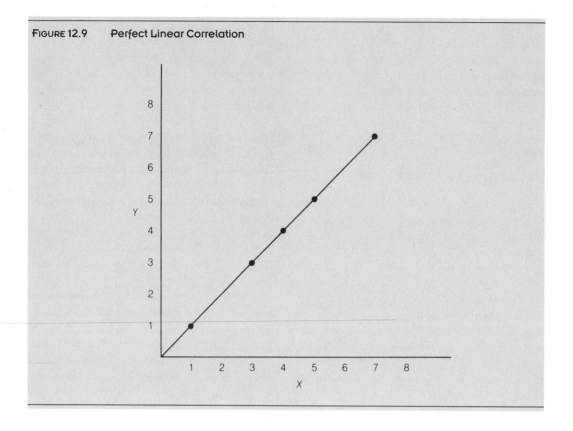

FIGURE 12.9   Perfect Linear Correlation

number of points. The computed line is then compared to the true, or perfect, line to determine the accuracy of the computed (predicted) line. The closer the computed line is to the true line, the more accurate the prediction.

The solid line in Figure 12.10(b) represents the best fitting line that passes through, or closest to, the greatest number of data points. The broken line connects the actual data points. It is clear that the broken line does not fall on the true line. The data points are some distance away from the true line (showing that the prediction is not perfect).

The principle of least squares involves measuring the distances from the data points to the perfect line, then *squaring* the distances to eliminate negative values, and adding the squared distances together. The computer does this over and over until the sum of the squared

distance is the smallest (least squares). The smaller the sum of squared distances, the higher the accuracy with which the computed formula predicts the dependent variable.

At this point it is necessary to review some basic analytical geometry. The general equation for a line is $\hat{Y} = a + bX$, where $\hat{Y}$ is the variable we are trying to predict and X is the variable we are predicting from. Furthermore, a represents the point at which the line crosses the y-axis (the vertical axis), and b is a measure of the slope (or steepness) of the line. In other words, b indicates how much $\hat{Y}$ changes for each change in X. Depending on the relationship between X and $\hat{Y}$, the slope can be positive or negative. To illustrate, Figure 12.9 (above) shows that every time X increases one unit, so does $\hat{Y}$. In addition, the a value is zero, since the line crosses the vertical axis at the origin.

FIGURE 12.10   (a) Scattergram of *X* and *Y*; (b) Scattergram with Regression Line

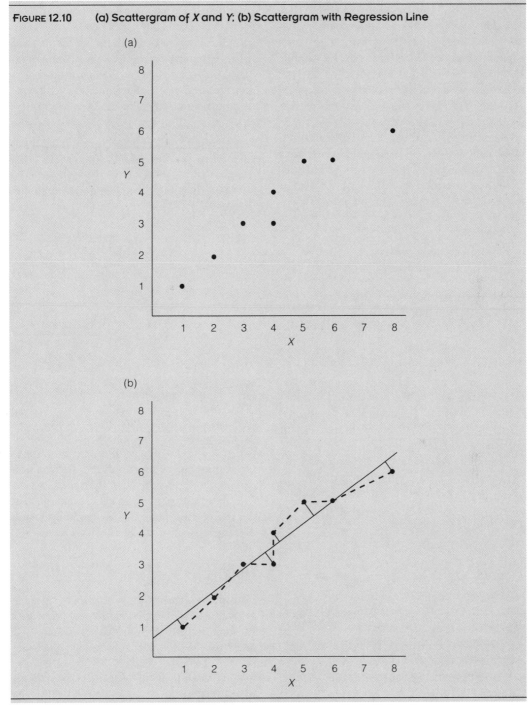

Note: The solid perpendicular lines connecting the data points to the computer line in (b) show the distances that must be determined and squared.

Strictly speaking, the equation for a *regression line* is the same as the general equation for a line, since the Y in the regression equation does not represent the actual variable Y but rather a predicted Y. Hence, the Y in the regression equation is usually symbolized $\hat{Y}$. Thus, the regression equation is written $\hat{Y} = a + bX$.

Now let us put this general equation into more concrete terms. Pretend that we have data on the relationship between years of education and number of minutes spent looking at the newspaper per day. The regression equation is

Minutes reading newspaper = 2 + 3 (education)

What can we deduce from this? In the first place, the *a* value tells us that a person with no formal education spends 2 minutes per day looking at the newspaper. The *b* value indicates that time spent with the newspaper increases 3 minutes with each additional year of education. What would be the prediction for someone with 10 years of education? Substituting, we have $\hat{Y} = 2 + 3(10) = 32$ minutes spent with the newspaper each day.

To take an additional example, consider the hypothetical regression equation predicting hours of TV viewed daily from a person's IQ score: $\hat{Y} = 5 - .01(IQ)$. How many hours of TV would be viewed daily by someone with an IQ of 100?

$$\hat{Y} = 5 - (.01)(100) = 5 - 1 = 4 \text{ hours}$$

Thus, according to this equation, TV viewing per day decreases 0.01 hour for every point of IQ.

The arithmetic calculation of the regression equation is straightforward. First, to find *b*, the slope of the line,

$$b = \frac{N\Sigma XY - (\Sigma X)(\Sigma Y)}{N\Sigma X^2 - (\Sigma X)^2}$$

Note that the numerator is the same as that for the *r* coefficient, and the denominator corresponds to the first expression in the denominator of the *r* formula. Thus, calculation of *b* is easily determined once the quantities necessary for *r* have been determined. To illustrate, using the data from Table 12.2 (page 255):

$$b = \frac{8(145) - (33)(29)}{[8(171) - 1,089]} = \frac{203}{279} = 0.73$$

The value of the Y intercept (*a*) is found by the following:

$$a = \bar{Y} - b\bar{X}$$

Again, using the data in Table 12.2 and the calculation of *b*,

$$a = 3.63 - (0.73)(4.125)$$
$$= 3.63 - 3.01$$
$$= 0.62$$

The completed regression equation is $\hat{Y} = 0.62 + 0.73X$.

Of course, as the name suggests, simple linear regression assumes that the relationship between X and Y is linear. If an examination of the scattergram suggests a curvilinear relationship, other regression techniques are necessary. The notion of regression can be extended to the use of multiple predictor variables to predict the value of a single criterion variable.

MULTIPLE REGRESSION

Multiple regression, an extension of linear regression, is another parametric technique used to analyze the relationship between two or more independent variables and a single dependent (criterion) variable. Although similar in some ways to an analysis of variance, multiple regression serves basically to *predict* the dependent variable, using information derived from an analysis of the independent variables.

In any research problem, the dependent variable is considered to be affected by a variety of independent variables. The primary goal of multiple regression is to develop a formula that accounts for, or explains, as much variance in the dependent variable as possible. It is widely used by researchers to predict success in college, sales levels, and so on. These dependent variables are predicted by *weighted linear combinations* of independent variables. A simple model of multiple regression is shown in Figure 12.11.

Linear combinations of variables play an important role in higher-level statistics. To understand the concept of a weighted linear combination, consider the following methods of classroom grading. One instructor determines each student's final grade by his or her performance on five exams: The scores on these exams are summed and averaged to obtain each final grade. A student might receive the following scores for the five exams: B (3.0), D+ (1.5), B (3.0), B+ (3.5), and A (4.0); thus the final grade would be a B (15/5 = 3.0). This grade is the dependent variable determined by the linear combination of five exam scores (the independent variables). No test is considered more important than another; hence, the linear combination is not said to be weighted (except in the sense that all the scores are "weighted" equally).

The second instructor also determines the final grades by students' performances on five exams; however, the first exam counts 30%, the last exam 40%, and the remaining three exams 10% each in the determination. A student with the same five scores as above thus would receive a final grade of 3.3. Again, the scores represent a linear combination, but it is a weighted linear combination: The first and last exam contribute more to the final grade than do the other tests. The second grading system above is used in multiple regression: The independent variables are weighted and summed to permit a prediction of a dependent variable. The weight of each variable in a linear combination is referred to as its *coefficient*.

A multiple regression formula may involve any number of independent variables, depending on the complexity of the dependent variable.

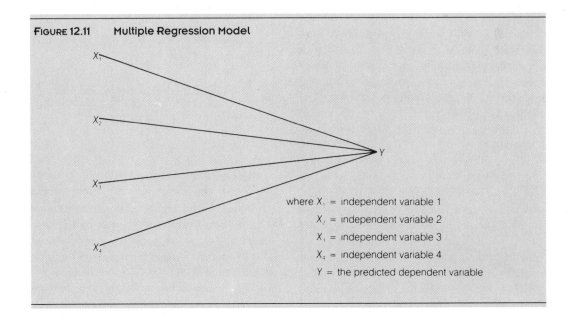

FIGURE 12.11   Multiple Regression Model

where X_1 = independent variable 1
X_2 = independent variable 2
X_3 = independent variable 3
X_4 = independent variable 4
Y = the predicted dependent variable

A simple formula of this type might look as follows (hypothetical values are used):

$$\hat{Y} = 0.89X_1 + 2.5X_2 - 3$$

where $\hat{Y}$ = the predicted score or variable; X_1 = Independent Variable 1; and X_2 = Independent Variable 2. The number 3 in the formula, a constant subtracted from each subject's scores, is derived as part of the multiple regression formula. All formulas produced by multiple regression analyses represent a line in space; that is, the dependent variable is interpreted as a linear combination, or line, of independent variables. The slope of this line is determined by the *regression coefficients* assigned to the variables (Cohen & Cohen, 1975; Thorndike, 1978). The goal of the researcher is to derive a formula for a line that coincides as nearly as possible with the *true* line (a mathematically determined line that represents a perfect prediction) of the dependent variable: The closer the computed line comes to the true line, the more accurate will be the prediction.

Another important value that must be calculated in a multiple regression analysis is the *coefficient of correlation* (R), which represents the product-moment correlation between the predicted $\hat{Y}$ score and the weighted linear combination of the X scores. The square of this coefficient (R_2) indicates the proportion of variance in the dependent variable that is accounted for by the predictor variables. The higher the R_2 (that is, the closer the figure is to 1.00), the more accurate the prediction is considered to be.

Drew and Reeves (1980) conducted a multiple regression analysis to determine what factors affect the way children learn from television news stories. They defined the dependent variable, "learning," in terms of performance on a 10-point questionnaire regarding a news program the children watched in an experimental setting. The selection of independent variables was based on the results of previous studies; they decided to measure: (1) whether

TABLE 12.3   Drew and Reeves' Multiple Regression Analysis

Predictor variables	Beta weights
Like program	.15**
Credibility	.10*
Informational content	.39***
Like story	.25***
Multiple R	.546
R^2	.298

*$p < .05$
**$p < .01$
***$p < .001$

the children liked the program, (2) whether the children liked the particular news story, (3) the credibility of the program, and (4) the informational content of the particular story.

The results, shown in Table 12.3, indicate that all the independent variables were statistically significant in their relation to learning. As the beta weights show, "informational content" seems to be the best predictor of learning, and "credibility" accounts for the least amount of variance. The multiple R of .546 could be considered highly significant; however, since it means that only 30% ($.546^2$) of the variance in the dependent variable was accounted for by the four predictor variables, this value may not substantially explain the variance.

SUMMARY

Mass media research has made great strides in terms of both number of research studies completed and types of statistical methods used. This chapter has introduced some of the more widely used basic statistical procedures involving one dependent variable and one or more independent variables. The information is intended to help beginning researchers in reading and analyzing published research.

The emphasis in this chapter is on using statistical methods rather than on the statistics themselves. The basic formula for each statistic is briefly outlined so that beginning researchers can understand how the data are derived; the goal, however, has been to convey a knowledge of how and when to use each procedure. It is important that researchers be able to determine not only what the problem or research question is, but also which statistical method most accurately fits the requirements of a particular research study.

QUESTIONS AND PROBLEMS FOR FURTHER INVESTIGATION

1. Design a mass media study for which a chi-square analysis is appropriate.

2. In the chi-square example of television set sales, assume that the observed sales frequencies are 210 (RCA), 350 (Sony), 200 (JVC), and 240 (Mitsubishi). What is the chi-square value? Is it significant?

3. What are the advantages of using an ANOVA over conducting several separate t-tests of the same phenomena?

4. How could multiple regression be used to predict a subject's television-viewing, radio-listening, and newspaper-reading behavior?

5. On page 255 we state that a Pearson r can be computed between any two sets of scores. Does that mean that all Pearson correlations will be logical?

6. Calculate r for the following set of scores:

X	Y
1	8
1	6
3	5
2	4
2	3
4	5
5	2
7	3

REFERENCES AND SUGGESTED READINGS

Atwood, L. E., & Sanders, K. R. (1976). Information sources and voting in a primary and general election. *Journal of Broadcasting, 20,* 291–301.

Champion, D. J. (1981). *Basic statistics for social research.* New York: Macmillan.

Cochran, W. G. (1976). Early development of techniques in comparative experimentation. In D. B. Owen (Ed.), *On the history of statistics and probability.* New York: Marcel Dekker.

Cohen, J., & Cohen, P. (1975). *Applied multiple regression/correlation analysis for the behavioral sciences.* Hillsdale, NJ: Lawrence Erlbaum.

Cutler, N. E., & Danowski, J. A. (1981). Process gratification in aging cohorts. *Journalism Quarterly, 57,* 269–276.

Drew, D., & Reeves, B. (1980). Learning from a television news story. *Communication Research, 7,* 121–135.

Garramone, G. (1985). Effects of negative political advertising: The roles of sponsor and rebuttal. *Journal of Broadcasting and Electronic Media, 29,* 147–159.

Genova, B. K. L., & Greenberg, B. S. (1979). Interests in news and the knowledge gap. *Public Opinion Quarterly, 43,* 79–91.

Idsvoog, K. A., & Hoyt, J. L. (1977). Professionalism and performance of television journalists. *Journal of Broadcasting, 21,* 97–109.

Jeffres, L. (1978). Cable TV and viewer selectivity. *Journal of Broadcasting, 22,* 167–178.

Kerlinger, F. N., & Pedhazur, E. J. (1973). *Multiple regression in behavioral research.* New York: Holt, Rinehart & Winston.

Krull, R., & Husson, W. (1980). Children's anticipatory attention to the TV screen. *Journal of Broadcasting, 24,* 35–48.

Metallinos, N., & Tiemens, R. (1977). Asymmetry of the screen: The effect of left versus right placement of television images. *Journal of Broadcasting, 21,* 21–34.

Nie, N. H., Hull, C. H., Jenkins, J. G., Steinbrenner, K., & Bent, D. H. (1975). *Statistical package for the social sciences.* New York: McGraw-Hill.

Nunnally, J. C. (1978). *Psychometric theory* (2nd ed.). New York: McGraw-Hill.

Presser, S., & Schuman, H. (1980). The measurement of a middle position in attitude surveys. *Public Opinion Quarterly, 44,* 70–85.

Reeves, B., & Miller, M. (1977). A multidimensional measure of children's identification with television characters. *Journal of Broadcasting, 22,* 71–86.

Roscoe, J. T. (1975). *Fundamental research statistics for the behavioral sciences.* New York: Holt, Rinehart & Winston.

Siegel, S. (1988). *Nonparametric statistics for the behavioral sciences.* New York: McGraw-Hill.

Thorndike, R. M. (1978). *Correlational procedures for research.* New York: Gardner Press.

Tukey, J. W. (1986). *The collected works of John W. Tukey,* Vols. III and IV. Belmont, CA: Wadsworth.

Wakshlag, J. J., & Greenberg, B. S. (1979). Programming strategies and the popularity of television programs for children. *Journal of Communication, 6,* 58–68.

Winer, B. J. (1971). *Statistical principles in experimental design.* New York: McGraw-Hill.

Winkler, R., & Hays, W. (1975). *Statistics: Probability, inference, and decision.* New York: Holt, Rinehart & Winston.

RESEARCH IN THE PRINT MEDIA

Methodologies used to study the print media are similar to those employed in most areas of research; academic and commercial research organizations often employ content analysis, experiments, focus groups, and surveys, among other procedures, to study newspapers and magazines. Print media research, however, tends to be more narrowly focused and more oriented toward practical application. This chapter provides a brief overview of the most common types of studies in newspaper and magazine research, with a special emphasis on the research most likely to be conducted by advertiser-supported publications.

This chapter does not address *basic market studies* and *advertising exposure studies*. A basic market study provides a demographic or psychographic portrait of the potential readers of a newspaper or magazine; this market research technique is more fully described by Green, Tull, and Albaum (1988). Advertising exposure studies (also called reader traffic studies) are conducted to determine which ads are noticed or read by a publication's audience; for more information on these studies, see Chapter 15.

BACKGROUND

Magazines and newspapers were one of the first subjects of mass media research. The initial interest in such research came from colleges and universities. In 1924 the *Journalism Bulletin* was first published by the Association of American Schools and Departments of Journalism. The first issue contained an article by William Bleyer entitled "Research Problems and Newspaper Analysis," which presented a list of possible research topics in journalism. Among them were the effects of form and typography on the ease and rapidity of newspaper reading, the effects of newspaper content on circulation, and the analysis of newspaper content. Bleyer's article was remarkably accurate in predicting the types of studies that would characterize newspaper and magazine research in the coming years.

Much of the content of early print media research was qualitative. The first volume of *Journalism Quarterly,* founded in 1928 to succeed the *Journalism Bulletin,* contained articles on press law, history, international comparisons, and ethics. Soon, however, quantitative research began to make its appearance in this academic journal: An article published in March 1930 surveyed the research interests of those currently working in the newspaper and magazine field and found the most prevalent type of study to be the survey of reader interest in newspaper content. The June 1930 issue contained an article by Ralph Nafziger, "A Reader Interest Survey of Madison, Wisconsin," which served as the prototype for hundreds of future research studies. The 1930s also saw the publication of many studies designed to assess the results of print media advertising. This led to studies in applied research, and several publications began sponsoring their own readership surveys. By and large, however, the results of these studies were considered proprietary.

As the techniques of quantitative research became more widely known and adopted, newspaper and magazine research became more empirical. This trend was first recognized by Wilbur Schramm (1957) in an article in *Public Opinion Quarterly* that reviewed 20 years of research as reported in *Journalism Quarterly*. Schramm found that only 10% of the 101 articles published between 1937 and 1941 concerned quantitative analyses; by 1952–1956, however, nearly half the 143 articles published were quantitative, a fivefold increase in only 15 years. The reasons for this trend, according to Schramm, were the growing availability of basic data, the development of more sophisticated research tools, and the increase in institutional support for research.

By 1960, newspapers and magazines were competing with television as well as radio for audience attention and advertiser investment. This situation greatly spurred the growth of private sector research. The Bureau of Advertising of the American Newspaper Publishers Association (subsequently called the Newspaper Advertising Bureau) began conducting studies on all aspects of the press and its audience. In the 1970s, it founded the News Research Center, which reports the results of research to editors. The Magazine Publishers Association also began to sponsor survey research at this time. The continuing interest of academics in print media research led to the creation of the *Newspaper Research Journal* in 1979, a publication devoted entirely to research that has practical implications for newspaper management.

In 1976 the Newspaper Readership Project was instituted to study the problems of declining circulation and sagging readership. As a major part of the 6-year, $5-million study, a news research center was set up at Syracuse University to abstract and synthesize the results of more than 300 private and published studies of newspaper reading habits. The Newspaper Advertising Bureau produced dozens of research reports and conducted extensive focus group studies. In addition, regional workshops were held across the country to explain to editors the uses and limitations of research. By the time the Readership Project ended, most editors had accepted research as a necessary tool of the trade. Bogart (1991) presents a thorough history of the Readership Project.

In 1977 the Newspaper Research Council (NRC), a subgroup of the Newspaper Advertis-

ing Bureau, was incorporated with 75 members. This group was involved with the American Society of Newspaper Editors in a circulation retention study and with the International Newspaper Marketing Association on how to convert Sunday-only readers to daily readers. In 1992, the Newspaper Advertising Bureau merged with the American Newspaper Publishers Association to create the Newspaper Association of America (NAA). The NAA continued the efforts of the NRC in the research area. In 1994, the NAA sponsored a study to determine how newspapers could attract younger readers. Another study, released in 1995, dealt with characteristics of readers of the editorial page.

Most newspapers with a circulation of at least 100,000 now have an in-house research department. The expansion of group-owned newspapers—about 75% of U.S. dailies in 1994—has also increased the trend toward research because many small papers can call upon their corporate research staffs for aid. Even some of the individually owned small papers have added researchers to their staff. The Vancouver, Washington, *Columbian* (circulation 48,000) recently hired a research manager, as did the Rochester, Minnesota, *Post-Bulletin* (circulation 39,000). A recent survey (Stein, 1991) of research directors of newspapers found that about half of the participating directors felt that research activity was enjoying increased influence at their papers. Experts estimate that the newspaper industry spent about $30–$40 million on research in 1992, a substantial increase since 1980.

As Veronis (1989) points out, research touches nearly every corner of the publishing industry: advertising, marketing, circulation, readership, and news-editorial. Print media research is conducted by commercial research firms, in-house research organizations, professional associations, and colleges. Print media research is likely to continue its growth. The Associated Press Managing Editors association recently released its "Year 2000" report in which it called for the establishment of an industry-wide research institute. A survey by

Schweitzer (1992) of 135 researchers at newspapers across the country revealed that two-thirds thought the importance their newspapers placed on research would increase in the next five years. Consensus among industry experts (Veronis, 1989) is that research will remain a vital element of the business as long as newspapers and magazines face heightened competition from other media.

TYPES OF PRINT MEDIA RESEARCH

Newspaper and magazine researchers conduct five basic types of studies: readership, circulation, management, typography/makeup, and readability. Most of their research focuses on readership; increasingly, however, studies are being conducted of circulation and management. Only a few studies have been conducted of typography/makeup and readability.

READERSHIP RESEARCH

Many readership studies were done in the United States in the years immediately preceding and following World War II. The George Gallup organization was a pioneer in developing the methodology of these studies—namely, a personal interview in which respondents were shown a copy of a newspaper and asked to identify the articles they had read. The most complete survey of newspaper readership was undertaken by the American Newspaper Publishers Association (ANPA), whose *Continuing Studies of Newspapers* involved more than 50,000 interviews with readers of 130 daily newspapers between 1939 and 1950 (Swanson, 1955).

Readership research became important to management during the 1960s and 1970s, as circulation rates in metropolitan areas began to level off or decline. Concerned with holding the interests of their readers, editors and publishers began to depend on surveys for the detailed audience information they needed to shape the content of a publication. The uncertain economy of the early 1990s and increasing competition from other media have made readership research even more important today.

Research into newspaper readership is composed primarily of five types of studies: reader profiles, item-selection studies, reader-nonreader studies, uses and gratifications studies, and editor-reader comparisons.

Reader Profiles. A reader profile provides a demographic summary of the readers of a particular publication. For example, a profile of the audience of a travel-oriented magazine might disclose that the majority of the readers earn more than $40,000 a year, are 25–34 years old, hold college degrees, possess six credit cards, and travel at least three times a year. This information can be used to focus the publication, prepare advertising promotions, and increase subscriptions.

Such information is particularly helpful when launching a new publication. For example, when *USA Today* debuted, a reader profile showed that 29% of its readers had annual incomes exceeding $35,000; 67% reported attending college; 32% were 18–29; and 26% had taken six or more round-trip plane trips in the past year. Obviously, such numbers would be of interest to both advertisers and editors.

Because there may be significant differences in the nature and extent of newspaper reading among individuals who have the same demographic characteristics, researchers recently have turned to psychographic and lifestyle segmentation studies to construct reader profiles. Both procedures go beyond the traditional demographic portrait and describe readers in terms of what they think or how they live. **Psychographic studies** usually ask readers to indicate their level of agreement or disagreement with a large number of attitudinal statements. Subsequently, patterns of response are analyzed to see how they correlate or cluster together. People who show high levels of agreement with questions that cluster together can be described with labels that summarize the substance of the questions. For example, people who tend to agree with statements such as "I like to think I'm a swinger," "I'm a night person," and "Sex outside marriage can be a healthy thing," might be called "Progressives." On the other hand, people who agree with items such as "Women's lib has gone too far," "Young people have too much freedom," and "The good old days were better," might be labeled "Traditionalists."

Lifestyle segmentation research takes a similar approach. Respondents are asked a battery of questions concerning activities, hobbies, interests, and attitudes. Again, the results are analyzed to see which items cluster together. Groups of individuals who share the same attitudes and activities are extracted and labeled. To illustrate, Guzda (1984) reported on a lifestyle segmentation study that resulted in the following group labels: young busy mothers, Mrs. traditionalist, ladder climbers, senior solid conservatives, midlife upscalers, and winter affluents. Similarly, Ruotolo (1988) identified five types of newspaper readers: instrumental readers, opinion-makers, pleasure readers, ego boosters, and scanners. Both psychographic and lifestyle segmentation studies are designed to provide management with additional insights about editorial aims, target

audiences, and circulation goals. Besides, they give advertisers a multidimensional portrait of the publications' readers. Two of the most popular scales designed to measure these variables are the List of Values (LOV) and the recently revised Values and Life Styles test (VALS II). Descriptions and comparisons of these scales are found in Novak and MacEvoy (1990). Other social factors might also be important. Loges and Ball-Rokeach (1993) note that newspaper readership is related to several sociological variables—including social understanding, self understanding, and action orientation—that explain more of the variation in readership than do traditional demographic variables.

Item-Selection Studies. A second type of newspaper readership study, the item-selection study, is used to determine who reads specific parts of the paper. The readership of a particular item is usually measured by means of **aided recall**, whereby the interviewer shows a copy of the paper to the respondent to find out which stories the respondent remembers. In one variation on this technique the interviewer preselects items for which readership data are to be gathered and asks subjects about those items only. Because of the expense involved in conducting personal interviews, some researchers now use phone interviews to collect readership data. Calls are made on the same day the issue of the paper is published. The interviewer asks the respondent to bring a copy of the paper to the phone, and together they go over each page, with the respondent identifying the items he or she has read. Although this method saves money, it excludes from study those readers who do not happen to have a copy of the paper handy.

Another money-saving technique is to mail respondents a self-administered readership survey. Hvistendahl (1977) described two variations of this type of study. In the "whole copy" method, a sample of respondents receives an entire copy of the previous day's paper in the mail, along with a set of instructions and a questionnaire. The instructions direct the respondents to go through the newspaper and mark each item they have read by drawing a line through it. A return envelope with postage prepaid is provided. In the "clipping" method, the procedure is identical except that respondents are mailed clippings of certain items rather than the whole paper. To save postage fees, the clippings are pasted up on pages, reduced 25%, and reproduced by offset. Hvistendahl reported a 67% return rate using this method with only one follow-up postcard. He noted that the whole copy and clipping methods produced roughly equivalent results, though readership scores on some items tended to be slightly higher when clippings were used. A comparison of the results of these self-administered surveys with the results of personal interviews also indicated an overall equivalence.

Stamm, Jackson, and Jacoubovitch (1980) suggested a more detailed method of item-selection analysis, which they called a tracking study. They supplied their respondents with a selection of colored pencils and asked them to identify which parts of an article (headline, text, photo, cutline) they had read, using a different colored pencil each time they began a new *reading episode* (defined as a stream of uninterrupted reading). The results showed a wide degree of variability in the readership of the elements that made up an item: For one story, 27% of the subjects had read the headline, 32% the text, and 36% the cutline. There was also variation in the length and type of articles read per reading episode.

The unit of analysis in an item-selection study is a specific news article (such as a front-page story dealing with a fire) or a specific content category (such as crime news, sports, obituaries). The readership of items or categories is then related to certain audience demographic or psychographic characteristics. For example, Larkin and Hecht (1979) found that readers of nonmetropolitan daily papers read news about local events the most and news about national events the least. In another readership study, Lynn and Bennett (1980) divided their sample according to residence in urban, rural, or farming areas. Their survey found that there was little difference in the type of news content read by farm and rural dwellers, but that urban residents were more likely to read letters to the editor, society items, and local news. More recently, Griswold and Moore (1989) found that readers of a small daily newspaper most often read local news, obituaries, police news, state news, and weather forecasts.

A 1991 study (Simmons Market Research Bureau, 1991) found that, among a national sample of adults, the general news and entertainment sections of the paper were read the most and the classified and "Home" sections were read the least. Item-selection studies are often used to help newspapers reach certain groups of readers. Gersh (1990), for example, reported that teenage readers have reading habits different from adults. The most popular sections of the newspaper among teens were comics, sports, and entertainment; finance, food, and home sections were the least popular.

Some item-selection studies have used comprehensive surveys that encompass many newspaper markets. Burgoon, Burgoon, and Wilkinson (1983) surveyed approximately 6,500 adults in 10 newspaper markets to identify clusters of items and topics that interested readers. Respondents were asked how often they typically read items dealing with about 30 topics normally found in the newspaper. Natural disasters/tragedies and stories about the national economy were the most read. A survey of 22,400 households sponsored by the Newspaper Association of America (Fisher, 1993) found that 92% of the audience read general news; the entertainment and sports section ranked second and third.

Reader-Nonreader Studies. The third type of newspaper readership research is called the reader-nonreader study. This type of study can be conducted via personal, telephone, or mail interviews with minor modifications. It is difficult, however, to establish an operational definition for the term *nonreader*. In some studies, a nonreader is determined by a "no" answer to the question, "Do you generally read a newspaper?" Others have used the more specific question, "Have you read a newspaper yesterday or today?" (The rationale being used here is that respondents are more likely to admit they have not read a paper today or yesterday than that they never read one.) A third form of this question uses multiple-response categories. Respondents are asked, "How often do you read a daily paper?" and they are given five choices of response: "very often," "often," "sometimes," "seldom," and "never." Nonreaders are defined as those who check the "never" response, or in some studies, "seldom" or "never." Obviously, the form of the question has an impact on how many people are classified as nonreaders. The largest percentage of nonreaders generally occurs when researchers ask, "Have you read a newspaper today or yesterday?" (Penrose, Weaver, Cole, & Shaw, 1974); the smallest number is obtained by requiring a "never" response to the multiple-response question (Sobal & Jackson-Beeck, 1981).

Once the nonreaders have been identified, researchers typically attempt to describe them by means of traditional demographic variables. For example, Penrose et al. (1974) found nonreading to be related to low education, low income, and residence in a nonurban area. Sobal and Jackson-Beeck (1981) reported that nonreaders tend to be older, to have less education and lower incomes, and to have more often been widowed or divorced than readers. And Bogart (1991) concluded that nonreaders are less likely to have voted in the last presidential election and to believe that their opinions had an impact on local government. A study by Stone (1994) found that education was a better predictor of newspaper readership than race among a sample of 18–34 year-olds.

Several studies of nonreaders have attempted to identify the reasons for not reading the newspaper. The data for these subjects have generally been collected by asking nonreaders to tell the interviewer in their own words why they do not read. Responses are analyzed and the most frequent reasons reported. Poindexter (1978) found that the three reasons named most often by nonreaders were lack of time, preference for another news medium (especially TV), and cost. Bogart (1991) identified four reasons: depressing news, cost, lack of interest, and inability to spend sufficient time at home. Lipschultz (1987) discovered that nonreaders relied more on radio and TV for news, found newspapers too costly, perceived papers as neither interesting nor useful, and thought that newspaper reading took up too much time. In addition, as revealed by the studies cited previously, people with less education were more likely to be nonreaders.

Broader studies in this area have included variables that are beyond the control of the newspaper. In a longitudinal study, Chaffee and Choe (1981) found that changes in marital status, residence, and employment had an impact on newspaper readership. Similarly, Einseidel and Kang (1983) found that reading habits are accounted for, at least in part, by civic attitudes. Finally, Cobb-Walgren (1990) focused on reasons why teenagers do not read the newspaper. She found that both teenagers' home environment and their image of the newspaper were important in determining why teens fail to read newspapers. Nonreaders perceived that reading the paper took up too much time and effort and were more likely to have parents who also did not read newspapers.

Uses and Gratifications Studies.   A uses and gratifications study is used to study all media content. For newspapers it is used to determine the motives that lead to newspaper reading and the personal and psychological rewards that result from it. The methodology of the uses and gratifications study is straightforward: Respondents are given a list of possible uses and gratifications and are asked whether any of these are the motives behind their reading. For example, a reader might be presented with the following items:

> Here is a list of some things people have said about why they read the newspaper. How much do you agree or disagree with each statement?

1. I read the newspaper because it is entertaining.
2. I read the newspaper because I want to kill time.
3. I read the newspaper to keep up to date with what's going on around me.
4. I read the newspaper to relax and to relieve tension.
5. I read the newspaper so I can find out what other people are saying about things that are important to me.

The responses are then summed and an average score for each motivation item is calculated.

Several studies have taken this approach to explain readership. For example, McCombs (1977) found three primary psychological motivations for reading newspapers: the need to keep up to date, the need for information, and the need for fun. Reading for information

seemed to be the strongest motivator. Similarly, Weaver, Wilhoit, and Reide (1979) found that the three motivations most common in explaining general media use are the need to keep tabs on what is going on around one, the need to be entertained, and the need to kill time. The authors also noted differences among demographic groups regarding which of these needs were best met by the newspaper. For example, young males, young females, and middle-aged males were most likely to say they read a newspaper to satisfy their need to keep tabs on things, but they preferred other forms of media for entertainment and killing time. A study done in Hawaii (Blood, Keir, & Kang, 1983) reinforced these conclusions. The two factors that were the best predictors of readership were "use in daily living" and "fun to read." In addition, gratifications from reading the newspaper seemed to differ across ethnic groups.

Elliott and Rosenberg (1987) took advantage of the 1985 newspaper strike in Philadelphia to survey the gratifications of readers during and after the strike. They found that people deprived of a daily newspaper turned to other media to fill the surveillance/contact function but no evidence of compensatory media behavior for the entertainment, "killing time," and advertising functions associated with newspaper reading. Payne, Severn, and Dozier (1988) studied uses and gratifications as indicators of magazine readership. They found three main classes of gratifications: surveillance, diversion, and interaction. In addition, readers' scores on these three categories were consistent with the magazines they chose to read. Bramlett-Solomon and Merrill (1991), in their study of newspaper usage in a retirement community, found that readers used the newspaper to keep them involved with the community. More recently, Perse and Courtright (1993) found that print media were seen as most useful in fulfilling learning needs but were not rated highly for social, arousal or companionship needs. As more and more print media move into on-line versions available over

Reading the Tabloids

Readership research can be either quantitative (as described in the text) or qualitative, as in the case of the book by Elizabeth Bird, *For Inquiring Minds: A Cultural Study of Supermarket Tabloids*. The author asked readers of the *National Examiner* to write letters explaining why they read the paper. She received more than 100 replies and conducted intensive interviews with 16 of the respondents. What sort of person reads the tabs? Many were middle-aged, white women with a high school education, but about one-third of those who replied were men. Do they actually believe the wild and bizarre stories that appear in the tabloids? Bird found that belief was selective. People who gave great credence to ESP, for example, were apt to put great faith in stories about its existence, but these same people might totally dismiss stories about UFOs or astrology. Some people, however, seemed completely gullible. One person traveled all the way to Guatemala in response to a report that a plant had been discovered there that would make people younger. Alas, the reader was unable to locate the plant.

electronic information services such as Prodigy or America On-line, future research will probably concentrate on comparing and contrasting the gratifications obtained from publications on this new channel of delivery with the traditional print versions.

Editor-Reader Comparisons. In the final area of newspaper readership research, editor-reader comparisons, a group of editors is questioned about a certain topic, and their answers are compared to those of their readers to see whether there is any correspondence between the two groups. Bogart (1989) presented two examples of such research. In one study, a group of several hundred editors was asked to rate 23 attributes of a high-quality newspaper. The editors ranked "high ratio of staff-written copy to wire service copy" 1st; "high amount of nonadvertising content" 2nd; and "high ratio of news interpretations . . . to spot news reports" 3rd. When a sample of readers ranked the same list, the editors' three top attributes were ranked 7th, 11th, and 12th, respectively. The readers rated "presence of an action line column" 1st; "high ratio of sports and feature news to total news" 2nd, and "presence of a news summary" and "high number of letters to

the editor per issue" in a tie for 3rd. In short, there was little congruence between the two groups in their perceptions of the attributes of a high-quality newspaper.

In a related study, Bogart gave readers an opportunity to design their own newspaper. Interviewers presented a sample of readers with 34 subjects and asked how much space they would give to each in a paper tailor-made to their own interests. Major categories of news were omitted from the listings because they were topics over which editors have little control. When the results were tabulated, the contents of a sample of newspapers were analyzed to see whether the space allocations made by editors matched the public's preferences. The resulting data indicated that readers wanted more of certain content than they were getting (consumer news; health, nutritional, and medical advice; home maintenance; travel) and that they were getting more of some topics than they desired (sports news; human interest stories; school news; crossword puzzles; astrology). More recently, Jones (1993) used a coorientation model to investigate the perceptions of a newspaper's editorial staff and its readers concerning the news selection process. The data revealed that the professionals' ranking of news items was significantly correlated with the readers' ranking.

Two studies indicate that this technique has been broadened to include journalist–reader comparisons as well as editor–reader matchups. Ogan and Lafky (1983) asked editors, reporters, and the general public to rank the most important news stories from the preceding year. These orderings were compared to the list of the top 10 stories compiled by the Associated Press and United Press International. The results demonstrated that local news stories seemed less important to readers than to professionals but, in general, consumers and newspaper staffers agreed on significant issues. Burgoon, Bernstein, and Burgoon (1983) asked 1,118 journalists (publishers, editors, reporters, and photographers), and 6,112 adults to rank-order statements describing the functions of a newspaper. Both the readers and the professionals agreed that the most important functions of a newspaper were to provide a timely account of significant events and to explain how important events and issues relate to the local community. There was one notable disagreement: Readers ranked the watchdog function of the press much lower than did journalists.

Magazine Readership Research. Magazine readership surveys are fundamentally similar to those conducted for newspapers but tend to differ in the particulars. Some magazine research is done by personal interview; respondents are shown a copy of the magazine under study and asked to rate each article on a four-point scale ("read all," "read most," "read some," or "didn't read"). The mail survey technique, also frequently used, involves sending a second copy of the magazine to a subscriber shortly after the regular copy has been mailed; instructions on how to mark the survey copy to show readership are included. For example, the respondents might be instructed to mark with a check the articles they scanned, to draw an X through articles read in their entirety, and to underline titles of articles that were only partly read.

Most consumer magazines use audience data compiled by the Simmons Market Research Bureau (SMRB) and Mediamark Research Inc. (MRI). Both companies select a large random sample of households (about 19,000 homes) and interview readers. Prior to 1994, SMRB and MRI used different techniques to measure readership. Simmons would screen its respondents by first showing them cards with magazine logos printed on them followed by stripped down issues of actual magazines. Those people who reported reading one or more magazines would then be interviewed again. Mediamark would present logo cards to respondents to identify readers and then gather more detailed data in a single interview. Since the two research companies used different techniques, their readership data did not always agree and the discrepancy was a source of some concern in the magazine industry. In 1994, however, partly as a money-saving strategy, SMRB announced that it was adopting a technique similar to that used by MRI.

Many magazines maintain *reader panels* of 25–30 people who are selected to participate for a predetermined period. All feature articles appearing in each issue of the magazine are sent to these panel members, who rate each article on a number of scales, including interest, ease of readership, and usefulness. Over time, a set of guidelines for evaluating the success of an article is drawn up, and future articles can be measured against that standard. The primary advantage of this form of panel survey is that it can provide information about audience reactions at a modest cost. Other publications might use surveys that are included with the magazine itself. The *Engineering News-Record,* for example, conducts periodic in-magazine surveys that ask readers about career issues. The results are then published in a special advertising section sponsored by recruiting firms (Katcher, 1995).

Readership profiles are commonly done at most magazines, particularly when a magazine has undergone a change of editors, design, or

---

Measuring Readership: Daily or Weekly?

Since it began, newspaper readership research has been geared to measuring the amount of readership garnered by daily newspapers. One of the most common questions used to measure readership has been, "Did you read a newspaper today or yesterday?" This question, however, is not adequate to measure weekly newspaper reading. Surveys done on Mondays, Tuesdays, Wednesdays, Saturdays, and Sundays would probably not accurately assess reading a weekly that appears on Thursday.

Thurlo and Milo (1993) suggest that more research should be devoted to the readership of weeklies. Their study of college students revealed that about half of them reported reading every issue of their campus weekly and a local weekly. In contrast, 56% of the students reported that they never read the local daily and only about 3% were classified as everyday readers. The authors note that it is important to track these students to see if they continue to favor the weekly over the daily or if they join the ranks of nonreaders.

---

focus. A readership profile done a year after Tina Brown assumed the editorship of *The New Yorker* revealed that not only had readership increased but that the median age of a *New Yorker* reader had dropped from 48 to 46 years while the median household income had increased by 12.5% (Janofsky, 1993).

Another procedure that is peculiar to magazine research is the *item pretest* (Haskins, 1960). A random sample of magazine readers is shown an article title, a byline, and a brief description of the content of the story. Respondents are asked to rate the idea on a scale from 0 to 100, where 100 represents "would certainly read this article" and 0 represents "would not read this article." The average ratings of the proposed articles are tabulated as a guide for editorial decisions. Note that this technique can be used in personal interviews or with a mail survey with little variation in approach. Haskins also reported a positive correlation between scores obtained using this technique and those determined by postpublication readership surveys.

Other magazine research involves item-selection and editor-reader comparisons. For example, for the last 25 years, *Glamour* has surveyed reader response to every issue (Smith,

1992). Questionnaires are mailed to readers asking them about the articles, the cover, and the respondents' general reading habits. *Travel & Leisure* follows a similar system. The McGraw-Hill magazine group spends approximately $250,000 a year on readership research. *Good Housekeeping* takes a random survey of its subscribers each month to determine what stories were enjoyed and what recipes were tried. Harcourt Brace Jovanovich does both pretesting and posttesting in its health care journals. The company sends the titles of 15 articles printed on a single sheet of paper to 400 or 500 physicians. The respondents are asked to rate each article as having high-, moderate-, or low-interest value. The Cahners magazine group, working with the Simmons Market Research Bureau, recently developed an Affinity Index for its trade publications; the index measures reader loyalty.

In addition to traditional readership studies, many magazines are conducting focus groups. Harcourt Brace Jovanovich depends particularly on focus groups to help fine-tune the content of new publications. Ziff Communications does the same. *Farmer* uses focus group sessions for reader reaction to headlines, graphics, and general editorial feedback. Other magazines use focus groups as supplements to their monthly questionnaires.

CIRCULATION RESEARCH

The term **circulation research** is applied to two different forms of newspaper and magazine study. The first type of circulation research uses a particular group of readers as its unit of analysis. It attempts to measure circulation in terms of the overall characteristics of a particular market—for example, to determine the proportion of households in a given market that are reached by a particular newspaper or the circulation pattern of a magazine among certain demographic groups or in specific geographic areas. Tillinghast (1981), who analyzed changes in newspaper circulation in four regions of the country, found that the greatest decrease had occurred in the East and the South. He also reported that the degree of urbanization in a region was positively related to circulation. In a study of 69 Canadian daily newspaper markets, Alperstein (1980) discovered that newspaper circulation was positively related to the proportion of reading households within the newspaper's home city. In addition, daily newspaper circulation was found to be inversely related to weekly newspaper circulation. More recently, two studies have examined the impact of newspaper content variables on circulation. Lacy and Fico (1991) demonstrated that measures of the content quality of a newspaper were positively related to circulation figures. Somewhat similarly, Lacy and Sohn (1990) found limited support for the hypothesis that the amount of space given to specific content sections in metropolitan newspapers correlates with circulation in suburban areas.

A recent trend in circulation research has been the identification of other market level or market structure variables that have an impact on circulation. Stone and Trotter (1981) found that the number of households in the local community and measures of broadcast media availability were the two best predictors of circulation. Blankenburg (1981) analyzed market structure variables and determined that county population and distance from the point of publication were strong predictors of circulation. Hale (1983) concluded from a regression analysis of Sunday newspaper sales in all 50 states that degree of urbanization, population density, and affluence were key predictors of circulation. Moore, Howard, and Johnson (1988) discovered that there was no relationship between viewing television news programs and afternoon newspaper circulation. Market size and location showed a stronger relation to circulation. In sum, it appears from these studies that many factors outside the control of the newspaper publisher have an impact on circulation.

Economic influences have also been examined. Blankenburg and Friend (1994) discovered that circulation figures were not related to the percentage of a newspaper's budget that was spent on news-editorial expenses nor was there a relationship between amount spent on promotion and circulation. There was, however, an influence due to newspaper price; papers that cost more tended to lose circulation. Similarly, Lewis (1995) found that increases in price were related to declines in circulation.

Some publications use computer models to predict circulation. *Playboy*, for example, collected data for 52 issues of its publication on number of copies sold, cover price, current unemployment statistics, dollars spent on promotion, number of days on sale, editors' estimates, number of full-page displays, and several other variables. These figures were subjected to a regression analysis to determine how each factor was related to total sales. Interestingly, the number of copies distributed, number of days an issue was on sale, and cover rating proved to be good predictors, but the amount of money spent on promotion was found to have little impact on sales.

Blankenburg (1987) generated a regression equation to predict circulation after newspaper consolidation. Guthrie, Ludwin, and Jacob

(1988) also developed a regression equation to predict metropolitan circulation in outlying counties. They found that the two most important predictor variables were an index of magazine circulation and an index of local newspaper competition for each county.

The second type of circulation research uses the individual reader as the unit of analysis to measure the effects of certain aspects of delivery and pricing systems on reader behavior. For example, McCombs, Mullins, and Weaver (1974) studied why people cancel their subscriptions to newspapers. They found that the primary reasons had less to do with content than with circulation problems, such as irregular delivery and delivery in unreadable condition. These reasons were substantiated in a 1992 Paragon Research study of circulation of the two newspapers in Denver, Colorado.

Magazine publishers often conduct this type of circulation research by drawing samples of subscribers in different states and checking on the delivery dates of their publication and its physical condition when received. Other publications contact subscribers who do not renew to determine what can be done to prevent cancellation (Sullivan, 1993). Studies have even been conducted to find out why some people do not pay their subscription bills promptly.

The Gannett Company's Newspaper Division conducted research that discovered that customer billing was a prime cause of their newspapers losing circulation. Subsequently, Gannett interviewed 1,000 subscribers and conducted several focus groups to devise a billing system that was more responsive to consumer needs. Some circulation research uncovers facts that management would probably never be aware of. For example, at the Wichita *Eagle,* management was puzzled over circulation losses. A survey found that many subscribers were canceling because the plastic delivery bags used by the paper on rainy days were not heavy enough, and many readers were fed up with soggy papers. In short, this type of circulation research investigates the effect on readership or subscription rates of variables that are unrelated to a publication's content.

NEWSPAPER MANAGEMENT RESEARCH

The fastest growing research area in the early 1990s examined newspaper management practices. This growth was due to several factors. First, newspaper companies expanded their holdings, which created a more complicated management structure. Second, media competition became more intense. Newspapers with efficient management techniques had more of an advantage in the new competitive environment. Third, the newspaper industry became more labor-intensive. Skilled and experienced personnel form the backbone of a successful newspaper. More and more managers turned to research to determine how to keep employees the most satisfied and productive. Finally, a weak advertising market during the early 1990s cut newspaper revenue and managers turned to research to find ways to operate more efficiently.

The techniques used to study newspaper management were the same as those used to study any business activity: surveys, case studies, descriptive content analysis, and mathematical models. The main topics that attracted the most research attention in the last five years were goal setting by management, employee job satisfaction, and effects of competition and ownership on newspaper content and quality.

Some representative examples of management research into goal setting include Demers and Wackman's (1988) study of the effect of chain (group) ownership on management's objectives. Secondary analysis of data collected from a sample of 101 newspaper managers revealed that editors at chain-owned daily newspapers were more likely to say that profit was a goal that was driving their organization. Analogous results were found in a follow-up study (Demers, 1991). In a similar study, Busterna (1989) administered a survey of 42 newspaper executives, most of them from weekly papers, asking them to rate several managerial goals in terms of their relative importance to their newspapers. Managers who also owned their papers placed less emphasis on maximizing profits as a goal, whereas nonowner managers ranked it first. Finally, Connery (1989) conducted a case study of several small daily newspapers and concluded that management commitment was necessary if a newspaper was to achieve its goal of journalistic excellence.

Job satisfaction among newspaper employees has been the topic of several studies. Bergen and Weaver (1988) conducted a secondary data analysis of a survey of 1,001 U.S. journalists. They found that the strongest correlate of individual job satisfaction was how satisfied the journalist was with the performance of his or her news organization. Stamm and Underwood's (1993) survey of 429 newsrooms revealed that job satisfaction was negatively related to a newspaper's emphasis on business over journalism but positively related to an emphasis on journalistic quality. Bramlett-Solomon (1993) discovered that the job satisfaction motivations of black journalists were not very different from those of white journalists.

A related issue that has garnered recent attention has been job burnout among journalists. Data collected from employees at five newspapers (Cook and Banks, 1993) revealed that the person most likely to suffer from burnout was a young, entry-level journalist working as a copy editor at a small daily newspaper. Not surprisingly, journalists with a high level of job satisfaction were unlikely to experience burnout. In a related study, Cook, Banks, and Turner (1993) reported that several work environment variables, including supervisor support and peer cohesion, were also related to burnout.

Research on the impact of concentration of ownership include Akhavan-Majid, Rife, and Gopinah's (1991) study of editorial positions taken by Gannett-owned papers. They found that the Gannett papers were more likely than

other newspapers to endorse similar editorial positions. Lacy (1990) found that local market monopoly newspapers used a smaller number of wire services than did papers in competitive markets, supporting earlier findings that competition encourages more spending on the news-editorial department. Coulson (1994) sampled 773 journalists at independent and group-owned papers about the quality of their publication. Reporters at independently owned papers were more likely to rate their paper's commitment to quality local coverage as excellent. Finally, Coulson and Hansen (1995) examined the news content of the *Louisville Courier-Journal* after its purchase by the Gannett organization. Results indicated that the total amount of news space increased but that the average length of stories and the amount of hard news coverage declined.

TYPOGRAPHY AND MAKEUP RESEARCH

Another type of print media research measures the effects of news design elements—specifically typeface and page makeup—on readership, reader preferences, and comprehension. By means of this approach, researchers have tested the effects of different typography and makeup elements, including amount of white space, presence of paragraph headlines, size and style of type, variations in column width, and use of vertical or horizontal page makeup.

The experimental method (Chapter 9) is used most often in typography and makeup studies. Subjects are typically assigned to one or more treatment groups, exposed to an experimental stimulus (typically in the form of a mock newspaper or magazine page), and asked to rate what they have seen according to a series of dependent variable measures.

Among dependent variables that have been rated by subjects are informative value of a publication, interest in reading a publication, image of a page, recall of textual material, readability, and general preference for a particular page. A common practice is to measure these variables by means of a semantic differential rating scale. For example, Siskind (1979) used a nine-point, 20-item differential scale with such adjective pairs as "messy/neat," "informative/uninformative," "unpleasant/pleasant," "easy/difficult," "clear/unclear," "bold/timid," and "passive/active." She obtained a general reader preference score by having subjects rate a newspaper page and summing their responses to all 20 items. Other studies have measured reader interest by using the rating scale technique or the 0–100 "feeling thermometer" (Figure 7.1, page 145). Comprehension and recall are typically measured by a series of true/false or multiple-choice questions on the content that is being evaluated.

Haskins and Flynne (1974) conducted a typical design study to test the effects of different typefaces on the perceived attractiveness of and reader interest in the women's section of a newspaper. They hypothesized that some typefaces would be perceived as more feminine than others and that headlines in such typefaces would create more reader interest in the page. The authors showed an experimental copy of a newspaper prepared specially for the study to a sample of 150 female heads of households: One subsample saw a paper with headlines in the women's section printed in Garamond Italic (a typeface experts had rated as feminine), while a second group saw the same page with Spartan Black headlines (considered to be a masculine typeface). A third group served as a control and saw only the headline copy typed on individual white cards. The subjects were asked to evaluate each article for reading interest. Additionally, each woman was shown a sample of 10 typefaces and asked to rate them on a semantic differential scale with 16 adjective pairs.

The researchers discovered that typeface had no impact on reader interest scores. In fact, the scores were about the same for the printed headlines as they were for those typed on white cards. Analysis of the typeface ratings revealed that readers were able to differentiate between typefaces; Garamond Italic was rated as the second most feminine typeface while Spartan Black was rated most masculine, thus confirming the judgment of the expert raters.

Studies of page layout have been used to help magazine editors make decisions about the mechanics of editing and makeup. Click and Baird (1979) provided a summary of the more pertinent research in this area. A few of their conclusions are listed here to illustrate the types of independent variables that have been studied:

1. Large illustrations attract more readers than small ones.
2. Unusually shaped pictures irritate readers.
3. A small amount of text and a large picture on the opening pages of an article increase readership.
4. Readers do not like to read type set in italics.
5. For titles, readers prefer simple, familiar typefaces.
6. Readers and graphic designers seldom agree about what constitutes superior type design.
7. Roman type can be read more quickly than other typefaces.

Wanta and Gao (1994) performed a similar study of newspaper design elements that young readers found desirable. They found that their sample of high school students preferred newspapers that used pull-out quotes, large graphics, and many small photographs.

The popularity of USA Today, with its ground-breaking illustrations and use of color, has prompted several studies. Two studies by Geraci (1984a, 1984b) compared the photographs, drawings, and other illustrations used by USA Today with those in traditional papers. Click and Stempel (1982) used seven front-page formats ranging from a modular page with a four-color halftone (the format favored by USA Today) to a traditional format with no color. Respondents were shown a slide of each page for 15 seconds and were asked to rate the page using 20 semantic differential scales. The results indicated that readers preferred modular pages and color.

More recent studies have continued along these same lines. Smith and Hajash (1988) performed a content analysis of the graphics used by 30 daily newspapers. They found that the average paper had 1 graphic per 17 pages compared to *USA Today's* average of 1.3 graphics per single page. The authors concluded that the influence of *USA Today* has not been overwhelming. Utt and Pasternack (1989) found that the influence of *USA Today* was more evident on the front-page design of American dailies. Most papers had increased their front-page use of color, photos, and informational graphics.

The impact of graphics on reader understanding and comprehension has also been examined, and the studies have had fairly consistent results. Kelly (1989) found that embellished graphic presentations of data (as commonly used by *USA Today*) were no better than unembellished graphics in helping readers retain information. Ward (1992) investigated whether using a sidebar graphic illustration along with a news story aided comprehension. He found that bar charts, tables, and an adorned bar chart were less effective in aiding comprehension than a straight sidebar story that accompanied the main story. On the other hand, Griffin and Stevenson (1992) reported that background material presented in both text and graphic forms increased readers' understanding of a complex story. These same researchers also found that including geographic information, either in the text or with a map, also raised comprehension scores on a news article (Griffin & Stevenson, 1994).

The advances in computerized pagination, layout, and graphics that occurred during the mid-1990s will probably make this area an important one in the future. In addition, the advent of many newspapers going online with services such as CompuServe and Prodigy, and many others having their own home pages on the World Wide Web, will mean that more research into the most effective design elements in electronic newspapers will also be likely.

READABILITY RESEARCH

Simply defined, readability is the sum total of all the elements and their interactions that affect the success of a piece of printed material. Success is measured by the extent to which readers understand the piece, are able to read it at an optimal speed, and find it interesting (Dale & Chall, 1948).

Several formulas have been developed to objectively determine the readability of text. One of the best known of these formulas is the **Flesch (1948) reading ease formula**, which requires the researcher to systematically select 100 words from the text, determine the total number of syllables in those words (wl), determine the average number of words per sentence (sl), and compute the following equation:

$$\text{Reading ease} = 206.835 - 0.846wl - 1.015sl$$

The score is compared to a chart that provides a description of style (such as "very easy") or a school grade level for the potential audience.

Another measure of readability is the **Fog Index**, which was developed by Gunning (1952). To compute the Fog Index, researchers must systematically select samples of 100 words each, determine the mean sentence length by dividing the number of words by the number of sentences, count the number of words with three or more syllables, add the mean sentence length to the number of words with three or more syllables, and multiply this sum by 0.4. Like the Flesch index, the Gunning formula suggests the educational level required for understanding a text. The chief advantages of the Fog Index are that the syllable count and the overall calculations are simpler to perform.

McLaughlin (1969) proposed a third readability index called **SMOG Grading** (for Simple

Measure Of Gobbledygook). The SMOG Grading is quick and easy to calculate: The researcher merely selects 10 consecutive sentences near the beginning of the text, 10 from the middle, and 10 from the end, and then counts every word of three or more syllables and takes the square root of the total. The number thus obtained represents the reading grade that a person must have reached to understand the text. McLaughlin's index can be quickly calculated using a small, easily measured sample. Although the procedure is related to that for the Fog Index, it appears that the SMOG grade is generally lower.

Taylor (1953) developed yet another method for measuring readability called the **Cloze procedure**. This technique departs from the formulas described above in that it does not require an actual count of words or syllables. Instead, the researcher chooses a passage of about 250–300 words, deletes every fifth word from a random starting point and replaces it with a blank, gives the passage to subjects and asks them to fill the blanks with what they think are the correct words, and then counts the number of times the blanks are replaced with the correct words. The number of correct words or the percentage of correct replacement constitutes the readability score for that passage. The paragraph below is a sample of what a passage might look like after it has been prepared for the Cloze procedure:

> The main stronghold of the far left _____ to be large _____ centers of north Italy. _____ is significant, however, that _____ largest relative increase in _____ leftist vote occurred in _____ areas where most of _____ landless peasants live-in _____ and south Italy and _____ Sicily and Sardinia. The _____ had concentrated much of _____ efforts on winning the _____ of those peasants.

Nestvold (1972) found that Cloze procedure scores were highly correlated with readers' own evaluations of content difficulty. The

Cloze procedure was also found to be a better predictor of evaluations than several other common readability tests.

Although they are not used extensively in print media research, readability studies can provide valuable information. For example, Fowler and Smith (1979), using samples from 1904, 1933, and 1965, found that text from magazines had remained constant in readability but that text from newspapers had fluctuated. For all years studied, magazines were easier to read than newspapers. Hoskins (1973) analyzed the readability levels of Associated Press and United Press International wire copy and found that both services scored in the "difficult" range; the Flesch indexes indicated that a 13th- to 16th-grade education was necessary for comprehension.

Fowler and Smith (1982) analyzed delayed-reward content (national affairs, science, medicine, business, and economy) and immediate-reward content (sports, people, newsmakers, and movies) in *Time* and *Newsweek*. In general, delayed-reward items were found to be more difficult to read than immediate-reward items. Smith (1984) also found differences in readability among categories of newspaper content, with features and entertainment more readable than national-international or state and local news. Smith also noted that three popular readability formulas did not assign the same level of reading difficulty to his sample of stories. Porter and Stephens (1989) found that a sample of Utah managing editors consistently underestimated the Flesch readability scores of five different stories from five different papers. They also found that the common claim that reporters write front-page stories at an 8th-grade level was a myth. The hard news stories they analyzed were written at an average 12th-grade level. Catalano (1990) discovered that wire service lead paragraphs were written in the "difficult" to "very difficult" range of readability. More recently, McAdams (1992/1993) computed a Fog Index for 14 news stories that were then given to a sample of readers. Results suggest that readers who found a story to have high overall quality were not adversely affected by a high Fog Index.

THE JOURNALIST AS RESEARCHER

Print media reporters and social scientists now have more in common with each other, thanks to two recent trends. The first trend is **precision journalism**, a technique of inquiry in which social science research methods are used to gather the news. Popularized by reporter and researcher Philip Meyer in his book, *Precision Journalism* (Meyer, 1973), the method relies primarily on the procedures of content analysis and survey research to generate quantitative data that are reported as news stories. For example, the *Detroit News* content analyzed almost 36,000 drunk-driving conviction records and discovered that big city judges gave more lenient penalties than rural judges. Similarly, the *Charlotte Observer* analyzed campaign finance reports and noted a link between voting patterns and contributions.

Precision journalism uses survey research to conduct polls designed to measure some aspect of public opinion. Many large newspapers such as *USA Today,* the *Washington Post,* and the *New York Times* regularly conduct public opinion polls on topics ranging from voting choices to attitudes about the environment. Other papers may sponsor a poll on a special topic to highlight a story. The *Dallas Times Herald,* for example, polled more than 1,200 passenger airline pilots as part of a series on the safety of air travel. Their survey noted that two-thirds of the pilots felt the skies were less safe now that the industry was deregulated.

There are, however, some disadvantages connected with precision journalism. First, lengthy content analyses and surveys take time and effort. Many of today's newspapers, faced with declining profits, may not be able to spare the people and the hours necessary to do precision journalism. Secondly, precision journalism can be costly. Phone bills, copying, computer software, and other supplies make this type of journalism more expensive than the usual reporting technique.

Nonetheless, the popularity of precision journalism suggests that competent journalists need a basic knowledge of social science techniques. To be specific, precision journalism requires a knowledge of measurement, research techniques, questionnaire design, sampling, sampling error, statistics, and data presentation. Demers and Nichols (1987) present a practical guide for journalists interested in this area.

The second trend is known as **database journalism**. Pioneered by reporter Elliot Jaspin, this form of reporting relies upon computer-assisted analysis of existing information files, an approach that has been accepted at many newspapers. Jaspin, for example, researching a story on school bus safety, studied computerized records of traffic citations over a three-year period and found that many bus drivers had frightful driving records. Koch (1991) lists several ways that reporters can use electronic databases:

- To help prepare informed questions prior to press conferences
- To compare the claims of news sources against existing information
- To find national information to complement a local story
- To generate original stories

An idea of the extent of database research done at most newspapers can be obtained from the results of a recent survey of 192 daily newspaper editors (Friend, 1994). This survey examined these papers' use of personal computers. The most common research use of PCs was to reanalyze secondary data appearing in on-line databases and libraries. The next most common use was the analysis of agency records. Almost every newspaper surveyed had done at least one database analysis in the past year, and 31% reported doing 11 or more, indicating that the PC has become a common research tool.

Database journalism can be costly, and learning to use these sources requires a good deal of time, particularly if reporters have little prior knowledge of the technique. Nevertheless, as more on-line information services become available and reporters learn to take advantage of the opportunities afforded by the Internet, most experts agree that database journalism will be a tool widely used by journalists in the future. Consequently, aspiring reporters will need to know more about data retrieval, data analysis, and data interpretation.

SUMMARY

Magazine and newspaper research began in the 1920s and for much of its early existence was qualitative in nature. Typical research studies dealt with law, history, and international press comparisons. During the 1930s and 1940s, readership surveys and studies of the effectiveness of print media advertising were frequently done by private firms. By the 1950s, quantitative research techniques became common in print media research. The continuing competition between television and radio for advertisers and audiences during the past three decades has spurred the growth of private sector research. Professional associations have started their own research operations.

✳ Research in the print media encompasses readership studies, circulation studies, management studies, typography and makeup studies, and readability studies. Readership research is the most extensive area; it serves to determine who reads a publication, what items are read, and what gratifications the readers obtain from their choices. Circulation studies examine the penetration levels of newspapers and magazines in various markets as well as various aspects of the delivery and pricing systems. Management studies look at goal setting and at job satisfaction.

Typography and makeup are studied to determine the impact of different newspaper and magazine design elements on readership and item preferences. Readability studies investigate the textual elements that affect comprehension of a message. Precision journalism and database journalism are two emerging techniques that highlight the importance of journalists' understanding of social science research.

QUESTIONS AND PROBLEMS FOR FURTHER INVESTIGATION

1. Assume that you are the editor of an afternoon newspaper faced with a declining circulation. What types of research projects might you conduct to help increase your readership?

2. Now suppose you have decided to publish a new magazine about women's sports. What types of research would you conduct before starting publication? Why?

3. Conduct a pilot uses and gratifications study of 15–20 people to determine why they read the local daily newspaper.

4. Using any five pages from this chapter as a sample, calculate the Flesch reading ease formula, the Gunning Fog Index, and McLaughlin's SMOG Grading.

5. Make a catalog of existing electronic databases that would be relevant to a local newspaper reporter.

REFERENCES AND SUGGESTED READINGS

Akhavan-Majid, A. M., Rife, A., & Gopinah, S. (1991). Chain ownership and editorial independence. *Journalism Quarterly, 68*(1/2), 59–66.

Alperstein, G. (1980). *The influence of local information on daily newspaper household penetration in Canada.* (ANPA News Research Report No. 26). Reston, VA: ANPA News Research Center.

Bergen, L. A., & Weaver, D. (1988). Job satisfaction of daily newspaper journalists and organization size. *Newspaper Research Journal, 9*(2), 1–14.

Blankenburg, W. R. (1981). Structural determination of circulation. *Journalism Quarterly, 58*(4), 543–551.

Blankenburg, W. R. (1987). Predicting newspaper circulation after consolidation. *Journalism Quarterly, 64*(3), 585–587.

Blankenburg, W. R., & Friend, R. (1994). Effects of cost and revenue strategies on newspaper circulation. *Journal of Media Economics, 7*(2), 1–14.

Bleyer, W. (1924). Research problems and newspaper analysis. *Journalism Bulletin, 1*(1), 17–22.

Blood, R., Keir, G., & Kang, N. (1983). Newspaper use and gratification in Hawaii. *Newspaper Research Journal, 4*(4), 43–52.

Bogart, L. (1989). *Press and public.* Hillsdale, NJ: Lawrence Erlbaum.

Bogart, L. (1991). *Preserving the press.* New York: Columbia University Press.

Bramlett-Solomon, S. (1993). Job satisfaction factors important to black journalists. *Newspaper Research Journal, 14*(3/4), 60–68.

Bramlett-Solomon, S., & Merrill, B. (1991). Newspaper use and community ties in a model retirement community. *Newspaper Research Journal, 12*(2), 60–68.

Burgoon, J., Bernstein, J., & Burgoon, M. (1983). Public and journalist perceptions of newspaper functions. *Newspaper Research Journal, 5*(1), 77–85.

Burgoon, J., Burgoon, M., & Wilkinson, M. (1983). Dimensions of content readership in ten newspaper markets. *Journalism Quarterly, 60*(1), 74–80.

Busterna, J. C. (1989). How managerial ownership affects profit maximization in newspaper firms. *Journalism Quarterly, 66*(2), 302–307.

Catalano, K. (1990). On the wire: How six news services are exceeding readability standards. *Journalism Quarterly, 67*(1), 97–103.

Chaffee, S., & Choe, S. (1981). Newspaper reading in longitudinal perspective. *Journalism Quarterly, 58*(2), 201–211.

Click, J. W., & Baird, R. (1979). *Magazine editing and production.* Dubuque, IA: William C. Brown.

Click, J. W., & Stempel, G. (1982). *Reader response to front pages with modular format and color.* (ANPA News Research Report No. 35). Reston, VA: ANPA News Research Center.

Cobb-Walgren, C. J. (1990). Why teenagers do not read all about it. *Journalism Quarterly, 67*(2), 340–347.

Connery, T. (1989). Management commitment and the small daily. *Newspaper Research Journal, 10*(3), 59–67.

Cook, B., & Banks, S. (1993). Predictors of job burnout in reporters and copy editors. *Journalism Quarterly, 70*(1), 108–117.

Cook, B., Banks, S., & Turner, R. (1993). The effects of work environment on burnout in the newsroom. *Newspaper Research Journal, 14*(3/4), 123–136.

Coulson, D. (1994). Impact of ownership on newspaper quality. *Journalism Quarterly, 71*(2), 403–410.

Coulson, D., & Hansen, A. (1995). The Louisville *Courier-Journal*'s news content after purchase by Gannett. *Journalism and Mass Communication Quarterly, 72*(1), 205–215.

Dale, E., & Chall, J. S. (1948). A formula for predicting readability. *Education Research Journal, 27*(1), 11–20.

Demers, D. P. (1991). Corporate structure and emphasis on profits and product quality at U.S. daily newspapers. *Journalism Quarterly, 68*(1/2), 15–26.

Demers, D. P., & Nichols, S. (1987). *Precision journalism: A practical guide.* Newbury Park, CA: Sage Publications.

Demers, D. P., & Wackman, D. B. (1988). Effect of chain ownership on newspaper management goals. *Newspaper Research Journal, 9*(2), 59–68.

Einseidel, E., & Kang, N. (1983). Civic attitudes among non-readers and non-subscribers. *Newspaper Research Journal, 4*(4), 37–42.

Elliott, W. R., & Rosenberg, W. L. (1987). The 1985 Philadelphia newspaper strike: A uses and gratifications study. *Journalism Quarterly, 64*(4), 679–687.

Fisher, C. (1993, July 26). Newspaper readers get choosier. *Advertising Age,* p. 22.

Flesch, R. (1948). A new readability yardstick. *Journal of Applied Psychology, 32*(2), 221–233.

Fowler, G., & Smith, E. (1979). Readability of newspapers and magazines over time. *Newspaper Research Journal, 1*(1), 3–8.

Fowler, G., & Smith, E. (1982). Readability of delayed and immediate reward content in *Time* and *Newsweek. Journalism Quarterly, 59*(3), 431–434.

Friend, C. (1994). Daily newspaper use of computers to analyze data. *Newspaper Research Journal, 15*(1), 63–72.

Geraci, P. (1984a). Comparison of graphic design and illustration use in three Washington, DC newspapers. *Newspaper Research Journal, 5*(2), 29–40.

Geraci, P. (1984b). Newspaper illustration and readership: Is *USA Today* on target? *Journalism Quarterly, 61*(2), 409–413.

Gersh, D. (1990, April 7). Reaching the teenage reader. *Editor & Publisher,* p. 18.

Green, P. E., Tull, D. S., & Albaum, G. (1988). *Research for marketing decisions.* Englewood Cliffs, NJ: Prentice-Hall.

Griffin, J., & Stevenson, R. (1992). Influence of text and graphics in increasing understanding of foreign news content. *Newspaper Research Journal, 13*(1/2), 84–98.

Griffin J., & Stevenson, R. (1994). The effectiveness of locator maps in increasing reader understanding of the geography of foreign news. *Journalism Quarterly, 71*(4), 937–946.

Griswold, W. F., & Moore, R. L. (1989). Factors affecting readership of news and advertising in a small daily newspaper. *Newspaper Research Journal, 10*(2), 55–66.

Gunning, R. (1952). *The technique of clear writing.* New York: McGraw-Hill.

Guthrie, T. L., Ludwin, W. G., & Jacob, S. B. (1988). A parsimonious regression model to predict metropolitan circulation in outlying counties. *Newspaper Research Journal, 9*(3), 59–60.

Guzda, M. (1984, June 9). Lifestyle segmentation. *Editor & Publisher,* p. 16.

Hale, D. (1983). Sunday newspaper circulation related to characteristics of the 50 states. *Newspaper Research Journal, 5*(1), 53–62.

Haskins, J. B. (1960). Pretesting editorial items and ideas for reader interest. *Journalism Quarterly, 37*(1), 224–230.

Haskins, J. B., & Flynne, L. (1974). Effects of headline typeface variation on reader interest. *Journalism Quarterly, 51*(4), 677–682.

Hoskins, R. (1973). A readability study of AP and UPI wire copy. *Journalism Quarterly, 50*(2), 360–362.

Hvistendahl, J. K. (1977). Self-administered readership surveys: Whole copy vs. clipping method. *Journalism Quarterly, 54*(2), 350–356.

Janofsky, M. (1993, July 22). A survey shows Tina Brown's *New Yorker* is attracting more and wealthier readers. *New York Times,* p. D21.

Jones, R. (1993). Coorientation of a news staff and its audience. *Communication Reports, 6*(1), 41–46.

Katcher, B. (1995, April 15). Readership surveys. *Folio,* pp. 33–34.

Kelly, J. D. (1989). The data-ink ratio and accuracy of newspaper graphics. *Journalism Quarterly, 66*(3), 623–639.

Koch, T. (1991). *Journalism for the 21st Century.* New York: Praeger.

Lacy, S. (1990). Newspaper competition and number of press services carried. *Journalism Quarterly, 67*(1), 79–82.

Lacy, S., & Fico, F. (1991). The link between content quality and circulation. *Newspaper Research Journal, 12*(2), 46–56.

Lacy, S., & Sohn, A. (1990). Correlations of newspaper content with circulation in the suburbs. *Journalism Quarterly, 67*(4), 785–793.

Larkin, E., & Hecht, T. (1979). Research assistance for the non-metro newspaper, 1979. *Newspaper Research Journal,* prototype edition, pp. 62–66.

Lewis, R. (1995). Relation between newspaper subscription price and circulation. *Journal of Media Economics, 8*(1), 25–41.

Lipschultz, J. H. (1987). The nonreader problem: A closer look at avoiding the newspaper. *Newspaper Research Journal, 8*(4), 59–70.

Loges, W., & Ball-Rokeach, S. (1993). Dependency relationships and newspaper readership. *Journalism Quarterly, 70*(3), 602–614.

Lynn, J., & Bennett, E. (1980). Newspaper readership patterns in non-metropolitan communities. *Newspaper Research Journal, 1*(4), 18–24.

McAdams, K. (1992/1993). Readability reconsidered. *Newspaper Research Journal, 13/14*(4/1), 50–59.

McCombs, M. (1977). *Newspaper readership and circulation.* (ANPA News Research Report No. 3). Reston, VA: ANPA News Research Bureau.

McCombs, M., Mullins, L. E., & Weaver, D. (1974). *Why people subscribe and cancel: A stop-start survey of three daily newspapers.* (ANPA News Research Bulletin No. 3). Reston, VA: ANPA News Research Center.

McLaughlin, H. (1969). SMOG grading: A new readability formula. *Journal of Reading, 22*(4), 639–646.

Meyer, P. (1973). *Precision journalism.* Bloomington, IN: Indiana University Press.

Moore, B. A., Howard, H. H., & Johnson, G. C. (1988). TV news viewing and the decline of the afternoon newspaper. *Newspaper Research Journal, 10*(1), 15–24.

Nafziger, R. (1930). A reader interest survey of Madison, Wisconsin. *Journalism Quarterly, 7*(2), 128–141.

Nestvold, K. (1972). Cloze procedure correlation with perceived readability. *Journalism Quarterly, 49*(3), 592–594.

Novak, T. P., & MacEvoy, B. (1990, June). On comparing alternative schemes: LOV and VALS. *Journal of Consumer Research, 17*(1), 105–109.

Ogan, C., & Lafky, S. (1983). 1981's most important events as seen by reporters, editors, wire services, and media consumers. *Newspaper Research Journal, 5*(1), 63–76.

Payne, G. A., Severn, J. J., & Dozier, D. M. (1988). Uses and gratifications motives as indicators of magazine readership. *Journalism Quarterly, 65*(4), 909–913.

Penrose, J., Weaver, D., Cole, R., & Shaw, D. (1974). The newspaper non-reader ten years later. *Journalism Quarterly, 51*(4), 631–639.

Perse, E., & Courtright, A. (1993). Normative images of communication media. *Human Communication Research, 19*(4), 485–503.

Poindexter, P. (1978). *Non-readers, Why they don't read.* (ANPA News Research Report No. 9). Reston, VA: ANPA News Research Center.

Porter, W. C., & Stephens, F. (1989). Estimating readability: A study of Utah editors' abilities. *Newspaper Research Journal, 10*(2), 87–96.

Ruotolo, A. C. (1988). A typology of newspaper readers. *Journalism Quarterly, 65*(1), 126–130.

Schramm, W. (1957). Twenty years of journalism research. *Public Opinion Quarterly, 21*(1), 91–108.

Schweitzer, J. (1992). Job opportunities in newspaper research for JMC masters graduates. *Newspaper Research Journal, 13*(1/2), 24–34.

Simmons Market Research Bureau (1991). *Page opening and reading style.* New York: Simmons Market Research Bureau.

Siskind, T. (1979). The effect of newspaper design on reader preference. *Journalism Quarterly, 56*(1), 54–62.

Smith, A. M. (1992, April). The measure of editorial success. *Folio,* pp. 95–98.

Smith, E. J., & Hajash, D. J. (1988). Information graphics in 30 daily newspapers. *Journalism Quarterly, 65*(3), 714–718.

Smith, R. (1984). How consistently do readability tests measure the difficulty of newswriting? *Newspaper Research Journal, 5*(4), 1–8.

Sobal, J., & Jackson-Beeck, M. (1981). Newspaper nonreaders: A national profile. *Journalism Quarterly, 58*(1), 9–13.

Stamm, K., Jackson, K., & Jacoubovitch, D. (1980). Exploring new options in newspaper readership methods. *Newspaper Research Journal, 1*(2), 63–74.

Stamm, K., & Underwood, D. (1993). The relationship of job satisfaction to newsroom policy changes. *Journalism Quarterly, 70*(3), 528–541.

Stein, M. L. (1991, April 27). Research for the newsroom. *Editor & Publisher,* p. 19.

Stone, G. (1994). Race yields to education as predictor of newspaper use. *Newspaper Research Journal, 15*(1), 115–126.

Stone, G., & Trotter, E. (1981). Community traits and predictions of circulation. *Journalism Quarterly, 58*(3), 460–463.

Sullivan, C. (1993, Nov. 1). Expire research is no dead end. *Folio,* pp. 39–40.

Swanson, C. (1955). What they read in 130 daily newspapers. *Journalism Quarterly, 32*(3), 411–421.

Taylor, W. (1953). Cloze procedure: A new tool for measuring readability. *Journalism Quarterly, 30*(4), 415–433.

Thurlow, G., & Milo, K. (1993). Newspaper readership. *Newspaper Research Journal, 14*(3/4), 34–43.

Tillinghast, W. (1981). Declining newspaper readership: Impact of region and urbanization. *Journalism Quarterly, 58*(1), 14–23.

Utt, S., & Pasternack, S. (1989). How they look: An updated study of American newspaper front pages. *Journalism Quarterly, 66*(3), 621–627.

Veronis, C. R. (1989, November). Research moves to center stage. *presstime,* pp. 20–26.

Wanta, W., and Gao, D. (1994) Young readers and the newspaper. *Journalism Quarterly, 71*(4), 926–936.

Ward, D. B. (1992). The effect of sidebar graphics. *Journalism Quarterly, 69*(7), 318–328.

Weaver, D., Wilhoit, C., & Reide, P. (1979). *Personal needs and media use.* (ANPA News Research Report No. 21). Reston, VA: ANPA News Research Center.

Chapter

||||||||||||||||||||||||||||||||||||||||

14

RESEARCH IN THE ELECTRONIC MEDIA

As this book goes to press, more than 100 companies and individuals are involved in some type of electronic media research. This count does not include hundreds of college and university professors and private citizens who also conduct studies for the electronic media. In addition, there are in-house research departments in most radio, television, and cable operations, as well as the networks. It is easy to understand why broadcasting and cable research is now a multimillion-dollar business.

Electronic media research continually changes due to advancements in technology as well as improved research methodologies. This chapter introduces some of the more widely used research procedures in this area.

BACKGROUND

Although broadcasting is relatively young compared with other mass media, the amount and sophistication of broadcasting research have grown rapidly. During the initial years of broadcasting (the 1920s), there was little or no concern for audience research. The broadcasters were experimenters and hobbyists who were interested mainly in making sure that their signal was being sent and received. The potential popularity of radio was unknown, and there was no reason to be concerned with audience size at that time.

This situation changed rapidly during the 1930s as radio became a popular mass medium. When broadcast stations began to attract large audiences, concern emerged over how radio would be financed. Eventually it was decided that advertising (as opposed to government financing or taxes on sales of equipment) was the most viable alternative. The acceptance of advertising on radio was the first step in the development of electronic media research.

Advertisers, not broadcasters, were the initiators of broadcast research. Once commercials began to be heard on the air, advertisers naturally wondered how many listeners were exposed to their messages and just how effective the messages were. Broadcasters were thus compelled to provide empirical evidence of the size and characteristics of their audience. This situation still exists—advertisers continually want more information about the people who hear and see their commercial announcements.

In addition to information about audience size, advertisers became interested in why people behave the way they do. This led to the development of the research area known as *psychographics*. But because psychographic data are rather vague, they were not adequate predictors of audience behavior; advertisers wanted more information. Research procedures were then designed to study *lifestyle* patterns and how they affect media use and buying behavior. Such information is valuable in designing advertising campaigns: If advertisers understand the lifestyle patterns of the people who purchase their products, they can design commercials to match those lifestyles.

Electronic media research studies today fall into two main categories: *ratings* and *nonratings* research. The remainder of this chapter is devoted to a discussion of these two areas.

RATINGS RESEARCH

When radio first became popular and advertisers began to grasp its potential for attracting customers, they were faced with the problem of documenting audience size. The print media were able to collect circulation figures, but broadcasters had no equivalent "hard" information—merely estimates. The early attempts at audience measurement failed to provide adequate data. Volunteer mail from listeners was the first source of data, but it is a well-known axiom of research that volunteers do not represent the general audience. Advertisers and broadcasters quickly realized that further information was urgently needed.

Since 1930, when a group called the Cooperative Analysis of Broadcasting conducted one of the first audience surveys for radio, several individuals and companies have attempted to provide syndicated audience information. The bulk of syndicated information for radio and television stations and cable is provided by two companies: A. C. Nielsen for local market and network television and cable TV, and The Arbitron Company for local market radio. The country is divided into over 200 markets, and no city is included in more than one market. In most markets, the Arbitron and Nielsen companies provide ratings data throughout the year (called *continuous measurement*), not just during certain times of the year as in the past. (A third local market radio ratings company, Birch Radio, entered radio research to compete with Arbitron, but went out of business on December 31, 1991. Currently, Strategic Radio, a radio research firm in Chicago, Illinois, is attempting to enter the radio ratings field with a service called *Accu-Ratings*.)

The A. C. Nielsen Company, founded in 1945, is a subsidiary of Dun and Bradstreet, with corporate headquarters in Northbrook, Illinois. Nielsen is one of the world's largest market research companies, and its television and cable ratings account for only a portion of its business even though the company's television measurements are conducted in eight foreign countries. The American Research Bureau (ARB) was founded in 1949. The name of the company was changed to The Arbitron Company in 1972,

then to The Arbitron Ratings Company in 1982, then back to The Arbitron Company in 1989. Arbitron is a subsidiary of the Ceridian Data Corporation and has headquarters in Laurel, Maryland. For more information about the history of broadcast ratings, see Beville (1988).

The Nielsen Company produces several television ratings reports. The *Viewers in Profile* are the basic market-by-market reports published under the category of *National Station Index* (NSI) estimates, which first appeared in 1954. These reports are produced from three to seven times per year, depending on the market, and are based on data collected by diaries (called the National Audience Composition, or NAC) and electronic meters. The data from these two collection procedures are combined to develop the ratings reports. *The National Television Index* (NTI), which was first produced in 1950, provides estimates of network television programs. Nielsen also publishes a summary of network estimates in a publication called *The Pocketpiece*. The *National Audience Demographics Report* (NAD) includes household and person estimates for various market segments (counties, households, and so on).

The Nielsen Company also produces a variety of specialized ratings reports such as measurements for cable services and for Turner Broadcasting's Airport Channel, and other out-of-home viewing measurements. It also produces a Hispanic television measurement service; begun in the fall of 1992, this is a people meter measurement system. (See Nielsen's *Media News* for up-to-date information.) Nielsen conducts national audience surveys four times a year, simultaneously surveying all of the more than 200 television markets. These ratings periods—February, May, July, and November—are called sweeps and are the year's most important surveys. Although other surveys are conducted throughout the year, most advertising rates set by networks and local stations are based on Nielsen's four "books." Blockbuster movies and special programs are aired during these four ratings periods because of the importance broadcast and cable executives place on the sweeps. The goal is to get the highest audience numbers possible.

Nielsen also has several markets that use electronic meters for data collection. The metered data are used for NTI and NSI reports, but also for overnights, which are preliminary ratings data gathered to give network and station executives, program producers, advertising agencies, and others an indication of the performance of the previous night's programs. Because the sample sizes involved in overnights are small, the actual ratings for the programs do not appear until several days later, when an additional sample is added to increase statistical reliability.

For several years, The Arbitron Company provided ratings for local market radio and television. However, it stopped producing television ratings in 1995. Currently, Arbitron produces only radio ratings by collecting information via diaries for its four major books—Winter, Spring, Summer, and Fall.

The only network radio ratings are gathered by Statistical Research, Inc., which is hired by networks to produce a RADAR report (Radio's All-Dimension Audience Research). Birch Radio used to collect radio information via telephone interviews.

Broadcast ratings create controversy in many areas: Viewers complain that "good" shows are canceled; producers, actors, and other artists complain that *numbers* are no judge of artistic quality (they are not intended to be); radio and television owners and operators complain that the results are not reliable; and advertisers often balk at the lack of reliable information. Although there may be merit to these complaints, one basic fact remains: Until further refinements are made, ratings as they currently exist will remain the primary decision-making tool in programming and advertising.

Since ratings will continue to be used for some time, it is important to understand several basic points about them. First, ratings are only approximations or estimates of audience size. They do not measure either quality of programs or opinions about the programs. Second, not all ratings are equally dependable: Different companies produce different ratings figures for the same market during the same time period.

The key point to remember when discussing or using ratings is that the figures are riddled with error. The data must be interpreted in light of several limitations (which are always printed in the last few pages of every ratings book). Individuals who depend on ratings as though they were facts are misusing the data.

RATINGS METHODOLOGY

The research methodologies used by Arbitron and Nielsen are complex; each company publishes several texts describing its methods and procedures that should be consulted for specific information (listed in the references at the end of this chapter). The data for ratings surveys are currently gathered by two methods: diaries and electronic meters (commonly called people meters). Each method has specific advantages and disadvantages.

Broadcast ratings provide a classic example of the need to sample the population. With about 95 million households in the United States, it would be impossible for any ratings company to conduct a census of media use. The companies naturally resort to sampling to produce data that can be generalized to the population. For example, Nielsen's national samples are selected using national census data and involve multistage area probability sampling that ensures that the sample reflects actual population distributions. That is, if Los Angeles accounts for 10% of the television households in the United States, Los Angeles households should comprise 10% of the sample as well. Nielsen uses four stages in sampling: selection of counties in the country, selection of block groups within the counties, selection of certain blocks within the groups, and selection of individual households within the blocks.

Nielsen claims that about 200 households in the NTI metered sample of approximately 4,000 households are replaced each month (Nielsen, 1992).

To obtain samples for producing broadcast listening and viewing estimates, Arbitron and Nielsen use recruitment by telephone, which includes calls to both listed and unlisted telephone numbers. Although all the ratings companies begin sample selection from telephone directories, each firm uses a statistical procedure to ensure the inclusion of unlisted telephone numbers, thus eliminating the bias that would be created if only persons or households listed in telephone directories were asked to participate in broadcast audience estimates (Chapter 4). Nielsen calls its procedure a Total Telephone Frame; Arbitron uses Expanded Sample Frame.

Target sample sizes for local audience measurements vary from market to market. Each ratings service uses a formula to establish a minimum sample size required for a specific level of statistical efficiency, but there is no guarantee that this number of subjects will actually be produced. Although many people may agree to participate in an audience survey, there is no way to force them all to complete the diaries they are given or to accurately use electronic meters. Additionally, completed diaries are often rejected because they are illegible or obviously inaccurate. The companies are often lucky to get a 50% response rate in their local market measurements.

In addition, since participation by minority groups in audience surveys is generally lower than for the remainder of the population, the companies make an extra effort to collect data from these groups by contacting households by telephone or in person to assist them in completing the diary. (These methods are generally used in high-density Hispanic (HDHA) and high-density African-American areas (HDBA); otherwise, return rates could be too low to provide any type of audience estimates.) When the return (or in-tab) rate is low, statistical weight-

---

Methods of Data Collection

- Electronic meters
- Diary
- Telephone
- People meters

---

ing or sample balancing is used to compensate for the shortfall. This topic is discussed later.

Perhaps the best known method of gathering ratings data from a sample is by means of electronic ratings-gathering instruments, in particular the Nielsen *audimeter,* which was introduced in 1936 to record radio usage on a moving roll of paper. (A. C. Nielsen purchased the audimeter from Robert Elder and Louis Woodruff, professors at the Massachusetts Institute of Technology.) Today's audimeter, the storage instantaneous audimeter (SIA), is a sophisticated device that automatically records the time each set in a household is turned on or off, the broadcasting station, the amount of time each set stays on a channel, and the channel switchings. Every day each household in the NTI sample is called by the central computer, located in Dunedin, Florida, which retrieves the stored data and stores them for computation of the National Television Index. All data collection is done automatically and does not require participation by persons in the NTI households.

For the second major form of data collection, subjects are asked to record in diaries the channels they watch or the stations they listen to, the time periods, and the number of people viewing or listening to each program or **daypart**, a segment of the broadcast day such as "prime time" (8:00 P.M.–11:00 P.M. EST). Arbitron uses diaries for radio; Nielsen uses diaries for the households in its NAC sample to supplement the information gathered from the SIA households because the audimeter cannot record the number of people watching each television set. An example of an Arbitron radio diary instruction page is shown in Figure 14.1. A Nielsen television diary is shown in Figure 14.2.

The third major type of data collection is by telephone. Although Birch Radio no longer operates, its methodology is still a viable alternative for broadcast ratings research. Tom Birch (1989), founder of Birch Radio, identified four reasons for selecting telephone interviewing when he started the company:

1. *Projectability*. Diary methods have high nonresponse rates (as high as 65%), whereas telephone interviews have about 40% nonresponse rates. According to Birch, the higher response rate yields a more reliable database.

2. *Reporting accuracy*. Unlike diaries, telephone calls do not give respondents time to think about (or plan) their answers. Respondents' answers are probably more accurate.

3. *Control*. Diaries kept in the home can be filled out by anyone, and may not be completed each day; or the diaries may be completed at the end of the 7–day diary period instead of each individual day. Significant error may be present because respondents rely on recall. The Birch method limits reports of listening to "yesterday."

4. *Speed*. A complete Birch Radio survey took only a few minutes to complete. In addition, the company installed CATI systems in all of its telephone centers, which allow for immediate access to data for any 24–hour period.

Nielsen and Arbitron also use the telephone to conduct a variety of special studies, allowing clients to request almost any type of survey research project. One of the most frequent types of custom work is the telephone **coincidental**. This procedure measures the size of the medium's audience at a given time—the survey coincides with actual viewing or listening. The method involves selecting a sample of households at random and calling these numbers during the viewing or listening period of interest. Individuals are simply asked what they are watching or listening to at that moment. This method avoids the necessity of trying to recall information from the previous day. Coincidentals are fairly inexpensive (generally a few thousand dollars) and are frequently used by station management to receive immediate feedback about the success of special programming. In most cases, coincidental data are used for advertising sales purposes.

The fourth method of ratings data collection, **people meters**, was started in the mid-1980s to attempt to improve the accuracy of ratings information and to obtain "*single-source data*," whereby research companies collect television ratings data, demographic data, and even household member purchasing behavior at one time.

Traditional television meters indicate only whether the television set is on or off, and the channel to which the set is tuned; there are no data about *who* is watching. Such information must be obtained by pooling TV meter data with information from households in the diary samples. People meters attempt to simplify this data collection task by requiring each person in the household, as well as all visitors, to push a specific button on a mechanical unit that records the viewing. Each person in the home is assigned a button on the meter. The meter instantaneously records information about how many people in the household are watching and the identity of each viewer. The data from each night's viewing is collected via computer. This specific information is valuable for advertisers and their agencies, who now can more accurately target their advertising messages.

Nielsen is convinced that using people meters is the way to obtain accurate television ratings information. The company's interest in people meters was spawned in 1987, when Audits of Great Britain (AGB) introduced the meters to the United States. However, AGB pulled out of the U.S. people meter service in 1988, which leaves only Nielsen to develop a universally accepted system of single-source data collection. In 1991, when Arbitron was involved

FIGURE 14.1   Instruction Page from Arbitron's Radio Diary

You count in the radio ratings!

No matter how much or how little you listen, you're important!

You're one of the few people picked in your area to have the chance to tell radio stations what you listen to.

This is *your* ratings diary. Please make sure you fill it out yourself.

Here's what we mean by "listening":

"Listening" is any time you can hear a radio — whether you choose the station or not.

When you hear a radio between Thursday, July 23, and Wednesday, July 29, write it down — whether you're at home, in a car, at work or someplace else.

When you hear a radio, write down:

TIME

Write the time you start listening and the time you stop.

If you start at one time of day and stop in another, draw a line from the time you start to the time you stop.

STATION

Write the call letters or station name. If you don't know either, write down the program name or dial setting.

Check AM or FM. AM and FM stations can have the same call letters. Make sure you check the right box.

PLACE

Check where you listening:
- at home
- in a car
- at work
- other place

Write down *all* the radio you hear. Carry your diary with you starting Thursday, July 23.

No listening? If you haven't heard a radio all day, check the box at the bottom of the page.

THURSDAY

Time		Station	Place				
Start	Stop	Call letters or station name. Don't know? Use program name or dial setting	AM	FM	At Home	In a Car	At Work	Other Place

Early Morning (from 5 AM)
5:45–7:15 KGTU ✓ ✓
7:15–7:40 Oldies on the dial ✓ ✓

Midday
9:30 WGXP ✓ ✓ | 3:00

Late Afternoon 4:20–4:25 Is Country Show ✓ ✓

Night (to 5 AM Friday) 11:30–12:15 KEM ✓ ✓

If you didn't hear a radio today, please check here. ☐

Questions? Call us toll-free at 1-800-638-7091.

© 1992 The Arbitron Company

THURSDAY

Time		Station			Place			
			Check (✓) one		Check (✓) one			
Start	Stop	Call letters or station name. Don't know? Use program name or dial setting.	AM	FM	At Home	In a Car	At Work	Other Place
Early Morning (from 5 AM)								
Midday								
Late Afternoon								
Night (to 5 AM Friday)								

If you didn't hear a radio today, please check here. ☐

4

FIGURE 14.2   Instruction Page from Neilsen's Television Diary

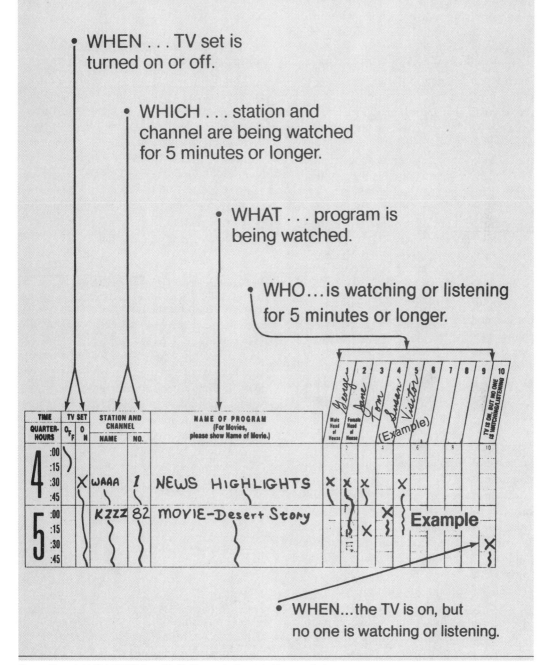

in television ratings, it tried to expand the concept of single-source data with a system called ScanAmerica. The plan was to collect household purchasing data and network television viewing from the same household. ScanAmerica was unsuccessful and was discontinued in late 1992.

In theory, people meters are quite simple—when a person begins or stops watching television, he or she pushes a button to document the behavior. The button may be located on a hand-held device or enclosed in a small box mounted on top of the television set. However, theory and reality are often misaligned. In late 1989, a survey funded by ABC, CBS, and NBC found that people meters "turned off" participants, especially with children's programming on Saturday mornings. Additional criticisms about low television-viewing numbers produced by the people meters continue in the mid-1990s.

The major problem with people meters is that participants tire of pushing buttons to record when they watch television, and children cannot be depended upon to push the necessary buttons when they turn on the set. The reality is that television ratings produced by people meters are lower than those produced by meters and diaries. Broadcasters and advertisers are concerned. Broadcasters claim the data underestimate actual viewing; advertisers claim the data are probably correct and they are paying too much money (CPM) for their commercials.

Each of the audience-estimate procedures has its critics—simple electronic meters because they do not provide specific audience information, and diaries because participants may fail to record viewing or listening as it happens and may rely on recall to complete the diary at the end of the week. In addition, many critics contend that diaries are used to "vote" for or against specific shows and that actual viewing is not recorded. Critics of data collection by telephone say that the method favors responses by younger people who are more willing to talk

on the phone; older respondents generally do not have the patience to answer the questions about their viewing or listening habits. Finally, people meters are condemned because of participant fatigue, and a failure by many participants (especially children) to remember to push the required buttons when they watch television.

One thing is certain: Debate about the accuracy of the various audience ratings methods will continue. Research companies, including Arbitron and Nielsen, will be forced to try to develop more valid and reliable research procedures. The next phase of ratings development will take the form of an electronic storage system for radio ratings. This is considered necessary by some researchers to eliminate the problems inherent in the hand-entry paper diaries used by Arbitron and Nielsen.

INTERPRETING THE RATINGS

The ratings interpretation process and its terminology can best be explained by an example. (This example uses television networks, but the procedures are the same for radio ratings. In addition, the example has been simplified by using only three commercial television networks; local market ratings books will always include many more stations.) Let's assume that Nielsen has collected the following data for a certain daypart on network television:

Network	Households viewing
ABC	880
CBS	800
NBC	716
Not watching	1,604
Total	4,000

Recall that Nielsen's NTI sample includes about 4,000 households in the United States, and the data collected from them are generalized to the *total* population of about 95 million television households.

Network rating	×	Population	=	Population HH estimate
ABC: 0.22	×	95 million	=	20,900,000
CBS: 0.20	×	95 million	=	19,000,000
NBC: 0.179	×	95 million	=	17,005,000

Rating. An *audience rating* is the percentage of people or households in a population with a television or radio tuned to a specific station, channel, or network. Thus, the rating is expressed as the station or network's audience divided by the total number of television households or people in the target population:

$$\frac{\text{People or households}}{\text{Population}} = \text{Rating}$$

For example, ABC's rating using the hypothetical data is computed as

$$\frac{880}{4,000} = 0.22, \text{ or } 22\%$$

This indicates that approximately 22% of the sample of 4,000 households was tuned to ABC at the time of the survey. (Note that even though ratings and related statistical values are percentages, when the data are reported, the decimal points are eliminated to ease reading.)

The combined ratings of all the networks or stations during a specific time period provide an estimate of the total number of homes using television (HUT). Since radio ratings deal with persons rather than households, however, the term *persons using radio* (PUR) is used. The HUT or PUR can be found either by adding together the households or persons using radio or television or by computing the total rating and multiplying that times the sample (or population when generalized). The total rating in the sample data is 59.9, which is computed as follows:

$$\text{ABC } \frac{880}{4,000} = 0.22, \text{ or } 22\%$$

$$\text{CBS } \frac{800}{4,000} = 0.20, \text{ or } 20\%$$

$$\text{NBC } \frac{716}{4,000} = 0.179, \text{ or } 17.9\%$$

$$\text{HUT} = 2,396 \quad \text{Total rating} = 59.9\%$$

In other words, about 59.9% of all households (HH) with television were watching one of the three networks at the time of the survey. As mentioned, the HUT can also be computed by multiplying the total rating times the sample size: $0.599 \times 4,000 = 2,396$. The same formula is used to project to the population. The population HUT is computed as follows: 0.599×95 million $= 56,905,000$

Stations, networks, and advertisers naturally wish to know the estimated number of households in the HUT tuned to specific channels. The data from the sample of 4,000 households are again generalized to find a rough estimate of the households viewing each network (or station).

Share. A *share* of the audience is the percentage of the HUT or PUR that is tuned to a specific station, channel, or network. It is determined by dividing the number of households or persons tuned to a station or network by the number of households or persons using their sets:

$$\frac{\text{People or households}}{\text{HUT or PUR}} = \text{Share}$$

Network share	×	HUT	=	Population HH exact	Rough Estimate
ABC: 36.7	×	56,905,000		20,884,135	20,900,000
CBS: 33.4	×	56,905,000		19,006,270	19,000,000
NBC: 29.9	×	56,905,000		17,014,595	17,005,000
				55,766,900	56,905,000

In the example, the sample HUT is 2,396 (880 + 800 + 716), or 59.9% of 4,000. The audience share for ABC would thus be

$$\frac{880}{2,396} = 0.367, \text{ or } 36.7\%$$

That is, of the households in the sample whose television sets were turned on at the time of the survey, 36.7% were tuned to ABC. (People may not have been *watching* the set but recorded that they did.) The shares for CBS and NBC are computed in the same manner: CBS share = 800/2,396, or 33.4%; NBC share = 716/2,396, or 29.9%.

Shares are also used to estimate the number of households in the target population. The previous example demonstrating how to compute households is considered a *rough estimate*. However, there is often need for a more exact method. This is achieved by multiplying the share times the HUT or PUR. The exact household estimates for each network are shown in the box above (rough estimates are for comparison).

Cost Per Thousand (CPM). Stations, networks, and advertisers need to be able to assess the efficiency of advertising on radio and television so that they can determine which advertising buy is the most cost-effective. One common way to express advertising efficiency is in **cost per thousand (CPM)**, or what it costs an advertiser to reach 1,000 households or persons. The CPM provides no information about

the effectiveness of a commercial message, only a dollar estimate of its reach. It is computed according to the following formula:

$$CPM = \frac{\text{Cost of advertisement}}{\text{Audience size (in thousands)}}$$

Using the hypothetical television survey, assume that a single 30-second commercial on ABC costs $175,000. The CPM for such a commercial would be

$$ABC \ CPM = \frac{\$175,000}{20,900(000)} = \$8.37$$

Computing the CPM in the same manner for CBS and NBC, we find CBS = $9.40 and NBC = $10.50.

The CPM is regularly used when buying commercial time. Advertisers and stations or networks often negotiate an advertising contract using CPM figures; the advertiser might agree to pay $8.50 per thousand households. In some cases, no negotiation is involved; a station or network simply offers a program to advertisers at a specified CPM.

The CPM is seldom the only criterion used in purchasing commercial time. Other information, such as audience demographics and type of program on which the advertisement will be aired, is considered before a contract is signed. An advertiser may be willing to pay a higher CPM to a network or station that is reaching a more desirable audience for its product. Cost per thousand should be used as the sole purchasing criterion only when all else is equal: demographics, programming, advertising strategy, and so on.

RELATED RATINGS CONCEPTS

Although ratings and shares are important in audience research, a number of other computations can be performed with the data. In addition, ratings, shares, and other figures are computed for a variety of survey areas and are split into several demographic categories. For an additional fee, ratings companies will also provide custom information such as ratings according to zip codes.

A **metro survey area (MSA)** generally corresponds to the Consolidated Metropolitan Statistical Areas (CMSA) for the country, as defined by the U.S. Office of Management and Budget. The MSA generally includes the town, the county, or some other designated area closest to the station's transmitter. The **designated market area (DMA)**, another area for which ratings data are gathered, defines each television or radio market in exclusive terms. (At one time Arbitron used the term *area of dominant influence,* or ADI, to describe the DMA, but has since changed to Nielsen's designation). Each county in the United States belongs to one and only one DMA, and rankings are determined by the number of television households in the DMA. Radio ratings use the DMAs established from television households; they are not computed separately.

The total survey area (TSA) includes the DMA and MSA as well as some other areas the market's stations reach (known as *adjacent DMAs*). Broadcasters are most interested in TSA data because they represent the largest number of households or persons. In reality, however, advertising agencies look at DMA figures when purchasing commercial time for television stations, and metro figures when purchasing radio time. The TSA is infrequently used in the sale or purchase of advertising time; it serves primarily to determine the reach

of the station, or the total number of people or households that listened to or watched a station or a channel. Nielsen's equivalent to Arbitron's TSA is the NSI area.

Ratings books contain information about the TSA/NSI, DMA, and the MSA. Each area is important to stations and advertisers for various reasons, depending on the type of product or service being advertised and the goals of the advertising campaign. For instance, a new business placing a large number of spots on several local stations may be interested in reaching as many people in the area as possible. In this case, the advertising agency or individual client may ask for TSA/NSI numbers only, disregarding the DMA and metro.

The **average quarter-hour (AQH)** is an estimate of the number of persons or households tuned to a specific station for at least 5 minutes during a 15-minute time segment. These estimates are provided for the TSA/NSI, DMA, and MSA in all ratings books. Stations are obviously interested in obtaining high AQH figures in all demographic areas, since these figures indicate how long an audience is tuned in, and thus how loyal the audience is to the station. The AQH data are used to determine the average listener's **time spent listening (TSL)** during a given day or daypart. All stations try to increase their audience TSL because it means that the audience is not continually changing to other stations.

The **cume** (cumulative audience) or **reach** is an estimate of the number of persons who listened to or viewed at least 5 minutes within a given daypart. The cume is also referred to as the "unduplicated audience." For example, a person who watches a soap opera at least 5 minutes a day Monday through Friday would be counted only once in a cume rating, whereas his or her viewing would be "duplicated" five times in determining average quarter-hours.

The **gross rating points (GRPs)** are a total of a station's ratings during two or more dayparts and represent the size of the gross audience. Advertising purchases are often made on

TABLE 14.1   Calculation of GRP for Five Dayparts

Daypart	Number of spots		Station rating		GRP (%)
M–F, 6A.M.–9A.M.	2	×	3.1	=	6.2
M–F, 12P.M.–3P.M.	2	×	2.9	=	5.8
M–F, 1P.M.–6P.M.	2	×	3.6	=	7.2
Sat, 6A.M.–9A.M.	2	×	2.5	=	5.0
Sun, 3P.M.–6P.M.	2	×	4.1	=	8.2
	10				32.4

TABLE 14.2   Computation of Turnover for Three Stations

Station	Cume audience		Average persons		Turnover
A	2,900	÷	850	=	3.4
B	1,750	÷	420	=	4.2
C	960	÷	190	=	5.1

the basis of GRPs. For example, a radio advertiser who purchases 10 commercials on a station may wish to know the gross audience he or she will reach. Using hypothetical data, the GRP is calculated as shown in Table 14.1. The gross rating point indicates that about 32.4% of the listening audience will be exposed to the 10 commercials.

A useful figure for radio stations is the **audience turnover**, or the number of times the audience changes during a given daypart. A high turnover is not always a negative factor in advertising sales; some stations have naturally high turnover (such as "Top 40" stations, whose audiences comprise mostly younger people who tend to change stations frequently). A high turnover factor simply means that an advertiser will need to run more spots to reach the station's audience. Usually such stations compensate by charging less for commercial spots than stations with low turnovers.

Turnover is computed by dividing a station's cume audience by its average persons total. (Both these figures are reported in ratings books.) Consider three stations in the Monday–Friday, 3:00–6:00 P.M. daypart, as shown in Table 14.2. In this market, an advertiser on Station C would need to run more commercials to reach all listeners than one who uses Station A. However, Station C, in addition to having a larger audience, may have the demographic audience most suitable for the advertiser's product.

READING A TV RATINGS BOOK

Reading a ratings book is relatively simple. As mentioned earlier, all decimal points are deleted and all numbers are rounded. A sample page from Nielsen's October 1995 Atlanta NSI ratings book is shown in Figure 14.3. The page is taken from the "Program Averages" section of the book. Only a portion of this page is used because the numbers in the actual book are very small. The page shows the 6:00 P.M. time period. On page 1 of the report, Nielsen states that the DMA audience estimates were based on an average in-tab sample of 372 DMA television households in which meter equipment provided information matching Nielsen's reporting standards.

We will use WSB-TV to describe how to read the data. First, notice that each column is numbered, beginning with columns 1 and 2 at the left under "Metro HH." During the 4–week rating period, WSB aired "Channel 2 Action News." The "AV5" line shows the average rating and share information for "Channel 2 Action News" during the 4 weeks: Columns 1 and 2 show the average metro rating and share as 17 and 31; the DMA multi-week averages for the program are listed as a 16 rating and a 30 share.

Columns 3–6 show the DMA ratings for each of the 4 weeks, columns 7 and 8 are the averages for the DMA for the survey, and column 14 shows the DMA HUT. The remaining columns (15–43) show the DMA ratings for specific age and gender cells. The letters *LT* mean that the number reported is less than 1%. Recall that this is only one page (of a total of 280 pages) from the October 1995 Atlanta NSI book.

Refer next to the Nielsen sample page. Notice that WSB-TV leads the time period. The data also show that the program is much stronger among women than among men. It is clear which station an advertiser would select in order to communicate with the largest Atlanta DMA audience.

Although information on ratings and shares is computed the same way for radio and television audience measurements, the information is presented very differently. Radio books usually contain more than 10 individual sections (such as Target Audience Estimates, Audience Composition, and various trend and rank data), and then concentrate on presenting audience estimates in terms of dayparts, not individual programs. Also, because there are so many radio stations in any given market, the emphasis in radio books is on shares, not ratings. Radio broadcasters rarely, if ever, use ratings to sell advertising. In addition, metro shares, not DMA or TSA shares, are the most important numbers in radio.

A sample page from an Arbitron radio book (for the Denver–Boulder area in Spring, 1995) is shown in Figure 14.4. The page is taken from the Metro Audience Trends for Persons 12+ (not all of the stations in the Denver market are shown on this sample page). Reading a radio ratings book is somewhat different from reading a television ratings book. We will use KOA, an AM news/talk station, to describe how to read this page.

First notice that the stations are listed from top to bottom in alphabetical order. Next are five columns of data that show the trends for Monday–Sunday, 6 A.M. to midnight. This is followed by an additional five columns of trends for Monday–Friday, 6 A.M. to 10 A.M.

Next notice that listed under each station are three pieces of information: SHARE, AQH, and CUME RTG. Note that AQH (average quarter hour) is listed in 100s; that is, "00" is eliminated from the reported data. For example, KOA's AQH for Spring 95 is listed as 202. This means that about 20,200 people age 12 and over were listening for at least 5 minutes during any given quarter hour between 6 A.M. and midnight (this is down from 21,800 in the previous book).

The CUME RTG (or rating) for KOA's Spring 95 book is 21.0, which means that the station attracts about 20% of all people 12+ Monday–Sunday, 6 A.M. to midnight (this is also down from the previous book).

The Arbitron book shows that KOA is having problems holding its audience. The 6 A.M. to midnight share data show an overall decline, from 8.8 in Spring 1994 to a 6.9 in Spring 1995. In broadcast terms, the station is "hurting." A similar trend is seen in the 6 A.M. to 10 A.M. columns. The trend is: 7.4, 10.0, 11.3, 10.4,

FIGURE 14.3 Sample Page from a Nielsen Television Ratings Book

ATLANTA, GA

WK1 9/28-10/04 WK2 10/05-10/11 WK3 10/12-10/18 WK4 10/19-10/25

The table below shows the sample Nielsen television ratings page for Atlanta, GA. Columns are grouped as METRO HH (RTG, SHR); STATION / DAY / PROGRAM; DMA HOUSEHOLD RATINGS by Weeks 1–4, MULTI-WEEK AVG (RTG, SHR), HUT; and DMA RATINGS broken into PERSONS, WOMEN, MEN, TNS, and CHILD demographic categories.

METRO HH RTG	METRO HH SHR	STATION / DAY / PROGRAM
2	1	R.S.E. THRESHOLDS 25+% (1 S.E.) 4 WK AVG 50+% 6:00PM
4	8	WATL MON FRESH PRINCE
5	10	TUE FRESH PRINCE
6	10	WED FRESH PRINCE
5	9	THU FRESH PRINCE
6	11	FRI FRESH PRINCE
5	10	AV5 FRESH PRINCE
4	7	SAT FLIX36 SAT 6PM
4	7	NOR FLIX36 SAT 6PM
6	12	SUN FRESH PRNCE WK
5	9	WGNX MON HOME IMPROV MF
5	8	TUE HOME IMPROV MF
4	8	WED HOME IMPROV MF
4	8	THU HOME IMPROV MF
5	9	FRI HOME IMPROV MF
4	8	AV5 HOME IMPROV MF
3	7	SAT HOME IMPROV WK
3	6	SUN 46 NWS-6 PM
<<	<<	WHSG SAT JACK GRAHAM
<<	<<	SUN BISHOP JAKES
<<	<<	WNGM MON EXTRA
<<	<<	TUE EXTRA
<<	<<	WED EXTRA
<<	<<	THU EXTRA
<<	<<	FRI EXTRA
<<	<<	AV5 EXTRA
<<	<<	SAT EXTRA WK
18	32	WSB MON CH2 ACTNWS 6PM
17	30	TUE CH2 ACTNWS 6PM
17	31	WED CH2 ACTNWS 6PM
17	32	THU CH2 ACTNWS 6PM
14	29	FRI CH2 ACTNWS 6PM
17	31	AV5 CH2 ACTNWS 6PM
12	23	SUN CH2 ACTNW SU 6
4	8	WTBS MON FAMILY MATTERS
4	8	TUE FAMILY MATTERS
4	8	WED FAMILY MATTERS
4	9	THU FAMILY MATTERS
3	6	THU GROWING PAINS
3	6	FRI FAMILY MATTERS
3	6	FRI GROWING PAINS
4	8	AV5 FAMILY MATTERS
3	6	AV2 GROWING PAINS
5	11	SAT WCW SA NIGHT
3	6	SUN WCW-MAIN EVENT
2	4	WVEU MON RICHARD BEY SH
2	4	TUE RICHARD BEY SH
2	3	WED RICHARD BEY SH
3	5	THU RICHARD BEY SH
2	4	FRI RICHARD BEY SH
2	4	AV5 RICHARD BEY SH
2	4	SAT LIVE SHOT
3	5	SUN OUTER LIMITS
4	8	WXIA MON 11 NEWS AT 6
5	9	TUE 11 NEWS AT 6
6	12	WED 11 NEWS AT 6
4	8	THU 11 NEWS AT 6
4	8	FRI 11 NEWS AT 6
5	9	AV5 11 NEWS AT 6
5	10	SAT 11 NEWS-6 SAT
4	9	NOR 11 NEWS-6 SAT
3	6	SUN 11 NEWS-6 SUN
		6:30PM
7	15	WAGA SAT ...
9	16	
6	10	

Source: Copyright 1995 Nielsen Media Research. Reprinted by permission.

and 7.2. The Spring 1995 share of 7.2 is very poor considering that the station was in the double digits less than a year ago.

The Arbitron data show that KOA's management needs to take a close look at the programming. What is driving the audience away? What changes, if any, were made on the station that would cause such an erosion of the audience?

ADJUSTING FOR UNREPRESENTATIVE SAMPLES

Since ratings are computed using samples for the population, there is always a certain amount of error associated with the data. This error, designated by the notation σ, is known as standard error (introduced in Chapter 4). Standard error must always be considered before interpreting ratings, to determine whether a certain gender/age group has been undersampled or oversampled.

There are numerous approaches to calculating standard error. One of the simpler methods is

$$SE(p) = \sqrt{\frac{p(100 - p)}{n}}$$

where p = sample percentage or rating, n = sample size, and SE = standard error. For example, suppose a random sample of 1,200 households produces a rating of 20. The standard error can be expressed as follows:

$$SE(p) = \sqrt{\frac{20(100 - 20)}{1,200}}$$
$$= \sqrt{\frac{20(80)}{1,200}}$$
$$= \sqrt{1.33}$$
$$= \pm 1.15$$

The rating of 20 has a standard error of ± 1.15 points, which means the rating actually ranges

from 18.85 to 21.15. Standard error formulas are included in all ratings books; Arbitron has simplified the procedure by publishing tables in the back of each book.

Weighting is another procedure used by ratings companies to adjust for samples that are not representative of the population. In some situations a particular sex/age group cannot be adequately sampled, and it becomes imperative that a correction be made.

Assume that population estimates for a DMA indicate that there are 41,500 men ages 18–34 and that this group accounts for 8.3% of the population over the age of 12. The researchers distribute diaries to a sample of the DMA population, of which 950 are returned and usable (known as *in-tab* diaries). They would expect about 79 of these to be from men ages 18–34 (8.3% of 950). However, they find that only 63 of the diaries are from this demographic group—16 short of the anticipated number. The data must be weighted to adjust for this deficiency. The weighting formula is:

$$\text{Weight}_{\text{MSA men, 18-34}} = \frac{0.083}{0.066}$$
$$= 1.25$$

This figure must be multiplied by the number of persons in the group that each diary would normally represent. That is, instead of representing 525 men (41,500 ÷ 79), each diary would represent 656 men (525 × 1.25). The ideal weighting value is 1.00, indicating that the group was adequately represented in the sample. On occasion, a group may be oversampled, in which case the weighting value will be a number less than 1.00.

Both Arbitron and Nielsen provide detailed explanations of error rates, weighting, and other methodological considerations. Each company includes pages of information in ratings books on how to interpret the data considering different sample sizes and weighting. In reality, however, the vast majority of people who interpret and use broadcast and cable ratings consider the printed numbers as gospel. If they are

FIGURE 14.4   Sample Page from an Arbitron Radio Book

Metro Audience Trends*
PERSONS 12+

	MONDAY-SUNDAY 6AM-MID					MONDAY-FRIDAY 6AM-10AM				
	SPRING 94	SUMMER 94	FALL 94	WINTER 95	SPRING 95	SPRING 94	SUMMER 94	FALL 94	WINTER 95	SPRING 95
KALC										
SHARE	3.7	3.8	4.3	3.5	4.2	2.8	3.4	4.2	3.7	4.6
AQH(00)	103	106	119	103	123	116	132	177	163	201
CUME RTG	11.5	13.8	13.4	12.2	13.5	5.6	6.8	7.6	6.6	7.3
KBCO										
SHARE		.1	.1	.2	.2		.1		.2	.1
AQH(00)	1	3	3	5	5		5	2	9	5
CUME RTG	.4	.6	.4	.5	.3	.1	.3	.2	.4	.2
KBCO-FM										
SHARE	5.6	4.4	3.9	3.6	3.9	5.0	4.0	3.3	2.7	3.7
AQH(00)	155	120	108	105	115	203	153	139	118	160
CUME RTG	12.8	10.5	9.7	11.8	10.6	7.4	6.2	5.2	6.1	6.0
KBNO										
SHARE	**	.7	.4	**	.7	**	.8	.5	**	.7
AQH(00)	**	20	10	**	21	**	32	19	**	29
CUME RTG	**	1.5	.9	**	1.7	**	.9	.5	**	1.0
KBPI										
SHARE	4.6	5.3	5.7	5.3	5.0	4.3	5.1	5.4	5.7	4.9
AQH(00)	129	147	158	153	147	175	195	228	251	212
CUME RTG	12.2	13.9	13.0	12.8	12.7	6.4	7.2	7.7	7.5	7.1
KCUV										
SHARE	.7	.5	.5	.6	1.5	.5	.3	.5	.7	1.2
AQH(00)	19	13	13	17	43	21	11	19	30	50
CUME RTG	1.0	1.5	1.2	1.3	2.0	.8	.6	.8	.9	1.5
KDKO										
SHARE	.8	.6	.5	1.0	.9	.6	.5	.5	1.1	.6
AQH(00)	23	16	15	29	27	25	19	21	50	28
CUME RTG	1.9	2.0	1.7	2.3	2.0	.8	1.0	.7	1.0	.9
KEZW										
SHARE	3.1	2.8	3.4	2.6	3.0	2.8	3.4	3.2	2.1	2.6
AQH(00)	85	78	93	75	88	115	131	133	90	115
CUME RTG	5.4	4.9	6.5	5.2	5.9	3.1	3.2	3.8	2.6	3.4
KHIH										
SHARE	4.1	2.9	3.3	4.5	3.5	3.6	2.5	2.6	3.7	3.1
AQH(00)	115	80	92	130	102	148	96	107	161	136
CUME RTG	10.0	8.7	8.0	10.7	10.4	5.1	3.9	4.3	5.3	4.7
KHOW										
SHARE	1.6	2.2	2.0	2.5	2.5	2.6	3.0	2.9	3.2	4.3
AQH(00)	44	60	55	72	72	106	115	122	142	186
CUME RTG	5.6	6.0	6.8	7.8	7.4	3.2	3.2	4.1	5.0	5.0
+KIMN-FM										
KMJI-FM										
SHARE	4.0	3.1	3.2	2.5	3.8	4.1	3.1	3.4	2.5	4.1
AQH(00)	111	86	89	74	112	170	120	143	111	179
CUME RTG	12.3	10.9	11.1	10.0	10.8	6.9	5.4	5.9	5.0	5.9
KJME										
SHARE	.8	.4	**	.3	.7	.9	.2	**	.4	.7
AQH(00)	21	12	**	9	19	36	9	**	17	29
CUME RTG	1.5	1.0	**	.9	1.7	1.0	.4	**	.5	1.2
KOA										
SHARE	8.8	9.5	9.9	7.5	6.9	7.4	10.0	11.3	10.4	7.2
AQH(00)	246	262	273	218	202	305	385	472	455	314
CUME RTG	26.2	24.4	27.5	22.2	21.0	12.4	12.8	14.3	13.9	11.0
KOSI										
SHARE	6.2	6.0	6.1	6.6	5.9	6.2	5.2	5.4	6.1	5.3
AQH(00)	171	166	168	193	172	255	202	228	268	229
CUME RTG	17.3	16.9	16.3	15.5	15.1	9.6	8.5	7.6	8.7	7.5
KQKS										
SHARE	4.9	3.9	4.1	4.5	4.5	4.0	2.9	2.9	3.5	3.1
AQH(00)	136	108	113	131	131	163	113	120	154	133
CUME RTG	15.3	12.9	14.2	13.7	13.9	8.2	5.5	7.3	6.9	6.6
KRFX										
SHARE	7.1	7.3	5.6	7.0	6.3	8.9	9.0	6.4	8.6	7.4
AQH(00)	198	202	156	203	185	363	348	267	379	322
CUME RTG	17.9	17.5	16.2	16.4	16.6	10.5	11.0	10.1	10.0	10.1
KTCL										
SHARE	2.1	1.6	1.9	1.9	1.2	1.7	1.5	1.4	1.4	.9
AQH(00)	58	45	52	54	36	68	57	58	62	41
CUME RTG	6.8	6.0	6.5	6.4	5.4	4.1	2.9	3.0	3.1	
KTLK										
SHARE	1.6	1.7	2.2	3.6	2.7	2.9	3.2	3.8		
AQH(00)	45	47	60	105	79			159		
CUME	4	5.5	6.2	10.1						
KVO										
		5	2.7 74							

considered at all, error rates, sample sizes, and other problems are important only when an owner or manager's station performs poorly in the ratings.

NONRATINGS RESEARCH

Although audience ratings are the most visible research data used in broadcasting, broadcasters, production companies, advertisers, and broadcast consultants use numerous other methodologies. Ratings yield estimates of audience size and composition. Nonratings research provides information about what the audience likes and dislikes, analyses of different types of programming, demographic and lifestyle information about the audience, and much more. All these data are intended to furnish decision makers in the industry with information they can use to eliminate some of the guesswork.

Nonratings research cannot solve all the problems broadcasters face, but it can be used to support decision making. Nonratings research is important to broadcasters in all markets, and one characteristic of all successful broadcast or cable operations is that the management uses research in all types of decision making. This section describes some of the nonratings research that is conducted in the electronic media.

PROGRAM TESTING

Research has become an accepted step in the development and production of programs and commercials. It is now common practice to test these productions in each of the following stages: initial idea or plan, rough cut, and post-production. A variety of research approaches can be used in each of these stages, depending on the purpose of the study, the amount of time allowed for testing, and the types of decisions that will be made with the results. A research

director must determine what the decision makers will need to know and design an analysis to provide that information.

Since major programs and commercials are very expensive to produce, producers and directors are interested in gathering preliminary reactions to a planned project. It would be ludicrous to spend thousands or millions of dollars on a project that would have little audience appeal.

Although most program testing is conducted by major networks, large advertising agencies, and production companies, there is an increasing interest in this area of research at the local level. Stations now test promotional campaigns, prime-time access scheduling, the acceptability of commercials, and various programming strategies.

One way to collect preliminary data is to show subjects a short statement summarizing a program or commercial and ask them for their opinions about the idea and their willingness to watch the program or buy the product on the basis of the description. The results may provide some indication about the potential success of a show or a commercial.

However, program descriptions cannot demonstrate the characters and their relationships to other characters in the program. This can be done only through the program dialogue and the characters' on-screen performance. For example, the NBC-TV program "ER" might have been described as follows:

> ER: A drama about a hospital emergency room showing the "real" events faced by doctors and nurses. Each week the program concentrates on a number of emergency situations and the relationships among the personnel in the hospital.

To many people this statement might seem to describe the type of show generally referred to as a "bomb." However, the indescribable on-screen relationship between the "doctors" and "nurses" and the other cast members, as well as the good story lines, made "ER" a hit in 1995.

If producers relied totally on program descriptions in testing situations, many successful shows would never reach the air.

If an idea tests well in the preliminary stages (or if the producer or advertiser wishes to go ahead with the project regardless of what the research indicates), a model or simulation is produced. These media "hardware" items are referred to as *rough cuts, storyboards, photomatics, animatics,* or *executions.* The **rough cut** is a simplistic production that usually uses amateur actors, little or no editing, and makeshift sets. The other models are photographs, pictures, or drawings of major scenes designed to give the basic idea of a program or commercial to anyone who looks at them.

Rough cuts or models are tested by several companies. The tests do not involve a lot of production expense, which is especially important if the tests show a lack of acceptance or understanding of the product. The tests provide information about the script, characterizations, character relationships, settings, cinematic approach, and overall appeal. They seldom identify the causes when a program or commercial is found to be unacceptable to the test audience; rather, they provide an overall indication that something is wrong.

When the final product is available, postproduction research can be conducted. Finished products are tested in experimental theaters, in shopping centers (where mobile vans are used to show commercials or programs), at subjects' homes in cities where cable systems provide test channels, or via telephone, in the case of radio commercials. Results from postproduction research often indicate that, for example, the ending of a program is unacceptable and must be reedited or reshot. Many problems that were not foreseen during production may be encountered in postproduction research, and the data usually provide producers with an initial audience reaction to the finished, or partially finished, product.

Each of the major commercial television networks uses its own approach to testing new programs. For example, according to Alan Wurtzel (1992), Senior Vice President of Marketing and Research for ABC, the network does not test program ideas or concepts. Wurtzel believes the approach is inadequate in evaluating a potential program. Instead, ABC begins by testing a completed pilot of the program. This is done by showing the pilot on cable television outlets throughout the country, where viewers are prerecruited to watch, or by sending viewers videotapes of the program to view at their leisure. Once a program is on the air, the show is continually tested with various qualitative and quantitative approaches such as focus groups and telephone interviews.

Other companies provide a variety of methods to test commercials or programs. Some companies test commercials and consumer products by showing different versions of commercials on cable systems. Test commercials can be cut in (that is, can replace a regularly scheduled commercial with a test spot) in certain target households. The other households on the cable system view the regular spot. Some time after the airing of the test commercial to the target households, follow-up research is conducted to determine the success of the commercial or the response to a new consumer product.

Commercials can also be tested in focus groups, shopping center intercepts, and auditorium-type situations. Generally speaking, commercials are not shown on television until they are tested in a variety of situations. The sponsors (even radio and television managers who wish to advertise their own station) do not want to communicate the wrong message to the audience.

MUSIC RESEARCH

Music is the product of a music radio station. To provide the station's listeners with music they like to hear and eliminate the songs that listeners do not like or are tired of hearing (*burned out*), radio programmers use a variety of research procedures.

Two of the most widely used music testing procedures are **auditorium music testing** and

call-out research. Auditorium tests are designed to evaluate *recurrents* (songs that were recently popular) and *oldies* (songs that have been around for years). Call-out research is used to test music on the air (*currents*). New music releases cannot be tested adequately in the auditorium or with call-out procedures. New music is often evaluated on the air during programs titled "Smash or Trash," or something similar, where listeners call in and voice their opinion about new releases.

Auditorium tests and call-out research serve the same purpose: to provide a program director and/or music director with information about the songs that are liked, disliked, burned, or unfamiliar. This information eliminates the gut feeling approach that many radio personnel once used in selecting music for their station.

Both music testing methods involve playing short segments, or hooks, of a number of recordings for the sample of listeners. A **hook** is a 5- to 15-second representative sample of the song—enough for respondents to identify the song if it is already familiar to them and to rate the song on some type of evaluation scale.

Several types of measurement scales are used in music testing research. For example, respondents can be asked to rate a hook on a 5- or 7-point scale, where 1 represents "hate" and 5 or 7 represents "like a lot" or "favorite." There are also choices of "unfamiliar" and "tired of hearing." Research companies and program directors use a variety of scales for listeners to use in evaluating the music they hear. Which scale is best? Research conducted over several years by the senior author indicates that the 7-point scale tends to provide the most reliable results.

Sometimes researchers ask the respondents to rate whether or not each song "fits" on their favorite radio station. These additional data help program directors determine which of the tested songs might not be appropriate for their station.

In addition, some research companies also ask listeners whether they would like radio stations in the area to play the song more, less, or the same amount as they currently do, but this is a highly inefficient and inaccurate method to determine the frequency with which a song should be played. The reason is that there is no common definition of *more, less,* or *same,* and listeners are extremely poor judges of how often a station currently plays the songs.

Auditorium Testing.   In this method, between 75 and 200 people are invited to a large room or hall, often a hotel conference room. Subjects are invited to the test because they meet specific requirements determined by the radio station and/or the research company (for example, people between the ages of 25 and 40 who listen to soft rock stations in the client's market). The recruiting of subjects for auditorium testing is handled by a field service that specializes in recruiting people for focus groups or other similar research projects. Respondents are generally paid $25–$100 for their cooperation.

The auditorium setting—usually a comfortable location away from distractions at home—enables researchers to test several hundred hooks in one 90- to 120-minute session. Usually between 200 and 400 hooks are tested, though some companies routinely test up to 600 hooks in a single session. However, after 400 songs, subject fatigue becomes evident by explicit physical behavior (looking around the room, fidgeting, talking to neighbors), and statistical reliability decreases. There is a great deal of evidence to show that scores for hooks after the 400 limit are not reliable (Wimmer, 1995).

Auditorium music testing is designed to test only songs that have been on the air for some time. It cannot be used on new releases because people cannot be expected to rate an unfamiliar recording on the basis of a 5- to 15-second hook.

Call-out Research.   The purpose of call-out research is the same as that for auditorium testing; only the procedure for collecting the data is changed. Instead of inviting people to a large hall or ballroom, randomly selected or prerecruited subjects are called on the telephone. Subjects are given the same rating instructions as in the auditorium test; they listen to the hook and provide a verbal response to the researcher making the telephone call. Call-out research is also used to test only newer music releases.

The major limitation of call-out research is that the number of testable hooks is limited to about 20, since subject fatigue sets in very quickly over the telephone. Further problems include the distractions that are often present in the home, and the frequently poor quality of sound transmission created by the telephone equipment. (The auditorium setting allows subjects to hear the hooks in stereo-quality sound.)

Even with such limitations, call-out research is used by many radio stations throughout the country. Since call-out research is fairly inexpensive compared with the auditorium method, the research can be conducted on a continual basis to track the performance of songs in a particular market. Auditorium research, which can cost about $20,000–$40,000 to test approximately 800 songs, is generally conducted only once or twice per year.

PROGRAMMING RESEARCH AND CONSULTING

Some of the largest mass media research companies are The Research Group, The Eagle Group, Frank N. Magid Associates, and Strategic Research. Although each company specializes in specific areas of broadcasting and uses different procedures, they all have a common goal: to provide management with data to be used in decision making. These companies offer custom research in almost any area of broadcasting, from testing call letters and slogans to air talent, commercials, music, importance of news programs, and the overall sound or look of a station.

Broadcast consultants can be equally versatile. The leading consultants have experience

in broadcasting and offer their services to radio and television stations. While some of their recommendations are based on research, many are made on the basis of past experience. A good consultant can literally "make or break" a broadcast station, and the task of a consultant is probably best described by a real consultant. E. Karl (1992, p. 1), a well-known and respected radio consultant, was asked to describe what a consultant does for a radio station. He states:

> A consultant works with research data to help plan a strategy for a station. A consultant puts research information into a package that will position the station correctly in listeners' minds, and helps market the station to bring listeners in to try out the station. The consultant does anything from designing music rotations, creating "clock hours" on the station, and selecting air talent . . . to developing television commercials to advertise the station, executing direct marketing campaigns to ask listeners to listen, to working with the station staff to make sure the "promise" of the station's position stays on track.

PERFORMER Q

Producers and directors in broadcasting naturally desire an indication of the popularity of various performers and entertainers. A basic question in the planning stage of any program is, "What performer or group of performers should be used to give the show the greatest appeal?" Not unreasonably, producers prefer using the most popular and likable performers in the industry to taking a chance on an unknown entertainer.

Marketing Evaluations, Inc., of Port Washington, New York, meets the demand for information about performers, entertainers, and personalities. The company conducts nationwide telephone surveys using three panels of about 1,250 households and interviewing about 5,400 people 6 years of age and older. The surveys are divided into three sections—Performer Q, Target Audience Rankings, and Demographic Profiles. The Performer Q portion of the analysis provides Familiarity and Appeal scores for more than 1,000 different personalities. The Target Audience Rankings provide a rank-order list of all personalities for several different target audiences, such as women 18–49. The target rank tells producers and directors which personalities appeal to specific demographic groups. In the third section, each personality is listed according to eight demographic profiles of the survey respondents. This section indicates the types of people that do and do not like the personalities in the survey.

Focus Groups

The focus group, discussed in Chapter 5, is a standard procedure in electronic media research, probably due to its versatility. Focus groups are used to develop questionnaires for further research and to provide preliminary information on a variety of topics, such as format and programming changes, personalities, station images, and lifestyle characteristics of the audience. Data in the last category are particularly useful when the focus group consists of a specific demographic segment.

Miscellaneous Research

The electronic media are unique, and each requires a different type of research. Examples of research conducted by and for stations include the following:

1. *Market studies.* A market study investigates the opinions and perceptions of the entire market, usually within a specific age range such as 25- to 54-year-olds. There are no requirements for respondents to meet in terms of station listening or viewing, and the sample matches the population distribution and makeup of the market.

2. *Format studies.* A format study for a radio station involves a sample of respondents who listen to or prefer a certain type of music.

These respondents are asked a series of questions to determine which stations provide the best service in a variety of areas such as music, news, traffic reports, and community activities.

3. *Program element importance.* Primarily used for radio, a program element importance study identifies the specific elements on radio that are most important to a group of listeners. Radio station managers use this information to design their radio station.

4. *Station image.* It is important for a station's management to know how the public perceives the station and its services; hence, "station image" has been mentioned throughout this chapter. Public misperception of management's purpose can create a decrease in audience size and, consequently, in advertising revenue. For example, suppose a radio station has been CHR for 10 years and switches to a country format. It is important that the audience and advertisers be aware of this change and have a chance to voice their opinions. This can be accomplished through a station image study, in which respondents to telephone calls are asked questions such as, "What type of music does radio station WAAA play?" "What types of people do you think listen to WAAA radio?" and "Did you know that WAAA now plays country music?" If research reveals that few people are aware of the change in format, management can develop a new promotional strategy. Or the station might find that the current promotional efforts have been successful and should not be changed. Station image studies are conducted periodically by most larger stations to maintain current information on how the audience perceives each station in the market. If station managers are to provide the services that listeners and viewers want, they must keep up to date with audience trends and social changes.

5. *Personality (talent) studies.* Radio and television managers of successful stations constantly test the on-air personalities. Announcers (DJs), news anchors, and all other personalities are tested for their overall appeal and fit

with other station personalities. Personality studies are often conducted for stations to find new talent from other markets, or even test personalities who are on other stations in the market with the intent of hiring them in the future.

6. *Advertiser (account) analysis.* To increase the value of their service to advertisers, many stations administer questionnaires to local business executives. Some typical questions include, "When did your business open?" "How many people own this business?" "How much do you invest in advertising per year?" "When are advertising purchase decisions made?" and "What do you expect from your advertising?" Information obtained from client questionnaires is used to help write more effective advertising copy, to develop better advertising proposals, and to allow the sales staff to know more about each client. Generally, the questionnaires are administered before a business becomes an advertiser on the station, but they can also be used for advertisers who have done business with the station for several years.

7. *Account executive research.* Radio and television station managers throughout the country conduct surveys of advertising agency personnel, usually buyers, to determine how their sales executives are perceived. It is vitally important to know how the salespeople are received by the buyers. The results of the survey indicate which salespeople are performing very well and which ones may need additional help. Many times a survey discloses that a problem between a sales executive and a buyer is purely a personality difference, and the station can easily correct the problem by assigning another salesperson to the advertising agency.

8. *Sales research.* In an effort to increase sales, many stations themselves conduct research for local clients. For example, a station may conduct a "banking image" study of all banks in the area to determine how residents perceive each bank and the service it provides. The results from such a study are then used in an advertising proposal for the banks in the

area. For example, if it is discovered that First National Bank's 24-hour automatic teller service is not well understood by local residents, the station might develop an advertising proposal to concentrate on this point.

9. *Diversification analyses.* The goals of any business are to expand and to achieve higher profits. In an effort to reach these goals, most larger stations, partnerships, and companies engage in a variety of studies to determine where investments should be made. Should other stations be purchased? What other types of activity should the business invest in? Such studies are used for forecasting, and represent a major portion of the research undertaken by larger stations and companies. The changes in broadcast ownership rules made by the FCC have significantly increased the level of acquisition research conducted by individuals, group owners, and other large companies in the broadcasting industry.

10. *Qualitative research.* Managers of successful broadcasting and cable operations leave nothing to chance—they test every aspect of their station. Research is conducted to test billboard advertising, logo designs, bumper stickers, bus advertising, direct mail campaigns, and programming interests.

SUMMARY

This chapter has introduced some of the more common methodologies used in broadcast research. Ratings are the most visible form of research used in broadcasting as well as the most influential in the decision-making process. However, nonratings approaches such as focus groups, music research, image studies, and program testing are all used frequently to collect data. The importance of research is fueled by an ever-increasing desire by management to learn more about broadcast audiences and their uses of the media.

Audience fragmentation is now an accepted phenomenon of the electronic media, and this competition for viewers and listeners has created a need for research data. Broadcast owners and managers realize that they can no longer rely on gut feelings when making programming, sales, and marketing decisions. The discussions in this chapter have been designed to emphasize the importance of research in all areas of broadcasting.

QUESTIONS AND PROBLEMS FOR FURTHER INVESTIGATION

1. Assume that a local television market has three stations: Channel 2, Channel 7, and Channel 9. There are 200,000 television households in the market. A ratings company samples 1,200 households at random and finds that 25% of the sample is watching Channel 2; 15%, Channel 7; and 10%, Channel 9.
   a. Calculate each station's share of the audience.
   b. Project the total number of households in the population watching each channel.
   c. Calculate the CPM for a $1,000, 30-second spot on Channel 2.
   d. Calculate the standard error involved in Channel 2's rating.

2. What are the major data-gathering problems associated with
   a. electronic meters
   b. diaries
   c. telephone interviews
   d. people meters

3. Find out what is happening in the development of electronic diaries. This information will be available in several of the weekly broadcasting trade publications. If you can develop a replacement for the paper diary on your own, please be sure to send an e-mail letter to the authors.

4. Examine a recent Arbitron market radio ratings book. Select a station and a daypart, and find that station's
   a. AQH
   b. cume
   c. turnover

5. Perform your own music call-out research. Edit several 15-second selections of recordings on a reel or cassette and ask people to rate them on a 7-point scale. Compute means and standard deviations for the results. What can you conclude?

REFERENCES AND SUGGESTED READINGS

The Arbitron Company. (1991). *How to read your Arbitron television market report*. New York: Arbitron.

The Arbitron Company. (1991). *Television universe estimates summary*. New York: Arbitron.

The Arbitron Company. (1991). *Tools for the trade*. New York: Arbitron.

The Arbitron Company. (1992). *A guide to some of the best buys in television and radio*. New York: Arbitron.

The Arbitron Company. (1992). *Arbitron's cable services: Making the connection*. New York: Arbitron.

The Arbitron Company. (1992). *Description of methodology*. New York: Arbitron.

The Arbitron Company. (1992). *Description of methodology: Radio market reports*. New York: Arbitron.

The Arbitron Company. (1994). *MediaWatch: The standard in commercial monitoring*. New York: Arbitron.

The Arbitron Company. (1995). *A guide to understanding and using radio audience estimates*. New York: Arbitron.

The Arbitron Company. (1995). *Electronic diary storage and review system*. New York: Arbitron.

Beville, H. M. (1988). *Audience ratings: Radio, television, cable*. (rev. ed.). Hillsdale, NJ: Lawrence Erlbaum.

Birch Radio. (1989a). *The Birch method of measurement and processing environment*. Birch Research Corporation.

Birch Radio. (1989b). *How Birch measures radio: The complete Birch radio sourcebook*. Birch Research Corporation.

Birch, T. (1989). Anatomy of the Birch radio telephone interview. *Radio & Records, 818*, 30.

Hawkins, W. J. (1990, February). TV views viewers. *Popular Science*, pp. 74–75.

Karl, E. (1992). Personal correspondence to Roger Wimmer.

Nielsen, A. C. (1989). *Reference supplement: Nielsen station index*. Nielsen Media Research.

Nielsen, A. C. (1989). *Reference supplement: Nielsen television index*. Nielsen Media Research.

Nielsen, A. C. (1992). *Media News*. New York: A. C. Nielsen.

Nielsen, A. C. (1992). *Nielsen Media Research . . . The quality behind the numbers*. Nielsen Media Research.

Webster, J., and Lichty, L. (1991). *Ratings analysis*. Hillsdale, N. J.: Lawrence Erlbaum.

Wimmer, R. D. (1995). An analysis of the reliability of auditorium music tests. Denver: The Eagle Group. (Proprietary data).

Wurtzel, A. (1992). Telephone conversation with Roger Wimmer.

Research in Advertising and Public Relations

For many years, research was not widely used in advertising and public relations; decisions were made on a more or less intuitive basis. However, with increased competition, mass markets, and mounting costs, more and more advertisers and public relations specialists have come to rely on research as a basic management tool (Haskins & Kendrick, 1993).

Much of the research in advertising and public relations is applied research, which attempts to solve a specific problem and is not concerned with theorizing or generalizing to other situations. Advertising and public relations researchers want to answer questions such as, "Should a certain product be packaged in blue or red?" "Is *Cosmopolitan* a better advertising buy than *Vogue*?" and "Should a company stress its environmental protection program in a planned publicity campaign?"

Advertising and public relations research does not involve any special techniques; the methods discussed earlier—laboratory, survey, field research, and content analysis—are in common use. They have been adapted, however, to provide specific types of information that meet the needs of these industries.

This chapter discusses the more common areas of advertising and public relations research and the types of studies they entail. In describing these research studies, the primary aim is to convey the facts the reader must know to understand the methods and to use them intelligently. A significant portion of the research in these areas involves market studies conducted by commercial research firms; these studies form the basis for much of the more specific research that follows in either the aca-

demic sector or the private sector. The importance of market research notwithstanding, this chapter does not have sufficient space to address this topic. Readers seeking additional information about market research techniques should consult Tull and Hawkins (1987) and Boyd, Westfall, and Stasch (1989).

There are three functional research areas in advertising: copy research, media research, and campaign assessment research. Each is discussed in turn, and the syndicated research available in each case is described when appropriate.

COPY TESTING

Everyone who does advertising research agrees that the term *copy testing* is misleading. The word *copy* implies that only the words in the ad are tested. This, of course, is not the case: Every element in an ad (layout, narration, music, illustration, size, length, and so on) is a possible variable in copy testing. Leckenby (1984) has suggested that the term *advertising stimulus measurement and research* (ASMAR) be substituted for *copy testing,* but the term has not gained wide usage. Likewise, the term *message research* is a less frequently used synonym. Thus we will continue to use the traditional term, despite its shortcomings.

Copy testing refers to research that helps develop effective advertisements and then determines which of several advertisements is the most effective. Copy testing takes place at every stage of the advertising process. Before a campaign starts, copy testing is used to determine what to stress and what to avoid. Once the content of the ad has been established, tests must be performed to ascertain the most effective way to structure these ideas. For example, in studying the illustration copy of a proposed magazine spread, a researcher might show to two or more groups of subjects an illustration of the product photographed from different angles. The headline might be evaluated by having potential users rate the typefaces used in several versions of the ad. The copy might be tested for readability and recall. In all cases, the aim is to determine whether the variable tested significantly affects the liking and/or the recall of the ad.

In TV, a rough cut of an entire commercial might be produced. The rough cut is a filmed or taped version of the ad in which amateur actors are used, locations are simplified, and the editing and narration lack the smoothness characteristic of broadcast (final cut) commercials. In this way, variations in the ad can be tested without incurring great expense.

The final phase of copy testing, which occurs after the finished commercials have appeared, serves to determine whether the campaign is having the desired effects. Any negative or unintended effects can be corrected before serious damage is done to a company's sales or reputation. This type of copy testing requires precisely defined goals. Some campaigns, for example, are designed to draw customers away from competitors; others are conducted to retain a company's present customers. Still others are intended to enhance the image of a firm and may not be concerned with consumers' purchase preferences. As will be discussed later, this type of copy testing blends in with campaign assessment research.

There are several different ways to categorize copy testing methods. Perhaps the most useful, summarized by Leckenby and Wedding (1982), suggests that there are appropriate copy testing methods for each of the three dimensions of impact in the persuasion process. Although, as represented in Table 15.1, the model suggests a linear process starting with the cognitive dimension (knowing) through the affective dimension (feeling) to the conative dimension (doing), it is not necessary for the steps to take place in this order. In any event, the model does serve as a convenient guide for discussing copy research testing methods.

THE COGNITIVE DIMENSION

Turning first to the cognitive dimension, the key dependent variables are attention, awareness, exposure, recognition, comprehension, and recall. Studies that measure attention to advertising can use various methods. One strategy involves a consumer jury. A group of 50–100 consumers are shown test ads and then asked which ad was best at catching their attention. A physiological measurement technique, known as an *eye tracking study*, is also used to determine what parts of an ad are noticed. An eye camera is a device that records the movement of the eye as it scans printed and graphic material. By analyzing the path the eye follows, researchers can determine which parts of the ad attracted initial attention.

A tachistoscope (or T-scope) is one way to measure recognition of an ad. The T-scope is actually a slide projector with adjustable levels

TABLE 15.1	Typology of Copy Testing Effects
Dimension of impact	**Typical dependent variables**
Cognitive	Attention
	Exposure
	Awareness
	Recognition
	Comprehension
	Recall
Affective	Attitude change
	Liking/disliking
	Involvement
Conative	Intention to buy
	Purchase behavior

Cigarette Ad Warnings and Eye-Tracking

An example of the use of the eye-tracking approach to measure attention and recall appeared in a recent issue of the *Journal of Advertising Research* (Krugman, Fox, Fletcher, Fischer & Rojas, 1994). The researchers were interested in determining how much attention adolescents paid to current warning messages in cigarette ads compared with possible new warnings.

At the beginning of the experiment, subjects were seated in a chair that was connected to the eye-tracking apparatus. They were then shown several magazine ads including two for cigarettes. The cigarette ads included either the current mandated warning or a new warning message. Subjects could view each ad as long as they pleased. The results showed that the new warnings were more effective than the old warnings in attracting attention and also held the subjects' attention longer. In addition, the amount of time a subject spent paying attention to the warning message was related to recall of the warning, thus providing a measure of validity for the eye-tracking technique.

of illumination and with projection speeds that can be adjusted down to a tiny fraction of a second. Ads are tested to determine how long it takes a consumer to recognize the product, the headline, or the brand name.

Ad comprehension is an important factor in advertising research. One study found that all 60 commercials used in a given test were miscomprehended by viewers (Jacoby & Hofer, 1982). To guard against results such as these, advertising researchers typically test new ads with focus groups (Chapter 5) to make sure their message is getting across as intended. The T-scope is also used to see how long it takes subjects to comprehend the theme of an ad—an important consideration for outdoor advertising, where drivers may have only a second or two of exposure.

Awareness, exposure, and recall are determined by several related methods. One measurement technique that taps these variables is used primarily by the print media: Subjects are shown a copy of a newspaper or magazine and are asked which advertisements they remember seeing or reading. The results are used to tabulate a "reader traffic score" for each ad.

This method is prone to criticism, however, because some respondents confuse the advertisements or the publications in which the ads

were seen, and some try to please the interviewer by reporting that they saw more than they actually did. To control this problem, researchers often make use of *aided recall* techniques; for instance, they might also show the respondent a list of advertisers, some of whose advertisements actually appeared in the publication and some of whose did not.

For obvious reasons, this type of **recall study** is not entirely suitable for testing radio and television commercials; a more commonly used method in such cases is the telephone survey. Two variations of this approach are sometimes used. In *aided recall*, the interviewer mentions a general class of products and asks whether the respondent remembers an ad for a specific brand. A typical question might be, "Have you seen or heard any ads for soft drinks lately?" In the *unaided recall technique*, researchers ask a general question such as, "Have you seen any ads that interested you lately?" Obviously, it is harder for the consumer to respond to the second type of question. Only truly memorable ads score high on this form of measurement. Some researchers suggest that the most sensitive way to measure recall is to ask consumers if they remember any recent advertising for each particular brand whose advertising is of interest (Haskins & Kendrick, 1993).

Perhaps a better understanding can be gained by examining the several research companies that offer syndicated services in this area. For example, Perception Research Services uses an eye-tracking camera to measure which parts of an ad were most noticed and the sequence in which consumers viewed the various elements of the ad. Gallup & Robinson conducts pilot testing of ads with their Rapid Ad Measurement (RAM) service. The ads to be tested are placed in special test issues of *Time* or *People,* and copies of the magazines are delivered to respondents in five urban areas. A phone interview takes place the following day, and the respondents are asked questions about the content of the ad, how much they remembered, and whether or not the ad changed their attitudes toward buying the product.

Video Storyboard Tests (VST) offers research concerning both print and television ads. For print, test ads are inserted into a specially prepared magazine that contains several articles and a number of control ads. Interviews with potential customers are conducted at shopping malls and focus on such topics as awareness and recall. For TV ads, VST conducts one-on-one interviews in central locations in several markets. Respondents are shown either a rough-cut of the ad or a storyboard that depicts key scenes from the ad and asked questions similar to those used in the testing of print ads.

Another method of posttesting television commercials is the In-View service provided by Gallup & Robinson. Gallup & Robinson measures the percentage of respondents who remember seeing the commercial and the percentage of those who can remember specific points. Additionally, they provide a score indicating the degree of favorable attitude toward the product, based on positive statements made by the subjects during the interview.

Gallup & Robinson also conducts pretests and posttests of magazine advertisements. Their Magazine Impact Research Service (MIRS) measures recall of advertisements appearing in general-interest magazines. Copies of a particular issue containing the advertisement under study are mailed to approximately 150 readers. (In the case of a pretest, the MIRS binds the proposed advertisement into each magazine.) The day after delivery of the magazines, respondents are telephoned and asked which advertisements they noticed in the magazine and what details they can remember about them. These results are reported to the advertiser.

One of the best known professional research firms is Starch INRA Hooper, Inc., which conducts posttest recall research. The company's Message Report Service routinely measures advertising readership in more than 100 magazines and newspapers. Using a sample of approximately 300 people, Starch interviewers take a copy of the periodical under study to respondents' homes. If a subject has already looked through that particular publication, he or she is questioned at length. The interviewer shows the respondents an advertisement and asks whether he or she has seen or read any part of it. If the answer is no, the interviewer moves on to another advertisement; if the answer is yes, more questions are asked to determine how much was read. This procedure continues until the respondent has been questioned about every advertisement in that issue up to 90 (at which point the interview is terminated to avoid subject fatigue). Starch places each respondent into one of four categories for each advertisement:

1. *Nonreader* (did not recall seeing the advertisement)
2. *Noted reader* (remembered seeing the advertisement)
3. *Associated reader* (not only saw the advertisement but also read some part of it that clearly indicated the brand name)
4. *Read most reader* (read more than half the written material in the advertisement)

The Starch organization uniquely reports the findings of its recall studies in a novel manner. Advertisers are given a copy of the magazine in which readership scores printed on yellow stickers have been attached to each advertisement. Figure 15.1 is an example of a "Starched" advertisement.

The Starch Message Report Service provides a measurement of recognition only; for an indication of an advertisement's success in getting its message across, advertisers can request a Starch Reader Impression Study. Such studies involve in-depth interviews with readers who have seen an advertisement in a particular newspaper or magazine and are asked a series of detailed questions about it, such as

1. "In your own words, what did this ad tell you about the product?"
2. "What did the pictures tell you?"
3. "What did the written material tell you?"

The responses are subjected to content analysis, and the results are summarized for clients. Additionally, Starch reports the percentage of favorable and unfavorable comments about each advertisement.

THE AFFECTIVE DIMENSION

The affective dimension usually involves research into whether a consumer's attitudes toward a particular product have changed because of exposure to an ad or a campaign. Techniques used to study the affective dimension include projective tests, theater testing, physiological measures, semantic differential scales, and rating scales. *Projective tests* provide an alternative to the straightforward "Do you like this ad?" approach. Instead, respondents are asked to draw a picture or complete a story that involves the ad or the product mentioned in the ad. Analysis of these responses provides additional insight and depth into the consumer's feelings.

Theater tests involve bringing an audience to a special facility where the audience is shown television commercials that are embedded in a TV show. Respondents are given electronic response indicators (similar to hand-

held calculators) that allow them to instantaneously rate each commercial they see. Fenwick and Rice (1991) describe five continuous measurement systems currently available and report the results of a reliability test using the Program Evaluation Analysis Computer (PEAC), a device with five buttons ranging from one labeled "feel very positive" to one labeled "feel very negative." The respondents press these buttons while watching a commercial. Fenwick and Rice report that the PEAC achieved high levels of test-retest reliability. The miniaturization of these hand-held rating devices allows tests to be conducted in focus room facilities or in specially equipped vans parked outside shopping malls. These tests have been criticized because they require respondents to make too many responses, analyze content that may be too minute to be put into practical use, and do not allow respondents to change their answers since they are recorded instantaneously in a computer. Sometimes a researcher's desire to use technology to impress clients overshadows the validity and reliability of a research approach.

Two *physiological tests* are commonly used in this area. In the *pupilometer test,* a tiny camera focused on the subject's eye measures the amount of pupil dilation that occurs while the person is looking at an ad. Changes in pupil diameter are recorded, because findings from psychophysiology suggest that people tend to respond to appealing stimuli with dilation (enlargement) of their pupils. Conversely, when unappealing, disagreeable stimuli are shown, the pupil narrows. The second test measures galvanic skin response, or GSR (that is, changes in the electrical conductance of the surface of the skin). A change in GSR rating while the subject is looking at an ad is taken to signify emotional involvement or arousal.

Semantic differential scales and *rating scales* (Chapter 3) are most often used to measure attitude change. For these measurements to be most useful, it is necessary to (1) obtain a picture of the consumer's attitudes before

FIGURE 15.1   A "Starched" Ad

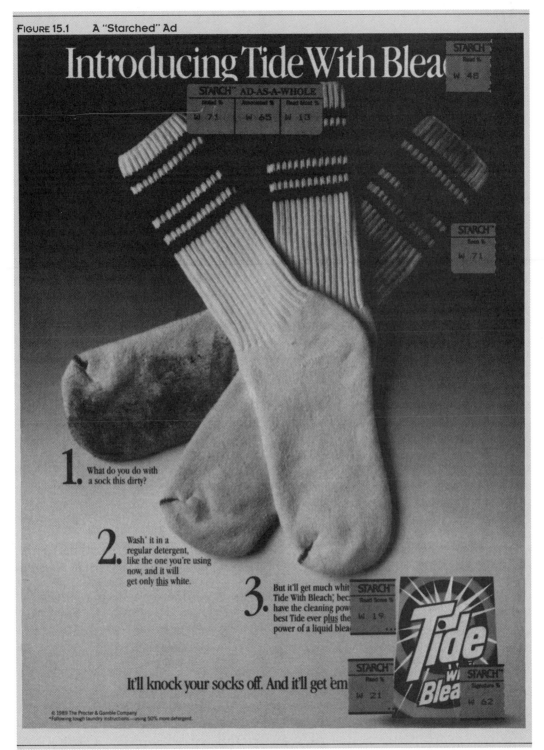

exposure to the ad, (2) expose the consumer to the ad or ads under examination, and (3) remeasure the attitude after exposure. To diminish the difficulties associated with achieving all three of these goals in testing television ads, many researchers prefer a **forced-exposure** method. In this technique, respondents are invited to a theater for a special screening of a TV program. Before viewing the program, they are asked to fill out questionnaires concerning their attitudes toward several different products, one of which is of interest to the researchers. Next, everyone watches the TV show, which contains one or more commercials for the product under investigation as well as ads for other products. When the show is over, all respondents again fill out the questionnaire concerning product attitudes. Change in evaluation is the key variable of interest. The same basic method can be used in testing attitudes toward print ads except that the testing is done individually, in each respondent's home. Typically, a consumer is interviewed about product attitudes, a copy of a magazine that includes the test ad (or ads) is left at the house, and the respondent is asked to read or look through the publication before the next interview. A short time later, the interviewer calls back the respondent, and asks whether the magazine has been read. If it has, product attitudes are once again measured.

The importance of the affective dimension was emphasized by Walker and Dubitsky (1994), who noted that the degree of liking expressed by consumers toward a commercial was significantly related to awareness, recall, and greater persuasive impact. Indeed, several advertising researchers have suggested that liking an ad is one of the most important factors in determining its impact (Haley, 1994).

Several research companies offer services designed to measure attitudes. As part of their In-View service, Gallup & Robinson test attitude change by calling eligible respondents and inviting them to participate in the viewing of a test program. During this call, the inter-

viewer records attitudes about six products, three of which will be advertised on the test show. Comparison data are collected from nonviewers of the program. After the program is viewed, respondents are called back and asked the same attitude questions. Changes in attitude are presumed to be the result of viewing the commercial. In magazine measurement, Gallup & Robinson constructs a special issue of a magazine containing the ads under consideration. Respondents are randomly selected from the phone book, visited at home, and given a copy of the magazine. The next day, to establish readership, respondents are asked questions about the magazine's contents. The interviewer next reads a list of products and asks whether the magazine contained ads for each product. Each time a respondent remembers seeing a product ad, the interviewer asks for a description of the ad, as well as the respondent's attitudes toward the product after reading the ad.

THE CONATIVE DIMENSION

The conative dimension deals with actual consumer behavior, and, in many instances, it is the most pertinent of all dependent variables. The two main categories of behavior that are usually measured are *buying predisposition* and *actual purchasing behavior.* In the first category, the usual design is to gather precampaign predisposition data and reinterview the subjects after the advertising has been in place. Subjects are typically asked a question along these lines: "If you were going shopping tomorrow to buy breakfast cereal, which brand would you buy?" This might be followed by, "Would you consider buying any other brands?" and "Are there any cereals you would definitely not buy?" (The last question is included to determine whether the advertising campaign has had any negative effects.) Additionally, some researchers (Haskins, 1976) suggest using a buying intention scale and instructing respondents to check the one position on the scale that best fits their intention. Such a scale might look like this:

_____ I'll definitely buy this cereal as soon as I can.

_____ I'll probably buy this cereal sometime.

_____ I might buy this cereal, but I don't know when.

_____ I'll probably never buy this cereal.

_____ I wouldn't eat this cereal even if somebody gave it to me.

The scale allows advertisers to see how consumers' buying preferences change during and after the campaign.

Perhaps the most reliable methods of post-testing are those that measure actual sales, direct response, and other easily quantifiable behavior. In the print media, direct response might be measured by inserting a coupon that readers might mail in for a free sample. Different forms of an ad might be run in different publications to determine which elicits the most inquiries. Another alternative suitable for use in both print media advertising and electronic media advertising consists of including a toll-free 800 number that consumers can call for more information or to order the product.

Some research companies measure direct response by means of a laboratory store. Usually used in conjunction with theater testing, this technique involves giving people chits with which they can buy products in a special store. (Most of the time this is a special trailer or field service conference room furnished to look like a store.) They are then shown a program containing some test commercials, given more chits, and allowed to shop again. Changes in pre- and postexposure choices are recorded.

Actual sales data can be obtained in many ways. They can be obtained directly by asking consumers, "What brand of breakfast cereal did you most recently purchase?" However, the findings would be subject to error due to faulty recall, courtesy bias, and so forth; for this reason, more direct methods are generally preferred. If enough time and money are available, direct observation of people's selections in the cereal aisles at a sample of supermarkets can be a useful source of data. Store audits that list the total number of boxes sold at predetermined times are another possibility. Lastly, and possibly most expensive, is the household audit technique whereby an interviewer visits the homes of a sample of consumers and actually inspects their kitchen cupboards to see what brands of cereals are there. In addition to the audit, a traditional questionnaire is used to gather further information about the respondent's feelings toward the commercials.

Many professional research firms conduct surveys that deal with purchasing behavior. The A. C. Nielsen Company uses advanced computer technology to monitor the viewing behavior of 4,000 households. The research company can electronically cut in test commercials without viewers being aware that something different is inserted. A tiny device attached to the TV set allows the set to accept these test commercials and to store viewing data for later retrieval. At the supermarket, members of Nielsen's sample present an ID card, and through the use of the UPC, all their purchases are electronically recorded and tabulated. Thus, clients are able to monitor actual buying behavior changes in response to test commercials.

Nielsen also offers a Scantrack service that monitors the TV viewing behavior of a panel of 40,000 households whose members also have their purchases recorded via electronic scanner. Information Resources Inc. (IRI) has a similar service called Infoscan.

In the print area, ASI-Market Research, Inc., uses a less expensive technique that measures pseudo-purchase behavior. A test magazine containing the client's ad is left at the house. The respondent is asked to read the magazine, told there will be a prize for participation, and asked which brands would be preferred if he or she is a grand prize winner. After the test ads have been looked at, the respondent is again asked about prize preferences. Changes in pre- and postexposure scores are carefully noted. In the television area, ASI offers Persuasion Plus, an ad-testing system that uses cable television. Respondents are contacted and asked to screen a new TV program over one of their cable channels. The day after, respondents are telephoned and asked questions about commercial recall and their intention to buy the product under examination. Finally, they are asked to select a brand that they would most like to receive as a prize.

COPY RESEARCH AND VALIDITY

All of the above methods of copy research are based on the assumption that this research identifies ads that will work well in the marketplace. To test this assumption, the Advertising Research Foundation (ARF) sponsored a research validity project to determine which copy testing measures were effective (Haley & Baldinger, 1991). To begin, ARF selected five pairs of TV commercials. Since one of the ads in each of these pairs had already been shown to have produced major sales differences in test markets, ARF researchers used the ads in a field experiment that included many common copy testing measures.

The experiment revealed a strong correlation between ads that copy tested well and ads that performed well in the marketplace. For example, measuring reaction to commercials on an affective scale (like/dislike) predicted the more effective ad of the pair 87% of the time. Top-of-mind awareness (unaided recall) measures correctly classified the more effective ad 73% of the time. Less effective were measures that asked respondents to recall the main point of the ad. In a reanalysis of the ARF data, Rossiter and Eagleson (1994) suggested that another measure—a pretest-posttest difference in replies to the item "I will definitely buy this product"—would also be a useful measure. In sum, it appears that copy testing research can help predict what ad will be most effective in generating sales.

MEDIA RESEARCH

The two key terms in media research are reach and frequency. **Reach** is the total number of households or persons that will be exposed to a message in a particular medium at least once over a certain period (usually 4 weeks). Reach can be thought of as the cumulative audience, and it is usually expressed as a percentage of the total universe of households that have been exposed to a message. For example, if 25 of a possible 100 households are exposed to a message, the reach is 25%. **Frequency** refers to the number of exposures to the same message that each household receives. Of course, not every household in the sample will receive exactly the same number of messages. Consequently, advertisers prefer to use the average frequency of exposure, expressed by the following formula:

$$\frac{\text{Total exposures for all households}}{\text{Reach}} = \text{Average frequency}$$

Thus, if the total number of exposures for a sample of households is 400 and the reach is 25, the average frequency is 16. In other words, the average household was exposed 16 times. Notice that if the reach were 80%, the frequency would be 5. As reach increases, average frequency drops. (Maximizing both reach and frequency would require an unlimited budget, something most advertisers lack.)

A concept closely related to reach and frequency is gross rating points (GRPs), introduced in Chapter 14. GRPs are useful when it comes to deciding between two media alternatives. For example, suppose Program A has a reach of 30% and an average frequency of 2.5, whereas Program B has a reach of 45% and a frequency of 1.25. Which program offers a better reach-frequency relationship? First, determine the GRPs of each program using the following formula:

$$\text{GRPs} = \text{Reach} \times \text{Average Frequency}$$

For A:

$$\text{GRPs} = 30 \times 2.5 = 75.00$$

For B:

$$\text{GRPs} = 45 \times 1.25 = 56.25$$

In this example, Program A scores better in the reach-frequency combination, and this would probably be a factor in deciding which was the better buy.

Media research falls into three general categories: studies of the size and composition of an audience of a particular medium or media (reach studies), studies of the relative efficiency of advertising exposures provided by various combinations of media (reach and frequency studies), and studies of the advertising activities of competitors.

AUDIENCE SIZE AND COMPOSITION

Analyses of audiences are probably the most commonly used advertising studies in print and electronic media research. Since advertisers spend large amounts of money in the print and electronic media, they have an understandable interest in the audiences for those messages. In most cases, audience information is gathered using techniques that are compromises between the practical and the ideal.

The audience size of a newspaper or magazine is commonly measured in terms of the number of copies distributed per issue. This number, which is called the publication's **circulation**, includes all copies delivered to subscribers as well as those bought at newsstands

or from other sellers. Because a publication's advertising rate is directly determined by its circulation, the print media have developed a standardized method of measuring circulation and have instituted an organization, the Audit Bureau of Circulations (ABC), to verify that a publication actually distributes the number of copies per issue that it claims. (The specific procedures used by the ABC are discussed later in this chapter.)

Circulation figures are used to compute the CPMs of various publications. For example, suppose Newspaper X charges $1,800 for an advertisement and has an ABC-verified circulation of 180,000; Newspaper Y, with a circulation of 300,000, charges $2,700 for the same size space. Table 15.2 shows that Newspaper Y is the more efficient advertising vehicle.

Note that this method considers only the number of circulated copies of a newspaper or magazine. This information is useful, but it does not necessarily indicate the total number of readers of the publication. To estimate the total audience, the circulation figure must be multiplied by the average number of readers of each copy of an issue. This information is obtained by performing audience surveys.

A preliminary step in conducting such surveys is to operationally define the concept *magazine reader* or *newspaper reader*. There are many possible definitions, but the one most commonly used is fairly liberal: A *reader* is a person who has read or at least looked through an issue.

Three techniques are used to measure readership. The most rigorous is the **unaided recall** method, in which respondents are asked whether they have read any newspapers or magazines in the past month (or other time period). If the answer is yes, subjects are asked to specify the magazines or newspapers they read. When a publication is named, the interviewer attempts to verify reading by asking questions about the contents of that publication. The reliability of the unaided recall method is open to question (as has been discussed)

TABLE 15.2 Determining Advertising Efficiency from Ad Cost and Circulation Data

	Newspaper X	Newspaper Y
Ad cost	$1,800	$2,700
Circulation	180,000	300,000
Cost per thousand circulated copies	$\dfrac{\$1,800}{180} = \$10.00$	$\dfrac{\$2,700}{300} = \$9.00$

TABLE 15.3 Determining Ad Efficiency from an Extended Database

	Newspaper X	Newspaper Y
Ad cost	$1,800	$2,700
Circulation	180,000	300,000
CPM	$10.00	$9.00
Number of people	630,000	540,000
who read the issue	(3.5 readers per copy)	(1.8 readers per copy)
Revised CPM	$2.86	$5.00

---

because of the difficulty respondents often have in recalling specific content.

A second technique involves **aided recall**. In this method, the interviewer names several publications and asks whether the respondent has read any of them lately. Each time the respondent claims to have read a publication, the interviewer asks whether he or she remembers seeing the most recent copy. The interviewer may jog a respondent's memory by describing the front page or the cover. Finally, the respondent is asked to recall anything that was seen or read in that particular issue. (In a variation on this process, masked recall, respondents are shown the front page or the cover of a publication with the name blacked out and are asked whether they remember reading that particular issue. Those who respond in the affirmative are asked to recall any items they have seen or read.)

The third technique, called the **recognition** method, entails showing respondents the logo or cover of a publication. For each publication the respondent has seen or read, the interviewer produces a copy and the respondent leafs through it to identify the articles or stories he or she recognizes. All respondents who definitely remember reading the publication are counted in its audience. To check the accuracy of the respondent's memory, dummy articles may be inserted into the interviewer's copy of the publication; respondents who claim to have read the dummy items thus may be eliminated from the sample or given less weight in the analysis. Many advertising researchers consider the recognition technique to be the most accurate predictor of readership scores.

Once the total audience for each magazine or newspaper has been tabulated, the advertiser can determine which publication is the

TABLE 15.4	Calculation of Ad Efficiency Incorporating Demographic Survey Results	
	Newspaper X	**Newspaper Y**
Ad cost	$1,800	$2,700
Circulation	180,000	300,000
CPM	$10.00	$9.00
Number of people who read average issue	630,000	540,000
Number of potential beer drinkers	150,000	220,000
Number of potential fast-food customers	300,000	200,000
CPM (beer drinkers)	$12.00	$12.27
CPM (fast-food customers)	$ 6.00	$13.50

most efficient buy. For example, returning to the example of Table 15.2, suppose that Newspaper X and Newspaper Y have the audience figures given in Table 15.3. On the basis of these figures, Newspaper X is seen to be the more efficient choice.

Another variable to be considered in determining the advertising efficiency (or media efficiency) of a newspaper or magazine is the number of times a person reads each issue. For example, imagine two newspapers or magazines that have exactly the same number of readers per issue. Publication A consists primarily of pictures and contains little text; people tend to read it once and not look at it again. Publication B, on the other hand, contains several lengthy and interesting articles; people pick it up several times. Publication B would seem to be a more efficient advertising vehicle, since it provides several possible exposures to an advertisement for the same cost as Publication A. Unfortunately, a practical and reliable method for measuring the number of exposures per issue has yet to be developed.

Perhaps the most important gauge for advertising efficiency is the composition of the audience. It matters little if an advertisement for farm equipment is seen by 100,000 people if only a few of them are in the market for such products. To evaluate the number of potential customers in the audience, an advertiser must first conduct a survey to determine certain demographic characteristics of the people who tend to purchase a particular product. For example, potential customers for beer might be typically described as males between the ages of 18 and 49; those for fast-food restaurants might be households in which the primary wage earner is between 18 and 35 and there are at least two children under 12. These demographic characteristics of the typical consumer are then compared with the characteristics of a publication's audience for the product. The cost of reaching this audience is also expressed in CPM units, as shown in Table 15.4. An examination of these figures indicates that Newspaper X is slightly more efficient as a vehicle for reaching potential beer customers and much more efficient in reaching fast-food restaurant patrons.

Due to the ephemeral nature of radio and television broadcasts, determining audience size and composition in the electronic media poses special problems for advertising researchers. One problem in particular involves the use of the CPM measure for media planning. The various measures of program audience discussed in Chapter 14 may or may not reflect the number of people actually viewing a TV program. Lloyd and Clancy (1991) suggest a new measure, the *CMPI,* or *cost per thousand involved persons,* as a solution. Constructing this measure consisted of asking viewers to respond to statements about their viewing such as:

> "There were parts in this show that really touched my feelings."
>
> "I was really involved in the program. I wished it had lasted longer."

Answers to these items revealed audience differences in program involvement, and the authors suggest that a program whose audience was small but involved might be a better advertising buy than a program with a large but marginally involved audience.

FREQUENCY OF EXPOSURE IN MEDIA SCHEDULES

An advertiser working within a strict budget to promote a product or service may be limited to the use of a single vehicle or medium. Often, however, an advertising campaign is conducted via several advertising vehicles simultaneously. But which combination of vehicles and/or media will provide the greatest reach and frequency for the advertiser's product? A substantial amount of recent media research has been devoted to this question, much of it concentrated on the development of mathematical models of advertising media and their audiences. The mathematical derivations of these models are beyond the scope of this book. However, the following material describes in simplified form the concepts underlying two computerized models: stepwise analysis and decision calculus. Readers who wish to pursue these topics in more rigorous detail should consult Aaker and Myers (1975), Moran (1963), and Rust (1986).

Stepwise analysis is called an iterative model because the same series of instructions to the computer is repeated over and over again with slight modifications until a predetermined best

or optimal solution is reached. The Young & Rubicam agency pioneered development in this area with its stepwise "high-assay" model. Stepwise analysis constructs a media schedule in increments, initially choosing a particular vehicle based on the lowest cost per potential customer reached. After this selection has been made, all the remaining media vehicles are reevaluated to determine whether the optimal advertising exposure rate has been achieved. If not, the second most efficient vehicle is chosen and the process is repeated until the optimal exposure rate is reached. This method is called the "high-assay" model because it is analogous to gold mining. The easiest-to-get gold is mined first, followed by less accessible ore. In like manner, the consumers who are the easiest to reach are first targeted, followed by those consumers who are harder to find and more costly to reach.

Decision calculus models make use of an **objective function**, a mathematical statement that provides a quantitative value for a given media combination (also known as a schedule). This value represents the schedule's effectiveness in providing advertising exposure. The advertising researcher determines which schedule offers the maximum exposure for a given product by calculating the objective functions of various media schedules.

Calculations of objective function are based on values generated by studies of audience size and composition for each vehicle or medium. In addition, a schedule's objective function value takes into account such variables as the probability that the advertisement will be forgotten, the total cost of the media schedule compared with the advertiser's budget, and the "media option source effect"—that is, the relative impact of exposure in a particular advertising vehicle. (For example, an advertisement for men's clothes is likely to have more impact in *Gentlemen's Quarterly* than in *True Detective.*)

Advertising planners realized early on that computer models would be helpful in calculating objective functions. The first, MEDIAC, calculated the probability that a given person within a market segment will be exposed to an ad (Little & Lodish, 1969). A second computer model, called ADMOD (Aaker, 1975), is designed to maximize favorable attitude changes among consumers toward the advertised product. ADMOD evaluates a media schedule by examining its likely impact on each individual in samples drawn from the market population. This impact is calculated by taking into account the number and source of exposures for each individual and the effect of these exposures on the probability of obtaining the desired attitude change. The results are then projected to the population. A unique ADMOD feature allows the researcher to include certain data about different message strategies that might be employed.

The years since these two models were developed have seen tremendous changes in both the media and the computer. In the first place, personal computers have become commonplace at advertising agencies, and a number of reach and frequency programs including MEDIAC and ADMOD have been developed for them. Leckenby and Kim (1994) surveyed media directors at the 200 largest ad agencies in the United States and found that at least 19 different programs were used to calculate reach and frequency schedules. At the same time, large-scale databases developed by research firms such as Nielsen, Simmons, and MRI have given advertisers much more data to analyze. Finally, new media have proliferated. Cable channels, VCRs, the Internet, and various out-of-home media have made the task of planning media buying campaigns even more complicated. In that connection, it is not surprising that the study by Leckenby and Kim found that the use of personal computers for media planning almost doubled in the last decade.

MEDIA RESEARCH BY PRIVATE FIRMS

As mentioned earlier, the Audit Bureau of Circulations (ABC) supplies advertisers with data on the circulation figures of newspapers and magazines. As of 1995, ABC measured the circulation of about 75% of all print media vehicles in the United States and Canada. ABC requires publishers to submit a detailed report of their circulation every 6 months; it verifies these reports by sending field workers to conduct an audit at each publication. The auditors typically examine records of the publications' press runs, newsprint bills, or other invoices for paper, as well as transcripts of circulation records and other related files.

The ABC audit results, as well as overall circulation data, coverage maps, press times, and market data, are published in an annual report and distributed to ABC members and advertisers. ABC now reports data on audience size for certain selected newspapers. Called the "Newspaper Audience Research Data Bank," this report consists of a collection of audience surveys conducted by newspapers in the top 100 markets.

The Simmons Market Research Bureau and Mediamark Research Inc. (MRI) provide comprehensive feedback about magazine readership. Both firms now use the same measurement technique, called the *recent reading method.* Each selects a large random sample of readers and shows them the logos of about 70 magazines to determine which ones they have recently read or looked through. At the same time, data are gathered about the ownership, purchase, and use of a variety of products and services. This information is tabulated by Simmons and MRI and released in a series of detailed reports on the demographic makeup and purchasing behavior of each magazine's audience. Using these data, advertisers can determine the cost of reaching potential buyers of their products or services. A portion of an MRI Magazine Total Audience Report is reproduced in Table 15.5.

Two companies—Arbitron and A. C. Nielsen—supply broadcast audience data for advertisers. Arbitron measures radio listening in about 200 markets across the United States, and Nielsen provides audience estimates for network

TABLE 15.5 Example of Mediamark Report

	AUDIENCE (000)			MEDIAN AGE			MEDIAN H/D INCOME			CIRCU-LATION	READERS PER COPY		
	TOTAL ADULTS	TOTAL MEN	TOTAL WOMEN	ADULTS	MEN	WOMEN	ADULTS	MEN	WOMEN	(000)	ADULTS	MEN	WOMEN
TOTAL ADULT POPULATION	180.974	86.307	94.667	40.8	39.9	41.7	31.717	33.829	29.538	·	·	·	·
AIR GROUP ONE (GR)	1.882	1.075	807	39.0	37.9	40.0	57.245	61.194	55.116	659	2.86	1.63	1.22
AMERICAN BABY	3.557	558	2.999	29.5	31.3	29.2	33.146	39.515	31.852	1.143	3.11	.49	2.62
AMERICAN HEALTH	3.851	1.175	2.676	40.8	42.7	40.2	37.115	35.287	37.483	1.102	3.49	1.07	2.43
AMERICAN LEGION	3.313	2.031	1.282	59.1	61.3	56.3	28.078	27.734	28.641	2.825*	1.17	.72	.45
AMERICAN WAY	1.062	528	534	45.2	44.3	47.7	59.750	61.967	52.500	245*	4.33	2.16	2.18
ARCHITECTURAL DIGEST	3.147	1.607	1.540	38.2	37.7	38.7	56.446	57.246	55.685	624	5.04	2.58	2.47
AUDUBON	1.580	616	964	42.7	41.7	44.5	38.528	33.737	43.117	453*	3.49	1.36	2.13
BABY TALK	2.258	403	1.855	27.9	31.6	27.2	23.636	33.096	21.667	.964*	2.34	.42	1.92
BASSMASTER	3.202	2.742	460	34.9	35.6	31.7	34.747	34.986	32.031	539	5.94	5.09	.85
BETTER HOMES & GARDENS	31.367	7.527	23.840	42.5	41.8	42.9	34.643	37.057	33.855	8.078	3.88	.93	2.95
BHG/LHJ COMBO (GR)	49.749	9.264	40.485	42.8	42.1	42.9	33.924	36.290	33.430	13.161	3.78	.70	3.08
BLACK ENTERPRISE	1.904	983	921	37.6	36.2	38.9	26.061	33.476	17.443	239	7.97	4.11	3.85
BON APPETIT	4.631	1.111	3.520	40.0	38.2	40.6	41.081	41.389	41.027	1.389	3.33	.80	2.53
BRIDE'S MAGAZINE	3.957	592	3.365	25.7	25.8	25.7	33.170	34.097	33.076	390	10.15	1.52	8.63
BUSINESS WEEK	6.136	4.341	1.795	37.4	38.1	36.3	45.881	48.094	42.012	929	6.60	4.67	1.93
THE CABLE GUIDE	14.852	7.401	7.451	36.5	35.5	37.3	39.966	40.799	39.102	7.684*	1.93	.96	.97
CAR & DRIVER	5.327	4.641	686	29.5	29.3	30.7	38.282	38.237	43.117	870*	6.12	5.33	.79
CAR CRAFT	2.506	2.257	249	29.1	28.4	33.7	31.271	31.576	28.092	435	5.76	5.19	.57
CHANGING TIMES	3.426	1.886	1.540	49.1	46.9	51.0	40.650	40.014	41.530	1.250	2.74	1.51	1.23
CHICAGO TRIBUNE MAGAZINE	2.336	1.143	1.193	42.7	42.4	43.0	44.888	46.855	43.154	1.130	2.07	1.01	1.06
COLONIAL HOMES	2.294	772	1.522	38.8	36.2	40.6	36.067	38.259	34.372	581*	3.95	1.33	2.62
CONDE NAST LIMITED (GR)	21.230	6.201	15.029	34.1	31.1	35.8	39.487	40.174	39.224	3.835	5.54	1.62	3.92
CONDE NAST WOMEN (GR)	28.258	3.178	25.080	30.0	30.5	29.9	36.392	42.740	36.035	5.936	4.76	.54	4.23
CONSUMERS DIGEST	4.676	2.682	1.994	40.7	40.9	40.4	39.012	38.900	39.132	935	5.00	2.87	2.13
COSMOPOLITAN	12.118	1.916	10.202	30.9	31.9	30.7	34.449	34.659	34.410	2.512	4.82	.76	4.06
COUNTRY HOME	5.762	1.563	4.199	38.3	37.5	38.6	38.741	42.211	37.851	976*	5.90	1.60	4.30
COUNTRY LIVING	10.372	2.700	7.672	39.5	38.0	40.1	37.262	40.876	36.359	1.748	5.93	1.54	4.39
CREATIVE IDEAS FOR LIVING	2.310	339	1.971	38.4	36.1	38.9	31.024	34.432	30.120	725	3.19	.47	2.72
DELTA SKY	1.255	691	564	40.2	38.2	41.6	57.540	56.905	57.861	397*	3.16	1.74	1.42
DIAMANDIS MAGAZINE NTWK (GR)	22.748	18.733	4.015	31.4	30.8	33.3	38.800	38.979	37.951	4.273	5.32	4.38	.94
DISCOVER	5.132	3.207	1.925	35.8	34.3	39.1	37.500	38.527	36.250	948	5.41	3.38	2.03
DISNEY CHANNEL MAGAZINE	5.710	2.389	3.321	36.2	36.5	36.0	40.547	43.816	37.874	4.664*	1.22	.51	.71
EAST/WEST NETWORK (GR)	3.849	2.244	1.605	39.1	38.7	39.6	52.133	58.272	43.262	1.329	2.90	1.69	1.21
EBONY	9.519	4.120	5.399	36.2	35.4	36.7	22.466	28.044	18.754	1.774	5.37	2.32	3.04
ELLE	2.298	299	1.999	29.7	36.1	29.1	45.038	47.961	43.562	751	3.06	.40	2.66
ESQUIRE	3.672	2.230	1.442	34.3	33.9	35.4	36.020	37.716	30.097	724	5.07	3.08	1.99
ESSENCE	3.484	987	2.497	34.3	32.0	35.0	25.205	31.369	22.592	921*	3.78	1.07	2.71
FAMILY CIRCLE	24.570	3.240	21.330	43.5	42.4	43.6	33.527	37.948	32.797	5.195	4.73	.62	4.11
FAMILY CIRCLE/MCCALLS (GR)	41.859	5.100	36.759	43.5	42.1	43.7	32.821	35.579	32.439	10.384	4.03	.49	3.54
FAMILY HANDYMAN	4.022	2.546	1.476	44.6	43.7	46.8	35.380	36.231	33.490	1.494	2.69	1.70	.99
FIELD & STREAM	13.794	10.385	3.409	37.0	37.0	37.0	32.582	33.383	29.889	2.104	6.56	4.94	1.62
FLOWER & GARDEN	3.620	1.007	2.613	43.1	42.9	43.1	28.540	29.911	27.370	606	5.97	1.66	4.31
FLOWER & GRDN/WORKBENCH (GR)	6.366	2.854	3.512	42.9	43.2	42.5	31.312	33.116	29.494	1.498	4.25	1.91	2.34
FOOD & WINE	2.722	1.184	1.538	38.7	38.3	38.9	40.618	43.936	39.581	884	3.08	1.34	1.74
FORBES	3.284	2.229	1.055	42.1	40.3	46.3	52.252	54.021	48.828	777	4.23	2.87	1.36
FORTUNE	3.307	2.254	1.053	38.5	36.6	42.5	51.495	50.956	52.516	704	4.70	3.20	1.50
4 WHEEL & OFF ROAD	2.816	2.423	393	25.7	26.0	24.4	32.862	33.353	28.786	331	8.51	7.32	1.19
FOUR WHEELER	2.046	1.799	247	25.9	25.3	31.8	34.565	35.342	23.565	311	6.58	5.78	.79
GAMES	1.648	816	832	36.1	32.6	39.1	34.495	34.033	35.000	682	2.42	1.20	1.22
GLAMOUR	8.984	768	8.216	30.6	31.4	30.5	35.591	47.444	34.890	2.141	4.20	.36	3.84
GOLF DIGEST	4.449	3.599	850	42.1	41.3	46.6	45.188	44.478	51.768	1.284	3.46	2.80	.66
GOLF DIGEST/TENNIS (GR)	6.076	4.618	1.458	40.1	39.2	42.6	44.297	43.726	47.703	1.826	3.33	2.53	.80
GOLF MAGAZINE	3.804	2.937	867	40.0	39.7	41.7	44.017	42.889	48.889	987	3.85	2.98	.88
GOOD HOUSEKEEPING	24.811	3.699	21.112	43.1	43.6	42.9	32.695	34.647	32.298	4.880	5.08	.76	4.33
GOURMET	2.850	741	2.109	43.0	41.2	43.9	47.023	50.198	45.833	767	3.72	.97	2.75
GQ (GENTLEMEN'S QUARTERLY)	4.369	3.185	1.184	26.1	26.3	25.7	37.190	38.196	33.278	633	6.90	5.03	1.87

Source: Mediamark Research Inc.

TV and local television markets. (Chapter 14 gives more information on the methods employed by these two companies and others.)

COMPETITORS' ACTIVITIES

It is often helpful to advertisers to know the media choices of their competitors. This information can help the advertiser to avoid making the mistakes of less successful competitors and to imitate the strategies of more successful competitors. Moreover, an advertiser seeking to promote a new product who knows that the three leading competitors are using basically the same media mix might feel that their consensus is worthy of consideration.

An advertiser can collect data on competitors' activity either by setting up a special research team or by subscribing to the services of a syndicated research company. Since the job of monitoring the media activity of a large number of firms advertising in several media is so difficult, most advertisers rely on the syndicated service. Such services gather data by direct observation—that is, by tabulating the advertisements that appear in a given medium. In addition to information about frequency of advertisements, cost figures are helpful; these estimates are obtained from the published rate cards of the various media vehicles.

Advertisers also find it helpful to know *what* competitors are saying. To acquire this information, many advertising agencies conduct systematic content analyses of the messages in a sample of the competitors' advertisements. The results often provide insight into the persuasive themes, strategies, and goals of competitors' advertising. It is because of such studies that many commercials look and sound alike: Successful commercial approaches are often mimicked.

The most comprehensive information about advertisers' activities and expenditures is provided by Competitive Media Reporting (CMR), a joint venture between VNU, a Dutch firm, and Arbitron. CMR tracks ad spending in 11 national consumer media.

For the electronic media, CMR's MediaWatch ranks spending on ads in network TV, national spot TV, cable TV, network radio, and spot radio. For network TV, MediaWatch tabulates every broadcast commercial minute on CBS, NBC, ABC, and Fox. Cable TV estimates come from observing 17 cable networks, such as CNN, USA, and MTV. Spot television estimates are obtained from monitoring the major stations in the top 75 markets. To obtain comparative advertising data about radio networks, MediaWatch monitors 13 networks. Spot radio data come from an examination of 3,500 radio stations in more than 200 markets.

Data for the print media are gathered by Leading National Advertisers (LNA), another division of CMR. LNA measures ad space in 129 newspapers in 50 of the country's top markets. National newspaper spending is determined by examining copies of *USA Today* and *The Wall Street Journal.* Comparative ad data for magazines come from the Publisher's Information Bureau (PIB), which measures ads in 210 consumer magazines and four Sunday supplements. The publishers of magazines that belong to the PIB mark all paid advertising in each issue and send the marked copies to LNA, where trained coders record detailed information about each advertisement. This information is recorded in a report sent to LNA subscribers. The data are arranged according to product type and brand name. By scanning the LNA reports, it is possible to determine which magazines competitors are using, the size of the advertisements they purchase, when they appear, and their approximate cost. CMR also provides data on outdoor and Yellow Pages advertising.

CAMPAIGN ASSESSMENT RESEARCH

Leckenby (1984) argues that the purpose of campaign assessment research is "to understand the overall response of the consumer to an integrated and executed advertising campaign which itself was the result of copy [and] media . . . research conducted previously." Campaign assessment research builds on copy and media research, but its research strategies are generally different from those used in the other areas. In general, there are two kinds of assessment research. The **pretest/posttest method** takes measurements before and after the campaign, and **tracking studies** assess the impact of the campaign by measuring effects at several points during the progress of the campaign. The major advantage of a tracking study is that it provides important feedback to the advertiser while the campaign is still in progress. This feedback might ultimately lead to changes in the creative strategy or the media strategy.

No matter what type of assessment research is chosen, one of the problems is deciding upon the dependent variable. The objective of the campaign should be spelled out before the campaign is executed so that assessment research is most useful. For example, if the objective of the campaign is to increase brand awareness, this measure should be the dependent variable rather than recall of ad content or actual sales increases. Schultz and Barnes (1994) list several campaign objectives that might be examined, including liking for the brand, ad recall, brand preference, and purchasing behavior.

Pretest/posttest studies typically use personal interviews for data collection. At times, the same people are interviewed before the campaign starts and again after its close (a panel study), or two groups are chosen and asked the same questions (a trend study; see Chapter 8). In any case, changes before and after the campaign are examined to gauge advertising effects. Winters (1983) reports several pretest/posttest studies done for a major oil company. In one study, a pretest showed that about 80% of the sample agreed that a particular oil company made too much profit. Five months later a posttest revealed that the percentage had dropped slightly among those who had seen an oil company newspaper ad but had remained the same among those who had not seen the ad. Additionally, the study disclosed that people who saw both print ads and TV ads showed less attitude change than those who saw only the TV ads, suggesting that the print ad might have had a dampening effect.

Tracking studies also rely on personal or telephone interviews as their main data collection devices. Technological developments have allowed researchers to track advertising and sales volume in a way not thought possible a few years ago. Of particular value are single-source research techniques. A single-source service, such as A. C. Nielsen, provides an advertiser with information on a household's exposure to advertising for a product and the purchases of that product within that household. For example, in an early study, Leckenby (1984) reported the results of a tracking study done for an instant coffee brand. It was determined that most of the TV commercials for the instant coffee were being seen by people who were regular coffee drinkers and, consequently, not good prospects. In response to this, the advertiser decided to shift the ads to reach more instant coffee drinkers. The single-source data allowed researchers to identify the times of day when a high proportion of instant coffee buyers were watching TV, and with this information it was easy to reschedule the ads in more favorable slots. Block and Brezen (1990) analyzed a tracking study of 223 households over 88 weeks concerning their spaghetti sauce purchases. They discovered that brand loyalty was the most important variable in predicting buying behavior. More recently, Jones (1995) reported the results of an elaborate tracking study of the advertising and purchasing behavior of 2,000 homes and 142 brands over an entire year. The study found evidence of pronounced short-term effects of advertising, but long-term effects were more difficult to isolate.

Tracking studies are tremendously useful but they are not without drawbacks. Perhaps the biggest problem is cost. Tracking studies typically require large samples; in fact, a sample of less than 1,500 cases per year is unusual. If detailed analysis of subgroups is needed, the sample size must be much larger. Furthermore, if the product is a national one, test markets across the country might be necessary to present a complete picture of the results. Finally, the use of sophisticated research methods, such as single-source data, makes the research even more expensive. For those who can afford it, however, the tracking study provides continuous measurement of the effects of a campaign and an opportunity to fine-tune the copy and the media schedule.

PUBLIC RELATIONS RESEARCH

Much like advertising, public relations, or PR, has become more research-oriented in recent years. As a leading text points out (Cutlip, Center, & Broom, 1994, p. 320):

> [A] research orientation is necessary for those practicing public relations in the information age . . . Modern managers are a fact-minded lot . . . When the public relations aspect of organizational problems must be brought home to them, the research-based approach is most effective.

This trend toward research is continuing. A 1990 issue of *Public Relations Review* was devoted to research, and several books concentrating on public relations research have been published in recent years. A study by Lindenmann (1990) found that 75% of public relations practitioners agreed that research was an integral part of the public relations process. Wiesendanger (1994) reported that of the 80 projects completed in 1993 by Ketchum Public Relations, 57% pertained specifically to PR evaluation research, up from 24% in 1988. Today techniques such as survey research, content analysis, and focus groups are widely employed in this field. A survey by Ryan and Martinson (1990) found that focus groups were used the most by PR professionals (61%), followed by mail surveys (60%), telephone surveys (57%), and personal interviews (55%). Used the least were content analysis (29%) and participant observation (23%). A more recent survey done by the industry newsletter *pr reporter* found that focus groups, surveys, and personal interviews were the three most frequently used techniques in 1993 (Wiesendanger, 1994). Public relations researchers, however, use these methods for a highly specific reason: to improve communication with various publics.

TYPES OF PUBLIC RELATIONS RESEARCH

Pavlik (1987) delineated three major types of public relations research: applied, basic, and introspective. **Applied research** examines specific practical issues; in many instances it is done to solve a specific problem. A branch of applied research, strategic research, is used to develop PR campaigns and programs. According to Broom and Dozier (1990), strategic research is "deciding where you want to be in the future . . . and how to get there." A second branch, evaluation research, is done to assess the effectiveness of a PR program and is discussed in more detail below.

Basic research in public relations creates knowledge that cuts across PR situations. It is most interested in examining the underlying processes and in constructing theories that explain the public relations process. For example, Everett (1993) suggested that the "ecological paradigm" deserved more attention as an explanatory model in public relations research. Similarly, Hallahan (1993) argued for consensus from PR practitioners and researchers concerning a dominant paradigm to be used in public relations theory and practice. Finally, Moffitt (1994) examined the utility of collapsing the concepts of "public" and "image" into a new theory.

The third major type of PR research is **introspective research**, which examines the field of public relations. Of all the media professions discussed in this book, public relations tends to be the most self-analytical. From mid-1992 to 1995, *Communication Abstracts* described nine studies in this area. To illustrate, Weaver-Lariscy, Cameron, and Sweep (1994) surveyed public relations in higher education to ascertain the status of women in the field. Lauzen (1995) compared the management attitudes of PR educators and practitioners and found that educators were more likely than professionals to hold an "outer-directed" view of management. Lastly, Kinnick and Cameron (1994) examined the efforts of PR educators to integrate management courses in their curriculum.

CORPORATE USES OF PUBLIC RELATIONS RESEARCH

As pointed out by Brody and Stone (1989), informal or exploratory methods are still widely used in public relations research despite the availability of highly developed social science methods. Lindenmann (1990) reported that about 70% of the respondents to his survey of PR professionals reported that they thought most research on the subject was informal rather than scientific. The major problem associated with these informal techniques lies in the selection of respondents. The representativeness of the samples is often questionable. In any event, these methods can be useful provided the researcher recognizes and appreciates their weaknesses. Some more common informal methods used in public relations research are personal contacts, expert opinion, focus groups, community forums, call-in telephone lines, mail analysis, and examination of media content.

The more formal methods of research provide objective and systematic information from representative samples. These methods include the familiar survey, tracking study, content analysis, secondary analysis of existing data, and panel studies. Table 15.6 contains a listing of the types of research done by PR professionals.

There are six major categories of public relations research: environmental monitoring programs, public relations audits, communication audits, social audits, evaluation research, and gatekeeping research. The first four were identified by Lerbinger (1977).

Environmental Monitoring Programs. Researchers use **environmental monitoring programs** to observe trends in public opinion and social events that may have a significant impact on an organization. Generally, two phases are involved. The "early warning" phase, an at-

tempt to identify emerging issues, often takes the form of a systematic content analysis of publications likely to herald new developments. For example, one corporation has conducted a content analysis of scholarly journals in the fields of economics, politics, and science; another company sponsors a continuing analysis of trade and general newspapers. An alternate method is to perform panel studies of community leaders or other influential and knowledgeable citizens. These individuals are surveyed regularly with regard to the ideas they perceive to be important, and the interviews are analyzed to pick out new topics of interest.

Brody and Stone (1989) list other forms of monitoring techniques. One technique is to have the people doing the monitoring look for a **trigger event**, an event or activity that might focus public concern on a topic or issue. For example, the Exxon oil spill in Alaska brought heavy visibility to environmental concerns, and the O. J. Simpson trial in Los Angeles concentrated public attention on racial relations. There is no scientific way, however, of determining what is or what may become a trigger event. Monitors are left to trust their instincts and judgment.

The technique of **precursor analysis** is similar to trigger events analysis. Precursor analysis assumes that leaders establish trends and that these trends ultimately trickle down to the rest of society. For example, Japanese businesses tend to lead in innovative management techniques, many of which have caught on in the United States. At home, California tends to be a leader in insurance concerns and Florida tends to lead in health issues. Monitors are instructed to pay particular attention to developments in these states.

The second phase of environmental monitoring consists of tracking public opinion on major issues. Typically this involves either a longitudinal panel study, in which the same respondents are interviewed several times during a specified interval, or a cross-sectional opinion poll, in which a random sample is surveyed

TABLE 15.6	Types of Research Done by PR Practitioners
Research conducting	**Percent**
Evaluating attitudes toward organization or issue	67
Identifying target audience	65
Identifying a program	58
Issue tracking	52
Measuring media use	38
Measuring changes in behavior	33
Pretesting messages	33

Abridged from Ryan & Martinson (1990)

only once. To illustrate, since 1959 the Roper organization has surveyed public attitudes about media credibility. AT&T, General Electric, General Motors, and the Dow Chemical Company have also conducted elaborate tracking studies. Most recently, DDB Needham reported the latest installment of its 16-year trend study of American lifestyles (Winski, 1992). Their data failed to support the popular idea that Americans were returning to traditional family values.

Monitoring studies have been made more efficient by the advent of on-line databases. Thomsen (1995) interviewed personnel at 12 PR firms to determine how these new research tools were used. He found that databases were most valuable to practitioners who specialized in issues management. Masterson (1992) lists seven databases that are useful for those doing monitoring studies, and Hauss (1995) describes how the new on-line technologies can be used to track news events.

Public Relations Audits. The public relations audit, as the name suggests, is a comprehensive study of the public relations position of an organization. Such studies are used to measure a company's standing both internally (in the eyes of its employees) and externally (with regard to opinions of customers, stock-

holders, community leaders, and so on). In short, as summarized by Simon (1986, p. 150), the public relations audit is a "research tool used specifically to describe, measure and assess an organization's public relations activities and to provide guidelines for future public relations programming."

The first step in a public relations audit is to list the segments of the public that are most important to the organization. This is generally accomplished through personal interviews with key management personnel in each department and by a content analysis of the company's external communications. The second step is to determine how the organization is viewed by each of these audiences. This involves conducting a corporate image study—that is, a survey of audience samples. The questions are designed to measure familiarity with the organization (Can the respondents recognize the company logo? Identify a product it manufactures? Remember the president's name?) as well as attitudes and perceptions toward it.

Ratings scales are often used. For example, respondents might be asked to rank their perceptions of the ideal electric company on a 7-point scale for a series of adjective pairs, as shown in Figure 15.2. Later, the respondents would rate a specific electric company on the same scale. The average score for each item

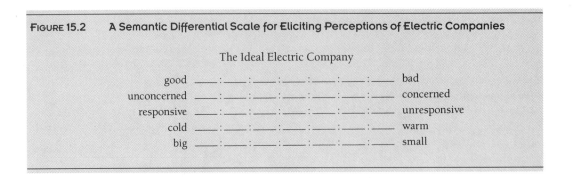

FIGURE 15.2   A Semantic Differential Scale for Eliciting Perceptions of Electric Companies

The Ideal Electric Company

good	___:___:___:___:___:___:___	bad
unconcerned	___:___:___:___:___:___:___	concerned
responsive	___:___:___:___:___:___:___	unresponsive
cold	___:___:___:___:___:___:___	warm
big	___:___:___:___:___:___:___	small

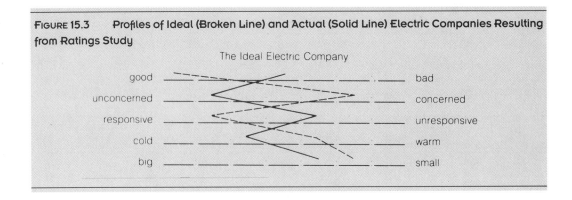

FIGURE 15.3   Profiles of Ideal (Broken Line) and Actual (Solid Line) Electric Companies Resulting from Ratings Study

The Ideal Electric Company

good		bad
unconcerned		concerned
responsive		unresponsive
cold		warm
big		small

would be tabulated, and the means connected by a zigzag line to form a composite profile. Thus, in Figure 15.3, the ideal electric company's profile is represented by a broken line and the actual electric company's standing by a solid line. By comparing the two lines, public relations researchers can readily identify the areas in which a company falls short of the ideal. Corporate image studies can also be conducted before the beginning of a public relations campaign and again at the conclusion of the campaign to evaluate its effectiveness.

To illustrate, because of bad publicity concerning logging, the New Hampshire paper industry was concerned about its image. A PR firm polled 800 residents and asked them questions regarding their perceptions of the industry and their attitudes toward the industry's efforts to fight pollution. Similar questions were then asked of key executives in the industry. The results (Six ways, 1994) showed that the consumers and the executives held widely different views. The executives thought that the general public would rate the industry's environmental programs poorly. Surprisingly, the study revealed that consumers were generally pleased with industry efforts to clean up the environment. As a result, the industry's PR program did not emphasize defensive messages but instead concentrated on more positive themes.

Communication Audits. The communication audit resembles a public relations audit but has narrower goals; it concerns the internal and external means of communication used by an organization, rather than the company's entire public relations program. The three research techniques generally used in conducting such an audit are readership surveys, content analyses, and readability studies. **Readership studies** are designed to measure how many people read certain publications (such as employee newsletters or annual reports) and/or remember the messages they contain. The results are used to improve the content, appearance, and method of distribution of the publications. For example, Pavlik, Vastyan, and Maher (1990) found that employees who felt comfortable within an organization were more apt to read organizational news and news about social relations. Pincus, Rayfield, and Cozzens (1991) audited the communication behaviors of corporate chief executive officers (CEOs) and found that CEOs spent about 20% of their working time communicating with their employees, favored face-to-face communication more than written memos or videotaped messages, and did most of their communication with top management.

Content analyses reveal how the media are handling news and other information about and from the organization; they may be conducted in-house or by private firms that provide computerized studies of press coverage. **Readability studies** help a company gauge the ease with which its employee publications and press releases can be read. An internal audit would also include an analysis of channels of communication within the organization.

Social Audits.

A social audit is a small-scale environmental monitoring program designed to measure an organization's social performance—that is, how well it is living up to its public responsibilities. The audit provides feedback on company-sponsored social action programs such as minority hiring, environmental cleanup, and employee safety. This is the newest form of public relations research and the most challenging. Researchers are currently studying such questions as what activities to audit, how to collect data, and how to measure the effects of the programs. Nevertheless, several large companies, including General Motors and Celanese, have already conducted lengthy social audits.

Evaluation Research.

A fifth major category of public relations research has recently achieved prominence and needs to be added to Lerbinger's list: evaluation research. **Evaluation research** refers to the process of judging the effectiveness of program planning, implementation, and impact. Rossi and Freeman (1982) have outlined some basic questions that occur at each of these stages. Here are three examples:

1. *Planning.* What is the extent of the target program? How do the costs of the program relate to the potential benefits?
2. *Implementation.* Is the program reaching the target population or target area?
3. *Impact.* Is the program effective in achieving its intended goals? Is the program having some effects that were not intended?

Lindenmann (1990) found that 75% of PR practitioners reported that they did research at the planning phase while 58% did implementation research and 56% did evaluation research. The specific research methods used at each of the three stages listed have been mentioned in other chapters. For example, at the planning stage, content analysis (Chapter 6) is used to determine how closely program efforts coincide with the actual plan. Readability tests (Chapter 13) are frequently used to determine whether the messages can be read and understood by the target group. During the implementation stage, content analysis is used again to count the number of messages that are placed in the media. Next, the number of people actually exposed to the message is determined by the methods of audience research mentioned earlier in this chapter. Circulation figures and audience estimates from the Audit

Research on Subliminal Advertising

You may be familiar with The Subliminal Man, the character on "Saturday Night Live" who utters saucy "subliminal" comments in between normal conversational statements, on the pretense that people will not notice that he is trying to program them with his "hidden" remarks. The word *subliminal* comes from a term used in perception research, *limen,* which means a perceptual threshold. Any message intended to be apprehended beneath the threshold of conscious perception is a subliminal message. Not surprisingly, **subliminal advertising** has received a lot of research attention. The reason for all the attention is this: If subliminal advertising works, advertisers might be using it to manipulate us into buying all sorts of things that we do not want.

One of the first studies (and certainly the most frequently cited) of subliminal advertising was done by Hawkins (1970). Using a tachistoscope, Hawkins exposed four groups to various stimuli in an experiment that purported to establish thresholds for the recognition of auto brand names. In one group, however, mixed in with the auto names was the message "Coke" that was flashed for 2.7 milliseconds, far below most people's limen of 20–25 milliseconds. Another group had the message "Drink Coke" flashed before them at the same speed. A third group had the nonsense message "NYTP" flashed before them. The fourth group, however, was allowed to recognize the message "Coke" on the screen and say it out loud. Hawkins then asked subjects to rate how thirsty they were. The groups that had the subliminal messages ("Coke," and "Drink Coke") flashed on the screen before them and the group that had said "Coke" out loud rated themselves as more thirsty than did the group that had the nonsense word flashed on the screen.

Hawkins's study was used for more than 15 years as evidence of the effectiveness of subliminal messages. A more recent study casts doubt upon the original findings. Beatty and Hawkins (1989) replicated Hawkins's experiment using the same procedures but with only three groups: one group that was exposed to the subliminal message "Coke," another to the message "NYTP," and another that was allowed to recognize "Coke" and say it aloud. The researchers found no differences in average thirst ratings among the groups, thus failing to replicate Hawkins's results. These findings suggest that any benefit from subliminal advertising is debatable. The experiment also points out the value of replicating the key studies in a given field.

Bureau of Circulations, Simmons Market Research Bureau, Nielsen, and Arbitron are helpful in measuring exposure.

At the impact level, public relations researchers are interested in the same three levels of effect that were mentioned in the discussion of copy research: cognitive, affective, and conative. At the cognitive level, researchers attempt to find out how much people learned

from the public relations campaign. At the affective level, measures of changes in attitudes, opinions, or perceptions are used quite frequently. Finally, behavioral change, at the conative level, is an important way to gauge public relations impact. Obviously, the techniques used in advertising campaign effectiveness studies—pretest/posttest and tracking studies—can be applied in measur-

dimension of public relations

~~lic relations professionals are relying more ~~~ the techniques of social science in their evaluation efforts. Bissland (1990) analyzed the evaluation techniques used by "Silver Anvil" award winners (the Silver Anvil is PR's equivalent of the Oscar). He found that only 25% of the winners used social science methods in 1980–1981 compared to more than 40% in 1988–1989.

Lindenmann (1988) discusses several examples of evaluation research used by corporations. The Aetna Life and Casualty Company has used before-and-after polling during the last few years as part of a campaign to introduce a long-term health care plan for elderly Americans. The company's precampaign polling revealed that a large majority of Americans incorrectly believed that Medicare coverage routinely extended to nursing home stays. After a communication campaign, the company's polls found that more people were aware of Medicare's limitations than had been before. The California Prune Board used the day-after recall method to gauge the effectiveness of its media campaign designed to promote prunes as a high-fiber food source. A survey of women in Detroit revealed that awareness of prunes as a fiber source increased from 50% to 65%. Rosser, Flora, Chaffee, and Farquar (1990) found that exposure to a PR campaign on reducing the risk of heart disease made a significant contribution to knowledge. Finally, the Miller Brewing Company conducted an extensive evaluation study of its involvement with the Harley Davidson Corporation's Reunion Ride (Six ways, 1994) and found that press coverage of the event was 98% positive.

Gatekeeping. A final area of PR research that has recently gained popularity can be termed **gatekeeping research.** This technique analyzes the characteristics of press releases and video news releases that allow them to "pass through the gate" and appear in a mass medium. Both content and style variables are typically examined. For example, Morton and Ramsey (1994) studied 129 national news releases carried over a PR wire service and found that 22 of the releases were carried by newspapers and that releases dealing with financial matters were more likely to be used than those dealing with other topics. News releases whose facts are localized—that is, rewritten to be of interest to the paper where it is being sent—were more apt to be published than general releases (Morton & Warren, 1992). The same authors also examined which type of artwork was preferred by newspaper gatekeepers. They found that hometown photos were favored, particularly by smaller-circulation newspapers. Finally, Walters, Walters, and Starr (1994) examined the differences between the grammar and syntax of original news releases and published versions. They found that editors typically shorten the releases and make them easier to read before publication. In sum, it appears that the news release most likely to pass through the gate would be one that is short, simply written, deals with localized financial matters, and is accompanied by a hometown photo.

SUMMARY

There are three main areas of advertising research: copy testing, media research, and campaign assessment research. Copy testing consists of studies that examine the advertisement or the commercial itself. The three main dimensions of impact examined by copy testing are cognitive (knowing), affective (feeling), and conative (doing). Media research helps determine which advertising vehicles are the most efficient and what type of media schedule will have the greatest impact. Campaign assessment studies examine the overall response of consumers to a complete campaign. The two main types of campaign assessment research are the pretest/posttest and the tracking study.

Many private firms spe   ing the impact
media, and assessment   campaign
Research in public   p
itoring relevant develop   o   ady-
ing the public relations   an organization, examining the m   produced by an
organization, measurir   ow well an organization is living up to its social responsibilities,
evaluating public relations campaigns, and determining what factors make it more likely for
PR material to be published.

QUESTIONS AND PROBLEMS FOR FURTHER INVESTIGATION

1. Assume that you have developed a new diet soft
   drink and are ready to market it. Develop a research study for identifying the elements and topics that should be stressed in your advertising.

2. A full-page advertisement costs $16,000 in Mag-
   azine A and $26,000 in Magazine B. Magazine A
   has a circulation of 100,000 and 2.5 readers
   per copy, and Magazine B has a circulation of
   150,000 and 1.8 readers per copy. In terms of
   CPM readers, which magazine is the most efficient advertising vehicle?

3. Select a sample of newspaper and magazine advertisements for two airlines. Conduct a content
   analysis of the themes or major selling points in
   each advertisement. What similarities and differences are there?

4. Assume you are the public relations director for a
   major automobile manufacturer. How would you
   go about conducting an environmental monitoring study?

5. How would you assess the public relations impact of an information campaign designed to
   persuade people to conserve water?

REFERENCES AND SUGGESTED READINGS

Aaker, D. (1975). ADMOD, an advertising decision
model. *Journal of Marketing Research, 12,* 37–45.

Aaker, D., & Myers, J. (1975). *Advertising management.* Englewood Cliffs, NJ: Prentice-Hall.

simulation: Some new da
Journal of Advertising, 18(3), 4–8

Bissland, J. H. (1990). Accountability gap.
tion practices show improvement. *Public Relations Review, 16*(2), 24–34.

Block, M. P., & Brezen, T. S. (1990). Using database
analysis to segment general media audiences.
Journal of Media Planning, 5(4), 1–12.

Boyd, H. W., Westfall, R., & Stasch, S. F. (1989). *Marketing research: Text and cases* (7th ed.). Home-
wood, IL: Irwin.

Brody, E. W., & Stone, G. C. (1989). *Public relations
research.* New York: Praeger.

Broom, G. M., & Dozier, D. M. (1990). *Using research in public relations.* Englewood Cliffs, NJ:
Prentice-Hall. .

Cutlip, S., Center, A., & Broom, G. (1994). *Effective
public relations* (7th ed.). Englewood Cliffs, NJ:
Prentice-Hall.

Dozier, D. M. (1984). Program evaluation and the
roles of practitioners. *Public Relations Review,
10*(2), 13–21.

Dunn, S. W., Barban, A. M., Krugman, D. K., & Reid,
L. N. (1990). *Advertising: Its role in modern marketing.* Chicago: Dryden.

Everett, J. (1993). The ecological paradigm in PR
theory and practice. *Public Relations Review,
19*(2), 177–185.

Fenwick, I., & Rice, M. D. (1991, February/March).
Reliability of continuous measurement copy
testing methods. *Journal of Advertising Research,
31*(1), 23–29.

Fletcher, A., & Bowers, T. (1991). *Fundamentals
of advertising research* (4th ed.). Belmont, CA:
Wadsworth.

Green, P. E., Tull, D. S., & Albaum, G. (1988). *Research for marketing decisions.* Englewood Cliffs,
NJ: Prentice-Hall.

Haley, R. (1994). A rejoinder to conclusions from
the ARF's copy research validity project. *Journal
of Advertising Research, 34*(3), 33–34.

Haley, R. I., & Baldinger, A. L. (1991, April/March).
The ARF copy research validity project. *Journal
of Advertising Research, 31*(2), 11–32.

Hallahan, K. (1993). The paradigm struggle and
public relations practitioners. *Public Relations
Review, 19*(2), 197–205.

Haskins, J. (1976). *An introduction to advertising research.* Knoxville, TN: Communication Research Center.

Haskins, J., & Kendrick, A. (1993). *Successful advertising research methods.* Lincolnwood, IL: NTC Business Books.

Hauss, D. (1995, May). Technology gives early warning on news breaks. *Public Relations Journal,* pp. 18–22.

Hawkins, D. (1970). The effects of subliminal stimulation on drive level and brand preference. *Journal of Marketing Research, 7*(3), 322–326.

Jacoby, J., & Hofer, W. D. (1982). Viewers' miscomprehension of televised communication. *Journal of Marketing, 46*(4), 12–27.

Jones, J. (1995). Single-source research begins to fulfill its promise. *Journal of Advertising Research, 35*(3), 9–11.

Katz, H. (1988). The role and function of media research at major U.S. advertising agencies. *Journal of Media Planning, 3*(2), 47–53.

Kinnick, K., & Cameron, G. (1994). Teaching PR management. *Public Relations Review, 20*(1), 69–84.

Krugman, D., Fox, R., Fletcher, J., Fischer, P., & Rojas, T. (1994). Do adolescents attend to warnings in cigarette advertising? *Journal of Advertising Research, 34*(6), 39–52.

Lauzen, M. (1995). A comparison of issues managers' and PR educators' worldviews. *Journalism Educator, 49*(4), 36–46.

Leckenby, J. (1984). *Current issues in the measurement of advertising effectiveness.* Paper presented to the International Advertising Association, Tokyo, Japan.

Leckenby, J., & Kim, H. (1994). How media directors view reach/frequency estimation: now and a decade ago. *Journal of Advertising Research, 34*(5), 9–21.

Leckenby, J., & Wedding, N. (1982). *Advertising management.* Columbus, OH: Grid Publishing.

Lerbinger, O. (1977). Corporate use of research in public relations. *Public Relations Review, 3*(4), 11–20.

Lindenmann, W. K. (1988). Beyond the clipbook. *Public Relations Journal, 44*(12), 22–26.

Lindenmann, W. K. (1990). Research, evaluation and measurement: A national perspective. *Public Relations Review, 16*(2), 8–16.

Little, J., & Lodish, L. (1969). A media planning calculus. *Operations Research, 17*(1), 1–35.

Lloyd, D. W., & Clancy, K. J. (1991, August/September). CPMs vs. CPMIs: Implications for media planning. *Journal of Advertising Research, 34*(4), 34–43.

Masterson, J. (1992, November). Discovering databases. *Public Relations Journal,* pp. 12–19.

McGee, M. (1988). Talking research. *Public Relations Journal, 44*(11), 10.

Moffitt, M. (1994). Collapsing and integrating concepts of public and image into a new theory. *Public Relations Review, 20*(2), 155–170.

Moran, W. (1963). Practical media decisions and the computer. *Journal of Marketing, 27*(3), 26–30.

Morton, L., & Ramsey, S. (1994). A benchmark study of the PR news wire. *Public Relations Review, 20*(2), 171–182.

Morton, L., & Warren, J. (1992). Proximity: Localization vs. distance in PR news releases. *Journalism Quarterly, 69*(4), 1023–1028.

Morton, L. & Warren, J. (1992/1993). Newspapers' art preferences from public relations sources. *Newspaper Research Journal, 13/14*(4/1), 121–129.

Pavlik, J. V. (1987). *Public relations: What the research tells us.* Beverly Hills, CA: Sage Publications.

Pavlik, J. V., Vastyan, J., & Maher, M. (1990). Using readership research to study employee views. *Public Relations Review, 16*(3), 250–261.

Pincus, J. D., Rayfield, R. E., & Cozzens, M. D. (1991). The chief executive officer: Internal communications role. In L. A. Grunig and J. E. Grunig, *Public Relations Research Annual* (Vol. 3). Hillsdale, NJ: Lawrence Erlbaum.

Rosser, C., Flora, J. A., Chaffee, S., & Farquar, J. W. (1990). Using research to predict learning from a PR campaign. *Public Relations Review, 16*(2), 61–77.

Rossi, P., & Freeman, H. (1982). *Evaluation: A systematic approach.* Beverly Hills, CA: Sage Publications.

Rossiter, J., & Eagleson, G. (1994). Conclusions from the ARF's copy research validity project. *Journal of Advertising Research, 34*(3), 19–32.

Rust, R. T. (1986). *Advertising Media Models.* Lexington, MA: D. C. Heath & Company.

Ryan, M., & Martinson, D. C. (1990). Social science research, professionalism and PR practitioners. *Journalism Quarterly, 67*(2), 377–390.

Schultz, D., & Barnes, B. (1994). *Strategic Advertising Campaigns*. Lincolnwood, IL: Business Books.

Six ways to use research. (1994, May). *Public Relations Journal*, pp. 26–27.

Simon, R. (1986). *Public relations: Concepts and practices*. Columbus, OH: Grid Publishing.

Thomsen, S. (1995). Using online databases in corporate issues management. *Public Relations Review, 21*(2), 103–122.

Tull, D. S., & Hawkins, D. I. (1987). *Marketing research* (4th ed.). New York: Macmillan.

Walker, D., & Dubitsky, T. (1994). Why liking matters. *Journal of Advertising Research, 34*(3), 9–18.

Walters, T., Walters, L., & Starr, D. (1994). After the highwayman: syntax and successful placement of press releases in newspapers. *Public Relations Review, 20*(4), 345–356.

Weaver-Lariscy, R., Cameron, G., & Sweep, D. (1994). Women in higher-education PR. *Journal of Public Relations Research, 6*(2), 105–124.

Wiesendanger, B. (1994, May). A research roundup. *Public Relations Journal*, pp. 22–24.

Winski, J. M. (1992, January 20). Who we are, how we live, what we think. *Advertising Age*, pp. 16–20.

Winters, L. (1983). Comparing pretesting and posttesting of corporate advertising. *Journal of Advertising Research, 23*(1), 33–38.

16

RESEARCH IN MEDIA EFFECTS

The preceding three chapters focused on research conducted in a professional or industry setting. However, a great deal of mass media research is conducted at colleges and universities. As mentioned in Chapter 1, there are several differences between research in the academic and the private sectors. To summarize briefly:

1. Academic research tends to be more theoretical in nature; private sector research is generally more applied.
2. The data used in academic research are public, whereas much industry research is based on proprietary data.
3. Private sector research topics are often determined by top management; academic researchers have more freedom in their choice of topics.
4. Projects in private sector research usually cost more to conduct than do academic investigations.

The two research settings also have some things in common:

1. Many research techniques and approaches used in the private sector emerged from academic research.
2. Industry and academic researchers use the same basic research methodologies and approaches.
3. The goal of research is often the same in both settings—to explain and predict audience and consumer behavior.

This chapter describes some of the more popular types of research carried out by aca-demic investigators and shows how this work relates to private sector research.

Obviously, not every type of scholarly research used in colleges and universities can be covered in one chapter. What follows is not an exhaustive survey, but rather an illustrative overview of the history, methods, and theoretical development of five research areas: the antisocial and prosocial effects of specific media content, uses and gratifications, agenda setting by the media, cultivation of perceptions of social reality, and advertising and the socialization of children.

ANTISOCIAL AND PROSOCIAL EFFECTS OF MEDIA CONTENT

The study of the *antisocial* effects of viewing television and motion pictures is one of the most heavily researched areas in mass media. Comstock, Chaffee, and Katzman (1978) reported that four times as many empirical studies focused on this topic as on all other problem areas, and this emphasis is still apparent almost 20 years later (Paik and Comstock, 1994).

The impact of *prosocial* content is a newer area and grew out of the recognition that the same principles underlying the learning of antisocial activities ought to apply to more positive behavior. Applied and academic researchers share an interest in this area: All the major networks have sponsored such research, and the effects of antisocial and prosocial content have been popular topics on college and university campuses for the past 30 years. Not surprisingly, there has been a certain amount of friction between academic researchers and industry executives.

HISTORY

Concern over the social impact of the mass media was evident as far back as the 1920s, when many critics charged that motion pictures had a negative influence on children. In 1928, the Motion Picture Research Council, with support from the Payne Fund, a private philanthropic organization, sponsored a series of 13 studies on aspects of the movies' influence on children. After examination of film content, information gain, attitude change, and influence on behavior, it was concluded that the movies were potent sources of information, attitudes, and behavior for children. Furthermore, many of the things that children learned had antisocial overtones. In the early 1950s, another medium, the comic book, was chastised for its alleged harmful effects (Wertham, 1954).

In 1960, Joseph Klapper summarized what was then known about the social impact of mass communication. In contrast to many researchers, Klapper downplayed the potential harmful effects of the media. He concluded that the media most often reinforced an individual's existing attitudes and predispositions. Klapper's viewpoint, which became known as the minimal effects position, was influential in the development of a theory of media effects.

In the late 1950s and early 1960s, concern over the antisocial impact of the media shifted to television. Experiments on college campuses by Bandura and Berkowitz (summarized in Comstock & Paik, 1991) showed that aggressive behavior could be learned by viewing violent media content and that a stimulation effect was more probable than a cathartic (or cleansing) effect. Senate subcommittees examined possible links between viewing of violence on television and juvenile delinquency, and in 1965, one subcommittee concluded that televised crime and violence were related to an-

tisocial behaviors among juvenile viewers. The civil unrest and assassinations in the middle 1960s prompted the formation of the National Commission on the Causes and Prevention of Violence, chaired by Milton Eisenhower. The staff report of the Eisenhower Commission, which concluded that television violence taught the viewer how to engage in violence, included a series of recommendations about reducing the impact of television violence.

The early 1970s saw extensive research into the social effects of the mass media. Just 3 years after the publication of the Eisenhower Commission report came the release of a multivolume report sponsored by the Surgeon General's Scientific Advisory Committee on Television and Social Behavior (1972, p. 10). In *Television and Growing Up,* the committee cautiously summarized its research evidence by stating the following:

> There is a convergence of fairly substantial evidence on short-run causation of aggression among children by viewing violence . . . and the much less certain evidence from field studies that . . . violence viewing precedes some long-run manifestation of aggressive behavior. This convergence . . . constitutes some preliminary evidence of a causal relationship.

The committee tempered this conclusion by noting that in accord with the reinforcement notion, "any sequence by which viewing television violence causes aggressive behavior is most likely applicable only to some children who are predisposed in that direction" (p. 10).

At about the same time, the three television networks were also sponsoring research in this area. CBS commissioned two studies: a field experiment that found no link between television viewing and subsequent imitation of antisocial behavior (Milgram & Shotland, 1973) and a longitudinal study in Great Britain that found an association between viewing of violence on television and committing antisocial acts such as property damage and hurting others (Belson, 1978). ABC sponsored a series of studies by two mental health consultants who concluded that television contributed only a tiny amount to the stimulation of aggression in children (Heller & Polsky, 1976). NBC began a large-scale panel study, but results were not released until 1983. In addition to television violence, the potential antisocial impact of pornography was under scrutiny. The Commission on Obscenity and Pornography, however, reported that this material was not a factor in determining antisocial behavior (Commission on Obscenity and Pornography, 1970). The commission's conclusions were somewhat controversial in political circles, but in general they supported the findings of other researchers in human sexuality (Tan, 1981). Subsequent efforts in this area were primarily directed toward examining links between pornography and aggression.

In contrast to violence and pornography, the prosocial effect of television was investigated as well. One stimulus for this research was the success of the television series "Sesame Street." A substantial research effort went into the preparation and evaluation of these children's programs. It was found that the series was helpful in preparing young children for school but not very successful in narrowing the information gap between advantaged children and disadvantaged children (Minton, 1975). Other studies by both academic researchers and industry researchers showed the prosocial impact of other programs. For example, the series "Fat Albert and the Cosby Kids" was found helpful in teaching prosocial lessons to children (CBS Broadcast Group, 1974).

Studies of these topics continued between 1975 and 1985, though there were far fewer than in the early 1970s. An update to the 1972 Surgeon General's Report, issued in 1982, reflected a broader research focus than the original document; it incorporated investigations of socialization, mental health, and perceptions of social reality. Nonetheless, its conclusions were even stronger than those of its predecessor:

"The consensus among most of the research community is that violence on television does lead to aggressive behavior" (National Institute of Mental Health, 1982, p. 8). Other researchers, notably Wurtzel and Lometti (1984) and Bear (1984), argue that the report does not support the conclusion of a causal relationship, while Chaffee (1984) and Murray (1984), among others, contend that the conclusions are valid. Not long after the Surgeon General's report was updated, the results of the NBC panel study begun in the early 1970s were published (Milavsky, Kessler, Stipp, & Rubens, 1983). This panel study, which used state-of-the-art statistical analyses, found a nonsignificant relationship between television violence viewing during the early phases of the study and subsequent aggression. The NBC data have been reexamined by others, and at least one article suggests that the data from this survey do show a slight relationship between violence viewing and aggression among at least one demographic subgroup—middle-class girls (Cook, Kendzierski, & Thomas, 1983). From 1985 to 1992 the controversy subsided, but this topic remained popular among academic researchers. Williams (1986) conducted an elaborate field experiment in three Canadian communities. One town was about to receive television for the first time, another received Canadian TV, and the third received both Canadian and U.S. programs. Two years later, Williams and her colleagues found that when compared to the other two communities, children in the town that had just received TV scored higher on measures of physical and verbal aggression.

Additional evidence on the topic of television and violence comes from a series of panel studies conducted by an international team of researchers (Huesmann & Eron, 1986). Data were gathered from young people in the United States, Finland, Australia, Israel, and Poland. Findings from the U.S. and Polish studies reached a similar conclusion: Early TV viewing was related to later aggression. The Finnish study found this relationship for boys but not for girls. The Israeli study found that TV viewing seemed related to aggression for children living in urban areas but not for those in rural areas. The Australian study failed to find a relationship. In all countries where a relationship between TV viewing and violence was found, the relationship was relatively weak. The practical implications of this weak relationship were examined by Rosenthal (1986), who concluded that even a weak relationship could have substantial social consequences.

In 1995, the issue of television violence was once again before Congress. A Congressional subcommittee held extensive hearings on the topic and a requirement for a V-chip, a computer chip that would allow parents to block out violent programming from their TV sets, was included in a proposed telecommunications act.

The increasing popularity of video games during the early years of the decade opened up another avenue of inquiry for researchers. Since more than 90% of young people report that they sometimes play these games, and since some of the more popular games feature graphic and explicit violence, social concern over their impact was widespread. Results of some of the early studies in this area (for example, Silvern & Williamson, 1987) suggest that playing video games can lead to increased aggression levels in young children.

Research interest in the antisocial effects of pornography increased in the late 1980s—averaging approximately eight studies per year as listed in *Communication Abstracts*—but declined by the mid-1990s, averaging only four studies. The most controversial research in this area examined whether prolonged exposure to nonviolent pornography had any antisocial effects (Donnerstein, Linz, & Penrod, 1987; Zillmann & Bryant, 1989; Allen, D'Alessio & Brezgel, 1995).

Research interest in the prosocial effects of media exposure decreased in the 1980s and early 1990s. Sprafkin and Rubinstein (1979) reported a correlational study in which the viewing of prosocial television programs accounted for only 1% of the variance in an index of prosocial behavior exhibited in school. The apparent lack of a strong relationship between these two variables, coupled with the absence of general agreement on a definition of *prosocial content*, might have discouraged researchers from selecting this area. In any case, an average of only one study per year appears in the 1986–1995 editions of *Communication Abstracts*, and many of these are content analyses (for example, Potter & Ware, 1989).

METHODS

Researchers studying the effects of mass media have used most of the techniques discussed in this book: content analysis, laboratory experiments, surveys, field experiments, observations, and panels. In addition, they have used some advanced techniques, such as meta-analysis, which have not been discussed. Given the variety of methods used, it is not possible to describe a typical approach. Instead, this section focuses on five of the methods as illustrations of some research strategies.

The Experimental Method. A common design to study the antisocial impact of the media consists of showing one group of subjects violent media content while a control group sees nonviolent content. This was the approach used by Berkowitz and Bandura in their early work. The dependent variable, aggression, is measured immediately after exposure—either by a pencil-and-paper test or by a mechanical device like the one described below. For example, Liebert and Baron (1972) divided children into two groups. The first group saw a 3.5-minute segment from a television show depicting a chase, two fistfights, two shootings, and a knifing. Children in the control group saw a segment of similar length in which athletes competed in track and field events. After viewing, the children were taken one at a time into another room that contained an apparatus with two buttons, one labeled "Help" and the other labeled "Hurt." An experimenter explained to the children that wires from the device were connected to a game in an adjacent room. The subjects were told that in the adjacent room, another child was starting to play a game. (There was, in fact, no other child.) At various times, by pressing the appropriate buttons, each child would be given a chance either to help the unseen child win the game or to hurt the child. The results showed that children who had seen the violent segment were significantly more likely than the control group to press the "Hurt" button.

Of course, there are many variations on this basic design. To list just a few, the type of violent content shown to the subjects can be manipulated (for example, cartoon versus live violence, entertainment versus newscast violence, justified versus unjustified violence). Also, some subjects may be frustrated before exposure. The degree of association between the media violence and the subsequent testing situation may be high or low. Subjects can watch alone or with others who praise or condemn the media violence. Media exposure can be a one-time event, or it can be manipulated over time. For a thorough summary of this research, see Comstock and Paik (1991) and Liebert and Sprafkin (1988).

Experimental studies examining the impact of media exposure on prosocial behavior have used essentially the same approach. Subjects see a televised segment that is either prosocial or neutral, and the dependent variable is then assessed. For example, Forge and Phemister (1987) randomly assigned preschoolers to one of four conditions: prosocial animated program ("The Get-along Gang"), neutral animated ("Alvin and the Chipmunks"), prosocial nonanimated ("Mr. Rogers' Neighborhood"), and neutral nonanimated ("Animal Express"). The children watched the program and were then placed in a free-play situation where their prosocial behaviors were observed and recorded. The results demonstrated an effect for the program variable (prosocial programs prompted more prosocial behaviors than did neutral programs) but no effect for the animated versus nonanimated variable.

The operational definitions of prosocial behavior have shown wide variation. Studies have examined cooperative behaviors, sharing, kindness, altruism, friendliness, creativity, and absence of stereotyping. Almost any behavior with a positive social value seems to be a candidate for study, as exemplified by the experiment by Baran, Chase, and Courtright (1979). Third graders were assigned to one of three treatment conditions. One group saw a condensed version of a segment of "The Waltons" demonstrating cooperative behavior. The second group saw a program portraying noncooperative behavior, and the third group saw no program. After answering a few written questions dealing with the program, each subject left the viewing room only to encounter a confederate of the experimenter who passed the doorway and dropped an armload of books. There were two dependent measures: whether the subject attempted to retrieve the books, and how much time elapsed until the subject began to help. The group that saw the cooperative content was found to be more likely to help, and their responses were quicker than those of the control group. Interestingly, there was no difference in helping behavior or in duration between the group seeing "The Waltons" and the group seeing the noncooperative content.

The Survey Approach. Most such studies have used questionnaires incorporating measures of media exposure (such as viewing television violence or exposure to pornography) and a pencil-and-paper measure of antisocial behavior or attitudes. In addition, many recent studies have included measures of demographic and sociographic variables that mediate the exposure-antisocial behavior relationship. Results are usually expressed as a series of correlations.

A survey by McLeod, Atkin, and Chaffee (1972) illustrates this approach. Their questionnaire contained measures of violence viewing, aggression, and family environment. Viewing was tabulated by giving respondents a list of 65 prime-time television programs with a scale measuring how often each was viewed. An index of overall violence viewing was obtained by using independent ratings of the violence level of each show and multiplying it by the frequency of viewing. Aggression was measured by seven scales. One measured respondents' approval of manifest physical aggression (sample item: "Whoever insults me or my family is looking for a fight"). Another examined approval of aggression ("It's all right to hurt an enemy if you are mad at him"). Respondents indicated their degree of agreement with each of the items comprising the separate scales. Family environment was measured by asking about parental control over television, parental emphasis on nonaggression punishment (such as withdrawal of privileges), and other variables. The researchers found a moderate positive relationship between the respondents' level of violence viewing and their self-reports of aggression. Family environment showed no consistent association with either of the two variables.

Sprafkin and Rubinstein (1979) used the survey method to examine the relationship between television viewing and prosocial behavior. They used basically the same approach as McLeod, Atkin, and Chaffee (1972), except that their viewing measure was designed to assess exposure to television programs established as prosocial by prior content analysis. Their measure of prosocial behaviors was based on peer nominations of persons who reflected 12 prosocial behaviors, including helping, sharing, rule-following, staying out of fights, and niceness. The researchers found that when the influence of the child's gender, the parents' educational level, and the child's academic level were statistically controlled, exposure to prosocial television explained only 1% of the variance in prosocial behaviors.

Prosocial effects are not limited to children. Brown (1990) studied the impact of an Indian TV show that was specifically produced to promote the status of women in Indian society.

Those who were frequent watchers of the program were aware of the show's prosocial messages and were more likely to believe in women's equality than were infrequent viewers.

Field Experiments. The imaginative and elaborate fieldwork used to study the antisocial effects of the media by Milgram and Shotland (1973) was discussed in Chapter 9. Parke, Berkowitz, and Leyens (1977) conducted a field experiment in a minimum-security penal institution for juveniles. The researchers exposed groups to unedited feature-length films that were either aggressive or nonaggressive. On the day after the last film was shown, in the context of a bogus learning experiment, the boys were told they had a chance to hurt a confederate of the experimenters who had insulted one group of boys and had been neutral to the other. The results on an electric shock measure similar to the one described previously revealed that the most aggressive of all the experimental groups were the boys who had seen the aggressive films and who had been insulted. In addition to this laboratory measure, the investigators collected observational data on the boys' aggressive interpersonal behavior in their everyday environment. These data showed that boys who saw the violent movies were more interpersonally aggressive. However, there was no apparent cumulative effect of movies on aggression. The boys who watched the diet of aggressive films were just as aggressive after the first film as after the last.

Figure 9.11 (page 201) illustrates the design of the Canadian field experiment (Williams, 1986) discussed earlier. The dependent variable of aggression was measured in three ways: observations of behavior on school playgrounds, peer ratings, and teacher ratings. On the observational measure, the aggressive acts of children in the town labeled A (the town that just received TV) increased from an average of .43 per minute in Phase 1 to 1.1 per minute in Phase 2. Children in the other towns showed only a slight and statistically insignificant rise in the same period. Peer and teacher ratings tended to support the behavioral data. As yet, there have been no large-scale field experiments examining prosocial behavior.

Panel Studies. Primarily because of the time and expense involved in panel studies, this analysis mode is seldom used to examine the media in relation to antisocial effects. Three studies relevant to this topic are briefly reviewed here. Lefkowitz, Eron, Waldner, and Huesmann (1972), using a catch-up panel design, reinterviewed 427 of 875 youthful subjects 10 years after they had participated in a study of mental health. Measures of television viewing and aggression had been administered to these subjects when they were in the third grade, and data on the two variables were gathered again a decade later. Slightly different methods were used to measure television viewing on the two occasions. Viewing in the third grade was established on the basis of mothers' reports of their children's three favorite television shows. Ten years later, respondents rated their own frequency of viewing. The data were subjected to cross-lagged correlations and path analysis. The results supported the hypothesis that aggression in later life was caused in part by television viewing during early years. However, the panel study by Milavsky et al. (1983), sponsored by NBC, found no evidence of a relationship.

The difference between the results of these studies might be due to several factors. The Milavsky study did not vary its measure of "violent television viewing" throughout its duration. In addition, the NBC researchers used LISREL (linear structural equations), a more powerful statistical technique that was not available at the time of the Lefkowitz study. Finally, the Lefkowitz measures were taken 10 years apart; the maximum time lag in the NBC study was 3 years.

Another panel study of the media and possible antisocial effects was conducted by Huesmann and Eron (1986). The investigators

followed 758 children who were in the first and third grades in 1977 and reinterviewed them in 1978 and 1979. Aggression was measured by both peer nominations and self-ratings. Multiple regression analyses disclosed that, for both boys and girls, watching TV violence was a significant predictor of aggression they would later demonstrate. Other variables that were also significant included the degree to which children identified with violent TV characters, the perceived reality of the violence, and the amount of a child's aggressive fantasizing. More recently, Valkenburg and Van Der Voort (1995) conducted a 1-year panel study that examined the influence of viewing TV violence on children's daydreaming. They found that exposure to violent programs stimulated an aggressive-heroic daydreaming style.

Meta-analysis. A complete description of the techniques of meta-analysis is beyond the scope of this book. For our purposes, meta-analysis is defined as the quantitative aggregation of many research findings and their interpretations. It allows researchers to draw general conclusions from an analysis of many studies of a definable research topic. Its goal is to synthesize an existing body of research. Given the large number of research studies that have been conducted on antisocial and prosocial behavior, it is not surprising that the mid-1990s saw the growth in popularity of meta-analytic research. Four examples of meta-analysis are summarized below.

Paik and Comstock (1994) performed a meta-analysis of 217 studies from 1959 to 1990 that tested 1,142 hypotheses. They concluded that the magnitude of the impact of exposure to media violence varied with the method used to study it. Experiments produced the strongest effects and time-series studies the weakest. Nonetheless, there was overall a highly significant positive association between exposures to portrayals of violence and antisocial behavior. In addition, they found that males were affected by exposure to media violence only slightly more than females and that violent cartoons and fantasy programs produced the greatest magnitude of effects. This latter finding is at odds with the conventional argument that cartoon violence does not affect viewers because it is so unrealistic.

A second meta-analysis—of the impact of exposure to pornography and subsequent aggressive behavior—was done by Allen, D'Alessio and Brezgel (1995). The researchers analyzed the results of 30 studies and found that there was indeed a connection between exposure to pornography and subsequent antisocial behavior. More specifically, they noted that exposure to nudity actually decreased aggressive behavior. In contrast, consumption of material depicting nonviolent sexual activity increased aggressive behavior while exposure to violent sexual activity generated the highest levels of aggression. These latter findings are in accord with those discussed by Paik and Comstock (1994). In a similar study (Allen, Emmers, Gebhardt & Giery, 1995), a meta-analysis of studies examining exposure to pornography and acceptance of rape myths revealed that experimental studies showed a positive effect between pornography and rape myth acceptance but nonexperimental studies displayed no effects.

Finally, Friedlander (1993) reported the results of a meta-analysis that compared the magnitude of effects reported by studies that looked at antisocial behavior with those that examined prosocial behavior. He found that, with few exceptions, the size of the effect found for prosocial media messages was larger than the effect found for antisocial messages.

Summary. Experiments and surveys have been the most popular research strategies used to study the impact of media on antisocial and prosocial behavior. The more elaborate techniques of field experiments and panel studies have been used infrequently. Laboratory experiments have shown a stronger positive relation between viewing media violence and aggression than have the other techniques. Meta-

analyses have offered general conclusions about the scope and magnitude of these effects.

THEORETICAL DEVELOPMENTS

One of the earliest theoretical considerations in the debate over the impact of media violence was the controversy of catharsis versus stimulation. The *catharsis* approach suggests that viewing fantasy expressions of hostility reduces aggression because a person who watches filmed or televised violence is purged of his or her aggressive urges. This theory has some obvious attraction for industry executives, since it carries the implication that presenting violent television shows is a prosocial action. The *stimulation* theory argues the opposite—that viewing violence prompts more aggression on the part of the viewer. The research findings in this area indicated little support for the catharsis position. A few studies did find a lessening of aggressive behavior after viewing violent content, but these results apparently were an artifact of the research design. The overwhelming majority of studies found evidence of a stimulation effect.

Since these early studies, many of the experiments and surveys have used social learning as their conceptual basis. As spelled out by Bandura (1977), the theory explains how people learn from direct experience or from observation (or modeling). Some key elements in this theory are attention, retention, motor reproduction, and motivations. According to Bandura, attention to an event is influenced by characteristics of the event and by characteristics of the observer. For example, repeated observation of an event by a person who has been paying close attention should increase learning. *Retention* refers to how well an individual remembers behaviors that have been observed. *Motor reproduction* is the actual behavioral enactment of the observed event. For example, some people can accurately imitate a behavior after merely observing it, but others need to experiment. The motivational component of the theory depends on the reinforcement or punishment that accompanies performance of the observed behavior.

Applied to the effects area, social learning theory predicts that antisocial or prosocial acts can be learned by watching films or television. The model further suggests that viewing repeated antisocial acts would make people more likely to perform these acts in real life. Yet another prediction involves *desensitization,* to account for the suggestion that people who are heavily exposed to violence and antisocial acts become less anxious about the consequences.

Bandura (1977) summarized much of the research concerning social learning theory. In brief, some key findings in laboratory and field experiments suggest that children can easily perform new acts of aggression after a single exposure to them on television or in films. The similarity between the circumstances of the observed antisocial acts and the postobservation circumstances is important in determining whether the act is performed. If a model is positively reinforced for performing antisocial acts, the observed acts will be more frequently performed in real life. Likewise, when children were promised rewards for performing antisocial acts, more antisocial behavior was exhibited. Other factors that facilitated the performance of antisocial acts included the degree to which the media behavior is perceived to be real, the emotional arousal of the subjects, and the presence of cues in the postobservation environment that elicit antisocial behavior. Finally, as predicted by the theory, desensitization to violence can occur through repeated exposure to violent acts.

Other research has continued to refine and reformulate some of the elements in social learning theory. For example, the arousal hypothesis (Tannenbaum & Zillmann, 1975) suggests that, for a portrayal to have a demonstrable effect, increased arousal may be necessary. According to this model, if an angered person is exposed to an arousing stimulus, such as a pornographic film, and is placed in a situation to which aggression is a possible response, the per-

son will become more aggressive. (*Excitation transfer* is the term used by the researchers.)

Zillmann, Hoyt, and Day (1979) offer some support for this model. Interestingly, it appears that subjects in a high state of arousal from seeing a violent film will perform more prosocial acts than nonaroused subjects. Like aggressive behavior, prosocial behavior seems to be facilitated by media-induced arousal (Mueller, Donnerstein, & Hallam, 1983).

Other research has shown that social learning theory can be applied to the study of the effects of viewing pornography. Zillmann and Bryant (1982) showed that heavy exposure to pornographic films apparently desensitized subjects to the seriousness of rape and led to decreased compassion for women as rape victims. A similar finding was obtained by Linz, Donnerstein, and Penrod (1984). Men who viewed five movies depicting erotic situations involving violence toward women perceived the films as less violent and less degrading to women than did a control group not exposed to the films. In sum, social learning theory is a promising framework for integrating many findings in this area.

Another promising theory, outlined by Berkowitz and Rogers (1986), is based on priming effects analysis. Drawing upon the concepts of cognitive-neoassociationism, priming effects analysis posits that elements of thought or feeling or memories are parts of a network connected by associative pathways. When a thought element is activated, the activation spreads along the pathways to other parts of the network. Thus, for some time after a concept is activated, there is an increased probability that it and other associated parts of the network will come to mind again, creating the priming effect. As a result, aggressive ideas prompted by viewing media violence trigger other semantically related thoughts, increasing the probability that associated aggressive thoughts will come to mind. Berkowitz and Rogers note that priming analysis can explain the fact that much exposure to media violence results in short-term, transient effects. They point out that the priming effect attenuates over time, lowering the probability of subsequent violent effects.

Van Evra (1990) suggests that "script theory" might also be useful in explaining the impact of TV violence. Since most viewers, particularly younger ones, have little real-life experience with violence but see a lot of it on TV, their behavior patterns or scripts might be influenced by the TV exposure. Those who watch a heavy amount of violent TV might store these scripts in their memory and display violence when an appropriate stimulus triggers the acting out of their scripts. Moreover, Huesmann and Eron (1986) argue that if a young child learns early in his or her developmental cycle that aggression is a potent problem-solving technique, it will be hard to change since the script has been well rehearsed by the child.

Drawing upon the above information, Comstock and Paik (1991) have proposed a three-factor explanation of the influence of media violence on antisocial and aggressive behavior:

1. Violent portrayals that are unusual, unique, and compelling are likely to prompt viewer aggression because of their high attention and arousal value.
2. Social cognition theory would suggest that repetitive and redundant portrayals of violence would prompt viewers to develop expectations and perceptions of violence.
3. Violent media content encourages the early acquisition of stable and enduring traits. Some violent scripts may be learned by children who are only 3 or 4 years old.

USES AND GRATIFICATIONS

The *uses and gratifications* perspective takes the view of the media consumer. It examines how people use the media and the gratifications they seek and receive from their media behaviors. Uses and gratifications researchers assume that audience members are aware of and can articulate their reasons for consuming various media content.

HISTORY

The uses and gratifications approach has its roots in the 1940s, when researchers became interested in why people engaged in various forms of media behavior, such as radio listening or newspaper reading. These early studies were primarily descriptive, seeking to classify the responses of audience members into meaningful categories. For example, Herzog (1944) identified three types of gratification associated with listening to radio soap operas: emotional release, wishful thinking, and obtaining advice. Berelson (1949) took advantage of a New York newspaper strike to ask people why they read the paper. The responses were placed in five major categories: reading for information, reading for social prestige, reading for escape, reading as a tool for daily living, and reading for a social context. These early studies had little theoretical coherence; in fact, many were inspired by the practical needs of newspaper publishers and radio broadcasters to know the motivations of their audience to serve them more efficiently. (Chapter 13 notes that the uses and gratifications approach is still one of the major types of research performed by those interested in understanding newspaper readership.)

The next step in the development of this research began during the late 1950s and continued into the 1960s. In this phase the emphasis was on identifying and operationalizing the many social and psychological variables that were presumed to be the antecedents of different patterns of consumption and gratification. For example, Schramm, Lyle, and Parker (1961), in their extensive study, found that children's use of television was influenced by individual mental ability and relationships with parents and peers, among other things. Gerson (1966) concluded

Listening to Rap Music and Antisocial Behavior

The 1990s are witnessing the increasing popularity of rap music and rap music videos. Critics charge that rap music denigrates women and glorifies violence. A study by Johnson, Jackson and Gatto (1995) investigated the short-term impact of exposure to rap videos. They divided a sample of 11- to 16-year-old African-American males into three groups. One group saw eight videos that contained violent acts and lyrics that glorified violence. A second group saw eight rap videos that did not contain violence, while a third group saw no videos.

After viewing, the youngsters were asked a series of questions. One set of questions described a situation in which a man behaved violently toward another man and toward a woman and asked the respondents to report their attitudes toward the violent acts and whether they, the young people, would engage in similar behavior. A second set of questions was based on the description of another situation in which two friends chose different paths in life. One elected to go to law school while the other decided to stay home. When the person in law school came home to visit his friend, he found that his friend was unemployed but was mysteriously able to afford an expensive car, expensive clothes, and other extravagant items. The youngsters were asked to indicate which friend they wanted to be like and whether the one friend would ever complete law school.

The results showed that the group seeing the violent rap videos was more likely to approve of violence than were the other two groups. In addition, the group seeing the violent rap video along with the group seeing the nonviolent videos were both more likely than the control group to indicate they wanted to be like the friend who stayed home and acquired the expensive belongings than the other friend who went to law school. In addition, when compared to the control group, both groups who saw the rap videos also expressed greater doubt that the one friend would ever finish law school. This study suggests that social scientists should consider content such as music videos along with conventional television programs when they investigate antisocial behavior.

---

that race was important in predicting how adolescents used the media. Greenberg and Dominick (1969) found that race and social class predicted how teenagers used television as an informal source of learning. These studies and many more conducted during this period reflected a shift from the traditional effects model of mass media research to the functional perspective.

According to Windahl (1981), a primary difference between the traditional effects approach and the uses and gratifications approach is that a media effects researcher usually examines mass communication from the perspective of the communicator, whereas the uses and grat-

ifications researcher uses the audience member as a point of departure. Windahl argues for a synthesis of the two approaches, believing that it is more beneficial to emphasize their similarities than to stress their differences. He has coined the term *conseffects* of media content and use to categorize observations that are partly results of content use in itself (a viewpoint commonly adopted by effects researchers) and partly results of content mediated by use (a viewpoint adopted by many uses and gratifications researchers).

Windahl's perspective serves to link the earlier uses and gratifications approach to the third phase in its development. Recently, uses and gratifications research has become more conceptual and theoretical as investigators have offered their data in explanation of the connections between audience motives, media gratifications, and outcomes. As Rubin (1985, p. 210) noted: "Several typologies of mass media motives and functions have been formulated to conceptualize the seeking of gratifications as variables that intervene before media effects." For example, Greenberg (1974) ascertained that a positive disposition to aggression characterized children who used television for arousal purposes. Rubin (1979) found a significant positive correlation between the viewing of television to learn something and the perceived reality of television content: Those using television as a learning device thought television content was more true to life. de-Bock (1980) noted that people who experienced the most frustration at being deprived of a newspaper during a strike were those who used the newspaper for information and those who viewed newspaper reading as a ritual. These and many other recent studies have revealed that a variety of audience gratifications are related to a wide range of media effects. These "uses and effects" studies (Rubin, 1985) have bridged the gap between the traditional effects approach and the uses and gratifications perspective.

The last few years have seen the uses and gratifications approach utilized to explore the impact of the new technologies on the audience For example, Lin (1993a) examined adolescents' viewing gratifications with the new media. She found that VCRs and remote control devices enhanced audience control of the viewing environment, which led to increased entertainment gratifications. In a similar study (Lin, 1993b), posited audience activity (planning viewing, discussion of content, remembering the program) would be an important intervening variable in the gratification seeking process because of the viewing options opened up by cable, VCRs, and remote controls. Her results supported her hypothesis. Viewers who were most active had a greater

level of gratification expectation and also reported a greater level of satisfaction obtained.

Perse and Ferguson (1993) also examined the impact of the new television technologies on satisfaction. They found that use of VCRs, remote controls, and cable viewing had an impact on the passing-time and companionship gratifications from TV watching. On a more general level, Perse and Courtright (1993) examined how 12 mass and interpersonal communication channels filled 11 communication needs. Interpersonal channels (conversation and telephone) were the most useful at filling various needs, while the computer was rated as least useful. The video and audio media were ranked highest in providing entertainment, while the print and interpersonal channels were the most useful for learning functions. Albarran and Dimmick (1993) combined the uses and gratifications approach with niche theory in their study of the utility of the video entertainment industries. They found that broadcast TV was the most diverse in serving the cognitive gratifications of the audience, while cable TV and the VCR were the most effective in meeting needs related to feeling and emotional states. All in all, the broad theoretical framework offered by the uses and gratifications framework makes it a popular technique for researchers interested in all forms of media content.

METHODS

Uses and gratifications researchers have relied heavily on the survey method to collect their data. As a first step, researchers have conducted focus groups or have asked respondents to write essays about their reasons for media consumption. Closed-ended Likert-type scales based on what was said in the focus group or written in the essays are then constructed. The closed-ended measures are typically subjected to multivariate statistical techniques such as factor analysis (Appendix 2), which identifies various dimensions of gratifications.

For example, in their study of the uses and gratifications of VCRs, Rubin and Bantz (1989) first asked selected groups of respondents to list 10 ways they used their VCRs and to provide reasons for those uses. This procedure resulted in a list of categories and statements describing VCR usage.

A questionnaire was then developed from this master list and administered to respondents who were asked to indicate how frequently they used their VCRs for these purposes and to rate how much importance they placed on the statements detailing the reasons for usage. After revisions, a final questionnaire was developed; it contained 95 motivational statements. This final questionnaire was administered to a sample of 424 VCR owners.

Through factor analysis, the 95 statements were then reduced to eight main motivational categories. Some examples of the factors and statements that went with them were as follows: "I want to keep a permanent copy of the program" (library storage); "I use music video for parties" (music videos); "I don't have to join an exercise class" (exercise tapes). Rubin and Bantz then correlated these factors with demographic and media exposure variables.

Note that the technique above assumes that the audience is aware of its reasons and can report them when asked. The method also assumes that the pencil-and-paper test is a valid and reliable measurement scale. Other assumptions include an active audience with goal-directed media behavior; expectations for media use that are produced from individual predispositions, social interaction, and environmental factors; and media selection initiated by the individual. Some researchers (see Becker, 1980) suggest that reliability and validity checks should be built into the uses and gratifications approach. For an example of how this has been accomplished, see Rubin (1985).

The experimental method has not been widely used in uses and gratifications research. When it has been chosen, investigators typically manipulated the subjects' motivations and measured differences in their media consumption. To illustrate, Bryant and Zillmann (1984) placed their subjects in either a state of boredom or a state of stress and then gave them a choice between watching a relaxing or a stimulating television program. Stressed subjects watched more tranquil programs and bored subjects opted for the exciting fare. McLeod and Becker (1981) had their subjects sit in a lounge area that contained public affairs magazines. One group of subjects was told that they would soon be tested about the current situation in Pakistan. A second group was told they would be required to write an essay on U.S. military aid to Pakistan, while a control group was given no specific instructions. As expected, subjects in the test and essay conditions made greater use of the magazines than did the control group. The two test groups also differed in the type of information they remembered from the periodicals. Experiments such as these two indicate that different cognitive or affective states facilitate the use of media for various reasons, as predicted by the uses and gratifications rationale.

THEORETICAL DEVELOPMENTS

As mentioned earlier, researchers in the academic sector are interested in developing theories concerning the topics they investigate. This tendency is well illustrated in the history of uses and gratifications research. Whereas early studies tended to be descriptive, later scholars have attempted to integrate research findings into a more theoretical context.

In an early explanation of the uses and gratifications process, Rosengren (1974) suggested that certain basic needs interact with personal characteristics and the social environment of the individual to produce perceived problems and perceived solutions. The problems and solutions constitute different motives for gratification behavior that can come from using the media or from other activities. Together the media use or other behaviors produce gratification (or nongratification) that has an impact on the individual or society, thereby starting the process anew. After reviewing the results of approximately 100 uses and gratifications studies, Palmgreen (1984) stated that "a rather complex theoretical structure . . . has begun to emerge." He proposed an integrative gratifications model that suggested a multivariate approach (Appendix 2).

The gratifications sought by the audience form the central concept in the model. There are, however, many antecedent variables such as media structure, media technology, social circumstances, psychological variables, needs, values, and beliefs that all relate to the particular gratification pattern used by the audience. Additionally, the consequences of the gratifications relate directly to media and nonmedia consumption behaviors and perceived gratifications that are obtained. As Palmgreen admits, this model is not sufficiently succinct and needs strengthening in several areas, but it does represent an increase in our understanding of the mass media process. Further refinements in the model will come from surveys and experiments designed to test specific hypotheses derived from well-articulated theoretical rationales and from carefully designed descriptive studies. For example, Levy and Windahl (1984) examined whether the audience was active, as is assumed by the uses and gratifications approach. They derived a typology of audience activity and prepared a model that linked activity to various uses and gratifications, thus further clarifying one important postulate in the uses and gratifications process.

Rubin (1986) pointed out that even though theory development had progressed, the uses and gratifications approach still had a long way to go. He argued that what was needed was a clearer picture of the relationship between media and personal channels of communication and sources of potential influence. In a similar vein, Swanson (1987) called for more research that would benefit the theoretical grounding of the uses and gratifications approach. Specifically, Swanson urged that research focus on (1) the role of gratification seeking in exposure to mass media, (2) the relationship between grat-

ification and the interpretive frames through which audiences understand media content, and (3) the link between gratifications and media content. Van Evra (1990) presents an integrated theoretical model of television's impact, in which the use of the medium is considered along with the amount of viewing, presence of information alternatives, and perceived reality of the medium. Her description highlights the complex interactions that need to be examined in order to understand the viewing process. Additionally, uses and gratifications researchers have recently incorporated a theory from social psychology, expectancy-value theory, into their formulations (Babrow, 1989). This theory suggests that audience attitude toward the media behavior is an important factor in media use. Rubin (1994) summarizes the growth of theory in the area and concludes that single-variable explanations of media effects are inadequate. He suggests that more attention be given to antecedent, mediating, and consequent exposure conditions. In sum, it is likely that the next few years will see an increased emphasis on theory building among uses and gratifications researchers.

The uses and gratifications approach also serves to illustrate the difference in emphasis between academic and applied research objectives. Newspaper publishers and broadcasting executives—who want guidance in attracting readers, viewers, and listeners—seem to be particularly interested in determining what specific content is best suited to fulfilling the needs of the audience. College and university researchers, on the other hand, are not only interested in content characteristics but want to develop theories that explain and predict the media consumption of the public based on sociological, psychological, and structural variables.

AGENDA SETTING BY THE MEDIA

Theory concerning agenda setting by the media proposes that "the public agenda—the kinds of things people discuss, think, and worry about (and sometimes ultimately press for legislation about)—is powerfully shaped and directed by what the news media choose to publicize" (Larson, 1986). This means that if the news media decide to give the most time and space to the budget deficit, this issue will become the most important item on the audience's agenda. If the news media devote the second most amount of coverage to unemployment, audiences, too, will rate unemployment as the second most important issue to them, and so on. Agenda-setting research examines the relationship between media priorities and audience priorities concerning the relative importance of news topics.

HISTORY

The notion of agenda setting by the media can be traced to Walter Lippmann (1922), who suggested that the media were responsible for the "pictures in our heads." Forty years later, Cohen (1963) further articulated the idea when he argued that the media may not always be successful in telling people what to think, but they are usually successful in telling them what to think about. Lang and Lang (1966, p. 468) reinforced this notion by observing, "The mass media force attention to certain issues. . . . They are constantly presenting objects, suggesting what individuals in the mass should think about, know about, have feelings about."

The first empirical test of agenda setting came in 1972, when McCombs and Shaw (1972) reported the results of a study done during the 1968 presidential election. They found strong support for the agenda-setting hypothesis. There were strong relationships between the emphasis placed on different campaign issues by the media and the judgments of voters regarding the importance of various campaign topics. This study inspired a host of others, many of them concerned with agenda setting as it occurred during political campaigns. For example, Tipton, Haney, and Baseheart (1975) used cross-lagged correlation (Chapter 8) to analyze the impact of the media on agenda setting during statewide elections. Patterson and McClure (1976) studied the impact of television news and television commercials on agenda setting in the 1972 election. They concluded that television news had minimal impact on public awareness of issues, but that television advertising accounted for a rise in the audience's awareness of candidates' positions on issues.

Lately, agenda-setting research has enjoyed increased popularity. *Communication Abstracts* has listed an average of 12 articles per year on agenda setting from 1994 to 1995. This is an increase from an average of 7.5 articles from 1978 to 1989. The more recent articles signal a shift away from the political campaign approach. In the years 1978–1981, about 30% of the agenda-setting articles were analyses of political campaigns; from 1982 to 1994, about 15% were of this type. In short, the agenda-setting technique is now being used in a variety of areas: history, advertising, foreign news, and medical news. McCombs (1994) presents a useful summary of this topic.

In recent years the biggest trends in agenda-setting research have been (1) how the media agenda is set (this research is also called *agenda building*) and (2) how the media choose to portray the issues they cover (this is called *framing analysis*). With regard to agenda building, Wanta, Stephenson, Turk, and McCombs (1989) noted some correlation between issues raised in the President's State of the Union address and the media coverage of those issues. Similarly, Wanta (1991) noted that the President can have an impact on the media agenda, particularly when presidential approval ratings are high. Turk and Franklin (1987) examined public relations efforts to set the news agenda, and Berkowitz and Adams (1990) explored how press releases and other "news subsidies" shaped the media agenda. Reese (1990) presents a thorough review of the agenda-building research.

Framing analysis recognizes that the media can impart a certain perspective or "spin" to the events that they cover and this, in turn, might influence public attitudes on an issue. For example, Page and Shapiro (1992) found that television news coverage of major foreign issues over 15 years predicted shifts in public opinion. Wanta and Hu (1993) found a similar pattern concerning coverage of international news. Finally, Iyengar and Simon (1993) found a framing effect in their study of news coverage of the Gulf War. Respondents who relied the most on television news, where military developments were emphasized, expressed greater support for a military rather than a diplomatic solution to the crisis.

METHODS

The typical agenda-setting study involves several of the approaches discussed in earlier chapters. Content analysis (Chapter 6) is used to define the media agenda, and surveys (Chapter 7) are used to collect data on the audience agenda. In addition, since determining the media agenda and surveying the audience are not done simultaneously, a longitudinal dimension (Chapter 8) is present as well. More recently, some studies have used the experimental approach (Chapter 9).

Measuring the Media Agenda.   Several techniques have been used to establish the media agenda. The most common method involves grouping coverage topics into broad categories and measuring the amount of time or space devoted to each category. The operational definitions of these categories are important considerations because the more broadly a topic area is defined, the easier it is to demonstrate an agenda-setting effect. Ideally, the content analysis should include all media, including television, radio, newspapers, and magazines. Unfortunately, this is too large a task for most researchers to handle comfortably, and most studies have been confined to one or two media, usually television and the daily newspaper. For example, Williams and Semlak (1978) tab-

ulated total air time for each topic mentioned in the three television network newscasts for a 19-day period. The topics were rank-ordered according to their total time. At the same time, the newspaper agenda was constructed by measuring the total column inches devoted to each topic on the front and editorial pages of the local newspaper. McLeod, Becker, and Byrnes (1974) content analyzed local newspapers for a 6-week period, totaling the number of inches devoted to each topic, including headlines and pertinent pictures on the front and editorial pages. Among other things, they found that the front and editorial pages adequately represented the entire newspaper in their topical areas.

The development of new technologies has created problems for researchers in measuring the media agenda. Cable TV, fax machines, e-mail, on-line computer services, and the Internet have greatly expanded the information outlets available to the public. The role of these new channels of communication in agenda setting is still unclear.

Measuring Public Agendas.   The public agenda is constructed in at least four ways. First, respondents are asked an open-ended question such as, "What do you feel is the most important political issue to you personally?" or "What is the most important political issue in your community?" The phrasing of this question can elicit either the respondent's intrapersonal agenda (as in the first example) or interpersonal agenda (the second example). A second method asks respondents to rate in importance the issues in a list compiled by the researcher. The third technique is a variation of this approach. Respondents are given a list of topics selected by the researcher and asked to rank-order them according to perceived importance. The fourth technique uses the paired-comparisons method. In this approach, each issue on a preselected list is paired with every other issue and then the respondent is asked to consider each pair and to identify the more important issue. When all the responses have been tabulated, the issues are ordered from the most important to the least important.

As with all measurement techniques, each has its associated advantages and disadvantages. The open-ended method gives respondents great freedom in nominating issues, but it favors those people who are better able to verbalize their thoughts. The closed-ended ranking and rating techniques make sure that all respondents have a common vocabulary, but they assume that each respondent is aware of all the public issues listed and restrict the respondent from expressing a personal point of view. The paired-comparisons method provides interval data, which allows for more sophisticated statistical techniques, but it takes longer to complete than the other methods, and this might be a problem in some forms of survey research.

Three important time frames are used in collecting the data for agenda-setting research: (1) the duration of the media agenda measurement period, (2) the time lag between measuring the media agenda and measuring the personal agenda, and (3) the duration of the audience agenda measurement. Unfortunately, there is little in the way of research or theory to guide the investigator in this area. To illustrate, Mullins (1977) studied media content for a week to determine the media agenda, but Gormley (1975) gathered media data for 4.5 months. Similarly, the time lag between media agenda measurement and audience agenda measurement has varied from no time at all (McLeod et al., 1974) to a lag of 5 months (Gormley, 1975). Wanta and Hu (1994a) discovered that different media have different optimal time lags. Television, for example, has a more immediate impact while newspapers are more effective in the long term.

Not surprisingly, the duration of the measurement period for audience agendas has also shown wide variation. Hilker (1976) collected a public agenda measure in a single day, while McLeod et al. (1974) took 4 weeks. Eyal, Winter, and DeGeorge (1981) suggested that methodological studies should be carried out to determine the optimal effect span or peak association period between the media emphasis and public emphasis. Winter and Eyal (1981), in an example of one of these methodological studies, found an optimal effect span of 6 weeks for agenda setting on the civil rights issue. Similarly, Salwen (1988) found that it took from 5 to 7 weeks of news media coverage of environmental issues before they became salient on the public's agenda.

In a large-scale agenda-setting study of German television, Brosius and Kepplinger (1990) found that the nature of the issue had an impact on the time lag necessary to demonstrate an effect. For general issues such as environmental protection, a lag of a year or two might be appropriate. For issues raised in political campaigns, 4 to 6 weeks might be the appropriate lag. For a breaking event within an issue, such as the Chernobyl disaster, a lag of a week might be sufficient.

Several researchers have used the experimental technique to study the causal direction in agenda setting. For example, Wanta (1988) showed groups of subjects newspaper stories with a dominant photograph, a balanced photograph, or no photograph. The results were mixed, but the dominant photograph did seem to have an effect on the subjects' agenda. Another experiment (Heeter, Brown, Soffin, Stanley, & Salwen, 1989) examined the agenda-setting effect of teletext. One group of subjects was instructed to abstain from all traditional news media for 5 consecutive days and instead spend 30 minutes each day with a teletext news service. The results indicated that a week's worth of exposure did little to alter subjects' agendas.

THEORETICAL DEVELOPMENTS

Despite the problems in method and time span mentioned above, the findings in agenda setting are consistent enough to permit some first steps toward theory building. To begin, the longitudinality of agenda setting has permitted some tentative causal statements. Most of this research has supported the interpretation that the media's agenda causes the public agenda; the rival causal hypothesis—that the public agenda establishes the media agenda—has not received much support (Behr & Iyengar, 1985; Roberts & Bachen, 1981). Thus, much of the recent research has attempted to specify the audience-related and media-related events that condition the agenda-setting effect.

It is apparent that constructing an agenda-setting theory will be a complicated task. Williams (1986), for example, posited eight antecedent variables that should have an impact on audience agendas during a political campaign. Four of these variables (voter interest, voter activity, political involvement, and civic activity) have been linked to agenda setting (Williams & Semlak, 1978). In addition, several studies have suggested that a person's "need for orientation" should be a predictor of agenda holding. (Note that such an approach incorporates uses and gratifications thinking.) For example, Weaver (1977) found a positive correlation between the need for orientation and a greater acceptance of media agendas.

These antecedent variables define the media-scanning behavior of the individual (McCombs, 1981). Important variables at this stage of the process include media use and the use of interpersonal communication (Winter, 1981). Other influences on the individual's agenda-setting behavior include the duration and obtrusiveness of the issues themselves and the specifics of media coverage (Winter, 1981). Three other audience attributes that are influential are the credibility given to the news media, the degree to which the audience member relies on the media for information, and the level of exposure to the media (Wanta & Hu, 1994b).

Despite the tentative nature of the theory, many researchers continue to develop models of the agenda-setting process. Manheim (1987), for example, developed a model of agenda setting that distinguished between content and salience of issues. VanLeuven and Ray (1988) presented a five-stage model of public issue development that includes agenda setting as one of its key dimensions.

Brosius and Kepplinger (1990) used time series analysis in their study of German news programs to test both a linear model and a nonlinear model of agenda setting. The linear model assumes a direct correlation between coverage and issue importance; an increase or decrease in coverage results in a corresponding change in issue salience. Four nonlinear models were also examined: (1) the threshold model—some minimum level of coverage is required before the agenda-setting effect is seen; (2) the acceleration model—issue salience increases or decreases to a larger degree than coverage; (3) the inertia model—issue importance increases or decreases to a lesser degree than coverage; and, (4) the echo model—extremely heavy media coverage will prompt the agenda-setting effect long after coverage recedes. Their data showed that the nature of the issue under study was related to what model best described the results. The acceleration model worked better for issues that were considered subjectively important by the audience (for example, taxes) and for new issues. The linear model seemed to work better with enduring issues (for example, the environment). Some support was also found for the threshold model. There was, however, little support for the inertia model, and not enough data were available for a convincing test of the echo model. In sum, these data suggest an agenda-setting process more complicated than that envisioned by the simple linear model.

CULTIVATION OF PERCEPTIONS OF SOCIAL REALITY

How do the media affect audience perceptions of the real world? The basic assumption underlying the cultivation, or enculturation, approach is that repeated exposures to consistent media portrayals and themes will influence our perceptions of these items in the direction of the media portrayals. In effect, learning from the media environment is generalized, sometimes incorrectly, to the social environment.

As was the case with agenda-setting research, most of the enculturation research has been conducted by investigators in the academic sector. Industry researchers are aware of this work and sometimes question its accuracy or meaning (Wurtzel & Lometti, 1984), but they seldom conduct it or sponsor it themselves.

HISTORY

Some early research studies indicated that media portrayals of certain topics could have an impact on audience perceptions, particularly if the media were the main information sources. Siegel (1958) found that children's role expectations about a taxi driver could be influenced by hearing a radio program about the character. DeFleur and DeFleur (1967) found that television had a homogenizing effect on children's perceptions of occupations commonly shown on television. On a more general level, Greenberg and Dominick (1969) discovered that lower-class teenagers were more likely than middle-class ones to believe that the middle-class world commonly portrayed on television programs was true to life.

The more recent research on viewer perceptions of social reality stems from the Cultural Indicators project of George Gerbner and his associates. Since 1968, they have collected data on the content of television and have analyzed the impact of heavy exposure on the audience. Some of the many variables that have been content analyzed include the demographic portraits of perpetrators and victims of television violence, the prevalence of violent acts, the types of violence portrayed, and the contexts of violence. The basic hypothesis of cultivation analysis is that the more time one spends living in the world of television, the more likely one is to report conceptions of social reality that

can be traced to television portrayals (Gross & Morgan, 1985).

To test this hypothesis, Gerbner and his associates have analyzed data from adults, adolescents, and children in cities across the United States. The first cultivation data were reported more than two decades ago (Gerbner & Gross, 1976). Using data collected by the National Opinion Research Center (NORC), Gerbner found that heavy television viewers scored higher on a "mean world" index than did light viewers. [Sample items from this index included the following: "Do you think people try to take advantage of you?" and "You can't be too careful in dealing with people" (agree/disagree).] Data from both adult and child NORC samples showed that heavy viewers were more suspicious and distrustful. Subsequent studies reinforced these findings that heavy television viewers were more likely to overestimate the prevalence of violence in society and their own chances of being involved in violence (Gerbner, Gross, Jackson-Beeck, Jeffries-Fox, & Signorielli, 1978). In sum, their perceptions of reality were cultivated by television.

Not all researchers have accepted the cultivation hypothesis. In particular, Hughes (1980) and Hirsch (1980) reanalyzed the NORC data using simultaneous rather than individual controls for demographic variables and were unable to replicate Gerbner's findings. Gerbner responded by introducing *resonance* and *mainstreaming,* two new concepts to help explain inconsistencies in the results (Gerbner, Gross, Morgan, & Signorielli, 1986). When the media reinforce what is seen in real life, thus giving an audience member a "double dose," the resulting increase in the cultivation effect is attributed to resonance. Mainstreaming is a leveling effect. Differences in perceptions of reality usually caused by demographic and social factors are offset by heavy viewing, resulting in a common viewpoint. These concepts refine and further elaborate the cultivation hypothesis, but they have not satisfied all the critics of this approach. Condry (1989) presents a comprehensive review of cultivation analysis and its literature, and an insightful evaluation of the criticisms directed against it.

Additional research into the cultivation hypothesis indicates that the topic may be more complicated than first thought. There is evidence that cultivation may be less dependent on the total amount of TV viewing than on the specific types of programs viewed (O'Keefe & Reid-Nash, 1987). Weaver and Wakshlag (1986) found that the cultivation effect was more pronounced among active TV viewers than among low-involvement viewers and that personal experience with crime was an important mediating variable that affected the impact of TV programs on cultivating an attitude of vulnerability toward crime. Additionally, Potter (1986) found that the perceived reality of TV content had an impact on cultivation. Other research (Rubin, Perse, & Taylor, 1988) demonstrated that the wording of the attitude and perceptual questions used to measure cultivation influenced the results. Potter (1988) found that variables such as identification with TV characters, anomie, IQ, and the informational needs of the viewer had differential effects on cultivation. In other words, different people react in different ways to TV content, and these different reactions determine the strength of the cultivation effect. In their study of possible cultivation effects following the 1989 Loma Prieta earthquake, Newhagen and Lewenstein (1992) suggested that it may be the quality as well as the quantity of the images presented on television that prompts cultivation. Finally, Perse, Ferguson and McLeod (1994) studied the impact of the new media technologies—cable TV, VCRs and remote control devices—on cultivation and found mixed results. Fear of crime was negatively related to VCR ownership and also negatively related to increased exposure to specialized cable channels. Watching channels that carried traditional broadcast network programs was positively related to feelings of interpersonal mistrust. The authors concluded that cable television might have altered the traditional impact of TV.

More recently, there have been three key trends in cultivation research. The first involves expanding the focus of cultivation into other countries and cultures. *Cultivation Analysis: New Directions in Media Effects Research* (Signorielli & Morgan, 1990) contains chapters on research done in Britain, Sweden, Asia, and Latin America. The results regarding the cultivation effect were mixed. The second trend, discussed in more detail in the next section, is typified by a closer examination of the measurements used in cultivation. Results suggest that the way TV viewing is quantified and the way the cultivation questions are framed all have an impact on the results. The final trend concerns explaining the conceptual mechanisms that result in the occurrence of the cultivation effect and will be discussed in the Theoretical Developments section.

METHODS

There are two discrete steps in performing a cultivation analysis. First, descriptions of the media world are obtained from periodic analyses of large blocks of media content. The result of this content analysis is the identification of the messages of the television world. These messages represent consistent portrayals of specific issues, policies, and topics that are often at odds with their occurrence in real life. The identification of the consistent portrayals is followed by the construction of a set of questions designed to detect a cultivation effect. Each question poses two or more alternatives. One alternative is more consistent with the world as seen on television, though another is more in line with the real world. For example, according to the content analyses performed by Gerbner et al. (1977), about 60% of television homicides are committed by strangers. In real life, according to government statistics, only 16% of homicides occur between strangers.

The question based on this discrepancy was, "Does fatal violence occur between strangers, or between relatives and acquaintances?" The "strangers" response was considered to be the answer most consistent with TV portrayals. Another question was, "What percentage of all males who have jobs work in law enforcement and crime detection? Is it 1% or 5%?" According to census data, 1% of males in real life have such jobs, compared to 12% in television programs. Thus, 5% is the television answer.

Condry (1989) points out that the cultivation impact seems to depend upon whether respondents are making judgments about society or about themselves. Societal-level judgments, such as the examples given above, seem to be more prone to the cultivation effect, but personal judgments (such as "What is the likelihood that you will be involved in a violent crime?") seem to be harder to influence. In a related study, Sparks and Ogles (1990) demonstrated a cultivation effect when respondents were asked about their fear of crime but not when they were asked to give their personal rating of their chances of being victimized. Measures of these two concepts were not related.

The second step involves surveying audiences with regard to television exposure, dividing the sample into heavy and light viewers (4 hours of viewing a day is usually the dividing line), and comparing their answers to the questions differentiating the television world from the real world. In addition, data are often collected on possible control variables such as gender, age, and socioeconomic status. The basic statistical procedure consists of correlational analysis between the amount of television viewing and the scores on an index reflecting the number of television answers to the comparison questions. Also, partial correlation is used to remove the effects of the control variables. Alternatively, sometimes the *cultivation differential* (CD) is reported. The CD is the percentage of heavy viewers minus the percentage of light viewers who gave the television answers. For example, if 73% of the heavy viewers gave the television answer to the question about violence being committed between strangers or acquaintances compared to 62% of the light viewers, the CD would be 11%. Laboratory experiments use the same general approach, but they usually manipulate the subjects' experience with the television world by showing an experimental group one or more preselected programs.

Measurement decisions can have a significant impact on cultivation. Potter and Chang (1990) gauged TV viewing using five techniques: (1) total exposure (the traditional technique used in cultivation analysis); (2) exposure to different types of television programs; (3) exposure to program types while controlling for total exposure; (4) measure of the proportion of each program type viewed, obtained by dividing the time spent per type of program by the total time spent viewing; and (5) a weighted proportion calculated by multiplying hours viewed per week by the proportional measure mentioned in the fourth technique.

The results showed that total viewing time was not a strong predictor of cultivation scores. The proportional measure proved to be the best indicator of cultivation. This suggests that a person who watches 20 hours of TV per week, with all of the hours being crime shows, will score higher on cultivation measures of fear of crime than a person who watches 80 hours of TV a week with 20 of them consisting of crime shows. The data also showed that all of the alternative measures were better than a simple measure of total TV viewing.

Potter (1991a) demonstrated that where the dividing point is set between heavy viewers and light viewers is a critical choice that can influence the results of a cultivation analysis. He showed that the cultivation effect may not be linear, as typically assumed. This finding may explain why cultivation effects in general are small in magnitude; simply dividing viewers into heavy and light categories cancels many differences among subgroups.

THEORETICAL DEVELOPMENTS

What does the research tell us about cultivation? After an extensive literature review of 48 studies, Hawkins and Pingree (1981) concluded that there was evidence of a link between viewing and beliefs regardless of the kind of social reality in question. Was this link real, or spurious? The authors concluded that the answer to this question did, in fact, depend on the type of belief under study. Relationships between viewing and demographic aspects of social reality held up under rigorous controls. As for causality, the authors concluded that most of the evidence indicated that television causes social reality to be interpreted in certain ways. Twelve years later, Shrum and O'Guinn (1993) echoed the earlier conclusion by stating that cultivation research has demonstrated a modest but persistent effect of television viewing on what people believe the social world is like.

How does this process take place? The most recent publications in this area have focused on conceptual models that explain the cognitive processes that cause cultivation. Potter (1993) presents an extensive critique of the original cultivation formulation and offers several suggestions for future research including developing a typology of effects and providing a long-term analysis. Van Evra (1990) posits a multivariate model of cultivation, taking into account the use to which the viewing is put (information or diversion), the perceived reality of the content, the number of information alternatives available, and the amount of viewing. She suggests that maximum cultivation occurs among heavy viewers who watch for information, believe the content to be real, and have few alternative sources of information. Potter (1991b) proposes a psychological model of cultivation incorporating the concepts of learning, construction, and generalization. He suggests that cultivation theory needs to be extended and revamped if it is to provide an explanation of how the effect operates.

Tapper (1995) divides a possible conceptual model of the cultivation process into two phases. Phase one deals with content acquisition and takes into account such variables as motives for viewing, selective viewing, the type of genre viewed, and perceptions of the reality of the content. Phase two, the storage phase, elaborates those constructs that might affect long-term memory. Tapper's model allows for various cultivation effects to be examined according to a person's viewing and storage strategies.

Shrum and O'Guinn (1993) present a psychological model of the cultivation process based on the notion of accessibility of information in a person's memory. They posit that human memory works much like a storage bin. When new information is acquired, a copy of that new information is placed on top of the appropriate bin. At some later time, when information is being retrieved for decision making, the contents of the bin are searched from the top down. Thus, information deposited most recently and most frequently stands a better chance of being recalled. A person who watches a lot of TV crime shows, for example, might file away many exaggerated portrayals of crime and violence in the appropriate bin. When asked to make a judgment about the frequency of real-life crime, the TV images are the most accessible and the person might base his or her judgment of social reality on them.

Shrum and O'Guinn reported the results of an empirical test of this notion. They reasoned that the faster a person is able to make a response, the more accessible is the information retrieved. Consequently, when confronted with a social reality judgment, heavy TV viewers should be able to make judgments faster than light viewers and their judgments should also demonstrate a cultivation effect. The results of their experiment supported this reasoning.

In sum, cultivation has proven to be an evocative and heuristic notion. It is likely that future research will concentrate on identifying key variables important to the process and on further specification of the psychological factors that underlie the process.

Advertising and the Socialization of Children

The concern over the impact of advertising on children stems from the sheer magnitude of their exposure to such communications. By the time a child reaches high school, he or she has been exposed to approximately 350,000 commercial messages. Not surprisingly, this area has drawn research attention from both academic researchers and applied researchers. There is a large body of applied research on samples of children being exposed to commercials to determine comprehensibility and persuasiveness (Griffin, 1976). Many of these studies are proprietary and not open for review. In the academic sector, the research has been conducted for two purposes: to develop a theory concerning children and consumer socialization and to provide guidelines for public policy. In fact, both the Federal Trade Commission (FTC) and the Federal Communications Commission (FCC) have undertaken inquiries into the impact of advertising on children, and academic research has played a key part in the deliberations of both agencies.

History

Concern over the effects of television advertising on children can be traced to the 1960s, when the National Association of Broadcasters adopted guidelines concerning toy advertising. It was not until the 1970s, however, that this issue gained wide attention. Action for Children's Television (ACT), a group of concerned parents, petitioned the FCC in 1970 for a new set of rules concerning children's television. Among other things, ACT requested a ban on

commercials on children's programs. At about the same time, members of the Council on Children, Media, and Merchandising appeared before Congress to complain about the advertising of high-sugar cereals on television.

This public concern was quickly followed by research into the effects of advertising directed at children. First to appear were content analyses of Saturday morning commercials (Winick, Williamson, & Chuzmir, 1973). The first behavioral studies were included as part of the Surgeon General's report on television and social behavior (Ward, 1972). A few additional studies appeared over the next few years, but research interest did not significantly increase until regulatory agencies used the results of existing studies to formulate new policy. The FTC, for example, cited research findings to support its prohibition of the use of premium offers in advertising.

The number of studies examining the socialization impact of television advertising increased markedly in the mid-1970s. A review of the literature of the period summarized 21 key studies in the area and reported that most were done between 1974 and 1976 (Adler et al., 1977). The main findings of these studies indicated that age was a crucial variable in determining children's understanding of television advertising. Young children (ages 3–5) had trouble separating the commercial messages from the program content. Older children (ages 6–8) could better identify commercials as distinct from the program but did not understand the selling motive behind their presentation. In 1978, in a report on children and television advertising, the FTC called for banning all commercials directed at children too young to understand their intent. In making this recommendation, the FTC used the results of many research studies that examined the age variable and its relationship to the understanding of commercials.

On the other hand, defenders of children's advertising have suggested that it helps the children become better consumers because it contributes to general economic understanding and knowledge of different products. Research into these claims conducted in the late 1970s was inconclusive (Ward, 1980).

The shift toward deregulation of the media during the early 1980s deemphasized the policy-making aspects of this research. Research interest in children's advertising leveled off during this period. Many of the more recent studies have been concerned with developmental influences on children's understanding of commercials and their relationship to Piaget's (1955) theory of cognitive development.

In 1984 the question of regulating ads directed at young people surfaced again, when congressional hearings were held concerning the impact of liquor commercials on adolescent drinking behavior. The research evidence in this area suggested that young people who were heavily exposed to liquor and beer ads drank more frequently or reported that they expected to start drinking sooner than did those who were not so heavily exposed (Atkin, Hocking, & Block, 1984). There was no immediate federal action as a result of these hearings, but broadcasters and advertisers promised to present messages that would promote the responsible use of alcohol.

These topics continued to receive research attention during the rest of the decade. Investigators were particularly interested in the impact of cognitive development on the understanding of commercials. Macklin (1985) found that improved nonverbal measures cast doubt on the idea that preschoolers understand the selling intent of commercials. Costley and Brucks (1987) compared the effects of age and knowledge of product on responses to deceptive advertising and found that age differences were more important. A more recent area of concern is program-length commercials. These are programs that are based on existing toys and, according to critics, are merchandising vehicles designed to increase sales of the fea-

tured toy or toys. Eaton and Dominick (1991) conducted a content analysis that found that cartoon shows based on existing toys contained more violent and antisocial acts than did other cartoons. Bryant (1985) conducted an experiment that disclosed that children who had seen a program featuring an existing toy with embedded commercials for the toy were more likely to show a preference for that toy than were children who had seen programs that were neutral with regard to a product.

On the policy front, the Children's Television Act took effect in 1992. Along with other provisions, this act limited the amount of commercial time during children's TV programming to 10.5 minutes per hour on weekends and 12 minutes per hour on weekdays. In addition, the act required stations to provide programming designed to meet the informational and educational needs of children. By 1995, the FCC had fined more than 20 stations for exceeding the commercial time limits. One station was fined $80,000 for 130 violations. Other stations were criticized for citing shows such as "GI Joe" as examples of educational and informational programming.

Tobacco advertising also received increased research attention in the early 1990s. Much like the earlier concern over alcohol ads, at issue was the impact of tobacco ads on encouraging young people to start smoking (see boxed material). Several studies seemed to suggest that, despite their claims to the contrary, tobacco advertisers were targeting their ads to a young audience. For example, Mazis, Ringold, Perry, and Denman (1992) asked respondents to judge the age of models in 50 magazine ads for cigarettes. The respondents perceived about one of every five models to be under age 25, an apparent violation of the tobacco industry's advertising code, which states that models in ads should not appear to be less than 25 years old. Klitzner, Greunwald, and Bamberger (1991) noted that adolescents who recognized advertised cigarette brands were also more likely to have experimented with cigarettes. Ward (1990), however, argued that, when compared to the family or peer groups, advertising plays a relatively minor role in the decision to start smoking.

METHODS

The most popular methods used to study this topic have been the survey and the laboratory experiment. Of the 26 key studies reviewed by Adler et al. (1980), half were surveys and half were done in the laboratory. Accordingly, this section examines several illustrative experiments and surveys.

The three dependent variables that have been examined by much of the research are (1) conditions concerning the identification and function of television advertising, (2) the impact of advertising on product preferences, and (3) the impact of advertising on the parent-child relationship. The survey technique has been widely used to study the first of these variables. Ward, Reale, and Levinson (1972) conducted a survey of 67 children, ranging in age from 5 to 12 years, concerning their knowledge of television commercials. Each child was asked a series of 16 questions, and the answers were transcribed. The responses were content analyzed and placed in categories according to the degree of awareness exhibited by the child. For example, children were asked, "What is a commercial?" Those whose answers showed confused perceptions and low discrimination between commercials and programs were categorized as having "low awareness." Answers from "medium-awareness" children showed an understanding of the advertising content and some information about the product. "High-awareness" children gave answers characterized by an understanding of the sponsor concept and the motive of the seller. The results of this analysis showed that more than 50% of those 5–7 years old, but only 13% of those 8–12 years old, were in the low-awareness cate-

gory, suggesting that understanding increases with age.

In a related study, Ward, Levinson, and Wackman (1972) used unobtrusive techniques to study children's attention to television commercials. Mothers were trained to record information about their children's normal TV viewing behaviors. Using code sheets, they noted whether the child was paying full attention, partial attention, or not watching commercials and programs. Analysis of the resulting data indicated a tendency of all children to exhibit a drop in attention when a commercial was shown, but the youngest group (5–7 years) showed the smallest drop. The researchers suggested that this more stable attention pattern among the youngest children demonstrated the difficulty they have in differentiating between programs and commercials. Wartella and Ettema (1974), however, in a more controlled situation with trained observers, found an increase in attention among their youngest age group (nursery children) when the commercials came on. This observation suggested that the discrepancy in findings with the study by Ward et al. might be due to the visual complexity of the ads that were shown in the respective investigations.

More recently, Kunkel (1988) performed an experiment that examined whether children understood a TV commercial that featured the same primary characters as those in the surrounding program content (a technique known as host selling). Kunkel looked at three dimensions of understanding: ability to differentiate the commercial from the program, ability to attribute persuasive intent to the ad, and attitudes about commercial appeals. In the experiment, younger children (ages 4–5) and older children (ages 7–8) saw either a cartoon and a commercial with the same characters or a cartoon with a commercial featuring other cartoon characters. The results indicated that both age groups were less likely to distinguish a commercial from a program when host sell-

"Old Joe" and New Smokers

The tobacco industry has maintained for many years that they do not want young people to smoke. Nonetheless, many critics insist that the industry runs ads featuring cartoon characters that encourage young people to smoke cigarettes. At the center of the controversy has been the "Old Joe" cartoon character used by Camel cigarettes. In late 1991, three studies appearing in the *Journal of the American Medical Association* demonstrated that the cartoon character was an effective weapon in Camel's marketing arsenal. One study estimated that Old Joe was in part responsible for increasing the sales of Camels to kids from $6 million to $476 million. Another study reported that 12- and 13-year-olds had the highest recognition of the character and that Camel's market share among 12–17-year-old boys was twice that of Camel's share among 18–24-year-old men. The third study found that Old Joe was as well known among 9-year-olds as was Mickey Mouse. For its part, R. J. Reynolds, Camel's parent company, questioned the studies' conclusions and restated its claim that Camel's advertising efforts were not targeting underage smokers. Despite R. J. Reynolds' claims, the American Medical Association and the Surgeon General of the United States urged the company to yank the cartoon character from its subsequent advertising campaigns. In October 1995, the tobacco company announced that it was dropping Joe Camel from its outdoor billboard ads but that the dromedary would continue in its print advertising.

ing was used, but that host selling had no impact on discerning commercial intent. Finally, older children were more influenced by commercials that used host selling. Kunkel concluded that concern about the effects of host selling should be expanded to older as well as younger children.

The second dependent variable, advertising impact, has been studied using both experimental and survey techniques. Experimental studies that contrast children exposed to television commercials with those not so exposed demonstrate some of the dimensions of this impact. Goldberg and Gorn (1978) showed one group of children commercials for a new toy, while a control group saw no commercials. To examine the ability of commercials to enhance the value of the toy in comparison with the value of being with peers, children were asked to choose between playing with a "nice" child without the advertised toy or with a "not so nice" child with the toy. Almost twice as many children in the control group chose to play with the nice child without the toy; those who saw the commercial more often opted to play with the other child who had the toy.

In a related experiment, Goldberg, Gorn, and Gibson (1978) showed different groups of children: (1) a television show with ads for products high in sugar content, (2) a television show with public service announcements stressing a balanced diet, or (3) an entire program stressing the value of eating a balanced diet. The children were then given a chance to select various snacks and breakfast foods that varied in nutritional value. The group that saw the entire program on a balanced diet selected only a few items that were low in nutrition. The group that saw the ads for the sugared products selected the least nutritional foods. Kohn and Smart (1984) showed college students a videotape edited into three different versions. One program had nine beer commercials, the second had four such commercials, and the third had none. Subjects could choose beer and other refreshments while watching. Exposure to the first beer commercials increased consumption, but continued exposure had no further effects.

The survey method investigates impact by correlating respondents' consumption patterns with exposure to ads. For example, Atkin, Reeves, and Gibson (1979) measured preferences in food brands among children 5–12 years old. There was a strong positive relationship between viewing television commercials for the food item and liking the food item. Atkin, Hocking, and Block (1984) sampled teenagers in four regions of the country. They measured exposure to liquor advertising in several ways. In one method respondents were shown specimen ads and asked how often they remembered seeing the commercial messages represented. Alcohol consumption was measured by asking how many different brands of liquor the respondent had drunk, or how much beer and wine were consumed in a typical week. A regression analysis showed that advertising exposure was the strongest correlate of liquor drinking and ranked second behind peer influence in predicting beer drinking. Advertising exposure showed little relation to wine drinking.

The survey approach has also been used to study the impact of advertising on parent-child relationships. To illustrate, Atkin (1975) found that children heavily exposed to Saturday morning commercials argued more with their parents when requests for an advertised product were turned down than did light viewers. Robertson, Ward, Gatignon, and Klees (1989) conducted a cross-cultural study in the United States, Japan, and Britain. In all three countries, mothers of young children kept diaries of TV viewing and purchase requests. Across cultures, the greater the TV viewing, the more the requests to parents and the greater the parent-child conflict. On the other hand, Isler, Popper, and Ward (1987) asked mothers of children ages 3–11 to keep a diary for a month and record purchase requests of an advertised product. They found that children made an average of about 14 requests in the 4-week period. About half of these requests were denied. When asked to report the child's reaction to these denials, the respondents reported that most of the time the kids took it without a protest but that older children argued a little. The authors suggest that advertising plays only a minor role in creating parent-child conflict.

Researchers have also relied upon the experimental approach. In the study by Goldberg and Gorn (1978), children were asked how a hypothetical child would respond if his/her parents denied his/her request to purchase a particular toy. A significantly greater proportion of children who saw ads for the toy reported that they would express rejection toward their parents than did those who did not see the ads. Galst and White (1976) allowed children in a nursery school setting to regulate their own viewing of commercials. Subsequently, trained observers followed the children and their mothers to the supermarket and recorded each time a child tried to influence a purchase. There was a significant relationship between the number of television commercials viewed and the number of purchase attempts made at the store.

In sum, both laboratory studies and survey studies of young consumers have demonstrated that age is an important factor in understanding the purpose of commercials, that ads do have an influence on product desirability, and that television commercials may be a source of friction in the parent-child relationship.

THEORETICAL DEVELOPMENTS

Two main theoretical perspectives have been associated with research dealing with advertising and young people. Predictions from the first, *social learning theory*, suggest that behaviors observed in the media, such as eating certain foods or playing with certain toys, will be imitated by observers, resulting in more con-

Channel One

In 1990, Whittle Communications began providing *Channel One,* a 10-minute newscast with 2 minutes of commercials, to cooperating middle and high schools across the country. In return for carrying the program, the schools received the free use of a satellite dish, two VCRs, and a TV set in each classroom.

Channel One caused an immediate controversy over the ethics and appropriateness of televising commercial messages in the school environment to a captive audience. Critics suggested that *Channel One* might create more materialistic and consumption-oriented attitudes among its audience members.

Brand and Greenberg (1994) tested some of these criticisms in their study of *Channel One's* impact on a sample of Michigan high schools. They surveyed schools that were receiving the program and compared their responses to a questionnaire to those of students in schools not carrying *Channel One.* The researchers found that students who were *Channel One* viewers evaluated products advertised on the program more favorably than their nonviewing counterparts. They also reported more consumption-oriented attitudes and that students were more likely to report that they intended to purchase the advertised items. When it came to actual purchases, however, the students were no more likely than the nonviewers to report buying the advertised items. These results suggest that in-school advertising may be just as or even more effective than advertising presented through more conventional channels.

sumption of advertised products. In addition, investigators expect to be able to discern conditions that either facilitate or inhibit the social learning process. As the foregoing discussion of research methods and results indicates, the main predictions of this theory are substantiated. Watching TV commercials for various products apparently leads to children's preferences for and consumption of the advertised products. Additionally, such factors as the presence of a celebrity endorser of the product (Atkin & Block, 1983) or specific audiovisual techniques (Meringoff & Lesser, 1980) can facilitate modeling. On the other hand, alerting the child audience to the persuasive intent of a commercial message seems to inhibit its effects (Sprafkin, Swift, & Hess, 1983). Further research that more accurately defines other contingent influences will make social learning theory more valuable as a predictive tool.

The other theoretical formulation is the *cognitive development theory* associated with

Swiss psychologist Jean Piaget (1955). This theory posits that children go through stages of development, one following another in a set pattern, but the age at which a child reaches any given stage depends on the individual. Thus these developmental stages are correlated with, but not synonymous with, chronological age. Piaget postulated four major stages in cognitive development: (1) the sensorimotor stage, characterized by the child defining his or her environment by behavior (grasping, sucking, and so on) without symbolic representation of objects; (2) the preoperational stage, during which the child develops some reasoning ability; (3) the concrete operations stage, characterized by the use of basic logical operations; and (4) the formal operations stage, in which the child achieves adult-like thought patterns such as abstract thought and hypothetical reasoning.

Much of the research in children's consumer socialization is devoted to applying this developmental mode to the comprehension of television messages. For example, Tada (1969) found that young children (those in the preformal operations stage) did not understand the various editing and production techniques used in an instructional film. Noble (1975) reported that preschool children had difficulty in understanding that television programs are "make believe" and that the characters seen on television are actors. Wartella (1980) summed up the results of many of the studies that looked at advertising and children. She reported that the development of an understanding of the differences between programs and commercials begins at about age 4, and that by kindergarten most children are able to distinguish between them. Higher-level understanding of the functional differences between programs and commercials occurs between kindergarten and third grade.

Recent research has been directed at modifying and refining Piaget's formulations. For example, although the theory suggests that the four stages of development are fixed and unchanging, some evidence suggests that there may be variation. In contrast to the findings of studies summarized by Adler et al. (1977), as well as his own earlier work with associates (Ward, 1972), Ward (1980) reported that some kindergarten children could identify the selling purpose of advertising and displayed other consumer-related skills beyond what would be expected from the cognitive stage typically observed in 5-year-olds. Soldow (1983) found greater cognitive ability than predicted by Piaget's theory among his subjects in a test of product recall. More recently, Stutts and Hunnicutt (1987) found evidence that supported Piaget's theory regarding verbal responses, but the evidence did not support it when nonverbal responses were considered. Acker and Tiemens (1981) found that logical operations concerning television images occurred among elementary school children at a later age than predicted. In addition, there is evidence that children can be taught to acquire some cogni-

tive abilities earlier than the theory's guidelines predict (Wackman, Wartella, & Ward, 1979). Sanft (1985) demonstrated that the child's knowledge base rather than chronological age is the important developmental variable. If a younger child is given the same knowledge base as an older child, he or she will perform equally well on information processing tasks. This finding suggests that knowledge rather than age will define the effects of advertising on children.

Comstock and Paik (1991) suggest that attention be focused on structural or outcome analyses that emphasize the effects and the role that advertising plays in the lives of young people. They present a model that examines (1) the stimulus properties of ads and (2) mediating variables from the child's social and psychological environment. They prefer this model because it is not tied to any specific stage of developmental theory and because it has policy implications. It is likely that future efforts in this area will continue to concentrate on further theoretical developments.

SUMMARY

Academic research and private sector research possess similarities and differences. They share common techniques and try to predict and explain behavior, but academic research differs from private sector research in that the former is public, more theoretical in nature, is generally determined more by the individual researcher than by management, and usually costs less than private sector research. Five main areas that exemplify mass media effects research conducted by the academic sector are (1) prosocial and antisocial effects of specific media content, (2) uses and gratifications, (3) agenda setting, (4) perceptions of social reality, and (5) advertising and the socialization of children. Each of these areas is typified by its own research history, method, and theoretical formulation.

QUESTIONS AND PROBLEMS FOR FURTHER INVESTIGATION

1. List some topics in addition to those mentioned in this chapter that might interest both private sector researchers and academic researchers.

2. What problems arise when the experimental technique is used to study agenda setting? Describe how this might be done.

3. Assume that as a consultant for a large metropolitan newspaper, you are designing a uses and gratifications study of newspaper reading. What variables would you include in the analysis? If you were instead an academic researcher interested in the same question, how might your investigation differ from the private sector study?

4. List some perceptions of social reality, in addition to those discussed in the chapter, that might be cultivated by heavy media exposure.

REFERENCES AND SUGGESTED READINGS

Acker, S., & Tiemens, R. (1981). Children's perception of changes in size of TV images. *Human Communication Research, 7*(4), 340–346.

Adler, R., Lesser, G. S., Meringoff, L. K., Robertson, T. S., Rossiter, J. R., & Ward, S. (1977). *Research on the effects of television advertising on children*. Washington, DC: U.S. Government Printing Office.

Adler, R., Lesser, G., Meringoff, L., Robertson, T., Rossiter, J., & Ward, S. (1980). *The effects of television advertising on children*. Lexington, MA: Lexington Books.

Albarran, A., & Dimmick, J. (1993). An assessment of utility and competition superiority in the video entertainment industries. *Journal of Media Economics, 6*(2), 45–51.

Allen, M., D'Alessio, D., & Brezgel, K. (1995). A meta-analysis summarizing the effects of pornography II. *Human Communication Research, 22*(2), 258–283.

Allen, M., Emmers, T., Gebhardt, L., & Geiry, M. (1995). Pornography and acceptance of rape myths. *Journal of Communication, 45*(2), 5–27.

Atkin, C. (1975). *Effects of TV advertising on children* (technical report). East Lansing, MI: Michigan State University.

Atkin, C., & Block, M. (1983). Effectiveness of celebrity endorsers. *Journal of Advertising Research, 23*(1), 57–62.

Atkin, C., Hocking, J., & Block, M. (1984). Teenage drinking: Does advertising make a difference? *Journal of Communication, 34*(2), 157–167.

Atkin, C., Reeves, B., & Gibson, W. (1979). *Effects of television food advertising on children*. Paper presented to the Association for Education in Journalism, Houston.

Babrow, A. J. (1989). An expectancy-value analysis of the student soap opera audience. *Communication Research, 16*, 155–178.

Bandura, A. (1977). *Social learning theory*. Englewood Cliffs, NJ: Prentice-Hall.

Baran, S. B., Chase, L., & Courtright, J. (1979). Television drama as a facilitator of prosocial behavior. *Journal of Broadcasting, 23*(3), 277–284.

Bear, A. (1984). The myth of television violence. *Media Information Australia, 33*, 5–10.

Becker, L. (1980). Measurement of gratifications. In G. Wilhoit & H. deBock (Eds.), *Mass communication review yearbook* (Vol. I). Beverly Hills, CA: Sage Publications.

Behr, R., & Iyengar, S. (1985). TV news, real-world clues and changes in the public agenda. *Public Opinion Quarterly, 49*(1), 38–57.

Belson, W. (1978). *Television violence and the adolescent boy*. Hampshire, England: Saxon House.

Berelson, B. (1949). What missing the newspaper means. In P. Lazarsfeld & F. Stanton (Eds.), *Communication research, 1948–49*. New York: Harper & Row.

Berkowitz, D., & Adams, D. B. (1990). Information subsidy and agenda building in local TV news. *Journalism Quarterly, 67*(4), 723–731.

Berkowitz, L., & Rogers, K. H. (1986). A priming effect analysis of media influences. In J. Bryant & D. Zillmann (Eds.), *Perspectives on media effects* (pp. 57–82). Hillsdale, NJ: Lawrence Erlbaum.

Brand, J., & Greenberg, B. (1994). Commercials in the classroom. *Journal of Advertising Research, 34*(1), 18–27.

Brosius, H. B., & Kepplinger, H. M. (1990). The agenda-setting function of TV news. *Communication Research, 17*(2), 183–211.

Brosius, H. B., & Kepplinger, H. M. (1992). Linear and non-linear models of agenda setting in television. *Journal of Broadcasting & Electronic Media, 36*(1), 5–24.

Brown, W. J. (1990). Prosocial effects of entertainment television in India. *Asian Journal of Communication, 1*(1), 113–135.

Bryant, J. (1985, October 28). Testimony at hearings before the U.S. House of Representatives Subcommittee on Telecommunications, Consumer Protection and Finance.

Bryant, J., & Zillmann, D. (1984). Using television to alleviate boredom and stress. *Journal of Broadcasting, 28*(1), 1–20.

Bryant, J., & Zillmann, D. (Eds.). (1994). *Media effects*. Hillsdale, NJ: Lawrence Erlbaum.

CBS Broadcast Group. (1974). Fat Albert and the Cosby kids. New York: CBS Office of Social Research.

Chaffee, S. (1984). Defending the indefensible. *Society, 21*(6), 30–35.

Cohen, B. (1963). *The press, the public and foreign policy*. Princeton, NJ: Princeton University Press.

Commission on Obscenity and Pornography. (1970). *The report of the commission on obscenity and pornography*. Washington, DC: U.S. Government Printing Office.

Comstock, G., Chaffee, S., & Katzman, N. (1978). *Television and human behavior*. New York: Columbia University Press.

Comstock, G., & Paik, H. (1991). *Television and the American child*. New York: Academic Press.

Condry, J. (1989). *The psychology of television*. Hillsdale, NJ: Lawrence Erlbaum.

Cook, T., Kendzierski, D., & Thomas, S. (1983). The implicit assumptions of television research. *Public Opinion Quarterly, 47*(2), 161–201.

Costley, C. L., & Brucks, M. (1987). The roles of product knowledge and age on children's responses to deceptive advertising. In P. N. Bloom (Ed.), *Advances in marketing and public policy*. Greenwich, CT: JAI Press.

deBock, H. (1980). Gratification frustration during a newspaper strike and a TV blackout. *Journalism Quarterly, 57*(1), 61–66.

DeFleur, M., & DeFleur, L. (1967). The relative contribution of television as a learning source for children's occupational knowledge. *American Sociological Review, 32*, 777–789.

Donnerstein, E., Linz, D., & Penrod, S. (1987). *The question of pornography: Research findings and policy implications*. New York: Free Press.

Eaton, B. C., & Dominick, J. R. (1991). Product-related programming and children's TV. *Journalism Quarterly, 68*(1/2), 67–75.

Eyal, C., Winter, J., & DeGeorge, W. (1981). The concept of time frame in agenda setting. In G. Wilhoit & H. deBock (Eds.), *Mass communication review yearbook* (Vol. II). Beverly Hills, CA: Sage Publications.

Forge, K. L., & Phemister, S. (1987). The effect of prosocial cartoons on preschool children. *Child Study Journal, 17*(2), 83–86.

Friedlander, B. (1993). Community violence, children's development and mass media. *Psychiatry, 56*(1), 66–81.

Galst, J., & White, M. (1976). The unhealthy persuader: The reinforcing value of television and children's purchase influence attempts at the supermarket. *Child Development, 47*(4), 1089–1096.

Gerbner, G., & Gross, L. (1976). Living with television: The violence profile. *Journal of Communication, 26*(2), 173–179.

Gerbner, G., Gross, L., Eleey, M. F., Jackson-Beeck, M., Jeffries-Fox, S., & Signorielli, N. (1977). TV violence profile no. 8. *Journal of Communication, 27*(2), 171–180.

Gerbner, G., Gross, L., Jackson-Beeck, M., Jeffries-Fox, S., & Signorielli, N. (1978). Cultural indicators: Violence profile no. 9. *Journal of Communication, 28*(3), 176–207.

Gerbner, G., Gross, L., Morgan, M., & Signorielli, N. (1986). Living with television: The dynamics of the cultivation process. In J. Bryant & D. Zillmann (Eds.), *Perspectives on media effects* (pp. 17–40). Hillsdale, NJ: Lawrence Erlbaum.

Gerson, W. (1966). Mass media socialization behavior: Negro-white differences. *Social Forces, 45*, 40–50.

Goldberg, M., & Gorn, G. (1978). Some unintended consequences of TV advertising to children. *Journal of Consumer Research, 5*(1), 22–29.

Goldberg, M., Gorn, G., & Gibson, W. (1978). TV messages for snack and breakfast foods. *Journal of Consumer Research, 5*(1), 48–54.

Gormley, W. (1975). Newspaper agendas and political elites. *Journalism Quarterly, 52*(2), 304–308.

Greenberg, B. S. (1974). Gratifications of television viewing and their correlates for British children. In J. G. Blumler & E. Katz (Eds.), *The uses of mass communication*. Beverly Hills, CA: Sage.

Greenberg, B., & Dominick, J. (1969). Racial and social class differences in teenagers' use of television. *Journal of Broadcasting, 13*(4), 331–344.

Griffin, E. (1976). What's fair to children? *Journal of Advertising, 5*(2), 14–18.

Gross, L., & Morgan, M. (1985). Television and enculturation. In J. Dominick & J. Fletcher (Eds.), *Broadcasting research methods*. Boston: Allyn & Bacon.

Hawkins, R., & Pingree, S. (1981). Using television to construct social reality. *Journal of Broadcasting, 25*(4), 347–364.

Heeter, C., Brown, N., Soffin, S., Stanley, C., & Salwen, M. (1989). Agenda-setting by electronic text news. *Journalism Quarterly, 66*(1), 101–106.

Heller, M., & Polsky, S. (1976). *Studies in violence and television*. New York: American Broadcasting Company.

Herzog, H. (1944). What do we really know about daytime serial listeners? In P. Lazarsfeld & F. Stanton (Eds.), *Radio research, 1942–43*. New York: Duell, Sloan & Pearce.

Hilker, A. (1976, November 10). Agenda-setting influence in an off-year election. *ANPA Research Bulletin*, pp. 7–10.

Hirsch, P. (1980). The "scary world" of the nonviewer and other anomalies. *Communication Research, 7*, 403–456.

Huesmann, L. R., & Eron, L. D. (1986). *Television and the aggressive child: A cross-national comparison*. Hillsdale, NJ: Lawrence Erlbaum.

Hughes, M. (1980). The fruits of cultivation analysis: A re-examination of some effects of television viewing. *Public Opinion Quarterly, 44*(3), 287–302.

Isler, L., Popper, E. T., & Ward, S. (1987). Children's purchase requests and parental response. *Journal of Advertising Research, 27*(5), 28–39.

Iyengar, S., & Simon, A. (1993). News coverage of the Gulf crisis and public opinion. *Communication Research, 20*(3), 265–283.

Johnson, J., Jackson, J., & Gatto, L. (1995). Violent attitudes and deferred academic aspirations. *Basic and Applied Social Psychology, 16*(1/2), 27–41.

Klapper, J. (1960). *The effects of mass communication*. Glencoe, IL: Free Press.

Klitzner, M., Gruenwald, D. J., & Bamberger, E. (1991). Cigarette advertising and adolescent experimentation with smoking. *British Journal of Addiction, 86*(3), 287–298.

Kohn, P., & Smart, R. (1984). The impact of TV advertising on alcohol consumption. *Journal of Studies on Alcohol, 45*(4), 295–301.

Kunkel, D. (1988). Children and host selling television commercials. *Communication Research, 15*(1), 71–92.

Lang, K., & Lang, G. (1966). The mass media and voting. In B. Berelson & M. Janowitz (Eds.), *Reader in public opinion and communication*. New York: Free Press.

Larson, C. U. (1986). *Persuasion* (4th ed.). Belmont, CA: Wadsworth.

Lefkowitz, M., Eron, L., Waldner, L., & Huesmann, L. (1972). Television violence and child aggression. In G. Comstock & E. Rubinstein (Eds.), *Television and social behavior: Vol. III. Television and adolescent aggressiveness*. Washington, DC: U.S. Government Printing Office.

Levy, M., & Windahl, S. (1984). Audience activity and gratifications. *Communication Research, 11*, 51–78.

Liebert, R., & Baron, R. (1972). Short-term effects of televised aggression on children's aggressive behavior. In J. Murray, E. Rubinstein, & G. Comstock (Eds.), *Television and social behavior: Vol. II. Television and social learning*. Washington, DC: U.S. Government Printing Office.

Liebert, R. M., & Sprafkin, J. (1988). *The early window*. New York: Pergamon Press.

Lin, C. (1993a). Adolescent viewing and gratifications in a new media environment. *Mass Comm Review, 20*(1/2), 39–50.

Lin, C. (1993b). Modeling the gratification-seeking process of television viewing. *Human Communication Research, 20*(2), 224–244.

Linz, D., Donnerstein, D., & Penrod, S. (1984). The effects of multiple exposure to film violence against women. *Journal of Communication, 34*(3), 130–147.

Lippmann, W. (1922). *Public opinion*. New York: Macmillan. (reprint, 1965). New York: Free Press.

Macklin, M. C. (1985). Do young children understand the selling intent of commercials? *Journal of Consumer Affairs, 19*(2), 293–304.

Manheim, J. B. (1987). A model of agenda dynamics. In M. L. McLaughlin (Ed.), *Communication yearbook* (Vol. 10, pp. 499–516). Beverly Hills, CA: Sage Publications.

Mazis, M. B., Ringold, D. J., Perry, E. S., & Denman, D. W. (1992, January). Perceived age and attractiveness of models in cigarette advertisements. *Journal of Marketing, 56*(1), 22–37.

McCombs, M. (1981). The agenda setting approach. In D. Nimmo & K. Sanders (Eds.), *Handbook of political communication*. Beverly Hills, CA: Sage Publications.

McCombs, M. (1994). News influence on our pictures of the world. In J. Bryant & D. Zillmann (Eds.), *Media effects*. Hillsdale, NJ: Lawrence Erlbaum.

McCombs, M., & Shaw, D. (1972). The agenda-setting function of mass media. *Public Opinion Quarterly 36*(2), 176–187.

McLeod, J., Atkin, C., & Chaffee, S. (1972). Adolescents, parents and television use. In G. Comstock & E. Rubinstein (Eds.), *Television and social behavior: Vol. III. Television and adolescent aggressiveness*. Washington, DC: U.S. Government Printing Office.

McLeod, J., & Becker, L. (1981). The uses and gratifications approach. In D. Nimmo & K. Sanders (Eds.), *Handbook of political communication*. Beverly Hills, CA: Sage Publications.

McLeod, J., Becker, L., & Byrnes, J. (1974). Another look at the agenda setting function of the press. *Communication Research, 1*(2), 131–166.

Meringoff, L., & Lesser, G. (1980). The influence of format and audiovisual techniques on children's perceptions of commercial messages. In R. Adler, G. Lesser, L. Meringoff, T. Robertson, J. Rossiter, & S. Ward (Eds.), *The effects of television advertising on children*. Lexington, MA: Lexington Books.

Milavsky, J., Kessler, R., Stipp, H., & Rubens, W. (1983). *Television and aggression*. New York: Academic Press.

Milgram, S., & Shotland, R. (1973). *Television and antisocial behavior*. New York: Academic Press.

Minton, J. (1975). The impact of "Sesame Street" on readiness. *Sociology of Education, 48*(2), 141–155.

Montgomery, K. (1995). Prosocial behavior in films. Unpublished master's thesis, University of Georgia.

Mueller, C., Donnerstein, E., & Hallam, J. (1983). Violent films and prosocial behavior. *Personality and Social Psychology Bulletin, 9*, 183–189.

Mullins, E. (1977). Agenda setting and the younger voter. In D. Shaw & M. McCombs (Eds.), *The emergence of American political issues*. St. Paul, MN: West.

Murray, J. (1984). A soft response to hard attacks on research. *Media Information Australia (33)*, 11–16.

National Institute of Mental Health. (1982). *Television and behavior: Ten years of scientific progress and implications for the 1980s*. Washington, DC: U.S. Government Printing Office.

Newhagen, J., & Lewenstein, M. (1992). Cultivation and exposure to television following the 1989 Loma Prieta earthquake. *Mass Communication Review, 19*(1/2), 49–56.

Noble, G. (1975). *Children in front of the small screen*. Beverly Hills, CA: Sage Publications.

O'Keefe, G. J., & Reid-Nash, K. (1987). Crime news and real world blues. *Communication Research, 14*(2), 147–163.

Page, B. & Shapiro, R. (1992). *The rational public*. Chicago: University of Chicago Press.

Paik, H. & Comstock, G. (1994). The effects of television violence on antisocial behavior: A meta-analysis. *Communication Research, 21*(4), 516–546.

Palmgreen, P. (1984). Uses and gratifications: A theoretical perspective. In R. Bostrom (Ed.), *Communication yearbook 8*. Beverly Hills, CA: Sage Publications.

Palmgreen, P., & Lawrence, P. A. (1991). Avoidances, gratifications and consumption of theatrical films. In B. A. Austin (Ed.), *Current Research in Film, Vol. 5* (pp. 39–55). Norwood, NJ: Ablex.

Parke, R., Berkowitz, L., & Leyens, J. (1977). Some effects of violent and nonviolent movies on the behavior of juvenile delinquents. *Advances in Experimental Social Psychology, 16*, 135–172.

Patterson, T., & McClure, R. (1976). *The unseeing eye*. New York: G. P. Putnam's.

Perse, E., & Courtright, J. (1993). Normative images of communication media. *Human Communication Research, 19*(4), 485–503.

Perse, E., & Ferguson, D. (1993). The impact of the newer television technologies on television satisfaction. *Journalism Quarterly, 70*(4), 843–853.

Perse, E., Ferguson, D., & McLeod, D. (1994). Cultivation in the new media environment. *Communication Research, 21*(1), 79–104.

Piaget, J. (1955). The language and thought of the child. New York: Meridian.

Porter, W. C., & Stephens, F. (1989). Estimating readability: A study of Utah editors' abilities. *Newspaper Research Journal, 10*(2), 87–96.

Potter, W. J. (1986). Perceived reality and the cultivation hypothesis. *Journal of Broadcasting and Electronic Media, 30*(2), 159–174.

Potter, W. J. (1988). Three strategies for elaborating the cultivation hypothesis. *Journalism Quarterly, 65*(4), 930–939.

Potter, W. J. (1991a). The linearity assumption in cultivation research. *Human Communication Research, 17*(4), 562–583.

Potter, W. J. (1991b). Examining cultivation from a psychological perspective. *Human Communication Research, 18*(1), 77–102.

Potter, W. (1993). Cultivation theory and research. *Human Communication Research, 19*(4), 564–601.

Potter, W. J., & Chang, I. C. (1990). Television exposure and the cultivation hypothesis. *Journal of Broadcasting and Electronic Media, 34*(3), 313–333.

Potter, W. J., & Ware, W. (1989). The frequency and context of prosocial acts on prime time TV. *Journalism Quarterly, 66*(2), 359–366.

Reese, S. D. (1990). Setting the media's agenda. In J. Anderson (Ed.), *Communication yearbook, No. 14.* Newbury Park, CA: Sage Publications.

Roberts, D., & Bachen, C. (1981). Mass communication effects. In M. Rosenzweig & L. Porter (eds.), *The uses of mass communication.* Beverly Hills, CA: Sage Publications.

Robertson, T. S., Ward, S., Gatignon, H., & Klees, D. M. (1989). Advertising and children: A cross-cultural study. *Communication Research, 16*(4), 459–485.

Rosengren, K. E. (1974). Uses and gratifications: A paradigm outlined. In J. G. Blumler & E. Katz (Eds.), *The uses of mass communication.* Beverly Hills, CA: Sage Publications.

Rosenthal, R. (1986). Media violence, antisocial behavior, and the social consequences of small effects. *Journal of Social Issues, 42*(3), 141–154.

Rubin, A. (1979). Television use by children and adolescents. *Human Communication Research, 5*(2), 109–120.

Rubin, A. (1985). Uses and gratifications: Quasi-functional analysis. In J. Dominick & J. Fletcher (Eds.), *Broadcasting research methods.* Boston: Allyn & Bacon.

Rubin, A. M. (1986). Uses, gratifications, and media effects research. In J. Bryant & D. Zillmann (Eds.), *Perspectives on media effects* (pp. 281–302). Hillsdale, NJ: Lawrence Erlbaum.

Rubin, A. M. (1994). Media uses and effects. In J. Bryant & D. Zillmann, (Eds.), *Media Effects.* Hillsdale, NJ: Lawrence Erlbaum.

Rubin, A. M., Perse, E. M., & Taylor, D. S. (1988). A methodological examination of cultivation. *Communication Research, 15*(2), 107–136.

Rubin, A. M., & Bantz, C. R. (1989). Uses and gratifications of videocassette recorders. In J. L. Salvaggio & J. Bryant (Eds.), *Media use in the information age.* Hillsdale, NJ: Lawrence Erlbaum.

Salwen, M. B. (1988). Effect of accumulation of coverage on issue salience in agenda setting. *Journalism Quarterly, 65*(1), 100–106.

Sanft, H. (1985). The role of knowledge in the effects of television advertising on children. In R. J. Lutz (Ed.), *Advances in consumer research* (pp. 147–152). Urbana, IL: Association for Consumer Research.

Schramm, W., Lyle, J., & Parker, E. (1961). *Television in the lives of our children.* Stanford, CA: Stanford University Press.

Shrum, L., & O'Guinn, T. (1993). Process and effects in the construction of social reality. *Communication Research, 20*(3), 436–471.

Siegel, A. (1958). The influence of violence in the mass media upon children's role expectations. *Child Development, 29,* 35–56.

Signorielli, N., & Morgan, M. (1990). *Cultivation analysis: New directions in media effects research.* Newbury Park, CA: Sage Publications.

Silvern, S., & Williamson, P. A. (1987). The effects of video game play on young children's aggressive, fantasy and prosocial behavior. *Journal of Applied Developmental Psychology, 8,* 453–462.

Soldow, G. (1983). The processing of information in the young consumer. *Journal of Advertising Research, 12*(3), 4–14.

Sparks, G., & Ogles, R. M. (1990). The difference between fear of victimization and the probability of being victimized. *Journal of Broadcasting and Electronic Media, 34*(3), 351–358.

Sprafkin, J., & Rubinstein, E. (1979). Children's television viewing habits and prosocial behavior. *Journal of Broadcasting, 23*(7), 265–276.

Sprafkin, J., Swift, C., & Hess, R. (1983). *Rx television: Enhancing the preventative impact of TV.* New York: Haworth Press.

Stutts, M. A., & Hunnicutt, G. G. (1987). Can young children understand disclaimers in television commercials? *Journal of Advertising, 16*(1), 41–46.

Surgeon General's Scientific Advisory Committee on *Television and Social Behavior.* (1972). *Television and social behavior. Television and growing up* (summary report). Washington, DC: U.S. Government Printing Office.

Swanson, D. L. (1987). Gratification seeking, media exposure, and audience interpretations. *Journal of Broadcasting and Electronic Media, 31*(3), 237–254.

Tada, T. (1969). Image cognition: A developmental approach. *Studies in Broadcasting, 7,* 105–174.

Tan, A. S. (1981). *Mass communication theories and research.* Columbus, OH: Grid Publications.

Tannenbaum, P., & Zillmann, D. (1975). Emotional arousal in the facilitation of aggression through communication. In L. Berkowitz (Ed.), *Advances in experimental social psychology.* New York: Academic Press.

Tapper, J. (1995). The ecology of cultivation. *Communication Theory, 5*(1), 36–57.

Tipton, L., Haney, R., & Baseheart, J. (1975). Media agenda setting in city and state election campaigns. *Journalism Quarterly, 52*(1), 15–22.

Turk, J. V., & Franklin, B. (1987). Information subsidies: Agenda setting traditions. *Public Relations Review, 13*(4), 29–41.

Valkenburg, P., & Van der Voort, T. (1995). The influence of television on children's daydreaming styles. *Communication Research, 22*(3), 267–287.

Van Evra, J. (1990). Television and child development. Hillsdale, NJ: Lawrence Erlbaum.

VanLeuven, J. K., & Ray, G. W. (1988). Communication stages and public issue coverage. *Newspaper Research Journal, 9*(4), 71–83.

Wackman, D., Wartella, E., & Ward, S. (1979). *Children's information processing of television advertising.* Washington, DC: National Science Foundation.

Wanta, W., (1988). The effects of dominant photographs: An agenda setting experiment. *Journalism Quarterly, 65*(1), 107– 111.

Wanta, W., (1991). Presidential approval ratings as a variable in the agenda-building process. *Journalism Quarterly, 68*(4), 672–679.

Wanta, W., & Hu, Y. (1993). The agenda setting effects of international news coverage. *International Journal of Public Opinion Research, 5*(3), 250–261.

Wanta, W., & Hu, Y. (1994a). Time-lag differences in the agenda-setting process. *International Journal of Public Opinion Research, 6*(3), 225–240.

Wanta, W., & Hu, Y. (1994b). The effects of credibility reliance and exposure on media agenda setting. *Journalism Quarterly, 71*(1), 90–98.

Wanta, W., Stephenson, M. A., Turk, J. V., & McCombs, M. E. (1989). How president's State of Union talk influenced news media agendas. *Journalism Quarterly, 66*(3), 537–541.

Ward, S. (1972). Effects of television advertising on children and adolescents. In E. Rubinstein, G. Comstock, & J. Murray (Eds.), *Television and social behavior: Vol. IV. Television in day-to-day life: Patterns of exposure.* Washington, DC: U.S. Government Printing Office.

Ward, S. (1980). The effects of television advertising on consumer socialization. In R. Adler, G. Lesser, L. Meringoff, T. Robertson, J. Rossiter, & S. Ward, (Eds.), *The effects of television advertising on children.* Lexington, MA: Lexington Books.

Ward, S. (1990). The effects of tobacco advertising on adolescent smoking initiation and smoking maintenance. *International Journal of Advertising, 9*(2), 85–91.

Ward, S., Levinson, D., & Wackman, D. (1972). Children's attention to television advertising. In E. Rubinstein, G. Comstock, & J. Murray (Eds.), *Television and social behavior: Vol. IV. Television in day-to-day life: Patterns of exposure.* Washington, DC: U.S. Government Printing Office.

Ward, S., Reale, G., & Levinson, D. (1972). Children's perceptions, explanations, and judgments of television advertising. In E. Rubinstein, G. Comstock, & J. Murray (Eds.), *Television and social behavior: Vol. IV. Television in day-to-day life: Patterns of exposure.* Washington, DC: U.S. Government Printing Office.

Ward, S., & Wackman, D. (1972). Television advertising and intrafamily influence. In E. Rubinstein, G. Comstock, & J. Murray (Eds.), *Television and social behavior: Vol. IV. Television in day-to-day life: Patterns of exposure.* Washington, DC: U.S. Government Printing Office.

Wartella, E. (1980). Children and television: The development of the child's understanding of the medium. In G. Wilhoit & H. deBock (Eds.), *Mass communication review yearbook.* Beverly Hills, CA: Sage Publications.

Wartella, E., & Ettema, J. (1974). A cognitive developmental study of children's attention to television commercials. *Communication Research, 1*(1), 46–49.

Weaver, D. (1977). Political issues and voter need for orientation. In M. McCombs & D. Shaw (Eds.), *The emergence of American political issues.* St. Paul, MN: West.

Weaver, J., & Wakshlag, J. (1986). Perceived vulnerability in crime, criminal victimization experience, and television viewing. *Journal of Broadcasting and Electronic Media, 30*(2), 141–158.

Wertham, F. (1954). *The seduction of the innocent.* New York: Holt, Rinehart & Winston.

Williams, T. B. (1986). *The impact of television.* New York: Academic Press.

Williams, W., & Semlak, W. (1978). Campaign '76: Agenda setting during the New Hampshire primary. *Journal of Broadcasting, 22*(4), 531–540.

Windahl, S. (1981). Uses and gratifications at the crossroads. In G. Wilhoit & H. deBock (Eds.), *Mass communication review yearbook.* Beverly Hills, CA: Sage Publications.

Winick, C., Williamson, L., & Chuzmir, S. (1973). *Children's television commercials: A content analysis.* New York: Praeger.

Winter, J. (1981). Contingent conditions in the agenda setting process. In G. Wilhoit & H. deBock (Eds.), *Mass communication review yearbook.* Beverly Hills, CA: Sage Publications.

Winter, J., & Eyal, C. (1981). Agenda setting for the civil rights issue. *Public Opinion Quarterly, 45*(3), 376–383.

Wurtzel, A., & Lometti, G. (1984). Researching TV violence. *Society, 21*(6), 22–30.

Zillmann, D., & Bryant, J. (1982). Pornography, sexual callousness, and the trivialization of rape. *Journal of Communication, 32*(4), 10–21.

Zillmann, D., & Bryant, J. (1989). *Pornography: Research advances and policy considerations.* Hillsdale, NJ: Lawrence Erlbaum.

Zillmann, D., Hoyt, J., & Day, K. (1979). Strength and duration of the effect of violent and erotic communication of subsequent aggressive behavior. *Communication Research, 1,* 286–306.

ANALYZING AND REPORTING DATA

Chapter

17

THE COMPUTER AS A RESEARCH TOOL

Researchers rely on computers for solving both simple problems and complex problems, for designing questionnaires, for building databases, and for retrieving and analyzing archival data such as Arbitron and Nielsen ratings. This reliance can be traced to the introduction of the personal computer (PC) in the early 1980s, a machine that literally reshaped scientific research in only a few years. PCs allow researchers at all levels access to powerful machines and software previously available only to a select group of scientists. Dramatically reduced prices, technological advances, and ease of use have made computers a necessity in all types of mass media research. Employers in any of the mass media consider computer experience a prerequisite for all job applicants; they expect new employees to know enough about computers to be able to quickly learn the system and software used by the company. More than 50% of a typical mass media researcher's day is spent on the computer (Wimmer, 1995).

Before the early 1980s, computers were generally perceived as intimidating devices used only by equally intimidating people. The machines were expensive, gigantic contraptions that had limited capabilities and ran according to sets of complex rules established by groups of computer scientists who had never heard the term *user-friendly*. Then came the personal computer. Advances in technology and a concern about computer *users* eliminated many of the early problems associated with computers. Easy-to-use PC systems, some of which cost well under $1,000, can quickly perform tasks that were tedious and sometimes impossible for their cumbersome ancestors. Using a computer no longer requires either a formal education in computer science nor a plastic shirt-pocket protector for pens and pencils.

As stated in previous editions of this book, this chapter is only an introduction to computers and data analysis; it is not intended to be an exhaustive discussion of these topics. Innovations in computer technology and the use of computers are announced daily, and no textbook can be completely up to date. Several publications listed at the end of the chapter will provide additional information for readers who are interested in learning more about the latest advances in computers and computer applications.

A Brief History of Computers

A very early type of computing instrument was the *abacus,* a Chinese invention used more than 2,000 years ago. The abacus is a wooden frame with several parallel wires on which beads are moved to perform a calculation (similar to the scoring system used for billiards). Around 1640 mathematician Blaise Pascal is said to have developed the first digital calculating machine, but it could perform only the addition function. Other earlier developers of calculating machines include Gottfried Wilhelm von Leibniz who, in the late 1600s, built a machine that could multiply; in 1820 Charles Xavier Thomas is said to have built the first commercially successful calculating machine; and around 1830, mathematics professor Charles Babbage presented ideas for a sophisticated steam-powered machine that was never built.

Computer development took a dramatic turn when Herman Hollerith and James Powers used punched data cards for the 1890 U.S. census. The data cards, used until the late 1970s, increased speed and decreased errors. Then, in the late 1930s, Howard Hathaway Aiken, along with IBM, developed the Harvard Mark I computer, which could handle as many as 23 decimal-place numbers. During World War II, the use of missiles and rockets led to the need for fast and accurate trajectory measurements. To solve the need, in 1946 John W. Mauchly and John Presper Eckert and their colleagues at the Moore School of Electrical Engineering at the University of Pennsylvania developed a high-speed computer called the ENIAC (Electrical Numerical Integrator And Calculator). Although the machine used 18,000 vacuum tubes, required about 1,800 square feet of space, and weighed about 30 tons, it was roughly 1,000 times faster than any previously built device.

Although some people credit the invention of the first computer to Mauchly and Eckert, a 1973 court ruling stated otherwise. After more than 50 years of uncertainty, credit for the invention of the computer was officially bestowed on John V. Atanasoff, a former Iowa State University professor. On November 13, 1990, President Bush presented a National Medal of Technology award to Atanasoff, then 87 years old, for his "invention of the electronic digital computer."

The court proceedings in the Atanasoff case produced interesting information about the development of Mauchly and Eckert's ENIAC. Around 1940, Atanasoff and Clifford Berry, a graduate student, developed a crude prototype of an electronic computer. For several days in 1941, John Mauchly visited Atanasoff in his Iowa home and learned about the new invention. Unfortunately, neither Atanasoff nor the University of Iowa applied for a patent for the machine. In 1946, Mauchly and Eckert unveiled the ENIAC (for which a patent was granted). However, the 1973 court ruling stated that the ENIAC was actually produced from Atanasoff and Berry's work. The title of "father of the modern computer" now officially belongs to John Atanasoff.

Computer enhancements grew rapidly during the 1950s with the invention of magnetic memory and transistors, which were then used in the 1960s to produce commercially available computers. During the 1960s, the development of the **printed circuit board** (a piece of flat plastic that contains electrical circuits) substantially increased the speed of the computer and decreased the size of its components. The advancements in electronic miniaturization continued in the 1970s and 1980s and brought the development of microcomputers, laptop computers, and even smaller machines. The early 1990s witnessed even more developments in computer speed with the introduction of chips such as Intel's Pentium. New printed circuit technology, fiber optics, laser optics, and other developments will allow manufacturers to produce machines in the future that we cannot even imagine today.

How a Computer Works

For all the mystique surrounding the computer, it is no less a tool than a hammer or a food processor. It is a device built to perform a specific task, and, like any other tool, it is necessary to understand how it works before it is possible to understand what to do with it. For example, understanding how a hammer works as well as having an idea of the many types of hammers available makes building something easier. Likewise, when a researcher understands the basic elements of a computer and how it works, it is much easier to use. Most of the problems people encounter with computers have less to do with the machine than with their expectations and fear of them.

At its most basic level, a computer very rapidly performs repetitive numeric tasks, or jobs dealing with the numbers 0 and 1 (binary).

However, regardless of the task, a computer is doing nothing more than performing a series of calculations. Computers do not think, though some people believe that recent developments in *artificial intelligence* (AI) may allow computers to do so on an elementary level. At this point in the development of computers, though, everything a computer "knows" must be input by a human. A computer simply performs human tasks with much greater speed, efficiency, and accuracy than a human typically can.

In short, computers save researchers time and energy—repetitive mathematical tasks, data manipulation, and word processing are perfect tasks for the computer. Many researchers wonder how their colleagues from the past (even the 1980s) got along without the computers we have today.

CLASSIFICATION OF COMPUTERS

Computers are generally classified in sizes: palmtop, subnotebook, notebook (laptop), micro, mini, mainframe, and super. Historically, a computer was classified by its physical size, but technological advancements have moved so rapidly that a computer's size is no longer relevant. Currently, the classification of a computer refers to its processing power rather than its physical size. All sizes of computers have multitasking (several jobs performed at once) or multiuser (many users on one machine) ability.

During the late 1980s, the personal computer, which is technically called a *microcomputer,* or micro, became the most widely used small computer. Probably the most popular micros are made by IBM and Apple. Several companies, such as Compaq, Dell, Zeos, and Texas Instruments, produce micros known as PC *compatibles,* or *clones,* because they copy the design and functions of the IBM PC. Until the mid-1990s there were no clones for Apple computers because the company did not wish to release the information necessary for other companies to copy its hardware configurations and specifications. Apple changed its position in 1995, probably because IBM-based machines far outnumber those made by Apple.

Laptop, notebook, subnotebook, and *palmtop* computers are the newest types of computers and are included in the PC category. Their small size and ability to run on batteries allows users to take them almost anywhere. The size of these computers often fools people, yet even the palmtop has the power of a typical microcomputer. These small computers have changed both the business field and the academic field (not only research), since complicated work can now be accomplished almost anywhere.

Minicomputers are about the size of a typical apartment or dormitory refrigerator. These are mostly used by small companies and usually run a network where all employees are "hooked" together.

The *mainframe* computer is the next largest computer. Mainframes can be large (as big as several large refrigerators), though they no longer occupy the huge amount of space that they did in the past. Mainframes are constructed by several companies including IBM and Control Data. They are used mostly by colleges, universities, and large companies because of their multi-user and data processing abilities.

The *supercomputer* is the most powerful of all computers and is considered the epitome of technological advancement. The "super" designation refers to the number of calculations it can perform, a rate that is measured in millions or billions of instructions per second (MIPS or BIPS). In late 1991, a new computer that could calculate a teraflop (1 trillion instructions) of information per second was announced. The physical size of supercomputers is deceiving, since they are often smaller than a typical mainframe.

Historically, the cost of supercomputers (from $2 million to $40 million) has limited their use to the federal government and large

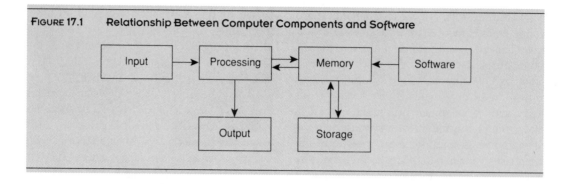

FIGURE 17.1   Relationship Between Computer Components and Software

companies involved in engineering, physics, chemistry, aerospace, and astronomy. However, recent developments in supercomputer technology may make them accessible to colleges, universities, and small businesses. The major breakthrough in technology relates to how supercomputers solve problems. For example, the typical Cray-2 supercomputer uses only one processor to solve calculations at an astonishing rate of about 1.2 billion instructions per second. The new supercomputer design uses a procedure known as **parallel processing**, where several small processors are connected together. These processors break down a problem or set of instructions into small parts and solve them simultaneously. The speed of these parallel processor supercomputers is currently substantially slower than a typical Cray-2, but the machine sells for only about $500,000. Some parallel processors can string together thousands of processors that can collectively handle hundreds of millions of instructions per second.

Regardless of the size of the computer a mass media researcher may use, it is necessary for anyone involved in research, or anyone who plans to become involved in research, to keep up to date with the new technology.

ANATOMY OF A COMPUTER

Any discussion of how computers operate involves two broad topics: **hardware**, which es-

sentially refers to the visible parts of a computer (the machinery), and **software**, which refers to the programs that allow the computer to operate. These two broad classes of elements are the basis for our discussion of the anatomy of a computer. All computers share certain characteristics. Regardless of size and specific engineering characteristics, every computer system has five basic components that are controlled by an operating system (OS).

Computer Components. The five basic computer system components are **input** and **output**, or input/output (I/O), **processing**, **memory**, and **storage**. The I/O components allow a user to put information into a computer and obtain results in some form. The processing component involves the computations a computer makes to solve a problem, which, in turn, requires memory to operate. Finally, the storage component saves data to allow for additional manipulation or retrieval. These five basic components, along with software, enable a computer to function. Figure 17.1 is a simple diagram demonstrating the relationship among the components and the software.

Additional hardware pieces help the computer operate and make using a computer easy. Some of these include the keyboard, the monitor (also known as a CRT, for cathode ray tube, or VDT, for video display terminal), printers, scanners, plotters, and cables. All hardware pieces, excluding the computer's central processing unit (CPU) and main memory, are called **peripherals**. A computer's CPU is the heart of a computer because it controls the entire system according to a set of guidelines provided by specialized software.

Operating Systems.   To allow the computer components to work together smoothly, a software operating system oversees the process. An **operating system (OS)**, is essentially a computer program that acts like a traffic cop: It translates user commands to computer language; designates when and how instructions should be interpreted, computed, and output; and controls the operation according to a specific set of guidelines. Operating systems are loaded into the computer's memory when the machine is turned on (or *booted*). Operating systems are machine-specific, which means that an OS for one type of machine will not work on another type. Software such as spreadsheets or word processors is usually written to operate with only one type of OS, which is why IBM software will not run on an Apple computer, and vice versa, without modification of the software or hardware. Some companies have developed hardware to allow programmers to write software that can be run on either a PC or an Apple.

The most common operating systems for PCs are **MS-DOS** (Microsoft disk operating system) and **PC-DOS** (personal computer disk operating system) developed by the Microsoft Corporation. In the late 1980s, Microsoft developed *Windows,* an *operating environment* and an extension of MS-DOS used to enhance a computer's operations. *Windows* is known as a graphical user interface, or GUI, which means, among other things, that directions to the computer are given by using a mouse (described in the next section) to click onto icons shown on the screen. With much fanfare, Microsoft introduced *Windows 95* to improve on the original Windows system. There are also several mainframe and microcomputer operating systems used for specific computers, such as Cyber NOS, UNIX, Xenix, and TSX.

THE COMPUTER SYSTEM

Input.   There are three broad categories of standard input devices for computers: keyboards, pointing devices, and scanners. A typical *keyboard* resembles a standard typewriter keyboard in form and function, but usually includes several other keys that perform specific functions, depending on the software being used. The more advanced *enhanced* keyboard includes a separate number pad for data entry and other unique keys. *A pointing device* allows users to select and manipulate characters and figures on the monitor. The most popular pointing device is the **mouse**, which is about the size of a deck of playing cards. Movement of the mouse corresponds to movement of a cursor on the monitor. Data are input, moved, or manipulated by buttons on top of the mouse. Most graphics packages, spreadsheets, and word processing programs are designed to be used with a mouse.

Scanners are versatile input devices that are available in a variety of styles and sizes. Mini-scanners are hand-held devices that, when passed over numbers, pictures, or other data, transmit the information to the computer. Large scanners allow for input of an entire page of information. One type of simple scanner is the **optical character reader (OCR)**, or **mark-sense reader,** which scans the types of sheets often used for educational exams. More advanced scanners are used to read Universal Product Codes (UPCs), pictures, and graphics. Scanners are incredibly quick. A typical OCR machine can read both sides of an 8-by-11-inch paper in about 2 seconds or less. Other input devices include pens, joysticks, magnetic strip readers (which read such things as the backs of credit cards), touch-sensitive screens (on which users enter data by touching areas of the monitor), and light pens and graphic pads (which users can use to draw or write information on an electronic pad). Input by speech recognition is under development and may be one of the major sources of data input in the future.

Processing. Computer processing is accomplished through the cooperation of the hardware and software. The primary hardware component is the **microprocessor chip** (microchip), or the CPU, which is the "brains" of the computer. The chip is a thin slice of silicon (or other element) about one-inch square that has electronic circuitry printed directly on it. Microchips are produced for various functions. For example, a chip called a math **coprocessor** is often installed by people who use their computer for complicated mathematical problems. The coprocessor speeds the computing process because the chip is designed only for "number crunching."

The type of microprocessor used in a computer is important because it designates the speed at which the computer operates. In 1979, the Intel Corporation developed the 8088 microprocessor, which processed about 330,000 instructions per second with 29,000 transistors. The 286 microprocessor was introduced in 1982 (3 MIPS, 134,000 transistors), then the 386 (11 MIPS, 275,000 transistors), the 486 (41 MIPS, 1.2 million transistors), and recently the Pentium (100+ MIPS, 3 million transistors). For IBM and IBM-clone machines, the type of chip identifies the type of computer, which is then simply called a 386, 486, or Pentium. The speed of a microchip is partly based on electrical speed, or *clock speed,* which is measured in megahertz (MHz). Megahertz is a measurement of transmission frequency, where 1 megahertz equals 1 million cycles per second. A computer designated as a Pentium/100 means that it has a Pentium microprocessor chip that operates at 100 megahertz. Intel's 486 and Pentium chips combine cache memory (where the most frequently used instructions are stored), data processing, and central pro-

cessing all on one chip. Before the 486, no computer chip contained more than 300,000 transistors, and the three processing operations required three individual microchips to communicate between each other to perform calculations.

Technological advances continually produce faster computers. The latest PC chips use a new technology called *reduced-instruction-set computing* (RISC), which offers another way to increase speed. The RISC chip gains speed over the typical chip by simplifying the instructions processed by the chip.

The microprocessor and its associated support circuitry comprise the computer's CPU. The CPU expresses and uses numbers in a *binary* system—a system of two numbers, 0 and 1. Each symbol in a binary number is called a *binary digit,* or bit. Bits have been coded into various schemes to represent specific numbers or characters. The most commonly used code is the **American Standard Code for Information Interchange,** or ASCII ('ask-ee). Each of the 128 codes uses 7 bits to represent one number, letter, or character. For example, the ASCII code for the number 4 is 0110100 and for the letter *D* it is 1000100. There is also an extended ASCII code that includes a variety of scientific and mathematical symbols.

Each letter, number, or character in an instruction is called a **byte,** which is made up of 8 bits. The original PCs were slow 8-bit systems, meaning that they read 8 bits in a single cycle. New computers can now simultaneously process 16, 32, or 64 bits.

Information is processed by computers in one of two basic ways: batch and interactive (also called on-line). **Batch processing** occurs when a list of instructions is given to the computer by one or more users. The individual instructions are executed in a priority order established by the computer, and the results are output to the user(s). A set of instructions executed in this way is known as a *batch job,* which is similar to being given a list of chores to do around the house and told not to come back until they are done. **Interactive processing**, or on-line processing, involves putting data directly into the computer, usually via a video screen. This type of processing is best exemplified by commercially available software packages that do not require users to enter program instructions. Using the software involves following a set of instructional menus that appear on the screen.

Batch processing is most common in a computer system where several people share the use of one CPU. *Time-sharing* describes batch processing when one mainframe is used by unrelated researchers who are at remote locations. The users are charged a fee for the amount of time spent on the computer. The term **local area network**, or **LAN**, refers to batch processing when one computer serves as a host for several users, usually located in one large office or in the same building.

Memory. Computer memory is described in terms of size, which is generally expressed in increments of 1,000 bytes (1,000 bytes = 1 kilobyte, expressed as Kb, or K). In reality, 1K of memory is actually 1,024 bytes, but it is rounded to 1,000 for convenience. A computer with a memory of 64K can store or work with 65,536 (64 × 1,024) bytes of data. A typical personal computer usually has between 4 and 8 megabytes (Mb) on its motherboard, but it is common for users to upgrade memory to 32Mb or more. (1 Mb, or 1 "meg" = one million bytes).

Computers use several types of memory systems. **Random access memory (RAM)** stores information and data input by the user. RAM is *volatile* memory, meaning that it is usable or addressable only when the computer is turned on; RAM memory is lost when the computer is off. RAM is the memory number used to identify the size of a computer (such as 64K or 640K). A second type of memory is **read-only memory (ROM)**, which is permanently stored in the computer and is nonvolatile; it is not erased when the computer is turned off. ROM

usually contains sets of operating instructions that are called upon when the computer is turned on, such as the computer's operating system information.

Another form of memory is called **programmable read-only memory (PROM)**, a microchip that is used to store information permanently. Generally speaking, users cannot write into PROMs, although some PROMs allow users to write on one occasion to set the chip to meet specific standards or uses. An **erasable programmable read-only memory (EPROM)** microprocessor allows users to change information as often as is necessary.

Storage. Because RAM information is lost when the computer is turned off, the ability to save information is important. The most popular forms of data storage are magnetic disks and tapes. Disks are usually associated with PCs, and tapes with larger computers, though all computers can use one or both media.

The types of disks most commonly used with computers are the floppy disk and the hard disk. Both are similar in that information is encoded on them by selectively magnetizing tiny particles of a metallic oxide bonded to a solid base material, similar to the process used in audiotape and videotape. The **floppy disk** is a thin piece of plastic material coated with an oxide and enclosed in either a flexible case or a rigid case that is inserted into a drive unit when needed. The disks are available in several sizes and storage capacities, ranging from 3.5 inches to 8 inches. A typical PC floppy is 3.5 inches and stores 1.44 Mb on a *double-sided, high-density disk*.

Hard disk storage capacity is almost unlimited. **Hard disks** are contained in airtight, dust-free, nonaccessible cases, though some companies make hard disks that are removable from the computer. Inside a hard disk unit, the disks look like typical audio CDs stacked one on another, and are rather fragile. A hard disk can "crash" and become unusable (in which case all the data are lost). For this reason, researchers who use hard disks make backup copies of the information. All disks must be formatted by the computer's OS before they can be used.

Some forms of data storage are not based on magnetic storage. One of the more common forms is *CD-ROM* (compact disc-read-only memory), which is similar to an audio CD. The CD-ROM uses a laser beam to read information from the disk, which currently stores about 650 Mb of information. CD-ROM users cannot change the data on the disk, but a device known as a *WORM* (write-once/read-many) allows users to write and permanently store information on the disc. WORMs are especially useful for libraries and other data archives that store information. The CD-ROM will probably have a major impact on computer use because of its flexibility and advanced storage capability. It is certain that one or more companies will soon produce a commercially available CD-ROM that can be used as a standard floppy or hard disk.

Tape backup systems are another form of storage system, though unlike floppy and hard disks they are not designed to be accessed. Tape backup systems are convenient—they can be set to automatically back up a computer's entire hard disk—and they save a great deal of agony if a hard disk crashes or a file is accidentally erased.

Output. The effort spent on input, processing, and storage is wasted if the output is not available to the user. Output from processing is usually sent to a monitor, printer, plotter, disk, videotape or audiotape, or a combination of devices.

Excluding the monitor and disk, all output devices provide a hard copy of the computed data. The most common type of **printer** is a laser printer, which produces high-quality print in a variety of fonts. Many computer users continue to use the reliable dot-matrix impact printer (characters are impacted onto the paper), which uses ribbons similar to a standard typewriter. Another popular type of printer is the ink jet, where characters and numbers are jet-sprayed onto paper.

COMPUTER COMMUNICATIONS

Computer systems can communicate with one another even if they are of differing types. This is useful when information stored on a PC needs to be transferred (uploaded) to a larger computer, or vice versa (downloaded). One way to transfer data from one computer to another, even over long distances, is with a **modem** (*mo*dulate-*dem*odulate), which uses standard telephone lines for communication purposes.

An important characteristic of a modem is the rate at which it sends or receives information, known as **bits per second (bps)**. Early modems operated at 300 BPS, but current modems now transfer data at rates up to 28,800 BPS. For two computers to exchange data successfully, they must use the same communication *protocol,* which means they must "speak" the same language. File exchange protocols are included in various telecommunications software packages. Not all telecommunications software supports all protocols.

Individual computers can also be connected together in a **network** so that the users can share information. A typical small network might consist of a *file server* and several *workstations*. The file server is a mass storage device that all users on the network can access. The file server acts as a processing device and storage system, where application programs are stored for users. (An individual user's private data files may be restricted to the person or persons who created them.)

Workstations may be special computer terminals built specifically for that purpose, or they may be PCs or Apples connected to the network. It is common to find several types of computers serving as workstations on the same network. Since a file server is generally available for data storage, processing speed and memory capacity are the most important considerations in choosing a workstation.

Computers operating as workstations on a network generally do not use modems to communicate with one another over standard phone lines. Rather, special communication hardware, cables, and software are installed in each workstation to allow the individual machines to communicate at much higher speeds than are possible using modems. One common type of networking system is called *Ethernet*. With the proper software, it is possible to design an Ethernet network that allows users to not only share files, but also send *electronic mail,* or *e-mail,* from workstation to workstation. Most networking arrangements also allow the workstation users to share output devices such as laser printers. (*Windows 95* is an example of current computer network capability.)

Networks that connect workstations and file servers within a few thousand yards of each other are called Local Area Networks, or **LAN**s. A network connecting computers in a classroom, or in an entire building for that matter, might all be part of a single LAN. A network connecting computers spread over an area (covering perhaps several buildings) is called a **VLAN**, for Very Large Area Network. Computers many miles apart, maybe hundreds or thousands, can be networked in arrangements called **WAN**s, for Wide Area Networks. Regardless of its size, a network's basic function is to allow users to share storage and output resources, as well as information.

A trend in computer networking over the past decade is the creation of *internetworks*. These systems allow users in one location (such as a college campus) to communicate to another location across the country by using a common communication pathway. As long as each LAN follows the same rules in terms of

how to access files, send e-mail, and locate individual users, a user can access a file server across the country as easily as one across the hall (with permission, of course).

The last decade has seen many universities, research organizations, corporations, and government agencies all over the world connect their in-house computer networks to high-speed "information super-highways" operated by governments and private industries alike. A set of communication protocols has been agreed to, and the result has been a worldwide interconnection of computer networks that is called the *Internet*. While people often refer to "The Net," it is useful to remember that there is no organization that goes by that name; indeed, it is only a convenient way to refer to the loose association of thousands of computer networks all over the world.

Mass media researchers can benefit from Internet access since a large number of resources are available *on-line*. For example, it is now possible to remotely access the library catalogs of universities across the country. Some organizations have created *on-line databases* that researchers can access to locate academic and professional journal abstracts. Other databases archive material ranging from news wire copy to the text of Supreme Court decisions. The evolution of the Internet has also allowed researchers across the country to collaborate much more easily than before, since information can be traded much more rapidly. And the development and acceptance of services such as *CompuServe, Prodigy,* and *America Online* have greatly expanded the use of the Internet.

USING COMPUTERS IN RESEARCH

Computers are well suited to statistical analysis because they are designed to make the same types of repetitive calculations found in statistical procedures. The ability to do these

FIGURE 17.2   First 10 Cases from Data Contained in Appendix 4

```
001  1  1  1  1  3  1  2  1  1  2  0  2  0  5  1  1  2  2  1  1  1  2  2  2  1  1  1  1  2  2  1  1  2  1
002  2  1  2  1  1  1  2  1  2  2  0  2  0  2  1  2  2  2  2  1  2  2  2  2  1  1  3  1  2  2  3  1  2  1
003  3  2  0  2  0  1  3  1  2  2  0  2  0  2  1  1  1  1  2  1  1  2  2  2  1  1  2  1  2  2  1  1  2  1
004  3  1  2  1  2  1  2  1  1  1  2  2  0  5  1  1  2  1  1  1  2  1  1  1  1  1  1  1  1  1  1  1  1  1
005  4  1  3  1  3  2  0  1  3  2  0  2  0  2  2  1  2  2  2  1  1  2  2  2  1  1  2  2  2  2  2  2  2  2
006  4  2  0  1  2  1  2  1  1  2  0  2  0  5  2  1  1  1  2  1  2  2  2  1  1  1  1  1  1  1  1  1  1  1
007  1  1  3  1  3  1  1  1  3  1  3  2  0  9  2  2  2  2  2  1  1  2  2  2  2  2  2  1  2  2  2  2  1  2
008  1  1  1  1  2  1  2  1  2  2  0  2  0  2  1  1  2  2  1  1  1  2  2  2  1  1  1  3  2  2  1  1  2  1
009  1  1  3  1  2  1  1  1  2  2  0  2  0  2  1  1  2  2  1  1  2  2  2  1  2  1  1  1  1  1  1  1  1  1
010  1  1  2  1  3  1  2  1  2  2  0  2  0  9  1  1  1  1  2  1  2  2  2  2  1  1  2  1  2  2  2  1  2  1
```

calculations rapidly can be either an advantage or a disadvantage to researchers, depending on their knowledge of the problem under consideration. The computer may be able to perform many intricate mathematical tasks, but the responsibility for its correct usage lies with those who use it. In short, it is always important for researchers to be sure that what is asked of a computer is actually what is needed.

The remainder of this chapter describes a widely available statistical software package designed specifically to analyze social science research data: *SPSS*. This software package, like all others available for commercial use, is constantly updated; new releases are announced periodically to reflect changes in the program. Major releases, called *versions,* usually involve substantial changes in the program. Minor releases, usually issued to eliminate "bugs" in the program or to add new features, are noted by a decimal digit added to the version number, such as Version 2.1 or 2.2. For this chapter, *SPSS* Version 6.1 was used. *SPSS* can be run on any type of computer, but regardless of the type of computer used, *SPSS* "looks and feels" essentially the same. The examples in this chapter used *SPSS* for *Windows.*

It is important for researchers to know which release of a software program is most current. Sometimes new releases are issued

without the knowledge of those who use the software. Computer users can update their knowledge by receiving newsletters published by computer centers at colleges and universities, or by being on the software company's mailing list. Although the previous version of a software manual can be used with a newer release, the manual will not describe the enhanced features made available by the new release. Because of the popularity of the *SPSS* software, the program is usually available at most large computing centers. If any problems are encountered in trying to rerun the data included in this chapter, readers are urged to consult the appropriate *SPSS* user's manual.

BASIC CHARACTERISTICS OF *SPSS*

Data analysis using the *SPSS* software package proceeds through four basic steps after data are collected and coded. First, the coded data are entered into the computer and stored as a file with a unique name. When the data are checked for accuracy, another file is written that tells *SPSS* how the data are entered and what they mean. Once the data are entered and properly defined in separate files, the two files are combined into one file. Finally, sets of commands are input that tell the computer to perform various analyses on the data. Each step involves some rules and concepts that must be understood before successfully using the software.

To help understand the *SPSS* process, the radio-listening study presented in Chapter 7 is used here to illustrate some of the rules and concepts. The data are included in Appendix 4 and are also available on diskette from Wadsworth Publishing. See Hedderson (1991) for more information about *SPSS*.

Data Entry. In the radio-listening survey, 200 respondents between the ages of 18 and 34 were asked 34 questions about their listening habits and preferences. Each person was also assigned an identification code, which means that a total of 35 pieces of information were coded for each respondent. In the parlance of *SPSS*, the data consist of 200 *cases* with 35 *variables* per case. Figure 17.2 shows the data for the first 10 cases taken from the complete data set in Appendix 4. The position of each number can be expressed in terms of its *record* and *column* position. Records are contained in rows; variables are contained in columns. In Figure 17.2 the data are arranged in 10 records and 34 columns.

The first three digits of each record represent the case identification number. Note that they increase by one for each record and that each lines up under one another. This shows how each column represents the value of one variable for 10 different people. In most situations, each record can contain no more than 80 columns of data. If each case required 96 columns for complete description, the columns would be split between two records—80 on the first record and 16 on the second. This is known as having two records per case. In this example, only one record is required because only 34 columns are used.

Figure 17.2 shows how *SPSS* data are generally entered. The file is an ASCII file containing nothing but rows and columns of numbers. Although this example leaves spaces between

columns of variables, *SPSS* does not require researchers to do so. As long as the values representing a single variable are not broken (such as the respondent's identification number), one or more spaces are usually included only for ease of reading by the researcher.

Data Definition. The process of reading this book is possible because we have learned specific rules on how to organize sets of symbols. If letters and words were randomly displayed, it would be impossible to decipher their meaning. Letters and words mean something to us only because we follow a specific set of rules.

This same situation is true for any software package. The letters and words must be arranged according to a set of guidelines established for the computer—all else is meaningless. *SPSS* communication rules are established with a computer through a set of instructions known as a *control file*, an example of which is shown in Figure 17.3.

The first *SPSS* command is the DATA LIST command, which designates how data are defined. DATA LIST tells *SPSS* where to find the relevant data file (\DATA/ASC) and how to read it once it does. It also establishes a unique name for each variable in the study (DEMO), and where to find the variable in the file ("5" = column 5). The variable name/column identification continues through all variables in the study. It is not always necessary to define the column numbers where the variables appear, but the explanations for the variations in defining data are left to the *SPSS* manuals.

Since commands can be longer than a single 80-character line, *SPSS* must be told when the end of a command has been reached. This is done with a period.

There are some general rules about naming variables. Names cannot exceed eight characters and must begin with a letter or one of a limited number of symbols. The *SPSS* manual lists the symbols that cannot be used for variable names. It is useful to use variable names

---

FIGURE 17.3   Control File for Radio Listening Survey

```
SET
  BLANKS=SYSMIS
  UNDEFINED=WARN.
DATA LIST
  FILE= 'C:\DATA.ASC' FIXED RECORDS=1 TABLE /    1 ID 1-3    DEMO 5    WAAA_LIS 7
  WAAA_AM 9    WBBB_LIS 11    WBBB_AM 13    WCCC_LIS 15    WCCC_AM 17    WDDD_LIS 19
  WDDD_AM 21 WEEE_LIS 23 WEEE_AM 25 WFFF_LIS 27 WFFF_AM 29 FAV_STA 31
  AMT_NEW 33 QUAL_NEW 35 AMT_OLD 37 QUAL_OLD 39 AM_SHOW 41 ENERGY 43
  CONTESTS 45 FRIENDS 47 PM_JOCKS 49 LOC_ACT 51 FAV_SONG 53 ATTITUDE 55
  AM_JOCKS 57 TEMPO 59 NEWS 61 TRAFFIC 63 NEW_MUS 65 SOURCE 69 AMT_MUS 71.
VARIABLE LABELS    ID        'CASE ID' /
                   DEMO      'DEMO GROUP' /
                   WAAA_LIS  'WAAA LISTENS' /
                   WAAA_AM   'WAAA MORNING' /
                   WBBB_LIS  'WBBB LISTENS' /
                   WBBB_AM   'WBBB MORNING' /
                   WCCC_LIS  'WCCC LISTENS' /
                   WCCC_AM   'WCCC MORNING' /
                   WDDD_LIS  'WDDD LISTENS' /
                   WDDD_AM   'WDDD MORNING' /
                   WEEE_LIS  'WEEE LISTENS' /
                   WEEE_AM   'WEEE MORNING' /
                   WFFF_LIS  'WFFF LISTENS' /
                   WFFF_AM   'WFFF MORNING' /
                   FAV_STA   'FAVORITE STATION' /
                   AMT_NEW   'AMOUNT OF NEW MUSIC' /
                   QUAL_NEW  'QUALITY OF NEW MUSIC' /
                   AM_SHOW   'MORNING SHOW' /
                   ENERGY    'UPBEAT FEELING' /
                   CONTESTS  'CONTESTS-PRIZES' /
                   FRIENDS   'FRIENDS LISTEN' /
                   PM_JOCKS  'PM ANNOUNCERS' /
                   LOC_ACT   'LOCAL ACTIVITIES' /
                   FAV_SONG  'FAVORITE SONG' /
                   ATTITUDE  'ATTITUDE-LISTENER' /
                   AM_JOCKS  'AM ANNOUNCERS' /
                   TEMPO     'PACE OR TEMPO' /
                   NEWS      'NEWS AND INFO' /
                   TRAFFIC   'TRAFFIC REPORTS' /
                   NEW_MUS   'HEAR NEW MUSIC' /.
VALUE LABELS       DEMO 1 'MALE 18-24'    2 'MALE 25-34'    3 'FEMALE 18-24'
                        4 'FEMALE 25-34' /
                   WAAA_LIS WBBB_LIS WCCC_LIS WDDD_LIS WEEE_LIS WFFF_LIS
                        1 'YES' 2 'NO' /
                   WAAA_AM WBBB_AM WCCC_AM WDDD_AM WEEE_AM WFFF_AM
                        1 'FREQUENTLY'    2 'SOMETIMES'    3 'NEVER' /
                   FAV_STA  2 'OTHER'   3 'WAAA'    4 'WBBB'    5 'WCCC'    6 'WDDD'
                        7 'WEEE'    8 'WFFF'    9 'WGGG/
                        AMT_NEW TO AMT_MUS   1 'AGREE'    2 'DISAGREE'.
MISSING VALUE      FAV_STA (1) /
                   AMT_NEW TO AMT_MUS (3).
SAVE OUTFILE=LISTENING.SYSTEM.
```

---

that are as descriptive as possible to make interpretation of the printout much easier.

The VARIABLE LABELS section in Figure 17.3 is optional in *SPSS*. This command, how-

ever, is useful for providing additional information for the variables in the study, and makes reading the printout much easier. VARIABLE LABELS is typed at the beginning of the command, followed by the variable to be labeled and the desired label enclosed in quotation marks ('DEMO GROUP'). A forward slash (/) separates each of the variables in the VARIABLE LABELS command section.

The VALUE LABELS command assigns additional information to each variable. For example, the value 1 of the variable DEMO means "male 18-24." If this value label were not included, the only way to know the meaning of the value would be to refer to the codebook. As with other commands, VALUE LABELS is typed first, followed by the names of variables to which the value labels will apply. Each value is then listed with its label immediately following in single quotation marks.

If several variables share the same value labels and are defined in order in the DATA LIST command, the word *TO* between the first and last similar variable is used to eliminate unnecessary typing. For example, the last 21 items defined in the DATA LIST command shown in Figure 17.3 share the same two value labels (1 = agree; 2 = disagree). Instead of naming all 21 variables in the VALUE LABELS command, it is only necessary to type AMT_NEW (the first variable in the group) TO AMT_MUS (the last variable) and define the value labels only once. The word *TO* can also be used in other commands.

Sometimes researchers wish to eliminate some answers given by respondents, such as the "Don't know/No answer" response to the Favorite Station question (FAVSTA). In this case, a value can be declared a missing value, which is done with the MISSING VALUES command (Figure 17.3).

The control file must be written very carefully. For example, the same spelling must be used for the variable names throughout the entire file. If *SPSS* were to encounter the variable AMTNEW in the DATA LIST command, but the variable AMTNEWS was found in the VARIABLE LABEL command, the program would interpret them as two different variables. In this case, *SPSS* would try to assign a variable

label to a variable that does not exist. This is not a serious problem (the label would simply be ignored), but forgetting to either enclose a label in single quotation marks or end a command with a period can cause serious (and extremely irritating) problems with a control file. Remember, *SPSS* does only what it is told, not what researchers intend.

System Files.   After the data are defined in one file and the control statements placed in another file, the information is combined into one file to make running the program more efficient for *SPSS* and the researcher if additional computations are necessary. With the use of the SAVE OUTFILE command, a special file containing the data and control files is created (shown as LISTENING.SYSTEM in Figure 17.3). It is a good idea to run a few test analyses to ensure that the data are defined correctly before combining the data file and the control file into a system file.

Procedure Command Structure.   The data analysis commands are made possible through the use of procedure commands, which include command key words and specifications. Command key words tell *SPSS* which statistical procedure(s) is/are to be performed. The specifications are instructions that appear with the command key word. These statements are used to modify the way the program operates or define which variables are to be analyzed.

There are three modes through which *SPSS* can be told to execute procedure commands: *batch, interactive,* and *Manager* modes. The batch mode requires that procedure commands be collected into a file called a *command file* that is submitted to *SPSS* by way of the computer's operating system. This mode is often used when memory-intensive analyses need to be executed on time-sharing systems. A batch program can be submitted and held in a *queue* until sufficient CPU memory resources are available to run the required analyses. The interactive mode allows users to start *SPSS* and issue

---

FIGURE 17.4 **SPSS 4.1 Crosstabs Command File for Radio Listening Survey**

```
GET FILE='LISTENING.SYSTEM'
CROSSTABS TABLES=WCCC_LIS BY DEMO/STATISTICS CHISQ.
```

---

procedure commands one at a time and see the results immediately. The Manager mode combines some of the features of batch and interactive modes. When *SPSS* is operating in the interactive mode, *pull-down menus* guide users through the possible commands and "smart help" screens make suggestions when problems are encountered. A *text editor* is included to create data, control, and command files. Entire series of procedure commands may be issued at once, as in the batch mode, but the results are immediately available on the screen, as in the interactive mode. There is no "best" way to use *SPSS* (though most will argue that the way *they* use it is "obviously" superior).

Before any data analysis is possible, *SPSS* must be told which file to analyze. In *SPSS* terminology, this is called defining the *active file*. This is accomplished by the GET FILE command shown in Figure 17.4. The command GET FILE is followed by an equals sign (=) and the name of the file to be called into memory. A GET FILE command must precede any procedure statement when a system file is being called into memory.

For batch and Manager mode jobs, the GET FILE command usually appears in the first line of the batch job and is followed by the other commands. Figure 17.4 is an example of a typical *SPSS* command file. In the interactive mode, the GET FILE command is issued and acknowledged by *SPSS*, then other commands are issued, one at a time. In the interactive and Manager modes, output is returned immediately to the screen and to another file called a *listing file*. The listing file is useful because it can be printed out after all the analyses are complete. Batch mode job output

is written only to a listing file that is defined somewhere in the command file.

Figure 17.4 shows the general structure of procedure commands. The command key word (for example, CROSSTABS) is followed by the first specification (TABLES=) separated by at least one space from the key word. Other specifications (for example, STATISTICS) are set apart by slashes. Procedure commands that are part of a command file (used in batch or Manager modes) may be indented or spaced in any way desired as long as the key words start in Column 1, specifications are separated by slashes, and the command ends with a period. Procedure commands issued in the interactive mode do not need to have the command key word in the first column, but should separate specifications by slashes and end commands with periods.

There is an important difference between commands written in the batch mode and those written in the interactive mode. This difference applies to the data definition commands mentioned earlier as well (for example, DATA LIST). The command key words of batch mode commands must begin in the first column of the line in which they appear. This is so the program can recognize where one command stops and another begins. If a command takes more than one line to write, which is often the case, other lines must be indented. To summarize, as a general rule, only command key words may appear in the first column if *SPSS* is being used in the batch mode.

Data Analysis. This section deals primarily with explaining the content of the command file shown in Figure 17.4 and showing the results of its execution. Data analysis is actually quite simple once the data are declared. It is not unusual for a procedure command to be only one line long, as is the case in Figure 17.4. SPSS offers a large number of analysis procedures, ranging from simple procedures such as CROSSTABS to more complex procedures such as FACTOR, the factor analysis command.

Other commonly used procedures are ANOVA, CORRELATIONS, FREQUENCIES, T-TEST, and REGRESSION. To keep the example simple, only CROSSTABS is used for illustration.

The command file in Figure 17.4 will produce a crosstabulation table to show the demographic characteristics of respondents who report listening to station WCCC. The command file accomplishes this in a relatively straightforward manner. First, the GET FILE command calls up the system file LISTENING.SYSTEM. On the next line the CROSSTABS key word is invoked. SPSS now knows that a crosstabulation procedure is desired. The next thing it needs is the variables involved in the analysis, which are provided by the TABLES specification followed by the two variable names. The analysis could stop here, but there is also an interest in determining whether a relationship exists between reported WCCC listening and demographic characteristics. This is accomplished by a STATISTICS specification.

The output for this procedure is shown in Figure 17.5. The top of the figure shows the names and variable labels for the two items included in the analysis. The numbers in each cell represent the number of respondents whose responses fit those categories. The numbers outside the right margin and below the lower margin of the table represent the number of responses and the percentage of total responses for each row and column. The chi-square results are located below the table. The chi-square statistic, its associated degrees of freedom, and its significance level are reported. The small significance level indicates that demographic characteristics are related to

WCCC listening habits in some manner. (Note that this analysis was chosen for its simplicity. These findings may or may not have practical significance.) The lowest expected frequency in any cell, as well as the number of cells with expected frequencies lower than 5, are also reported. These figures are useful for assessing the appropriateness of the chi-square procedure for a particular distribution. Since all the cells shown here have expected values greater than 5, this procedure appears to be acceptable. Finally, the number of missing cases is shown on the last line of the output.

The preceding is a simple example of an analysis procedure, but it is not too far removed from the most sophisticated procedures. All the commands are similar. For example, let us suppose we wanted a frequency distribution of our data. We would examine the manual and find that what we want is a procedure command called FREQUENCIES. We would then write the command "FREQUENCIES VARIABLES=AMT_NEW TO AMT_MUS." The wide variety of specifications available on most commands requires that researchers have a clear understanding of the procedure. Otherwise, it is easy to produce mountains of output that mean nothing.

SUMMARY

Because of the complex nature of computer technology, students in mass media research must continually pursue up-to-date materials to keep abreast of current developments. Much of the information discussed in this chapter will become obsolete shortly after it is written.

Like other areas of media research, computers may initially appear to be difficult or confounding. Once some exposure is gained, however, computers and their applications usually become less intimidating. This chapter discussed the various components of computers and how they work together to form a system. Learning the vocabulary related to computers

FIGURE 17.5   Crosstabs Produced by SPSS 4.1

```
WCCC_LIS  WCCC LISTENS  by  DEMO  DEMO GROUP

                 DEMO                              Page 1 of 1
          Count  |
                 |MALE 18- MALE 25- FEMALE 1 FEMALE 2
                 |24        34       8-24      5-34      Row
                 |     1 |      2 |      3 |      4 | Total
WCCC_LIS  -------+--------+--------+--------+--------+
               1 |    22 |    24 |    53 |    40 |   139
     YES         |       |       |       |       |  69.5
                 +--------+--------+--------+--------+
               2 |     3 |    14 |    13 |    31 |    61
     NO          |       |       |       |       |  30.5
                 +--------+--------+--------+--------+
          Column      25      38      66      71     200
          Total      12.5    19.0    33.0    35.5   100.0

    Chi-Square                Value          DF         Significance
----------------------     -----------      ----       ------------

Pearson                     14.19371          3            .00265
Likelihood Ratio            14.87619          3            .00193
Mantel-Haenszel test for     5.92421          1            .01493
     linear association

Minimum Expected Frequency -     7.625

Number of Missing Observations:   0
```

is necessary for media researchers to understand and use computers.

The final portion of the chapter described how to run an *SPSS* program. As indicated, readers should consult the appropriate *SPSS* user's manual for additional information because the discussion presented here was very brief. Knowledge of statistical software packages is best acquired through experience.

QUESTIONS AND PROBLEMS FOR FURTHER INVESTIGATION

1. Consult the following list of magazines for further information:
   PC World
   Personal Computing
   MacUser
   MacWorld
   Computerworld
   PC Computing
   PC Magazine

2. Use the data in Appendix 4 to run additional *SPSS* analyses.

3. When can computers hinder mass media research?

4. The following computer-related terms were *not* used in this chapter. Find the definition for each in a computer textbook or in periodicals.
   • BIOS
   • Bulletin boards (BBS)
   • Carpal tunnel syndrome
   • COBOL
   • Compiler
   • Computer virus
   • Dynamic data exchange (DDE)
   • Expansion slots
   • Flash memory
   • Icon
   • Multimedia PC

- Object Linking and Embedding (OLE)
- Soft boot

REFERENCES AND SUGGESTED READINGS

Asimov, I. (1984). *How did we find out about computers?* New York: Walker.

Burks, A. R. (1988). *The first electronic computer: The Atanasoff story*. Ann Arbor: University of Michigan Press.

Hedderson, J. (1991). *SPSS/PC+ made simple*. Belmont, CA: Wadsworth.

Lawlor, S. C. (1990). *Computer information systems*. New York: Harcourt Brace Jovanovich.

Ritchie, D. (1986). *The computer pioneers: The making of the modern computer*. New York: Simon & Schuster.

Shurkin, J. N. (1984). *Engines of the mind. A history of the computer*. New York: W. W. Norton.

Wimmer, R. D. (1995). A researcher's reliance on the computer. Denver: The Eagle Group. (Proprietary data).

18

RESEARCH REPORTS, ETHICS, AND FINANCIAL SUPPORT

Chapters 13–16 discussed mass media research from the planning stages of a study to the selection of the most appropriate statistical methods for testing purposes. Chapter 17 introduced the computer as a research tool. This chapter focuses on three other areas that are not part of the research process itself but are nevertheless vital to the execution of any research project: reporting, ethics, and financial support.

RESEARCH REPORTS

The first step in writing any research report is to identify the intended readers. This is an important decision because the organization, style, and even the mode of presentation depend on the target audience. In mass media research, there are typically two types of audiences and research reports:

1. Reports aimed at colleagues and intended for publication in scholarly and professional journals or for presentation at a convention.
2. Reports aimed at decision makers and intended for in-house use only.

The format, length, style, and organization of a published report must conform to the guidelines of the journal in which it appears. Since colleagues are the target audience for such reports and papers, writers must pay close attention to the theory underlying the research, the methods used, and the techniques of analysis. For the second group of readers, there is more flexibility. Some decision makers prefer to be briefed orally by the researcher. In such cases, a verbal presentation might be supplemented by written summary handouts, visual aids, and on request, a detailed report. In other circumstances, the researcher might prepare a written report with a short executive summary, confining most of the technical material to appendixes. No matter what the situation or audience, the primary goals in all research reports are accuracy and clarity.

THE NEED FOR ACCURATE REPORTING PROCEDURES

Researchers need to report research accurately for two reasons. First, a clear explanation of the investigator's methods provides an opportunity for readers to more completely understand the project. Researchers should keep in mind that most readers' knowledge of a given project is based solely on the information contained in the report. Since readers do not instinctively understand each procedure used in a study, these details must be supplied. Second, an accurate report provides the necessary information for those who wish to replicate the study. As Rummel (1970) suggested:

> In non-proprietary research, enough information must be included or stored somewhere to allow for replication of the study without the necessity of personal contact with the researcher. This is to ensure that a study is always replicable despite the decades or generations that may pass.

Rummel has even argued that researchers should be able to replicate a published study from the information contained therein. Realistically, however, this is not always possible. Mass media journals have limited space, and journal editors do not have the luxury of printing all raw data, tables, and graphs generated by a study; they are forced to eliminate some essential information. Therefore, Rummel's alternative—**data archives**—is very important. Unfortunately, the mass media field has yet to establish its own data archive service for researchers to use. Thus, individual researchers must take full responsibility for accurately reporting and storing their own research data. To facilitate this task, the following subsections describe the important elements of research that should be included in a published study. Some of the lists may appear to be long, but most of the information can be expressed in a few short sentences. At any rate, it is better to include too much information than too little.

THE MECHANICS OF WRITING A RESEARCH REPORT

Beginning researchers may find the writing style used for research reports awkward or cumbersome, but there is a definite purpose for the rules governing scientific writing: clarity. Every effort must be made to avoid ambiguity. Here are some suggestions, adapted from Saslow (1994), that are helpful in achieving clarity in a research report. First, don't assume that the audience has much prior knowledge about the topic. Research articles and reports are generally quite specialized, but a report written as though it were intended for *only* those readers with particular expertise will appeal to a limited readership. Researchers should make a distinct effort to make their writing accessible and understandable to all; overly technical language should be avoided. Second, remember that the audience may not have much time to ponder the intricacies of the research. Decision makers may have many reports to read; scholars may be reading the article as part of a lengthy literature review. In both cases it is necessary to present the rationale, methods,

and findings in a clear, coherent, and organized fashion. Finally, remember that readers may not grasp the implications of the report as readily as you do. As the person closest to the data, the researcher has the responsibility to integrate the research findings into a larger conceptual and social framework. Putting the results into a larger context is more helpful than simply reporting the findings.

Given the wide variety of approaches to research, it stands to reason that the approaches to writing a research report are equally varied. Most research reports, however, include only seven basic sections: abstract, introduction, literature review, methods, results, discussion, and references.

Abstract. An abstract is a short (100–150-word) summary of the key points of the research. Most readers scan the abstract to decide whether they want to read the rest of the article.

Introduction. The introduction should alert the reader to what is to follow. Most introductions usually contain the following information:

1. *Statement of the problem.* The first job of the report writer is to provide some information about the background and the nature of the problem under investigation. If the research topic has a long history, then a short summary is in order. This section should also discuss any relevant theoretical background that pertains to the research topic.

2. *Justification.* This section should address the question of why it is important for us to spend time and energy researching this particular problem. Research can be important because it deals with a crucial theoretical issue, because it has practical value, or because it has methodological value.

3. *Aims of the current study.* Most introductory sections conclude with an unequivocal statement of the hypothesis or research question to be answered by the study.

Literature Review. The second major section is the review of the literature. (In some formats, the literature review is incorporated into the introduction.) As the name suggests, the literature review section briefly recapitulates the work done in the field. The review need not be exhaustive; the writer should summarize only those studies most relevant to the current project. Accuracy and relevance are explained below:

1. *Accuracy.* A concise and accurate distillation of each study is a prerequisite for any literature review. The main points of each study—hypotheses that were tested, sample, method, findings, and implications—should be briefly summarized. The review should be selective but thorough.

2. *Relevance.* A literature review should be more than a rote recitation of research studies. It must also contain analysis and synthesis. The writer is obligated to discuss the relevance of the past work to the current study. What theoretic development can be seen in past work? What major conclusions have recurred? What were some common problems? How do the answers to these questions relate to the current study? The ultimate aim of the review is to show how your study evolved out of past efforts and how the prior research provides a justification for your study.

Methods. The methods section describes the approach used to confront the research problem. Topics that are usually mentioned in this section are as follows:

1. *Variables used in the analysis.* This includes a description of both independent and dependent variables, explaining how the variables were selected for the study, what marker variables (Chapter 3), if any, were included, and how extraneous variables were controlled. Each variable also requires some justification for its use—variables cannot be added without reason. The mean and the standard deviation for each variable should be reported when necessary.

2. *Sample size.* The researchers should state the number of subjects or units of study and also explain how these entities were selected. Additionally, any departure from normal randomization must be described in detail.

3. *Sample characteristics.* The sample should be described in terms of its demographic, lifestyle, or other characteristics. When human subjects are used, at least their age and sex should be indicated.

4. *Methodology.* Every research report requires a description of the methods used to collect and analyze data. The amount of methodological description to be included depends on the audience; articles written for journals, for instance, must contain more detailed information than reports prepared in private sector research.

5. *Data manipulation.* Often the collected data are not normally distributed, and researchers must use data transformation to achieve an approximation of normality. If such a procedure is used, a full explanation should be given.

Results. The results section presents the findings of the research. It typically contains the following:

1. *Description of the analysis.* The statistical techniques used to analyze the data should be mentioned. If the analysis used common or easily recognized statistics, a one-sentence description might be all that is needed, such as "Chi-square analyses were performed on the data," or "Analysis of variance was performed. . . ." If appropriate, the particular statistical program used by the researcher should be identified. Finally, this part should include an overview of what is to follow: "This section is divided into two parts. We will first report the results of the analysis of variance and then the results of the regression analysis."

2. *Description of findings.* The findings should be tied to the statement of the hypotheses or research questions mentioned in the introduction. The author should clearly state whether the results supported the hypotheses

or whether the research questions were answered. Next, any peripheral findings can be reported. Many researchers and journal editors suggest that interpretation and discussion of findings be omitted from this section and that the writer stick solely to the bare facts. Others believe that this section should contain more than numbers, suggesting the implications of the findings as well. In fact, for some short research articles, this section is sometimes called "Findings and Discussion." The choice of which model to follow depends upon the purpose of the report and the avenue of publication.

3. *Tables.* Tables, charts, graphs, and other data displays should be presented concisely and, if the article is being submitted to a journal, in the proper format. Remember that many readers turn first to the tables and may not read the accompanying text; consequently, tables should be explicit and easily understood by themselves. Visual materials for any research report can be easily produced with a variety of commercially available software packages. In combination with a color printer or plotter, the visual materials can be the predominant part of a research report, especially in reports for the private sector.

Discussion. The last section of a research report is the discussion. The contents of this section are highly variable, but the following elements are common:

1. *Summary.* A synopsis of the main findings of the study often leads off this section.

2. *Implications/discussion/interpretations.* This is the part of the report that discusses the meaning of the findings. If the findings are in line with current theory and research, the writer should include a statement of how they correspond with what was done in the past. If the findings contradict or do not support current theory, some explanation for the current pattern of results should be provided.

3. *Limitations.* The conclusions of the study should be tempered by a report of some of its constraints. Perhaps the sample was limited, or the response rate was low, or the experimental manipulation was not as clean as it could have been. In any case, the researcher should list some of the potential weaknesses of the research.

4. *Suggestions for future research.* In addition to answering questions, most research projects uncover new questions to be investigated. The suggestions for research should be relevant and practical.

References. The authors, article titles, sources, and publication dates of the research mentioned in the research report are contained in the references. Each academic journal has a particular style for listing references. Some journals prefer listing all the references at the end of the article, and others use a system of footnotes that appear throughout the article.

WRITING STYLE

Since the writing requirements for journal articles and business or government reports vary in several ways, the following guidelines are divided into two sections.

Scholarly Journals. There are nine principal guidelines for writing for scholarly journals:

1. Avoid using first person pronouns: *I, me, mine, we,* and so on. Research reports are almost always written in the third person ("Subjects were selected randomly," "Subject A told the researcher . . . ," and so on). First-person pronouns should be used only when the article is a commentary.

2. When submitting a paper for professional publication, place each table, graph, chart, and figure on a separate page. This is done because, if the article is accepted, these pages will be typeset by one department of the printing company and the text by another. (In management reports, tables, graphs, and other displays are included in the text unless they are too large, in which case they should be placed on separate pages.)

3. Read the authors' guidelines published by each journal. They provide specific rules concerning acceptable writing style, footnote and bibliography formats, number of copies to submit, and so forth. A researcher who fails to follow these guidelines may decrease the chance that his or her report will be accepted for publication—or at least substantially delay the process while alterations are made.

4. Be stylistically consistent with regard to tables, charts, graphs, section headings, and so forth. All tables, for example, should follow the same format and should be numbered consecutively.

5. Clearly label all displays with meaningful titles. Each table, graph, chart, or figure caption should accurately describe the material presented and its contribution to the report.

6. Keep language and descriptions as simple as possible by avoiding unnecessary and overly complex words, phrases, and terms. The goal of scientific writing is to explain findings clearly, simply, and accurately.

7. When possible, use the active rather than the passive voice. For example, "The researchers found that . . ." is preferable to "It was found by the researchers that . . ." Writing in the active voice makes reading more pleasant and also requires fewer words.

8. Proofread the manuscript carefully. Even researchers who are meticulous in their scientific approach can make errors in compiling a manuscript. All manuscripts, whether intended for publication or for management review, should be proofread several times to check for accuracy. It is not enough to run a computer spelling or grammatical check. There our many errors that spilling checkers will not ketch, as this sentence proves.

9. Miscellaneous considerations:
   a. Avoid phrases or references that could be interpreted as sexist or racist.
   b. Check all data for accuracy. Even one misplaced digit may affect the results of a study.

c. Use acceptable grammar; avoid slang.
d. Provide acknowledgments whenever another researcher's work is included in the report.
e. Include footnotes to indicate where further information or assistance can be obtained.

Business and Government Reports. Guidelines for writing a report for business or government decision makers include the following:

1. Provide an executive summary at the beginning of the report. Since decision makers may not read anything else in the report, great care must be taken in constructing this section. Here are three useful hints:
   a. Get right to the point and state conclusions quickly.
   b. Keep the language simple and concise. Do not use jargon, clichés, or overly technical terms.
   c. Be brief. Keep the summary to a page or two. Anything more ceases to be a summary.

2. Place detailed and complicated discussions of methods in a technical appendix. Summarize the procedures in the body of the report.

3. Use clearly defined and easily understood quantitative analysis techniques. Most decision makers are not familiar with complicated statistical procedures. Keep the basic analysis simple. If advanced statistical procedures must be used, explain in the body of the report what was done and what the results mean. Include another technical appendix that describes the statistical technique in detail.

4. Use graphs and charts wherever appropriate to make numerical findings more understandable and meaningful. Never let tabular material stand alone; to ensure that its importance is not overlooked, mention or explain each such item.

5. Decision makers like research that answers their questions. Put the conclusions

reached by the investigators and, if appropriate, recommendations for action, in the last section of the report.

RESEARCH ETHICS

Most mass media research involves observations of human beings—asking them questions or examining what they have done. In this probing process, however, the researcher must ensure that the rights of the participants are not violated. This requires a consideration of ethics: distinguishing right from wrong and proper from improper. Unfortunately, there are no universal definitions for these terms. Instead, several guidelines, broad generalizations, and suggestions have been endorsed or at least tacitly accepted by most in the research profession. These guidelines do not provide an answer to every ethical question that may arise, but they can help make researchers more sensitive to the issues.

Before discussing these specific guidelines, let's pose some hypothetical research situations involving ethics.

1. A researcher at a large university hands questionnaires to the students in an introductory mass media course and tells them that if they do not complete the forms, they will lose points toward their grade in the course.

2. A researcher is conducting a mail survey about attendance at X-rated motion pictures. The questionnaire states that responses will be anonymous. Unknown to the respondents, however, each return envelope is marked with a code that enables the researcher to identify the sender.

3. A researcher recruits subjects for an experiment by stating that participants will be asked to watch "a few scenes from some current movies." Those who decide to participate are shown several scenes of bloody and graphic violence.

4. A researcher shows one group of children a violent television show and another group a nonviolent program. After viewing, the

children are sent to a public playground, where they are told to play with the children who are already there. The researcher records each instance of violent behavior exhibited by the young subjects.

5. Subjects in an experiment are told to submit a sample of their newswriting to an executive of a large newspaper. They are led to believe that whoever submits the best work will be offered a job at the paper. In fact, the "executive" is a confederate in the experiment and severely criticizes everyone's work.

These examples of ethically flawed study designs should be kept in mind while reading the following guidelines to ethics in mass media research.

GENERAL ETHICAL PRINCIPLES

General ethical principles are difficult to construct in the research area. There are, however, at least four relevant principles. First is the principle of autonomy, or self-determination. Basic to this concept is the demand that the researcher respect the rights, values, and decisions of other people. The reasons for a person's action should be respected and the actions not interfered with. This principle is exemplified by the use of informed consent in the research procedure.

A second ethical principle important to social science research is nonmaleficence. In short, it is wrong to intentionally inflict harm on another. A third ethical principle—beneficence—is usually considered in tandem with nonmaleficence. Beneficence stipulates a positive obligation to remove existing harms and to confer benefits on others. These two principles operate together, and often the researcher must weigh the harmful risks of research against its possible benefits (for example, an increase in knowledge or a refinement of a theory).

A fourth ethical principle that is sometimes relevant to social science is the principle of justice. At its general level, this principle holds that people who are equal in relevant respects should be treated equally. In the research context, this principle should be applied when new programs or policies are being evaluated. The positive results of such research should be shared with all. It would be unethical, for example, to deny the benefit of a new teaching procedure to children because they were originally chosen to be in the control group rather than in the group that received the experimental procedure. Benefits should be shared with all who are qualified.

Although difficult to generalize, it is clear that mass media researchers must follow some set of rules to fulfill their ethical obligations to their subjects and respondents. Cook (1976), discussing the laboratory approach, offers one such code of behavior:

1. Do not involve people in research without their knowledge or consent.
2. Do not coerce people to participate.
3. Do not withhold from the participant the true nature of the research.
4. Do not actively lie to the participant about the nature of the research.
5. Do not lead the participant to commit acts that diminish his or her self-respect.
6. Do not violate the right to self-determination.
7. Do not expose the participant to physical or mental stress.
8. Do not invade the privacy of the participant.
9. Do not withhold benefits from participants in control groups.
10. Do not fail to treat research participants fairly and to show them consideration and respect.

To this list the authors add:

11. Always treat every respondent or subject with *unconditional human regard*. (That is, accept and respect a person for what he or she is, and do not criticize the person for what he or she is not.)

Are ethical principles transmitted from one generation of researchers to another? A study by McEuen, Gordon and Todd-Mancillas (1990) that examined Ph. D. programs in communication found that no program offered a graduate-level course devoted to the study of research ethics. About 70% of the programs, however, did offer one or more courses that were partly devoted to ethics instruction. Their survey also revealed that the four ethical issues that received the most attention were subjects' confidentiality, subjects' right of withdrawal, informed consent, and dealing with institutional review boards.

VOLUNTARY PARTICIPATION AND INFORMED CONSENT

An individual is entitled to decline to participate in any research project or to terminate participation at any time. Participation in an experiment, survey, or focus group is always voluntary, and any form of coercion is unacceptable. Researchers who are in a position of authority over subjects (as when the researcher handed questionnaires to the university students) should be especially sensitive to *implied* coercion: Even though the researcher might tell the class that failure to participate will not affect their grades, many students may not believe this. In such a situation, it would be advisable to keep the questionnaires anonymous and for the person in authority to be absent from the room while the survey is administered.

Voluntary participation is a less pressing ethical issue in mail and telephone surveys, since respondents are free to hang up the phone or to throw away the questionnaire. Nonetheless, a researcher should not attempt to induce subjects to participate by misrepresenting the organization sponsoring the research or by exaggerating its purpose or importance. For example, phone interviewers should not be instructed to identify themselves as representatives of the "Department of Information" to mislead people into thinking the survey is government-sponsored. Likewise, mail questionnaires should not be constructed to mimic census forms, tax returns, social

How Informed Is Informed Consent?

For subjects to be sufficiently informed to give their consent, they have to understand what it is they are consenting to. Usually, researchers accomplish this task by asking each research participant to sign a consent form, one that typically has been approved by the institution's review board. As most researchers can attest, these forms tend to be long and contain complicated language that is included to fulfill federal guidelines. Some researchers have expressed doubts that their research subjects receive much information from the consent forms about the risks involved or their legal rights.

A study by Mann (1994) suggests that some of these concerns are well founded. She gave two versions of a consent form to 83 undergraduates to read and sign before participating in an experiment. One version was the standard long form that had been used before in studies of this type. The second was a short form constructed by removing redundancy and detail from the long form. Both forms were matched for readability and graphic appearance. The students were then asked questions about the contents of the forms they had just read. The results indicated that the short form was more effective at conveying specific information about the upcoming experiment, while the short and long forms performed about equally in conveying general information about the students' rights as research participants. This suggests that federal regulations that add more and more information to these forms might actually impede understanding. In addition, no matter what form was used, many of the subjects did not understand important aspects of the study. More than half could not name the risks associated with the experiment; about 40% were unable to report what they could do if they had a complaint about the study. This study raises the question of whether the informed consent that subjects provided was actually valid.

security questionnaires, or other official government forms.

Closely related to voluntary participation is the notion of *informed consent*. For people to volunteer for a research project, they need to know enough about the project to make an intelligent choice. Researchers have the responsibility to inform potential subjects or respondents of all features of the project that can reasonably be expected to influence participation. Respondents should understand that an interview may take as long as 45 minutes, that a second interview is required, or that after completing a mail questionnaire they may be singled out for a telephone interview.

In an experiment, informed consent means that potential subjects must be warned of any possible discomfort or unpleasantness that

might be involved. Subjects should be told if they are to receive or administer electric shocks, be subjected to unpleasant audio or visual stimuli, or undergo any procedure that may cause concern. Any unusual measurement techniques that may be used also must be described. Researchers have an obligation to answer candidly and truthfully, as far as possible, all the participants' questions about the research.

Experiments that involve deception (as described in the following subsection) cause special problems with regard to obtaining informed consent. If deception is absolutely necessary to conduct an experiment, is the experimenter obligated to inform subjects that they may be deceived during the upcoming experiment? Will such a disclosure affect participation in the experiment? Will it also affect the experimental results? Should the researcher compromise by telling all potential subjects that deception will be involved for some participants but not for others?

A second problem is deciding exactly how much information about a research project must be disclosed in seeking to achieve informed consent. Is it enough to explain that the experiment involves rating commercials, or is it necessary to add that the experiment is designed to test whether subjects with high IQs prefer different commercials from those with low IQs? Obviously, in some situations the researcher cannot reveal everything about the project for fear of contaminating the results. For example, if the goal of the research is to examine the influence of peer pressure on commercial evaluations, alerting the subjects to this facet of the investigation might change their behavior in the experiment.

Problems might occur in research examining the impact of mass media in nonliterate communities—for example, if the research subjects did not comprehend what they were told regarding the proposed investigation. Even in literate societies, many people fail to understand the implications for confidentiality of the storage of survey data on computer disks or tape. Moreover, an investigator might not have realized in advance that some subjects would find part of an experiment or survey emotionally disturbing.

In 1992, the American Psychological Association (APA) released its statement on "Ethical Principles of Psychologists and Code of Conduct," which addresses a wide range of ethical issues of relevance to that discipline. Since many of the ethical issues faced by psychologists are also faced by mass communication researchers, it seems useful to quote from that document several provisions with regard to informed consent. Researchers should:

- Use language understandable to participants to obtain consent.

- Tell participants they can withdraw from the research.
- Inform participants of the important things that might affect their decision (such as discomfort and loss of confidentiality.)
- If participation in a research project is a course requirement or opportunity for extra credit, students should be given a choice of alternate activities.
- Prior consent must be obtained if participants will be filmed, taped, or recorded in any form unless the research involves natural observation in public places.

Research findings provide some indication of what research participants should be told in order to ensure informed consent. Epstein, Suedefeld, and Silverstein (1973) found that subjects wanted a general description of the experiment and what was expected of them; they wanted to know whether danger was involved, how long the experiment would last, and the experiment's purpose. As for informed consent and survey participation, Sobal (1984) found wide variation among researchers about what to tell respondents in the survey introduction. Almost all introductions identified the research organization and the interviewer by name and described the research topic. Less frequently mentioned in introductions were the sponsor of the research and guarantees of confidentiality or anonymity. Few survey introductions mentioned the length of the survey or that participation was voluntary. More recently, Greenberg and Garramone (1989) reported the results of a survey of 201 mass media researchers that disclosed that 96% usually provided guaranteed confidentiality of results, 92% usually named the sponsoring organization, 66% usually told respondents that participation is voluntary, and 61% usually disclosed the length of the questionnaire.

Finally, one must consider the form of the consent to be obtained. Written consent is a requirement in certain government-sponsored research programs and may also be required by many university research review committees, as discussed next in connection with guidelines promulgated by the federal government. In several generally recognized situations, however, signed forms are regarded as impractical. These include telephone surveys, mail surveys, personal interviews, and cases in which the signed form itself might represent an occasion for breach of confidentiality. For example, a respondent who has been promised anonymity as an inducement to participate in a face-to-face interview might be suspicious if asked to sign a consent form after the interview. In these circumstances, the fact that the respondent agreed to participate is taken as implied consent.

CONCEALMENT AND DECEPTION

Concealment and deception techniques are encountered most frequently in experimental research. *Concealment* is the withholding of certain information from the subjects; *deception* is deliberately providing false information. Both practices raise ethical problems. The difficulty in obtaining consent has already been mentioned. A second problem derives from the general feeling that it is wrong for experimenters to lie to or otherwise deceive subjects.

Many critics argue that deception transforms a subject from a human being into a manipulated object and is therefore demeaning to the participant. Moreover, once subjects have been deceived, they are likely to expect to be deceived again in other research projects. At least two research studies seem to suggest that this concern is valid. Stricker and Messick (1967) reported finding a high incidence of suspicion among subjects of high school age after having been deceived. Fillenbaum (1966) found that about one-third to one-half of subjects were suspicious at the beginning of an experiment after experiencing deception in a prior research project.

On the other hand, some researchers argue that certain studies could not be conducted at all without the use of deception. They claim that the harm done to those who are deceived is outweighed by the benefits of the research to scientific knowledge. Indeed, Christensen (1988) suggests that it may be immoral to fail to investigate important areas that cannot be investigated without the use of deception. He also argues that much of the sentiment against deception in research exists because deception has been analyzed only from the viewpoint of abstract moral philosophy. The subjects who were "deceived" in many experiments did not perceive what was done to them as deception but viewed it as a necessary element in the research procedure. Christensen suggests that any decision regarding the use of deception should take into account the context and aim of the deception. Research suggests that subjects are most disturbed when deception violates their privacy or increases their risk of harm.

Obviously, deception is not a technique that should be used indiscriminately. Kelman (1967) suggested that before the investigator settles on deception as an experimental tactic, three questions should be examined:

1. How significant is the proposed study?
2. Are alternative procedures available that would provide the same information?
3. How severe is the deception? (It is one thing to tell subjects that the experimentally constructed message they are reading was taken from the *New York Times*; it is another to report that the test a subject has just completed was designed to measure latent suicidal tendencies.)

Another set of criteria was put forth by Elms (1982), who suggested five necessary and sufficient conditions under which deception can be considered ethically justified in social science research:

1. When there is no other feasible way to obtain the desired information

Dangers of Deception

The use of deception in an experiment can have practical as well as ethical consequences. A well-known story in social science research concerns an experiment done with the cooperation of a convenience store owner. A confederate of the experimenter would enter the convenience store along with an unsuspecting subject. When the proprietor went into a back room, the confederate, in full view of the subject, stole several cartons of cigarettes and walked out of the store. If the subject made no attempt to call the proprietor, a second confederate then entered the store and said, "I was outside and I saw that guy steal those cigarettes. Didn't you see him?" One subject, obviously disturbed, answered no and rushed out of the store before anybody could explain what was happening. A few minutes later police arrived and arrested the first confederate, who was hanging around outside the store waiting for another unsuspecting subject. It seems the subject who had rushed out the door had called the police and reported the crime. The experiment had to be halted while everyone explained to a judge what was going on.

2. When the likely benefits substantially outweigh the likely harm
3. When subjects are given the option to withdraw at any time without penalty
4. When any physical or psychological harm to subjects is temporary
5. When subjects are debriefed about all substantial deception and the research procedures are made available for public review

Together the suggestions of Kelman and Elms offer researchers good advice for the planning stages of investigations.

When an experiment is concluded, especially one involving concealment or deception, it is the responsibility of the investigator to debrief subjects. Debriefing should be thorough enough to remove any lasting effects that might have been created by the experimental manipulation or by any other aspect of the experiment. Subjects' questions should be answered and the potential value of the experiment stressed. How common is debriefing among mass media researchers? In the survey cited in Greenberg and Garramone (1989), 71% of the researchers reported they usually debrief subjects, 19% debrief sometimes, and 10% rarely or never debrief subjects. Although an ethical requirement of most experiments, the practice of debriefing has yet to be embraced by all investigators.

The APA's 1992 statement of principles contains the following provisions concerning deception:

- Deception should not be used unless it is justified by the study's scientific value and other nondeceptive techniques are not feasible.
- Subjects should never be deceived about factors that might have an impact on their informed consent.
- If deception is used, subjects should be debriefed as promptly as possible.

There are no data available on how often deception is used in mass media research. Some information, however, is available from the psychology field. In a study of 23 years of articles published in a leading psychology journal, Sieber (1995) found that 66% of all studies published in 1969 employed deception compared to 47% in 1992. Since a good deal of psychological research utilizes the experimental approach (see Chapter 9), a strategy not used nearly as often in mass communication research, the comparable percentages for media research would probably be significantly lower.

PROTECTION OF PRIVACY

The problem of protecting the privacy of participants usually occurs more often in survey research than in laboratory studies. Subjects have a right to know whether their privacy will be maintained and who will have access to the information they provide. There are two ways to guarantee privacy: by assuring anonymity and by assuring confidentiality. A promise of *anonymity* is a guarantee that a given respondent cannot possibly be linked to any particular response. In many research projects, anonymity is an advantage, since it encourages respondents to be honest and candid in their answers. Strictly speaking, personal and telephone interviews cannot be anonymous because the researcher can link a given questionnaire to a specific person, household, or telephone number. In such instances, the researcher should promise *confidentiality*; that is, the respondents should be assured that even though they can be identified as individuals, their names will never be publicly associated with the information they provide. A researcher should never use "anonymous" in a way that is or seems to be synonymous with "confidential."

Additionally, respondents should be told who *will* have access to the information they provide. The researcher's responsibility for assuring confidentiality does not end once the data have been analyzed and the study concluded. Questionnaires that identify persons by name should not be stored in public places, nor should other researchers be given permission to examine confidential data unless all identifying marks have been obliterated. The APA's statement does not contain much guidance on issues of privacy and confidentiality. It does say that researchers should inform subjects if they are planning to share or use further data that are personally identifiable.

FEDERAL REGULATIONS CONCERNING RESEARCH

In 1971 the Department of Health, Education, and Welfare (HEW) drafted rules for obtaining informed consent from research participants, which included full documentation of informed consent procedures. In addition, the government set up a system of institutional review boards (IRBs) to safeguard the rights of human subjects. In 1995 there were more than 700 IRBs at medical schools, colleges, universities, hospitals, and other institutions. At most universities, IRBs have become part of the permanent bureaucracy. They hold regular meetings and have developed standardized forms that must accompany research proposals that involve human subjects or respondents.

In 1981 the Department of Health and Human Services (successor to HEW) softened its regulations concerning social science research. The Department's Policy for the Protection of Human Research Subjects exempted studies using existing public data, research in educational settings about new instructional techniques, research involving the use of anonymous education tests, and survey, interview, and observational research in public places, provided the subjects are not identified and sensitive information is not collected. Signed consent forms were deemed unnecessary if the research presented only a minimal risk of harm to subjects and involved no procedures for which written consent was required outside the research context. This meant that signed consent forms were no longer necessary in the interview situation, because a person did not usually seek written consent before asking a question.

Although the new guidelines apparently exempt most nonexperimental social science research from federal regulation, IRBs at some

Implications of Pledging Confidentiality

Researchers who tell respondents that the information they provide will be held confidential need to understand the consequences of that statement. Consider the case of Rik Scarce, a sociologist who specializes in ethnographic research (see Chapter 9).

In the early 1990s, Scarce's research interest was the sociology of the radical environmentalist movement. One of the people Scarce interviewed at length was a suspect in a 1992 bombing at a mink research facility at Michigan State University. When a federal grand jury learned that Scarce had spoken with the suspect, the researcher was summoned and asked to reveal the content of his talks with the suspect. Scarce refused, citing a portion of the ethics code of the American Sociological Association, which requires that scholars maintain confidentiality even if the information they have gathered "enjoys no legal protection or privilege and legal force is applied." He was then cited for contempt and placed in jail. He maintained his pledge of confidentiality for 159 days while being held in a Washington state prison. Eventually, the judge relented and released him.

institutions still review all research proposals that involve human subjects, and some IRBs still follow the old HEW standards. In fact, some IRB regulations are even more stringent than the federal guidelines. As a practical matter, a researcher should always build a little more time into the research schedule to accommodate IRB procedures.

ETHICS IN DATA ANALYSIS AND REPORTING

Researchers are also responsible for maintaining professional standards in analyzing and reporting their data. The ethical guidelines in this area are less controversial and more clearcut. One cardinal rule is that researchers have a moral and ethical obligation to refrain from tampering with data: Questionnaire responses and experimental observations may not be fabricated, altered, or discarded. Similarly, researchers are expected to exercise reasonable care in processing the data to guard against needless errors that might affect the results.

Another universal ethical principle is that authors should not plagiarize. The work of someone else should not be reproduced with-

out proper credit to the original author. Somewhat relatedly, only those individuals who contribute significantly to a research project should be given authorship credit. This last statement addresses the problem of piggybacking, when a subordinate is pressured by someone in authority to include the superior's name on a manuscript even though the superior had little input into the finished product. The definition of a "significant contribution" might be fuzzy at times; generally, however, to be listed as an author, a person should play a major role in the conceptualizing, analysis, or writing of the final document.

Researchers should never conceal information that might influence the interpretation of their findings. For example, if 2 weeks elapsed between the testing of an experimental group and the testing of a control group, this delay should be reported so that other researchers can discount the effects of history and maturation on the results. Every research report should contain a full and complete description of method, particularly of any departure from standard procedures.

Since science is a public activity, researchers have an ethical obligation to share their

---

American Association for Public Opinion Research
Code of Professional Ethics and Practices

I. Principles of Professional Practice in the Conduct of our Work
   A. We shall exercise due care in gathering and processing data, taking all reasonable steps to assure the accuracy of results.
   B. We shall exercise due care in the development of research designs and in the analysis of data.
      1. We shall recommend and employ only research tools and methods of analysis which, in our professional judgment, are well suited to the research problem at hand.
      2. We shall not select research tools and methods of analysis because of their capacity to yield a misleading conclusion.
      3. We shall not knowingly make interpretations of research results, nor shall we tacitly permit interpretations, which are inconsistent with the data available.
      4. We shall not knowingly imply that interpretations should be accorded greater confidence than the data actually warrant.
   C. We shall describe our findings and methods accurately and in appropriate detail in all research reports.
II. Principles of Professional Responsibility in Our Dealings with People
   A. The Public
      1. We shall cooperate with legally authorized representatives of the public by describing the methods used in our studies.
      2. When we become aware of the appearance in public of serious distortions of our research we shall publicly disclose what is required to correct the distortions.

---

findings and methods with other researchers. All questionnaires, experimental materials, measurement instruments, instructions to subjects, and other relevant items should be made available to those who wish to examine them.

Finally, all investigators are under an ethical obligation to draw conclusions from their data that are consistent with those data. Interpretations should not be stretched or distorted to fit a personal point of view or a favorite theory, or to gain or maintain a client's favor. Nor should researchers attribute greater significance or credibility to their data than the data justify. For example, when analyzing correlation coefficients obtained from a large sample, it is possible to achieve statistical significance with an r of only, for example, .10. It would be

perfectly acceptable to report a statistically significant result in this case, but the investigator should also mention that the predictive utility of the correlation was not large, and specifically, that it explained only 1% of the total variation. In short, researchers should report results with candor and honesty.

ETHICS IN THE PUBLICATION PROCESS

Publishing the results of research in scholarly journals is an important part of the process of scientific inquiry. Science is a public activity, and publication is the most efficient way to share research knowledge. In addition, success in the academic profession is often tied to a

B. Clients and Sponsors
  1. When undertaking work for a private client we shall hold confidential all proprietary information obtained about the client's business affairs and about the findings of research conducted for the client, except when the dissemination of the information is expressly authorized by the client or becomes necessary under terms of Section II-A-2.
  2. We shall be mindful of the limitations of our techniques and facilities and shall accept only those research assignments which can be accomplished within these limitations.
C. The Profession
  1. We shall not cite our membership in the Association as evidence of professional competence, since the Association does not so certify any persons or organizations.
  2. We recognize our responsibility to contribute to the science of public opinion research and to disseminate as freely as possible the ideas and findings which emerge from our research.
D. The Respondent
  1. We shall not lie to survey respondents or use practices and methods which abuse, coerce, or humiliate them.
  2. Unless the respondent waives confidentiality for specified uses, we shall hold as privileged and confidential all information that tends to identify a respondent with his or her responses. We shall also not disclose the names of respondents for nonresearch purposes.

Reprinted by permission of the American Association for Public Opinion Research.

successful publication record. Consequently, certain ethical guidelines are usually followed with regard to publication procedures. From the perspective of the researcher seeking to submit an article for publication, the first ethical guideline comes into play when the article is ready to be sent off for review. The researcher should submit the proposed article to only one journal at a time because simultaneous submission of the report to several sources is inefficient and wasteful. When an article is submitted for review to an academic journal, it is usually sent to two or three (or more) reviewers for evaluation. Simultaneous submission means that several sets of referees spend their time pointing out the same problems and difficulties that could have been reported by a single set. This duplication of effort is unnecessary and might delay consideration of other potential articles waiting for review.

A related ethical problem concerns attempts to publish nearly identical or highly similar articles based on the same data set. For example, suppose a researcher has data concerning the communication patterns in a large organization. The investigator writes up one article emphasizing the communication angle for a communication journal and a second article with a management slant for a business journal. Both articles draw upon the same database and contain comparable results. Is this practice ethical? This is not an easy question to answer. Some journal editors apparently do not approve of writing multiple papers from the same data; others suggest that this practice is acceptable, provided submissions are made to journals that have no overlapping audiences. In addition, there is also the sticky question of how different one manuscript has to be from another in order to be considered a separate entity. Campbell (1987) discusses these and other vexing issues.

On the other side of the coin, journal editors and reviewers also have ethical obligations to those who submit manuscripts to be evaluated. Editors and reviewers should not let the decision process take an inordinate amount of time; a prompt and timely decision is owed to all contributors. (Most editors of mass communication journals try to notify their contributors of their decision within 3 months.) Reviewers should try to provide positive and helpful reviews; they should not do "hatchet jobs" on articles submitted to them. Moreover, reviewers should not unjustly squelch manuscripts that argue against one of their pet ideas or contradict or challenge some of their own research. Each contributor to a journal is due an objective and impartial review. Neither should reviewers quibble needlessly over minor points in an article or demand unreasonable changes. Reviewers also owe contributors consistency. Authors find it frustrating to revise their manuscripts according to a reviewer's wishes only to find that, on a second reading, the reviewer has a change of mind and prefers the original version.

A PROFESSIONAL CODE OF ETHICS

Formalized codes of ethics have yet to be developed by all professional associations involved in mass media research. One organization that has developed a code (shown in the box on pages 412–413) is the American Association for Public Opinion Research.

THE RIGHTS OF STUDENTS AS RESEARCH PARTICIPANTS

Much of the data in social research is provided by college students. In psychology, for example, more than 70% of studies use students (Korn, 1988). In fact, it is the rare liberal arts major who has not participated in (or had a request to participate in) social science research. The ethical dimensions of this situation have not been overlooked. Korn (1988) suggests a "bill of rights" for students who agree to be research subjects:

1. Participants should know the general purpose of the study and what they will be expected to do. Beyond this, they should be told everything a reasonable person would want to know in order to participate.
2. Participants have the right to withdraw from a study at any time after beginning participation in the research.
3. Participants should expect to receive benefits that outweigh the costs or risks involved. To achieve the educational benefit, participants have the right to ask questions and to receive clear, honest answers. If they don't receive what was promised, they have the right to remove their data from the study.
4. Participants have the right to expect that anything done or said during their participation in a study will remain anonymous or confidential, unless they specifically agree to give up this right.
5. Participants have the right to decline to participate in any study and may not be coerced into research. When learning about research is a course requirement, an equivalent alternative to participation should be available.
6. Participants have the right to know when they have been deceived in a study and why the deception was used. If the deception seems unreasonable, participants have the right to withhold their data.
7. When any of these rights is violated or participants have objections about a study, they have the right and responsibility to inform the appropriate university officials.

FINDING SUPPORT FOR MASS MEDIA RESEARCH

Research costs money. Finding a source of research funds is a problem that confronts both quantitative and qualitative researchers in all fields of mass media. This section cites some organizations that have supported mass media research projects. A researcher in need of funding should contact these organizations for details about the types of studies they support and the amount of funds available, as well as instructions for preparing research proposals.

University or college researchers should determine whether their institution has a program of research grants for individual faculty members. Many colleges award such grants, often on a competitive basis, for research in mass media. Typically these grants are modest in size—usually under $5,000—but they are among the easiest to apply for and to administer. In many cases, grants are available for student research as well.

Several philanthropic foundations sponsor mass media research. Among the better known are the Ford Foundation, the John and Mary Markle Foundation, the Kellogg Foundation, and the Alfred P. Sloan Foundation. The amounts these organizations give to support research range from about $5,000 to as much as $150,000. Competition is stiff, and the researcher should be certain that his or her research area is one for which these foundations provide funding. As an alternative, there may be smaller foundations located near the researcher's base of operations that could be investigated.

Certain departments of the federal government sponsor mass media research. Among the agencies that have been active in supporting media research are the National Institute of Mental Health, the National Science Foundation, and the National Endowment for the Humanities. Other funding agencies can be identified by looking through the *Federal Grant Register*. Applying for a government grant tends to be complicated, and there are many guidelines and regulations. In addition, there is the usual problem of government red tape. Nonetheless, these agencies have been known to make sizable grants to investigators. The availability of these grants, however, is tied to the political situation. Should Congress be in a cost-cutting mood, as it has been in the mid-

1990s, the research budgets of these organizations are likely to be reduced.

Many professional media associations sponsor continuing programs to support research relevant to their particular field. In radio and television, the National Association of Broadcasters awards annual grants for research in broadcasting. The competition is keen: Approximately half a dozen grants of $5,000 are made each year to professors and students interested in broadcasting research. The Dowden Center for Telecommunication Studies at the University of Georgia offers awards to support dissertation research on cable TV and other new electronic media. In the print media, ANPA sponsors research on readership and circulation. The Gannett Foundation also provides research funding, and the Magazine Publishers Association (MPA) sponsors magazine-related research.

The American Academy of Advertising sponsors an annual competition to award a $1,500 grant to a new faculty member (one who has been teaching less than 5 years) to conduct research studies in the field of advertising. The American Association of Advertising Agencies has also funded research projects. Similarly, the Foundation for Research in Education and Public Relations has a program of small grants ($1,000–$3,000) to support research in public relations.

Many researchers have financed their research by working with the media industry. The four major television networks have research departments that are willing to examine proposals from outside investigators that might be of interest to them. Occasionally, they will even sponsor a research program themselves. The American Broadcasting Company in the mid-1970s funded five research projects submitted by academic researchers, providing $20,000 for each. The Columbia Broadcasting System sponsored a lengthy audience survey conducted among British youngsters. In the mid-1990s both the broadcasting industry and the cable industry funded elaborate content analyses that examined violence on television. In addition, the larger group owners in broadcasting have research departments that might be approached. The Corporation for Public Broadcasting, for example, has sponsored several audience studies relating to their programs. Similarly, large newspaper chains are potential funding sources. In the public relations field, many researchers have obtained support by contacting the professional organization of the industry they are studying or by working with a private company or corporation.

Industry support can be a mixed blessing. On the one hand, working with industry backing makes it easier for a researcher to enlist the cooperation of people or organizations within that industry and also facilitates obtaining data about the inner workings of the industry. On the other hand, many media industries are interested in limited research areas that may not have much theoretical attraction for the researcher. A company may specify the focus of the study and the variables to be examined. Therefore, when approaching a media organization or any other private company for support, it is wise to determine in advance what control, if any, the private organization will have over the design, execution, and subsequent publicizing of the project.

Finally, most colleges and universities have an Office of Contracts and Grants (or some similar title) that can be of great help to researchers. In addition to helping the researcher meet the bureaucratic requirements for a grant application, this office can offer valuable assistance in other areas. For example, this office might offer computerized searches of sponsoring agencies, information about current grants, budget advice, preparation of abstracts, and even word processing services. Researchers in the academic setting should take advantage of this resource.

Summary

Writing a research report is naturally an important step in the scientific process, since the re-

port places the research study in the public domain for consideration and confirmation. Beginning researchers generally find the process much easier after they have completed one or two studies. A key to successful writing is to follow the guidelines developed by journal editors or styles developed by individual companies or businesses. The same basic seven-section format is used for all reports.

Ethical considerations in conducting research should not be overlooked. Nearly every research study could affect subjects in some way, either psychologically or physically. Researchers dealing with human subjects must ensure that all precautions are taken to preclude any potential harm to subjects. This includes carefully planning a study and debriefing subjects upon completion of a project.

The final part of this chapter described financing research projects. This topic is relevant to all researchers because lack of funds often cancels good research projects. The chapter described a variety of sources that provide financial assistance; none should be overlooked.

Questions and Problems for Further Investigation

1. Read an article in a recent academic journal of mass media research. See how well the authors follow the reporting guidelines discussed in this chapter.

2. Using the five examples on page 404, suggest alternative ways of conducting a study that would be ethically acceptable.

3. In your opinion, what types of media research are unfair to respondents? What types of studies would encroach on the guidelines discussed in this chapter?

4. In your opinion, is it wrong for researchers to give respondents the impression that they are being recruited for a particular study when the researchers actually have another purpose in mind? What are the limits?

REFERENCES AND SUGGESTED READINGS

Beauchamp, T., Faden, R., Wallace, R. J., & Walters, L. (Eds.). (1982). *Ethical issues in social science research.* Baltimore: Johns Hopkins University Press.

Bower, R., & deGasparis, P. (1978). *Ethics in social research.* New York: Praeger.

Campbell, D. J. (1987). Ethical issues in the publication process. In S. L. Payne & B. H. Charnov (Eds.), *Ethical problems for academic professionals.* Springfield, IL: Charles C. Thomas.

Christensen, L. (1988). Deception in psychological research. *Personality and Social Psychology Bulletin, 14*(4), 664–675.

Cook, S. (1976). Ethical issues in the conduct of research in social relations. In C. Sellitz, L. Wrightsman, & S. Cook (Eds.), *Research methods in social relations.* New York: Holt, Rinehart & Winston.

Elmes, D. G., Kantowitz, B. H., & Roediger, H. L. (1992). *Research methods in psychology.* New York: West Publishing.

Elms, A. (1982). Keeping deception honest. In T. Beauchamp, R. Faden, R. J. Wallace, & L. Walters (Eds.), *Ethical issues in social science research.* Baltimore: Johns Hopkins University Press.

Epstein, Y., Suedefeld, P., & Silverstein, S. (1973). The experimental contract. *American Psychologist, 28,* 212–221.

Fillenbaum, S. (1966). Prior deception and subsequent experimental performance. *Journal of Personality and Social Psychology, 4,* 532–537.

Greenberg, B. S., & Garramone, G. M. (1989). Ethical issues in mass communication research. In G. H. Stempel & B. H. Westley (Eds.), *Research methods in mass communication* (2nd ed.). Englewood Cliffs, NJ: Prentice-Hall.

Kelman, H. (1967). Human use of human subjects: The problem of deception in social psychological experiments. *Psychological Bulletin, 67,* 111.

Kelman, H. (1982). Ethical issues in different social science methods. In T. Beauchamp, R. Faden, R. J. Wallace, & L. Walters (Eds.), *Ethical issues in social science research.* Baltimore: Johns Hopkins University Press.

Korn, J. H. (1988). Students' roles, rights, and responsibilities as research participants. *Teaching of Psychology, 15*(2), 74–78.

Mann, T. (1994). Informed consent for psychological research. *Psychological Science, 5*(3), 140–143.

McEuen, V., Gordon, R., & Todd-Mancillas, W. (1990). A survey of doctoral education in communication research ethics. *Communication Quarterly, 38*(3), 281–290.

Rubin, R. B., Rubin, A. M., & Piele, L. J. (1990). *Communication research: Strategies and sources* (2nd ed.). Belmont, CA: Wadsworth.

Rummel, R. J. (1970). *Applied factor analysis.* Evanston, IL: Northwestern University Press.

Saslow, C. (1994). *Basic research methods.* New York: McGraw-Hill.

Sieber, J. (1992). *Planning ethically responsible research.* Newbury Park, CA: Sage.

Sieber, J. (1995). Deception methods in psychology. *Ethics & Behavior, 5*(1), 67–85.

Sobal, J. (1984). The content of survey introductions and the provision of informed consent. *Public Opinion Quarterly, 48*(4), 788–793.

Stricker, L., & Messick, J. (1967). The true deceiver. *Psychological Bulletin, 68,* 1320.

APPENDIXES

Appendix

1

TABLES

TABLE 1   Random Numbers

```
0 8 9 5 6 4 4 8 9 4 0 7 5 9 7 0 4 5 3 1 2 7 8 6 6
8 2 4 4 8 8 0 2 6 5 5 0 3 5 9 1 3 8 6 8 8 3 1 8 5
3 1 2 3 7 6 4 1 1 4 3 5 2 7 4 9 3 2 7 5 5 4 7 6 2
2 3 8 1 8 6 6 1 0 8 4 1 0 5 0 4 8 5 3 7 8 7 6 5 7
0 0 4 3 6 5 5 2 3 5 2 4 3 3 9 3 2 5 2 0 8 4 6 2 1
1 2 8 9 7 5 8 9 7 8 6 7 4 0 4 0 4 9 7 8 5 0 2 9 8
9 8 4 6 9 9 0 8 0 2 3 2 8 0 5 4 5 0 6 7 6 2 3 9 8
0 7 3 6 9 5 1 6 3 8 0 5 9 0 0 2 0 9 3 6 8 8 2 4 3
2 2 3 9 5 7 9 4 0 6 7 3 6 9 6 4 1 7 3 6 5 1 8 2 6
4 9 5 6 9 3 1 4 7 8 1 5 6 7 2 2 4 6 3 6 5 4 2 1 2
4 0 6 6 8 5 4 3 7 8 3 2 6 8 1 2 2 7 0 6 5 3 5 8 4
6 3 3 2 0 3 9 7 0 2 3 6 9 5 3 4 1 6 1 8 3 9 4 3 3
0 6 1 8 4 2 1 8 6 7 5 4 1 9 0 3 2 4 1 5 7 7 4 0 8
2 2 4 2 9 6 8 5 8 2 6 1 0 7 6 1 7 9 2 0 9 2 8 7 8
8 3 2 3 0 7 4 3 5 8 9 0 8 0 5 8 8 7 1 3 6 0 1 3 9
2 3 1 8 2 3 1 0 9 0 0 8 9 1 2 0 3 7 0 2 0 1 8 1 7
0 8 7 3 4 4 5 1 8 7 4 5 1 9 9 0 3 2 2 3 1 2 6 4 6
5 8 5 6 7 6 1 0 1 6 7 0 2 1 9 1 6 3 2 0 1 1 5 5 9
6 1 1 0 5 1 3 6 7 7 7 8 2 4 5 9 3 0 7 6 7 9 1 1 6
5 3 6 1 2 7 2 6 2 7 3 3 6 8 2 6 5 5 8 4 2 4 2 1 8
8 7 3 9 5 1 1 8 4 1 8 5 6 6 0 6 9 2 2 6 8 2 5 8 5
2 9 1 9 9 5 6 1 8 6 6 4 0 5 0 0 8 8 2 5 9 2 0 1 2
8 1 0 2 1 7 2 0 2 7 6 8 4 8 0 2 6 2 8 0 8 3 6 0 7
9 7 1 5 5 7 4 6 1 5 6 5 9 9 2 2 7 1 2 7 0 0 5 0 9
6 3 7 9 8 8 7 4 9 5 0 3 3 0 3 7 0 7 5 8 1 2 8 3 1
9 4 2 2 1 3 2 0 5 6 0 6 0 9 0 9 3 1 7 8 1 2 3 1 1
5 2 8 5 1 0 2 4 6 0 8 3 4 2 9 0 2 4 0 5 2 7 8 8 8
7 9 7 1 3 7 2 4 6 3 8 4 0 2 5 5 4 6 1 6 5 4 6 3 0
0 1 5 0 6 5 1 1 8 0 9 4 1 1 2 6 1 4 2 0 8 6 3 1 0
5 8 1 7 4 7 5 6 2 1 9 3 7 4 0 4 6 4 6 9 6 7 5 0 6
2 5 0 7 5 1 6 0 4 0 4 1 9 4 9 8 3 6 3 8 0 0 1 7 9
8 8 3 7 8 1 4 6 3 8 0 5 6 4 4 3 5 0 6 9 5 5 0 6 0
4 3 1 8 7 3 4 1 7 1 6 1 5 2 7 9 4 0 2 9 9 6 8 7 6
9 1 4 7 7 4 3 7 4 2 5 5 0 2 1 1 1 4 0 6 4 7 5 9 6
8 6 0 8 2 9 3 4 3 4 7 6 9 6 1 8 2 3 3 8 3 4 6 8 3
3 3 0 6 2 3 8 7 4 3 8 3 1 1 5 9 7 4 4 4 9 7 6 0 9
1 8 2 0 2 9 8 8 0 1 6 8 0 7 5 6 0 8 3 9 2 1 1 2 0
4 7 4 1 1 8 5 9 6 9 7 7 8 0 8 0 8 5 7 2 6 9 4 6 7
7 2 8 1 1 0 4 0 5 0 0 8 2 5 7 4 9 4 0 6 9 7 1 8 0
8 4 0 0 8 1 8 7 1 5 0 1 3 7 3 1 1 4 1 9 7 1 7 8 5
1 5 0 5 3 1 9 7 5 0 3 7 6 3 4 7 2 2 0 5 0 0 7 5 1
6 8 5 1 2 4 1 0 4 6 2 5 9 9 3 2 5 6 0 1 2 0 6 7 7
7 6 5 5 4 6 1 9 1 1 7 9 9 9 6 6 7 1 3 7 7 4 8 8 2
7 8 2 4 2 1 6 4 3 9 7 2 6 6 5 7 0 1 2 8 9 7 1 4 5
9 0 3 3 8 1 3 5 1 4 2 8 7 7 0 3 5 8 0 8 4 2 6 6 4
5 5 4 8 6 5 6 8 0 3 2 0 4 8 4 5 6 6 5 4 7 1 3 1 2
0 6 4 9 7 7 9 8 0 6 4 0 9 2 4 7 8 2 5 1 7 2 3 5 2
6 0 6 7 8 0 8 7 6 8 5 0 1 3 4 3 0 4 7 0 5 2 4 1 3
1 6 3 6 4 9 6 5 3 5 5 3 0 3 3 8 3 7 9 1 1 5 8 2 2
2 1 5 9 7 1 2 6 4 4 5 0 2 1 4 5 1 1 7 0 4 0 1 3 0
```

TABLE 1   Random Numbers (*continued*)

```
5 0 3 9 1 8 3 8 9 5 5 6 7 3 0 6 7 9 7 1 4 9 2 3 3
3 5 8 1 8 1 6 3 4 7 0 6 7 7 8 9 6 2 0 8 5 0 4 3 7
7 0 6 4 0 6 9 0 5 9 3 3 7 7 1 1 4 4 3 8 0 6 2 1 8
1 0 4 9 2 7 8 1 6 4 4 9 3 2 9 6 7 3 2 4 2 6 4 9 6
7 7 7 0 3 2 5 7 9 3 0 5 6 6 5 8 7 6 2 8 5 2 5 3 8
3 1 4 2 0 1 2 3 5 8 0 4 9 9 9 5 6 4 8 6 4 3 5 0 8
8 7 9 8 4 6 4 1 7 0 8 6 0 0 6 1 7 0 9 0 2 9 8 4 2
5 0 6 9 7 6 4 6 4 9 6 6 0 5 3 2 7 9 2 4 4 4 0 6 5
0 9 7 6 2 3 7 3 6 5 7 7 4 8 5 9 4 9 6 6 0 9 5 6 3
1 1 2 9 9 4 6 0 0 6 3 7 1 3 1 9 1 2 6 6 0 8 7 5 2
9 5 5 5 1 9 7 5 9 0 3 2 1 5 6 1 1 1 2 8 3 5 9 5 5
5 6 2 2 6 5 2 0 4 0 5 8 1 8 6 1 2 3 9 0 3 4 3 0 3
3 0 8 5 5 8 7 5 1 7 1 0 7 0 2 7 4 9 9 5 4 9 3 4 6
1 9 4 1 2 5 8 1 2 4 4 9 7 5 9 7 5 8 8 6 2 2 2 4 0
1 6 0 1 7 5 6 9 4 1 7 3 2 2 6 5 1 4 5 9 8 9 9 2 4
9 4 3 4 6 5 3 2 3 0 8 5 6 6 1 1 0 6 6 6 9 6 0 1 1
3 8 5 2 2 5 3 1 3 4 8 8 2 8 7 5 4 6 4 6 4 0 3 3 4
6 5 9 8 7 5 1 5 0 1 3 1 3 5 7 1 1 7 6 6 6 6 8 4 5
9 9 7 6 9 8 8 7 0 6 1 5 7 9 7 1 5 9 7 9 2 6 7 1 1
3 2 8 0 3 7 7 6 8 3 1 2 6 3 0 8 1 4 8 6 1 2 6 6 8
8 9 9 2 9 7 7 4 2 3 3 5 9 2 3 5 8 6 7 3 0 6 4 9 9
5 2 2 0 3 2 8 7 3 4 1 2 6 8 9 6 8 9 4 1 7 6 8 2 9
9 3 7 1 9 8 3 6 0 2 8 6 3 5 3 0 1 6 1 3 3 8 3 4 8
0 6 7 9 9 0 3 7 7 2 6 0 7 7 1 1 8 1 2 9 9 7 8 0 6
6 5 3 1 0 4 2 4 5 1 4 9 5 3 9 0 2 2 4 5 9 9 9 0 0
4 1 8 9 1 7 4 3 6 4 4 6 6 6 0 7 6 3 2 5 8 2 0 6 8
4 5 4 7 1 1 4 5 0 4 7 9 4 0 6 1 2 1 9 4 9 9 0 2 3
2 5 4 3 3 6 3 1 4 0 9 3 7 9 1 1 8 8 1 8 0 3 1 9 5
4 3 6 4 0 1 7 8 2 0 4 9 5 9 7 9 0 3 3 7 2 9 9 4 0
2 3 8 5 4 4 3 3 0 6 1 0 7 3 5 3 1 3 2 0 6 0 9 1 7
1 6 4 8 7 9 9 9 1 3 1 0 8 6 7 5 6 9 0 3 1 6 8 2 0
4 8 1 6 3 4 5 0 2 7 5 7 0 8 3 2 4 8 5 3 2 9 6 8 1
4 2 1 9 4 6 2 3 0 1 1 6 1 0 7 2 2 3 4 8 7 9 1 4 6
4 0 7 6 5 4 2 9 5 3 3 9 0 6 3 0 2 5 4 9 5 3 6 0 8
8 4 9 3 0 8 2 8 4 0 4 5 6 9 0 6 8 1 1 4 6 7 4 8 1
1 7 6 3 8 1 4 6 2 2 9 4 5 0 3 5 7 0 0 2 4 1 7 1 2
5 6 4 6 9 0 1 5 1 5 5 0 3 1 4 5 1 2 7 0 2 4 9 9 6
0 3 6 0 7 1 4 8 0 3 5 4 8 8 0 4 0 6 7 3 3 1 1 7 4
6 7 2 9 0 4 2 9 2 6 4 6 4 6 4 6 9 4 6 2 3 9 4 8 8
0 3 1 4 5 9 5 0 8 2 6 5 0 8 5 8 0 7 5 0 9 5 3 1 5
7 3 0 9 3 6 1 9 3 1 3 9 8 3 9 7 7 6 6 5 3 0 2 6 8
8 6 7 9 6 6 8 3 4 0 5 9 5 1 7 8 0 1 0 8 9 7 1 4 6
4 9 5 8 6 8 0 4 4 4 5 6 7 4 8 1 7 1 4 9 2 9 5 1 9
6 0 3 9 9 5 8 4 4 1 5 4 0 6 8 6 0 2 0 0 1 8 8 8 0
4 1 0 5 3 6 3 5 0 6 4 0 0 1 2 1 8 2 9 5 4 8 7 2 5
5 2 7 9 6 5 7 4 5 1 3 3 8 8 4 4 0 4 1 8 9 1 1 6 5
3 4 6 1 2 1 8 7 4 7 6 3 3 5 0 0 7 9 1 6 4 0 7 4 6
8 2 2 0 8 8 8 7 3 8 3 1 5 8 4 9 5 1 9 1 7 9 7 9 9
4 8 7 0 7 8 9 4 3 0 9 2 3 5 4 7 2 1 4 6 6 8 6 3 2
9 0 4 3 8 0 1 5 7 6 7 1 6 3 0 5 7 3 7 1 0 9 5 6 6
```

TABLE 1 Random Numbers (*continued*)

```
8 2 8 9 7 9 6 9 7 9 0 8 2 9 8 1 5 6 9 3 2 9 2 3 3
9 4 6 9 2 6 8 4 4 7 8 3 5 1 0 1 3 9 9 2 9 0 4 0 8
5 6 7 4 2 7 4 1 2 7 3 1 5 8 3 1 0 7 3 8 7 5 2 5 1
8 0 9 9 8 3 2 9 7 5 5 8 0 5 2 1 3 4 2 3 8 6 8 3 6
6 7 0 3 7 9 8 8 2 0 9 1 0 6 0 7 2 4 5 1 3 3 5 1 0
8 1 3 0 0 8 3 4 8 8 3 4 8 9 9 2 0 4 3 9 6 7 6 5 7
1 7 6 2 5 8 6 2 6 6 8 0 8 3 9 8 8 7 4 2 1 3 3 3 2
9 9 7 1 7 5 9 1 3 2 4 6 0 5 9 0 7 3 8 2 3 5 4 7 1
0 4 6 4 0 1 7 9 9 3 6 8 1 5 3 7 1 1 9 5 1 0 1 4 8
9 7 8 2 1 2 9 7 2 0 6 4 2 5 2 7 0 8 1 1 9 7 7 7 0
2 4 6 4 6 3 6 7 5 2 0 0 5 4 7 3 3 4 1 0 7 4 4 0 9
8 5 4 5 4 7 7 4 0 0 5 0 6 4 2 8 8 0 8 0 9 9 0 5 8
5 8 6 7 6 6 4 7 0 1 4 9 9 5 7 2 1 4 1 1 9 7 7 3 5
1 3 8 1 4 7 0 7 4 8 8 4 4 0 1 2 5 1 4 8 1 7 7 3 2
4 1 5 9 7 9 5 6 6 7 4 5 6 1 8 8 8 2 8 9 0 0 9 2 5
9 5 4 7 0 6 8 1 2 1 4 0 4 5 8 3 1 6 0 1 9 7 5 6 0
3 7 2 7 4 1 4 8 3 6 4 1 6 1 9 0 4 1 3 2 6 8 9 2 5
9 7 1 8 1 0 8 3 6 0 1 7 5 0 6 3 2 7 9 2 5 6 2 9 9
9 9 9 9 1 9 4 2 6 9 5 8 5 6 8 3 9 8 6 9 9 6 8 2 5
9 3 0 1 8 1 5 8 8 1 1 4 4 6 6 4 1 0 9 6 6 7 5 5 8
7 9 4 6 8 9 0 6 6 9 5 4 3 1 9 5 1 9 5 6 2 8 2 7 4
3 5 5 4 5 2 5 2 2 1 4 8 2 0 9 1 8 4 3 5 0 3 2 6 5
6 7 2 1 9 0 5 4 3 3 9 8 9 0 1 2 6 6 1 3 0 4 5 4 1
4 0 5 3 9 2 6 3 2 2 0 4 2 0 9 1 0 0 8 8 8 0 2 8 1
2 1 5 7 3 7 3 6 2 8 9 3 2 8 7 9 6 7 9 5 1 9 5 5 4
8 2 9 1 7 6 5 0 5 7 4 2 4 7 5 1 4 2 8 4 0 2 0 4 5
0 4 9 2 5 9 9 8 7 4 7 3 2 2 1 7 7 1 9 5 1 4 4 9 4
3 8 6 7 5 6 1 5 3 0 9 0 8 4 0 4 6 7 2 2 6 8 4 3 5
7 1 8 8 3 6 3 7 4 3 6 3 3 0 1 3 4 9 7 3 8 9 2 3 6
2 3 0 4 7 4 6 9 9 9 8 7 4 4 2 8 1 4 4 4 0 0 6 0 8
8 6 4 4 0 7 1 2 9 6 3 1 3 4 9 1 6 2 9 3 7 6 1 1 0
0 5 5 4 6 7 7 9 6 9 0 2 5 5 3 5 8 5 1 2 9 6 9 3 9
5 7 4 3 2 8 8 4 4 2 0 8 9 6 3 0 5 1 1 2 7 3 7 8 0
8 3 2 7 1 2 7 0 2 9 1 1 7 1 5 4 8 1 9 1 2 5 0 5 3
3 1 2 1 0 7 7 3 0 4 7 1 3 8 9 3 8 7 2 7 5 1 4 8 9
0 7 9 7 0 6 4 5 3 0 5 8 2 7 3 7 3 0 6 2 4 3 3 9 1
9 0 3 4 4 3 1 8 2 1 0 4 5 9 7 2 9 0 5 5 4 7 1 5 9
1 5 7 9 2 9 5 2 8 9 1 8 6 4 2 3 4 0 6 1 4 1 7 9 9
7 3 8 2 7 8 4 7 5 9 3 4 2 9 9 4 8 3 1 1 6 5 1 5 6
2 4 0 4 4 0 4 5 0 7 6 4 9 2 0 5 3 9 2 8 1 1 8 0 2
2 9 9 9 6 6 8 0 6 9 4 0 8 4 2 4 0 4 6 0 2 1 2 2 4
5 8 2 2 2 1 7 7 2 5 9 4 2 1 7 2 1 7 7 9 3 3 5 9 8
7 3 7 4 3 6 3 0 9 9 1 6 3 9 2 3 0 2 6 8 9 8 9 0 7
8 8 9 7 6 2 9 9 0 1 2 0 0 1 0 2 4 7 8 9 6 6 9 7 8
1 4 0 9 6 1 0 9 8 7 0 5 8 0 6 5 8 0 5 0 1 9 3 0 1
1 6 4 2 4 7 6 7 7 3 5 9 3 2 2 9 2 7 8 6 3 7 7 8 1
1 2 9 8 1 2 5 7 7 9 6 8 4 4 0 6 3 3 1 1 6 7 2 5 8
5 7 7 5 3 5 5 5 6 7 9 4 3 1 5 7 2 7 6 9 7 6 1 0 3
2 4 7 9 1 7 2 8 3 4 4 1 1 1 3 0 6 9 1 4 8 8 7 5 6
0 2 5 9 4 0 8 2 5 6 0 4 7 1 6 3 6 5 5 6 1 1 6 7 6
```

TABLE 1   Random Numbers (*continued*)

```
8 9 0 8 8 8 7 4 1 9 9 9 5 5 1 8 2 1 3 7 5 7 8 7 1
1 1 0 4 2 7 2 3 9 9 5 7 5 0 9 5 3 9 6 8 6 7 4 9 0
0 0 6 6 6 3 1 5 6 3 8 9 7 2 9 0 9 8 4 9 4 2 5 0 0
2 8 5 9 9 3 5 2 5 2 1 1 7 4 0 7 9 0 1 4 9 1 9 8 9
7 5 8 0 7 9 4 5 7 9 3 2 0 7 6 3 2 6 3 6 0 9 7 8 5
2 8 1 2 4 9 9 2 0 1 9 7 9 7 2 0 8 1 4 9 2 8 6 5 9
1 6 5 9 5 2 6 8 5 8 1 8 0 6 1 2 2 7 1 0 8 6 1 9 9
3 8 0 2 2 2 0 4 5 5 5 4 5 6 9 9 1 4 2 6 7 3 9 3 5
7 0 7 8 2 1 9 6 3 1 1 8 1 1 7 8 1 6 0 3 9 6 7 1 0
9 5 9 2 6 6 6 7 4 1 9 5 1 9 8 4 2 7 9 3 8 5 5 0 8
9 9 3 7 7 0 5 3 1 2 2 4 7 0 2 2 4 0 2 1 4 5 2 6 9
2 8 6 7 5 0 2 8 7 0 4 2 5 4 1 5 3 3 7 0 7 8 8 0 8
5 8 4 6 5 0 3 6 4 5 2 4 7 9 6 7 7 3 1 5 9 7 7 4 2
2 7 9 4 0 0 1 7 0 7 2 0 0 5 1 8 6 4 9 7 9 7 0 4 8
3 2 0 4 1 5 9 2 4 0 8 3 9 0 6 9 8 3 7 7 2 6 0 6 8
9 4 4 2 4 3 1 3 1 3 0 2 2 8 2 7 5 6 8 5 3 2 9 9 9
1 4 7 7 0 3 1 3 3 5 9 6 5 1 6 4 0 6 9 7 3 9 2 1 6
2 7 4 6 7 2 6 2 7 2 5 1 3 8 7 7 8 2 1 9 2 5 0 9 0
5 3 2 1 6 4 9 4 4 6 2 5 3 3 3 5 2 5 4 9 5 7 4 4 6
6 0 9 6 4 0 0 9 3 2 7 7 6 6 7 9 7 8 1 8 0 4 1 8 1
6 8 6 5 0 5 3 4 2 3 3 7 5 7 7 9 7 4 7 0 5 6 5 1 3
7 2 1 3 4 1 7 8 1 8 4 4 1 6 6 6 2 5 6 6 2 0 4 1 9
7 5 9 1 3 2 7 1 2 6 3 1 3 3 1 2 9 0 9 8 9 8 6 9 8
8 7 7 6 8 8 8 1 6 8 6 1 8 8 6 1 7 5 6 8 6 4 3 6 9
0 4 6 4 6 1 9 6 1 4 5 9 1 1 3 6 1 4 5 7 0 8 2 5 4
9 6 8 6 1 6 3 0 3 7 0 4 9 8 8 7 7 6 8 1 7 1 5 0 8
7 6 9 7 0 9 8 7 1 2 0 9 0 3 8 5 3 9 3 7 4 1 1 5 7
3 2 7 0 9 2 7 5 8 0 4 7 8 1 4 2 4 0 0 9 6 5 9 2 5
4 2 6 8 9 1 9 0 4 2 1 3 4 3 2 0 6 7 4 7 1 3 9 7 9
6 8 6 5 1 4 1 3 0 6 7 0 9 5 2 8 7 0 9 3 8 5 1 3 5
6 3 5 7 2 0 2 8 6 3 3 8 5 3 1 0 4 6 6 3 1 7 9 9 7
7 3 7 7 3 4 5 2 3 6 2 3 6 5 5 3 9 2 1 7 0 6 4 2 0
6 0 1 2 5 0 2 9 4 9 8 3 5 9 5 7 4 5 2 8 4 7 6 6 4
2 6 6 8 6 5 0 7 7 5 5 4 9 1 2 0 3 4 8 9 6 4 9 8 9
3 6 8 7 2 9 9 2 7 5 6 0 9 0 6 5 8 8 2 8 3 4 7 4 0
4 2 5 5 7 2 6 5 9 4 3 8 7 5 6 5 3 6 3 4 3 8 5 4 7
3 2 3 1 1 5 6 5 8 3 9 6 2 2 0 2 9 0 9 3 1 1 3 1 4
0 2 3 6 6 9 4 4 6 6 0 9 9 7 4 0 1 3 2 5 6 9 4 5 1
6 5 6 9 4 1 6 8 8 6 7 0 0 6 0 8 8 3 9 7 8 4 1 7 6
7 3 1 3 9 1 2 0 7 1 5 2 1 2 0 7 0 1 7 8 6 4 6 6 3
3 5 2 5 5 9 9 0 1 5 3 2 1 7 0 1 9 3 6 3 3 4 5 0 9
2 7 6 2 3 9 6 7 5 3 6 1 5 0 2 0 3 2 9 1 6 2 1 4 6
7 8 9 1 3 0 3 0 0 2 8 5 5 4 3 8 9 6 8 2 2 1 8 8 1
1 1 0 8 2 7 9 9 8 5 5 1 9 0 7 1 2 5 7 6 8 5 8 2 8
9 6 3 9 6 2 1 1 1 0 3 2 1 7 5 0 6 9 0 6 2 0 9 5 1
1 0 3 2 4 6 1 9 9 8 8 6 5 7 6 9 8 9 1 2 4 9 1 3 5
2 3 7 1 5 7 2 5 8 1 1 7 6 6 4 9 1 3 0 3 5 2 6 3 3
2 3 6 4 7 5 3 4 7 7 7 6 4 3 5 9 6 3 8 7 8 0 1 3 2
9 3 6 1 5 4 4 5 3 3 5 4 1 5 2 3 4 6 4 5 3 7 6 9 2
0 4 0 4 6 7 0 2 9 4 3 5 9 9 7 4 9 0 6 8 7 5 9 3 6
```

TABLE 1   Random Numbers (continued)

```
9 3 6 4 8 6 5 9 2 6 4 5 1 6 9 9 0 8 6 7 4 5 7 2 8
1 1 5 8 8 6 9 0 3 3 6 8 4 1 8 1 3 9 0 8 3 4 5 6 5
7 2 8 1 8 8 3 7 4 4 3 5 0 2 1 3 1 9 9 1 1 1 7 0 0
1 8 4 9 4 8 6 2 6 5 1 7 6 9 5 8 8 2 8 4 0 6 2 7 8
2 7 3 0 6 1 3 6 4 1 9 2 4 5 4 4 9 5 4 7 1 4 2 0 0
2 1 0 3 9 9 3 2 8 0 0 3 4 6 2 9 2 5 5 9 6 5 0 7 8
5 1 2 1 7 3 1 5 7 1 5 8 7 7 5 7 9 8 0 8 5 3 2 5 8
2 5 3 5 4 8 4 5 2 5 7 7 2 8 7 1 8 2 3 9 3 1 5 9 9
0 6 1 5 3 1 9 8 0 4 3 2 0 1 4 5 4 2 9 8 2 9 1 5 5
4 7 0 9 2 7 5 8 6 1 5 4 0 9 9 7 3 9 6 5 5 4 0 1 4
4 6 1 4 8 5 7 1 9 7 0 9 4 2 8 0 1 3 6 4 0 4 9 7 2
8 5 2 7 5 0 5 6 6 3 3 1 8 1 6 7 3 2 4 9 6 6 8 9
1 9 5 1 2 4 1 4 7 2 9 8 7 7 4 9 5 1 2 8 6 7 0 0 7
1 1 7 5 2 6 4 7 5 9 2 9 2 7 0 9 3 3 1 6 2 1 0 8 2
6 0 4 0 7 7 9 9 5 0 3 8 6 9 8 9 1 2 5 2 6 3 3 6 5
4 2 8 8 4 2 2 6 5 9 7 6 4 5 2 4 4 4 7 2 3 3 8 0 1
6 3 1 3 5 0 4 8 3 4 1 7 2 9 0 6 3 3 5 0 4 0 4 5 1
4 9 9 6 2 8 3 1 8 4 8 1 1 0 9 4 6 4 2 1 5 9 4 8 6
5 5 8 5 7 3 5 3 1 0 8 9 8 0 1 0 6 2 1 6 9 7 3 5 1
0 8 3 6 4 9 7 5 6 2 8 7 3 8 9 0 2 2 0 0 4 9 9 0 9
5 6 2 1 3 3 7 4 0 7 1 9 3 8 7 6 5 8 9 0 8 3 7 1 4
6 7 6 6 5 2 7 1 5 0 1 5 8 3 1 5 3 5 5 2 2 4 2 5 4
1 0 2 9 2 0 9 5 4 1 6 9 6 8 4 0 2 6 5 3 2 2 1 3 9
9 7 3 0 4 1 8 8 6 5 9 3 9 1 2 2 0 7 2 3 8 9 9 7 8
3 6 6 7 1 6 5 6 6 9 6 7 8 6 2 1 4 1 1 0 8 8 5 4 0
2 4 3 9 7 6 0 0 6 2 8 4 3 4 4 1 1 5 9 3 7 9 4 8 3
0 4 7 0 4 1 0 7 2 9 6 4 5 2 7 2 9 8 3 4 5 6 8 8 2
6 0 5 9 1 1 1 4 4 6 9 7 8 8 6 3 6 7 6 0 5 1 0 5 5
1 1 5 1 6 6 0 5 1 5 6 0 7 5 2 7 3 7 2 4 8 6 2 5 4
3 4 2 3 2 5 9 4 7 1 7 8 4 1 3 8 8 5 3 7 6 8 8 6 4
8 3 3 6 5 8 0 5 9 6 6 1 3 4 5 4 2 8 3 9 5 0 8 9 1
9 2 1 2 4 7 6 5 9 3 6 0 5 0 7 5 3 7 9 3 8 5 1 7 6
2 6 6 8 4 7 5 4 7 0 8 4 2 6 8 3 1 4 5 9 8 7 5 0 6
6 6 4 6 5 8 8 5 9 8 5 9 4 6 5 2 4 0 7 1 4 1 8 7 0
1 1 6 5 4 5 4 0 4 1 7 2 1 5 7 5 8 5 7 4 4 8 2 6 2
3 0 8 3 7 1 3 1 9 0 7 7 5 2 2 7 6 3 9 9 9 0 3 8 6
8 0 2 6 1 8 5 9 3 1 7 9 4 7 5 5 4 9 6 4 6 1 6 0 1
4 5 2 7 5 1 0 6 4 2 1 6 2 4 9 1 8 3 1 8 8 2 7 4 1
0 5 6 1 3 8 3 9 8 3 6 9 4 9 1 5 2 5 6 5 8 4 5 1 9
7 4 1 5 0 4 4 3 4 8 7 4 8 7 4 5 1 3 9 2 4 1 2 2 5
7 4 5 7 0 9 8 3 4 9 7 8 1 3 2 2 8 3 7 3 8 5 2 6 1
5 8 8 2 4 5 4 9 5 6 5 5 0 1 7 6 3 6 1 6 6 5 6 8 9
1 4 9 9 2 0 5 4 1 2 6 4 3 8 4 3 4 3 2 4 4 2 9 5 6
2 3 5 4 3 3 6 9 2 8 2 1 1 5 5 0 7 1 4 5 0 5 6 3 0
9 6 1 5 9 9 1 2 9 2 5 3 9 9 4 1 6 2 3 4 0 8 8 6 9
0 7 2 9 3 7 5 5 5 0 5 7 3 3 6 8 6 2 7 2 1 5 0 0 3
6 2 8 1 5 1 1 4 8 2 9 5 5 6 5 2 0 6 7 3 3 9 2 2 2
2 7 8 8 9 0 4 1 4 6 9 7 5 4 9 2 4 4 0 6 9 5 4 4 4
4 3 3 9 1 2 1 3 6 3 4 3 4 8 8 6 9 3 2 3 3 4 7 1 2
8 8 0 5 2 2 8 0 8 5 3 0 3 7 4 9 6 0 1 8 5 3 8 6 4
```

TABLE 2   Distribution of *t*

	Level of significance for one-tailed test					
	10	05	025	01	005	0005
df	Level of significance for two-tailed test					
	20	10	05	02	01	001
1	3 078	6 314	12 706	31 821	63 657	636 619
2	1 886	2 920	4 303	6 965	9 925	31 598
3	1 638	2 353	3 182	4 541	5 841	12 941
4	1 533	2 132	2 776	3 747	4 604	8 610
5	1 476	2 015	2 571	3 365	4 032	6 859
6	1 440	1 943	2 447	3 143	3 707	5 959
7	1 415	1 895	2 365	2 998	3 499	5 405
8	1 397	1 860	2 306	2 896	3 355	5 041
9	1 383	1 833	2 262	2 821	3 250	4 781
10	1 372	1 812	2 228	2 764	3 169	4 587
11	1 363	1 796	2 201	2 718	3 106	4 437
12	1 356	1 782	2 179	2 681	3 055	4 318
13	1 350	1 771	2 160	2 650	3 012	4 221
14	1 345	1 761	2 145	2 624	2 977	4 140
15	1 341	1 753	2 131	2 602	2 947	4 073
16	1 337	1 746	2 120	2 583	2 921	4 015
17	1 333	1 740	2 110	2 567	2 898	3 965
18	1 330	1 734	2 101	2 552	2 878	3 992
19	1 328	1 729	2 093	2 539	2 861	3 883
20	1 325	1 725	2 086	2 528	2 845	3 850
21	1 323	1 721	2 080	2 518	2 831	3 819
22	1 321	1 717	2 074	2 508	2 819	3 792
23	1 319	1 714	2 069	2 500	2 807	3 767
24	1 318	1 711	2 064	2 492	2 797	3 745
25	1 316	1 708	2 060	2 485	2 787	3 725
26	1 315	1 706	2 056	2 479	2 779	3 707
27	1 314	1 703	2 052	2 473	2 771	3 690
28	1 313	1 701	2 048	2 467	2 763	3 674
29	1 311	1 699	2 045	2 462	2 756	3 659
30	1 310	1 697	2 042	2 457	2 750	3 646
40	1 303	1 684	2 021	2 423	2 704	3 551
60	1 296	1 671	2 000	2 390	2 660	3 460
120	1 289	1 658	1 980	2 358	2 617	3 373
∞	1 282	1 645	1 960	2 326	2 576	3 291

Table abridged from Table III of Fisher and Yates, *Statistical Tables for Biological, Agricultural, and Medical Research*, published by Longman Group Ltd., London (previously published by Oliver and Boyd Ltd., Edinburgh), by permission of the authors and publishers.

TABLE 3   Areas Under the Normal Curve. Proportion of Area Under the
Normal Curve Between the Mean and a z Distance from the Mean

$\frac{x}{\sigma}$ or z	00	01	02	03	04	05	06	07	08	09
0	0000	0040	0080	0120	0160	0199	0239	0279	0319	0359
1	0398	0438	0478	0517	0557	0596	0636	0675	0714	0753
2	0793	0832	0871	0910	0948	0987	1026	1064	1103	1141
3	1179	1217	1255	1293	1331	1368	1406	1443	1480	1517
4	1554	1591	1628	1664	1700	1736	1772	1808	1844	1879
5	1915	1950	1985	2019	2054	2088	2123	2157	2190	2224
6	2257	2291	2324	2357	2389	2422	2454	2486	2517	2549
7	2580	2611	2642	2673	2704	2734	2764	2794	2823	2852
8	2881	2910	2939	2967	2995	3023	3051	3078	3106	3133
9	3159	3186	3212	3238	3264	3289	3315	3340	3365	3389
1.0	3413	3438	3461	3485	3508	3531	3554	3577	3599	3621
1.1	3643	3665	3686	3708	3729	3749	3770	3790	3810	3830
1.2	3849	3869	3888	3907	3925	3944	3962	3980	3997	4015
1.3	4032	4049	4066	4082	4099	4115	4131	4147	4162	4177
1.4	4192	4207	4222	4236	4251	4265	4279	4292	4306	4319
1.5	4332	4345	4357	4370	4382	4394	4406	4418	4429	4441
1.6	4452	4463	4474	4484	4495	4505	4515	4525	4535	4545
1.7	4554	4564	4573	4582	4591	4599	4608	4616	4625	4633
1.8	4641	4649	4656	4664	4671	4678	4686	4693	4699	4706
1.9	4713	4719	4726	4732	4738	4744	4750	4756	4761	4767
2.0	4772	4778	4783	4788	4793	4798	4803	4808	4812	4817
2.1	4821	4826	4830	4834	4838	4842	4846	4850	4854	4857
2.2	4861	4864	4868	4871	4875	4878	4881	4884	4887	4890
2.3	4893	4896	4898	4901	4904	4906	4909	4911	4913	4916
2.4	4918	4920	4922	4925	4927	4929	4931	4932	4934	4936
2.5	4938	4940	4941	4943	4945	4946	4948	4949	4951	4952
2.6	4953	4955	4956	4957	4959	4960	4961	4962	4963	4964
2.7	4965	4966	4967	4968	4969	4970	4971	4972	4973	4974
2.8	4974	4975	4976	4977	4977	4978	4979	4979	4980	4981
2.9	4981	4982	4982	4983	4984	4984	4985	4985	4986	4986
3.0	4987	4987	4987	4988	4988	4989	4989	4989	4990	4990
3.1	4990	4991	4991	4991	4992	4992	4992	4992	4993	4993
3.2	4993	4993	4994	4994	4994	4994	4994	4995	4995	4995
3.3	4995	4995	4995	4996	4996	4996	4996	4996	4996	4997
3.4	4997	4997	4997	4997	4997	4997	4997	4997	4997	4998
3.5	.4998									
4.0	.49997									
4.5	.499997									
5.0	.4999997									

TABLE 4   Distribution of Chi-Square

	Probability					
df	.20	.10	.05	.02	.01	.001
1	1.642	2.706	3.841	5.412	6.635	10.827
2	3.219	4.605	5.991	7.824	9.210	13.815
3	4.642	6.251	7.815	9.837	11.345	16.266
4	5.989	7.779	9.488	11.668	13.277	18.467
5	7.289	9.236	11.070	13.388	15.086	20.515
6	8.558	10.645	12.592	15.033	16.812	22.457
7	9.803	12.017	14.067	16.622	18.475	24.322
8	11.030	13.362	15.507	18.168	20.090	26.125
9	12.242	14.684	16.919	19.679	21.666	27.877
10	13.442	15.987	18.307	21.161	23.209	29.588
11	14.631	17.275	19.675	22.618	24.725	31.264
12	15.812	18.549	21.026	24.054	26.217	32.909
13	16.985	19.812	22.362	25.472	27.688	34.528
14	18.151	21.064	23.685	26.873	29.141	36.123
15	19.311	22.307	24.996	28.259	30.578	37.697
16	20.465	23.542	26.296	29.633	32.000	39.252
17	21.615	24.769	27.587	30.995	33.409	40.790
18	22.760	25.989	28.869	32.346	34.805	42.312
19	23.900	27.204	30.144	33.687	36.191	43.820
20	25.038	28.412	31.410	35.020	37.566	45.315
21	26.171	29.615	32.671	36.343	38.932	46.797
22	27.301	30.813	33.924	37.659	40.289	48.268
23	28.429	32.007	35.172	38.968	41.638	49.728
24	29.553	33.196	36.415	40.270	42.980	51.179
25	30.675	34.382	37.652	41.566	44.314	52.620

TABLE 4   Distribution of Chi-Square (*continued*)

	Probability					
df	.20	.10	.05	.02	.01	.001
26	31.795	35.563	38.885	42.856	45.642	54.052
27	32.912	36.741	40.113	44.140	46.963	55.476
28	34.027	37.916	41.337	45.419	48.278	56.893
29	35.139	39.087	42.557	46.693	49.588	58.302
30	36.250	40.256	43.773	47.962	50.892	59.703
32	38.466	42.585	46.194	50.487	53.486	62.487
34	40.676	44.903	48.602	52.995	56.061	65.247
36	42.879	47.212	50.999	55.489	58.619	67.985
38	45.076	49.513	53.384	57.969	61.162	70.703
40	47.269	51.805	55.759	60.436	63.691	73.402
42	49.456	54.090	58.124	62.892	66.206	76.084
44	51.639	56.369	60.481	65.337	68.710	78.750
46	53.818	58.641	62.830	67.771	71.201	81.400
48	55.993	60.907	65.171	70.197	73.683	84.037
50	58.164	63.167	67.505	72.613	76.154	86.661
52	60.332	65.422	69.832	75.021	78.616	89.272
54	62.496	67.673	72.153	77.422	81.069	91.872
56	64.658	69.919	74.468	79.815	83.513	94.461
58	66.816	72.160	76.778	82.201	85.950	97.039
60	68.972	74.397	79.082	84.580	88.379	99.607
62	71.125	76.630	81.381	86.953	90.802	102.166
64	73.276	78.860	83.675	89.320	93.217	104.716
66	75.424	81.085	85.965	91.681	95.626	107.258
68	77.571	83.308	88.250	94.037	98.028	109.791
70	79.715	85.527	90.531	96.388	100.425	112.317

Table 4 is taken from Table IV of Fisher and Yates, *Statistical Tables for Biological, Agricultural, and Medical Research,* published by Longman Group UK Ltd., 1974.

TABLE 5 Distribution of F: .05 Level

df_2 \ df_1	1	2	3	4	5	6	7	8	9	10	12	15	20	24	30	40	60	120	∞
1	161.4	199.5	215.7	224.6	230.2	234.0	236.8	238.9	240.5	241.9	243.9	245.9	248.0	249.1	250.1	251.1	252.2	253.3	254.3
2	18.51	19.00	19.16	19.25	19.30	19.33	19.35	19.37	19.38	19.40	19.41	19.43	19.45	19.45	19.46	19.47	19.48	19.49	19.50
3	10.13	9.55	9.28	9.12	9.01	8.94	8.89	8.85	8.81	8.79	8.74	8.70	8.66	8.64	8.62	8.59	8.57	8.55	8.53
4	7.71	6.94	6.59	6.39	6.26	6.16	6.09	6.04	6.00	5.96	5.91	5.86	5.80	5.77	5.75	5.72	5.69	5.66	5.63
5	6.61	5.79	5.41	5.19	5.05	4.95	4.88	4.82	4.77	4.74	4.68	4.62	4.56	4.53	4.50	4.46	4.43	4.40	4.36
6	5.99	5.14	4.76	4.53	4.39	4.28	4.21	4.15	4.10	4.06	4.00	3.94	3.87	3.84	3.81	3.77	3.74	3.70	3.67
7	5.59	4.74	4.35	4.12	3.97	3.87	3.79	3.73	3.68	3.64	3.57	3.51	3.44	3.41	3.38	3.34	3.30	3.27	3.23
8	5.32	4.46	4.07	3.84	3.69	3.58	3.50	3.44	3.39	3.35	3.28	3.22	3.15	3.12	3.08	3.04	3.01	2.97	2.93
9	5.12	4.26	3.86	3.63	3.48	3.37	3.29	3.23	3.18	3.14	3.07	3.01	2.94	2.90	2.86	2.83	2.79	2.75	2.71
10	4.96	4.10	3.71	3.48	3.33	3.22	3.14	3.07	3.02	2.98	2.91	2.85	2.77	2.74	2.70	2.66	2.62	2.58	2.54
11	4.84	3.98	3.59	3.36	3.20	3.09	3.01	2.95	2.90	2.85	2.79	2.72	2.65	2.61	2.57	2.53	2.49	2.45	2.40
12	4.75	3.89	3.49	3.26	3.11	3.00	2.91	2.85	2.80	2.75	2.69	2.62	2.54	2.51	2.47	2.43	2.38	2.34	2.30
13	4.67	3.81	3.41	3.18	3.03	2.92	2.83	2.77	2.71	2.67	2.60	2.53	2.46	2.42	2.38	2.34	2.30	2.25	2.21
14	4.60	3.74	3.34	3.11	2.96	2.85	2.76	2.70	2.65	2.60	2.53	2.46	2.39	2.35	2.31	2.27	2.22	2.18	2.13
15	4.54	3.68	3.29	3.06	2.90	2.79	2.71	2.64	2.59	2.54	2.48	2.40	2.33	2.29	2.25	2.20	2.16	2.11	2.07
16	4.49	3.63	3.24	3.01	2.85	2.74	2.66	2.59	2.54	2.49	2.42	2.35	2.28	2.24	2.19	2.15	2.11	2.06	2.01
17	4.45	3.59	3.20	2.96	2.81	2.70	2.61	2.55	2.49	2.45	2.38	2.31	2.23	2.19	2.15	2.10	2.06	2.01	1.96
18	4.41	3.55	3.16	2.93	2.77	2.66	2.58	2.51	2.46	2.41	2.34	2.27	2.19	2.15	2.11	2.06	2.02	1.97	1.92
19	4.38	3.52	3.13	2.90	2.74	2.63	2.54	2.48	2.42	2.38	2.31	2.23	2.16	2.11	2.07	2.03	1.98	1.93	1.88

20	4.35	3.49	3.10	2.87	2.71	2.60	2.51	2.45	2.39	2.35	2.28	2.20	2.12	2.08	2.04	1.99	1.95	1.90	1.84
21	4.32	3.47	3.07	2.84	2.68	2.57	2.49	2.42	2.37	2.32	2.25	2.18	2.10	2.05	2.01	1.96	1.92	1.87	1.81
22	4.30	3.44	3.05	2.82	2.66	2.55	2.46	2.40	2.34	2.30	2.23	2.15	2.07	2.03	1.98	1.94	1.89	1.84	1.78
23	4.28	3.42	3.03	2.80	2.64	2.53	2.44	2.37	2.32	2.27	2.20	2.13	2.05	2.01	1.96	1.91	1.86	1.81	1.76
24	4.26	3.40	3.01	2.78	2.62	2.51	2.42	2.36	2.30	2.25	2.18	2.11	2.03	1.98	1.94	1.89	1.84	1.79	1.73
25	4.24	3.39	2.99	2.76	2.60	2.49	2.40	2.34	2.28	2.24	2.16	2.09	2.01	1.96	1.92	1.87	1.82	1.77	1.71
26	4.23	3.37	2.98	2.74	2.59	2.47	2.39	2.32	2.27	2.22	2.15	2.07	1.99	1.95	1.90	1.85	1.80	1.75	1.69
27	4.21	3.35	2.96	2.73	2.57	2.46	2.37	2.31	2.25	2.20	2.13	2.06	1.97	1.93	1.88	1.84	1.79	1.73	1.67
28	4.20	3.34	2.95	2.71	2.56	2.45	2.36	2.29	2.24	2.19	2.12	2.04	1.96	1.91	1.87	1.82	1.77	1.71	1.65
29	4.18	3.33	2.93	2.70	2.55	2.43	2.35	2.28	2.22	2.18	2.10	2.03	1.94	1.90	1.85	1.81	1.75	1.70	1.64
30	4.17	3.32	2.92	2.69	2.53	2.42	2.33	2.27	2.21	2.16	2.09	2.01	1.93	1.89	1.84	1.79	1.74	1.68	1.62
40	4.08	3.23	2.84	2.61	2.45	2.34	2.25	2.18	2.12	2.08	2.00	1.92	1.84	1.79	1.74	1.69	1.64	1.58	1.51
60	4.00	3.15	2.76	2.53	2.37	2.25	2.17	2.10	2.04	1.99	1.92	1.84	1.75	1.70	1.65	1.59	1.53	1.47	1.39
120	3.92	3.07	2.68	2.45	2.29	2.17	2.09	2.02	1.96	1.91	1.83	1.75	1.66	1.61	1.55	1.50	1.43	1.35	1.25
∞	3.84	3.00	2.60	2.37	2.21	2.10	2.01	1.94	1.88	1.83	1.75	1.67	1.57	1.52	1.46	1.39	1.32	1.22	1.00

TABLE 6 Distribution of F: .01 Level

df_2 \ df_1	1	2	3	4	5	6	7	8	9	10	12	15	20	24	30	40	60	120	∞
1	4052	4999.5	5403	5625	5764	5859	5928	5982	6022	6056	6106	6157	6209	6235	6261	6287	6313	6339	6366
2	98.5	99.00	99.17	99.25	99.30	99.33	99.36	99.37	99.39	99.40	99.42	99.43	99.45	99.46	99.47	99.47	99.48	99.49	99.50
3	34.12	30.82	29.46	28.71	28.24	27.91	27.67	27.49	27.35	27.23	27.05	26.87	26.69	26.60	26.50	26.41	26.32	26.22	26.13
4	21.20	18.00	16.69	15.98	15.52	15.21	14.98	14.80	14.66	14.55	14.37	14.20	14.02	13.93	13.84	13.75	13.65	13.56	13.46
5	16.26	13.27	12.06	11.39	10.97	10.67	10.46	10.29	10.16	10.05	9.89	9.72	9.55	9.47	9.38	9.29	9.20	9.11	9.02
6	13.75	10.92	9.78	9.15	8.75	8.47	8.26	8.10	7.98	7.87	7.72	7.56	7.40	7.31	7.23	7.14	7.06	6.97	6.88
7	12.25	9.55	8.45	7.85	7.46	7.19	6.99	6.81	6.72	6.62	6.47	6.31	6.16	6.07	5.99	5.91	5.82	5.74	5.65
8	11.26	8.65	7.59	7.01	6.63	6.37	6.18	6.03	5.91	5.81	5.67	5.52	5.36	5.28	5.20	5.12	5.03	4.95	4.86
9	10.56	8.02	6.99	6.42	6.06	5.80	5.61	5.47	5.35	5.26	5.11	4.96	4.81	4.73	4.65	4.57	4.48	4.40	4.31
10	10.04	7.56	6.55	5.99	5.64	5.39	5.20	5.06	4.94	4.85	4.71	4.56	4.41	4.33	4.25	4.17	4.08	4.00	3.91
11	9.65	7.21	6.22	5.67	5.32	5.07	4.89	4.74	4.63	4.54	4.40	4.25	4.10	4.02	3.94	3.86	3.78	3.69	3.60
12	9.33	6.93	5.95	5.41	5.06	4.82	4.64	4.50	4.39	4.30	4.16	4.01	3.86	3.78	3.70	3.62	3.54	3.45	3.36
13	9.07	6.70	5.74	5.21	4.86	4.62	4.44	4.30	4.19	4.10	3.96	3.82	3.66	3.59	3.51	3.43	3.34	3.25	3.17
14	8.86	6.51	5.56	5.04	4.69	4.46	4.28	4.14	4.03	3.94	3.80	3.66	3.51	3.43	3.35	3.27	3.18	3.09	3.00
15	8.68	6.36	5.42	4.89	4.56	4.32	4.14	4.00	3.89	3.80	3.67	3.52	3.37	3.29	3.21	3.13	3.05	2.96	2.87
16	8.53	6.23	5.29	4.77	4.44	4.20	4.03	3.89	3.78	3.69	3.55	3.41	3.26	3.18	3.10	3.02	2.93	2.84	2.75
17	8.40	6.11	5.18	4.67	4.34	4.10	3.93	3.79	3.68	3.59	3.46	3.31	3.16	3.08	3.00	2.92	2.83	2.75	2.65
18	8.29	6.01	5.09	4.58	4.25	4.01	3.84	3.71	3.60	3.51	3.37	3.23	3.08	3.00	2.92	2.84	2.75	2.66	2.57
19	8.18	5.93	5.01	4.50	4.17	3.94	3.77	3.63	3.52	3.43	3.30	3.15	3.00	2.92	2.84	2.76	2.67	2.58	2.49

df_2																			
20	8.10	5.85	4.94	4.43	4.10	3.87	3.70	3.56	3.46	3.37	3.23	3.09	2.94	2.86	2.78	2.69	2.61	2.52	2.42
21	8.02	5.78	4.87	4.37	4.04	3.81	3.64	3.51	3.40	3.31	3.17	3.03	2.88	2.80	2.72	2.64	2.55	2.46	2.36
22	7.95	5.72	4.82	4.31	3.99	3.76	3.59	3.45	3.35	3.26	3.12	2.98	2.83	2.75	2.67	2.58	2.50	2.40	2.31
23	7.88	5.66	4.76	4.26	3.94	3.71	3.54	3.41	3.30	3.21	3.07	2.93	2.78	2.70	2.62	2.54	2.45	2.35	2.26
24	7.82	5.61	4.72	4.22	3.90	3.67	3.50	3.36	3.26	3.17	3.03	2.89	2.74	2.66	2.58	2.49	2.40	2.31	2.21
25	7.77	5.57	4.68	4.18	3.85	3.63	3.46	3.32	3.22	3.13	2.99	2.85	2.70	2.62	2.54	2.45	2.36	2.27	2.17
26	7.72	5.53	4.64	4.14	3.82	3.59	3.42	3.29	3.18	3.09	2.96	2.81	2.66	2.58	2.50	2.42	2.33	2.23	2.13
27	7.68	5.49	4.60	4.11	3.78	3.56	3.39	3.26	3.15	3.06	2.93	2.78	2.63	2.55	2.47	2.38	2.29	2.20	2.10
28	7.64	5.45	4.57	4.07	3.75	3.53	3.36	3.23	3.12	3.03	2.90	2.75	2.60	2.52	2.44	2.35	2.26	2.17	2.06
29	7.60	5.42	4.54	4.04	3.73	3.50	3.33	3.20	3.09	3.00	2.87	2.73	2.57	2.49	2.41	2.33	2.23	2.14	2.03
30	7.56	5.39	4.51	4.02	3.70	3.47	3.30	3.17	3.07	2.98	2.84	2.70	2.55	2.47	2.39	2.30	2.21	2.11	2.01
40	7.31	5.18	4.31	3.83	3.51	3.29	3.12	2.99	2.89	2.80	2.66	2.52	2.37	2.29	2.20	2.11	2.02	1.92	1.80
60	7.08	4.98	4.13	3.65	3.34	3.12	2.95	2.82	2.72	2.63	2.50	2.35	2.20	2.12	2.03	1.94	1.84	1.73	1.60
120	6.85	4.79	3.95	3.48	3.17	2.96	2.79	2.66	2.56	2.47	2.34	2.19	2.03	1.95	1.86	1.76	1.66	1.53	1.38
∞	6.63	4.61	3.78	3.32	3.02	2.80	2.64	2.51	2.41	2.32	2.18	2.04	1.88	1.79	1.70	1.59	1.47	1.32	1.00

Note: df_1 = rows of table (for degrees of freedom in denominator) – within
df_2 = columns of table (for degrees of freedom in numerator) – between

Appendix

2

MULTIVARIATE STATISTICS

The discussions of statistics in Chapters 10–12 dealt with *univariate* procedures, which are used to investigate the relationship between one or more independent variables and a single dependent variable. This appendix is an introductory discussion of multivariate statistics, methods that allow analysis of several independent variables *and* several dependent variables in a single study.

The rationale for using multivariate statistics in mass media research is quite simple. Both human behavior and the media are complex systems of interacting variables. There are few situations in which one dependent variable accurately represents a phenomenon or is solely responsible for a particular attitude or behavior. Instead, a series of dependent variables, correlated to some degree, act together to produce or represent a phenomenon, or create an attitude or behavior.

Because they accept the idea of interacting variables affecting interrelated phenomena, many researchers select multivariate statistical methods to analyze data rather than the more traditional, and limited, univariate approaches. This does not mean that univariate procedures are invalid, but rather that multivariate statistics are generally more useful in media research.

The reliance on multivariate analysis in research is based on insights formulated several years ago: (1) Any given experimental manipulation affects several different, but partially related, areas of an individual's behavior, and univariate analysis is capable of investigating only one of these relationships at a time (Harris, 1975); (2) Because human beings are multidimensional, it seems reasonable to study them on several dimensions simultaneously, rather than to focus on a single, often arbitrarily chosen variable (Tucker, 1982); (3) Measurements taken on the same individual are correlated by virtue of their common origin and thus lend themselves to simultaneous study (Tucker, 1982); (4) Multivariate statistical methods save time, money, and resources, since it is much simpler to investigate several correlated variables simultaneously than to study them one at a time; and (5) Multivariate analysis allows researchers to investigate variables as *structures* or *constructs* rather than as the individual components of a structure or construct (Cattell, 1966).

However, multivariate statistics have some disadvantages. First of all, they are more difficult to use than univariate methods. Unlike a *t*-test, for example, multivariate methods require extensive reading and trial-and-error work with a computer. The interpretation of multivariate results is also difficult in many instances. Whereas the results of a *t*-test are relatively straightforward—two groups are either similar or different—in multivariate procedures, researchers are often faced with dozens of variable combinations to interpret, and intuitive abilities may become taxed.

Another disadvantage of the multivariate approach is that it is easy to include too many variables so that no sense can be made of the results. Although researchers are often tempted to include many potentially relevant variables in a multivariate study, guidelines must be established and followed to restrain this tendency. Finally, multivariate statistics are useful when a research question calls for such analysis, but they are not a panacea for all research problems.

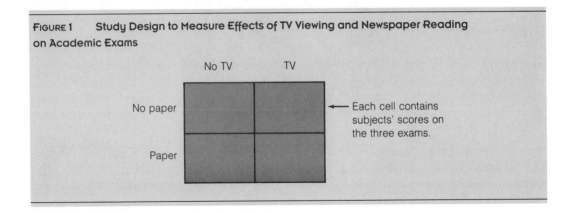

FIGURE 1   Study Design to Measure Effects of TV Viewing and Newspaper Reading on Academic Exams

This appendix is devoted to discussions of the most widely used multivariate statistical methods and examples of how they are used in mass media research. The simplified explanations ignore many controversial aspects of each method for the sake of brevity. Readers interested in learning more about multivariate statistics should consult the works listed in the "References and Suggested Readings" section.

BASICS OF MULTIVARIATE STATISTICS

The usefulness of multivariate statistics can be demonstrated by an example using the method called **multivariate analysis of variance (MANOVA)**. Assume that researchers are interested in measuring the effects of television viewing and newspaper reading on academic exams in English, history, and economics. Their study design would look like Figure 1, which depicts four situations: "No paper/No TV," "No paper/TV," "Paper/No TV," and "Paper/TV." MANOVA allows the researchers to investigate the effects of the independent variables on all three exams simultaneously; univariate ANOVA would require three individual studies of each exam. It is clear that the multivariate procedure represents a significant savings in time, money, and resources.

All multivariate statistics are designed to reduce an original "test space," or group of data, into a minimum number of values or dimensions that describe the relevant information contained in the data. Thus, instead of using 20 dependent variables to describe a phenomenon, a researcher might use multivariate methods to reduce the number to 3 summary variables (weighted linear combinations) that are nearly as accurate as the original 20. Data reduction involves little loss of information and makes the data easier to handle. It is an especially useful process in mass media studies dealing with almost limitless numbers of variables.

MATRIX ALGEBRA

Multivariate procedures solve the problem of comparing multiple criterion variables by establishing *weighted linear combinations* of two or more such scores. These composite scores are represented as lines in space called **vectors**. Thus in multivariate statistics one or more vectors are manipulated, usually in an attempt to predict an outcome or event through the principle of least squares. This manipulation of vectors requires a different type of analysis, involving what is known as *matrix algebra*.

Because all multivariate statistics deal with multiple measurements of data in multidimensional space, they depend on matrix algebra. A complete knowledge of matrix algebra is not necessary to understand multivariate statistics, but familiarity with several frequently used terms is essential.

A **scalar** is a single-digit number, such as 6, 9, or 7. A column of scalars is called a *column vector* and is denoted by a lowercase letter:

$$a = \begin{bmatrix} a_1 \\ a_2 \\ \cdot \\ \cdot \\ \cdot \\ a_n \end{bmatrix}$$

(The subscript represents the scalar's location in the column.)

A row of scalars is referred to as a **row vector** and is denoted by a lowercase letter followed by a prime symbol:

$$a' = [a_1 a_2 \cdots a_n]$$

A **matrix** is a two-dimensional array of scalars, having p rows and n columns, and is denoted by a capital letter:

$$A = \begin{bmatrix} a_{11} & a_{12} & \cdots & a_{1n} \\ a_{21} & a_{22} & \cdots & a_{2n} \\ a_{p1} & a_{p2} & \cdots & a_{pn} \end{bmatrix}$$

The most common matrix used in multivariate statistics is the **intercorrelation** (or simply correlation) **matrix**, which is denoted as R. This matrix contains the coefficients of correlation between pairs of variables. For example, a 3 × 3 correlation matrix (the first number refers to the number of rows, the second to the number of columns) is used to display the relationship between three variables:

$$R = \begin{bmatrix} 1.0 & .64 & .29 \\ .64 & 1.0 & .42 \\ .29 & .42 & 1.0 \end{bmatrix}$$

This is a **square matrix**: the number of rows equals the number of columns. It contains the value 1.00 in the principal diagonal (top left to bottom right) because the correlation of a variable with itself is usually considered to be 100%. The term *usually* is necessary because in some multivariate models, it is assumed that even a correlation of a variable with itself includes some error and hence must be valued at less than 1.00.

A **diagonal matrix** is a square matrix whose elements equal zero except in the principal diagonal. If in addition all the elements in the principal diagonal are 1, the array is known as an **identity matrix** and is denoted by a capital *I*:

$$I = \begin{bmatrix} 1 & 0 & 0 \\ 0 & 1 & 0 \\ 0 & 0 & 1 \end{bmatrix}$$

An identity matrix indicates that there are no correlations between the variables in the analysis except for the correlation of each variable with itself. Essentially, the identity matrix form implies that the data are of poor quality. Identity matrices are common in research studies that use random numbers (usually in demonstrations of statistical procedures).

Associated with every square matrix is a single number that represents a unique function of the numbers contained in the matrix. This scalar function is known as a **determinant** and is denoted as *A*. In addition, each square matrix has an associated characteristic equation that represents the information contained in the matrix. The results from the characteristic equation (when computed) reproduce the matrix from which the equation was developed. Several values can be used to calculate a characteristic equation for a matrix; each of these includes a value or number known as an **eigenvalue**. Each eigenvalue has an associated eigenvector (a column of numbers); the eigenvalue is actually the sum of the squared elements in the eigenvector. In short, eigenvalues and eigenvectors are used to construct a formula that duplicates the information contained in a matrix. Each matrix has a number of characteristic equations, but only one is appropriate for a particular type of analysis.

Multivariate statistics involve two basic algebraic operations. The first is *partitioning* of a matrix, whereby the original matrix is divided into submatrices for analysis. The second operation, *transposition,* involves changing the matrix columns to rows and the rows to columns for further analysis (Horst, 1966). For example, the "transpose" of Matrix *A* is Matrix *A'*:

$$A = \begin{bmatrix} 1 & 4 \\ 2 & 5 \\ 3 & 6 \end{bmatrix} \qquad A' = \begin{bmatrix} 1 & 2 & 3 \\ 4 & 5 & 6 \end{bmatrix}$$

SIX MULTIVARIATE PROCEDURES

Although there are several multivariate statistics available, six methods appear to be used most often in mass media research. These are factor analysis, canonical correlation, discriminant analysis, multivariate analysis of variance (MANOVA), cluster analysis, and multidimensional scaling. Each method is discussed in terms of how it works and what it can do in media research.

FACTOR ANALYSIS

Factor analysis is a generic term for a variety of statistical procedures developed for the analysis of the intercorrelations *within* a set of variables. These relationships are represented by weighted linear combinations known as factor scores (or variates), which, in turn, are used in the development of constructs and theories. Factor analysis is divided into several techniques, each of which is appropriate to a specific type of investigation. However, two major techniques are used most often in mass media research: *R-technique* and *Q-technique*. The R-

technique is used to factor a set of variables collected at the same time from a number of individuals. The Q-technique is used to factor a number of individuals from variables collected at the same time from those individuals.

Each technique includes a variety of approaches. Types of R-technique factor analysis include common factor analysis (CFA), principal components analysis (PC or PCA), and minimum residuals (minres). The most often used procedure in the Q-technique is cluster analysis, which seeks to identify types of individuals, not groups of variables as in the R-technique.

Because of its flexibility, factor analysis is the most widely used multivariate statistic in mass media research. Some of the more common uses for factor analysis include the following (Rummel, 1970).

1. Investigating patterns of variable relationships
2. Reducing data
3. Analyzing the structure of a phenomenon
4. Classifying or describing individuals, groups, or variables
5. Developing measurement scales (Chapter 3)
6. Testing hypotheses or research questions
7. Making preliminary investigations in new areas of research

Developing Theories. As Rummel suggested, factor analysis is appropriate in any phase of research, from pilot studies to theory development. This is not true of other multivariate statistical procedures. Researchers who use factor analysis assume that any group of variables has some inherent order that, once discovered, can make the description of a concept or construct less complicated. As Thurstone (1947) noted:

A factor problem starts with the hope or conviction that a certain domain is not so chaotic as it looks. Factor analysis was developed primarily for the purposes of identifying principal dimensions or categories of mentality; but the methods are general, so that they have been found useful for other psychological problems and in other sciences as well. . . . Factor analysis is especially useful in those domains where basic and fruitful concepts are essentially lacking and where experiments have been difficult to achieve.

As Thurstone suggested, factor analysis is useful in all types of scientific research. This does not imply, however, that the results of a factor analysis in any particular area are necessarily *meaningful;* any matrix of variables can be factorially analyzed, but not all will yield scientifically useful or meaningful information (Gorsuch, 1974). It is necessary to understand the purpose of factor analysis in order to determine its appropriateness for a specific mass media problem.

Factor analysis includes a wide variety of alternatives. Because of the complexity of many of these methods, it is not possible to discuss each one here. This is left to multivariate statistics books and other more detailed texts.

The two most widely used forms of factor analysis are *principal components* and *principal factors* (also called common factor analysis). The methods are identical except for the initial step: The principal components model uses *unities* (1.00) in the principal diagonal of the correlation matrix, while the principal factors technique assumes that each variable's correlation with itself contains some degree of error and therefore cannot be 100%. These correlations, called *communalities*, replace the unities in the principal diagonal of the original matrix. Communalities are a bit more complicated than unities, since they are only *estimates* of the correlations of variables and themselves. Although choosing the communality estimates to insert into the principal diagonal may sound simple, it is one of the most controversial decisions in factor analysis.

A typical factor analysis begins with the collection of data on a number of different variables (usually at the interval or ratio level). These quantified variables are then transformed via computer into a *product-moment correlation matrix,* the matrix that is usually chosen for factoring. To illustrate, consider the problem of determining which medium, or combination of media, a subject uses for news and information. A questionnaire is designed to collect this information with regard to five media sources: radio, television, magazines, newspapers, and books. The correlation matrix developed from these data may look like Figure 2. The matrix shows the correlations between all five variables. The principal diagonal divides the matrix into two parts, each a mirror image of the other. The diagonal itself is composed of unities, indicating that the method of principal components is being employed.

Note that although any matrix can be factored, even a matrix of random numbers, certain procedures can help researchers determine whether a particular correlation matrix is valid. Two tests are particularly useful: Bartlett's sphericity test and Kaiser's measure of sampling adequacy (MSA). Both are used to determine the quality of the correlation matrix and to indicate whether the information is adequate for analysis.

In mathematical terms, factoring a matrix consists of extracting eigenvectors and their associated eigenvalues. These two sets of values are used to mathematically reproduce the correlation matrix. Eigenvectors are factor loadings, or numerical values from -1.00 to $+1.00$, indicating each variable's relative contribution toward defining a factor. A factor loading is a quantified relationship—the farther its value is from zero, the more relevant the variable is to the factor. The eigenvalues are used to determine which factors are relevant, and hence should be analyzed. (Recall that an eigenvalue is computed by squaring and summing the elements in its eigenvector.) One common procedure is to interpret only the factors with eigenvalues greater than 1.00 (though other methods are used).

The eigenvectors and eigenvalues for the hypothetical study are displayed in Table 1. This example shows that two factors "fell out"

FIGURE 2   Example of Correlation Matrix (*R*)

	1	2	3	4	5
1	1.00	.92	.70	.38	.05
2	.92	1.00	.95	.71	.26
3	.70	.95	1.00	.88	.33
4	.38	.71	.88	1.00	.14
5	.05	.26	.33	.14	1.00

(were significant as determined by the eigen-value cutoff of greater than 1.00) and may be used in explaining the media used for news and information. The eigenvalues are computed by squaring and summing each element in the eigenvector:

The analysis does not stop with this initial extraction of factors; the initial factor loadings are generally too complex to be used for interpretation. Instead, researchers generally perform a second step, factor *rotation,* which essentially involves changing the multidimensional space in which the factors are located. Recall that eigenvectors (a vector of factor loadings) represent lines in space—a space visually constructed by *x*- and *y*-axes. The unrotated factor loadings are often in complex form; that is, there may be several complex variables such that one variable loads significantly on more than one factor. Rotation attempts to clear this problem by changing the space in which the factor loadings are placed. The new factor loadings are mathematically equivalent to the original unrotated matrix, but more often they represent a more meaningful set of factors—where the goal is to have each variable load significantly on only one factor. This additional ease of interpretation

makes rotation appealing in behavioral research. A rotated factor matrix is shown in Table 2.

The rotated factor matrix is mathematically equivalent to the unrotated matrix, as witnessed by identical eigenvalues, and the factors are now easier to interpret. The first step in interpretation is to identify the variables that are associated with one and only one factor. Here, it is evident that Variables 1, 2, and 3 "load" more heavily on Factor 1, while Variables 4 and 5 load more heavily on Factor 2. Three variables (1, 2, 3) are said to "define" Factor 1, and two variables (4, 5) define Factor 2.

The next step is to categorize the factors on the basis of the variables that define it. In this case, Factor 1 might be classified as "print media" and Factor 2 as "electronic media." In reality, however, Factor 2 might be eliminated altogether at this point, since it is defined by just two variables. When classifying factors it is customary to select only those that have at least three variables with significant loadings. Some researchers consider this practice controversial, but three significant loadings are necessary to establish the direction of the factor. If a factor has only two significant variable load-

TABLE 1	Unrotated Factor Matrix		
Medium	**Factor 1**	**Factor 2**	
Newspaper	.85	.53	
Magazines	.66	−.09	
Books	.37	.73	Eigenvectors
Radio	−.52	.34	
Television	.29	.63	
	1.65	1.33	Eigenvalues

ings—one positive and the other negative—it cannot be determined whether the factor itself is positive or negative; a third variable is required to provide the direction. Even when both variables are positive or both are negative, however, a two-variable factor may be inadequate to explain the variance in the factor. As a general rule, it is best to consider only factors that are defined by at least three variables.

Researchers must also consider which type of rotation to use. Although many procedures are available, the two used most often by behavioral researchers are *orthogonal* and *oblique* rotation. The names refer to the angles of the axes on which the data points (factor loadings) are located. Orthogonal rotation keeps the angles at 90° and assumes that the factors are not intercorrelated (that is, orthogonal = uncorre-

lated). Oblique rotation allows the axes to take any angle that will produce the most interpretable results; researchers using this approach assume that the factors are correlated to some degree (that is, oblique = correlated). The choice of a rotation method depends on the researcher's likes and dislikes as well as the purpose of the study.

Of the many possible uses of factor analysis mentioned earlier, the three that are most prominent in research studies are data reduction, the search for order in variable structures, and the exploration of uncharted phenomena.

1. *Data reduction,* as noted earlier, is essential when investigating research problems that contain large numbers of variables. Factor analysis is often used as a preliminary narrowing device because it allows the salient variables to be selected from a large group: It provides a simplification of a particular domain of variables by replacing them with a small number of hypothetical variates (weighted linear sums of the original variables, or factor scores). These variates can then be used in other analyses that employ different statistical methods without a substantial loss of information. For example, consider a 50-item questionnaire designed to measure attitudes toward commercials on television and their effects on buying habits. A factor analysis of the 50 variables would produce a substantially smaller number of representative variates, or factor

TABLE 2	Rotated Factor Matrix	
Medium	**Factor 1**	**Factor 2**
Newspaper	.87	.15
Magazines	.66	−.03
Books	.61	.22
Radio	.17	.85
Television	.20	.74
	1.63	1.34

scores, thus providing an opportunity for a much simpler explanation of the phenomenon being investigated.

2. *The search for order* in a domain of variables via factor analysis is referred to by several different names: It can be said that factor analysis identifies variable patterns, dimensions of variable domains, underlying constructs, factor dimensions, or factor structures. Whatever terminology is used, the meaning is the same: Factor analysis allows the identification from a large group of variables of a smaller number of composite variables that help order and define the phenomenon under study.

A construct such as "program success" may be defined by an infinite number of variables. It may be difficult, if not impossible, to intuitively determine which variables contribute significantly to the construct. Factor analysis, by reducing the number of variables, makes it easier to identify patterns and underlying structures. However, one factor analysis does not produce conclusive results concerning the composition of a construct; different samples, different factor analysis methods, and different variables must be used to verify that the initial results were not sample- or method-specific. That is, replication is necessary to ensure that results are not dependent on some condition external to the relationship among the variables.

3. Finally, factor analysis can help to provide *explanations of previously unstudied phenomena*. Every research area has many concepts and constructs that have eluded investigation. One reason for this is that the concepts are obscured by large numbers of variables. An example is the question of what characterizes a successful television program. Television executives still do not know; there are simply too many variables. Factor analysis can play a significant (albeit preliminary) role in solving problems of this nature by isolating salient variables from those that will add nothing to the accuracy of a prediction.

Factor analysis allows researchers to take a panoramic view of a variable domain and to isolate important variables. However, it should be used only when a research project is well constructed and meets the prerequisite assumptions discussed above. It should *not* be used in an attempt to salvage a poorly planned study. As mentioned earlier, any matrix of variables can be factorially analyzed, but there is no guarantee that the results will be meaningful.

CANONICAL CORRELATION

Canonical correlation (R_c) is essentially a multivariate extension of linear multiple regression: A group of independent variables is analyzed to predict multiple criterion variables. However, no distinction is actually made between independent and dependent variables; there are simply two *sets* of variables.

A canonical correlation begins with the formation of an intercorrelation "supermatrix" composed of both sets of variables. For example, if three variables are included in one set and two variables in the second set, the intercorrelation matrix is formed as in Figure 3.

Note that the correlation matrix is divided into four areas: R_{11} represents the intercorrelations among the elements of Set 1; R_{22} denotes intercorrelations among the elements of Set 2; and R_{12} and R_{21} are the cross-correlations between the elements of Sets 1 and 2. This "supermatrix" of intercorrelations provides the information necessary to compute the basic R_c relationship matrix by means of the formula:

$$R_c = [R_{22}^{-1} R_{21} R_{11}^{-1} R_{12}]$$

The canonical correlation matrix formed by the formula is a square matrix and therefore contains eigenvectors and eigenvalues (each unique solution is called a *root*; each root has a canonical correlation). A *pair* of eigenvectors is extracted from each variable set and normalized; the resulting scalar values are the sets' beta weights. Finally, for each variable set, the subject's standardized raw scores are multi-

FIGURE 3 R_c Intercorrelation "Supermatrix"

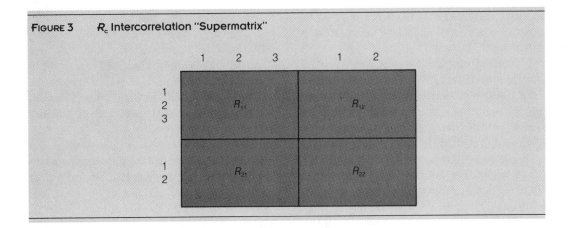

plied by the beta weight and the products summed. This process yields a pair of scores called *composite canonical variates* (weighted linear combinations of variables). The R_c is the product-moment correlation between these variates.

A researcher interprets three basic values in canonical correlation analysis: The canonical correlation for each root, the canonical components, and the redundancy index. The canonical correlation, since it is merely a product-moment correlation, is interpreted in the same way as any correlation value: The closer the value to 1.00, the stronger the relationship between the composite variates (canonical correlations cannot be negative). The R_c model allows the extraction of as many roots as there are variables in the smaller of the two sets (in the example above, the researcher could extract two unique roots), and each of these is orthogonal (uncorrelated) to all other roots in the analysis. This can provide several possibilities for interpretation (though not all the roots may be statistically significant).

Interpretation of the individual variables in a canonical correlation involves analyzing their *canonical components,* that is, each variable's correlation with the canonical variate corresponding to its particular set. Thus, the canonical components are also correlations and

interpreted as such: The components whose values are farthest from zero are considered most significant. However, not all researchers agree on what constitutes a significant component value; many consider .30 to be significant, while others use .35, .40, or some different value.

The redundancy index provides the direction in which the canonical results should be interpreted; that is, it determines whether the R_c is to be interpreted as "Set 1 given Set 2" or "Set 2 given Set 1," or, possibly, whether it should be interpreted in both directions. The redundancy index increases the interpretive value of canonical correlation by allowing researchers to interpret relationships within canonical components, as well as between the variable sets. In fact, relationships between sets should never be interpreted without first computing the redundancy index.

The formula for computing a redundancy index (R) is simple: Square each component value in a variable set, add the squares, divide the sum by the number of variables in the set, and multiply this value by the canonical correlation squared:

$$\overline{R} = \frac{\Sigma (R_{cc})^2}{M} (R_c^2)$$

where $\bar{R}$ = the redundancy index; R_{cc} = a canonical component; and M = the number of variables in the set.

The importance of these three values in canonical correlation analysis can be illustrated by the research problem shown in Table 3, which asked the question, "What, if any, relationship exists between the mass media actually used for political information and the media considered to be most informative?"

First consider the four canonical correlations for the four roots. Each root has a value of at least .30, indicating that all may be interpreted unless the component loadings and redundancy index indicate otherwise (.30 is usually the cutoff value for interpretation of a canonical root; however, this depends on the nature of the study and the requirements established by the researcher). In most cases not all the roots in a canonical analysis have a value of .30 or higher, but such values are common in studies using extremely large samples.

The second step is to examine the significant canonical components, which are considered to be those with absolute values of .30 or greater. (Again, this limit is at the discretion of the researcher.) Referring to Root 1, the variables in Set 1 (also known as the *left set*) show a high positive component value for television (.53) and a very low value for the variable "none" ($-.30$); the remaining variables have values too minimal to be considered significant. The left variable set of Root 1 thus suggests a degree of dichotomy: A great many subjects considered television the most informative medium for political information, but a smaller number indicated that none was most informative, possibly meaning that all were regarded as equally informative. (The negative value means that those subjects who responded "television" as most informative did not respond "none".) All the variables in Set 2 (the *right set*) surpassed the .30 cutoff value for Root 1, indicating that the subjects in the study used all these media for political information.

Before the computation can be continued,

redundancy indexes must be computed. Without redundancy figures, one can interpret only the relationships within sets, not those between sets. This point is repeated because of its importance: Many researchers incorrectly interpret the relationships between sets because they have neglected to compute redundancy indexes.

The general cutoff level for redundancy is .05. That is, a canonical root must account for at least 5% of the variance in the set before interpretation can continue. The redundancy indexes displayed in Table 3 indicate that only Set 2 of the first root achieved a high enough value to qualify for further interpretation; this means that Root 1 is to be interpreted from the right set (media used), given the left set (media considered most informative).

The remaining three roots in the analysis did not receive significant redundancy indexes (even though their R_c values met minimum requirements); these roots must therefore either be eliminated from further discussion or interpreted for heuristic value only. This demonstrates how the redundancy index serves as a cross-validation for the canonical roots extracted from the analysis; it serves as a back-up test for significance.

Applying this information to the data, the results show that individuals who used all the media for political information tended to feel that television was the most informative. In addition, a smaller group of individuals who used all the media felt that all were equally important.

Discriminant Analysis

Mass media researchers frequently are interested in examining or predicting the attitudes or behavior of subjects who are members of a particular group. For example, a researcher might wish to examine the differences between subjects who subscribe to certain magazines or newspapers, or to predict the characteristics of individuals occupying management-level

TABLE 3	Canonical Correlation Example			
Variables	**Root 1** ($R_c = .85$)	**Root 2** ($R_c = .45$)	**Root 3** ($R_c = .31$)	**Root 4** ($R_c = .31$)
Left set (media considered most informative)				
Newspaper	.28 (1.00)*	−.63 (−.29)	−.33 (−.07)	−.06 (−.03)
Radio	.02 (.35)	−.08 (.01)	.42 (.50)	−.87 (−.84)
Television	.53 (1.30)**	.53 (.62)	−.30 (.10)	.01 (.02)
Magazines	.16 (.54)	−.46 (−.31)	.64 (.72)	.46 (.45)
Paper and TV	.07 (.27)	−.02 (.03)	−.15 (−.10)	.05 (.05)
2 Combination	.06 (.22)	−.10 (−.05)	.13 (.17)	−.10 (.09)
3 Combination	.04 (.13)	−.09 (−.01)	.10 (.12)	−.02 (−.02)
People	.01 (.08)	.06 (.09)	−.05 (−.03)	.01 (.01)
None	−.30 (.50)**	.49 (.65)	.46 (.59)	.19 (.18)
Right set (media used for political information)				
Newspaper	.85 (.41)**	−.41 (−.82)	−.30 (−.99)	.02 (−.05)
Radio	.62 (.15)**	−.03 (.07)	.32 (.43)	−.70 (−1.10)
Magazines	.63 (.52)**	−.38 (.45)	.56 (.97)	.35 (.57)
Television	.90 (.52)**	.41 (1.10)	.02 (−.05)	.11 (.39)

Root 1: $x^2 = 5,460.32$; $df = 36$; $p < .01$
Root 2: $x^2 = 1,358.26$; $df = 24$; $p < .01$
Root 3: $x^2 = \ 635.01$; $df = 14$; $p < .01$
Root 4: $x^2 = \ 313.93$; $df = \ 6$; $p < .01$

Redundancy indexes

Left set		Right set	
Root 1:	.0470	Root 1:	.4308
Root 2:	.0273	Root 2:	.0258
Root 3:	.0117	Root 3:	.0126
Root 4:	.0111	Root 4:	.0154

*Canonical components are listed first with corresponding beta weights in parentheses.
**Indicates a significant canonical component value.

positions in the media. Discriminant analysis can be a useful tool in research situations of these types.

In **discriminant analysis**, linear combinations of continuously scaled variables are derived from measurements of groups of subjects. The model is used to define a vector that represents the variables for each group so that the separation between groups is maximized. In other words, the researcher uses all the variables in the discriminant analysis to compute a weighted linear combination (variate) for each group, from which it can be determined which of the variables are most helpful in separating or distinguishing the groups. These variables are known as the *discriminating variables*.

The discriminant analysis procedure is shown in graphic form in Figure 4. Here, a bivariate example is used (two groups). The two ellipses represent data *swarms* for each group, and the dot at the center of each ellipse denotes the group mean, or *centroid*. The two points at which the ellipses intersect define a line, designated as A. If a second line, B, is constructed perpendicular to Line A, and the points from the intersection of Groups 1 and 2 are projected onto Line B, the overlap between the groups is smaller along Line B (indicated as *a*) than any other possible line (Cooley & Lohnes, 1971). The discriminant analysis procedure attempts to define this *true* line along which the groups are maximally separated.

Discriminant analysis can serve two purposes, analysis and classification. The data are analyzed by means of statistical tests designed to measure the significance of the combined variables. In classification, which takes place after the data have been analyzed, categories of membership are created for the subjects in the study. A particular study may involve one or both procedures.

Discriminant analysis is closely related to factor analysis and canonical correlation in that each model extracts "factors" from a battery of variables. The factors, which are linear combinations in all models, are referred to as *discriminant functions*. Each discriminant function is orthogonal to all others in the analysis; that is, each function is an independent representation of the analysis in question. In discriminant analysis, the number of functions is one less than the number of groups involved, unless the number of variables in the analysis is smaller. In that case, the number of discriminant functions is equal to the number of original variables.

Interpreting a discriminant analysis involves examining the discriminant functions and the weights assigned to each of the variables used in forming those functions. Taken together, these observations allow researchers to analyze the nature of group differences. As in factor analysis, the dimensions represented by the discriminant functions may be susceptible to meaningful interpretation. However, even if the interpretation is not meaningful, conciseness is achieved by reducing the original space in which the group differences existed (Tatsuoka, 1971).

Another procedure involved in discriminant analysis is plotting the centroids of the discriminant functions. Each group has a mean for the linear combination it creates; these means are plotted to determine the nature of the distance between the groups—the plot provides a visual representation of group differences. Tests are also available to indicate whether the distance separating the groups is statistically significant (Klecka, 1980; Tatsuoka, 1970).

Haynes (1978) used discriminant analysis to test two hypotheses related to children's perceptions of comic and authentic violence in cartoons. A "comic" cartoon was defined as one that portrayed a violent act in a comical manner, and the victim suffered no true or lasting ill effects. An "authentic" cartoon depicted a violent act as "true to life," with no comic effect intended. The two hypotheses were (1) that children would perceive the violence in a comic cartoon as being more violent than that in an

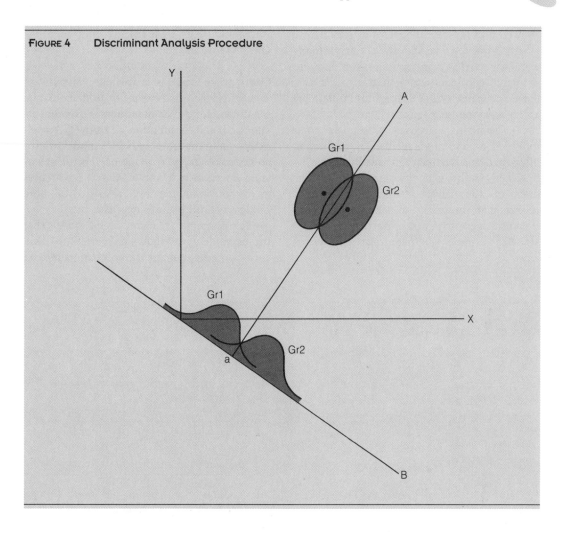

FIGURE 4   Discriminant Analysis Procedure

authentic cartoon, and (2) that females would perceive all the cartoons as being more violent than would males. Haynes's first step was to administer a 12-item questionnaire to a group of 120 children, asking them to describe how they felt about a cartoon they viewed in an experimental situation. These responses were factor analyzed and the factor scores used in the discriminant analysis to determine whether group differences existed. (In this study, Haynes used discriminant analysis solely as a classification procedure, since he had no knowledge about group membership beforehand.)

The first discriminant function (DF I, Table 4) revealed that the males and females who viewed the comic cartoons (Group 1) were most clearly distinguishable from the males and females who viewed the authentic cartoons (Group 2) in terms of a function described as "perceived violence" (so named because of the nature of the most significantly weighted variables in the function). The second discriminant function, DF II, showed that Group 1 was most different from Group 2 with regard to a function described as "acceptability of violence." The centroids for each group showed that no sex differences existed. However, Haynes did find that the comic cartoons were perceived as being more violent than the authentic cartoons, and that the comic violence was perceived as being more unacceptable than authentic violence.

Discriminant analysis is a useful research tool in all areas of mass media. The method is often used as a secondary phase of research, as it was by Haynes, whereby the researcher conducts a factor analysis or other statistical procedure that produces summary scores, and then uses these scores in a discriminant analysis to determine whether group differences exist.

MULTIVARIATE ANALYSIS OF VARIANCE

Multivariate analysis of variance (MANOVA) was introduced briefly earlier to demonstrate the utility of multivariate statistics over univariate methods. As mentioned, MANOVA is an extension of the simple ANOVA model to situations involving more than one dependent variable. Specifically, MANOVA allows researchers to test the differences between two or more groups on multiple response data.

The distinctive feature of MANOVA is that the dependent variables are represented as a vector, or weighted linear combination, instead

TABLE 4 Haynes's Discriminant Analysis of Male and Female Perceptions of "Comic" and "Authentic" Cartoon Violence		
	Discriminant function coefficients	
	Function I	**Function II**
Perceived violence	−.997	.079
Acceptability of violence	.093	.994
DF 1-perceived violence	**Centroids**	
Male/authentic	.35	
Female/authentic	.42	
Male/comic	−.48	
Female/comic	−.51	
DF II-acceptability	**Centroids**	
Male/authentic	.61	
Female/authentic	.65	
Male/comic	−.17	
Female/comic	−.12	

Source: "Children's Perception of 'Comic' and 'Authentic' Cartoon Violence" by Richard B. Haynes, Winter 1978, *Journal of Broadcasting,* p. 68. Reprinted by permission.

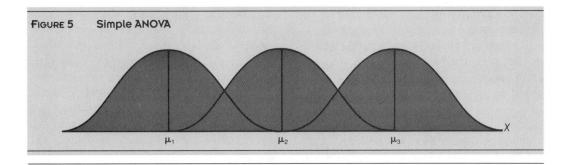

FIGURE 5   Simple ANOVA

of as a single value, as in ANOVA. ANOVA involves testing for group differences along a continuum formed by the dependent variable, as is shown in Figure 5 (Cooley & Lohnes, 1971).

The MANOVA model extends this idea by testing for group differences in a multidimensional space, as depicted in Figure 6.

The test used in MANOVA to determine the equality of centroids (compared to the test for equality of group means in ANOVA) involves forming an F-ratio between the within

groups' and total groups' *dispersion matrices*. This concept is beyond the scope of an introductory text; suffice it to say that the procedure is similar to that used in ANOVA except that matrices are used instead of sums of squares.

Lambert, Doering, Goldstein, and McCormick (1980) performed a study that illustrates how several dependent variables can be simultaneously analyzed using MANOVA. The project demonstrates that not only are time and resources saved, but also several characteristics of an individual can be considered simultaneously,

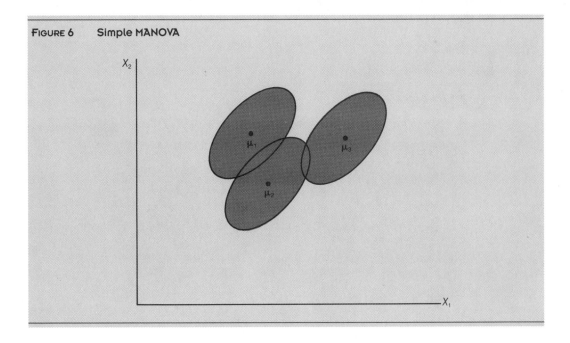

FIGURE 6   Simple MANOVA

thus providing a closer approximation of reality than could a univariate statistical approach.

Lambert and his colleagues were interested in examining the attitudes of consumers generally, and of the elderly in particular, about opportunities to save money by substituting lower-priced generic drugs for brand name products prescribed by their physicians. The authors used a multistage quota sampling procedure to select 510 respondents from four cities in Florida. The subjects completed a questionnaire containing 18 dependent variables. An interesting aspect of the study was the refusal of several of the respondents over age 65 to cooperate with the researchers for one reason or another (such as poor eyesight or fear of being victimized by salespeople). The study offers excellent examples of the problems that can occur in some research studies.

The authors divided the sample into two groups: people who accepted the idea that generic drugs are equivalent to brand name drugs, and those who did not. The groups were compared with respect to their scores on the 18 variables, which included demographics, mobility, general drug knowledge, age, and income. The design is illustrated in Figure 7.

The MANOVA results indicated a significant difference ($p < .0001$) between the two groups on the 18 variables taken as a whole. The study allowed the authors to discuss the influence of many variables on consumers' attitudes toward generic drugs and to recommend how drug education programs might help individuals, especially older people, take advantage of the lower-cost generic drugs that are available.

CLUSTER ANALYSIS

Cluster analysis refers to a variety of methods used by researchers when the goal is to classify phenomena into similar groups, or clusters. For example, radio listeners in a given market can be placed in clusters according to their evaluations of various types of music.

Cluster analysis analyzes variables and determines their similarity or dissimilarity, and then places similar variables in groups. The procedure is similar to factor analysis. Most people differentiate between the two methods by stating that factor analysis analyzes columns of data in a data set, whereas cluster analysis investigates the rows of data. However, a few

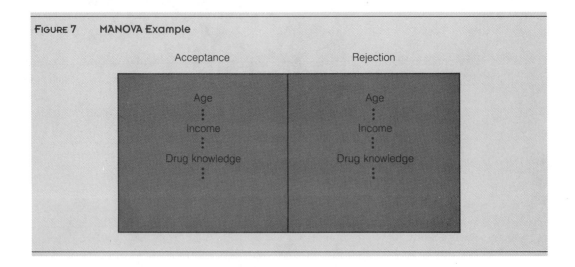

FIGURE 7   MANOVA Example

FIGURE 8   Classic Rock Cluster: MDS Graph of Radio Stations

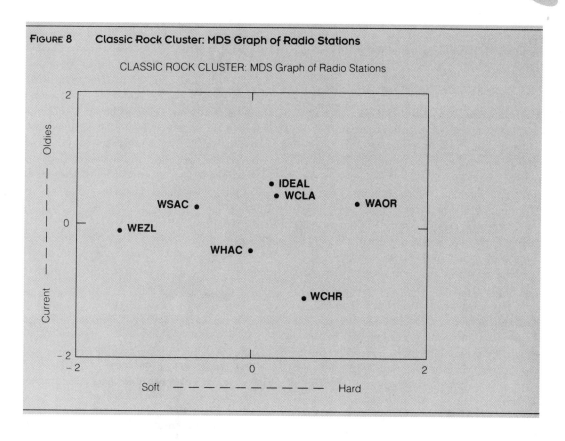

CLASSIC ROCK CLUSTER: MDS Graph of Radio Stations

cautions should be taken when using the various types of cluster analysis. Aldenderfer and Blashfield (1984) discuss three problems. First, most cluster analysis procedures are simple and are not supported by an extensive body of statistical reasoning. Unlike most other multivariate statistics, cluster analysis requires researchers to make a wide variety of subjective judgments regarding the procedures for conducting the study and the interpretation of the results. In other words, cluster analysis is highly subjective: Some researchers view it as more "art" than science.

Second, cluster analysis is used by many research disciplines, and each discipline has interpreted what is and what is not required in conducting such a study. These discipline biases mean that cluster analysis in one area of research may not be the same as in another area.

Another problem with cluster analysis is that different clustering methods can generate different solutions to the same set of data. There are at least seven different methods of searching for clusters in a data set. Each one can produce a different analysis of the data. Obviously, the choice of the clustering procedure is important. In fact, using several clustering methods is generally suggested in order to determine which analysis is the most logical.

The final major problem with cluster analysis is that the method imposes clusters on any data set. It is possible to uncover clusters in data that are not actually there. As Aldenderfer and Blashfield state, "The key to using cluster analysis is knowing when these groups are real and not merely imposed on the data by the method." The problem is finding the key.

MULTIDIMENSIONAL SCALING

Multidimensional scaling (MDS) is a multivariate technique that identifies proximities, or distances, among a set of data by searching for similarities and differences among objects or phenomena. MDS results are displayed in spatial graphs such as the one shown in Figure 8. This figure shows an actual proprietary data set produced by The Eagle Group. In this case, 400 respondents were questioned about a variety of radio stations in a midwestern city.

The first step of the study used cluster analysis to place people in categories according to their favorite type of music. The groups were then asked several questions about the radio stations in their market. The graph in Figure 8 shows the evaluations by listeners who prefer only "classic rock" music. Similar graphs were produced for listeners who prefer other types of music. The stations' call letters were changed to reflect the type of music played: WEZL = beautiful music; WSAC = soft AC; WHAC = hot AC; WCLA = classic rock; WCHR = CHR; WAOR = AOR; and IDEAL represents the classic rock listeners' evaluations of what an ideal classic rock station would be.

Two dimensions are represented in the graph. The x-axis represents the continuum of "soft to hard" music; the y-axis represents the "current to oldies" continuum. The graph shows that these classic rock listeners rate the local classic rock station very close to their ideal station. (Notice the proximity of IDEAL and WCLA on the graph.) However, WAOR plays music that is somewhat too hard (it is to the right of the ideal on the x-axis), but has a good mix of currents and oldies (it is close to the ideal on the y-axis); WCHR plays music that is slightly too hard and too current; WHAC, WSAC, and WEZL all play music that has about the right mix of currents and oldies, but all (especially WEZL) are considered too soft.

This graph, and others like it in the analysis, allow the radio station management to visually inspect how their station is perceived by listeners, and what needs to be done to move closer to the ideal. For example, if this study were for WEZL, the management would know immediately that the station would need to play harder music in order to meet the needs of listeners who prefer classic rock music.

REFERENCES AND SUGGESTED READINGS

Aldenderfer, M. S., & Blashfield, R. K. (1984). *Cluster analysis.* Beverly Hills, CA: Sage Publications.

Cattell, R. B. (Ed.). (1966). *Handbook of multivariate experimental psychology.* Skokie, IL: Rand McNally.

Comrey, A. L. (1973). *A first course in factor analysis.* New York: Academic Press.

Cooley, W. W., & Lohnes, P. R. (1971). *Multivariate data analysis.* New York: John Wiley.

Duncan, O. D. (1966). Path analysis: Sociological examples. *American Journal of Sociology, 72,* 1–16.

Gorsuch, R. L. (1974). *Factor analysis.* Philadelphia: W. B. Saunders.

Harris, R. (1975). *A primer of multivariate statistics.* New York: Academic Press.

Haynes, R. B. (1978). Children's perceptions of "comic" and "authentic" cartoon violence. *Journal of Broadcasting, 22,* 63–70.

Horst, P. (1966). An overview of the essentials of multivariate analysis methods. In R. B. Cattell (Ed.), *Handbook of multivariate experimental psychology.* Skokie, IL: Rand McNally.

Joreskog, K. G. (1973). A general model for estimating a linear structural equation system. In A. S. Goldberger & O. D. Duncan (Eds.), *Structural equation models in the social sciences.* New York: Seminar Press.

Joreskog, K. G., & Sorbom, D. (1984). *LISREL VI.* Mooresville, IN: Scientific Software.

Klecka, W. R. (1980). *Discriminant analysis.* Beverly Hills, CA: Sage Publications.

Kruskal, J. B., & Wish, M. (1989). *Multidimensional scaling.* Beverly Hills, CA: Sage Publications.

Lambert, Z. V., Doering, P., Goldstein, E., & McCormick, W. (1980). Predisposition toward generic drug acceptance. *Journal of Consumer Research, 7,* 14–23.

Rummel, R. J. (1970). *Applied factor analysis.* Evanston, IL: Northwestern University Press.

Tatsuoka, M. M. (1970). *Discriminant analysis.* Champaign, IL: Institute for Personality and Ability Testing.

Tatsuoka, M. M. (1971). *Multivariate analysis.* New York: John Wiley.

Thurstone, L. L. (1947). *Multiple factor analysis.* Chicago: University of Chicago Press.

Torgerson, W. (1958). *Theory and methods of scaling.* New York: John Wiley.

Tryon, R. C., & Bailey, D. E. (1970). *Cluster analysis.* New York: McGraw-Hill.

Tucker, R. K. (1982). *Basic multivariate research models.* San Diego, CA: College Hill Press.

Brief Guide for Conducting Focus Groups

Although a popular research method for many decades and a very valuable research tool, focus groups are double-edged swords. The method looks deceptively simple: Invite 6–12 people to a research location, hold a controlled discussion for 2 hours, and write a report. However, despite their simplicity, focus groups have gremlins hiding around dozens of corners. Researchers who are unaware of the potential problems in conducting a focus group may reap disastrous results. Even the simplest focus group topic can become impossible to handle under certain circumstances. Here we discuss some of the problem areas that should be considered both before a focus group meets and while the group is in progress. The comments are based on the authors' experiences while conducting over 2,000 focus groups during the past 20+ years.

ARE FOCUS GROUPS THE CORRECT METHOD?

First, the researcher must be sure that the focus group methodology is the correct approach for the research problem at hand. Focus groups are intended to collect qualitative information—nothing more. All too often, however, this intention is altered, and people (including some researchers) attempt to interpret focus group data as quantitative information. Indeed, the most egregious error associated with conducting focus groups is using the method for the wrong reason(s). Focus groups should be used to collect indications of what may exist—they should not be used to answer quantitative questions.

ASSEMBLING THE GROUPS

A research project requires a great deal of careful planning to anticipate any condition or situation that might complicate its completion. Two important considerations in assembling focus groups are date and time.

DATE

Focus groups are similar to surveys and experiments in that they must be carefully scheduled. Any conflict with major holidays or other officially recognized days away from work may cause extreme difficulty in recruiting participants. In addition to religious holidays, the Fourth of July, Labor Day, and other long-established holidays, researchers need to anticipate problems that may be created by less-well-known events.

Depending on the city and the time of year, some or all of the following may create havoc with recruiting: *Monday Night Football,* the World Series, the Stanley Cup, or even local high school or college sports events. There are also blockbuster television shows or other widely publicized TV programs that create a great deal of viewer interest; county or state fairs, major musical events or concerts; and political elections.

Conducting focus groups on Friday is generally not recommended. It might be a good idea in an "emergency" research situation, but usually most respondents do not want to give up one of their weekend nights to participate in a research project. While some recruiting companies may be willing to accept a Friday night focus group, most frown on the practice **455** and will try to convince the researcher to consider another day of the week. If Friday night groups are scheduled, researchers should plan to pay participants more incentive money and should expect the field service to charge more for recruiting because more telephone calls will be required to recruit participants.

TIME

The time selected to conduct focus groups depends completely on the type of participants desired. If housewives are needed, late morning or early afternoon is satisfactory. People who work outside the home are best scheduled for evenings. In most cases, back-to-back night focus groups begin at 6:00 P.M. and 8:00 P.M. Since most groups last about 2 hours, some researchers schedule the second group for 8:15 or 8:30 to allow some time for tidying the facility and resetting equipment. Also, the additional time gives the moderator a few minutes to relax before the second group starts.

Just as the date of focus groups can affect the turnout, so can the time. If business travelers are the target group, it might be wise to schedule their group to begin at 8:30 P.M. Researchers need to put themselves in the position of the type of person who is being recruited and try to anticipate the time that would be most convenient.

THE UNEXPECTED

Sometimes researchers consider every possible scheduling conflict and still encounter unforeseen problems.

Problems created by nature obviously cannot be controlled, but consideration should be given to the weather conditions that may exist at the time the groups are scheduled. For example, focus groups planned in the northern part of the United States from January to March may need to be cancelled because of snow storms. If the research cannot wait until spring, it is wise to plan for an alternative day and

possibly an alternative site. Experienced research companies that recruit for focus groups often ask the people recruited about their availability at a later time if the weather forces cancellation of the originally scheduled group.

Then there are the completely unanticipated events that force a cancellation. For example, in the past 20+ years of conducting focus groups around the United States, the authors have had to cancel focus groups because of an earthquake, riots after the Rodney King decision in Los Angeles, a hurricane, loss of electrical power at the research facility, and a field service hostess who mistakenly turned respondents away because she "rescreened" the respondents with the wrong screener. Researchers should always assume that something unexpected will happen and prepare for unforeseen events.

CHOOSING A FIELD SERVICE AND A FACILITY LOCATION

A researcher who frequently conducts focus groups in the same city usually uses the same field service for respondent recruiting and facility use. In addition to establishing a rapport with the company, the researcher is accustomed to the facilities and is generally not surprised by anything when the groups begin. However, it is extremely important to make a complete investigation of *any* company used for the first time. A researcher who does not follow through on this simple task may be headed for a major "surprise" in the long run.

Veteran researchers have learned that just because a company calls itself a research firm does not mean that the people who own and operate the firm know what they are doing. There are incompetents and charlatans in the research field, just as in any other business. Many researchers who plan to use a company new to them usually contact other researchers for a recommendation. In addition, some researchers consult the lists of recruiting facilities prepared by marketing research organizations such as the American Marketing Association (AMA). However, don't assume that a research facility listed by an association will conducts its business in a professional manner. The only requirement for listing in an association directory is payment of annual membership dues. A caveat in the research field is: Beware of any marketing, research, or consulting association whose members can join by simply paying a fee.

Once satisfactory references about a field service have been received, the focus group facility should be investigated. Is the facility easily accessible, or will participants have difficulty finding the building? Is parking nearby and safe? If the focus group sessions are to be held in a motel room, it is important to find out about the motel itself. Obviously, a run-down and poorly located motel will hinder recruitment and make it difficult for the researcher to moderate a serious discussion with respondents. Respondents will base their perceptions of the status of the research project on the quality of the facilities, so every effort should be made to select a facility that communicates "professionalism."

The focus room should provide enough seating space for up to 14 adults, and the table should allow for easy discussion among all members of the group. The viewing room should have comfortable seating for the observers.

Finally, the researcher must find out about the recording equipment the research company plans to use. The microphones must be sensitive enough to pick up all levels of sound in the room, and a backup system should be provided in the event that the main recording system fails during the group sessions.

RECRUITING

The recruiting questionnaire, or screener, used to select people to participate in the groups is one of the most important aspects of the focus group methodology. The screener defines who will be allowed to participate in the discussion. If the screener questions do not adequately identify the type of person who should attend, the results of the research will probably be worthless.

Researchers usually work very closely with the recruiting firm in developing the screener. Every characteristic desired for the participants needs to be covered (age, sex, race, location of residence, type of employment, knowledge of the topic under discussion, and so on). All relevant characteristics must be addressed by the questions in the screener, and the interviewers who will make the recruiting phone calls must understand the requirements precisely. Good research companies will carefully review the screener with their recruiting staff, but it never hurts to ask whether the procedure (known as "briefing") is planned.

Guidelines for recruiting include the following.

1.   Always overrecruit. The number of excess people generally depends on the type of person desired. There is no rule of thumb, but if a researcher needs 10 participants in a group, 14 or 15 should be recruited.

2.   Determine the amount of co-op money to be paid during the initial discussions of recruiting with the research company. As mentioned earlier, co-op fees can range between $10 and $500. Most research companies ask that the co-op money be provided in advance; this is standard procedure. The respondents, however, are always paid after the group, not before or during the session.

3.   Make sure the guidelines for recruiting participants are clearly understood by the field service. These companies usually use a database to recruit for focus groups so it is best to specify that only one person from each such club, organization, or other group will be allowed to participate. (Otherwise a field service might simply call the local PTA and ask for volunteers.) In addition, it must be emphasized that relatives of participants will not be

allowed in the groups. Finally, it is good practice to insist that no person be recruited for a group if he or she has participated in related focus groups during the past year (or other time period the researcher feels is appropriate). This restriction serves to eliminate the "professional" focus group member—the person who is constantly called by the field service to participate.

4. Just before the groups start, or shortly after, always ask the field service for the screeners used in recruiting the groups. Professional field services will not hesitate to provide researchers with the screeners; companies that claim screeners are private property, have been destroyed, or are proprietary information are generally trying to hide something (such as recruiting members from the same club or organization).

BEFORE THE GROUPS BEGIN

The major items researchers must attend to before the focus groups begin are enumerated below. Although the items are numbered, they need not be completed in this particular order. Moreover, some jobs involve a great deal of time, while others can be completed in a few minutes.

1. Prepare the moderator's guide. The moderator uses the guide to ensure that all relevant questions are asked, not to force a group into a set pattern of questioning and answering. Researchers must be prepared to skip among the prepared questions, depending on how the group reacts. In many cases, respondents mention interesting points that should be pursued.

2. Make arrangements with the field service for any audiotaping or videotaping that will be required. While audiotaping is generally considered standard for all groups, videotaping is an option. Most research companies do not charge for audiotaping, but there is usually a substantial fee for videotaping.

3. Check all electronic equipment and other mechanical devices that will be used during the groups. Assume that nothing will work and check everything. The items (for example, tape machines) that aren't checked are the ones that will not work when they are supposed to (Murphy's law).

4. In most focus group situations, respondents are offered a light dinner or snack. Catering arrangements need to be discussed with the recruiting company and depend on how much money the client wishes to spend.

5. Although respondents are reminded several times of the group's starting time, one or two people are sure to arrive late. It is the researcher's responsibility to instruct the recruiting company on how to handle late arrivals. Some focus groups may suffer no harm if one or two respondents arrive a few minutes late. However, if the session begins with showing or playing some type of information (audiotapes, videotapes, placards), a late respondent cannot participate meaningfully in the group. In such cases, it is best to pay the late respondent the co-op money and allow the person to go home.

Many "professional" focus group respondents have learned that if they arrive about 15 minutes late they will still receive the co-op money. It is up to the researcher to decide the time limit. The authors' practice is that if respondents are more than 15 minutes late for the session, they are not paid the co-op.

6. Researchers need to establish with the recruiting company what will happen if not enough respondents "show" for a group. The course of action (such as not paying for the recruiting of the group) depends on the reason for the low turnout. If bad weather or another unpredictable natural event makes it difficult for people to get to the facility, the recruiting company should not be penalized. However, if the weather is fine and there are no unexpected

disrupting influences, the researcher may request that recruiting charges be waived. Fortunately for researchers, good field services who face shortfalls generally offer to reschedule the groups for no additional charge.

7.   There is one rule for the people who view the groups behind the one-way mirror: no loud noises. The only thing that separates the viewing room from the focus room is a thin sheet of glass, and loud talking, laughing, or other noises from behind the mirror are annoying to the moderator as well as to the respondents. Viewers should also refrain from lighting cigarettes, cigars, or pipes if the flame may be detected by those on the other side of the mirror. This sounds like a minor detail, but the quick flash of light can distract a respondent who may be unaware of the presence of viewers behind the mirror. Other rules for the viewers are established by the moderator on an ad hoc basis. For example, the authors do not allow viewers to send in more than one or two notes during the group (the notes contain other questions to ask).

CONDUCTING THE GROUPS

The type of introduction to a focus group and the amount of information provided to the respondents depend on the purpose of the group and the sponsor of the research. In some cases it is important for the respondents to receive no preliminary information during the introduction; in other cases concepts or procedures must be explained before actual questioning can begin.

The moderator usually starts a focus group by explaining the purpose of the group (the amount of detail depends on the reason for the group). Some of the information the authors tell respondents in a focus group introduction is summarized below:

1.   There are no right or wrong answers to the questions that will be asked. Everyone should feel free to make relevant comments, whether positive or negative.

2.   The group is being audiotaped (or videotaped) for future reference. None of the comments made in the group will be used outside the group without prior written permission.

3.   There is at least one person behind the mirror watching the group. In the author's case, this person is usually a coworker, so the respondents would be told that, "A person who works with me is behind the mirror watching the group. If you hear any noises back there, that's him falling off his chair or something." Some researchers don't like to tell respondents that there are viewers behind the mirror for fear of making the respondents nervous. However, in moderating many thousands of focus groups, the authors have never found this to be a problem.

4.   The group is informal and there is no need to raise a hand to say something. No one should hesitate to ask questions, and the respondents should feel free to speak up without being invited to do so.

After the brief introduction, the respondents are asked to introduce themselves and give a bit of information about their background, such as occupation, length of time living in the area, and so forth.

A focus group will not fail if the moderator has a thorough understanding of the goals of the group, a detailed moderator's guide, and an acute interest in listening to the respondents' answers. A moderator should not feel restricted to the order of questioning in the moderator's guide. If respondents raise a relevant point, it is important to ask follow-up questions.

HANDLING RESPONDENTS

As a rule, people who participate in focus groups tend to be one of five types:

1.   The *active* participant, who is interested in providing relevant answers to the

moderator's questions. A group of 10 of this type would make a moderator's job easy.

2. The *shy* person who is embarrassed to speak out or feels inhibited for some reason. This person can be included simply by calling on him or her for a response, such as, "Bob, what do you think about that?"

3. The *know-it-all,* who has an answer to every question and tries to dominate the group. This person can be handled by saying something like, "Bob, before you answer, let me find out what Jim thinks."

4. The *over-talker,* who cannot answer a question in one or two sentences. This person can be controlled by saying something like, "Bob, very briefly, what do you think about that?" If "Bob" continues, cut him off.

5. The *obnoxious* person, who does not really wish to participate and tries to make life difficult for the moderator by making sarcastic remarks or irrelevant comments. This person is also easy to control simply by cutting him off, or by saying, "My purpose in conducting this group is to get a variety of opinions about [the focus group topic]. I'm not interested in listening to sarcastic remarks or degrading comments. If that is what you wish to do, I'll allow you to leave now." (If the person continues to be obnoxious, it is easy to have the person removed from the group.)

Eliminating people from a group that is already in session calls for a prior arrangement with the field service. For example, it may be agreed that when the moderator believes it is necessary to eliminate a respondent, the moderator will leave the focus room and give the name of the offending person to the field service representative. A few minutes after the moderator has returned to the group, the unwanted group member is summoned by the field service representative for a "phone call." Outside the focus room, the company representative very politely dismisses the person. ("You seem to be an expert in the area, and your input may affect the other respondents' answers" is one approach.)

The goal is to eliminate the problem respondent quickly. The moderator cannot allow one person to destroy the group. Speed is most important in getting rid of an unwanted respondent.

PROCEDURAL STEPS IN CONDUCTING A FOCUS GROUP

The authors tend to follow the same procedure consistently when arriving at a focus group facility to conduct a group. This series of steps ensures that all potential problems have been addressed ahead of time. Upon arriving at the facility (usually one hour before the start of the first group), each of the authors will:

1. Introduce himself to the receptionist, show an appropriate picture I. D. card, and ask for the host or hostess in charge of the group.
2. Ask which focus room will be used.
3. Determine entrances and exits for respondents and viewers.
4. Examine the focus room for the appropriate equipment, space, number of chairs around the focus table, writing instruments, pads of paper, and other materials needed for the group.
5. Explain to the host/hostess that it will be all right for respondents to bring food into the room.
6. Review the procedures for eliminating an unwanted respondent.
7. Review the procedures for handling respondents who show up late for the group (either allow them to enter the room, or pay them and send them home).
8. Check for air conditioning and heating controls.
9. Ask for the screeners for the respondents recruited for the group.
10. Review the procedures for starting the audiotape and/or videotape.

11. Review the procedures for allowing notes to be sent in from viewers behind the mirror.
12. Check to see that meals or snacks have been prepared for respondents and viewers.
13. Explain any unique aspects, such as whether a break will be taken after one hour, to the host or hostess.
14. Determine how long after the scheduled starting time the group will actually start. This is based on how many respondents arrive at the scheduled starting time.

FOCUS GROUP CRITICISMS

Some researchers claim that focus groups are not a good research methodology because of the potential influence of one or two respondents on the remaining members of the group. These critics say that a "dominant" respondent can negatively affect the outcome of the group, and that group "pressures" may influence the comments made by individuals.

It is the authors' experience that those who criticize focus groups because of the potential influence of respondents do not have enough experience moderating focus groups to allow them to deal with the range of respondents who participate in the groups. A professional moderator never encounters problems with difficult respondents. A professional moderator can identify almost immediately a "problem" respondent and can solve the problem in a matter of minutes. If a moderator has problems with respondents, the moderator should consider another occupation.

CAVEAT

This section is not intended to scare novice researchers. Rather, the intention is to explain a situation that must be considered by any researcher who plans to conduct focus groups.

The problem relates to the cheating that some companies do to recruit respondents for focus groups. In some cases, it is difficult for field services to find enough qualified respondents for a project because the screener requirements are too stringent. Instead of calling the client and explaining the recruiting difficulty, some recruiters simply use "standbys" for the group. These people are usually friends of the company owner or company personnel who are called at the last minute to meet the goal of a focus group's "show rate."

Does this mean that inferior research is conducted in some cases? The sad truth is, yes. During their research careers the authors have caught several field services and recruiting companies in the act of cheating. However, most field services and recruiting companies are owned and operated by hard-working professionals who sincerely care about the quality of their work. As always, it is a minority of operators who spoil the process for all companies. It is the researcher's responsibility to check everything about a focus group to ensure that all is in order. A researcher should never assume that what he or she sees is real.

SUMMARY

Properly conducted focus groups are a valuable research tool. They are exciting to conduct and they can provide a great deal of useful information. Yet it is important for a novice researcher to view several groups before jumping into the moderator's seat. Although focus groups can be easy to conduct, they can also turn into nightmares if the moderator does not have enough experience dealing with the multitude of respondent types who will be involved. At one time or another, all moderators will face respondents who are drunk, high on drugs, physically sick, angry, happy, sad, tired, or have any one of several psychological problems.

Sample Data

SAMPLE DATA

Note: The codebook for the following data is included in Chapter 7.

Respondent	4	5	6	7	8	9	10	11	12	13	14	15	16	17	18	19	20	21	22	23	24	25	26	27	28	29	30	31	32	33	34	35	36	37
001	1	1	1	1	3	1	2	1	1	2	0	2	0	5	1	1	2	2	1	1	1	2	2	2	2	1	1	1	2	2	1	1	2	1
002	2	1	2	1	1	1	2	1	2	2	0	2	0	2	2	2	2	2	2	1	2	2	2	2	1	1	3	1	2	2	1	1	2	1
003	3	2	2	1	1	1	3	1	2	2	0	2	0	2	1	1	1	1	1	1	2	2	2	2	1	1	2	1	1	2	3	1	2	1
004	3	1	0	2	0	1	2	1	1	1	0	2	0	5	1	1	2	1	1	1	1	1	2	1	1	1	1	1	1	2	1	1	2	1
005	4	1	2	1	2	2	1	1	3	2	0	2	0	2	2	2	2	2	2	1	1	2	2	2	1	1	1	2	2	2	2	2	2	1
006	4	2	3	1	2	2	2	1	3	2	0	1	0	5	2	1	1	2	2	1	2	1	2	2	1	1	2	1	2	2	2	2	2	2
007	1	1	1	3	3	1	1	1	3	1	3	2	0	9	2	1	2	1	1	1	1	2	2	2	2	1	1	3	1	1	1	1	1	1
008	1	1	3	1	2	2	2	1	2	2	0	2	0	2	2	2	2	2	2	1	2	2	2	2	1	1	2	1	2	2	2	2	1	2
009	1	1	1	1	3	1	1	1	2	2	0	1	2	2	1	1	1	2	1	1	2	2	2	2	2	2	2	1	2	2	2	1	1	1
010	1	1	3	1	2	2	1	1	2	2	0	2	0	2	1	1	1	2	2	1	1	2	2	2	1	3	1	1	2	3	1	1	1	1
011	2	2	2	1	2	1	2	1	2	2	1	1	2	2	1	2	1	1	2	1	2	2	2	2	2	2	1	1	1	1	1	2	1	1
012	2	1	2	1	2	2	0	1	1	1	0	1	0	5	1	1	1	2	1	1	1	2	2	2	1	1	2	1	2	3	1	1	1	1
013	2	2	2	1	2	2	1	1	2	2	0	2	0	9	1	2	2	2	1	1	2	2	2	2	1	1	2	1	1	1	1	1	1	1
014	3	2	2	1	2	2	1	1	1	1	1	1	3	5	1	1	1	1	2	1	1	2	1	2	2	1	2	1	1	1	2	2	1	2
015	3	1	2	1	3	1	2	1	2	1	0	2	0	5	1	1	2	2	2	1	2	2	2	2	2	2	1	3	1	1	1	1	1	1
016	3	2	2	1	3	2	0	1	3	2	0	2	3	8	1	1	1	1	1	1	2	1	1	1	1	1	2	2	2	1	1	1	1	1
017	3	2	2	1	2	1	2	1	2	2	0	2	0	2	1	1	2	2	2	1	2	2	2	2	2	1	2	1	1	1	1	2	1	1
018	3	1	1	1	2	1	0	1	1	2	0	2	0	5	1	1	2	2	2	2	1	2	2	2	1	1	2	2	2	1	1	1	1	1
019	3	2	2	1	2	2	2	1	2	2	0	2	0	5	1	1	2	2	2	1	2	2	2	2	1	1	2	1	2	2	1	1	1	1
020	3	1	0	1	1	2	0	1	1	1	0	2	0	2	1	1	2	2	1	1	1	1	2	3	1	1	1	1	1	1	1	1	1	1
021	3	2	2	1	3	2	3	1	1	2	0	2	3	2	1	1	2	2	1	1	2	1	1	1	1	1	2	1	2	2	1	1	2	1
022	3	1	2	1	2	2	2	1	2	2	0	2	1	2	1	1	2	1	2	1	2	2	2	2	1	1	2	1	2	3	1	1	1	1
023	3	2	0	1	2	1	0	1	2	2	0	2	0	5	1	1	2	2	2	1	1	2	2	3	1	1	1	1	3	3	1	1	2	1
024	3	1	3	1	2	1	2	1	2	2	0	2	0	3	1	1	2	1	1	1	2	1	2	2	1	1	2	1	3	3	1	1	2	1
025	4	1	1	1	2	1	2	1	1	1	2	1	2	9	1	1	1	1	1	1	2	1	2	1	1	1	1	1	1	1	1	1	1	1

056	057	058	059	060	061	062	063	064	065	066	067	068	069	070	071	072	073	074	075	076	077	078	079	080	081	082	083	084	085
1	1	1	1	1	2	1	1	1	1	2	2	2	1	1	2	1	1	1	1	2	2	1	1	2	2	1	1	1	1
1	1	2	2	1	2	1	2	2	1	2	2	2	1	2	1	2	1	2	2	1	2	2	1	2	2	1	1	2	1
1	2	1	1	2	1	2	1	1	2	1	1	1	1	1	2	1	2	1	1	2	1	2	1	2	1	2	1	2	1
1	1	1	1	2	2	2	2	1	1	1	2	1	1	1	1	2	1	1	2	2	2	1	2	2	1	2	1	2	1
1	1	1	2	1	2	1	1	1	1	2	2	2	1	1	1	2	1	2	2	2	1	2	2	2	1	2	1	2	1
1	1	1	2	1	2	1	1	1	1	2	2	1	2	1	1	2	2	1	2	2	2	1	2	2	1	2	1	2	1
2	1	1	3	1	2	1	1	1	1	1	2	1	1	1	1	2	1	2	1	1	2	1	2	1	1	2	1	1	1
2	1	1	2	2	2	2	1	1	1	2	1	1	2	1	2	2	2	1	3	1	1	2	1	2	1	2	1	1	1
1	1	1	2	1	2	2	2	1	1	1	2	1	1	1	2	1	2	2	1	3	2	1	1	1	1	1	2	1	1
1	1	1	1	2	2	1	1	1	1	2	1	1	1	1	2	1	1	1	1	1	1	1	2	1	2	1	2	1	1
1	3	2	1	2	2	1	1	1	1	2	1	1	2	1	2	1	2	1	2	2	1	2	1	2	1	1	1	1	1
2	1	2	2	2	1	2	2	1	1	2	1	2	1	1	2	1	2	2	2	1	2	1	2	2	1	1	1	1	1
2	2	2	2	2	2	2	2	2	1	2	2	2	2	2	1	2	2	2	2	2	2	2	2	2	2	2	2	2	2
2	2	2	2	2	2	2	2	2	2	2	2	2	2	1	2	2	2	2	2	2	2	2	2	2	2	2	2	2	1
2	1	1	2	1	2	2	1	1	1	2	1	2	1	2	1	1	2	1	1	2	1	2	1	1	1	1	1	1	1
2	1	1	2	2	2	2	2	1	3	1	2	1	2	1	2	1	2	1	2	2	1	2	1	2	1	1	1	1	1
1	1	2	2	2	1	1	1	1	1	2	1	1	2	1	2	1	2	1	1	1	1	1	2	1	1	1	2	2	1
1	2	2	2	2	2	1	2	1	2	1	2	1	2	1	2	1	2	1	2	1	2	1	2	1	2	2	1	2	2
1	1	2	1	2	1	2	1	1	2	1	2	1	1	2	2	1	2	1	1	1	1	2	1	2	1	1	1	1	1
1	1	1	1	2	2	2	1	1	2	1	2	1	1	2	1	1	1	1	1	2	1	2	1	2	1	1	1	1	1
2	3	5	3	6	7	2	3	2	3	2	2	9	5	5	6	5	5	2	2	3	9	2	2	3	3	5	5	2
0	0	0	0	1	3	0	0	1	2	0	1	0	3	0	0	0	0	0	2	0	0	0	0	2	0	0	2	0	0
2	2	2	2	1	1	2	2	1	1	2	1	2	1	2	2	2	1	2	2	2	2	1	2	2	1	2	2	2
0	0	0	0	2	2	3	3	1	2	0	1	3	0	0	0	0	3	0	0	0	0	0	2	3	3	2	3	0
2	2	2	2	1	1	1	1	1	1	1	2	1	2	2	1	1	2	1	1	2	1	1	1	1	1	1	2	2
3	1	2	3	3	3	3	2	3	3	2	3	1	1	2	1	2	3	2	2	2	1	3	2	3	2	1	3	2
1	1	1	1	1	1	1	1	1	1	1	1	1	1	1	1	1	1	1	1	1	1	1	1	1	1	1	1	1
2	2	3	0	3	3	3	2	2	0	3	0	3	2	2	3	3	0	0	0	0	2	3	0	0	0	0
1	1	1	2	1	1	1	2	1	1	2	1	1	2	1	2	1	2	2	2	2
3	1	2	2	3	3	3	3	1	3	3	2	0	2	3	0	2	1	2	3	3	3	3	1	2
1	1	1	1	1	1	1	2	1	2	1	1	1	1	1	1	1	1	1	1	1	1
2	2	0	3	2	3	3	3	3	2	3	2	3	0	0	2	0	0	0	3	0	2
1	1	2	1	1	1	1	1	1	1	1	1	2	2	1	2	2	2	1	1	2	1
1	1	1	2	2	2	2	2	2	2	3	3	3	3	3	3	3	4	4	4	4	4	4	4	1	2	2	2	2

	116	117	118	119	120	121	122	123	124	125	126	127	128	129	130	131	132	133	134	135	136	137	138	139	140	141	142	143	144	145
	2	1	1	1	1	1	1	1	1	1	1	1	1	1	1	1	1	1	1	1	1	1	1	2	2	1	1	1
	2	1	2	2	1	1	2	1	1	1	1	1	1	1	1	1	2	1	1	1	1	2	2	2	2	2
	1	1	1	2	1	2	1	1	1	1	1	1	1	1	1	1	1	1	2	1	2	2	2
	2	1	1	1	1	1	2	1	1	1	1	1	2	2	1	1	1	1	1	1	1	2	1	1	2
	1	1	2	3	2	1	2	1	1	1	3	1	2	1	2	1	2	2	2	1	2	1	1	1	3	2
	1	1	2	2	2	1	2	1	1	1	1	1	2	2	2	2	1	1	1	1	1	2	1	2
	2	1	1	1	1	2	1	1	1	3	1	1	1	1	1	1	2	1	2	1	1	2	1	2
	2	2	2	2	2	1	2	1	1	1	2	1	2	1	2	1	1	2	2	2	2	1	2	2	1	2	1	2	2
	2	1	2	1	1	1	2	1	1	3	1	1	1	1	3	1	2	2	1	1	1	2	1	2	1
	1	1	1	1	1	1	2	1	1	1	1	1	1	1	1	1	1	1	1	1
	2	2	2	1	1	2	1	1	1	1	1	1	2	1	1	2	1	1	2	2	2	2
	2	2	2	1	2	1	2	1	1	2	2	1	2	1	2	1	2	2	2	2	2	2	1	3	2	2	2
	2	2	2	2	2	1	2	2	1	2	2	2	1	2	1	2	2	2	2	2	2	2	2	2
	2	2	2	1	2	1	1	1	3	1	2	1	2	2	1	2	2	1	2	1	3	2
	2	1	1	2	1	1	2	1	1	1	1	1	1	1	1	1	1	1	1	2	1	2
	1	2	1	2	2	1	2	1	1	2	3	2	1	2	1	2	2	1	1	1	2	1	2
	2	2	2	1	1	1	2	2	1	2	1	2	1	2	1	2	1	2	2	2	2
	2	2	2	1	1	1	2	2	1	2	1	2	1	2	1	2	1	2	2	2	2	2
	1	2	1	1	1	1	2	1	1	1	1	1	1	1	1	2	1	2	1	1	1	1	1	2
	1	1	1	2	1	2	1	1	1	1	1	2	1	1	1	2	1	2	1	1	1	1	1	2
	3	2	3	3	3	5	9	5	2	2	3	5	5	5	2	9	5	5	2	2	3	2	8	5	5	3	2	9	2	2
	0	0	0	0	0	0	0	3	0	2	0	0	0	0	0	2	0	3	0	0	0	0	0	3	0	0	0	0	0	3
	2	2	2	2	2	2	2	1	2	1	2	2	2	2	1	2	1	2	2	2	2	1	2	2	2	2	1
	0	0	0	0	0	0	0	3	0	2	0	0	0	0	0	2	3	0	0	0	0	0	0	2	0	0	0	0	0	2
	2	2	2	2	2	2	1	1	2	1	2	2	2	2	1	2	2	2	2	1	2	2	2	2	1
	2	2	1	3	3	1	3	1	2	2	3	3	2	1	2	1	1	2	3	2	3	1	2	2	2	2	1	3	3
	1	1	1	1	1	1	1	1	1	1	1	1	1	1	1	1	1	1	1	1	1	1	1	1	1
	0	2	2	0	1	2	0	2	0	3	2	2	2	1	2	0	2	3	3	2	0	2	0	1	1	3	0
	2	1	1	2	1	1	2	1	2	1	1	1	1	2	1	1	1	2	1	1	1	1	2
	1	2	1	2	2	3	0	2	2	2	1	3	2	3	0	2	2	0	2	0	0	2	1	0	3	3	2
	1	1	1	1	2	1	1	1	1	2	1	2	1	2	2	1	1	2	1	1
	3	3	3	0	0	3	3	0	0	3	3	3	1	2	2	3	0	2	2	2	2	0	1	2	0
	1	1	2	2	1	2	1	2	1	1	1	1	1	1	2	1	1	1	1	1	2	1	1	2
	4	4	4	4	4	1	1	2	2	2	3	3	3	3	3	4	4	4	4	4	4	4	4	1	1	2	3

146	147	148	149	150	151	152	153	154	155	156	157	158	159	160	161	162	163	164	165	166	167	168	169	170	171	172	173	174	175
1	1	1	1	1	1	1	2	1	2	1	1	1	1	1	1	1	1	1	1	2	2	1	1	1					
1	1	2	2	2	1	1	1	1	2	1	2	3	2	1	1	1	1	1	2	1	1	1	2	1					
1	1	2	1	1	1	1	1	1	2	1	1	2	2	1	1	1	2	1	1	2	2	2	1						
1	1	1	1	2	1	1	1	1	1	1	1	2	1	1	1	2	1	1	2	1	1	1							
2	1	2	1	2	1	2	1	1	1	1	1	2	2	1	1	1	1	1	1	1	1	1	1						
1	1	2	2	2	2	1	1	1	2	1	2	2	1	2	2	1	1	1	1	1	2	2	1						
1	1	2	1	1	1	2	1	1	1	1	1	3	1	1	1	1	1	1	1	1	1	1	1						
2	1	2	1	1	1	2	1	2	2	1	2	1	2	3	1	1	1	1	1	2	1	1	2						
1	1	1	1	1	1	1	3	1	1	1	1	1	1	1	1	1	1	1	1	1	1	3	2						
1	1	1	1	1	1	2	2	1	1	1	2	1	1	2	1	1	1	2	1	1	3	1							
2	2	2	3	1	1	1	1	1	1	2	3	2	1	3	1	1	1	1	1	1	2	2	2						
2	2	1	1	2	1	1	1	1	2	3	2	1	1	2	1	1	2	2	2	2	2	1	2						
2	2	1	1	2	2	1	2	2	2	2	2	1	2	1	2	2	2	2	2	2	2	2	2						
2	2	2	1	2	1	2	1	1	3	2	2	1	1	1	2	1	1	2	2	1	2	2	2						
1	1	1	1	1	1	1	2	1	1	1	1	2	1	1	2	1	2	1	2	1									
2	1	1	2	1	1	2	1	2	1	2	1	1	1	1	1	2	2	1	2	1	2								
1	1	2	1	2	2	1	1	2	1	2	1	1	2	2	2	1	1	1	1	2	1	2							
1	1	2	2	2	1	2	1	2	1	1	2	1	2	2	1	1	1	1	2	1	2								
1	1	1	1	1	2	1	1	1	1	1	1	1	1	1	1	1	2	1											
1	1	1	1	1	2	1	2	1	2	1	1	1	1	2	1	1	1	2	1										
5	5	6	5	5	5	5	2	2	6	8	5	2	6	2	2	5	5	5	5	2	2	2	5	5	5	5	5	5	2
3	0	0	1	3	2	0	0	0	0	0	2	0	0	0	0	3	0	0	0	2	0	2	0	0	0	0	0	0	0
1	2	2	1	1	2	2	2	2	2	2	2	2	2	1	2	2	2	2	2	2	1	2	2	2	2	2	2	2	2
3	0	0	1	3	2	0	2	3	0	3	1	0	0	0	0	3	0	0	1	3	0	0	2	0	0	0	0	0	0
1	2	2	1	1	1	1	1	2	1	2	2	2	2	1	2	2	2	1	1	2	1	2	2	2	2	2	2	2	2
3	1	1	1	1	2	3	2	3	2	2	2	2	3	2	1	2	2	3	2	2	1	3	1	1	1	1	1	1	2
1	1	1	1	1	1	1	1	1	1	1	1	1	1	1	1	1	1	1	1	1	1	1	1	1	1	1	1	1	1
2	2	2	0	3	2	2	2	0	3	0	3	0	1	2	3	2	3	3	3	1	3	2	0	0	0	2	0	3	3
1	1	1	2	1	1	2	1	2	1	1	1	1	1	1	1	2	2	2	1	2	1	1
3	0	0	3	0	2	0	0	0	0	2	3	2	3	2	0	3	3	3	0	3	2	1	2	2	2	3	2
1	2	2	1	2	1	1	2	2	1	1	1	1	2	1	1	2	1	1	1	1	1	1
3	0	2	3	0	2	0	1	1	2	1	3	0	1	1	3	3	3	3	0	3	1	2	3	2	1	2	0	3
1	2	1	2	1	2	1	2	2	1	1	1	1	1	1	2	1	1	1	1	1	2	2
3	3	3	3	3	3	4	2	2	2	2	2	2	3	3	3	3	3	4	4	4	4	4	4	4	4	4

176	177	178	179	180	181	182	183	184	185	186	187	188	189	190	191	192	193	194	195	196	197	198	199	200
1	1	1	1	1	1	1	1	2	1	1	1	1	1	2	1	1	1	1	1	2	1	1	1	1
1	1	1	2	1	1	1	1	1	1	1	2	2	2	1	2	1	1	1	1	2	1	2	2	1
2	1	2	2	1	1	1	1	1	2	1	1	1	1	1	1	1	1	1	1	2	2	1	1	1
1	2	2	1	1	1	1	1	1	1	2	1	1	1	1	1	1	1	1	1	1	1	1	1	3
1	1	2	1	1	2	1	1	2	1	1	2	2	2	1	1	1	1	2	1	1	1	1	1	1
2	2	1	1	1	2	1	1	1	1	1	1	2	2	1	2	1	2	1	2	1	1	1	1	3
1	1	1	1	1	1	1	1	1	2	1	2	1	1	1	1	1	1	1	1	2	1	1	1	1
2	2	2	2	1	1	1	2	1	2	1	1	1	3	1	1	2	1	2	1	2	2	1	1	3
1	2	2	2	1	1	1	1	1	1	2	1	1	2	1	1	1	1	1	2	1	1	1	1	1
1	2	2	1	1	1	1	1	2	1	1	1	1	2	1	1	1	1	1	1	1	1	1	1	1
1	2	1	2	1	2	2	1	2	1	2	1	1	2	1	1	1	1	2	1	2	1	2	1	1
2	2	1	1	2	2	2	2	1	1	2	1	2	1	2	1	2	1	2	2	1	2	2	2	1
2	2	2	2	2	2	2	2	2	1	2	1	2	2	2	1	2	1	2	2	2	2	2	2	2
2	1	1	1	2	2	3	2	2	2	1	1	2	1	1	1	2	1	2	2	2	2	1	1	2
1	1	2	1	1	1	1	1	1	2	1	1	1	1	1	1	1	1	1	1	1	1	1	1	3
2	1	2	2	2	1	1	2	1	2	1	1	2	2	1	2	1	2	1	2	1	1	2	1	1
2	2	2	2	1	2	2	1	2	1	1	2	1	1	1	2	1	2	1	1	2	1	2	1	1
2	2	2	2	1	2	2	1	2	1	2	1	1	2	1	1	2	1	1	2	1	2	2	2	1
1	2	1	1	1	1	1	1	1	2	1	1	1	1	1	1	1	1	1	1	1	1	1	1	1
1	2	1	1	1	1	1	2	1	1	1	1	1	1	1	1	1	1	1	1	1	1	1	1	1
5	2	6	5	2	5	5	3	9	5	6	2	5	9	5	2	5	3	5	3	5	5	3	5	5
3	2	1	3	0	0	0	0	3	0	1	0	1	0	0	0	0	0	2	0	3	0	0	0	0
1	1	1	1	2	2	2	2	1	2	1	2	2	2	2	1	2	1	2	1	2	2	2	2	2
0	1	2	3	2	0	0	3	3	0	1	0	2	0	2	0	0	3	0	2	0	2	0	0	0
3	2	1	1	1	2	2	1	2	1	2	1	2	2	2	1	2	1	2	1	2	2	2	2	2
3	2	3	3	2	1	3	3	2	1	3	3	1	2	2	3	1	2	3	1	2	3	1	1	1
1	1	1	1	1	1	1	1	1	1	1	1	1	1	1	1	1	1	1	1	1	1	1	1	1
0	3	0	3	1	2	2	2	0	1	0	2	2	2	2	3	3	3	3	0	3	0	3	0	2
2	1	2	1	1	1	1	1	1	2	1	1	1	1	1	1	1	1	1	1	2	1	2	1	1
0	2	0	3	3	2	2	2	3	2	1	2	3	2	3	1	2	3	2	3	1	3	3	3	2
2	1	3	2	1	1	1	1	1	1	1	1	1	1	1	1	1	1	1	1	1	1	1	1	1
1	2	3	3	1	3	2	0	1	0	2	1	2	0	0	2	3	1	0	2	0	2	3	0	2
1	1	1	1	1	2	1	2	1	1	2	2	1	1	1	2	1	1	2	1	1	2	1
4	4	1	1	1	1	2	2	2	2	4	3	3	3	3	3	4	4	4	4	4	4	4

SAMPLE QUESTIONNAIRE

The sample questionnaire in this section contains several types of questions that can be asked in a telephone interview for a radio station. The questionnaire is based on one designed by The Eagle Group in Denver, Colorado. However, because the original questionnaire was proprietary, it has been edited and "masked" so that the exact location and nature of the questions cannot be identified. In addition, the actual questionnaire included more questions. Note that the format of the response options does not exactly match those shown in Chapter 7. This is because of the conventions and styles of the CATI-based interviewing system used by The Eagle Group.

Review the questionnaire and then answer the following questions:

1. What is the advantage of numbering the pages "Page 2 of 6," "Page 3 of 6," and so on?
2. What is important about the way the introduction is worded?
3. What type of person is interviewed? (Check the screener questions.)
4. Why are questions 5 and 6 screening questions? Why are they located near the beginning of the questionnaire?
5. Why are there two apparently redundant race-related questions (7 and 8)?
6. Which questions have quotas that the interviewers (or CATI system) must consider?
7. Why do questions 10, 11, 12, and 18 use "when you choose" or "when you have the choice" in the wording?
8. Analyze the skip patterns. Who answers each of the questions?
9. Why is question 28 included? What information can be gained from this question?
10. What other questions would you add to this questionnaire? (The goal of the questionnaire is to find out how the station is perceived by listeners and nonlisteners.)

CONFIDENTIAL BIG CITY PROPRIETARY (N = 400) ©1995 The Eagle Group

Hi. We're conducting an opinion survey about radio in the Big City area and would like to ask you a few questions. This is _____ from The Eagle Group. We're not selling anything and this is not a promotion or a contest. For quality control purposes, this interview may be monitored. Please tell me which of the following age categories you fall into . . . Under 25, 25 to 34, 35 to 44, 45 to 54, or over 54. [QUOTAS]

1.　　　　　　　　Under 25 .... [QUOTA FILLED. TERM]

1 = M 25–34	4 = F 25–34
2 = M 35–44	5 = F 35–44
3 = M 45–54	6 = F 45–54

　　　　　　　　Over 54.................................. [QUOTA FILLED. TERM]

2. I'd like to describe a type of radio station by reading a brief list of artists the station might play. I'd like to know if you do listen, or if you would listen, to the station often, sometimes, or never. How frequently would you listen to a station that plays music by artists such as Wendy Whitman, Carl Anthony, Larry Barnes, and Jeremy Scott?

    1 = Often.................................... [ASK Q. 3]
    2 = Sometimes............................ [ASK Q. 3]
    3 = Never ....[TERM]
    4 = DK/NA ....[TERM]

3. Is there a station like this in the Big City area now? [DON'T READ]

    1 = Yes.. [ASK Q. 4]
    2 = No .... [SKIP TO Q. 5]
    3 = DK/NA .... [SKIP TO Q. 5]

4. Which station is that? [RECORD] _____

5. Considering that you can listen to radio at home, in your car, at work, and elsewhere, about how much time during a *typical day* do you spend listening to the radio? [TERM IF LESS THAN 1 HOUR]

6. Including yourself, how many members of your household or friends are employed by a radio or TV station, a company that *owns* a radio or TV station, a newspaper, advertising agency, record company, or market research company? [IF ANY, TERM]

7. For classification purposes, are you of Spanish or Hispanic origin?

    1 = Yes
    2 = No
    3 = Refused

8. To be sure that we represent all people fairly, how do you classify your race? [DON'T READ]

    1 = White/Anglo
    2 = Black/African American
    3 = Hispanic/Spanish
    4 = Asian
    5 = Refused
    6 = Other _____

9. Which county do you live in? [DON'T READ. TERM IF ONE OF BELOW NOT NAMED OR REFUSED

Page 3 of 6 ©1995 The Eagle Group

>   1 = Harley
>   2 = Davidson .... [BASED ON ZIP CODE DISTRIBUTION]

10. During a typical week, which radio stations do *you choose* to listen to for music? [PROBE:] Any others?

   _____   _____   _____

11. When *you have the choice*, which station do you listen to most often for music?

   Station: _____

12. When *you have the choice*, which station do you listen to second most often for music?

   Station: _____

13. Now I'd like to read a list of items about radio stations and have you tell me how important each item is OVERALL when you listen to the radio. Use a scale of 1 to 10, where the *higher the number, the more important the item is* to you when you listen to the radio. [1-10. X=DK/NA. ROTATE]

   Overall, how important is it to you that a radio station . . .

   a. plays a lot of music without a lot of talk
   b. has DJs who tell you interesting things about the music they play
   c. has DJs who are upbeat and fun, but don't overshadow the music
   d. has local weather reports
   e. has traffic reports

14. During a typical week, do you usually listen to the radio in the mornings between 6 and 10 A.M.? [DON'T READ]

   >   1 = Yes .... [ASK Q. 15]
   >   2 = No .... [SKIP TO Q. 17]
   >   3 = DK/NA .... [SKIP TO Q. 17]

15. Which station do you choose to listen to most often weekday mornings between 6 and 10 A.M.?

   Station: _____

16. I'd like to read a list of items that a radio station can include in its weekday morning show between 6 and 10 A.M. Please tell me how important each item is to you when you listen to

the radio weekday mornings. Use a scale of 1 to 10, where the higher the number, the more important the item is to you. [1-10. X=DK/NA]

How important is it to you that a radio station's weekday morning show has. . . .

a. local news coverage
b. weather reports and forecasts
c. traffic reports
d. a lot of music without a lot of talk
e. a team of DJs instead of one personality
f. international news reports

17. During a typical week, Monday through Friday, do you usually listen to the radio while working at your job. [DON'T READ]

    1 = Yes...................................... [ASK Q. 18]
    2 = No................................ [SKIP TO Q. 19]
    3 = DK/NA......................... [SKIP TO Q. 19]

18. Which station do you choose to listen to most often while working?

    Station: _____

19. Next, to save time, I'd like to ask you a few questions about only one station . . . So that I may be sure, do you listen to KAAA-FM during a typical week? [DON'T READ]

    1 = Yes................................ [SKIP TO Q. 21]
    2 = No...................................... [ASK Q. 20]
    3 = DK/NA......................... [SKIP TO Q. 28]

20. Why don't you listen to KAAA-FM? [PROBE:] What else?

    [RECORD AND SKIP TO Q. 28]

21. How long have you been listening to KAAA-FM? [DON'T READ]

    1 = Less than 1 month
    2 = Between 1 month and 3 months
    3 = More than 3 months
    4 = DK/NA

22. How did you find out about KAAA-FM? [DON'T READ]

Page 5 of 6 ©1995 The Eagle Group

> 1 = By accident/scanning dial
> 2 = Billboard
> 3 = Friend/relative
> 4 = TV commercial
> 5 = Other
> 6 = DK/NA

23. What, if anything, do you like most about KAAA-FM? [PROBE:] What else?

24. What, if anything, do you like least about KAAA-FM? [PROBE:] What else?

25. During a typical week, Monday through Friday, do you listen to the morning show on KAAA-FM between 6 and 10 A.M.? [DON'T READ]

> 1 = Yes .... [ASK Q. 26]
> 2 = No .... [SKIP TO Q. 27]
> 3 = DK/NA .... [SKIP TO Q. 27]

26. I'd like to read a list of items about the weekday morning show on KAAA-FM and have you tell me if it has enough, too much, or not enough of each item. [ROTATE. USE CODE]

> 1 = ENOUGH . . .   2 = TOO MUCH . . .   3 = NOT ENOUGH . . .   4 = DK/NA

Referring to KAAA's weekday morning show . . . would you say there is enough, too much, or not enough . . .

a. number of songs in a row
b. weather reports and forecasts
c. humor
d. traffic reports

27. Next, I'd like to read a few of the words and slogans that might describe the type of music KAAA-FM plays and find out how well you think each one fits. Use a scale of 1 to 10, where the higher the number, the better the word or slogan describes KAAA-FM's music. [READ. 1-10. X=DK/NA]

a. Best Mix of Yesterday and Today
b. The Oldies Station
c. The Best of Yesterday and Today

28. Earlier I asked your age. I would like to get a narrower age range. Would you please tell me your exact age? [IF "NO," READ CATEGORIES]

Page 6 of 6 ©1995 The Eagle Group

$$1 = 25 \text{ to } 27$$
$$2 = 28 \text{ to } 30$$
$$3 = 31 \text{ to } 33$$
$$4 = 34 \text{ to } 36$$
$$5 = 37 \text{ to } 39$$
$$6 = 40 \text{ to } 42$$
$$7 = 43 \text{ to } 45$$
$$8 = 46 \text{ to } 48$$
$$9 = 49 \text{ to } 51$$
$$0 = 52 \text{ to } 54$$

29. Thanks for participating in the survey. For verification purposes, may I have your name?

GLOSSARY

acceptance rate: the percentage of the target sample that agrees to participate in a research project.

agenda setting: the theory that the media provide topics of discussion and importance for consumers.

aided recall: a survey technique in which the interviewer shows the respondent a copy of a newspaper, magazine, television schedule, or other item that might help him or her to remember a certain article, program, advertisement, and so on.

algorithm: a statistical procedure or formula.

American Standard Code for Information Interchange (ASCII): the standard machine language used by microcomputers; each letter, number, or special character is represented by 7 bits of information.

analysis of variance (ANOVA): a statistical procedure used to decompose sources of variation in two or more independent variables.

analytical survey: a survey that attempts to describe and explain why certain conditions exist (usually by testing certain hypotheses).

antecedent variable: (1) in survey research, the variable used to predict another variable; (2) in experimental research, the independent variable.

applied research: research that attempts to solve a specific problem rather than to construct a theory.

area of dominant influence (ADI): a region composed of a certain number of television households; every county is assigned to one and only one ADI.

artifact: a variable that creates an alternative explanation of results (a confounding variable).

audience turnover: in radio research, an estimate of the number of times the audience changes stations during a given daypart.

auditorium music testing: a testing procedure where a group of respondents simultaneously rates music hooks.

available sample: a sample selected on the basis of accessibility.

average quarter-hour (AQH): the average number of persons or households tuned in to a specific channel or station for at least 5 minutes during a 15-minute time segment.

bar chart: *see* histogram.

batch processing (batch job): a computer operating procedure in which several users input instructions that are computed in order of input or priority.

baud rate: the rate at which a modem sends or receives information.

beta weight: a mathematically derived value representing a variable's contribution to a prediction or weighted linear combination (also called *weight coefficient*).

bit: a single piece of information in computers; 8 bits typically represent one character or number, called a *byte*.

bit processing: term used to identify the type of information processing system used by a computer; most common is the 8–bit processor in microcomputers.

bits per second (BPS): measurement used to quantify the speed of a computer chip.

byte: a unit of computer storage, which is typically one character or number; a byte consists of 8 bits.

call-out research: a procedure used in radio research to determine the popularity of recordings; *see also* hook.

canonical correlation: a multivariate statistic used to investigate the relationship between two sets of variables.

case study: an empirical inquiry that uses multiple sources of data to investigate a problem.

catch-up panel: members of a previous cross-sectional sample who are relocated for subsequent observation.

CATI: computer-assisted telephone interviewing; video display terminals are used by interviewers to present questions and enter responses.

census: an analysis in which the sample comprises every element of a population.

central limit theorem: the sum of a large number of independent and identically distributed random variables that has an approximate normal distribution.

central location testing (CLT): research conducted with respondents who are invited to a field service facility or other research location.

central processing unit (CPU): the control and coordination system of a computer that decides the order in which computations are made and where to store information, sends information to peripherals, and regulates the entire system operation.

central tendency: a single value that is chosen to represent a typical score in a distribution, such as the mean, the mode, or the median.

checklist question: a type of question in which the respondent is given a list of items and is asked to mark those that apply.

chi-square statistic: a measurement of observed versus expected frequencies; often referred to as crosstabs.

circulation: in the print media, the total number of copies of a newspaper or magazine that are delivered to subscribers plus all copies bought at newsstands or from other sellers.

circulation research: (1) a market-level study of newspaper and magazine penetration; (2) a study of the delivery and pricing systems used by newspapers and magazines.

closed-ended question: a question the respondent must answer by making a selection from a prepared set of options.

Cloze procedure: a method for measuring readability or recall in which every *n*th word is deleted from the message and readers are asked to fill in the blanks.

cluster analysis: a multivariate statistic that classifies phenomena into groups or segments.

cluster sample: a sample placed into groups or categories.

codebook: a menu or list of responses used in coding open-ended questions.

coding: the placing of a unit of analysis into a particular category.

coefficient of determination: in correlational statistics, the amount of variation in the criterion variable that is accounted for by the antecedent variable.

coefficient of nondetermination: in correlational statistics, the amount of variation in the criterion variable that is left unexplained.

cohort analysis: a study of a specific population as it changes over time.

communication audit: in public relations, an examination of the internal and external means of communication used by an organization.

computer-assisted telephone interviewing (CATI): questionnaires are designed for the computer; inter-

viewers enter respondents' answers directly into the computer for tabulation; question skips and response options are controlled by the computer.

concept: a term that expresses an abstract idea formed by generalization.

confidence interval: an area within which there is a stated probability that the parameter will fall.

confidence level: probability (for example, .05 or .01) of rejecting a null hypothesis that is in fact true; also called the *alpha level*.

constitutive definition: a type of definition in which other words or concepts are substituted for the word being defined.

construct: a combination of concepts that is created to describe a specific situation (for example, "authoritarianism").

constructive replication: an analysis of a hypothesis taken from a previous study that deliberately avoids duplicating the methods used in the previous study.

continuous variable: a variable that can take on any value over a range of values and can be meaningfully broken into subparts (for example, "height").

control group: subjects who do not receive experimental treatment and thus serve as a basis of comparison in an experiment.

control variable: a variable whose influence a researcher wishes to eliminate.

convenience sample: a nonprobability sample consisting of respondents or subjects who are available, such as college students in a classroom.

co-op (incentive): a payment given to respondents for participating in a research project.

coprocessor: a computer microchip designed for a specific function.

copy testing: research used to determine the most effective way of structuring a message to achieve desired results; also known as *message research*.

cost per interview (CPI): the dollar amount required to recruit or interview one respondent.

cost per thousand (CPM): the dollar cost of reaching 1,000 people or households by means of a particular medium or advertising vehicle.

criterion variable: (1) in survey research, the variable presumed to be the effects variable; (2) in experimental research, the dependent variable.

cross-lagged correlation: a type of longitudinal study in which information about two variables is gathered from the same sample at two different times. The correlations between variables at the same point in time are compared with the correlations at different points in time..

cross-sectional research: the collection of data from a representative sample at only one point in time.

cross-tabulation analysis (crosstabs): *see* chi-square statistic.

cross-validation: a procedure whereby measurement instruments or subjects' responses are compared to verify their validity or truthfulness.

cultivation analysis: a research approach that suggests that heavy television viewing leads to perceptions of social reality that are consistent with the view of the world as presented on television.

cume: an estimate of the number of different persons who listened to or viewed a particular broadcast for at least 5 minutes during a given daypart; *see also* reach.

data archives: data storage facilities where researchers can deposit data for other researchers to use.

database journalism: a form of journalism that relies on computer-assisted analysis of existing information.

database marketing: research conducted with respondents whose names are included in databases, such as people who recently purchased a television set, or members of a club or organization.

daypart: a given part of the broadcast day (for example, prime time = 8:00 P.M.–11:00 P.M. EST).

demand characteristic: the premise that subjects' awareness of the experimental condition may affect their performance in the experiment; also known as the *Hawthorne effect.*

dependent variable: the variable that is observed and whose value is presumed to depend on the independent variable(s).

descriptive statistics: statistical methods and techniques designed to reduce data sets to allow for easier interpretation.

descriptive survey: a survey that attempts to picture or document current conditions or attitudes.

design-specific results: research results that are based on, or specific to, the research design used.

determinant: a scalar that represents a unique function of the numbers in a square matrix.

diagonal matrix: a square matrix whose elements all equal zero, except for those along the principal diagonal.

discrete variable: a variable that can be conceptually subdivided into a finite number of indivisible parts (for example, the number of children in a family).

discriminant analysis: a multivariate statistic used to classify groups according to variable similarities or to analyze the statistical significance of a weighted linear combination of variables.

disk-by-mail (DBM) survey: a survey questionnaire on computer disk sent to respondents to answer at their leisure.

disk operating system (DOS): computer program that controls the operation of the CPU.

dispersion: the amount of variability in a set of scores.

disproportionate stratified sampling: overrepresenting a specific stratum or characteristic.

distribution: a collection of scores or measurements.

double-barreled question: a single question that in reality requires two separate responses (for example, "Do you like the price and style of this item?").

double-blind experiment: a research study in which experimenters and others do not know whether a given subject belongs to the experimental group or the control group.

dummy variable: the variable created when a variable at the nominal level is transformed into a form more appropriate for higher order statistics.

editor-reader comparison: a readership study in which the perceptions of editors and readers are solicited.

eigenvalue: the sum of the squared elements in an eigenvector; total variance.

eigenvector: a vector comprised of beta weights characteristically found in multivariate statistics such as factor analysis or canonical correlation.

environmental monitoring program: in public relations research, a study of trends in public opinion and events in the social environment that may have a significant impact on an organization.

equivalency: the internal consistency of a measure.

error variance: the error created by an unknown factor.

evaluation apprehension: a fear of being measured or tested, which may result in invalid data.

evaluation research: a small-scale environmental monitoring program designed to measure an organization's social performance.

exhaustivity: a state of a category system such that every unit of analysis can be placed into an existing slot.

experimental design: a blueprint or set of plans for conducting laboratory research.

external validity: the degree to which the results of a research study are generalizable to other situations.

factor analysis: a multivariate statistical procedure used primarily for data reduction, construct development, and the investigation of variable relationships.

factorial design: a simultaneous analysis of two or more independent variables or factors.

factor score: a composite or summary score produced by factor analysis.

feeling thermometer: a rating scale patterned after a weather thermometer on which respondents can rate their attitudes on a scale of 0 to 100.

field service: a research company that conducts interviews and/or recruits respondents for research projects.

field observation: a study of a phenomenon in a natural setting.

filter question: a question designed to screen out certain individuals from further participation in a study; also called *screener question.*

Flesch reading ease formula: an early readability formula based on the number of words per sentence and the number of syllables per word.

floppy disk: an external computer storage device.

focus group: an interview conducted with 6–12 subjects simultaneously and a moderator who leads a discussion about a specific topic.

Fog Index: a readability scale based on sentence length and the number of syllables per word.

follow-back panel: a research technique in which a current cross-sectional sample is selected and matched with archival data.

forced-choice question: a question that requires a subject to choose between two specified responses.

forced exposure: a test situation in which respondents are required to be exposed to a specific independent or dependent variable.

frequency: in advertising, the total number of exposures to a message that a person or household receives.

frequency curve: a graphical display of frequency data in the form of a smooth, unbroken curve.

frequency distribution: a collection of scores, ordered according to magnitude, and their respective frequencies.

frequency polygon: a series of lines connecting points that represent the frequencies of scores.

gross incidence: the percent of qualified respondents reached of all contacts made.

gross rating points: the total of audience ratings during two or more time periods, representing the size of the gross audience of a radio or television broadcast.

group administration: conducting measurements with several subjects simultaneously.

hard disk: an external computer storage device capable of storing several million bytes of information.

hardware: any type of computer equipment; the physical components of a computer.

histogram: a bar chart that illustrates frequencies and scores.

homogeneity: equality of control and experimental groups prior to an experiment; also called *point of prior equivalency.*

hook: a short representative sample of a recording used in call-out research.

hypothesis: a tentative generalization concerning the relationship between two or more variables that predicts an experimental outcome.

identity matrix: a square matrix whose elements equal zero except for those along the principal diagonal, which equal one.

incidence: the percentage of a population that possesses the desired characteristics for a particular research study.

independent variable: the variable that is systematically varied by the researcher.

input: data placed into a computer.

instrumental replication: the duplication in a research study of the dependent variable of a previous study.

instrument decay: the deterioration of a measurement instrument during the course of a study, which reduces the instrument's effectiveness and accuracy.

intensive interview: a hybrid of the one-on-one personal interview.

interaction: a treatment-related effect dependent on the concomitant influence of two independent variables on a dependent variable.

interactive processing (on-line processing): inputting data directly into a computer, usually via a cathode ray tube.

intercoder reliability: in content analysis, the degree of agreement between or among independent coders.

intercorrelation matrix: a matrix composed of correlations between pairs of variables.

internal consistency: the level of consistency of performance among items within a scale.

internal validity: a property of a research study such that results are based on expected conditions rather than on extraneous variables.

interval level: a measurement system in which the intervals between adjacent points on a scale are equal (for example, a thermometer).

isomorphism: similarity of form or structure.

item pretest: a method of testing subjects' interest in reading magazine or newspaper articles.

item-selection study: a readership study used to determine who reads specific parts of a newspaper.

laptop computer: a computer that is smaller than a personal computer; larger than a palmtop; about the size of an average telephone book; also includes notebook computers.

leading question: a question that suggests a certain response or makes an implicit assumption (for example, "How long have you been an alcoholic?").

Likert scale: a measurement scale where respondents strongly agree, agree, are neutral, disagree, or strongly disagree with the statements.

literal replication: a study that is an exact duplication of a previous study.

local area network (LAN): computer batch processing when one computer serves as a host for several others.

longitudinal research: the collection of data at different points in time.

magazine readership survey: a survey of readers to determine which sections of the magazine were viewed and/or read.

mailing list: a compilation of names and addresses, sometimes prepared by a commercial firm, that is used as a sampling frame for mail surveys.

mail survey: the mailing of self-administered questionnaires to a sample of people; the researcher must rely on the recipients to mail back their responses.

main effect: the effect of the independent variable(s) on the dependent variable (no interaction is present).

mainframe: a computer that is larger than a mini or micro, but smaller than a supercomputer.

manipulation check: a test to determine whether the manipulation of the independent variable actually had the intended effect.

marker variable: a variable that highlights or defines the construct under study.

mark-sense reader: *see* optical character reader.

masked recall: a survey technique in which the interviewer shows respondents the front cover of a newspaper or magazine with the name of the publication blacked out to test unaided recall of the publication.

matrix: a two-dimensional array of scalars.

mean: the arithmetic average of a set of scores.

measurement: a procedure whereby a researcher assigns numerals to objects, events, or properties according to certain rules.

measurement error: an inconsistency produced by the instruments used in a research study.

media efficiency: reaching the maximum possible audience for the smallest possible cost.

median: the midpoint of a distribution of scores.

medium variables: in a content analysis, the aspects of content that are unique to the medium under consideration (for example, typography to a newspaper or magazine).

memory: the amount of information a computer can store and work with, excluding external storage devices.

method of authority: a method of knowing whereby something is believed because a source perceived as an authority says it is true.

method of intuition: a method of knowing whereby something is believed because it is "self-evident" or "stands to reason"; also called *a priori reasoning*.

method of tenacity: a method of knowing whereby something is believed because a person has always believed it to be true.

method-specific results: research results based on, or specific to, the research method used.

metro survey area (MSA): a region representing one of the Consolidated Metropolitan Statistical Areas (CMSA), as defined by the U.S. Office of Management and Budget.

microcomputer: *see* personal computer.

microprocessor chip (microchip): primary computer hardware processing component.

minicomputer: a computer that is larger than a microcomputer but smaller than a mainframe.

mode: the score that occurs most often in a frequency distribution.

modem: an electronic device used to transfer computer data via telephone lines (acronym for *modulate-de*modulate).

monitor: a television-type screen that allows a user to view what is entered into the computer as well as the results of any calculations or word processing; also known as a CRT (cathode ray tube).

mortality: in panel studies and other forms of longitudinal research, the percent of original sample members who drop out of the research project for one reason or another.

motherboard: a computer's factory-installed primary memory board.

mouse: a computer device used to input and manipulate data.

MS-DOS: Microsoft disk operating system.

multidimensional scaling: a multivariate statistic that identifies distances among a set of data by searching for similarities and differences among objects.

multiple regression: an analysis of two or more independent variables and their relationship to a single dependent variable; used to predict the dependent variable.

multistage sampling: a form of cluster sampling in which individual households or persons, not groups, are selected.

multitasking (multiuser): a computer system designed to allow for simultaneous use by several users.

multivariate analysis of variance (MANOVA): an extension of analysis of variance used to study more than one dependent variable.

multivariate statistics: statistical methods that investigate the relationship between one or more independent variables and more than one dependent variable.

mutually exclusive: a category system in which a unit of analysis can be placed in one and only one category.

net incidence: the number of respondents or subjects who actually participate in a research project.

network: several computers connected to a server (central computer).

nominal level: the level of measurement at which arbitrary numerals or other symbols are used to classify persons, objects, or characteristics.

nonparametric statistics: statistical procedures used with variables measured at the nominal or ordinal level.

nonprobability sample: a sample selected without regard to the laws of mathematical probability.

normal curve: a symmetrical, bell-shaped curve that possesses specific mathematical characteristics.

normal distribution: a mathematical model of how measurements are distributed. A graph of a normal distribution is a continuous, symmetrical, bell-shaped curve.

notebook computer: a computer whose dimensions are about 8" × 11"—the most popular of the sub-PC computers.

null hypothesis: the denial or negation of a research hypothesis.

objective function: a mathematical formula that provides various quantitative values for a given media schedule of advertisements; used in computer simulations of advertising media schedules.

one-on-one interviews: sessions in which respondents are interviewed one at a time.

open-ended question: a question to which respondents are asked to generate an answer or answers with no prompting from the item itself (for example, "What is your favorite type of television program?").

operating system (OS): the set of instructions that controls a computer's operation.

operational definition: a definition that specifies patterns of behavior and procedures in order to experience or measure a concept.

operational replication: a study that duplicates only the sampling methodology and experimental procedures of a previous study.

optical character reader (OCR): an input device that electronically reads information from a printed page for entering into a computer.

ordinal level: the level of measurement at which items are ranked along a continuum.

output: information a computer computes and displays.

overnights: ratings surveys of a night's television viewing computed in five major U.S. cities by the A. C. Nielsen Company.

palmtop computer: the smallest computer in the PC family.

panel study: a research technique whereby the same sample of respondents is measured at different points in time.

parallel processing: computer system design where several small processors are connected together to act as one unit.

parameter: a characteristic or property of a population.

parametric statistics: statistical procedures appropriate with variables measured at the interval or ratio level.

parsimony principle: the premise that the simplest method is the most preferable; also known as *Occam's razor*.

partial correlation: a method used to control a confounding or spurious variable that may affect the relationship between independent variables and dependent variables.

PC-DOS: a personal computer disk operating system.

people meter: an electronic television audience data-gathering device capable of recording individual viewing behavior.

periodicity: any form of bias resulting from the use of a nonrandom list of subjects or items in selecting a sample.

peripheral: any add-on device to a computer system such as a printer.

personal computer (PC): IBM or IBM clone; technically called a microcomputer.

personal interview: a survey technique in which a trained interviewer visits a respondent and administers a questionnaire in a face-to-face setting.

pilot study: a trial run of a study conducted on a small scale to determine whether the research design and methodology are relevant and effective.

population: a group or class of objects, subjects, or units.

population distribution: the frequency distribution of all the variables of interest as determined by a census of the population.

power: the probability of rejecting the null hypothesis when an alternative is true.

precision journalism: a technique of inquiry in which social science research methods are used to gather the news.

precursor analysis: a study that assumes that leaders establish trends, and that these trends ultimately trickle down to the rest of society.

predictor variable: *see* antecedent variable.

prerecruits: respondents who are recruited ahead of time to participate in a research project.

prestige bias: the tendency of a respondent to give answers that will make him or her seem more educated, successful, financially stable, or otherwise prestigious.

printed circuit board: a piece of flat plastic that contains electrical circuits.

printer: a typewriterlike device controlled by a computer.

probability level: a predetermined value at which researchers test their data for statistical significance.

probability sample: a sample selected according to the laws of mathematical probability.

processing: calculations made by a computer.

programmable read-only memory (PROM): information stored on a computer chip that is used over and over again, as in cable television channel converters.

proportionate stratified sampling: representing population proportions of a specific stratum or characteristic.

proposition: a statement of the form "if A then B," which links two or more concepts.

proprietary data: research data gathered by a private organization that are available to the general public only if released by that organization.

protocol: a document containing the procedures to be used in a field study.

psychographics: an area of research that examines why people behave and think as they do.

public relations audit: a comprehensive study of the public relations position of an organization.

purposive sample: a sample deliberately chosen to be representative of a population.

qualitative research method: a description or analysis of a phenomenon that does not depend on the measurement of variables.

quantitative research method: a description or analysis of a phenomenon that involves specific measurements of variables.

quasi-experiment: a research design that does not involve random assignment of subjects to experimental groups.

quota sample: a sample selected to represent certain characteristics of interest.

random access memory (RAM): a computer's main memory, which is erased when the computer is turned off.

random digit dialing: a method of selecting telephone numbers that ensures that all telephone households have an equal chance of being selected.

random error: error in a research study that cannot be controlled by the researcher.

random sample: a subgroup or subset of a population selected in such a way that each unit in a population has an equal chance of being selected.

range: a measure of dispersion based on the difference between the highest and lowest scores in a distribution.

rating: an estimate of the percentage of people or households in a population that are tuned to a specific station or network.

ratio level: a level of measurement that has all the properties of an interval level scale and also has a true zero point.

reach in advertising: the total number of people or households exposed to a message at least once during a specific period of time; *see also* cume.

reactivity: a subject's awareness of being measured or observed and its possible impact on that subject's behavior.

readability: the total of all elements in a piece of printed material that affect the degree to which people understand the piece and find it interesting.

reader-nonreader study: a study that contrasts non-readers of newspapers or magazines with regular readers.

reader profile: a demographic summary of the readers of a particular publication.

read-only memory (ROM): permanent memory stored in a computer.

recall study: a study in which respondents are asked to remember which advertisements they remember seeing in the medium being investigated.

recognition: a measurement of readership in which respondents are shown the logo of a magazine or newspaper.

redundancy index: a mathematical procedure used in canonical correlation to aid in interpreting relationships between variable sets.

region of rejection: the proportion of an area in a sampling distribution that equals the level of significance; the region of rejection represents all the values of a test statistic that are highly unlikely, provided the null hypothesis is true.

reliability: the property of a measure that consistently gives the same answer at different points in time.

repeated-measures design: a research design wherein numerous measurements are made on the same subjects.

replication: an independent verification of a research study.

research question: a tentative generalization concerning the relationship between two or more variables.

research supplier: a company that provides various forms of research to clients, from data collection only to a final written analysis and summary of the data.

retrospective panel: a study in which each respondent is asked questions about events and attitudes in his or her lifetime.

rough cut: a model or simulation of a final product.

sample: a subgroup or subset of a population or universe.

sample distribution: the frequency distribution of all the variables of interest as determined from a sample.

sample-specific results: research results that are based on, or specific to, the research sample used.

sampling distribution: a probability distribution of all possible values of a statistic that would occur if all possible samples of a fixed size from a given population were taken.

sampling error: the degree to which measurements obtained from a sample differ from the measurements that would be obtained from the population.

sampling frame: a list of the members of a particular population.

sampling interval: a random interval used for selection of subjects or units in the systematic sampling method.

sampling rate: the ratio of the number of people chosen in the sample to the total number in the population (for example, if 100 fraternity members were systematically chosen from a sampling frame of 1,000 fraternity members, the sampling rate would be 10%, or 1/10).

scalar: a single digit (used in matrix algebra).

scale: a form of measurement such as 10-point scales, Likert, Guttman, or semantic differential.

scattergram: a graphic technique for portraying the relationship between two variables.

scientific method: a systematic, controlled, empirical, and critical investigation of hypothetical propositions about the presumed relations among natural phenomena.

screener: a short survey or a portion of a survey designed to select only appropriate respondents for a research project.

secondary analysis: the use of data collected by a previous researcher or another research organization; also called *data reanalysis*.

semantic differential: a rating scale consisting of seven spaces between two bipolar adjectives (for example, "good- - - - - - -bad").

share: an estimate of the percentage of persons or households tuned to a specific station, channel, or network.

shopping center interview (intercept): a nonprobability study where respondents are recruited and interviewed in a shopping mall.

sigma (Σ): the Greek capital letter symbolizing "the sum of".

skewness: the degree of departure of a curve from the normal distribution (curves can be positively or negatively skewed).

SMOG Grading: a measure of readability based on the number of syllables per word.

social audit: in public relations research, an analysis of the social performance of an organization.

software: any type of ready-to-use computer program designed for mathematical computations, word processing, graphics, spreadsheets, and so on.

square matrix: a matrix in which the number of rows equals the number of columns.

stability: the degree of consistency of the results of a measure at different points in time.

staged manipulation: a situation whereby researchers construct events and circumstances so they can manipulate the independent variable.

standard deviation: the square root of the variance (a mathematical index of dispersion).

standard error: an estimate of the amount of error present in a measurement.

standard score: a measure that has been standardized in relation to a distribution's mean and standard deviation.

statistics: a science that uses mathematical methods to collect, organize, summarize, and analyze data.

storage: forms of saving computer data, such as magnetic disks and tapes.

straightforward manipulation: a situation whereby materials and instructions are simply presented to respondents or subjects.

stratified sample: a sample selected after the population has been divided into categories.

structured interview: an interview in which standardized questions are asked in a predetermined order.

subnotebook computer: a palmtop or "downsized" notebook computer.

summary statistics: statistics that summarize a great deal of numerical information about a distribution, such as the mean and the standard deviation.

supercomputer: the most powerful computer currently made; computes billions of instructions per second (BIPS).

sweep: a nationwide survey conducted by the A. C. Nielsen Company and Arbitron of every television market.

systematic random sampling: a procedure to select every nth subject for a study, such as every 10th person in a telephone directory.

systematic variance: a regular increase or decrease in all scores or data in a research study by a known factor.

telephone coincidental: a broadcasting research procedure in which random subjects or households are called and asked what they are viewing or listening to at that moment.

telephone survey: a research method in which survey data are collected over the telephone by trained interviewers who ask questions and record responses.

theory: a set of related propositions that presents a systematic view of phenomena by specifying relationships among concepts.

time spent listening (TSL): a quantitative statement about the average time a listener spends listening to a radio station (or several stations); stated in hours and minutes.

total observation: in field observation, a situation in which the observer assumes no role in the phenomenon being observed other than that of observer.

total participation: field observation in which the observer becomes a full-fledged participant in the situation under observation.

total survey area (TSA): a region in which an audience survey is conducted.

tracking study: a special readership measurement technique in which respondents designate material they have read (using a different color of pencil for each reading episode).

trend study: a longitudinal study in which a topic is restudied using different groups of respondents (for example, the Roper studies of the credibility of the media).

triangulation: using a combined quantitative and qualitative approach to solve a problem.

trigger event: an event or activity that might focus public concern on a topic or issue.

t-test: a statistic used to determine the significance between group means.

Type I error: rejection of the null hypothesis when it should be accepted.

Type II error: acceptance of the null hypothesis when it should be rejected.

unit of analysis: the smallest element of a content analysis; the thing that is counted whenever it is encountered.

unstructured interview: an interview in which the interviewer asks broad and general questions but retains control over the discussion.

uses and gratifications study: a study of the motives for media usage and the rewards that are sought.

validity: the degree to which a test actually measures what it purports to measure.

variable: a phenomenon or event that can be measured or manipulated.

variance: a mathematical index of the degree to which scores deviate from the mean.

vector: a series of data points represented by a line in space.

very large area network: a group of computers connected over great distances.

volunteer sample: a group of people who go out of their way to participate in a survey or experiment (for example, by responding to a newspaper advertisement).

weighting: a mathematical procedure used to adjust a sample to meet the characteristics of a given population; also called *sample balancing*.

Name Index

Subject Index